Advanced Topics in Global Information Management

Volume 5

M. Gordon Hunter, The University of Lethbridge, Canada

Felix B. Tan, Auckland University of Technology, New Zealand

IDEA GROUP PUBLISHING
Hershey • London • Melbourne • Singapore

Acquisitions Editor:	Michelle Potter
Development Editor:	Kristin Roth
Senior Managing Editor:	Amanda Appicello
Managing Editor:	Jennifer Neidig
Copy Editor:	Susanna Svidunovich
Typesetter:	Jessie Weik
Cover Design:	Integrated Book Technology
Printed at:	Integrated Book Technology

Published in the United States of America by
    Idea Group Publishing (an imprint of Idea Group Inc.)
    701 E. Chocolate Avenue, Suite 200
    Hershey PA 17033
    Tel: 717-533-8845
    Fax: 717-533-8661
    E-mail: cust@idea-group.com
    Web site: http://www.idea-group.com

and in the United Kingdom by
    Idea Group Publishing (an imprint of Idea Group Inc.)
    3 Henrietta Street
    Covent Garden
    London WC2E 8LU
    Tel: 44 20 7240 0856
    Fax: 44 20 7379 0609
    Web site: http://www.eurospanonline.com

Advanced Topics in Global Information Management, Volume 5 is part of the Idea Group Publishing series named *Advances in Global Information Management* Series, formerly known as the *Advanced Topics in Global Information Management* Series (ISSN: 1537-9302).

ISBN 1-59140-923-3
Paperback ISBN 1-59140-924-1
eISBN 1-59140-925-X

British Cataloguing in Publication Data
A Cataloguing in Publication record for this book is available from the British Library.

All work contributed to this book is new, previously-unpublished material. The views expressed in this book are those of the authors, but not necessarily of the publisher.

Advanced Topics in
Global Information Management Series

ISSN: 1537-9302

Series Editors
M. Gordon Hunter
University of Lethbridge, Canada

Felix B. Tan
Auckland University of Technology,
New Zealand

Advanced Topics in Global Information Management, Volume 5
1-59140-923-3 (h/c) • 1-59140-924-1 (s/c) • copyright 2006

Advanced Topics in Global Information Management, Volume 4
1-59140-468-1 (h/c) • 1-59140-469-X (s/c) • copyright 2005

Advanced Topics in Global Information Management, Volume 3
1-59140-251-4 (h/c) • 1-59140-294-8 (s/c) • copyright 2004

Advanced Topics in Global Information Management, Volume 2
1-59140-064-3 (h/c) • 1-59140-101-1 (s/c) • copyright 2003

Advanced Topics in Global Information Management, Volume 1
1-930708-43-2 (h/c) • copyright 2002

Visit us today at www.idea-group.com !

IDEA GROUP PUBLISHING
Hershey • London • Melbourne • Singapore

Advanced Topics in Global Information Management
Volume 5

Table of Contents

Preface

Many businesses exist today in a global environment. Whether they are large or small companies, they may have suppliers or customers that reside in a different geographical location. The ability to function in this global environment has been facilitated by the use of information technology.

Large companies may decide to place significant portions of their operations physically close to resources or markets. Thus, a manufacturing process for glass containers could be situated in a remote location in near proximity to sand and natural gas. However, the sales function for this particular product could be located in urban centers with large populations of potential customers. Other corporations may establish operations near to where they may access skilled personnel. This is evident in the establishment of various versions of "silicon valley" locations throughout the world. Whatever the reason, employing information technology facilitates this process of internationalization.

Small businesses are also able to establish a global presence. It is possible, through the creation of a Web site, for small businesses to present their products and services to a global market. Thus, through the Internet, it is possible for potential customers to access information from small wineries in southeast Australia or even western Canada. Many of these sites support the purchase of product and subsequent international delivery.

Through the use of information technology, governments are now better able to provide information and services to citizens. Thus, governments at the national as well as local levels are employing information technology. Even within a country, aspects of intra-national culture must be addressed. Differences may exist between urban and rural residents. There will most certainly be inter-generational differences. Further, the ethnic mix will also contribute to cultural variability.

The ability of business, both large and small, and government, from the national level to the local level, to function in these altered environments has been facilitated by the introduction and use of information technology. In all of these situations, both business and government must be able to function and respond to various stakeholders by adopting the appropriate and necessary cultural perspective. The research projects included in this volume address many of these issues. The chapters presented here are organized into themes relating to manuscripts that take a global or regional perspective.

Global Themes

The chapters in this section report the results of investigations which have adopted a global perspective. In Chapter I, Ein-Dor, Myers, and Raman analyze the production of information technology over a five-year period in Finland, Israel, New Zealand, and Singapore. Karahanna, Evaristo, and Srite, in Chapter II, present a conceptual discussion of cultural variability. In Chapter III, Corbittt, Peszynski, Inthanond, Hill, and Thanasankit explore various ways of framing information system research within the context of national culture. Then Grant and Chau, in Chapter IV, present a generic e-government framework that supports the identification of strategic initiatives. In Chapter V, Gefen, Rose, Warkentin, and Pavlou investigate trust-related perceptions of electronic voting by comparing results of investigation in the United States of America and the Republic of South Africa. Sagi, Carayannis, Dasgupta, and Thomas, in Chapter VI, examine differences in attitude toward e-commerce among different cultural groups. In Chapter VII, Chin conducted an exploratory investigation of the impact in information technology governance structures related to mergers and acquisitions in developing countries. Finally, Edwards and Sridhar, in Chapter VIII, investigate virtual teams based in Canada and India to understand the complexities of determining information system requirements.

Regional Themes

The chapters in this section are the results of research which has concentrated upon one or a few countries in a specific region. In Chapter IX, Doolin, Dillon, and Corner focus on New Zealand and present a research model of consumer risk in online shopping. Vasisht and Gutierrez, in Chapter X, also present the results of an investigation in New Zealand of the revenue streams of Internet content providers. In Chapter XI, Kawalek and Wastall present three UK-based case studies regarding the transformation of local government authorities. Mbarika, Meso, and Musa, in Chapter XII, document the telecommunications capabilities in sub-Saharan countries. In Chapter XIII, Elbeltagi, McBride, and Hardaker analyze senior managers' use of decision support systems in Egyptian local authorities. Chan and Lu, in Chapter XIV, investigate adoption and use of Internet banking in Hong Kong. In Chapter XV, Dologite, Mockler, Bai, and Viszhanyo present a case study of change agent roles played during information system implementation in China. Finally, in Chapter XVI, Tan, Lim, and Pan base their investigation of the aspects of governance in e-government in Singapore.

Acknowledgments

We thank the many authors of the chapters included in this volume. We appreciate your thorough and excellent investigations into the topic of global information management. We also wish to recognize all those individuals from Idea Group Inc., for their patience and assistance in this project. We would specifically like to thank Dr. Mehdi Khosrow-Pour, Ms. Jan Travers, Kristin Roth, and Michelle Potter for their valuable guidance.

We dedicate this book to our parents, Malcolm and Mary Hunter, and Michael and Laura Tan. We are extremely grateful for all that you have done for us.

Thank you all very much.

M. Gordon Hunter
Felix B. Tan
February 2006

Section I: Global Themes

Chapter I

IT Industry Development and the Knowledge Economy:
A Four Country Study

Phillip Ein-Dor, Tel-Aviv University, Israel

Michael Myers, University of Auckland, New Zealand

K. S. Raman, National University of Singapore, Singapore

ABSTRACT

It is generally accepted that knowledge has become a third major factor of production, in addition to the traditional factors — labor and capital. Information technology production is a significant factor in the knowledge economy both because it is a major enabler of that economy and because it is itself highly knowledge intensive. Many countries around the world are looking for ways to promote the development of the knowledge economy, and information technology industries in particular. An important question is to what extent — and how — small developed countries might succeed in this endeavor. This study suggests a modified and more comprehensive version of the Ein-Dor et al. (1997) model of IT (information technology) industry success in small developed countries. Whereas the earlier model of IT industry success was based solely on the macro-economic theory of Grossman and Helpman (1991), the revised model suggested here incorporates Romer's (1990) work in New Growth economics. A significant advance over earlier work in this area is the use of both longitudinal and time slice data. This article provides an in-depth analysis of the IT industry in four countries over a five-year period: Finland, Israel, New Zealand and Singapore. It analyses some changes that occurred over the period 1994 through 1998 and thus provides a reasonably comprehensive picture of the factors affecting the production of IT in these small developed countries. Our study reveals that four of the five endogenous variables studied have a close relationship to the development of IT industries in small developed countries. These variables are research and development, technological infrastructure, firm strategies, and capital availability. On the other hand, domestic IT use does not seem to be a major factor in IT industry development. Our analysis thus largely supports the more comprehensive model of IT industry success. These findings should be of interest to both researchers and policy makers seeking to develop the knowledge economy and information technology industries in particular.

INTRODUCTION

For countries in the vanguard of the world economy, the balance between knowledge and resources has shifted so far towards the former that knowledge has become perhaps the most important factor determining the standard of living — more than land, than tools, than labor. Today's most technologically advanced economies are truly knowledge-based. (World Bank, 1999)

Some contemporary economists have suggested that knowledge has become a third factor of production in leading economies. Paul Romer, in particular, has proposed his "New Growth Theory" as an alternative to the neo-classical model of economics (Romer, 1990). Whereas neo-classical economics recognised just two factors of production (labor and capital), Romer has suggested that technology (and the knowledge on which it is based) is an intrinsic part of today's economic system.

Consequently, many governments around the world are looking for ways to promote the development of the knowledge economy, and information technology industries in particular. According to many New Growth economists, information technology is best regarded as the facilitator of knowledge creation in innovative societies (OECD, 1996). Information technologies do not by themselves create transformations in society, but they are the enablers of change. New information technologies are tools for releasing the creative potential and knowledge embodied in people. Particularly important from the perspective of this study is the fact that IT industries are themselves knowledge industries in the sense that they employ knowledge intensive research, design, and production processes.

Using the macro-economic work of Grossman and Helpman (1991) and Romer (1990) as a base, this study attempts to provide a comprehensive picture of the factors affecting the production of IT in small developed countries. It does so by providing an in-depth analysis of the IT industry in four countries — Finland, Israel, New Zealand and Singapore — the last three over a five-year period. These four countries were chosen because they are comparable in many ways, making it easier to identify the factors leading to differential development of their IT industries. Given that IT industries provide a technical platform for innovation and are a key component in fostering the development of the knowledge economy, we believe it is important to identify the key drivers in fostering IT industry success. The primary purpose of this article is to identify what these drivers might be.

This study analyses the relative changes that occurred over the period 1994 through 1998. We believe that our use of both longitudinal and time slice data represents a considerable advance over earlier studies of a similar nature. Furthermore, an effort has been made to identify and employ consistent bodies of data wherever possible.

Earlier studies (Dedrick et al., 1995; Ein-Dor et al., 1997) were based mainly on 1993 and 1994 data. However, developments in IT industries were extremely rapid in the period between the two studies and it was assumed that this would help in identifying the relevant factors. This study revisited the earlier studies in order to determine whether their conclusions still held five years later and whether changes may have occurred in the explanatory factors. Admittedly, the data are not particularly recent, but it should be remembered that the objective of this study is to identify IT industry success factors; as these factors do not change rapidly, the particular time period studied is of little consequence, as long as it is one in which development has occurred and the factors can be identified.

The article is organised as follows. It begins by exhibiting some background data of the four countries. As the dependent variable in our study is IT industry success, it then develops a measure of such success and determines the level of success of the countries studied. Next, it presents the macro-economic model underlying this study. Attention then shifts to a presentation of the data regarding the respective countries' IT industries and an attempt is made to relate the changes in performance over time to the variables in our model. In the final concluding section, directions for future research and implications for policy makers are suggested.

BACKGROUND DATA

Previous studies have suggested a number of exogenous variables over which countries have little control. There are two main groups of exogenous variables; the first relates to ethnic and quality of life factors, while the second encompasses economic factors. The current values of these items for the four countries are exhibited in Table 1. Some obvious facts arising from the table are:

1. The ethnic composition of the four countries is very different, the predominant groups being Semitic for Israel, European for New Zealand and Finland, and Asian in Singapore.
2. The religious affiliations of the four countries differ widely.
3. The predominant languages of all four are different, although English plays a major role in all of them: as the mother tongue in New Zealand, as the official language of administration and most public activity in Singapore, and as a widely used second language in Finland and Israel.

Of the four countries, only New Zealand is well endowed with raw materials. The countries differ widely in their proximity to market regions and their trade patterns might be expected to be markedly different.

Given that any changes in the exogenous variables tend to be very slow, we believe that it is highly unlikely that any changes that may have occurred in the IT industries are attributable to them.

Table 1. Summary of exogenous variables – 1997

Exogenous variables	Finland		Israel		New Zealand		Singapore	
People:								
Ethnic groups	Finn	93%	Jewish	82%	European, mostly British	88%	Chinese	76%
	Swede	6%	Non Jewish (mostly Arab)	18%	Polynesian	9%	Malay	15%
	Lapp	0.11%					Indian	6%
	Gypsy	0.12%						
	Other	0.02%						
Official languages	Finnish, Swedish		Hebrew, Arabic		English, Maori		Chinese, Malay, Tamil, English	
Religions	Evangelical Lutheran	89%	Jewish	82%	Anglican	24%	Buddhist	
	Greek Orthodox	1%	Muslim	14%	Presbyterian	18%	Taoist	
	None	9%	Other	4%	Roman Catholic	15%	Muslim	
	Other	1%					Christian	
							Hindu	
Human development:								
UNDP Human Development Index (1999 rank of 174 countries)[3]	13		23		18		22	
Life expectancy	Male 74		male 76		male 74		male 75	
	Female 81		female 80		female 80		female 81	
Infant mortality/1000 live births	3.8		9		7		5	
Literacy	100%		95%		100%		(1993) 91%	
Newspaper circulation	455 per 1000 pop.[2]		242 per 1000 pop.		304 per 100 pop.		350 per 1000 pop.	
Leading export partners[4]								
	Germany	11.0%	USA	32.1%	Australia	20.2%	USA	18.4%
	UK	10.0%	UK	6.2%	Japan	14.5%	Malaysia	17.5%
	Sweden	9.8%	Hong Kong	5.3%	USA	10.4%	Hong Kong	9.6%
	Russia	7.3%	Belgium/Luxembourg	5.0%	UK	6.2%	Japan	7.1%
			Japan	4.6%			Thailand	4.6%
			Netherlands	4.4%			Taiwan	4.5
raw materials	few		few		many		none	

Sources. (1) Unless otherwise stated: K-III Reference Corporation (1997). (2) Finnish Newspapers Association (2000). (3) United Nations Development Program (1999). (4) The Economist. Pocket World in Figures (1999).

Table 2. Population and economic indicators and changes therein

Country	Population (millions) 1994/1998 [1]	Population Rank 1994/1998 [1]	GDP (US$bn) [2]	Per Capita GDP (US$) [3]	Per Capita GDP Rank of 53 countries [3]
Finland – 1994	5.1	103		$19,221	16
Finland – 1998	5.1	105	125.1	$24,292	14
Change	0	-2		+26%	+2
NZ – 1994	3.5	122		13,006	22
NZ – 1998	3.6	121	52.7	15,470	24
Change	+2.8%	+1		+19%	-2
Israel – 1994	5.1	104		13,727	23
Israel – 1998	5.6	100	98.8	16,330	22
Change	+9.8%	+4		+19%	+1
Singapore – 1994	3.3	124		24,187	9
Singapore – 1998	3.5	118	84.4	21,789	17
Change	+6%	+6		-10%	-8

Sources. (1) U.S. Bureau of the Census (1999). (2) World Economic Forum (1999). (3) IMD (1999).

Table 2 exhibits some data that will be frequently used in the following analyses, particularly population and GDP data. (Note: Data are generally presented by development rank where that emphasizes relevant relationships; otherwise they are presented by alphabetical order of country names.)

The data show some quite significant demographic and economic changes in the countries under consideration during the period studied. The populations of New Zealand and Singapore grew by about 6% over five years and that of Israel by about 10%; only the population of Finland remained unchanged during the period considered. In Israel and Singapore, these changes were due to natural growth and, especially, to significant levels of immigration. In New Zealand, immigration was less dominant and the growth is attributable to natural increase. No matter what the causes, the growth that occurred moved the three countries up one to six places in the world population rankings. Only Finland receded in the population rankings as a consequence of its zero population growth.

The changes in per capita GDP (Gross Domestic Product) are more dramatic. The increase in this datum varied from 19% in New Zealand and Israel to a remarkable 26% in Finland; Singapore alone exhibited negative growth resulting from the Asian economic crisis of the late 1990s. The positions of the countries in the international ranking by GDP were little changed, except for the 8-place decline of Singapore for the reason given. In the context of the present article, the interesting question, of course, is to what extent the per capita GDP changes can be linked to IT industries.

RESEARCH METHOD

In most earlier studies of this type, a major weakness has been the inadequacy and limited availability of good statistical data. Some of the most serious problems have been as follows:

- Lack of availability of consistent data from a single source. For example, reported data concerning domestic IT expenditure may have been gathered from various national sources. The inconsistent definitions of data make accurate comparisons impossible.
- Data from a single source may not convey exactly the meaning that is desired. Whereas the statistical categories for traditional industries may have been provided in great detail, those for IT are more likely to have been defined less precisely. The standard statistical classifications suffer from low granularity in the IT context. Thus, for example, it may be difficult to differentiate between different kinds of communication costs; software might be considered a service, and the data not related to that on hardware; computers may be lumped together with office machines.

Our solution to these problems has been to use *single sources* wherever possible, and to use sources with good quality reporting of IT usage. We are fortunate that such sources have become available in recent years. These sources include *The Economist Pocket World in Figures, The Global Competitiveness Report, UNESCO Statistical Yearbook,* and *The World Competitiveness Yearbook.* Our use of these global sources strengthens the article and, we believe, represents a significant advance over much of the earlier work in this area, which generally relied on inconsistent national sources.

In those instances where data from single sources are not available, an attempt has been made to use official national sources such as the US Census Bureau and the Singapore National Computer Board. As a last resort, journal and newspaper data were occasionally utilized. In some cases, where it was not possible to obtain a data item for all four countries from a single source, multiple sources were used that may relate to proximate years rather than to a single year.

Considerable use has been made here of survey data published by the World Economic Forum in *The Global Competitiveness Yearbook 1999*. "The survey questions were selected to provide a reasonably comprehensive view of what leading businessmen perceive to be happening in their countries, with special emphasis on questions for which alternative quantitative data are not available." Responses were obtained from about 4,000 executives in the 59 countries reported.

The data points in the surveys are much closer for the different countries than for the objective data. Apparently, most managers surveyed tend to see the situation in their own countries in a relatively favorable light. In order to compensate for this and to make the differences more obvious, we have normalized the survey data in some of the charts. The same has been done for other data where necessary. In each case, the normalization is explained for the specific chart displayed.

THEORETICAL MODEL

The relationship between production and use of information technology (IT) and economic development of countries has received increasing attention in recent years. The role of IT in the rapid economic growth of some Asia-Pacific countries has received particular attention (Blanning et al., 1997; Dedrick & Kraemer, 1995, 1998; Kraemer et al., 1992). These studies show that Hong Kong, New Zealand, and Singapore are economically developed and advanced in IT production and use even though they are small countries with less than 10 million population. Beyond the Asia-Pacific region, Ireland, Israel, and Nordic countries with populations of less than 10 million are major IT producers and/or sophisticated users (Dedrick et al., 1995). Production and use of IT in these countries are out of proportion to their size and natural resources.

Of the numerous country level studies on IT production and use, three focus on small developed countries with populations of less than 10 million. In a descriptive study of nine geographically and culturally diverse small developed countries, Dedrick et al. (1995) suggest that the likely success factors are the level of economic development, a basic education system, sophistication in IT use, telecommunications infrastructure, and government policies towards trade, investment, and IT. In a detailed study of Israel, New Zealand, and Singapore, Ein-Dor et al. (1997) built on the macroeconomic theoretical framework provided by Grossman and Helpman (1989, 1991). They concluded that although the three countries are very similar in terms of the level of economic development, the IT industry seemed most developed in Israel, followed by Singapore and New Zealand. Exogenous variables such as geographical location, availability of raw materials, and national culture did not seem to provide explanations for the different levels of

IT industry development. Of the endogenous variables, local IT use and firm strategies did not seem to explain the differential levels of IT industry development. The dominant factor, which seemed to provide some explanation, was government policy towards promoting IT industries directly, in supporting IT industry R&D, and in education policies providing appropriately trained labor pools. More recently, Watson and Myers (2001) used the Ein-Dor et al. (1997) model to study the IT industry and IT use in Finland and New Zealand based on 1998 data. They found that Finland and New Zealand are very similar in terms of economic development and country size. Despite this similarity, Finland's IT industry is more developed than New Zealand's, particularly in the hardware sector. Their research suggests that government promotion of IT, high levels of private sector R&D investment, and an education system that produces IT-literate graduates are the most important factors in IT industry success.

The theoretical basis of this article is a modified and more comprehensive version of the model suggested earlier by Ein-Dor et al. (1997). It is a more general version of the Grossman and Helpman (1991) model but now incorporates Romer's (1990) work.

Grossman and Helpman analyse how governments can help in promoting technology and knowledge via research and development (R&D) subsidies. Romer suggests that technology and knowledge are a third factor of production together with labor and capital. He adds human capital, defined as the cumulative effect of formal education and on-the-job training, as an important factor that affects growth. In addition to the variables suggested by Grossman and Helpman's model and Romer, our model includes national culture and firm strategies.

The elements of the model are as follows:

1. *Control variables:* those which define country size
2. *Dependent variables:* those which define IT industry success
3. *Independent variables:*
    (a) Exogenous variables — those over which countries have little or no control:
        i.   Resources,
        ii.   Proximity to markets,
        iii. National culture
    (b) Endogenous mediating factors:
        i.   Domestic IT use
        ii.   Human capital development
        iii. Research & development; technological sophistication
        iv.   Firm strategies
        v.   Availability of capital

In this model, government policies are not considered as a separate variable but are discussed within the context of the other factors. Graphically, our model may be represented as in Figure 1.

Figure 1. Model of IT industry success factors

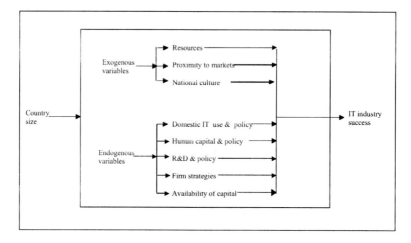

DATA

IT Industry Development Measures

As the countries under consideration are small, one cannot expect to find in them broad coverage of the spectrum of IT products. Furthermore, being as small as they are, their internal IT markets are also necessarily small. Thus, IT product exports have been chosen as a measure of the development of IT industries for those countries. Since they have only limited product lines and small internal markets, exports are a good indicator of total IT production. This measure does not specify the quality of the exports, whether locally designed and manufactured products, vertical production, or products assembled from imported components and re-exported. Unfortunately, such data are not available.

The second measure is the number of firms engaged in the IT industry and their size relative to firms in other industries. While there are no consistent data on this item, it does provide some indication of industry development.

The third measure chosen was the number of IT firms listed on local and foreign stock exchanges. This measure is somewhat more problematic, for at least three reasons:

1. It reflects financing strategies chosen by entrepreneurs and firms. These strategies are influenced by factors such as availability and attractiveness of other types of funding, interest rates, exchange rates and so forth. Thus, they do not directly reflect the condition of a country's IT industry.
2. It reflects investor perceptions of the country in question and of its IT industry and is not necessarily an objective measure, especially in the short run until markets have learned the attributes of the industries involved.

3. The question arises whether the ability of an IT industry to raise capital on stock markets is an indicator of development, or perhaps rather a reason for success. At the very least, there is something of a reinforcing effect in which successful IPOs breed an industry that, if successful, in turn encourages the market.

In spite of these shortcomings, we nevertheless feel that this is a useful indicator of industry development, or at least the degree to which it is perceived to be a success.

The data for 1998 on the three measures for the four countries studied are exhibited in Table 3.

From Table 3 we see that IT exports relative to GDP vary from 0.87% for New Zealand up to 9.5 % for Israel with Finland at 6.19%, and Singapore with 4.14%. This ranking is repeated for IT exports per capita which range from $133 for New Zealand to $1,756 for Israel with Finland and Singapore at $1,518 and $1,191 respectively.

An additional measure in Table 3 is stock market listings. In spite of the reservations mentioned above, this measure is some indication of the level of activity in the IT industries and the number of firms active in them. Again, the data indicate Israel in the top ranking followed by Finland, Singapore, and New Zealand, in that order.

The final measure in Table 3 is the number of IT firms among the largest firms in the country. Here, again, the same rankings are evident as in the previous two measures. Israel and Finland rank first and second; New Zealand and Singapore have nearly the same ranking. Table 4 summarises the rank orders of the four countries on the measures used.

The consistency of the results would seem to support the conclusion that in terms of success in developing IT industries, the overall ranking is Israel, Finland, Singapore, and New Zealand, in that order.

In conclusion, it seems that all four countries in the study have developed indigenous IT industries, albeit with varying levels of prominence. The remainder of this article attempts to tease out the causes of the differences in level of IT industry development.

The model presented in Figure 1 has much in common with that of the Global Competitiveness Yearbook (IMD, 1999). Because of this similarity, it is of interest to consider whether the global competitiveness factors can explain the observed differences in IT industry success in the countries studied. The comparison in Table 5 of the global competitiveness rankings with the IT industry development rankings defined previously indicates little correlation. This is true of the overall rankings and holds by and large for the detailed competitiveness factors. Thus, Israel and New Zealand have about the same competitiveness rankings (24 and 20 respectively) but are at opposite ends of the IT industry development ranking. We can only conclude that the global competitiveness factors, while making sense at the level of the total economy, are probably too coarse to capture the specific items which contribute to IT industry development as defined above. It is the objective of the rest of this paper to identify these specific items.

Next we compare the development data from 1994 with the current data. Unfortunately, the 1994 data for Finland were not available in the earlier study (Ein-Dor et al., 1997). Data for the three countries for which data are available for both 1994 and 1998 (Table 6) indicate rapid growth during that period. Total IT exports grew by 250% for

Table 3. IT industry development and success measures

IT Industry Development	Finland	Israel	New Zealand	Singapore
Number and size of IT firms				
Firms in IT:	4200[1]	n.a.	2529[4]	5500[1]
IT firms/largest firms	4/50 = 8%[2]	40/150 = 27%	12/200[5] = 6%	25/400 = 6%[2]
IT industry employment	5.5%[3]	4.0%[2.6]	2.6% (1996)[1]	6.1%
locally developed products		H/W & S/W	SW/HW	H/W & S/W
IT exports:				
Hardware	7,255m[4]	$7,784m[1]	$281m[1]	$3,710m[3]
Software	$488[1]	$1,601m[5]	$198m[1]	$0.46bn[3]
Total	$7,743	$9,385m	$479m	$4.17bn[3]
IT exports per capita	$1518	$1756.3	$133.1	$1191.4
IT exports/GDP	6.19%	9.50%	0.87%	4.94%
IT stock market listings				
Domestic	27[5]	ca. 80[3]	3[2]	35[4]
Foreign	1	ca. 80[4]		2[5]

Sources. **Finland (1)** *Nygard, Ann Marie and Kunnas, Tarja. (1998).* Computer Networking Hardware/ Software. *Finland: International Trade Administration. (2) Finnfacts. (12/11/1999).* 50 Largest Finnish Companies. *www.finnfacts.com/Ffeng0399/record_profits.htm (3) Statistics Finland. (1999a).* On the Road to the Finnish Information Society - Summary. *www.stat.fi/tk/yr/tttietoti_en.html (4) Statistics Finland. (1999b).* Production and Foreign Trade of High-Technology Products. *www.stat.fi/tk/yr/tthuippu1_en.html. (5) Helsinki Stock Exchange. (1999).* Listed Companies. *www.hex.fi/eng/listed_companies/*

Israel (1) *Central Bureau of Statistics. (August 1999). (2) Central Bureau of Statistics. (October 1999). (3) Tel-Aviv Stock Exchange (1999). (4) NASDAQ lists 96 Israeli companies (http://www.nasdaq.com/ reference/israel_companies.stm). A quick scan of the list indicates that 76 of these are in IT. A few Israeli companies are listed on other exchanges, so 80 is probably a good estimate of the current total number of Israeli IT companies listed abroad. (5) Koren. (January 25, 2000), Keren, Tsuriel . (Jan 25, 2000). (6) Breakdown of IT industry employees (7) Dun & Bradstreet Israel Ltd.*

New Zealand (1) *Ministry of Commerce.* Statistics on Information Technology in New Zealand. *Wellington (April, 1999). (2) The New Zealand Company Registrar 1996-97 – 35th Edition (April 1999), Prepared by Headliner Publishing Co. Published by Mercantile Gazette Marketing Ltd., Christchurch. (3) Government web page. www.govt.nz. Stats from Statistics NZ. (4) NZ Computer Industry Directory 1999. A Computerworld publication. Published by IDG Communications (5) 1998 Top 200 New Zealand Companies. Deloitte & Touche Consulting Group.* Management Magazine *(1999), 45(11), 74-87.*

Singapore *(1) IDC Singapore. The classification covers computer and telecommunication hardware and software; IT and telecommunication services; and high-tech office equipment. Nearly 87% are small enterprises that employ less than 25 people. (2) Several large IT firms are subsidiaries of large multinationals. (3) National Computer Board, Singapore.* IT Focus, *(1998). This gives 1997 figures. Flat growth for 1998 is assumed due to the Asian economic crisis. (4) This figure was obtained by studying the background and activities of companies in the Stock Exchange of Singapore database. (5) Two more Singapore companies, Chartered Semiconductors and Pacific Internet, were listed on NASDAQ in 1999.*

Table 4. IT development rankings for four countries

	IT exports/ GDP	IT exports per capita	Stock market listings	IT firms/ largest firms
Finland	2	2	2	2
Israel	1	1	1	1
New Zealand	4	4	4	3
Singapore	3	3	3	3

Table 5. Global competitiveness rankings versus IT industry development rank

	IT industry development rank	Overall competitiveness	Domestic economy	Internationalization	Government	Finance	Infrastructure	Management	Science & technology	People	Mean (columns 3-10)
Israel	1	24	22	23	29	24	25	14	15	19	21.375
Finland	2	3	4	11	10	8	2	3	6	1	12.500
Singapore	3	2	18	2	1	9	13	4	12	4	6.750
New Zealand	4	20	31	33	9	18	14	10	24	16	20.375

Table 6. Changes in IT industry development measures

Industry Development	Israel 1994	Israel 1998	New Zealand 1994	New Zealand 1998	Singapore 1994	Singapore 1998
IT product sales:						
IT industry sales	$4.15bn	$7.78bn	$1.5bn	$3.46bn	$1.56bn	$4.17bn
IT sales/GDP	6% of GDP	9.5%	3.5% of GDP	3.5%	3.8% of GDP	4.9%
Number and size of IT firms						
firms in IT:	350		300	2529	600	5500
IT firms/largest firms	34/200=17%	40/150=27%	15/200=7.5%	12/200=6%	6/400=1.5%	25/400=6%
IT industry employment	3.3%	4.0%[2,6]	2.8%	2.6%	10%	6.1%
IT exports:						
Hardware	$2.50bn	$7.78bn[1]	$58m	$281m	n.a.	$3.71bn
Software	$0.17bn	$1.60bn[5]	$59m	$198m	n.a.	$0.46bn
Total	$2.67bn	$9.38bn	$117m*	$479m	$494	$4.17bn
stock market listings	35	ca. 80[3]	2	3	7	35
domestic	30	ca. 80[4]	-		2	2
foreign						

Table 7. Population and economic development

Country	Population (millions)	Per Capita GDP	Land area km^2
Finland	5.1	22,121	337,030
Israel	5.6	17,276	21,950
NZ	3.6	15,470	267,800
Singapore	3.5	25,059	625

Sources. The International Program Center (IPC) of the US Bureau of the Census (1998) and World Economic Forum (1999).

Israel, 310% for New Zealand, and a remarkable 744% for Singapore. It is true that the total world IT market expanded rapidly during this period, but it would seem that these three countries expanded their roles within it more than proportionately.

Control Variable — Country Size

Country size is the control variable in this study. By country size, we are referring mostly to population and economic development figures, rather than land area. We believe that land area is unlikely to be significant with regard to the IT industry. The data for 1998 for all four countries are summarized in Table 7 (more detail is provided in Table 2).

It can be seen that all four countries are quite alike in terms of population and all fall within European levels of per capita GDP.

Exogenous Variables

Resources

Of the countries studied, only New Zealand has significant quantities of natural resources. However, as was found in previous studies, natural resources are not a significant requirement for IT industry development. In fact, many of the countries with successful IT industries tend to be resource-poor. Examples not in our study are Taiwan, Hong Kong, and Ireland. Thus, this is a factor that may be dropped from future considerations of IT industry development.

Proximity to Markets

For bulky goods, proximity to markets is still an important factor determining trade patterns. Even with the advent of the global economy, it appears that most countries still trade mainly with others in their own region. This is reflected in Table 8, which exhibits the trading patterns for the countries in this study.

The foreign trade patterns of the four countries are very different. The USA is the major export market for Israel and Singapore and an important one for New Zealand, but not for Finland. Beyond that, two of the countries trade mainly with their nearest neighbours — Europe for Finland, the Pacific area for New Zealand. Israel and Singapore differ from this pattern in that their main trading partner is the USA; beyond that, Singapore trades mainly with neighboring Asian countries while Israel trades further afield because of political tensions between Israel and its nearest neighbors. In general,

Table 8. Leading export partners — 1999

Finland		Israel		New Zealand		Singapore	
Germany	11.0%	USA	32.1%	Australia	20.2%	USA	18.4%
UK	10.0%	UK	6.2%	Japan	14.5%	Malaysia	17.5%
Sweden	9.8%	Hong Kong	5.3%	USA	10.4%	Hong Kong	9.6%
Russia	7.3%	Belgium/Lux.	5.0%	UK	6.2%	Japan	7.1%
		Japan	4.6%			Thailand	4.6%
		Netherlands	4.4%			Taiwan	4.5%

Source. The Economist. Pocket World in Figures (1999).

Table 9. Hofstede scores for countries studied

	Finland	Israel	New Zealand	Singapore
power distance (PDI)	33	13	22	74
uncertainty avoidance (UAI)	59	81	49	8
individuality (IDV)	63	54	79	20
masculinity (MAS)	26	47	58	48

Source. Hofstede (1980).

the pattern is one of countries trading with their nearest neighbours, despite the current rhetoric associated with globalisation.

In the context of this article, the question is whether proximity to markets has any effect on the development of IT industries. From the above data, it would appear not. Finland is the only country in the study close to all its major markets. The other three countries trade with a mix of countries near and far. This is the case for *total* exports. Given the ease with which almost all IT products can be rapidly delivered anywhere in the world, the conclusion would seem to apply even more forcibly to IT products.

Culture

In most previous papers, researchers have concluded that culture is not a major factor explaining differences in IT industry development. However, the evidence provided has been largely circumstantial and so we decided to examine this conclusion further. Hofstede (1980) has frequently been to the basis for studies of the effect of cultural differences in the IS setting. Table 9 and Figure 2 exhibit Hofstede's scores for the four countries in this study on the four factors he examined — power distance, uncertainty avoidance, individualism, and masculinity.

Figure 2 exhibits the scores by IT industry development ranking. The most striking feature of these data is the almost total lack of consistency. Individuality and masculinity show no relationship to our development ranking. Power distance and uncertainty avoidance suggest a relationship to the success ranking for ranks 1 to 3. However, fourth ranked New Zealand controverts that suggestion by being the closest to first ranked Israel on those two factors. We conclude that these particular measures of culture are not closely related to IT industry success.

Figure 2. Hofstede's international differences in work-related values (Hofstede, 1980)

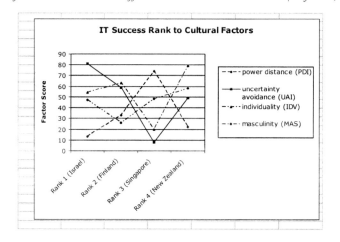

Given the considerable cultural differences between the countries and the fact that all four have substantial IT industries, this supports previous studies showing the relatively unimportant role of culture (Ein-Dor et al., 1997). It should be noted, however, that Hofstede did find some correlations between his dimensions and levels of economic activity. For example "the one consistent correlate (of UAI with economic activity) is faster economic growth with higher UAI" (p. 154). The UAI curve does not support this with respect to IT industry development.

Other studies have begun to question the importance of culture in economic development. Thus, a recent article argues that what are frequently known as "Asian" or "Confucian" values are not the dominant force in Asia's recent economic success that they are often held out to be (*The Economist,* 2000). Rather, cultural values of the type quoted may be a result of a level of economic development, not its determinant. Thus, personal and family connections (*guanxi*), frequently identified with Asian entrepreneurship, were equally representative of earlier stages of European economic development; the Rothschild, Thyssen, Siemens, and Wallenberg families are just a few examples that come to mind. It is argued that, with their development, Asian economies are now beginning to emulate the modern capitalist structures of the West, thereby emulating its historical development.

However, the seeming lack of connection between Hofstede's four dimensions of culture and IT industry development does not necessarily mean that culture is unimportant. There may be other cultural dimensions that come into play or cultural factors that are mediated by other variables such as the role of government. At the very least, there is a need to consider the interplay between culture and government policies that attempt to change it. However, a consideration of culture at this level of analysis is outside the scope of this article.

SUMMARY OF
EXOGENOUS VARIABLES

In summarising our discussion of exogenous variables, we can conclude that the existence of natural resources and proximity to major markets has little effect on IT industry success. The effects of national culture are less clear-cut. However, given the variety of cultures exhibited by the countries studied, it seems that there is no obvious relationship between cultural factors and IT industry development. If this is so, then exogenous factors play a minor role in IT industry success and we must look for endogenous factors to explain some of the findings on IT industry success.

Endogenous Variables

Domestic IT Use

High levels of domestic IT use might be assumed to be a factor promoting the domestic IT industry. In fact, the government of Singapore has for many years now encouraged IT use for precisely that reason. However, the data do not seem to support this assumption very strongly.

Our analysis is based on two objective items and two opinion survey items. The objective data are the number of PCs and number of Internet servers relative to population; these are generally considered good measures of levels of IT use. The opinion data are from surveys of managers reported in The Global Competitiveness Report 1999 and refer to diffusion of computer use and management use of computers.

Addressing first the objective data, these are exhibited in Table 10 and Figure 3 (which is a graphic representation of the levels of IT use relative to IT industry development rankings); there seems to be no consistent relationship between the two. Israel, with the highest IT industry development ranking, has the lowest domestic use of IT. Finland, second in the success rankings is first in domestic IT use.

The subjective data provide some insight into the perceptions of managers concerning the use of IT in their countries. These data are exhibited in Table 11.

Table 12 combines the objective and subjective data. These data have been normalised to permit simultaneous presentation of different dimensions and scaling. In every case in which data have been normalised, the normalisations are specified after the table. The normalised data are exhibited in Figure 4. The figure shows that Finland completely dominates the other three countries in terms of domestic IT use. On every dimension except diffusion, Israel is dominated by at least two other countries.

Table 10. Measures of domestic IT use by IT industry development rankings

	Israel	Finland	Singapore	New Zealand
Development ranking	1	2	3	4
Internet hosts/1M[1]	14692.3	94581.5	18561.3	44676.0
PCs/1000 pop.[1]	219.3	354.0	315.5	319.6

Source. World Economic Forum (1999)

Figure 3. Domestic IT use to IT success ranking

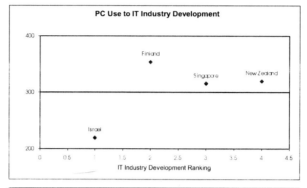

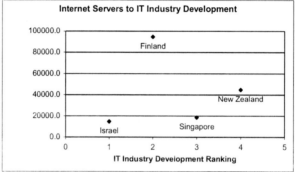

Table 11. Perceptions of IT use by IT industry development rankings

	Israel	Finland	Singapore	New Zealand
Development ranking	1	2	3	4
Diffusion of IT use[1]	6.61	6.84	6.58	6.51
Management use[2]	5.87	6.21	6.02	6.52

Source. World Economic Forum (1999). (1) The use of computers is highly sophisticated and widespread (2) Managers personally use computers and information technology extensively.

These results merit some thought. It is quite possible that domestic IT use plays an important role in promoting IT industries in large countries; this is almost certainly the case with respect to the US, and probably also applies to China. However, when the local market is small, firms wishing to play a role in the IT industries must perforce look for markets elsewhere and the level of domestic use may be irrelevant. Further evidence for this argument may be supplied by India, which has a burgeoning IT industry but a relatively low level of domestic IT use.

Table 12. Computer use

	Development rank	Diffusion[1] - actual	Diffusion[1] normalized	Management use[2] actual	Management use[2] normalized	Internet hosts per 1 million population	PCs per 1000 population
Israel	1	6.61	5.56	5.87	5.51	1.09	3.41
Finland	2	6.84	6.84	6.21	6.21	7.00	5.50
Singapore	3	6.58	5.39	6.02	5.82	1.37	4.91
New Zealand	4	6.51	5.00	5.62	5.00	3.31	4.97

Source. World Economic Forum (1999). (1) The use of computers is highly sophisticated and widespread (2) Managers personally use computers and information technology extensively. Normalization: Diffusion and Management Use extended to the range 5 to the maximum value for the item. Internet hosts and PCs per 1000 population proportionately normalized to the range 0 to 7.

Figure 4. Dimensions of domestic IT use

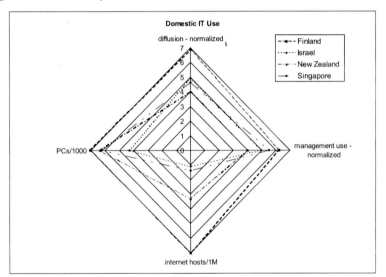

This is not to imply that encouragement of domestic use is wasted effort. While encouraging domestic IT use of itself may not directly encourage IT industries, it may play an important role in preparing cadres of people with the requisite skills to permit development of such an industry. In any case, it is hardly likely that a policy of encouraging domestic IT use would have any negative effects on IT industry development; in the worst case, it may not be quite as beneficial as supposed.

Table 13. Education data

	Development rank	Education expenditure as % of GDP[1]	Math and Science Education - score[2]	Math and Science Education - rank	Tertiary education Enrolment - rank[3]
Israel	1	7.2	5.10	12	23
Finland	2	7.6	6.48	12	4
Singapore	3	3.0	5.49	1	26
New Zealand	4	7.3	4.00	35	7

Source. Item 1. UNESCO, Items 2-3. World Economic Forum (1999). (1) Percent of GDP. (2) "The school system excels in math and basic science education. (1=strongly disagree, 7 = strongly agree)". (3) Enrolment as % of population of designated age.

Table 14. Education data — Normalized

	Development rank	Education expenditure as % of GDP[1]	Math and Science Education[2]	Tertiary education Enrolment[3]
Israel	1	6.63	5.10	4.28
Finland	2	7.00	6.48	7.00
Singapore	3	2.76	5.49	4.00
New Zealand	4	6.72	4.00	5.88

Source. Item 1. UNESCO, Items 2-3. World Economic Forum (1999). (1) Percent of GDP - normalized on interval 0-7. (2) The school system excels in math and basic science education. (1=strongly disagree, 7 = strongly agree) Given a top score close to 7, left unnormalized. (3) Enrolment as % of population of designated age. Normalized on interval 4-7.

Human Capital

As defined earlier, human capital is a set of skills a population can acquire by education and training. The data presented here on education are from the World Economic Forum's (1999) rankings and survey of managers and from UNESCO's data on education budgets. The data are exhibited in Tables 13 and 14 and in Figure 5. Please note that the math and science education ranks represent managers' subjective feelings about the state of education in their countries, whereas the education expenditure and tertiary enrolment data are objective findings. The data in Table 14 and Figure 5 have been normalised as specified following the table.

Figure 5. Education system dimensions

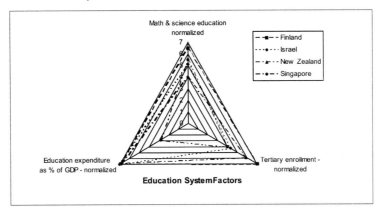

According to Figure 5, Finland leads in all three dimensions, although the education expenditures of Israel and New Zealand are, in percentage, very close. These data contain some surprising elements.

First is the very low percentage of GDP spent by Singapore on education. (It should be noted, however, that education accounts for 23% of the total government budget.) This is even more surprising when taken together with the high score on math and science education. One can only conclude that Singapore's education system must be remarkably efficient compared to the others.

A second surprise is that New Zealand's high rate of tertiary enrolment does not seem to have had a great impact on its IT industries. This might be explained by the way tertiary students are distributed across the various disciplines.

A third surprise is that Israel scores third on math and science education and yet has managed to lead the four countries studied in IT industry development. One plausible explanation is the large number of well-trained scientists and engineers who immigrated to Israel in the 1990s and may have compensated for deficiencies in the education system. Thus, Israel may be living on borrowed time unless it can upgrade its educational system. On the other hand, it should be noted that much of Israel's IT industry is in the hands of start-up ventures with young managers, many of them graduates of ICT training in the Israel Defence Forces (Ariav & Goodman, 1994). Thus, relevant military training and experience are probably also factors compensating for the less developed public education system.

R&D and Technological Infrastructure

Research and development are usually acknowledged as important underpinnings of high tech industry success. This is often buttressed by evidence that "Silicon Valley" type development is at least partly due to the proximity of high standard academic institutions. Data on percent of GNP devoted to research and number of researchers relative to population are exhibited in Table 15. Table 16 exhibits sources of R&D funds.

Table 15. National R&D outlays and numbers of researchers

	Rank	Research as % of GNP				Researchers/1M inhabitants			
Israel	1	2.23	(1989)	2.35	(1997)	4,828	(1984)	5087	(1997)
Finland	2	1.20	(1987)	2.70	(1997)	2,146	(1987)	2,799	(1995)
Singapore	3	0.91	(1984)	2.32	(1995)	930	(1984)	2,318	(1995)
New Zealand	4	0.95	(1989)	1.04	(1995)	1,450	(1989)	1,663	(1995)

Source. UNESCO Statistical Yearbook 1999. *Selected R&D Indicators.*
Note: Data for the number of researchers in Israel are not available for recent years. The number for 1997 was computed by multiplying the number of researchers in 1984 by the increase in % of GDP devoted to R&D between 1989 and 1997 (5.4%); this is clearly a very conservative estimate.

Table 16. Distribution of R&D funds by sector of origin

	IT Industry Rank	Business enterprise	Government	Higher education	Private non-profit	Funds from abroad
Israel 1995	1	35.7	40.7	10.2	7.0	6.5
Finland 1995	2	57.7	37.4	0.4	—	4.5
Singapore 1995	3	62.5	31.4	2.4	—	3.7
New Zealand 1993	4	33.9	54.7	8.9	—	2.4

Table 15 indicates that the development rankings closely reflect the number of researchers per million population. Table 16 shows that Israel has a higher percentage of its R&D outlay originating in universities and that it also has a higher percentage of its research funded from abroad than do the other countries. This presumably has a twofold effect; foreign funded R&D is frequently also channelled to universities from bi-national funds (e.g., joint Israel-German and Israel-US funds) and international organisations such as the European Union research programs. On the basis of the perception that high-tech industries develop in proximity to clusters of universities, we speculate that university R&D provides the greatest spur to IT industrial development. It should also be noted that in 1989, Israel spent a much larger portion of its GNP on R&D than did the other countries at that time, so there may well be a cumulative effect which was still being felt. It is also quite possible that the substantial growth in the R&D expenditures of Finland and Singapore will be reflected in their industries when more recent data become available.

In the other two dimensions — research institutions and scientists and engineers — Finland is second to Israel. While it is intuitively obvious that these dimensions promote IT industry development, the data underscore this perception. It is not clear why Finland's lead in the educational factors and technological sophistication does not translate into a lead in the other two dimensions. One plausible explanation is, again, the

Figure 6. IT industry development relative to government R&D funding

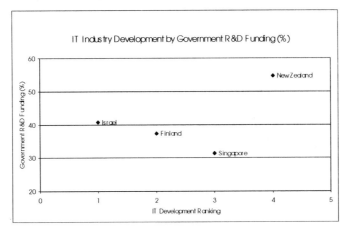

Table 17. Technology infrastructure scores

	Development Ranking	Technological Sophistication[1]	Scientists and Engineers[2]	Research Institutions[3]	Technological Sophistication[1] Normalized	Scientists and Engineers[2] Normalized	Research Institutions[3] Normalized
Israel	1	5.82	6.32	6.32	5.58	6.32	6.32
Finland	2	5.95	5.89	5.79	5.95	5.77	5.51
Singapore	3	5.65	5.62	4.80	5.10	5.42	4.00
New Zealand	4	5.26	4.52	5.10	4.00	4.00	4.46

Source. World Economic Forum (1999). (1) Overall, your country is a world leader in technology. (2) Scientists and engineers are prevalent and of high quality. (3) Scientific research institutions are truly world class.
Normalization. All data normalized on the interval 4-7.

large number of scientists and engineers who immigrated to Israel in the 1990s, many of whom gravitated to research institutions and so may have compensated for its less developed education sector.

These data do not accord very well with the model of Grossman and Helpman (1989, 1991). Their analysis found that the first-best growth path "can be attained with subsidies to both R&D and the production of intermediates". The second-best growth path can be achieved with subsidies to R&D alone. However, the success rankings developed here bear only a tenuous relationship to the portion of R&D funding provided by the

Table 18. Technology infrastructure rankings

	Development Ranking	Technological Sophistication[1]	Scientists and Engineers[2]	Research Institutions[3]
Israel	1	7	1	2
Finland	2	5	9	7
Singapore	3	9	13	21
New Zealand	4	16	44	17

Source. World Economic Forum (1999). (1) Overall, your country is a world leader in technology. (2) Scientists and engineers are prevalent and of high quality. (3) Scientific research institutions are truly world class.

Table 19. Innovation rankings

	UIF[1]	DIF[2]	Innovation Factor
Finland	2	5	3
Israel	4	19	16
New Zealand	20	16	18
Singapore	10	17	16

Source. World Economic Forum (1999). (1) Upstream Innovation Factor rank. (2) Downstream Innovation Factor Rank

Figure 7. R&D and technological sophistication

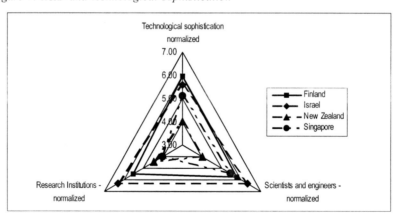

Source. The International Program Center (IPC) of the US Bureau of the Census (1998) and World Economic Forum (1999).

Table 20. Elements of firm strategies

	Development rank	MCI[1]	Obtaining Technology[2]	International Brands[3]	Absorbing new technology[4]	Competitive Advantage[5]	Exporting Companies[6]
Score							
Israel	1	20	5,74	4.66	5.79	5.86	5.59
Finland	2	2	5.74	5.84	6.16	5.84	5.58
Singapore	3	12	4.33	4.56	5.53	5.21	5.21
New Zealand	4	16	4.72	5.39	5.35	4.62	4.82
Rank							
Israel	1	20	3	22	6	7	11
Finland	2	2	3	7	2	10	13
Singapore	3	12	23	25	16	21	16
New Zealand	4	16	14	15	9	14	20

Source. World Economic Forum (1999). (1) Microeconomic Competitiveness Index rank. (2) Companies obtain technology by pioneering their own new products or processes. (3) Companies, which sell internationally, have developed their own international brands. (4) Companies are aggressive in absorbing new technology. (5) Competitive advantages of your nations companies in international markets are due to unique products and processes. (6) Exporting companies conduct not only production, but product development, distribution, and marketing.

government; this is highlighted by the fact that New Zealand has the highest proportion of government R&D funding, as exhibited in Figure 6. Another point of interest in the data is that the highest business and lowest government contributions to R&D are in Singapore.

In addition to R&D outlays, an important factor in developing high-tech industries is the nature of the technological infrastructure, the environment within which R&D take place. Table 17 exhibits survey data on managerial perceptions of three infrastructure items — national technological sophistication, availability and quality of scientists and engineers, and quality of research institutions. Table 18 exhibits country rankings on the same items. The data are displayed graphically in Figure 7.

The data on technological sophistication appear to paint a clear picture in which Israel leads in scientists and engineers and research institutions and is second on technological sophistication. As mentioned, Israel has been fortunate in the influx of trained personnel it experienced with the break up of the Soviet Union and also has highly regarded research institutions. Thus it would seem that there is a clear relationship between these items and IT industry development.

As a final element of technological infrastructure, Table 19 exhibits innovation rankings. These indicate that Israel, New Zealand and Singapore are ranked very closely

Figure 8. Firm strategy dimensions

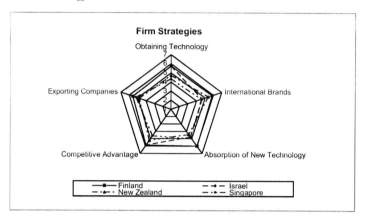

on this factor while Finland is ranked much more highly. The case of Israel is rather interesting as its ranking is composed of a very high upstream innovation factor (UIF) and a rather low downstream innovation factor (DIF). This apparently reflects the nature of Israeli R&D, which is very innovative, but less successful in marketing the resulting innovations.

Firm Strategies

Firm strategies are characterised here by five elements — the method by which technology is obtained, the development of international brands, absorption of new technology, the uniqueness of products, and the breadth of the value chain. These data, together with the questions asked are exhibited in Table 20. As a matter of interest, the microeconomic competitiveness index ranks are also exhibited. The data are displayed graphically in Figure 8.

The picture arising in this connection is rather an interesting one. Finnish firms clearly have the best-rounded strategy, scoring highly on all five dimensions. Singapore's strategy is concentrated on export companies managing a large portion of the value chains for their products. New Zealand's strategies are based on internationally known brand names and on unique products and processes. Israel is roughly equal to Finland on three of the dimensions — pioneering own technologies, unique products and processes, and coverage of the value chain, while scoring much lower than Finland on absorption of new technology and brand names. Thus, it would seem that firms concentrating on the three dimensions common to Finland and Israel are best placed in terms of IT industry development.

Availability of Capital

The availability of capital to fund new start-ups and to maintain existing firms and their growth is clearly a major factor in IT industry development. This is not a purely

Table 21. Availability of capital rankings

	Development rank	Venture Capital Availability[1]	Gross domestic investment rank[2]	R&D Spending[3]	Domestic IT Stock Market Listings[4]	Foreign Stock Market Listings[4]
Israel	1	5.51	20.71	5.32	80	80
Finland	2	5.05	19.00	5.53	27	1
Singapore	3	3.77	32.10	4.59	35	2
New Zealand	4	4.59	20.12	3.85	3	0
normalized						
Israel	1	5.51	4.1	5.32	6.7	6.7
Finland	2	5.05	3.8	5.53	2.5	0.1
Singapore	3	3.77	6.4	4.59	3.2	0.1
New Zealand	4	4.59	4.0	3.85	0.3	0

Source. Items 1-3 World Economic Forum (1999), Items 4 see Table 3. (1) Venture capital is readily available for new business development - not normalised. (2) Percent of GDP (top part of column). Normalised to 0-7 interval by division by 5 (bottom part of column). (3) "The business sector spends heavily on R&D." (4) Normalised in chart by division by 12.

endogenous factor as, in addition to local availability of capital, it also depends on exogenous factors such as the availability of foreign direct investment, ability to raise capital overseas, and so forth. However, foreign capital is most readily available when the internal situation is favorable and, in that sense, even foreign investment may be viewed, at least in part, as an endogenous factor. Data on some elements of capital availability are exhibited in Table 21 and charted in Figure 9. The elements listed are availability of venture capital, gross domestic investment, R&D spending, and IT stock market listings, both domestic and foreign. It should be noted that only the last of these relate directly to IT industries; however, in countries with important IT sectors, much of other sources are invested in IT.

Based on these data, it appears that, overall, capital is more readily available in Israel than elsewhere, especially by means of stock offerings. Singapore is clearly endowed with high domestic investment, but overall availability is about on a par with Finland. Capital seems to be least available in New Zealand.

As the capital availability data seem to follow the IT industry ranking quite closely, it would appear that this is indeed an important factor determining IT industry success.

CONCLUSIONS

In this article we have provided an in-depth analysis of the IT industry in four countries: Finland, Israel, New Zealand and Singapore. We have also presented the relative changes that occurred over the period 1994 through 1998. We believe that our use of both longitudinal and time slice data represents a considerable advance over

Figure 9. Availability of capital

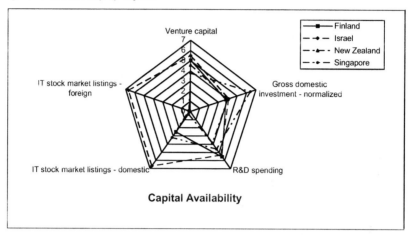

Capital Availability

earlier studies of a similar nature. As such, this paper represents one of the first attempts to provide a comprehensive picture of the factors affecting IT production in small developed countries over time. The findings are probably also more broadly applicable to knowledge use and knowledge based industries in general and to small countries in particular.

The primary purpose of this article has been to identify the key drivers in fostering IT industry success in these countries. Given that IT industries provide a technical platform for innovation and are a key component in fostering the development of the knowledge economy, we believe that such a quest is well justified.

Our study has revealed that four of the six endogenous variables have a close relationship to the success of IT industries in small developed countries. Our analysis thus largely supports the model of IT industry success developed earlier (Figure 1). Research and development, technological infrastructure, firm strategies, and capital availability all appear to have significant impacts on the development of IT industries.

Rather surprising are our findings that domestic IT use and education seem to have little impact. In the case of domestic use we surmise that this is because of the nature of IT industries in small countries, in which the local market is not a dominant factor. In the case of education, the finding may be an artefact of the small sample size and of the special case of Israel with massive immigration of scientists and engineers within that small sample. It may also indicate that education is a necessary but not a sufficient factor in IT industry success.

We believe our findings have important implications for researchers and policy makers interested in the relationship between the production and use of information technology (IT) and economic development. Many countries around the world are looking for ways to promote the development of the knowledge economy, and information technology industries in particular. Our article suggests that policy makers need to concentrate on fostering research and development, the technological infrastructure, firm strategies and capital availability if they wish to promote the development of indigenous IT industries.

Finally, we recommend that our findings should be treated with caution. The constructs that we have developed need further refinement and additional efforts need to be made to develop universal and consistent data sources. Much additional research is required, and especially research which looks at a broader range of countries, both small and large. Given a large enough sample, it should be possible to apply statistical testing, thus lending greater credibility to any relationships found. We do believe, however, that our present findings represent one step towards understanding the factors that affect the development of IT industries in small developed countries, and may be relevant to other countries as well.

REFERENCES

Ariav, G., & Goodman, S.E. (1994). Israel: Of swords and software plowshares. *Communications of the ACM, 37*(6), 17-21.

Blanning, R.W., Bui, T.X., & Tan, M. (1997). National information infrastructure in Pacific Asia. *Decision Support Systems, 21,* 215-227.

Central Bureau of Statistics (Israel). (1999, August). Exports by economic branch. *Monthly Bulletin of Statistics, 50*(8).

Central Bureau of Statistics (Israel). (1999, October). K. labour and wages. *Monthly Bulletin of Statistics, 50*(10).

Dedrick, J.L., Goodman, S.E., & Kraemer, K.L. (1995). Little engines that could: Computing in small energetic countries. *Comm. of the ACM, 38*(5), 21-26.

Dedrick, J.L., & Kraemer, K.L. (1995). National technology policy and computer production in Asia-Pacific countries. *Information Society, 11,* 29-58.

Dedrick, J.L., & Kraemer, K.L. (1998). *Asia's computer challenge: Threat or opportunity for the United States and the world?* New York: Oxford University Press.

Deloitte & Touche Consulting Group. (1998). 1998 top 200 New Zealand companies. *Management Magazine, 45*(11), 74-87.

Dun & Bradstreet Israel Ltd. (n.d.). *Leading industrial companies by sales revenue: 150 Companies.*

The Economist. (1999). *Pocket world in figures.* London: Profile Books.

The Economist. (2000, April 29-May 5). *Asian capitalism: The end of tycoons.*

Ein-Dor, P., Myers, M.D., & Raman, K.S. (1997). IT in three small developed countries. *Journal of Management Information Systems, 13*(4), 61-89.

Finnfacts. (1999). *50 largest Finnish companies.* Retrieved November 11, 1999: *www.finnfacts.com/Ffeng0399/record_profits.htm*

Finnish Newspapers Association. (2000). Facts about the Finnish press. Retrieved May 17, 2000: *http://www.sanoma lehdet.fi/en/tietoa/graafi1.shtml#3*

Grossman, G., & Helpman, E. (1989). Growth and welfare in a small open economy. Working paper no. 2970. National Bureau of Economic Research. Cambridge, MA.

Grossman, G., & Helpman, E. (1991). *Innovation and growth in the global economy.* Cambridge, MA: MIT Press.

Hofstede, G. (1980). *Culture's consequences: International differences in work-related values.* Beverly Hills, CA: Sage Publications.

IMD. (1999). *The world competitiveness yearbook 1999.* Lausanne.

K-III Reference Corporation. (1997). *The world almanac and book of facts 1997.*

Keren, T. (2000, January 25). 99 software exports up 33% to $2 Bln. *Globes.*

Koren, O. (1999, November 22). The export institute: 2000 will be a turning point in exports; will grow by 6% - to 17 billion dollars. *Ha'aretz.*

Kraemer, K.L., King, J.L., & Gurbaxani, V. (1992). Economic development, government policy, and the diffusion of computing in Asia-Pacific countries. *Public Administration Review, 52*(2), 146-156.

Ministry of Commerce. (1999, April). *Statistics on information technology in New Zealand.* Wellington.

National Computer Board, Singapore. (1998). *IT Focus.*

New Zealand Company Registrar 1996-97 (35th ed.). (1999, April). Prepared by Headliner Publishing Co. Published by Mercantile Gazette Marketing Ltd., Christchurch.

Nygard, A.M., & Kunnas, T. (1998). *Computer networking hardware/software.* Finland: Int. Trade Administration.

NZ Computer Industry Directory 1999. (1999) A Computerworld publication. Published by IDG Communications.

Romer, P.M. (1990). Endogenous technological change. *The Journal of Political Economy, 98*(5), Part 2, S71-S102.

Statistics Finland. (1999a). *On the road to the Finnish information society - Summary.* Retrieved from http://www.stat.fi/tk/yr/tttietoti_en.html

Statistics Finland. (1999b). *Production and foreign trade of high-technology products.* Retrieved from http://www.stat.fi/tk/yr/tthuippu1_en.html

Statistics New Zealand. (1998). *New Zealand official yearbook* (101st ed.). Wellington, NZ: Department of Statistics.

Tel-Aviv Stock Exchange. *Electronics and computer listings.* Retrieved November 17, 1999, from http://www.tase.co.il/qsystem/index.cgi?subsection

UNESCO Institute for Statistics. *Public expenditure on education as percentage of gross national product and as percentage of government expenditure.* Retrieved September 28, 2000, from http://unescostat.unesco.org/i_pages/IndPGNP.asp

UNESCO Institute for Statistics. *UNESCO statistical yearbook 1999.* Science and technology: III.1 Selected R&D indicators. Retrieved from http://unescostat.unesco.org/statsen/statistics/yearbook/tables/

UNESCO Institute for Statistics. *UNESCO statistical yearbook 1999. Science and technology: III.3 Percentage distribution of gross domestic expenditure on R&D by source of funds.* Retrieved from http://unescostat.unesco.org/statsen/statistics/yearbook/tables\SandTec\

United Nations Development Program. (1999). Human Development Index (HDI). *Human development report 1999.* Retrieved July 7, 2000, from http://www.undp.org/hdro/HDI.html

U.S. Bureau of the Census. (1999). Report WP/98. *World population profile, 1998.* Washington, D.C.: U.S. Government Printing Office. Retrieved from http://www.census.gov/ftp/pub/ipc/www

Watson, R., & Myers, M.D. (2001). IT industry success in small countries: The case of Finland and New Zealand. *Journal of Global Information Management, 9*(2), 4-14.

World Bank. (1999). *World development report 1998/99: Knowledge for development.* Washington: World Bank. Retrieved from http://www.worldbank.org/wdr/wdr98/

World Economic Forum. (1999). *The global competitiveness report 1999.* Geneva, Switzerland.

This article was previously published in the *Journal of Global Information Management,* 12(4), pp. 23-49, © 2004.

Chapter II

Levels of Culture and Individual Behavior:
An Integrative Perspective

Elena Karahanna, University of Georgia, USA

J. Roberto Evaristo, University of Illinois, USA

Mark Srite, University of Wisconsin - Milwaukee, USA

ABSTRACT

In an organizational setting, national culture is not the only type of culture that influences managerial and work behavior. Rather, behavior is influenced by different levels of culture ranging from the supranational (regional, ethnic, religious, linguistic) level through the national, professional, and organizational levels to the group level. The objective of this study is to integrate these different levels of culture by explicitly recognizing that individuals' workplace behavior is a function of all different cultures simultaneously. It is theorized that the relative influence of the different levels of culture on individual behavior varies depending on the nature of the behavior under investigation. Thus, for behaviors that include a strong social component or include terminal and moral values, supranational and national cultures might have a predominant effect. For behaviors with a strong task component or for those involving competence values or practices, organizational and professional cultures may dominate. These propositions are illustrated with examples from the IS field. This paper is a conceptual study and therefore extends theory and the current understanding of how culture is examined by not only explicitly recognizing that behaviors are simultaneously influenced by multiple levels of culture but by also specifying conditions under which certain levels of culture dominate. Such an approach has the potential to inform researchers and practitioners about the generalizability or universality of theories and techniques across national, organizational, and professional borders.

INTRODUCTION

The significant changes in the work environment of the past two decades have highlighted the importance of cross-cultural variables in management theories. These changes include the globalization of the market, the emergence of the virtual organization whose members do not meet face-to-face but are linked through computer technology, the increased focus on teamwork, the emergence of high technology telecommunication systems, increased immigration, and unification and separatism in the political arena. As a result, cultural differences have become a focus of attention and their effect on work behavior is becoming increasingly evident (Erez & Earley, 1993). Theories developed in one country have met with limited success when applied to other settings (Hofstede, 1993). Thus, a major question that cross-cultural research in business attempts to answer is: "Why are successful managerial theories and techniques not found to be uniformly effective across cultural borders?" To understand why managerial practices and techniques differ in multiple cultures and why the transfer of certain techniques across cultures is not always effective, we should learn more about the role that culture plays in our theories of work behavior. Toward this end, some research has focused on examining the impact of national culture on work behaviors.

Clearly, however, in an organizational setting, national culture is not the only culture that influences managerial and work behavior. Culture can be defined on different levels of analysis ranging from the national level through the professional and organizational levels to the group level (Hofstede, 1991). Thus, research has focused on these other levels of analysis. For example, organizational culture can have a strong effect on beliefs, attitudes, and behavior of individuals within the organizational boundaries (Martin, 1992; Schein, 1985; Schein, 1990). Furthermore, since within one nation or within one organization there can be many subcultures (e.g., professional associations, political parties, ethnic groups), individuals' work behavior may also be influenced by the norms and values of these subcultures (Schein, 1990; Triandis, 1972). Recent research (Straub et al., 2002) based on Social Identity Theory (SIT) has proposed that these levels interact. They propose that different layers of culture can influence an individual's behavior and that each individual is influenced more by certain layers and less by other layers depending on the situation and their own personal values.

Additionally, a recent issue of *IEEE Transactions on Engineering Management* focused on cultural issues. Of the eight articles, three (Ford, Connelly, & Meister, 2003; Loch, Straub, & Kamel, 2003; Rose, Evaristo, & Straub, 2003) focused on national culture, while three (Doherty & Doig, 2003; Huang, Newell, Galliers, & Pan, 2003; Ngwenyama & Nielsen, 2003) focused on organizational culture. However, the remaining two articles examined more than one type of culture. Tan, Smith, Keil, and Montelegre (2003) looked at the impact of organizational climate on two different national cultures (individualistic and collectivistic). Finally, Weisinger and Trauth (2003) discussed IT management issues and how they are affected by national culture, IT industry (professional) culture, and organizational culture. Though not exhaustive, Table 1 presents the various levels of culture studied in IS research and illustrates the rareness of multilevel cultural studies.

In a similar vein, based on evidence in the literature (e.g., Gregory, 1983; Martin & Siehl, 1983; Maynard-Moody, Stull, & Mitchell, 1986; Meyer, 1982; Reynolds, 1986; Rose, 1988; Smircich, 1983; Trice & Beyer, 1984; Van Maanen & Barley, 1984, 1985), Jermier, Slocum, Fry, and Gaines (1991) question the assumption that organizations comprise monolithic cultures. Instead, they suggest that multicultural models consisting of multiple cultures, subcultures, and countercultures better represent contemporary organizations.

Although the monolithic cultural perspective explanation employed by the majority of the studies is clearly better than no explanation at all, a deeper understanding and better predictive and prescriptive power will be gained by recognizing, utilizing, and integrating the different cultural perspectives that exist (Evaristo & Mullins, 1994).

The objective of this study is to integrate these different levels of analysis by explicitly recognizing that individuals' workplace behavior is a function of all different cultures simultaneously. However, it is theorized that the relative influence of the different levels of culture on individual behavior varies depending on the nature of the behavior under investigation. This study has the potential to inform researchers and practitioners about the

Table 1. Levels of culture studied in representative IS studies

Author	Year	Level(s) Studied
Cougar	1986	National
Delong & Fahey	2000	Organizational
Dohery & Doig	2003	Organizational
Ford, Connelly, & Meister	2003	National
Gold, Malhotra, & Segars	2001	Organizational
Grover, Teng, & Fiedler	1998	Organizational
Hasan & Ditsa	1999	National
Hill, Loch, Straub, & El-Sheshai	1998	National
Huang, Newall, Galliers, & Pan	2003	Organizational
Jarvenpaa & Leidner	1998	National
Jarvenpaa & Staples	2001	Organizational
Keil et al.	2000	National
Leidner and Carlsson	1999	National
Loch, Straub, & Kamel	2003	National
Meijas, Shepherd, & Morgan	1996	National
Ngwenyama & Nielsen	2003	Organizational
Png, Tan, & Wee	2001	National
Rose, Evaristo, & Straub	2003	National
Straub	1994	National
Tan, Smith, & Keil	2003	National & Organizational
Tan, Watson, & Wei	1995	National
Tan, Wei, Watson, & Walczuch	1998	National
Tan, Wei, Watson, Clapper, & McLean	1998	National
Watson, Ho, & Raman	1994	National
Weisinger & Trauth	2003	National, Professional, & Organizational

generalizability or universality of theories and techniques across national, organizational, and professional borders. The influence of culture on individual behavior has been illustrated with examples from the IS field.

In particular, the research will focus on behaviors of individuals with respect to information technology. Even though great progress has been made in cross-cultural research in information systems, more studies are needed to develop theories that make *à priori* predictions on the influence of culture on the transfer of IS software, hardware, and practices (Gallupe & Tan, 1999). This study is conceptual in nature and aims at enhancing our understanding of the cross-cultural applicability of our theories and at informing the practice of technology transfer (Boyacigiller & Adler, 1991). As noted above, cultural research, with some exceptions, has been primarily conducted at a single cultural level. This is the driver behind the manuscript's integrated focus at a conceptual level. This paper can be seen as a first step in a more complex conceptualization of culture. Suggestions for empirically testing our model are provided at the end of the paper.

THEORETICAL FRAMEWORK

Before discussing and integrating different levels of culture, a general definition of culture that encompasses all of its different levels needs to be provided. Kroeber and Kluckholn (1952) define culture as:

Patterned ways of thinking, feeling and reacting, acquired and transmitted mainly by symbols, constituting the distinctive achievements of human groups, including their embodiments in artifacts; the essential core of culture consists of traditional (i.e., historically derived and selected) ideas and especially their attached values. (p. 86)

Another definition of culture is given by Triandis (1972).[1]

[Subjective] culture is defined as an individual's characteristic way of perceiving the man-made part of one's environment. It involves the perception of rules, norms, roles, and values, is influenced by various levels of culture such as language, gender, race, religion, place of residence, and occupation, and it influences interpersonal behavior. (p. 4)

The above definitions are presented to show the variability across cultural definitions. For a more extensive discussion on how culture has been defined and conceptualized, see Straub et al. (2002). Although the definitions by Kroeber and Kluckholn (1952) and Triandis (1972) enfold the various levels of culture, they are somewhat complex and unwieldy. A similar but more parsimonious definition of culture provided by Hofstede (1984) will be used in this research. Hofstede defines culture as "the collective programming of the mind which distinguishes the members of one human group from another" (p. 260). He further suggests that several layers of cultural programming exist that encompass the range of cultures operative on one's behavior (Hofstede, 1991). These layers of culture consist of national, regional/ethnic/religious/linguistic, gender, generation, social class, and organizational cultures.

Table 2. Levels of culture

Level	Definition
Supranational • Regional • Ethnic • Religious • Linguistic	Any cultural differences that cross national boundaries or can be seen to exist in more than one nation. Can consist of: • Regional – Pertaining to a group of people living in the same geographic area • Ethnic – Pertaining to a group of people sharing common and distinctive characteristics • Linguistic – Pertaining to a group of people speaking the same tongue
National	Collective properties that are ascribed to citizens of countries (Hofstede, 1984)
Professional	Focus on the distinction between loyalty to the employing organization versus loyalty to the industry (Gouldner, 1957)
Organizational	The social and normative glue that holds organizations together (Siehl & Martin, 1990)
Group	Cultural differences that are contained within a single group, workgroup, or other collection of individuals at a level less than that of the organization

We elaborate further on these layers to create a hierarchy of cultural layers, as shown in Table 1. Regional, ethnic, religious, and linguistic affiliations can span national cultures and, as a result, can be considered as supranational dimensions of culture, constituting the highest level in the hierarchy. Social class, as defined by Hofstede (1991), is associated with educational opportunities and a person's occupation or profession. In an organizational environment, this is likely to refer to one's professional culture, and it is defined as such in Table 1. In addition to organizational culture, group culture has also been added to the hierarchy of cultures. Ongoing groups develop their own values and norms over time and thus have their own culture. With the increasing importance and frequency of teamwork in both traditional and virtual groups, group culture is likely to become an important factor in the interactions and effectiveness of groups. The various layers of culture and their definitions are shown in Table 2.

As can be inferred by the definitions presented above, the various levels of culture are both hierarchically and laterally related (Figure 1). For example, ethnic culture can span nations (such as people of Irish descent having immigrated but somewhat kept the culture of their home country) or be a smaller part of a single country (Maoris in New Zealand). Similar arguments can be made for religious, linguistic, and other levels of culture. This relationship across levels of culture is not necessarily hierarchical from the more general (supranational) to the least general (group). For instance, in the case of multinational corporations, organizational culture can span national, religious, ethnic, regional, linguistic, and professional cultures. Furthermore, groups may include members from several organizations, professions, nations, religions, ethnic backgrounds, regions, and linguistic backgrounds. These interrelations are shown diagrammatically in Figure 1 using overlapping and nested ellipses.

In Figure 1, the ellipse labeled *Individual* does not represent another layer of culture but rather shows how an individual's culture is the product of several levels of culture. Each individual belongs to a specific ethnic, linguistic, and national culture. Individuals may also have a religious orientation, a professional degree, and work in an organization. Some of these cultures may dominate depending on the situation. The cultures that enfold the individual interact and derive the individual's unique culture, eventually influencing the individual's subsequent actions and behavior.

Figure 1. Interrelated levels of culture (Adapted from Karahanna, Evaristo, & Srite, 1998)

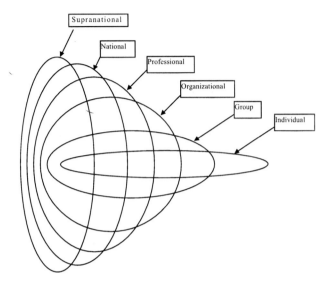

VALUES AND PRACTICES

Looking back at the definitions of culture presented earlier, two critical components are the presence of values (other cultural definitions that include values are Kroeber, 1952; Parsons & Shils, 1951; McClelland, 1961; Kluckholn & Strodbeck, 1961; Murdock, 1965; and Lachman, 1983) and practices. Values refer to relationships among abstract categories that are characterized by strong affective components and imply a preference for a certain type of action. According to Rokeach (1973, p. 5), a value is an enduring belief that a specific mode of conduct or end-state of existence is personally or socially preferable to an opposite or converse mode of conduct or end-state of existence. A value system is an enduring organization of beliefs concerning preferable modes of conduct or end-states of existence along a continuum of relative importance.

Values are acquired through lifestyle altering experiences, such as childhood and education. Typically, values are acquired early on in life through the family and neighborhood and later through school. They provide us with fundamental assumptions about how things are. Once a value is learned, it becomes integrated into an organized system of values where each value has a relative priority. This value system is relatively stable in nature but can change over time reflecting changes in culture (e.g., migration or values imparted by a professional culture, such as the professional values of physicians or accountants) as well as personal experience. Therefore, individuals based on their unique experiences not only differ in their value systems, but also in the relative stability of these value systems.

Figure 2. Values and practices

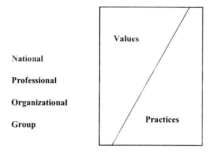

Practices are learned later through socialization at the workplace after an individual's values are firmly in place. They provide us with learned ways of doing things, such as facts about the world, how it works, and cause-effect relationships. Among others, symbols, heroes, and rituals are all learned practices (Hofstede, 1991). Whereas values are fairly hard to change, practices can be altered. A similar distinction between values and practices is made by Erez and Earley (1993). They make the distinction between peripheral values (i.e., practices) that can change through life and core values (i.e., values) that are acquired in youth and are difficult to change. Similarly, Jermier et al. (1991) make a distinction between an organizational culture's *ideational* component that consists of covert layers of meaning anchored in shared values, beliefs, and assumptions and its *material* component that consists of the tangible manifestations of the ideational component (e.g., rituals) and is anchored in norms and practices.

A key issue that emerges is the relationship between values and practices (or core and peripheral values or the ideational and material components). The literature suggests that the two are intertwined. Values are affected by practices (or the environment) during the formative years in which values are starting to form. Later on in life, practices do not influence values. Conversely, practices are always evolving. Ideally, practices should reflect values and be in sync with them, but that is not always the case. We suggest that this discontinuity typically occurs when practices dictated by one level of culture (e.g., organizational) are at odds with values comprising another level of culture (e.g., national). In fact, practices are much more related to current environmental conditions.

A good example of national values being out of sync with organizational or professional practices might exist in software development teams. Individualism is a national cultural value that is generally prominent in the United States. However, software is typically developed by project teams, an organizational and professional practice that is contrary to a national culture with individualistic values. Supranational and national cultural differences are composed primarily of differences in values and, to a lesser extent, of differences in practices (Hofstede, 1991). These values are acquired early in childhood in one's family, neighborhood, and school. Progressively, however, as we transcend the various levels of culture shown in Figure 1, the balance between

Figure 3. Theoretical model

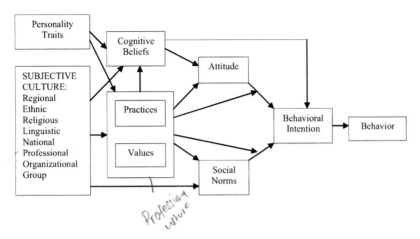

values and practices changes, and practices become a more predominant component of lower level cultures. For example, professional culture implies the acquisition of both values and practices, whereas organizational culture is composed primarily of shared perceptions of organizational practices and, to a lesser extent, of values. Figure 2, adapted from Hofstede (1991) illustrates the relative importance of values and practices at various levels of culture. Values are more important than practices in the higher level cultures (i.e., supranational), and practices and norms dominate for the lower level cultures (i.e., group). Consequently, it is likely that an individual's *values* are predominantly influenced by supranational (e.g., ethnic or religious) and national levels of culture. An individual's *practices*, on the other hand, would be influenced primarily by professional and organizational cultures.

In addition to the relative balance of values and practices across different levels of culture, we also suggest that the nature of values promoted by different levels of culture may also vary. For instance, Rokeach (1973) suggests various categories of values, such as terminal values that are further subdivided into personal and social values and instrumental values that are further subdivided into moral and competence values. As we elaborate in the next section, different levels of culture are likely to influence different types of values.

We stated above that various levels of culture interact to form an individual's culture and to shape behavior. It is our contention, however, that depending on the behavior, different levels of culture will have a dominant influence on an individual's actions. Building on the fact that national and supranational levels of culture influence one's values, then it follows that behaviors that involve consideration of values as a major component of the decision as to whether to engage in a behavior will be influenced by national and supranational cultures. On the other hand, behaviors that involve practices will more likely be influenced by professional and organizational cultures.

Theoretical Model

The theoretical model for the study ensuing from the above discussion is presented next and shown in Figure 3. The model derives its structure from theories of behavior in social psychology, such as the Theory of Reasoned Action (Fishbein & Ajzen, 1975) and the model of subjective culture (Triandis, 1972).

Consistent with the Theory of Reasoned Action (TRA), which has received considerable empirical support, we suggest that behavioral intentions toward a specific behavior are the best predictors of the behavior. In turn, intentions are determined by one's attitude toward the behavior (e.g., Davis, Bagozzi, & Warshaw, 1989; Fishbein & Ajzen, 1975; Karahanna, Straub, & Chervany, 1999; Mathieson, 1991; Morris & Venkatesh, 2000; Taylor & Todd, 1995; Thompson, Higgins, & Howell, 1994) and the normative pressures one feels from important referents to perform or not perform the behavior (indicated as the social norms box in Figure 3) (e.g., Fishbein & Ajzen, 1975; Karahanna et al., 1999; Morris & Venkatesh, 2000; Taylor & Todd, 1995; Venkatesh & Davis, 2000; Venkatesh & Morris, 2000; Venkatesh, Morris, & Ackerman, 2000; Venkatesh, Morris, David & Davis, 2003). While the Theory of Reasoned Action (Fishbein & Ajzen, 1975) states that attitude fully mediates the influence of cognitive beliefs on behavioral intention, studies in information systems (e.g., Davis, 1989; Venkatesh & Davis, 2000) have shown that some cognitive beliefs, such as perceived usefulness, also have a direct effect on behavioral intention over and above their effect via attitude. Thus, consistent with the literature, a direct link is posited between cognitive beliefs and intended behavior. In turn, attitude, or one's positive or negative affect toward the behavior, is influenced by one's cognitive beliefs about the consequences of the behavior. For example, there is abundant empirical evidence (e.g., Adams, Nelson, & Todd, 1992; Agarwal & Karahanna, 2000; Davis, Bagozzi, & Warshaw, 1989; Gefen & Straub, 2000; Gefen, Karahanna, & Straub, 2003; Karahanna et al., 1999; Plouffe, Hulland, & Vandenbosch, 2001; Straub, Limayem, & Karahanna, 1995; Taylor & Todd, 1995; Venkatesh & Davis, 2000) that perceptions of usefulness and ease of use, the key constructs in the widely used Technology Acceptance Model (Davis, 1989), are antecedent cognitive beliefs to attitude toward using information technology and to behavioral intention. Additional cognitive beliefs used in the literature include characteristics of innovations (Rogers, 1983), such as compatibility, image, result demonstrability, and visibility (Agarwal & Prasad, 1997, 1998; Karahanna et al., 1999; Moore & Benbasat, 1991, 1996; Plouffe et al., 2001; Taylor & Todd, 1995; Venkatesh & Davis, 2000).

In this study and consistent with Triandis (1972), we propose that values are also important antecedents (or moderators) of cognitive beliefs, attitudes, and social norms and thus of behavior (also see Bandura, 1977). The role of values in attitude models in IS research has been largely ignored, possibly due to the fact that most research was performed in single cultures (both organizational and national). Therefore, values might have been of little consequence for explaining variation due to the fact that they differed little among the subjects. However, given the prominence of values in national and supranational cultures, we believe that values should be a central construct in our model. Two notable exceptions are Seligman (2001) and Srite and Karahanna (2000). Seligman (2001) examined the effect of the professional values of physicians, nurses, and administrators on acceptance of a new information system. Srite and Karahanna (2000) examined the effect of espoused national cultural values on the acceptance of information systems. Their results indicate that these values moderate the relationship between social norms and acceptance behaviors as well as the relationship between cognitive beliefs and acceptance behaviors.

In addition to values, existing practices may also be important antecedents or moderators of technology acceptance constructs and relationships. For instance, in the case of adoption of an innovation, existing practices will determine the relative advantage of the innovation and also its compatibility, which have been consistently shown to be significant antecedents of attitude toward adopting the innovation. Additional support derives from the Task-Technology Fit Theory (Goodhue, 1995; Goodhue & Thompson, 1995), which suggests that perceptions of usefulness, as well as the performance impact of the technology, will depend on the fit between the task and practices at hand and the capabilities afforded by the technology.

We propose that values and practices are in turn influenced by culture and personality traits. Social learning theory (Bandura, 1977) suggests that one's behavior is a function of one's personality and environment. Consistent with the Theory of Reasoned Action, we posit that these effects of environment (which consist of culture among other factors) and personality on behavior are mediated by values and the constructs in the TRA, that is, attitudes and social norms. Finally, the causal link between culture on one hand and values and practices on the other has been discussed extensively in the previous section. Specifically, as we argued in the previous section, a person's value set that eventually determines behavior does not merely consist of the values dictated by a specific culture. Rather, it is an amalgamation or function of all the various levels of culture (e.g., national, organizational, professional) to which the individual belongs:

$$\text{Subjective Cultural Values} = \Sigma(W)c_i Vc_i$$

where C_i is a particular layer of culture to which an individual belongs, Wc_i is the weight or level of influence of the specific culture for the behavior in question, and Vc_i is the specific value set that the specific culture espouses. The cultures included (C_i) depend on an individual's specific background, whereas their weights (Wc_i) depend on the particular behavior in question. In other words, the relative influence of a specific level of culture on behavior (i.e., its $(W)c_i$) will vary depending on the specific nature of the behavior. In the next section, we elaborate further on this topic and present specific propositions and hypotheses.

THEORETICAL PROPOSITIONS

Work behavior involves both a task dimension, concerned with the technical aspects of performing the behavior, and a relationship or social dimension, concerned with interactions with others in the organization as part of the behavior. For example, using electronic mail involves both the actual technical knowledge of how to use the system and a social component dealing with communicating with colleagues. The social component of behaviors is influenced to a large extent by an individual's value system. Individuals learn how to socialize and interact with others early on in life, and thus national culture plays an important role in acquiring values regarding socialization (Hall,

1981, 1982). The task component primarily refers to the "how to" of a behavior, and thus it predominantly involves practices. Therefore, one would expect national and supranational cultures to predominantly influence behaviors that involve a social dimension and professional, organizational, and group cultures to predominantly influence behaviors involving task dimensions. Most of the IS-related behaviors, such as adoption, display a mix of social elements and task components. Therefore, it is imperative to understand, for the particular product or service in question, which one may be prevalent. For instance, for the adoption of a new virtual work environment, the social component is likely to be more prevalent, whereas for the adoption of a new word processor, the task component is likely to dominate.

For example, the national cultural dimension of individualism/collectivism might play an important role in the adoption of group-based technologies, such as LotusNotes (a technology that has social implications) or, as empirically shown by Ho, Raman, and Watson (1989), for GDSS. However, a strong organizational culture might influence the adoption, acceptance, and use of a mandated new technology, such as an ERP system that is more task-focused.

Proposition 1: Behaviors involving a social element will be primarily influenced by national and supranational cultures, whereas behaviors involving a task component will be primarily influenced by professional, organizational, and group cultures.

A deeper understanding of the interplay between values and culture can be gained by referring to Rokeach's (1973) typology of values. Values are prescriptive or proscriptive types of beliefs[2] that denote if some means or end of action is judged to be desirable and undesirable. As such, like all beliefs, they have a cognitive, affective, and connative or behavioral component. If an individual has a value then that individual cognitively knows the correct way to behave or the correct end-state to strive for. The individual also feels emotional about the value, affectively either for or against it, and approving or disapproving of others who exhibit positive or negative instances of it. Finally, values lead to action. Values can be either instrumental or terminal. Instrumental values refer to desirable modes of conduct. Terminal values refer to desirable end-states. Instrumental values can be further subdivided into moral values and competence values. Whereas moral values (e.g., honesty, forgiveness, salvation, helpfulness) have an interpersonal focus and arouse feelings of guilt when violated, competence (or self-actualization) values are personal in nature (e.g., behaving logically and intelligently, imaginative, independent), and their violation leads to feelings of shame about personal inadequacy rather than feelings of guilt about wrongdoing (see Appendix A for a more comprehensive list of values). Similarly, terminal values are subdivided into personal and social values (Rokeach, 1973). Personal values are self-centered and intrapersonal (for instance, peace of mind, true friendship, self-respect, inner harmony), whereas social values are society-centered and interpersonal in nature (such as world peace, equality, national security, freedom).

More recent research on values has elaborated on Rokeach (1973) to derive motivational domains of values (Schwartz & Bilsky, 1987). This theoretical structure was tested cross-culturally with Israeli and German respondents. In both samples, there was

Table 3. Specific predictions

Practices[*]	Terminal Values		Instrumental Values	
	Personal Values	Social Values	Moral Values	Competence Values
Supranational	√	√	√	√	
National	√	√	√	√	
Professional	√			√	√
Organizational	√				√
Group	√				√

* A smaller check mark indicates a smaller indirect effect as indicated by Proposition 5

a clear empirical distinction between terminal and instrumental values. Even though there was general agreement between the two samples as to the domains, some differences emerged in the placement of specific values in the various domains, that is, evidence of the effect of culture on values. For instance, in Israel, freedom was considered to be part of the security domain, whereas in Germany it was viewed as a self-direction value indicating perhaps that freedom has a different meaning in the two countries.

In this study, we chose to use Rokeach's (1973) typology of values. Although other classifications exist, this is the most widely accepted and used classification of values. For example, even though the theoretical classification suggested by Schwartz and Bilsky (1987) has face validity and has received some empirical support in their study, there is insufficient empirical evidence at this point to support their theoretical classification (as compared to the Rokeach's typology).

Based on Rokeach's (1973) typology of values, we can make more specific predictions on the level of culture that influences behavior. In the previous set of propositions, we had indicated that professional culture predominantly influences task-heavy behaviors. Clearly, however, professional culture may in some instances also influence one's values (e.g., physicians, lawyers). Table 3 helps us make a distinction between values influenced solely by supranational and national cultures and values influenced by professional, organizational, and group cultures. Based on Table 3, we posit that the types of values involved at different levels of culture differ. For instance, we know that terminal values include both personal values, such as inner harmony and peace of mind, and social values, such as world peace, freedom, and equality. All these values are clearly related to the supranational level of culture (for instance, inner harmony may be an objective in certain religious cultures) and to the national level as well (freedom and equality are needs at a national level analogous to Hofstede's (1991) power distance dimension of national culture). Power distance could influence the level of computer monitoring accepted by individuals. In a high power distance culture, people will be more willing to allow others to monitor their IT-related behaviors. Additionally, collectivistic and feminine cultures strive for harmony, and consequently, in these cultures one may expect a higher influence of social norms on technology acceptance behaviors (Srite & Karahanna, 2000).

Analogously, the examination of moral values, such as honesty and salvation, suggest that they are also related to supranational and national levels of culture. For instance, at the supranational cultural level, religious principles might invoke moral values that could influence Internet adoption behaviors. For instance, certain individuals might be unwilling to use the Internet due to the possibility of viewing images of a profane nature. Indeed, some countries, based on moral values, have imposed restrictions on sites that can be viewed via the Internet (e.g., China and certain Middle Eastern countries).

On the other hand, we posit that professional cultures involve the acquisition of predominantly moral (i.e., forgiveness) and competence values (i.e., creativity, independence, logical, and intelligent behavior), whereas organizational and group cultures involve predominantly the acquisition of competence values. For example, the nurses' professional culture centers on patient care (a moral value of helpfulness). Adoption of any information system that is perceived to interfere or not contribute toward providing quality patient care is resisted (Seligman, 2001). Competence values, particularly those pertaining to valuing creativity and imagination, may be very pertinent to postadoptive behaviors, such as encouraging exploratory use of the system to find new innovative uses or to employ additional features. Naturally, professional, organizational, and group cultures have strong influences on practices. For instance, software production practice in an organization is strongly influenced by the professional software engineering practices, by the culture of the organization, and for a specific project, by the culture of the project team. Thus:

Proposition 2: Behaviors involving terminal values are primarily influenced by supranational and national levels of culture.

Proposition 3: Behaviors involving moral values are primarily influenced by supranational, national, and professional cultures.

Proposition 4: Behaviors involving competence values are primarily influenced by professional, organizational, and group cultures.

Proposition 5: Behaviors involving practices are primarily influenced by professional, organizational, and group cultures (which are in turn influenced by the national culture within which they operate).

Given a behavior of interest, we can dissect it into its component values and practice dimensions. This determination enables predictions about the specific combination of cultural layers that predominantly influence the behavior.

CONCLUSIONS

The current paper has important theoretical and practical implications. In terms of theory, this is the first paper we are aware of that attempts to integrate and make predictions as to the relative importance of different layers of culture on behavior. Moreover, this essay goes beyond prior discussions of the cultural levels mostly as level of analysis issues (e.g., Hofstede, 1993; Klein & Kozlowski, 2000). It extends the discussion presented by Straub et al. (2002) by identifying conditions that favor dominance of one cultural layer over the others. This breaks new ground by extending the explanatory power of the culture construct in multifarious behaviors. In order to do so, we examine the structure of behaviors along two separate facets: degree of task and social content, and degree to which it encompasses practices, terminal values, and instrumental values. We believe that this extends theory and our understanding of the effects of culture on individual behavior. The most practical aspect of this theoretical advance is to enable future research on the effect of culture on behavior to be more level focused and therefore enhance the chances of not only finding more significant results but also of eliminating possible cultural cross-level behavior confounds that have plagued much of the cross-cultural research in the past.

In terms of contributions to practice, understanding how culture influences behavior, if at all, will increase the efficacy of technology transfer. Based on the type of technology transfer, one can determine whether national and supranational cultures will play a dominant role in individuals' reactions to the technology. If they do, then the firm may need to infuse a cultural component into the new practice to make it more compatible with the extant cultural values. Moreover, a critical consideration is the resulting increased understanding of the dominant cultural level and associated mindset expected in the adoption of a particular innovation or any other managerial behavior of interest. A consequence is that appropriate implementation interventions, localization of the technology, framing of the behavior, and incentives can be designed that address the salient value concerns raised by the introduction of the new technology. This will enable more effective management of potential resistance to the introduced procedure or technology and consequently higher acceptance and utilization.

DIRECTIONS FOR
FUTURE RESEARCH

In this paper, we have developed some high-level propositions derived from an overarching conceptual model linking levels of culture and individual behavior. Clearly, further theoretical development is needed both to elaborate and refine these propositions as well as to define the model at a lower level of abstraction. For instance, national culture can be disaggregated into certain cultural values (e.g., Hofstede, 1984; Hofstede, Bond & Luk, 1993), masculinity/femininity, individualism/collectivism, power distance, uncertainty avoidance, and long-term orientation). Similarly, organizational culture can be disaggregated into certain values, for example, involvement, consistency, adaptability, and mission (Denison & Mishra, 1995), practices (e.g., Hofstede, Neuijen, Ohayv, & Sander, 1990), dimensions of work practices of loose vs. tight control, process vs. results oriented, employee vs. job oriented, parochial vs. professional, open vs. closed environment, and normative vs. pragmatic. These can then be incorporated into a model similar to the one illustrated in Figure 3. Specific hypotheses based on the propositions we have posited and the specific cultural values and practices identified can be developed and then empirically tested across acceptance of two dissimilar IT systems (e.g., acceptance of a system that encompasses a large social component, such as collaborative technologies, versus a system that encompasses a large task component, such as an ERP). To the extent that national and organizational values have significantly different impacts across the two systems (along the lines specified by the propositions), the study can provide empirical evidence to validate the conceptual framework presented above. Similarly, the propositions can be tested through a case study or a series of case studies that can richly examine how the various levels of culture interact and influence IS-related behaviors within an organization.

We hope that the paper can provide other researchers with a new theoretical lens through which to study the impact of culture on behavior. Clearly, to assess the validity of the conceptual framework presented, the model needs to be empirically validated across a number of different levels of culture (national, professional, and organizational) and a number of different behaviors.

REFERENCES

Adams, D., Nelson, R.R., & Todd, P. (1992). Perceived usefulness, ease of use, and usage of information technology: A replication. *MIS Quarterly, 16*(2), 227-248.

Agarwal, R., & Karahanna, E. (2000). Time flies when you're having fun: Cognitive absorption and beliefs about information technology usage. *MIS Quarterly, 24*(4), 665-694.

Agarwal, R., & Prasad, J. (1997). The role of innovation characteristics and perceived voluntariness in the acceptance of information technologies. *Decision Sciences, 28*, 557-582.

Agarwal, R., & Prasad, J. (1998). A conceptual and operational definition of personal innovativeness in the domain of information technology. *Information Systems Research, 9*, 204-215.

Bandura, A. (1977). *Social learning theory*. Englewood Cliffs, NJ: Prentice Hall.

Boyacigiller, N.A. & Adler, N.J. (1991). The parochial dinosaur: Organization science in a global context. *Academy of Management Review, 16*(2), 262-290.

Couger, J.D. (1986). Effect of cultural differences on motivation of analysts and programmers: Singapore vs. the United States. *MIS Quarterly, 10*(2), 198-196.

Davis, F.D. (1989). Perceived usefulness, perceived ease of use, and user acceptance of information technology. *MIS Quarterly, 13*(3), 319-340.

Davis, F.D., Bagozzi, R., & Warshaw, P.R. (1989). User acceptance of computer technology. *Management Science, 35*(8), 982-1003.

DeLong, D.W., & Fahey, L. (2000). Diagnosing cultural barriers to knowledge management. *Academy of Management Executive, 14*(4), 113-127.

Denison, D.R., & Mishra, A.K. (1995). Toward a theory of organizational culture and effectiveness. *Organization Science, 6*(2), 204-223.

Doherty, N.F., & Doig, G. (2003). An analysis of the anticipated cultural impacts of the implementation of data warehouses. *Transactions on Engineering Management, 50*(1), 78-88.

Erez, M., & Earley, P.C. (1993). *Culture, self-identity, and work*. New York: Oxford University Press.

Evaristo, J.R., & Mullins, J. (1994, March). Cross-cultural research in entrepreneurship: A research agenda. *Proceedings of the Fourth Global Entrepreneurial Research Conference, INSEAD,* Fontainbleau, France.

Fishbein, M., & Ajzen, I. (1975). *Belief, attitude, intention, and behavior: An introduction to theory and research*. Reading, MA: Addison-Wesley.

Ford, D.P., Connelly, C.E., & Meister, D.B. (2003). Information systems research and Hofstede's Culture's Consequences: An uneasy and incomplete partnership. *IEEE Transactions on Engineering Management, 50*(1), 8-25.

Gallupe, R.B., & Tan, F.B. (1999, July-September, 5-18). A research manifesto for global information management. *Journal of Global Information Management*.

Gefen, D., & Straub, D.W. (2000). The relative importance of perceived ease-of-use in IS adoption: A study of e-commerce adoption. *Journal of the AIS, 1*(8), 1-30.

Gefen, D., Karahanna, E., & Straub, D.W. (2003). Trust and TAM in online shopping: An integrated model. *MIS Quarterly, 27*(1), 51-90.

Gold, A.H., Malhotra, A., & Segars, A.H. (2001). Knowledge management: An organizational capabilities perspective. *Journal of Management Information Systems, 18*(1), 185-214.

Goodhue, D.L. (1995). Understanding user evaluations of information systems. *Management Science, 41*, 1827-1844.

Goodhue, D.L., & Thompson, R.L. (1995). Task-technology fit and individual performance. *MIS Quarterly, 19*, 213-236.

Gouldner, A.W. (1957). Cosmopolitans and locals: Toward an analysis of latent social roles. *Administrative Science Quarterly, 2*, 281-306.

Gregory, K.L. (1983). Native-view paradigms: Multiple cultures and culture conflicts in organizations. *Administrative Science Quarterly, 28*, 359-376.

Grover, V., Teng, J.T.C., & Fiedler, K.D. (1998). IS investment priorities in contemporary organizations. *Communications of the ACM, 41*(2), 40-48.

Hall, E.T. (1981). *The silent language*. New York: Anchor Books, Doubleday.

Hall, E.T. (1982). *The hidden dimension*. New York: Anchor Books, Doubleday.

Hasan, H., & Ditsa, G. (1999). The impact of culture on the adoption of IT: An interpretive study. *Journal of Global Information Management, 7*(1), 5-15.

Hill, C.E., Loch, K.D., Straub, D., & El-Sheshai, K. (1998). A qualitative assessment of Arab culture and information technology transfer. *Journal of Global Information Management, 6*(3), 29-38.

Ho, T.H., Raman, K.S., & Watson, R.T. (1989, December 10-13). Group decision support systems: The cultural factor. *Proceeedings of the 10th International Conference on Information Systems*, Boston (pp. 119-129).

Hofstede, G. (1984). *Culture consequences*. Newbury Park, CA: Sage.

Hofstede, G. (1991). *Cultures and organizations: Software of the mind*. London: McGraw-Hill.

Hofstede, G. (1993). Cultural constraints in management theories. *Academy of Management Executive, 7*(1), 81-105.

Hofstede, G., Bond, M.H., & Luk, C. (1993). Individual perceptions of organizational cultures: A methodological treatise on levels of analysis. *Organization Studies, 14*(4), 483-503.

Hofstede, G., Neuijen, B., Ohayv, D.D., & Sander, G (1990). Measuring organizational culture: A qualitative and quantitative study across twenty cases. *Administrative Science Quarterly, 35*, 286-316.

Huang, J.C., Newell, S., Galliers, R.D., & Pan, S. (2003). Dangerous liaisons? Component-based developement and organizational subcultures. *Transactions on Engineering Management, 50*(1), 89-99.

Jarvenpaa, S., & Leidner, D.E. (1998). An information company in Mexico: Extending the resource-based view of the firm to a developing country context. *Information Systems Research, 9*(4), 342-361.

Jarvenpaa, S.L., & Staples, S.D. (2001). Exploring perceptions of organizational ownership of information and expertise. *Journal of Management Information Systems, 18*(1), 151-183.

Jermier, J.M., Slocum, J.W., Fry, L.W., & Gaines, J. (1991). Organizational subcultures in soft bureaucracy: Resistance behind the myth and façade of an official culture. *Organization Science, 2*(2), 170-194.

Karahanna, E., Evaristo, J.R., & Srite, M (1998, December 13). Levels of culture and individual behavior: An integrative perspective. *Proceedings of the Annual Cross-Cultural Research Workshop,* ICIS, Helsinki, Finland.

Karahanna, E., Straub, D.W., & Chervany, N.L. (1999). Information technology adoption across time: A cross-sectional comparison of pre-adoption and post-adoption beliefs. *MIS Quarterly, 23*, 183-213.

Keil, M., Tan, B.C.Y., Wei, K., Saarinen, T., Tuunainen, V., & Wassenaar, A. (2000). A cross-cultural study on escalation of commitment behavior in software projects. *MIS Quarterly, 24*(2), 295-325.

Klein, K., & Kozlowski, S. (2000). *Multilevel theory, research, and methods in organizations.* San Francisco: Jossey-Bass.

Kluckholn, C., & Strodbeck, F.L. (1961). *Variations in value orientations.* Evanston, IL: Row and Peterson.

Kroeber, A.L. (1952). *The nature of culture.* Chicago: Chicago University Press.

Kroeber, A.L., & Kluckholn, C. (1952). *Culture: A critical review of concepts and definitions.* New York: Vintage Books.

Lachman, R. (1983). Modernity change of core and peripheral values of factory workers. *Human Relations, 36*, 563-580.

Leidner, D.E., & Carlsson, S. (1999). Mexican and Swedish managers. Perceptions of the impact of EIS on organizational intelligence. *Decision Sciences, 30*(3), 633-661.

Loch, K.D., Straub, D.W., & Kamel, S. (2003). Diffusing the Internet in the Arab world: The role of social norms and technological culturation. *Transactions on Engineering Management, 50*(1), 45-63.

Martin, J. (1992). *Cultures in organizations: Three perspectives.* Oxford, UK: Oxford University Press.

Martin, J., & Siehl, C. (1983). Organizational culture and counterculture: An uneasy symbiosis. *Organizational Dynamics, 12*(2), 52-64.

Mathieson, K. (1991). Predicting user intentions: Comparing the technology acceptance model with the theory of planned behavior. *Information Systems Research, 2*, 173-191.

Maynard-Moody, S., Stull, D.D., & Mitchell, J. (1986). Reorganization as status drama: Building, maintaining, and displacing dominant subcultures. *Public Administration Review, 46*, 301-310.

McClelland, D.C. (1961). *The achieving society.* Princeton, NJ: Van Nostrand.

Mejias, R.J., Shepherd, M.M., & Morgan, M. (1996). Consensus and perceived satisfaction and consensus levels: A cross cultural comparison of GSS and non-GSS outcomes within and between the US and Mexico. *Journal of Management Information Systems, 13*(3), 137-161.

Meyer, A.O. (1982). How ideologies supplant formal structures and shape responses to environments. *Journal of Management Studies, 19*, 45-61.

Moore, G.C., & Benbasat, I. (1991). Development of an instrument to measure the perceptions of adopting an information technology innovation. *Information Systems Research, 2*, 192-222.

Moore, G.C., & Benbasat, I. (1996). Integrating diffusion of innovations and theory of reasoned action models to predict utilization of information technology by end-users. In K. Kautz & J. Pries-Hege (Eds.), *Diffusion and adoption of information technology* (pp. 132-146). London: Chapman and Hall.

Morris, M.G., & Venkatesh, V. (2000). Age differences in technology adoption decisions: Implications for a changing workforce. *Personnel Psychology, 53*, 375-403.

Murdock, G.P. (1965). *Culture and society*. Pittsburgh: University of Pittsburgh Press.

Ngwenyama, O., & Nielsen, P.A. (2003). Competing values in software process improvement: An assumption analysis of CMM from an organizational culture perspective. *Transactions on Engineering Management, 50*(1), 100-112.

Parsons, T., & Shils, E.A. (1951). *Toward a general theory of action*. Cambridge, MA: Harvard University Press.

Plouffe, C.R., Hulland, J.S., & Vandenbosch, M. (2001). Research report: Richness versus parsimony in modeling technology adoption decisions—Understanding merchant adoption of a smart card-based payment system. *Information Systems Research, 12*, 208-222.

Png, I.P.L., Tan, B.C.Y., & Wee, K. (2001). Dimensions of national culture and corporate adoption of IT infrastructure. *IEEE Transactions on Engineering Management, 48*(1), 36-45.

Reynolds, P.D. (1986). Organizational culture as related to industry, position and performance. *Journal of Management Studies, 23*, 333-345.

Rogers, E. (1983). *Diffusion of innovations* (3rd ed.). New York: Free Press.

Rokeach, M. (1972). *Beliefs, attitudes and values*. San Francisco: Jossey-Bass.

Rokeach, M. (1973). *The nature of human values*. New York: Free Press.

Rose, G.M., Evaristo, R., & Straub, D. (2003). Culture and consumer responses to Web download time: A four-continent study of mono and polychronism. *Transactions on Engineering Management, 50*(1), 31-44.

Rose, R. (1988). Organizations as multiple cultures: A rules theory analysis. *Human Relations, 41*, 139-170.

Schein, E.H. (1985). *Organizational culture and leadership*. San Francisco: Jossey-Bass.

Schein, H.E. (1990). Organizational culture. *American Psychologist, 45*(2), 109-119.

Schwartz, S.H., & Bilsky, W. (1987). Toward a universal psychological structure of human values. *Journal of Personality and Social Psychology, 53*(3), 550-562.

Seligman, L. (2001). *Perceived value impact as an antecedent of perceived usefulness, perceived ease of use, and attitude*. Unpublished doctoral dissertation, University of Texas at Austin.

Siehl, C., & Martin, J. (1990). Organizational culture: A key to financial performance? In B. Schneider (Ed.), *Organizational climate and culture*. San Francisco: Jossey-Bass.

Smircich, L. (1983). Concepts of culture and organizational analysis. *Administrative Science Quarterly, 28*, 339-358.

Srite, M., & Karahanna, E. (2000, December 10). A cross-cultural model of technology acceptance. *Proceedings of the Annual Diffusion of Innovations Group in Information Technology (DIGIT)*, Charlotte, North Carolina.

Straub, D. (1994). The effect of culture on IT diffusion: Email and fax in Japan and the U.S. *Information Systems Research, 5*(1), 23-47.

Straub, D., Limayem, M., & Karahanna, E. (1995). Measuring system usage: Implications for IS theory testing. *Management Science, 41*, 1328-1342.

Straub, D., Loch, K., Karahanna, E., Evaristo, J.R., & Srite, M. (2002). Toward a theory based measurement of culture. *The Journal of Global Information Management, 10*(1) 13-23.

Tan, B.C.Y., Smith, H.J., Keil, M., & Montelegre, R. (2003). Reporting bad news about software projects: Impact of organizational climate and information asymmetry in an individualistic and a collectivistic culture. *Transactions on Engineering Management, 50*(1), 64-77.

Tan, B.C.Y., Watson, R.T., & Wei, K. (1995). National culture and group support systems: Filtering communication to dampen power differentials. *European Journal of Information Systems, 4*, 82-92.

Tan, B.C.Y., Wei, K.K., Watson, R.T., Clapper, D.L., & McLean, E. (1998). Computer-mediated communication and majority influence: Assessing the impact in an individualistic and a collectivist culture. *Management Science, 44*(9), 1263-1278.

Tan, B.C.Y., Wei, K., Watson, R.T., & Walczuch, R.M. (1998). Reducing status effects with computer-mediated communication: Evidence from two distinct national cultures. *Journal of Management Information Systems, 15*(1), 119-141.

Taylor, S., & Todd, P.A. (1995). Understanding information technology usage: A test of competing models. *Information Systems Research, 6*(2), 144-176.

Thompson, R.L., Higgins, C.A., & Howell, J.M. (1994). Influence of experience on personal computer utilization: Testing a conceptual model. *Journal of Management Information Systems, 11*, 167-187.

Triandis, H.C. (1972). *The analysis of subjective culture*. New York: John Wiley & Sons.

Trice, H.M., & Beyer, J.M. (1984). Studying organizational cultures through rites and ceremonials. *Academy of Management Review, 9*, 653-669.

Van Maanen, J., & Barley, S.R. (1984). Occupational communities: Culture and control in organizations. *Research in Organizational Behavior, 6*, 287-65.

Van Maanen, J., & Barley, S.R. (1985). Cultural organization: Fragments of a theory. In P. Frost et al. (Eds.), *Organizational culture* (pp. 31-53). Beverly Hills, CA: Sage.

Venkatesh, V., & Davis, F.D. (2000). A theoretical extension of the technology acceptance model: Four longitudinal field studies. *Management Science, 46*, 186-204.

Venkatesh, V., & Morris, M.G. (2000). Why don't men ever stop to ask for directions? Gender, social influence, and their role in technology acceptance and usage behavior. *MIS Quarterly, 24*, 115-139.

Venkatesh, V., Morris, M.G., & Ackerman, P.L. (2000). A longitudinal field investigation of gender differences in individual technology adoption decision making processes. *Organizational Behavior and Human Decision Processes, 83*, 33-60.

Venkatesh, V., Morris, M.G., David, G.B., & Davis, F.D. (2003). User acceptance of information technology: Towards a unified view. *MIS Quarterly, 27*(3), 425-478.

Watson, R.T., Ho, T.H., & Raman, K.S. (1994). Culture: A fourth dimension of group support systems. *Communications of the ACM, 37*(10), 45-55.

Weisinger, J.Y., & Trauth, E.M. (2003). The importance of situating culture in cross-cultural IT management. *Transactions on Engineering Management, 50*(1), 26-30.

ENDNOTES

[1]   Triandis' definition of subjective culture referred to a cultural *group's* characteristic way of perceiving the environment. We extend this definition in this study to refer to an *individual's* characteristic way of perceiving one's environment.

[2]   As opposed to descriptive (or existential) beliefs (those capable of being true or false) and evaluative beliefs (wherein the object of belief is proven to be good or bad) (see Rokeach, 1972 for a discussion). More recent work in social psychology distinguishes between cognitive or behavioral beliefs which refer to an individual's beliefs about the consequences of a behavior and normative beliefs which refer to an individual's perceptions of normative pressures to perform or not perform a behavior imposed by salient referents.

APPENDIX A: VALUES

TERMINAL	INSTRUMENTAL
A Comfortable Life	Ambitious
An Exciting Life	Broadminded
A Sense of Accomplishment	Capable
A World of Peace	Cheerful
A World of Beauty	Clean
Equality	Courageous
Family Security	Forgiving
Freedom	Helpful
Happiness	Honest
Inner Harmony	Imaginative
Mature Love	Independent
National Security	Intellectual
Pleasure	Logical
Salvation	Loving
Self-respect	Obedient
Social Recognition	Polite
True Friendship	Responsible
Wisdom	Self-controlled

This article was previously published in the *Journal of Global Information Management,* 13(2), pp. 1-20, © 2005.

Chapter III

Cultural Differences, Information and Code Systems

Brian J. Corbitt, Deakin University, Australia

Konrad J. Peszynski, Deakin University, Australia

Saranond Inthanond, Deakin University, Australia

Bryon Hill, Deakin University, Australia

Theerasak Thanasankit, Varakit Textiles & Kasetsart University, Thailand

ABSTRACT

This paper explores an alternative way of framing information systems research on the role and impact of national culture. It argues that the widely accepted structural framework of Hofstede reduces interpretation to a simplistic categorical description which in many cases ignores differentiation within cultures. The alternative model suggests, that national culture can be better understood by seeking out the dominant codes that frame the discourse pervasive in a culture and understanding how that discourse affects the obvious social codes of ritual, custom and behavior and the textual codes which express the nature of that culture. This framework is applied to two different case studies — one in New Zealand and one in Thailand — to demonstrate its applicability.

INTRODUCTION

IS researchers have been interested to explain differences in adoption and/or usage of IT/IS by considering the impact of culture — primarily national culture on human behaviour and the way humans use the IT (Myers & Tan, 2002; Straub, Loch, Evaristo, Karahanna, & Srite, 2002; Thanasankit, 2002; Peszynski & Thanasankit, 2002; Hanisch, Thanasankit, & Corbitt, 2002; Thanasankit & Corbitt, 2000; Burn, Saxena, Ma, & Cheung, 1993; Burn, 1995; Burn, Davison, & Jordan, 1997; Davison & Jordan, 1996; Ho, Raman, & Watson, 1989; Korpela, Soriyan, Olufokunbi, & Mursu, 1998; Malling, 1998; Nelson & Clark, 1994). Researchers have examined differences in the adoption and use of information systems, knowledge systems and the business processes that are generated by and support information systems and information technology (IT). The purpose of this paper is to discuss a different view of culture, culture as code systems.

This article adopts a different approach. We examine the construction and meaning of information in its cultural context through the use of code systems and reconceptualise a framework to understand national culture and then apply that framework to two previously published studies, one from Thailand and one from New Zealand. One of the countries studied represents a Western culture and the other an Asian or Oriental culture which Said (1995) suggests are significantly differentiated in the practice of cultural norms. The results of these applications are analyzed and briefly discussed as a means of understanding the complexities involved with the application and understanding of national culture and of progressing the debate leading to a less structured and formalistic framework for dealing with the concept of national culture.

Despite several limitations, the recent phenomenon of a National State has dominated the understanding and measurement of cultural factors in IS literature (Myers & Tan, 2002; Straub, Loch, Evaristo, Karahanna, & Srite, 2002). Although many authors have accepted the existence of a single National Culture for each country (Scarborough, 1998; Burn, Saxena, Ma, & Cheung, 1993; Hofstede, 2000), the adoption of such a rigid definition neglects many of the facts presented throughout history (Myers & Tan, 2002) and oversimplifies the measurement of culture (Straub et al., 2002). Furthermore, many political boundaries defining a National State fail to represent actual cultural boundaries; a single National Culture does not reflect the true cultural beliefs present within many countries (Myers & Tan, 2002). Many agree with Straub and conclude that an "...individual's membership in a cultural group, such as their national culture, defines the nature of values they espouse" (Straub et al., 2002, p. 13).

Due to the complex nature of measuring culture, much research adopts specific (and often predefined) parameters to capture and understand cultural differences (Hofstede, 2000; Scarborough, 1998; Burn & Szeto, 1998; Xing, 1995; Burn et al., 1993). Despite these rigid techniques to measure culture some authors recognise the need to understand the process of how cultures are formed (Myers & Tan, 2002) and employ suitable methodologies to do so (Trauth, 2000). A summary of alternative methodologies found in the literature, including an examination of research employing Hofstede's behaviour principles follows. Cultural dimensions explored though the literature have varied, although Hofstede's principles have dominated. The study of Individualism, Uncertainty Avoidance, Power Distance and Masculinity has been closely observed (Burn, Saxena, Ma, & Cheung, 1993; Mcleod, Saunders, Jones, Schreel, & Estrada, 1997; Cummings & Guynes, 1994; Hofstede, 2000; Hunter & Beck, 2000; Mejias, Shepherd, Vogel, & Lazanco, 1997;

Milberg, Burke, Smith, & Kallman, 1995; Niederman, 1997; Palvia & Hunter, 1996; Walczuch, Singh, & Palmer, 1995; Watson & Bracheau, 1991; Watson, Kelly, Galliers, & Brancheau, 1997). Harvey (1997) adopts an ethnographic approach when considering Masculinity dimensions, while Hansan and Ditsa (1999) broadened Hofstede's principles concentrating on Time Orientation, Context, Mono/Polymorphic and Mono/ Polychrony. Adopting a slightly focused approach, Garfield and Watson (1998), Shore and Venkatachalam (1994, 1995) and Png, Tan, and Wee (2004) centre on Power Distance and Uncertainty Avoidance, though Straub (1994) considers Language Style in addition to Uncertainty Avoidance. Moreover, Uncertainty Avoidance is considered by Keil, Tan, Wei, Saarinen, Tuunainen, and Wassenaar (2000) and Keil, Mixon, Saarinen, and Tuunainen (1994/1995), while Tan, Watson, and Wei (1995) and Tan, Wei, Watson, and Walczuch (1998) look at Power Distance. Lally (1994) and Tan, Wei, Watson, Clapper, and McLean (1998) examine Individualism, as do Watson, Ho, and Raman (1994), who further consider Power Distance.

Others have taken into account alternative methods, including Hill, Loch, Straub, and El-Sheshai (1998), Thanasankit and Corbitt (2000) and Trauth (2001) who have not adopted predefined cultural dimensions. Robey and Rodriguez-Diaz (1989) and Martinsons and Westwood (1997) consider a general focus on culture, while Ein-Dor, Segev, and Orgad (1993) look at Economic, Demographic and Socio-Psychological dimensions. The literature considers Objective/Subjective factors (Menou 1983), Bottom up/Top Down issues (Trauth and Thomas, 1993), Family Orientation (Tricker 1988), while Moores and Gregory (2000) explore issues surrounding avoidance of group debates and the use of multiple languages. Xing (1995), Scarborough (1998) and Straub et al. (2002) have made progress towards a cultural comparison between Western and Eastern society by considering the process and foundation of culture development. Even though Xing (1995) and Scarborough (1998) consider how culture is coded when examining aspects of Eastern society, their research employs a limited set of parameters from which culture differences are generalised, and simplified conclusions are drawn. Such an approach is criticised by both Myers and Tan (2002) and Straub et al. (2002), as it overlooks and generalises many of the complex attributes of culture. Similar criticisms are present in other research; Burn et al. (1993) adopts Hofstede's model of national culture to compare cultural attributes of several nations. Despite the inherent criticisms of the model (Myers & Tan, 2002) several generalisations are drawn from the research. Hofstede (2000) compares several synthetic cultural profiles, although the research, not intended to reflect real-world cultures, appears rigid and one-dimensional. The research lists several parameters for each synthetic cultural profile (based on Hofstede's previous work), and seems simplistic.

Considering the limitations of an approach incorporating set parameters, several authors have advocated process-based methods to examine the codification of culture (Myers & Tan, 2002; Trauth, 2000; Straub et al., 2002). Existing research methods are inadequate when focusing on culture, an assessment of specific parameters is likely to lead to an inaccurate conclusion. Such techniques do not clearly reflect or measure a culture (Straub et al., 2002). (Myers & Tan, 2002, p. 30) agree that culture should be seen as "...contested, temporal and emergent..." and propose IS researchers adopt more in-depth approaches to study culture. Moreover, measurement of culture must occur at an "...individual level even though it is assumed that it is a group-level phenomenon" (Straub et al., 2002, p. 16).

A dynamic, multi-layer approach is therefore necessary when considering the codification of culture. Straub et al. (2002, p. 3) enlist a dynamic "virtual onion" model to represent the various layers of culture; the layers nearest to the core are considered more important, but layers can interact and trade places with outer layers (Straub et al., 2002). Such an approach allows for the conceptualisation of the process in which cultures are developed, thus moving away from the parameter-based methods.

Both Myers and Tan (2002) and Straub et al. (2002) have recognised the importance of examining the process of culture creation. However, these authors have presented theoretical reasoning to justify such positions without sufficient evidence. Despite such shortcomings, these authors have highlighted future research topics and possible directions suitable to support the presented theory.

In contrast to the quantitative approach proposed by Straub et al. (2002), qualitative research has been adopted as a popular means of measuring culture (Myers & Tan, 2002; Trauth, 2000). Rather than conducting research with pre-defined questions and parameters, Trauth (2000, p. 383) adopts an ethnographic approach with interviews, participant observations and document analysis. Such an approach allows the researcher to "...directly experience many [of] the social-cultural factors..." being studied. Trauth examines the process of culture codification, yet a series of classic socio-cultural parameters are the focus of early interviews. Despite using set parameters to measure culture, Trauth (2000, p. 380) uncovers further parameters (through open interviews) as determined by the "...particular 'expertise' or inclination of the respondent", and allows each participant to control the flow of the interview session.

While others have not fully described data analysis techniques, Trauth (2000) avoids using specific categories to analyse the collected data. Instead of inheriting set parameters from interviews, Trauth permits categories of interest to evolve throughout the entire analysis process. Such an approach avoids missing important factors when examining culture and allows the "...coding categories [to] emerge..." (Trauth, 2000, p. 386) from the data during analysis.

In spite of several recommendations, the most notable from Myers and Tan (2002), the majority of literature focuses on a parameter based means of measuring and examining cultures. Limited research has focused on understanding the process of how cultures are actually developed. Trauth (2000) presents a major contribution stemming from in-depth ethnographic research conducted in Ireland. While Trauth examines the process of culture from a qualitative perspective, Straub et al. (2002) have described a suitable quantitative method, although the authors have not supplied evidence resulting from a study; rather a call for further research is presented. From the examination of the extant literature, it is evident that further research is required to focus on understanding the process of how cultures are developed within societies, rather than a parameter based method of measurement.

CULTURE AND CODE SYSTEMS

Recently, the extant body of IS literature has paid limited attention to the impact of cultural differences on the development and use of information and communications technologies (e.g., Myers & Tan, 2002; Straub, Loch, Evaristo, Karahanna, & Srite, 2002; Thanasankit, 2002; Peszynski & Thanasankit, 2002; Hanisch, Thanasankit, & Corbitt,

2002; Thanasankit & Corbitt, 2000; Burn, 1995; Burn, Davison, & Jordan, 1997; Davison & Jordan, 1996; Ho, Raman, & Watson, 1989). The need to understand the management of organizations that span different nations and cultures is increasingly important in the age of globalization, through what Sheil (2001) suggests is reconciled with the denationalization of ownership and power. In innovative multinational organizations, information technology must be employed to achieve efficiencies, coordination, and communication. Because many organizations are now doing business beyond their national boundaries — and these global activities are facilitated and supported to a large extent by current communication and information technologies — it is important to understand the impact of cultural differences on these activities. A study of cultural differences, therefore, is of significant importance for transnational organizations and for IT researchers (Applegate, McFarlan, & McKenney, 1999; Harris & Davison, 1999; Tan, Watson, & Wei, 1995).

In a recent survey of global IT research, Gallupe and Tan (1999) found that a wide variety of cultural differences have been studied from a national culture perspective. However, most of this research into the impact of national culture has relied on Hofstede's (1980, 1991) dimensions to test and validate propositions relating to a variety of IS issues. Hofstede defines national culture as "the collective programming of the mind which distinguishes the members of one group or category of people from another" (Hofstede, 1991, p. 5). He argues that people share a collective national character that represents their cultural mental programming. This mental programming shapes values, beliefs, assumptions, expectations, perceptions and behavior.

Hofstede's concept of national culture focuses on shared values as the central feature and distinguishing characteristic of a culture. According to Sarbaugh (1988, p. 16), values refer to "the beliefs about what is important or unimportant, good or bad, and right or wrong. They are broad and fundamental norms, which are generally shared by groups. As such, they serve to guide, integrate, and channel the organized activities of the members. They are expressed in the norms of overt behavior and role expectation".

Hofstede's concept of national culture suggests that culture consists of patterned ways of behaviour that are shared across people in a society. These patterns are based on values. These values or mental programming shape individuals' cognitions, beliefs, expectations, assumptions, attitudes, and behaviors, judged within a structured framework, with strictly defined dimensions. Kroeber and Kluckholn (1952, p. 181) had initiated this perspective arguing that "culture consists of patterns, explicit and implicit, of and for behaviour, acquired and transmitted by symbols constituting the distinctive achievement of human groups..."

Straub et al. (2002) suggest that Hofstede's (1980) work is unique because it offers a simple mechanism whereby a cultural value can be assigned to a particular group of people, which exemplifies a rather reductionist approach. This group is determined by a nation-state boundary. Straub et al. (2002) also suggest that one of the shortcomings of conceptualizing culture as a value system is that there are recognized subcultures that span national geographical boundaries and nations which have strong internal cultural differences or recognized intra-regional differences. Fundamentally, these instantiations of culture are all value-based. The key distinction is the boundary, e.g., the nation-state/ geographic borders, organization or profession. In addition, by seeing culture as a value system, IS scholars have missed other characteristics of culture such as cultural change, cultural dynamics and cultural flows. Hofstede's model of culture is structural and categorical. It is essentially reductionist and favors binary categories of one truth against another. It avoids process and internal difference and those elements of society which frame the subcultures which Straub et al. (2002) address. Objects in the real world are initiated by identity and social position rather than by structure. We would argue then that objects are given meaning in culture by the way in which they are socially constructed and accepted.

The information systems literature on the social construction of meaning is limited. Most IS references to communication are based on a transmission model in which a sender transmits a message to a receiver. The simplistic process reduces meaning to 'content' which is delivered like a parcel (Reddy, 1979). This is a basis of Shannon and Weaver's well-known model of communication, which makes no allowance for the importance of social contexts and code (Shannon & Weaver, 1949). For instance, although Reichwald (cited in Wigand, Picot, & Reichwald, 1997) developed an analysis of information transmission at pragmatic, semantic, and syntactic levels, the notion of meaning of information in this framework is not different from Shannon and Weaver's model.

An alternative view of the concept of culture is code systems, which is based on social construction theory. Social construction of reality theory (Berger & Luckman, 1967) holds that the concept of reality is not given, rather reality is socially constructed. Thus different people would see the world differently. Social constructionists believe that there are two levels of the world in a human society. The first level is a physical world, which is composed of natural things such as trees, skies, rivers, etc. The other world is a social world in which different persons give meanings to things in a physical world differently. Every society develops a set of ideas, values, and rules that come to be useful for achieving its goals and solving the problems with which it must deal. According to this view, culture can be defined in terms of the production and exchange of meaning (Hall, 1997). It focuses on shared meanings among people who belong in the same culture.

The meanings humans make of things in the world they receive strongly depend on their social worlds, social context and culture. For example, a New Zealand Mäori tribe and a tribal group in Africa have different social worlds. The worship of specific living creatures and artifacts such as animals, plants, volcanoes, particular places or objects by some social groups in their environment may seem strange to other social groups. One group derives meanings from these totems, which are different for other social groups. This results in building their cultural identity.

This concept has useful implications to IS research where the same information or the same information technologies may take on different meanings for people whose social context is different. For example, data with the same sets of symbols may generate different meanings to different users according to their different social context or social world (Shanks & Corbitt, 1999). However we need to address the theory that supports this.

The theoretical grounding of the social construction of reality is derived from two schools of thoughts: sociology and linguistics. Sociologists suggest that humans create a reality based upon what tools they find available in their culture — the meanings they sustain and create in their daily interactions (Berger & Luckman, 1967). What seems strange and unfamiliar to one person may be normal to another from a different culture or subculture or counterculture. Charon (2001) argues that reality never tells us exactly what is; facts do not fill empty heads. Instead, human beings must interpret reality as it is, and that interpretation begins with the culture we use to guide us. That culture in turn arises from our groups and from society.

Another explanation of this reality comes from linguistics. Sapir (1958) and Whorf (1956) argue that the way in which we see the world is influenced by the kind of language we use. Whorf (1956) claims that one's language influences what one perceives and how it is interpreted. Precise measures of time are very important to persons in highly technological cultures, while in less industrialized societies, there is less emphasis on time, and the language codes are less precise for time.

Hall (1997) explains the notion of the social world, culture, in terms of a conceptual map. He argues that there is a conceptual map or 'system' by which all sorts of objects, people and events are correlated with a set of concepts which people carry around in their heads. People who belong to the same culture share a broadly similar conceptual map, so they too also share the same ways of interpreting the signs within language.

Thayer suggests that "what we learn is not the world, but particularly codes into which it has been structured" (Thayer, 1982, p. 30). Constructivist theorists argue that linguistic codes play an important role in the construction and maintenance of social reality. Berger and Luckman (1967) point out that the reality of everyday life is the intersubjective world — with language as a vehicle needed to objectify meanings so they can be shared by more than one person. Similarly Hall (1997) argues that language is the privileged medium in which we 'make sense' of things, in which meaning is produced and exchanged.

We would argue that social constructionist theory is useful in that we can understand culture by investigating codes that establish those social meanings and construct social realities. The concept of code is fundamental to understanding culture, since people in a society learn to read and understand the world in terms of codes and conventions which are dominant within the specific socio-cultural context and roles within which they are socialized. They adopt the values, assumptions and 'world view' which are built into them without normally being aware of their intervention in the construction of reality (Chandler, 2001). Understanding such codes, their relationships and the contexts in which they are appropriate is part of what it means to be a member of a particular culture. People who belong to the same culture can interpret the world in broadly the same ways and can express themselves, their thoughts and feeling about the world, in ways which will be understood by each other (Hall, 1997). Codes vary not only between different places but also different time periods. This suggests that cultural codes are historically and geographically situated.

There are a variety of codes in a culture. These codes are multi-layered. There must be dominant codes at the macro-level and subordinate codes, or sub-codes at the micro level. Danesi (1994) has suggested that a culture can be defined as a kind of macro code, consisting of the numerous codes which a group of individuals habitually use to interpret reality. Charon (2001) argues that a culture is a context within which experience is perceived and interpreted. People socialize the codes in a society and take them for granted. People do not simply learn from experience — they interpret what they experience through the lens of culture (Charon, 2001). Berger and Luckman (1967) argue that these realities are intersubjective. That is, each person's meaning relates to, and to some extent depends on, the meaning of others. They point out that people's personal habits become public, and that these shared habits eventually become so widely and strongly accepted that the are taken for granted, and passed on from generation to

Figure 1.   Tripartite framework of codes

Textual codes
- Scientific codes, including mathematics
- Aesthetic codes within the various expressive arts (poetry, drama, painting, sculpture, music, etc.) — including classicism, romanticism, realism
- Genre, rhetorical and stylistic codes: narrative (plot, character, action, dialogue, setting, etc.), exposition, argument and so on
- Mass media codes including photographic, televisual, filmic, radio, newspaper and magazine codes, both technical and conventional (including format)

Social codes
- Verbal language (phonological, syntactical, lexical, prosodic and paralinguistic subcodes)
- Bodily codes (bodily contact, proximity, physical orientation, appearance, facial expression, gaze, head nods, gestures and posture)
- Commodity codes (fashions, clothing, cars)
- Behavioural codes (protocols, rituals, role-playing, games)

Interpretative codes
- Perceptual codes: e.g., of visual perception
- Ideological codes: More broadly, these include codes for 'encoding' and 'decoding'. More specifically, we may list the 'isms', such as individualism, liberalism,

Source: Chandler (2001)

---

generation as always having been true. They create the cultural codes at the same time as they are created by them.

Thus, we would argue that it would be useful to understand cultural code systems. A number of scholars have sought to identify codes, and the tacit rules and constraints which underlie the production of meaning and interpretation of meaning within that society. Chandler (2001) suggests a tripartite framework of codes—textual codes, social codes and interpretive codes. This framework is communication-oriented. It deals with the production and interpretation of meaning because codes are interpretive frameworks which are used by producers and interpreters of texts. Nevertheless, codes listed here are not exhaustive. Chandler suggests that these three types of codes correspond broadly to three key types of knowledge required by the interpreter of a text/data, namely knowledge of (1) the world (social knowledge), (2) the medium and the genre (textual knowledge), and the relationship between (1) and (2) (modality judgments) (Figure 1). This framework suggests that culture is dominated by ideological codes such as orientalism, individualism, feminism, nationalism, capitalism, etc. Subordinate to these dominant codes, and informed by them, are social codes such as rituals, customs and protocols, which have also interested the anthropologists and which framed the structuralist, Hofstede model.

Also in a subordinate context are the textual codes which frame technologies, social practice and genre, and which many perceive as expressive as identities of culture. We would argue that the social and textual codes prevalent in what we as researchers perceive are actually encompassed by discourse and behaviors generated by the dominant ideological codes.

Textual Codes

Textual codes refer to a set of conventions that a group of people use to produce and interpret a text. Textual codes are the most arbitrary. The user must be trained to use and understand them. Scientific codes such as mathematics are one example of textual codes. Aesthetic codes for Chandler (2001) include the various expressive arts such as poetry, drama, painting, sculpture, music, films; and their sub-codes such as classicalism, romanticism and realism, etc. Genre, rhetorical and stylistic codes involve narrative, exposition, argument and so on. Each medium has its own codes. Information too generates codes according to its orientation. Codes are created about business information, commercialism, marketing, consumer behavior, business processing and change. The codes generated about each of these information concepts will be defined and redefined within different social contexts generating different cultural definitions. Once defined they become recontextualised (Corbitt, 1997) and redefined within subgroups according to their historical practices, creating subcultures. In the business context, information interpretation becomes ontological depending then on the nature of the business at any one time, subject to trade cycles and political decision-making. The textual code of "dot.com" was interpreted as successful until their continued demise from 2000. From that time that text has taken on a more negative connotation. The ontological basis of the text has changed for business and for technology investors.

Social Codes

Social codes refer to a set of conventions that a group of people in a society use to produce and interpret their social interactions and cultural practices. This kind of code is socially and culturally learned with or without training through the process of socialization. Therefore people are less aware when they are using these codes than when they use textual codes. Chandler suggests that there are four kinds of social codes: verbal, body, commodity and behavioral codes. Verbal language involves using linguistic codes such as phonological, syntactical, lexical, prosodic and paralinguistic subcodes. Bodily codes include bodily contact, proximity, physical orientation, appearance, facial expression, gaze, head nod, gesture and posture. Commodity codes include fashion and clothing. Behavioral codes, for Chandler, deal with protocols, rituals, role-playing and games. The meaning of information is interpreted via the use of social codes within a culture. What is an accepted business process in one cultural context is often reinterpreted and adopted differently in a different setting. For example, business in Asian cultures is dominated by *guanxi*, connections (Corbitt & Thanasankit, 2001; Scarborough, 1998; Xing, 1995). Some interpret these connections as offering favours, even as corrupt practices. Leung, Wong, and Wong (1996, p. 749) suggest that *guanxi* is not just about social networking and good relationships. They state that *guanxi* goes deeper than connection. It necessitates very personal interactions with other people and always involves a reciprocal obligation. *Guanxi* is developed with ingenuity, creativity, supplementing by flexibility. It is cultivated through a person's network of connections.

Guanxi is also important to any culture that has been influenced by Chinese culture (e.g., Thailand (Jirechiefpattana, 1996) and Taiwan (Hwang, 1987)) where good relationships and personal connections influence the success of business. In those countries, business negotiations are preferred to be done by using personal interaction where rich communication is a chosen, almost exclusive method. This is different from the trusted relationships for business owners who trust people they know better. This is a behaviour that is inherently imbedded within the practice of business. It is constructed and created person-to-person, and is expected.

These types of code interpretation sometimes reflect misunderstanding and often a different cultural or social ontology which informs an alternative or different perspective. On other occasions they reflect an ideological difference or political stance designed to gain advantage or create negative reflection for business advantage.

Interpretive Codes

Interpretive codes refer to a set of social conventions which engender meaning to appear real and natural. These codes operate in the human mind at the level of virtual unconsciousness. According to Chandler, interpretive codes include perceptual and ideological codes. Perceptual codes are visual. In the physical world, things are perceived as three dimensional and they must be coded into two dimensions according to the visual representation (Hall 1980). One of these interpretative codes encompasses ideology.

Chandler (2001) suggests that individualism, liberalism, feminism, racism, materialism, capitalism, progressivism, conservativism, constitute ideological codes. An ideology is a set of ideas that structure a group's notion of reality, a system of representations or a code of meanings governing how individuals and groups see the world (Littlejohn, 1992). A group of people who share an ideology share a common set of ideas as to what the world is like. Every society displays a general or 'dominant' ideology, a code of general values most of its people share, consciously and unconsciously, and within various groups. From this, individual ideologies arise. Berger and Luckman (1967) argue that ideologies serve to legitimize a society's institutions. Ideologies manifest themselves as rules which constrain thought and speech. Ideologies frame the culture in which they are set. They become the taken-for-granted truths, which members of a society accept without serious question. All information in any cultural context derives meaning from the rules established by the various ideologies grounded in that context. Any information system includes established rules and frames the way the systems are constructed, interpreted and used.

Codes provide useful insights into the concept of culture as value systems, a mechanistic pattern that governs people's beliefs and behaviors, expresses only partial truth about culture. We can also view culture as a code system with sets of social conventions for production and interpretation of meanings. Codes are variable according to time and place. Culture is always changing and dynamic through people's interaction in a society and a culture involves multi-layers of codes within which experience is perceived, interpreted and recontextualised. Understanding code systems organizes 'shared meanings' in a society and enables researchers to understand intracultural differences, which Straub et al. (2002) noted.

To try and gain an understanding of the applicability of this type of framework to research in information systems, we have applied the framework to data obtained in two other studies of culture and information, one in Thailand and the other in New Zealand.

RESEARCH METHOD

The studies reported below were originally independently undertaken, one in Thailand using an ethnographic methodology (Thanasankit, 1999) and the other in New Zealand using interpretative interviews (Peszynski, 2001). Each study focused on one element of information technology with the express aim of trying to understand the impact of national culture. Each study relied on Hofstede's typology of cultural analysis and used that extensively to interpret the data collected. Each study has been reported elsewhere in some detail (Thanasankit, 2002; Peszynski & Thanasankit, 2002; Thanasankit & Corbitt 2001; Hanisch, Thanasankit, & Corbitt, 2002).

For this study the authors revisited the data within the context of the framework suggested above, looking for exemplars of social codes as a means of extracting meaning and creating an alternative interpretation of what was happening in each case. The raw data was originally captured on tape and as transcripts, so its use and reinterpretation became possible. The interpretative epistemology used enables reinterpretation as the driver of understanding meaning derived from the socially constructed framework as a lens through which the researchers make sense of the data. Like all interpretative research, we acknowledge that this lens is imbued with the cultural bias of the researchers. We have tried to deal with this in having two Thai researchers and three New Zealand/Australian researchers deal with the data. Even then we accept that there are still limitation to this as a methodology.

Case Study 1:   New Zealand and B2C E-Commerce

Using Hofstede's (1980) classification, the Mäori community (in New Zealand) is classed as a collective society, that is, they depend heavily on their relationships with immediate family members (*whanau*) and tribal (*iwi*) elders (Gregory, 2001). As a result, Mäori are likely to help and trust people in their in-group, as opposed to someone outside of their family and tribe structure (Yamagishi & Yamagishi, 1994; Thanasankit, 1999). In a study of trust and B2C eCommerce, it was found that Mäori respondents prefer to speak to someone they know and trust, who has been to a Web site and made a purchase from it, rather than read customer testimonials left on the Web site by unknown customers (Peszynski & Thanasankit, 2002).

Using the framework outlined above (interpretive codes, social codes and textual codes), the classification of Mäori in the Peszynski and Thanasankit (2002) study can be reinterpreted (Figure 2).

Using Hofstede's (1980) national concept of culture, Mäori are categorized as collectivist. However, applying the concept of ideological codes, different dominating structures emerge. Mäori may have nationalism, but other "ism's" can be applied, such as *Iwi* (tribal) nationalism and *Whanau* (family) nationalism[1]. That is, Mäori can be identified as being Mäori (Mäori nationalism), which then leads to their *Whanau* (identity in terms of their family background). This is also an association with their *Iwi* (identity in terms of their tribal background), and lastly, Mäori then identified by the nationalism as being from *Aoteoroa* (New Zealand).

Trust and respect is earned through the status of the individual in relation to their *whanau, iwi* or *hapu*. Patterson (2000) states, "In Mäori eyes a person without family is scarcely a person at all, and the *mana* of any member of a family extends to all members"

Figure 2. Social and text codes in Mäori B2C e-commerce

Social codes

• **Verbal language**	• Use of Mäori words to replace English equivalent. For example, *Te Reo Mäori* for 'the Mäori language', *Iwi* (tribe), *Hapu* (sub-tribe), *Whanau* (family). • Words such as 'we' were often used by interviewees during the interviews as Mäori culture is classified as a collective society (Hofstede, 1991).
• **Bodily codes**	• When carrying out the interviews, body position is important for the Mäori interviewee. Facing the interviewee when sitting and maintaining good eye contact by way of spontaneous glances to express interest helps create a better, more trustful relationship between the interviewer and the interviewee.
• **Commodity codes**	• Interviewees were either in the public or private sector, so no specific dress code is enforced, however, many wear *pounamu* necklaces (Mäori greenstone carvings).
• **Behavioural codes**	• Protocols need to be respected. Even when conducting the interviews, the use of Mäori terms throughout the interview showed sincerity on behalf of the interviewer and helped create trust in the interviewer, and again, eye contact was very important in maintaining the trusting relationship.

(p. 232). *Mana* is a (supernatural) power that can be present in a person, place, object or spirit. It is commonly understood as prestige, power, or authority. The connections are about relationships to people and to place (Patterson, 2000; Light, 1999; Peszynski & Thanasankit, 2002).

In terms of social codes, Mäori prefer to communicate face-to-face (Light, 1999), as this helps build trust in a relationship. One can increase the trust and respect by facing the Mäori when sitting and maintaining good eye contact by way of spontaneous glances to express interest (OPRA Limited, 1998). In terms of the model proposed in this paper, the dominant ideology framing the use of information by Mäori in e-Commerce is Mäori nationalism rather than the dominant ideologies of New Zealand which are New Zealand nationalism, capitalism and social justice. This dominant ideology frames those practices, as social and textual codes, which are enactments of the discourse of Mäori nationalism, like the more obvious *hongi's* (greeting by 'kissing' noses); *haka powhiri* (a mass welcome — speeches, chants and *haka's*); language (pronounciation of vowels), their *moko* (tattoo's), dress (traditional grass skirts), rituals for funerals and so on.

This brief analysis from what is a larger and more complex study of the use of B2C eCommerce by Mäori would suggest that the alternative perspective on culture, proposed in the paper, offers an enticing and perhaps more satisfying response. The generalizations of the Hofstede analysis are replaced by culturally formed ontologies like *iwi* and *whanau*, which in themselves reflect both sameness as Mäori, but also difference according to which *iwi* and more specifically still, which *whanau* they associate with.

Differentiation relates to various forms of codes which create the meanings generated for and by information in this context. The codes not only enable this differentiation to be explored, but they suggest explanation about why information is generated and why it is used.

Case Study 2: Requirements Engineering Processes in Thailand

This research attempted to investigate how Thai culture and value influence the requirements engineering process from three Thai software houses (Thanasankit, 1999). The study employed Hofstede's (1991) framework to interpret the impact of Thai culture. The study argued that by using Hofstede's model, one could argue that Thai culture framed the interactional behavior between clients and system analysts, who were perceived as service providers. The clients, especially at the management level, were then perceived by the systems analysts as their superiors. The behaviour of systems analysts mirrored how they behaved towards their own superiors. Power played an important role in this (Thanasankit, 2002). The high power distance in Thai society (Hofstede) influenced the requirements engineering process where clients were allowed to request changes throughout the development processes, even after agreements had been reached. One of the Thai values that was presented as a significant influence on requirements engineering processes in Thai software houses was that of an upward delegation, where lower ranked employees preferred not to take any initiative in decision-making as decision-making brought uncertainty in results and unpredictable outcomes. Hofstede's (1991) classification identifies Thai culture as being high in uncertainty avoidance. Therefore, any decisions about requirements need to be passed up to higher levels of management for making final decisions and signing off the requirements specification.

Instead of examining these codes, we reexamined the data transcripts and the literature to seek out dominant codes and discourse across Thai culture, and in Thai business and IT industries. In Thailand the dominant ideologies are Thai nationalism derived from respect and social status. The discourse derives from the status of the king and the status of wealth and political power. Respect and social position are inherent in title and expectation, and manifests as discourse which Thai accept to varying degrees. Understanding this discourse and its impact enables the researcher to better understand and explain the expression of the discourse through social and textual codes rather than through the structured classification of Hofstede, which reduces all Thais to being submissive, which many are not, to being hierarchical and subordinate, which many are not, and to being sure about avoiding uncertainty, which many, especially in business are not. Risk in business and investment has always characterized many Thais and the necessity to reduce their behavior to one form does not represent the reality. Understanding all of the codes and especially the roles of the dominant codes ensures that the researcher is able to more fully understand what is supporting perceived action and behavior, and enables a less rigid and less categorical view of that behavior.

Using the culture code framework suggested in this paper, the textual and social codes identified from the previous research (Thanasankit, 1999; Thanasankit & Corbitt, 2000; Peszynski & Thanasankit, 2002) can be listed and described as a means to understand what we observe as researchers (Figure 3). However, the codes do not tell us what is informing and framing those behaviors, nor explain the differences between various actors involved. The Hofstede model was not able to explain difference, nor does

Figure 3. Social and text codes in the Thai RE software house context

Textual codes	
• Scientific codes	• Data Flow Diagrams were used for requirements modelling. The systems analysts stated that two different models were required. The first model was for the systems developers and the second model, which employed more simplified notations relevant to the real world, was developed for communication with clients, because clients found that it was simpler for them to relate to notation, which can represent real-world objects.
• Aesthetic codes	• Many verses in Thai and Confucian philosophy were used for expression
• Genre, rhetorical and stylistic codes	• The Thai script and style of printed and scripted writing were used within the normal formal setting out of forms
Social codes	
• Verbal language	• Many words such as 'we' were often used by system analysts during the interviews as Thai culture was classified as a collective society (Hofstede, 1991).
	• Many English words such as OK, requirements, specification, DFD, complaints, etc. were used by the systems analyst, which represented their high level of education and understanding of good English commands. Speaking and using good English commands are one of the prestige symbols in Thai education. This symbol is represented in many families sending their children to be educated in overseas countries.
• Bodily codes	• Different types of smiles were used by the systems analysts. Thais' smiles can be interpreted in different ways. Most Thais understand these different smile types eg. a smile for when they do not understand, or a smile for when they do not want to answer questions, etc.
• Commodity codes	• Staff have to be well dressed to represent respect and politeness.
• Behavioural codes	• Protocols need to be respected. In establishing the interview, the researcher needs to approach the CEO of the organisation for permission. He/she then assigns a unit for the researcher to study. The head of the unit is required to be briefed by the researcher. The project manager also needs to be briefed.

it explain why people do behave differently even in the same context. That difference is inevitably associated with the degree of influence of the discourse in the dominant codes.

DISCUSSION

These case studies of information elements, within two different information systems and two contrasting scenarios and cultures, focused on the role of national culture. The brief analysis presented suggests that using Hofstede's culture model enables the researchers to classify according to the items in the classification schema. However, this leads to oversimplification and reductionism, and does not address the internal differences noted by Straub et al. (2002). This paper's alternative analysis using codes enables a more reflective understanding of both subtle intercultural differences and intracultural differentiation.

The intricacies that distinguish the intracultural differentiation within Mäori are represented not only in obvious ways like *moko*, but more especially in the way information is constructed, interpreted, represented and made systemic through the use of other codes within the culture. Information is constructed based on social norms. Interpretations of information are not based on an individual appraisal. Rather the interpretations are imbedded in the social structure of family, tribe and Maori nationhood. These represent the social codes that frame how information meaning and application are constructed. In the systems context, these social codes frame the ways then that Maori will undertake business or shop online. They will react to information and to systems based on their/its relevance to their needs. If the information or system challenges their social norms, there is every likelihood that they will reject the system or not use it. The connections have to be about relationships to people and to place (Patterson, 2000; Light, 1999; Peszynski & Thanasankit, 2002). Where a system or process does not enable that connection, then there will be rejection, irrespective of economic or social reality. This is a more incisive view about the impact of culture than the over simplistic Hofstede modeling, which creates uniform paradigm of behavior. Where culture is not differentiated by race or nation — as is the case with the Maori, but is differentiated by much smaller units of tribe, and family — then, we would argue, a more accurate representation of the impact of culture can be developed. If this work is then grounded in multiple cases, a deontic modeling of culture might emerge rather than being imposed. Reductionism associated with existing culture modeling would be replaced by emergent theory based on practice and the fine grain actions of differentiated social groupings.

Intracultural differentiation, we would suggest, frames the ontological structures that enable development, implementation and evaluation of information systems in business within that culture. The differences identified enable explanation and comparison without having to resort to oversimplification, parody, reductionism or stereotyping.

This analysis of cultural practices using information framed by codes is also useful in explaining the differential behaviour noted in the Thai Systems Analysts. Too often in information systems we accept the apparently obvious — 'Thai software analysts behave differently from software analysts from other nations.' What we often do not accept, or even know, is *why,* other than resorting again to the oversimplified models of cultural differences. Thai social codes are formed within multiple contexts. The Thai people identify as 'Thai' but are also officially and unofficially differential as 'white Thai', black Thai, Thai, Thai Jin (Chinese Thai), Hill Tribes, Malays, etc. Each of these tribal forms or groups create their own social codes, and these inform the systems in which they work and frame their own and social interpretations of information. In the study reported in this paper, one analyst noted that he wanted to do things like the Chinese. But in the Thai context that means absorption: doing it the Thai way with a Chinese flavour, what ever Chinese means to that person. This creates in the Thai context multiple differentiated and recontextualised constructions about what information means and how systems are used. The apparent simplicity of the Maori structures are not applicable in the Thai context and there are multiple layers of meanings, each affording interpretation and collectively creating differentiated construction of meaning based on the context of the person, the social context and status of the person, and in the case of systems, the organizational context. While this latter point is invariably reflected across the globe,

Hofstede if anything demonstrated that clearly for IBM in this massive study, the complexity and chaos created by the multiple layer in the Thai social context creates multiple levels of codes, each creating their own 'culture'. In a sense, while there is a recognizable 'Thai culture', there is not one set of codes that enables people in that culture to behave or frame applications or develop systems in any sort of unified way. The generalized 'Thai culture' only provides a malleable skin which captures and encompasses the multitude of smaller scale, differentiated 'cultures' that together create the 'Thai". The software engineers that formed the study reported in this paper reflected that differentiation. Each of them used different sets of codes, some informed by Thai culture, some informed by their ethnicity and race, some informed by their organizational context, some informed by their clients, some informed by their international experience, and some informed by the content and ontology of their IT practice. This analysis has shown why differences exist between the level of individual systems analysts. The behaviour associated with each set of codes from the underlying ontological structures explain the differentiated behaviour patterns and practices evident in the larger study (Thanasankit, 1999). The codes offer the researcher a means by which to compare different sets of behaviours and a means with which to explain why differences actually exist.

CONCLUSIONS

This paper has not created a new theory to replace that of Hofstede. That was not the intention. We wanted to add to the debate highlighted most recently by Myers and Tan (2002) and Straub et al. (2002) by suggesting an alternative perspective drawn from other studies of culture and semiotics within sociology. This perspective adds newer, richer dimensions and offers a broader means to construct meanings of culture as part of the process of explaining the behaviors associated with information systems research. This reconceptualisation frees the researcher from the impositions of structure and the need to categorize. It enables various interpretations which will support other generalizations and a deeper understanding of what is being observed or indeed described. The ontologies which emerge become better representations of the information because they are formed out of a more coherent and socially supportable perspective, which addresses the discourse and ideologies which drive different cultures. The emphasis then re-emerges into understanding and better explanation, rather than on the ultimate need for reductionism and categorization. These ontologies can then be re-evaluated in different studies to enable support for clear descriptions of what culture and its component parts might be. As information systems researchers, we must develop better epistemology and better understand the nature of what we do. This paper has advanced both that search and the understanding of that a little.

REFERENCES

Applegate, L. M., McFarlan, F. W., & McKenney, J. L. (1999). *Corporate information systems management: Text and cases* (5th ed.). Chicago: Irwin.
Berger, P., & Luckman, T. (1967). *The social construction of reality.* New York: Anchor/ Doubleday.

Burn, J. M., Saxena, K. B. C., Ma, L., & Cheung, H. K. (1993). Critical issues in IS management in Hong Kong: A cultural comparison. *Journal of Global Information Management, 1*(4), 28-37.

Burn, J. M., & Szeto, C. (1998). Information systems management issues in Hong Kong: A contingency analysis and comparison with the United Kingdom. *Journal of Global Information Technology Management, 1*(1), 5-17.

Chandler, D. (2001). *Codes.* University of Wales, Aberystwyth. Retrieved April 14, 2001, from http://www.aber.ac.uk/media/Documents/S4B/sem08.html

Charon, J. M. (2001). *Ten questions: A sociological perspective.* Wadsworth.

Corbitt, B. J. (1999). Exploring the social construction of IT Policy – Thailand and Singapore. *Prometheus, 17*(3), 309-321.

Corbitt, B.J., & Thanasankit, T. (2001). The challenge of trust and 'Guanxi' in Asian e-Commerce. In M. Singh & T. Teo (Eds.), *E-commerce diffusion: Strategies and challenges* (pp.141-158). Melbourne: Heidelberg Press.

Cummings, M. L., & Guynes, J. L. (1994). Information system activities in transnational corporations: A comparison of U.S. and non-U.S. subsidiaries. *Journal of Global Information Management, 2*(1), 12-27.

Danesi, M. (1994). *Message and meaning: An introduction to semiotics.* Toronto: Canadian Scholars' Press.

Ein-Dor, P., Segev, E., & Orgad, M. (1993). The effect of national culture on IS: Implications for international information systems. *Journal of Global Information Management, 1*(1), 33-44.

Gallupe, R. B., & Tan, F. B. (1999). A research manifesto for global information management. *Journal of Global Information Management, 7*(3), 5-18.

Garfield, M. J., & Watson, R. T. (1998). The impact of national culture on national information infrastructure. *Journal of Strategic Information Systems, 6*(4), 313-338.

Gregory, R. J. (2001). Parallel themes: Community psychology and Mori culture in Aotearoa. *Journal of Community Psychology, 29*(1), 19-27.

Hall, S. (1980). Encoding and decoding. In S. Hall et al. (Eds.), *Culture, media, language.* London: Hutchinson.

Hall, S. (1997). The work of representation. In S. Hall (Ed.). *Representation: Cultural representations and signifying practices (Culture, Media and Identity series).* London: Sage.

Hanisch, J., Thanasankit, T., & Corbitt, B. (2002). Exploring the cultural and social impacts on the requirements engineering processes: Highlighting some problems challenging virtual team relationship with clients. *Journal of Systems and Information Technology, 5*(2), 1-20.

Harris, R., & Davison, R. (1999). Anxiety and involvement: Cultural dimensions of attitudes toward computers in developing countries. *Journal of Global Information Management, 7*(1), 26-38.

Harvey, F. (1997). National cultural differences in theory and practice: Evaluating Hofstede's national cultural framework. *Information Technology & People, 10*(2), 132-146.

Hasan, H., & Ditsa, G. (1999). The impact of culture on the adoption of IT: An interpretive study. *Journal of Global Information Management, 7*(1), 5-15.

Hill, C. E., Loch, K. D., Straub, D. W., & El-Sheshai, K. (1998). A qualitative assessment of Arab culture and information technology transfer. *Journal of Global Information Management, 6*(3), 29-38.

Hofstede, G. (1980). *Cultural consequences: International differences in work related values.* Beverly Hills, CA: Sage.

Hofstede, G. (1991). *Cultures and organizations: Software of the mind.* New York: McGraw-Hill.

Hofstede, G. J. (2000). You must have been at a different meeting. Enacting culture clash in the international office of the future. *Journal of Global Information Technology Management, 3*(2), 42-58.

Hunter, M. G., & Beck, J. E. (2000). Using repertory grids to conduct cross-cultural information systems research. *Information Systems Research, 11*(1), 93-101.

Ives, B., & Jarvenpaa, S. L. (1991). Applications of global information technology: Key issues for management. *MIS Quarterly, 15*(1), 32-49.

Keil, M., Mixon, R., Saarinen, T., & Tuunainen, V. (1994/1995). Understanding runaway information technology projects: Results from an international research program based on escalation theory. *Journal of Management Information Systems, 11*(3), 65-86.

Keil, M., Tan, B. C. Y., Wei, K. K., Saarinen, T., Tuunainen, V., & Wassenaar, A. (2000). A cross-cultural study on escalation of commitment behavior in software projects. *MIS Quarterly, 24*(2), 299-325.

Lally, L. (1994). The impact of environment on information infrastructure enhancement: A comparative study of Singapore, France and the United States. *Journal of Global Information Management, 2*(3), 5-12.

Light, E. (1999). Market to Maori: Key mistakes, key remedies. *Marketing, 18*(6), 10-17.

Littlejohn, S. W. (1992). *Theories of human communication* (4th ed.). Wadsworth Publishing.

Martinsons, M. G., & Westwood, R. I. (1997). Management information systems in the Chinese business culture: An explanatory theory. *Information & Management, 32*(5), 215-228.

McLeod, R., Kim, C. N., Saunders, C., Jones, J. W., Schreel, C., & Estrada, M. C. (1997). Information management as perceived by CIOs in three Pacific Rim countries. *Journal of Global Information Management, 5*(3), 5-16.

Mejias, R. J., Shepherd, M. M., Vogel, D. R., & Lazaneo, L. (1997). Consensus and perceived satisfaction levels: A cross-cultural comparison of GSS and non-GSS outcomes within and between the United States and Mexico. *Journal of Management Information Systems, 13*(3), 137-161.

Menou, M. (1983). Cultural barriers to the international transfer of information. *Information Processing & Management, 19*(3), 121-129.

Milberg, S. J., Burke, S. J., Smith, H. J., & Kallman, E. A. (1995). Values, personal information privacy, and regulatory approaches. *Communications of the ACM, 38*(12), 65-74.

Moores, T. T., & Gregory, F. H. (2000). Cultural problems in applying SSM for IS development. *Journal of Global Information Management, 8*(1), 14-19.

Myers, M.D., & Tan, F.B. (2002). Beyond models of national culture in information system research. *Journal of Global Information Management, 10*(1), 24-32.

Niederman, F. (1997). Facilitating computer-supported meetings: An exploratory comparison of U.S. and Mexican facilitators. *Journal of Global Information Management, 5*(1), 17-26.

OPRA Limited. (1998). Mäori knowledge assessment: Technical support manual. *OPRA consulting.* Retrieved July 16, 2001, from http://www.opra.co.nz/downloads/manuals/MKAManual.pdf

Palvia, S., & Hunter, M. G. (1996). Information systems development: A conceptual model and a comparison of methods used in Singapore, USA and Europe. *Journal of Global Information Management, 4*(3), 5-17.

Patterson, J. (2000). Mana: Yin and Yang. *Philosophy East & West, 50*(2), 229-240.

Peszynski, K. J. (2001). *Trust and the Mäori Internet shopper: An exploratory study.* Honours Thesis (unpublished), Victoria University of Wellington.

Peszynski, K. J., & Thanasankit, T. (2002, June 6-8). *Exploring trust in B2C e-commerce – An exploratory study of Mäori culture in New Zealand.* European Conference on Information Systems (ECIS), Gdansk, Poland.

Png, I. P. L., Tan, B. C. Y., & Wee, K. L. (2004). Dimensions of national culture and corporate adoption of IT infrastructure. *IEEE Transactions on Engineering Management.*

Reddy, M.J. (1979). The conduit metaphor: A case of frame conflict in our language about language. In A. Ortony (Ed.), *Metaphor and thought.* Cambridge: Cambridge University Press.

Robey, D., & Rodriguez-Diaz, A. (1989). The organizational and cultural context of systems implementation: Case experience from Latin America. *Information & Management, 17*, 229-239.

Said, E.W. (1995). *Orientalism.* Penguin Books

Sapir, E. (1958). *Culture, language and personality* (Ed. Mandelbaum, D.G). Berkeley: University of California Press.

Sarbaugh, L.E. (1988). *Intercultural communication.* NJ: Transaction.

Scarborough, J. (1998). Comparing Chinese and Western cultural roots: Why East is East and.... *Business Horizons, 41*(6), 15-24.

Shanks, G., & Corbitt, B.J. (1999, November). *Understanding data quality: social and cultural aspects.* Australian Conference on Information Systems, Wellington, NZ.

Shannon, C.E., & Weaver, W. (1949). *The mathematical theory of communication.* Urbana: University of Illinois Press.

Shore, B., & Venkatachalam, A. R. (1994). Prototyping: A metaphor for cross-cultural transfer and implementation of IS applications. *Information & Management, 27*, 175-184.

Shore, B., & Venkatachalam, A. R. (1995). The role of national culture in systems analysis and design. *Journal of Global Information Management, 3*(3), 5-14.

Straub, D. (1994). The effect of culture on IT diffusion: E-mail and FAX in Japan and the U.S. *Information Systems Research, 5*(1), 23-47.

Straub, D., Loch, K., Evaristo, R., Karahanna, E., & Srite, M. (2002.). Toward a theory-based measurement of culture. *Journal of Global Information Management, 10*(1), 13-23.

Tan, B. C. Y., Watson, R. T., & Wei, K. K. (1995). National culture and group support systems: Filtering communication to dampen power differentials. *European Journal of Information Systems, 4*, 82-92.

Tan, B. C. Y., Wei, K. K., Watson, R. T., Clapper, D. L., & McLean, E. R. (1998). Computer-mediated communication and majority influence: Assessing the impact of an individualistic and a collectivistic culture. *Management Science, 44*(9), 1263-1278.

Tan, B. C. Y., Wei, K. K., Watson, R. T., & Walczuch, R. M. (1998). Reducing status effects with computer-mediated communications: Evidence from two distinct national cultures. *Journal of Management Information Systems, 15*(1), 119-141.

Te Puni Kokiri. (1994). *Privacy of health information.*

Thanasankit, T. (1999). *Exploring social aspects of requirements engineering – An ethnographic study of Thai software houses.* PhD Thesis, (unpublished), University of Melbourne.

Thanasankit, T. (2002). Requirements engineering – Exploring the influence of power and Thai values. *European Journal of Information Systems, 11*, 128-141.

Thanasankit, T., & Corbitt, B. (2000). Thai culture and communication of decision-making processes in requirements engineering. *Second International Conference on Culture Attitudes Towards Technology and Communication 2000*, Murdoch University, Australia (pp. 217-242).

Theyer, L. (1982). Human nature: Of communication, of structuralism, of semiotics. *Semiotica, 41*(1/4), 25-40.

Tractinsky, N., & Jarvenpaa, S. L. (1995). Information systems design decisions in a global versus domestic context. *MIS Quarterly, 16*(4), 507-534.

Trauth, E. M. (2000). *The culture of an information economy: influences and impacts in the Republic of Ireland.* Dordrecht; London: Kluwer Academic.

Trauth, E. M. (2001). *Qualititive research in IS: Issues and trends.* Hershey, PA: Idea Group Publishing.

Trauth, E. M., & Thomas, R. S. (1993). Electronic data interchange: A new frontier for global standards policy. *Journal of Global Information Management, 1*(4), 6-27.

Tricker, R. I. (1988). Information resource management - A cross cultural perspective. *Information & Management, 15*, 37-46.

Walczuch, R. M., Singh, S. K., & Palmer, T. S. (1995). An analysis of the cultural motivations for transborder data flow legislation. *Information Technology & People, 8*(2), 37-58.

Watson, R. T., & Bracheau, J. C. (1991). Key issues in information systems management: An international perspective. *Information & Management, 20*, 213-223.

Watson, R. T., Ho, T. H., & Raman, K. S. (1994). Culture: A fourth dimension of group support systems. *Communications of the ACM, 37*(10), 44-55.

Watson, R. T., Kelly, G. G., Galliers, R. D., & Brancheau, J. C. (1997). Key issues in information systems management: An international perspective. *Journal of Management Information Systems, 13*(4), 91-115.

Whorf, B.L. (1956). *Language, thought and reality* (Ed. John B. Carroll). Cambridge, MA: MIT Press.

Wigand, R., Picot, A., & Reichwald, R. (1997). *Information, organization and management: Expanding markets and corporate boundaries.* Chichester, UK: John Wiley & Sons.

Xing, F (1995). The Chinese cultural system: Implications for cross-cultural management, *S.A.M. Advanced Management Journal, 60*(1), 14-23.

Yamagishi, T., & Yamagishi, M. (1994). Trust and commitment in the United States and Japan. *Motivation and Emotion, 18*, 129-165.

ENDNOTE

[1]   Nationalism rather than tribalism reflects the use of the words within the culture itself. The Mäori refer to their own tribes as nations and their families as sub-nations.

This article was previously published in the *Journal of Global Information Management,* 12(3), pp. 65-85, © 2004.

Chapter IV

Developing a
Generic Framework for
E-Government

Gerald Grant, Carleton University, Canada

Derek Chau, Carleton University, Canada

ABSTRACT

Electronic government (e-government) initiatives are pervasive and form a significant part of government investment portfolio in almost all countries around the world. However, understanding of what is meant by e-government is still nascent and becomes complicated because the construct means different things to different people. Consequently, the conceptualization and implementation of e-government programs are diverse and are often difficult to assess and compare across different contexts of application. This paper addresses the following key question: Given the wide variety of visions, strategic agendas, and contexts of application, how may we assess, categorize, classify, compare, and discuss the e-government efforts of various government administrations? In answering this question, we propose a generic e-government framework that will allow for the identification of e-government strategic agendas and key application initiatives that transcend country-specific requirements. In developing the framework, a number of requirements are first outlined. The framework is proposed and described; it is then illustrated using brief case studies from three countries. Finally, findings and limitations are discussed.

INTRODUCTION

E-government (electronic government) is increasingly a global phenomenon that is consuming the attention of politicians, policy makers, and even ordinary citizens. Governments around the world have made and continue to make massive financial and political commitments to establishing e-government (Accenture, 2004). A report by the United Nations (UN World Public Sector Report, 2003) indicates that by 2003, over 173 countries had developed government Web sites. Additionally, many countries (including Canada, Germany, Malaysia, Norway, the UK, and the U.S.) have embarked on ambitious multi-year programs to create more citizen-centered, effective, and efficient governments (Accenture, 2004).

E-government is predicated on leveraging the capabilities and power of IT to deliver services provided by governments at local, municipal, state, and national levels. While early conceptions of e-government have largely focused on electronic service delivery as the key feature of the phenomenon, a closer examination suggests a more complex set of circumstances. Beyond service delivery, e-government offers additional channels of interaction among governments, businesses, and citizens, separately or collectively. For example, individual citizens may interact with government electronically by filing their income tax documents online. Governments in delivering services may do so directly or indirectly through intermediaries such as banks, postal outlets in private businesses, and by other means. Consequently, any e-government effort must meet the needs of a diverse set of stakeholders that operate in the political, business, or civic spheres of influence. E-government, however, is more than a technological phenomenon. Whether through deliberate choice or passive acceptance, it is transformative in nature, affecting the management of human, technological, and organizational resources and processes. Consequently, the implementation of e-government is a monumental change effort.

The drive to implement e-government has resulted in the adoption of many e-government visions and strategic agendas (Accenture, 2004). However, each vision is driven by its own unique set of social, political, and economic factors and requirements. Consequently, the mission and objectives that emanate from these e-government visions variously manifest strong focus on one or two elements. For example, the United States has placed a major focus on service delivery and on increasing cross-functional efficiencies (OMB, 2003). The South African government's e-government program is heavily weighted towards service delivery, while e-government efforts in the United Kingdom have tended to balance several strategic objectives.

A key factor driving the achievement of any e-government program is the vision of e-government, articulated and adopted by a government administration. Coupled with actual developments undertaken by the administration, the articulated vision (expressed in documents, objectives, frameworks) greatly helps to describe the e-government space. However, these efforts are not necessarily well articulated nor well coordinated. In large part, this is due to how electronic government is conceptualized. With each administration articulating its own view, it becomes difficult to identify, assess, and understand what is being accomplished under the e-government aegis. While some e-government strategic agendas focus primarily on service delivery issues, others may focus more on creating internally efficient systems and processes. Still others may adopt a more comprehensive view, incorporating issues such as constituent relationship management and e-democracy. Understanding what is meant by e-government becomes complicated because the construct means different things to different people. Although each of these views of e-government may be legitimate, there is a need for some common understanding to allow for assessment, comparison, and explanation of current efforts vis-à-vis past and future investment in the e-government enterprise.

This article addresses the following key question: Given the wide variety of visions, strategic agendas, and contexts of application, how may we categorize, classify, assess, compare, and discuss the e-government efforts of various government administrations? In answering this question, we see the need for a mechanism that will facilitate the articulation and discussion of current issues and concepts related to e-government. We believe this instrument would ideally transcend country-specific requirements and identify experiences and elements that could be transferred across contexts of application. For example, we should be able to describe and discuss the e-government efforts in a country such as Malaysia and make some broad comparisons with similar efforts in the United Kingdom. Therefore, we propose the development of a generic framework that can be used to categorize, classify, and compare electronic government visions, strategic agendas, and application initiatives. Such a framework, rather than seeking to rigidly constrain or categorize e-government activities, should act as a lens to focus attention and awareness on underlying issues and elements that could be debated, discussed, and further developed. Clearly, our main objective is to find a way to make sense of the plethora of perspectives and developmental agendas populating the e-government space. Our proposed framework should be viewed as a first step in this process. It represents another way to consider e-government efforts and provide a starting point for integrating current experiences and knowledge.

This article is organized as follows. Following this introduction, section one (Literature Review) focuses on developing a working operational definition for e-government that will underpin the development of a generic e-government framework. Key requirements for the development of such a framework are identified and discussed. A framework is proposed. Section two (Methodology) provides insight into the development of the framework. We illustrate, in section three, the application of the framework. Here, we use it to categorize, classify, and discuss the e-government visions and implementation efforts of three nations: the United States, the United Kingdom, and Malaysia. Section four presents the findings from the case studies. In section five we discuss the practical and theoretical implications of applying the framework. Possible future roles and directions will also be considered.

LITERATURE REVIEW

Defining E-Government

Definitions of e-government abound in the literature. Some definitions narrowly focus on using ICTs, particularly the Internet, to deliver more efficient and effective government services, while others view e-government as a broad-based effort to transform government and governance. In the examples below, e-government is characterized as:

- the use of technology to enhance the access to and delivery of government services to benefit citizens, business partners, and employees (Deloitte Research, 2000, p. 4);
- electronic information-based services for citizens (e-administration) with reinforcement of participatory elements (e-democracy) to achieve objectives of balanced e-government (Bertelsmann Foundation, 2001, p. 4);
- the use of information and communication technologies, particularly the Internet, as a tool to achieve better government (OECD, 2003, p. 63); and
- the use of information and communication technologies in all facets of the operations of a government organization (Koh & Prybutok, 2003, p. 34).

These definitions, while useful in describing e-government in a broad-based manner, offer little insight into deeper issues and considerations relating to the construct. On the one hand, those definitions that focus exclusively on the service delivery component of e-government efforts, fail to capture the more complex aspects of transforming government or acknowledge the role of the information and information technology elements. Such a one-sided focus tends to skew the e-government development and deployment agenda. Consequently, most implementation activities center around service delivery concerns with little emphasis on real transformation of the services themselves or the processes associated with their delivery (Poostchi, 2002). On the other hand, definitions that are too broad make it difficult to determine what really constitutes e-government and, as a consequence, may confuse the treatment of the issue.

For e-government to be properly understood and applied, we believe that it needs to be more comprehensively conceptualized (Caldow, 2001). However, the nascence of the e-government phenomenon, coupled with the complexities associated with the public sector context, contribute to the multiple interpretations and confusion surrounding the concept. Our review of academic, practitioner, and a variety of government publications suggests that any conceptualization of e-government needs to address a variety of concerns beyond the service delivery elements (Chadwick & May, 2003; Marche & McNiven, 2003; OECD, 2003). E-government is a detailed and complex development that is difficult to conceptualize. What is known and understood is mostly of a descriptive and anecdotal nature. The end result is that e-government implementations have yet to realize the upper stages of maturity and that the understanding and knowledge of the area is still in the process of formation.

Developing an Operational Definition for E-Government

Our review of the e-government literature (frameworks, models, white papers, government documents, etc.) suggests several characteristics that should be taken into consideration when defining e-government. These are identified and listed in Table 1.

Strong Service Delivery and Information Component

Most e-government programs emphasize a strong service delivery and information provision component, particularly in the initial stages (Accenture, 2004; Bertelsmann Foundation, 2001; Deloitte Research, 2000; World Markets Research Centre, 2001). Citizen experiences with customer-centric information and service offerings via the Internet have resulted in an increased demand on government administrations to

Table 1. E-government operational definition

Characteristic	Description	References
Strong service delivery and information provision component	• Electronic services and information provision provides the chief mode of interaction • Transaction and feedback effected via services and information provision components	Deloitte Research, 2000; Bertelsmann Foundation, 2001; World Markets Research Centre, 2001; Accenture, 2002, 2004; Koh & Prybutok, 2003; Layne & Lee, 2001; Reddick, 2004; OECD, 2003
E-government is a transformation effort	• Represents multiple levels of engagement • Cuts across functional and organizational boundaries • Digital age public sector reform • Demands new forms of interaction between citizens and government	Osborne & Gaebler, 1992; Rais Abdul Karim, 1999; OECD, 2003; Accenture, 2004
Diverse number of solutions and patterns of development	• Country-specific • Implementation differs across contexts of application (political, social, economic) • Multiple patterns of development prevail	UK Cabinet Office, 2000a; Corrocher & Ordanini, 2002; OMB, 2001; OMB, 2003; Accenture, 2002, 2004; OECD, 2003
IS/IT-Based development, but not limited to IS/IT	• IS/IT infrastructure essential in deploying an e-government program • Leverages IS/IT capabilities to deliver systems and services • Overlapping functionality and knowledge • Added complexities from public sector context • IS/IT knowledge insufficient to explain and predict future trends	Box, 1999; Guy, 2001; Heeks, 1999; UK Cabinet Office, 2000a; Chadwick & May, 2003
Convergence of integration, sophistication, and maturity	• Extends beyond service automation and efficiencies to integrated service offering • Integrative efforts and requirements increasing with added functionality and citizen-centric design • Increasing complexity and functionality requires commensurate development of understanding and knowledge of relationships among e-government and other functional areas and organizational concepts, including IS/IT contributions • Asymptoting towards higher levels of service interaction and maturity	Deloitte Research, 2000; Bertelsmann Foundation, 2001; Accenture, 2002, 2004; Koh & Prybutok, 2003; Layne & Lee, 2001; Working Group on E-Government, 2002
International Phenomenon	• Diversity of e-government realizations • Crosses geographic boundaries • Adaptable to country-specific requirements • Growing number of implementations and developments worldwide	Accenture 2002, 2004; Deloitte Research, 2000; Basu, 2004; Ke & Wei, 2004

organize information, services, and government functions around the citizen (Deloitte & Touche, 2000). The breadth and maturity of information and service offerings are also increasing where a significant number of nations with high levels of maturity have been measured (Accenture, 2002, 2004). For example, transaction level services have been observed, categorized, and represented in several measurement frameworks (Accenture, 2002; Koh & Prybutok, 2003) and models (Layne & Lee, 2001). These include services such as tax filing and payment, postal agency bill payments, and license renewal and registration. Portals such as the U.S. www.consumer.gov and the Canadian www.canada.gc.ca, provide access to a broad range of information and services, reflecting a "cradle to grave" philosophy that supports citizens' information and service needs throughout their lives.

E-Government as a Transformational Endeavor

Most operational definitions of e-government betray an underlying transformational or reformation theme that ranges from more effective services delivery to greater participation through relationship building with stakeholders. They embrace many aspects of the transformational agenda promoted under the rubric of the "new public management," which calls for the reinvention of government (Osborne & Gaebler, 1992). The transformation agenda focuses on the need for governments to more effectively manage inputs, processes, and outputs of the public administration organization, and envisions broad classes of institutional reform (Osborne & Gaebler, 1992; Rais Abdul Karim, 1999). These include:

- increased efficiencies in government operations;
- decentralization of services and administration;
- increased accountability;
- improved resource management; and
- marketization and leveraging of market forces to enhance public sector and private sector relationships

Research by the OECD (2003b) suggests that e-government can be an important catalyst to public sector reform agendas, whether as a tool of reform, a catalyst for change initiatives, or an instrument for improving processes and governance. The recent report by Accenture (2004) implies that to get more value from e-government investments, governments will need to embrace a more ambitious transformation agenda.

Diverse Number of Solutions and Contexts of Application

Changes and transformational efforts can be undertaken across many dimensions and are often a reflection of the unique political, social, and economic needs and capacities of the hosting nation or government administration. We refer to this as the context of application. Corrocher and Ordanini (2002) suggest that different patterns (asymmetric and symmetric) of development exist, depending on the particular economic and administrative situation of the nations in question.

We anticipate that e-government as a public sector and technology-enabled initiative will be subject to contextual factors similar to those experienced by other public sector initiatives, and also will exhibit multiple patterns of development. We see examples of this in the differing foci and patterns of development in nations such as the U.S., the UK, Malaysia, and South Africa. In some nations, e-government developments have a market and efficiencies emphasis (OMB, 2001, 2003). In others, increasing citizen awareness and access to services are given priority. Still others take a balanced approach to e-government development (UK Cabinet Office, 2000).

Electronic Government, Information, and IT

There is a special relationship among e-government, information, and IT. Information permeates all organizational activities and is used by all members of the organization, from the front line to back room, impacting every organizational function (Lacity & Willcocks, 1998; Ward & Peppard, 2002). This is particularly true for government organizations that are charged with managing (in the public interest) multiple stakeholders across the social, political, and economic domains. Information is a key resource for the operation of government and generates key inputs for producing the outputs of policy and public action (Box, 1999; Guy, 2001). Accurate and timely information about the external environment and stakeholder requirements are at the heart of effective decision-making, policy development, and administration.

A strong relationship also exists between e-government and the use of information technology and systems. E-government, like e-business, would be impossible without the technological platform provided by modern information and communication technologies. Perhaps the most significant capability that is enabled by IT is the creation of a new interaction and communication channel. The connectivity element of IT provides another conduit for information and feedback between government agencies, departments, and stakeholders through the application of standardized Web browsers, workflow, project management, and customer relationship management technologies, among others (Koh & Prybutok, 2003). The use of real time communication and data processing technology also allows for almost instantaneous exchange and feedback that cuts across geography, time, and organizational boundaries. The IT infrastructure effectively enables the rapid propagation of information and data throughout the e-government network to all connected parties, increasing both the quality and quantity of information received.

This unique combination of increased efficiency, information quality and quantity, and organization-wide distribution and connectivity creates an effect that goes beyond the support of government operations. The use of IT creates the potential for change and reinforces the transformation elements of e-government, providing a medium for the realization of electronic ideas, goals, and objectives (Heeks, 1999). However, e-government is not principally driven by technology concerns, but rather must reflect the operational context and obligations of the public sector (Chadwick & May, 2003; UK Cabinet Office, 2000). IT systems are enablers of e-government. The inclusion of these systems and technologies within e-government is not the final objective.

Integration, Service Sophistication, and Maturity

Electronic service delivery is undoubtedly a key component of any electronic government effort. However, governments have begun to recognize the need to move beyond front end efficiencies to a more sophisticated model where saving "money should not be the broad vision that motivates e-government" and where the implementation is more than just automated service delivery and a series of Web presences (Pacific Council on International Policy, 2002). The ultimate goal of many government efforts is to present one view of government, regardless of the point of access, through an integrated and secure service and interaction environment. This represents an evolution of the service contract between citizens and government and is also driven by constituent relationship management (CRM) efforts aimed at serving citizens and other stakeholders better (Accenture, 2002). Consequently, e-government is expected to impact every area of the organization (Bertelsmann Foundation, 2001; Deloitte Research, 2000) and crosses political and functional boundaries. The effort is beyond the scope of any one agency, and ultimately, the degree of integration an administration achieves will strongly determine how much value is brought to itself and its citizens (Bertelsmann Foundation, 2001).

Integration of applications and services across governments are relatively more complex and problematic than similar integration in private businesses. Integration efforts in government require cross agency cooperation, which is not necessarily forthcoming or legally permitted (Marche & McNiven, 2003). In many governments, individual ministers and agencies are charged with executing the responsibilities assigned to them through legislation and are, therefore, not eager or able to expend resources on cross-agency arrangements that were not anticipated or provided for in budgetary allocations and mandates (OECD, 2003). The difficulty encountered in deploying an integrated services platform is partly responsible for the slowdown in e-government advances in many countries (Accenture, 2004). Any definition of e-government, therefore, needs to encompass a whole-of-government view that envisions an integrated network of applications and services that will provide a seamless service delivery and transaction environment to which there is 'no wrong door.'

The maturity and breadth of e-government services are on the rise (Accenture, 2002, 2004). The reach and range of e-government applications and other developments are increasing in terms of both scope and functionality. Implementations have begun to move towards full transaction level experiences between citizens and government where communication can occur in duplex mode (i.e., feedback is given bi-directionally by both government and citizens). Transaction level services, such as tax filing and payment and postal-agency-based bill payments, have been observed, categorized, and represented in measurement frameworks (Accenture, 2002, Koh & Prybutok, 2003) and models (Layne & Lee, 2001). Service sophistication and maturity in the e-government area parallel developments in the IS/IT sphere (Nolan & Gibson, 1974; Somogyi & Galliers, 1987). There has also been a shift from an internal to an external focus. This includes the creation of citizen-centric services in response to citizen demands that stem from Internet-based encounters (Deloitte Research, 2000). This shift is evidenced in the growing focus on CRM efforts, which seek to organize services and government functions around the citizen. Emerging initiatives in service personalization extends this trend (Accenture, 2004).

E-government service maturity will continue to change and evolve in keeping with changing stakeholder requirements. This maturation process suggests that conceptualizations of e-government should not be limited to the services and applications that currently exist. Any definition or framework that seeks to describe or explain e-government phenomena must be sufficiently robust to accommodate the evolution of activities and applications without requiring a total reconstitution of the frameworks or models previously developed.

International Phenomenon

E-government is an international phenomenon that is undertaken by a diverse array of government administrations (Basu, 2004; Chadwick & May, 2003; Ke & Wei, 2004; OECD, 2003). Studies from independent consultants detail the efforts of both developed and developing nations to deploy e-government services and applications (Accenture, 2002, 2004; Deloitte Research, 2000). These initiatives have inherent benefits that apply to all administrations, regardless of economic and social background, although there is great variability in how the implementation is undertaken. Governments around the world are convinced that e-government efforts can provide that engine for deep and valuable economic, social, political, technological, and strategic transformation due to its broad scope (OECD, 2003). Consequently, we are now witnesses to the proliferation of e-government implementation around the world, superseding geographical as well as cultural boundaries. This means, therefore, that as we conceptualize e-government, we need to be cognizant of its international dimension and that it has implications for more substantive economic, social, political, and cultural impacts.

Based on the preceding discussion and our understanding of published material on the subject, we propose a working operational definition of e-government that expands the limited view present in most practitioner definitions. We define electronic government as follows:

A broad-based transformation initiative, enabled by leveraging the capabilities information and communication technology; (1) to develop and deliver high quality, seamless, and integrated public services; (2) to enable effective constituent relationship management; and (3) to support the economic and social development goals of citizens, businesses, and civil society at local, state, national, and international levels.

Developing a Generic Framework for E-Government

The operational definition of electronic government implies a number of complex issues. From our research, we have observed that every government has its own vision of what constitutes the construct and its own approach to implementing that vision. However, we feel that there is a common need to characterize and identify the direction and dimensions of each of these approaches. Certain commonalities and challenges exist in every e-government undertaking. Our goal is to develop a generic e-government framework (GEF) that will help to overcome and to restate these challenges. To do this, we first identify key requirements for developing the framework. We then propose a framework, identifying and discussing its various features and functionality.

Requirements for a Generic E-Government Framework

E-government deployment is influenced by diverse factors. Consequently, in developing a generic framework, we need to establish a set of criteria that should inform and shape what factors constitute the framework, its requirements, and features, and how they are arranged and relate to each other. We believe a generic e-government framework should meet the following requirements.

a.   *Provide a "noise free" representation of e-government*

To respond to and represent the desires of a variety of stakeholder groups, an e-government program must embrace and satisfy the desires of citizens, businesses, civil society, and policymakers, while taking into consideration the requirements of existing political structures and operating processes. As a result, a significant amount of "noise" and interference generated by political, social, and technological factors and agendas, are injected into the process of identifying, analyzing, and deciding what projects and processes to adopt in executing the e-government program.

E-government efforts inherit problems similar to those found in the IS/IT field, where technical jargon and definitions are confusing and a large number of terms are used inconsistently for the same concepts (Ward & Peppard, 2002). Technology issues, including technology jargon, can also obscure the true situation (Luftman, 1996; Keen, 1991). As a result, there are often disconnects between the points of view of key participants (i.e., policymakers and technology experts). The resulting interference makes it difficult to determine the true situation surrounding the overall strategy and transformation effort (Osborne & Gaebler, 1992). A nonpartisan view would aid greatly in optimizing planning and implementation activities. Therefore, it is vital to have a high-level framework that has the ability to capture a more objective representation of e-government. Such a framework can then be shared and easily referenced across political, ideological, and technological boundaries, providing a common basis for informed discourse about issues relating to the e-government agenda.

b.   *Enable identification and articulation of e-government goals and objectives*
Effective coordination and organization of an e-government program requires clear understanding of goals and objectives. The power of setting clear goals and a shared mission statement is potentially one of the most significant acts that an administration can undertake in the reform process (Osborne & Gaebler, 1993). These are not always easy to ascertain, given the many vagaries involved in the vision development and realization process. In order to maximize support and success, the vision must be shared and communicated effectively (Cufaude, 2003). The articulation of goals and objectives also helps to meet the requirement of creating a shared vision and has the powerful effects of (1) communicating the fundamental purpose and mission of the effort; (2) creating a common understanding and commitment to the overall effort; and (3) integrating and aligning different functional areas. Therefore, a framework that will aid in the articulation and identification of common goals and objectives will have significant benefits.

c.   *Identify the gap between the present and the future states of e-government deployment*
Understanding and identifying the gap between current and future states are key elements in the strategic management process and provide an effective way of monitoring the progress of e-government initiatives. The distance between reform initiatives and the current realities of the public sector is often of vital importance in determining the success and failure of reform initiatives (Heeks, 1999). Mapping the progress from "the way things are now" to "the way things ought to be" also allows decision makers to weigh the potential progress of each area against the level of future development required by the e-government vision. It can also assist policymakers and administrators in analyzing the potential benefits and impacts of committing resources and implementation effort as they engage in the planning process.

Beyond the determination of success and failure, the mapping of current reality against the mission statement of the future also generates the energy for change that is a requirement for any transformation process. In effect, the transformation process needs both a vision and a picture of the present to move forward. Therefore, we have another compelling argument for the creation of a new representation of e-government efforts that allows planners and implementers to measure and map the current state of the implementation against its intended result.

d.   *Support prediction of future trends affecting e-government initiatives*

Electronic government is a reform effort that is breaking new ground in many areas. For example, beyond the ability to access information and perform basic electronic transactions, citizens in some jurisdictions are demanding more customized products and services rather than acceding to the traditional public institution 'one size fits all' approaches (Osborne & Gaebler, 1992). The emphasis of technology-enabled service delivery has shifted towards providing the right systems and services that users need and want rather than purely emphasizing operational efficiencies (Friedman, 1994). Trends are towards increasing functionality, specialization, and integration (Bertelsmann, 2001; Nolan & Gibson, 1974). New funding arrangements and horizontal and vertical integration are some of the many new elements that are being implemented (Accenture, 2001; Layne & Lee, 2001). As a result, there are no pre-established roadmaps; an international standard or format does not exist (Bertelsmann, 2001).

Beyond citizen-focused initiatives, electronic government also requires the balancing of diverse elements across strategic and operational domains. Changes in the technology field can significantly affect the direction and progress of applications development by either enhancing or limiting choices or functionality. Planners and decision makers must maintain a high level of awareness of required technology and applications change (Nolan & Gibson, 1974). Strategic foresight, coupled with an understanding of the technology and application changes required, is essential to managing internal and external operational and strategic constraints. Consequently, a framework for e-government, acting as a diagnostic tool, should be helpful in predicting the impact of future trends and requirements. In this way, the potential effect of future events can be anticipated and taken into account throughout the entire development life cycle.

e.   *Be transferable across different contexts of application*

Every nation has its own functional, social, and administrative objectives to fulfill. As a result, each nation's vision will differ with respect to the strategic priorities of the policymakers and the jurisdiction they represent, giving a unique flavor and direction for each e-government endeavor. Therefore, every e-government program should be viewed and assessed with respect to its context of application (Corrocher & Ordanini, 2002). A greater understanding of motivations and resulting patterns of development in different settings can facilitate the process of comparing approaches and provide a rational means of setting the reform of public administration on course for efficiency and transparency, with clear orientation towards its citizens (Bertelsmann, 2001). It is vitally important to distinguish patterns of development and motivations for e-government and identify transferable elements. Common experiences and practices from one nation's realization could be incorporated into another's, resulting in the creation of a synergistic learning capability. This would be invaluable, given that electronic government is an evolving and pioneering effort where all countries can be considered as being in the early stages of development (Pacific Council on International Policy, 2002). The ability to leverage the experiences and lessons learned by other administrations and selectively identify the applicable elements of other nations would create a synergistic learning and knowledge network that would reduce planning and strategizing efforts. A generic framework that encapsulates these principles would go a long way to improve the discourse about how e-government is being developed across different jurisdictions and contexts.

f.   *Support a system representation of strategic agendas and implementation efforts*

A system representation of e-government is required to capture the system's nature of the concept. Systems are one of the common units of analyses within the e-government endeavor. Systems must be balanced across the implementation and are also an area where mapping efforts can be applied and gaps can be identified. The impact and effects of future needs and requirements also have a direct effect on the e-government systems. Given that the operation of e-government depends significantly on the effective management of a variety of systems, a generic framework should capture details of electronic government at this level.

g.   *Provide a functional representation of e-government objectives*

Another common unit of analysis is at the functional level. Goals, objectives, and future needs and requirements are typically articulated in the form of functional capacities. In addition, gaps in functionality provide the first indicators that the realization of the e-government vision is not on course. Functional capacities are also used in the comparison of international efforts. To account for these realities the framework must maintain a capability to identify functional capabilities at a high level in a way that reflects the primary motivations and objectives of the overall e-government program. Therefore, a functional representation of e-government is a necessary requirement, supporting several types of analytical efforts.

h.   *Support reusability and expandability of framework constructs*

The analysis and consideration of electronic government also has an implicit requirement for reusability and expandability. E-government is an evolving phenomenon that reflects the changing needs and requirements of a society. The mapping of current development against the future is an ongoing effort and must be periodically reviewed and revised. As a result, the generic framework also must be able to capture new data and information about new developments on an ongoing basis. In brief, the framework must classify and describe the ongoing activities at a high level and provide a functional representation that can aid in the planning and implementation process. With regards to the changing nature of e-government, the framework should act as a "sliding window" that reveals the relationship between current initiatives and the overall vision. By meeting these requirements, we are seeking to create a new model for viewing e-government programs as a contiguous whole, while providing a starting point for discussing current knowledge and practices and extending the boundaries of these two areas.

A Generic E-Government Framework (GEF): A Proposal

In Figure 1, we present a proposal for a generic framework for e-government. The framework comprises a number of features that attempt to provide a comprehensive representation of e-government endeavors that meet the requirements identified and discussed earlier. Following a discussion of some of the key features of the framework presented in Figure 1, we discuss how the framework was developed.

Figure 1. Generic framework for electronic government

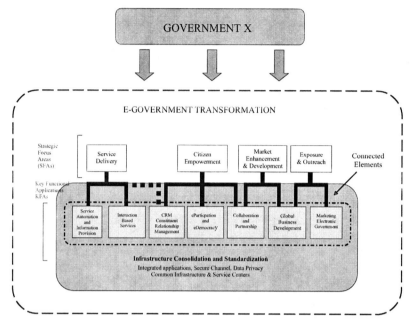

GEF Framework Features

The GEF model presented in Figure 1 displays a number of features that, we believe, enhance its usefulness.

Graphical Representation

A graphical representation was chosen, since it provided the best balance between detail and abstraction of e-government visions and implementation activities. From our analysis of other models and frameworks in the IS/IT and e-government areas, a graphical representation or hybrid representation (text plus graphics) was often utilized to better illustrate key details and concepts, including:

- levels of abstraction;
- complex relationships and interactions;
- multiple dimension spanning developments; and
- systems and functional perspective.

For example, the four-stage EDP model (Nolan & Gibson, 1974) uses a combination of text and graphical elements to provide varying levels of abstraction with respect to growth elements and management techniques over the model's four development stages. Graphical illustrations were also used to describe the dynamics of the IS function within user organizations (Friedman, 1994), as well as the interconnection between technology, human, and business elements (Alter, 2002). With respect to e-government developments, the graphical representation is more direct. Koh and Prybutok (2003) directly depict the three-ring model for measuring the dimensions of e-government functions in graphical form. Similarly, Layne and Lee (2001) provide a graphical representation of functional development mapped against overall integration and development complexity in their four-stage model of fully functional e-government. A pictorial view was also deemed to be the most effective way of communicating in a common language that provides a functional perspective free of technical language jargon and document-based artifacts. Such a framework would be easier to share and disseminate across administrations and development contexts, and it reduces the number of implicit assumptions and uncertainties. Our hope is that such a representation would be subject to less interpretation errors and could be debated and discussed with greater facility than a traditional text-based document.

Modularity, Flexibility, and Scalability

The model illustrated in Figure 1 provides a system level representation of a generic Government X's implementation or vision. Strategic focus areas (SFAs) and key functional applications (KFAs) are represented as stand-alone blocks and sub-blocks that represent vertical and horizontal elements of electronic government vision and implementation. The basic security and computing infrastructure platform was also designed to meet the same requirements. These are stand-alone elements that can be reused and interconnected in a variety of ways. This modularity enables reuse and ease of modification and also significantly supports scalability and flexibility capabilities.

By virtue of its flexibility and modularity, the framework can be expanded and modified to represent a diverse array of e-government visions of developments through the selection of SFA clusters and by interconnecting these with relevant developmental areas. In this way, customized views can be built to provide a contingency capability that allows for differentiation and representation of different development perspectives and development patterns. This allows for multiple applications of the framework to different implementations and vision plans and also meets the requirement for transferability across contexts. Note also that the model classifies efforts by function or end objective and not by departmental or agency boundaries, and thus provides additional flexibility in considering electronic government developments.

Application of the framework is not limited to the predefined SFAs and key application areas. New SFA and KFA blocks can be created or interchanged, and interconnections between elements also can be readily changed to reflect new relationships and developments as they arise over time. The framework is not a static construct with rigid classifications; the key application areas and SFAs given are only meant as starting points for future investigations. The framework is customizable, not only across contexts of application, but also across different development periods where it can be reapplied to the same implementation periodically. This scalability and ease of reapplication underline the need for longitudinal analysis and continual monitoring and environmental scanning.

Table 2. Identification of e-government functional applications

E-Government Functional Applications (Initial)	Sources
· Interaction based services · Seamless service delivery and automation · Integration of information, services and agencies · Information organization and content aggregation · CRM – Constituent Relationship Management · Democracy and Participation · Transparency and Constituent Connectivity · Exposure and outreach · Global Business Development · Data and security protection	-Bertilsmann, 2001, Layne, & Lee, 2001; OECD, 2003 Accenture 2001, 2002; Working Group E-gov., 2002; Word Markets Research, 2001 -Accenture 2002, Government of Canada, 2002, Koh & Prybutok, 2003 Layne, & Lee, 2001, Koh & Prybutok, 2003, Working Group E-gov., 2002 -Accenture, 2001, Deloitte Research, 2000, Government of Canada, 2002 -UK Online Action Plan, 2001, Government of Canada, 2002, Accenture, 2001, Heeks, 1999; Chadwick & May, 2003; OECD, 2003 -MAMPU Flagship Applications, 2002, CIMU White Paper, 2002, Accenture, 2002, Working Group E-gov., 2002 -Accenture, 2002, Working Group E-gov., 2002, Government of Canada, 2002, UK Online Action Plan, 2001

METHODOLOGY

Formulating Key Application Areas and Identifying Strategic Agenda Clusters

The conceptualization of the generic framework was a multi-phased process and began with the study of information age agendas proposed by Heeks (1999). These were identified as increased efficiency, decentralization, increased accountability, improved resource management, and marketization. These agenda items are, in effect, the horizontal motivating elements that are shared across functional and departmental lines. We inferred from this that every electronic government initiative could be considered in some way to fulfill one or more of these agendas.

To build upon these findings, we then identified prominent areas of electronic government development by analyzing e-government vision and white paper documents of various nations, along with independent consulting reports and academic research. Initially, we focused on developed nations (U.S., Canada, France, Denmark), but further expanded the analysis to include developing and developed nations (Malaysia, Singapore, Malta, Mauritius, South Africa, United Kingdom). This level of analysis highlighted a number of key functional applications and represents a progression in the framework development process from high-level motivations to more concrete implementation aspects. Table 2 outlines the e-government applications initially identified from the literature investigated.

The next step was the refinement of the application areas to include operational and infrastructure components, and human and collaborative elements that were not explicitly identified in the reviewed material. These components act as bridging and enabling elements to many of the other areas and must necessarily be acknowledged as essential areas of e-government development. See Appendix 1 for a detailed description of the application areas.

In Table 3 some key refinements introduced into the conceptualization of the framework at this stage were:

- Separation of services into interactive and automation and information based efforts. This demarcation parallels the evolutionary progression of services towards greater maturity and sophistication and allows for the measurement of efforts with differing levels of each.
- Recognition of a common infrastructure and security platform that provides a baseline for developing internal efficiency, reliability, and acceptance for IT and human systems. This platform addresses the need for a high degree of integration between technology, organizational and human systems.
- Recognition of ICT as a determining factor in the participation and democracy developmental areas by the inclusion of the "e" prefix
- Recognition of collaborative elements involved in the planning, rollout and adoption of e-government initiatives and services. This can also be seen as the acknowledgment of soft integration elements not defined in the basic infrastructure platform.
- Addition of marketing of e-government as another key area that supports the adoption and diffusion of initiatives but is not intended to replace the marketization agenda presented earlier.

At this stage, we have identified the generic areas of development that an administration can potentially undertake. However, the framework, as it stood, did not meet the requirements for transferability across different contexts of application. To meet this exigency, we created a classification scheme entitled Strategic Focus Areas (SFAs) that could be used to identify high-level e-government vision objectives that would be applicable across different government administrations. Each group incorporates a number of relevant functional applications. The SFAs are identified in Figure 1 as:

- Service Delivery
- Citizen Empowerment
- Market Enhancement and Development
- Exposure and Outreach

Each SFA provides a suggestive mapping between KFA and higher-level agendas. SFA clustering represents an initial interpretation of the strategies and directions employed in current e-government programs and, at best, is an informed estimate of

Table 3. E-government functional applications (refined)

E-Government Functional Applications (Initial)	E-Government Key Functional Applications (Refined)
· Interactive services · Seamless service delivery & automation · Integration of information, services and agencies · Information organization & content aggregation · CRM – Constituent Relationship Management · Democracy & Participation · Transparency & Constituent Connectivity · Exposure & outreach · Global Business Development · Data & Security protection	· Interactive Services · Service Automation & Information Provision · *Infrastructure consolidation & Standardization* · CRM Development · eDemocracy & eParticipation · Collaboration & Partnership Programs · Marketing E-Government · Global Business Development

current efforts. In addition to these four groupings, we introduce the horizontal dimension of the infrastructure consolidation and standardization. Given the level of coupling between groupings and an integrated and secure infrastructure, each SFA's associated developmental area is interconnected with the integrated platform. We note one caveat, however. The growing importance and impact of security and privacy concerns within e-government may soon merit their own Strategic Focus Area.

SFA Analytical Capabilities

The model is designed to provide the flexibility to consider developments at different levels of abstraction. Figure 1 represents a high-level categorization of general trends and directions that could be used to generate awareness and discussion. Lower-level differentiation would consist of analyzing actual implementation initiatives and nesting them within the appropriate key functional application areas. This ability to decompose the elements of the functional application areas is useful for operational and strategic analyses. This decomposition technique can be applied for the following:

a.   Verification of direction and strategy against actual implementation activities on an ongoing basis

This constitutes a top down application of the GEF. An objective view of e-government is created when implementation activities are nested within SFAs. This view provides a measure of the progress of the implementation relative to strategic objectives and can be used in conjunction with predefined qualitative or quantitative criteria (e.g., usage rates or degree of operational readiness). If applied on a continuing basis, this application can be utilized as a dynamic check that reveals how far strategic objectives have been realized, based on the degree of completion within key application areas.

b.   Vision identification for emerging e-government efforts

This represents a bottom-up application. Key initiatives can be identified and used to form functional application areas. These can then be used to create appropriate SFA clusters that can be used to define vision objectives and directions. The application of GEF in such a manner would be ideal for situations where e-government initiatives are ad hoc and an overall vision or strategy has not yet been articulated.

In Table 4, we provide some examples of the decomposition of the GEF using e-government initiatives and activities from five nations. Various activities are identified and placed under the appropriate SFA and KFA headings. This mapping then gives the relative degree of activity in each SFA and KFA. As presented, the depiction gives an overall view of e-government initiatives internationally. However, each nation's relative activity level could also be determined only by considering its specific activities. For example, South African efforts focus mainly on Service Delivery and Exposure and Outreach SFAs, with minor activity elsewhere.

Consolidated GEF Features and Requirements

A mapping between the requirements and GEF features is given in Table 5 to conclude our discussion.

E-government is an ongoing endeavor that is constantly evolving. We expect that the rate of change will continue to accelerate, given the potential for new technological advances and the complexity of government processes and citizen needs and requirements. To accommodate the fluid nature of the effort, future oriented tools and methodologies must be scalable and have the capability to measure progress on a continuing basis. The framework must act as a sliding window that can be used to update key stakeholders of the current state of the vision. Therefore, a framework or conceptual model also must have the freedom to classify and reclassify ongoing developments as the implementation and vision mature.

CASE STUDIES

To further illustrate the application of the framework, we used it to study the e-government programs of three countries: the United States; the United Kingdom; and Malaysia. The case studies are presented in brief and should not be considered as the complete representation of all the e-government efforts in the countries selected. Our aim is simply to illustrate the main features of the framework. In Table 6, we outline the key features of each of the cases. Information used in the table was gleaned from published government documents (white papers, reports, etc.) typically found on government Web sites and from other publicly available sources. Data presented here were gathered in 2002 and 2003. Note that some of the information since might have been updated since then.

We begin the table by first identifying the published title for e-government vision and the principal agency responsible for executing the vision. We then briefly outline key e-government initiatives undertaken by each government administration under the rubric of the SFAs. We should note that the visions and initiatives here represent activities at the national/federal level only. Once the initiatives have been listed, we

Table 4. Illustration of GEF decomposition using e-government initiatives from five nations

Service Delivery — Service Auto & Info, Interactive Services, CRM	Citizen Empowerment — eParticipation/ Democracy, Collaboration, Partnership, CRM	Market Enhancement & Development — Collaboration/ Partnership, Globalization	Exposure and Outreach — Globalization, Marketing E-Gov	Infrastructure Consolidation and Standardization
Service Automation & Info	**eParticipation/Democracy**	**Collaboration/Partnership**	**Global Business Development**	**Internal efficiencies and procurement**
SA-PIT – public information	US-Census/Library Congress: www.census.gov, www.thomas.loc.gov	US-Bus/Agency Proc. Portal: procurement portal for business and agencies: www.FedBizOpps.gov	MAL- Cyber Jaya, technology showcase, integrated infrastructure, open invitation to international firms to share knowledge openly…	SA- Consolidate buying power of state, common procurement platform
SA-Transport – www.transport.gov.za train schedules, road construction update)	UK-Democracy: Citizen space	MAL- Government Supplier and Vendor Commerce site http://home.eperolehan.com.my		US – 24 month high pay off initiatives, internal efficiencies and federal infrastructure
US-Central Gov't Portal: www.FirstGOv.gov (figures, account driven/ legislative docs search)	UK-Democracy: live debate coverage of parliament + feedback encouraged, 12 month trial: www.parliament.uk/	**Global Business Development**	**Marketing E-Gov**	US – Internal Efficiency and Effectiveness Portfolio
UK-WAP wireless services (Land Registry)	SA- Voting and registration services and information and results updates: www.elections.org.za	MALTA- Partnering w/ Global firm to develop common ICT infrastructure	SA –Alternative Technologies ITV, WAP, KIOSK	MAL – Generic Office Environment (Paperless)
Interactive Services		UK-digital key infrastructure to enable eCommerce, one certification authority	SA-Multilanguage and Literacy Level delivery mechanisms	MAL – Electronic Procurement (Internal Supply Chain initiative)
SA-Education – www.education.pwv.gov.za www.unisa.ac.za (online 'cente + fees)	**Collaboration/Partnership**		SA-Smartcard & Population Registry → an example of Reach focus and enabling access to e-government services	
SA-Taxes –www.mytax.co.za (filing public/private, view correspondence, forms)	Fin: interactive public discussion forum hosted by ministry: www.otakantaa.fi/kavynissa.fin		SA-PIT – public information terminal → an example of Reach focus and enabling access to e-government services	
US-Postal: www.moverguide.com (follow-up procedure)			UK- Online Media Campaign coincides w/ 2005 service launch	
CAN- Revenue Netfile – private/ citizen filing, paperless: www.netfile.gc.ca				
CRM				
SA-Multilanguage and Literacy Level delivery mechanisms				
US-CRM ** Labor: www.aib.org				
MAL-Citizen Central, user group focused info (community, young adult, parent) http://www.mcsc.com.my				

provide a qualitative assessment of how much emphasis is placed on them by the government administration in question. We classify the emphases as major, balanced, or minor. As noted earlier, each government administration may place a different emphasis on an application area. The emphasis placed depends on the strategic objectives being pursued, the history and context influencing the choices being made, as well as the level of e-government implementation experience and maturity. Most government administrations give priority to service delivery efforts because they are able to deliver "quick wins" in this area (Accenture, 2002, 2004). However, as they grow in e-government deployment maturity and the service delivery application areas become more fully functional, they tend to move on to other areas of focus.

FINDINGS

We now present some general observations and comments with respect to overall e-government development. From the above, the generic framework was applied to the three nations and provided a good initial mapping of their e-government development efforts. The modularity feature provided a high degree of freedom in classifying the different initiatives and strategic objectives of each vision, which mapped well to the predetermined and SFA and KFA clusters. The case outlines also uncovered a number of potentially key developmental themes including:

- varying degree of centralization
- lack of balanced development
- service delivery SFA as the most prevalent development cluster

Table 5. GEF features and requirements

Framework Features	Key Benefits	Requirements Supported
Graphical representation	- Differing levels of abstraction - Illustration of complex relationships and interactions - Multi-dimensional view - Common alignment medium	- System perspective - Noise free representation - Transferability and across contexts of application - Functional representation of E-government
Modularity Flexibility Scalability	- Stand alone vertical and horizontal elements - Flexible interconnection - Customizable - Capture capability (strategic developments, developments) - Longitudinal analysis and ease of reapplication	- System perspective - Functional Representation of E-government - Reusability and Expandability - Mapability of present against overall objectives - Transferability across contexts of application
Breakout Capability	- Differing levels of abstraction - Strategic & operational Applications - Diagnostic capabilities	- Reusability and expandability - Mapability of present against overall objectives

Similar to the measurement of digital divide dimensions by Corrocher and Ordanini (2002), there were significant differences in how administrations choose to develop their visions of electronic government. Development efforts were undertaken in both symmetric and asymmetric fashions. Certain nations, such as the United Kingdom, focused on more integrated and distributed efforts (symmetric) across all SFAs, while others focused only on a few of the SFA efforts to meet specific contexts of application (asymmetric).

Patterns of development also reflected the degree of centralized direction that each nation followed. Most nations followed a long-term approach, with the exception of the United States, which drives its implementation based on a 24-month-long initiative with clear and measurable returns.

There is also a distinct lack of balanced development. SFA development was more prevalent in areas with more well defined and measurable impacts and benefits. Most nations did not pursue a balanced development across all dimensions, but chose one or more key areas on which to concentrate their efforts. The overall US and UK visions for e-government represented the two endpoints of the centralization spectrum. Service Delivery SFA initiatives were present for all nations, however. Exposure and Outreach and Market Enhancement SFA clusters were the next most prevalent. The weakest SFA was Citizen Empowerment. This supports the observation made by Chadwick and May (2003) that the consultative and participatory focus of e-government efforts were the least developed and often overlooked. We believe that the development and performance of the former are more measurable (usage rates, penetration levels, revenue generated) than the latter, and that a relationship exists between measurability and the frequency of implementation. Additionally, there may be a relationship between the maturity of the vision (infrastructure, service sophistication and diversity, degree of articulated centralized direction) and the level of symmetric development. From our findings, therefore, we can confirm the following:

- There is a strong services component in e-government visions and realizations.
- There is a prevalence of a practitioner perspective that focuses on "quick wins."
- There are many different ways to conceptualize and implement e-government.

DISCUSSION AND CONCLUSIONS

Framework Capabilities and Requirements

We now discuss the implications of findings on framework capabilities and requirements. Six initial requirements were suggested and incorporated into the framework design. Of these, five were fully or partially demonstrated by the first application of the generic framework, and one was not.

From this application, we observed that the framework provided:

- a mapping of diverse electronic government elements to a common perspective;
- the ability to compare and differentiate underlying goals and themes between different implementations; and
- the ability to draw general conclusions and compare differences and similarities across implementations.

Table 6. Case study summaries

	United States	United Kingdom	Malaysia
Vision Title:	Information Super Highway Updated with Expanded Electronic Government 2001 (1993-present)	Information age Government (1998-present)	Electronic Government (1997-present)
Principal Driver:	Office of Management and Budget	Office of the e-Envoy	Malaysian Administrative Modernization and Management Planning Unit (MAMPU)
Strategic Focus Area			
Service Delivery	**Major** **Government to Citizen Portfolio** – consumer portal with diverse free and pay based benefits & services (Education, tax, forms, postal) **Government to Business Portfolio** Expanded tax products for business, international trade licensing and regulation	**Balanced** -*UK Online Centers – 6000 online centers introduce e-Government services by 2002* -Transaction based services – Postal & Education -Alternate technology services - WAP wireless services	**Major** -**PMO Office: Paperless environment** - Internally focused program to create electronic seat of Government. -**Centralized public service offerings** – Human Resources, Electronic Procurement -**Automated service pilot programs** – including interaction public service/citizen based services (knowledge sharing, labour, licensing)
Citizen Empowerment	**Minor** eVoting Service oriented based segmentation Business centric collaboration & partnership	**Balanced** -**PIU web based policy making and parliament web TV** –governance and public participation integration efforts -Web access to Government legislation and initiative status - **UK Online Centers** basic skills training and framework for bringing e-Government to a national audience.	**Minor** -KIOSK development principally to meet service delivery objectives -Articulated CRM efforts – Rough segmentation of targeted groups
Market Enhancement & Development	**Major** **Government to Business Portfolio** – Streamlined support process, E-Business communication enhancement, one-stop business compliance provision. **Core Process Identification and High Payoff Initiatives** – Twenty-four (24) high payoff initiatives across twenty-eight (28) lines of business	**Balanced** -**Citizen focused development** –Extensive government wide CRM efforts to identify and segment user groups -**Collaboration and Partnership** – Dedicated E-Commerce group to develop E-Commerce environment with public, private stakeholders -Action plans to overcome regulatory/legal barriers and enhance connectivity to the global community	**Minor** -Marketing of Malaysia as a technological R&D Center for international development. -Technology component of E-Government is significantly articulated.
Exposure & Outreach	**Minor** Consumer portal – a single point of access to federal information sources online.	**Balanced** **Strategic marketing plan** – Online media campaign for 2005 service launch, E-Government branding & high profile marketing of services to users at local and international arenas	**Major** -**Cyberjaya: Smart City** Multimedia fully wired oasis designed to attract innovative companies from around the world -**PMO Office: Generic Office Environment** –Showcase a fully integrated, distributed and scalable deployment of multimedia information technology -**Multimedia Super Corridor (MSC)** – Twenty (20) year transformation effort to build and create a knowledge based society and technology utopia

Table 6. (continued)

	United States	United Kingdom	Malaysia
Infrastructure consolidation and standardization	Major Government to Government Portfolio – Integrated Federal Architecture for IT efficiency (information, processes, resources) Internal Efficiency and Effectiveness Portfolio Commercial best practices application	Minor E-government interoperability framework.	
Overall Assessment	A market driven vision with high pay off applications developed on a case by case basis to maximize internal efficiencies across 28 lines of business. Strong focus on support services and streamlining processes to develop the business environment. A diverse and large array of services offered with citizen engagement predominantly focused on linking users with product offerings.	A balance and integrated approach supported by a wide variety of services for private citizens, business and the public service coupled to extensive segmentation and customization CRM efforts. A clearly articulated and integrated marketing strategy to maximize exposure and outreach at local and international levels along with ongoing collaboration to create a conducive E-Commerce framework.	An outreach and exposure based vision that is also service oriented. Integrated with the Multimedia Super Corridor (MSC) transformation effort to build and create a knowledge-based society and technology utopia. Significant showcasing and marketing of technological areas of excellence and innovation including paperless environments, cyber smart cities at the international level. Centralized services and pilot applications serve both public service and private citizens.

In our application of the framework, we were able to represent higher-level objectives as Strategic Focus Areas and Key Functional Applications. These provide the common elements that are flexible enough to classify the specific elements of each initiative, yet not introduce too great a level of detail. As a result, interpretation and jargon "noise" effects were minimized. The profiles are highly customizable and allow for the creation of a common view of electronic government that could be easily shared and compared.

For example, in the U.S. and Malaysian profiles, we were able to identify key areas of strategic focus. Both nations had a similarly strong focus on the service delivery component, but differed on the other dimensions. The U.S. e-government program has a strong market enhancement and infrastructure consolidation and standardization focus, whereas the Malaysian development's other area of concentration lay in the exposure and outreach area. Therefore, different areas of strategic focus and activities were captured, and different patterns of development were observed by comparing levels of strategic concentration (minor, major) and related key functional application activities. U.S. development tended to be more internalized and focused on providing maximum efficiencies and economic benefits over a shorter period (24-month high payoff initiatives), while Malaysian efforts reflected a more externalized approach to raise global awareness of Malaysian society and technology offerings over an extended period (20 years). Some potential contextual factors were also highlighted during this process. Perhaps U.S. efforts reflect a more established base of applications and development, while Malaysian efforts are more focused on growth and enhancement of emerging technical and social conditions.

In a similar fashion, country profiles were created for all three nations and used to identify patterns of development that highlighted both similarities and differences in implementation activities and strategic areas of focus. We observed a number of general trends and developments:

Table 7. Framework requirement evaluation

Framework Requirement	Successfully Demonstrated
• Noise free representation	Partial
• Transferability and across context of application	Yes
• Functional representation of E-government objectives	Yes
• System representation	Partial
• Reusability and Expandability	Partial
• Mapability of present against overall objectives	No, untested

- differing patterns of development;
- varying degrees of centralization;
- lack of balanced development; and
- service delivery SFA as the most prevalent development cluster.

We were able to identify these because the framework was expandable and reusable across the e-government programs studied. We successfully used the breakout capabilities to analyze and classify the activities and articulated objectives. In this manner, we were able to perform a mixed analysis with some qualitative (articulated objectives) and quantitative (achievements, implementations) elements. The built-in modularity, scalability, and flexibility features then provided the means to identify patterns of development in a simplified yet inclusive manner. As a result, we were able to consider these patterns at a manageable level of abstraction and draw general conclusions that transcend the specific activities of each e-government endeavor and that could be shared across contexts of application.

Limitations

However, we also observed the following shortcomings of the framework:

- lack of support for a full systems representation;
- potential noise effects could be present; and
- case study represents a static application.

The generic framework only provides partial systems representation of e-government. The interconnection of key application areas and SFAs provides a high-level system representation of overall objectives and some of the relationships between different areas of development. By its very nature, it is more functionally orientated and not optimized towards representing system connections and interrelationships. Profiles are designed to provide a common perspective based on analyzing findings from material that tends to describe developments from a functional or capabilities viewpoint. Consequently, these common elements are abstracted from the actual systems and relationships employed by the administrations under study. For example, the relationships and connectivity of the IS/IT function with the executive and public service branch of government are not detailed. Only high-level objectives and relationships are depicted as interconnected SFAs and KFAs. This level of abstraction is required in order to maintain the common perspective and ability to transcend application contexts. Therefore, for an analysis of the actual systems, additional models and tools will be required to complement the application of the GEF.

Another post application discovery was the lack of filtering for potential bias and inconsistencies in vision claims and achievements included in the country-specific profiles. The profiles did present a common view that filtered out technical jargon and multiple interpretation artefacts, but did not provide any checks on the validity of the data that was used in profile construction. Initially, our intention was that a "noise-free" representation would be achieved by virtue of reviewing several sources from both involved and independent parties; additionally, profiles were envisioned to be generated based on a substantial body of achieved, as well as articulated, objectives. However, most developments were in the initial stages, and, therefore, profiles were based almost exclusively on the latter. Consequently, this application may contain political noise artefacts and inconsistencies and only offers a best attempt at "noise-free" depiction based on the data available.

The case studies only represent a static application at one point in time. The expandability and reusability requirement has only been confirmed with respect to the application to different e-government efforts, but not over the dimension of time. As a result, the measurability of e-government maturity requirement is untested, given that vision objectives and achievements were combined instead of measuring the current state against the intended vision. In conclusion, the framework was successful in providing a common perspective that transcends any one e-government offering, but must be supported by additional analytical tools to provide a full systems perspective. It must also be reapplied to fully test its applicability over time.

In addition to these shortcomings, there are a number of questions still to be addressed. For example, if service delivery and a practitioner perspective are the basis for e-government developments, what direction will future developments take? Is balanced development across all areas necessary for superior performance? Additionally, what are the ultimate potential and benefits of application areas such as Citizen Empowerment? Currently, initiatives in this area are the weakest (Chadwick & May, 2003). We argue that, in the end, some form of balanced development will be necessary. There are only a limited number of "quick-win" initiatives available, and most of these have already been exploited in advanced countries (Accenture, 2004).

Ultimately, electronic government development and maturity must reflect the changes in the political, social, and economic orientation of the hosting nation. Therefore, it must evolve beyond its current state. However, this will require additional knowledge, experience, and deliberation. New technology and organizational infrastructure will also need to be developed. We hope that the generic framework can be refined and reapplied to identify some of these upcoming trends and developments, and we look forward to the emergence of additional tools and models that will move the e-government consciousness closer to this point of maturity.

REFERENCES

Accenture (2001). eGovernment leadership: Innovation delivered.

Accenture (2002). eGovernment leadership: Realizing the vision.

Accenture (2004, May). *eGovernment leadership: High performance, maximum value.* E-Government Executive Series.

Alter, S. (2002). *Information systems: Foundations of e-business* (4th ed.). Upper Saddle, NJ: Prentice Hall.

Basu, S. (2004). E-government and developing countries: An overview. *International Review of Law, Computers & Technology, 18*(1), 109-132.

Bertelsmann Foundation (2001). Balanced e-government: E-government– Connecting efficient administration and responsive democracy.

Box, R. (1999). Running government like a business: Implications for public administration theory and practice. *American Review of Public Administration, 29*(1), 19-43.

Brodie, J. (1999). *Critical concepts: An introduction to politics.* Scarborough, Canada: Prentice Hall; Allyn and Bacon.

Caldow, J. (2001). *Seven e-Government leadership milestones.* Working paper - Institute of Electronic Government, IBM Corporation.

Chadwick, A., & May, C. (2003, April 27). Interaction between states and citizens in the age of the Internet: "E-government" in the United States, Britain, and the European Union. *Governance, 16*(2), 271-300.

Corrocher, N., & Ordanini, A. (2002). Measuring the digital divide: A framework for the analysis of cross-country differences. *Journal of Information Technology, 17*(1), 9-19.

Cufaude, J. (2003). Creating the future while managing the present. *Association Management, 55*(8), 28-34.

Davies, A., & Heeks, R. (1999). Different approaches to information age reform. In R. Heeks (Ed.), *Reinventing government in the information age* (pp. 9-12). London; New York: Routledge.

Deloitte Research – Public Sector Institute. (2000). *At the dawn of e-government: The citizen as customer.*

Friedman, A. (1994). The stages model and the phases of the IS field. *Journal of Information Technology, 9*, 76-88.

Guy, J.J. (2001). *People, politics and government: A Canadian perspective.* Scarborough, Ontario: Prentice Hall.

Heeks, R. (1999). Reinventing government in the information age. In R. Heeks, (Ed.), *Reinventing government in the information age* (pp. 9-12). London; New York: Routledge.

Ke, W., & Wei, K.K. (2004, June). Successful e-government in Singapore. *Communications of the ACM, 47*(6), 95-99.

Keen, P.G.W. (1991). *Shaping the future: Business design through information technology.* Boston: Harvard Business School Press.

Koh, C.E., & Prybutok, V.R. (2003). The three ring model and development of an instrument for measuring dimensions of e-government functions. *Journal of Computer Information Systems, 43*(3), 34-39.

Lacity, M.C., & Willcocks, L.P. (1998). *Strategic sourcing of information systems: Perspectives and practices.* Chicester, UK; New York: Wiley.

Layne, K., & Lee, J. (2001). Developing fully functional e-government: A four stage model. *Government Information Quarterly, 18*, 122-36.

Luftman, J.N. (1996). *Competing in the information age: Strategic alignment in practice.* New York: Oxford University Press.

Marche, S., & McNiven, J.D. (2003). E-government and e-governance: The future isn't what it used to be. *Canadian Journal of Administrative Sciences, 20*(1), 74-86.

Nolan, R., & Gibson, C. (1974). Managing the four stages of EFP growth. *Harvard Business Review, 52*(1), 76-78.

OECD (2003). The case for e-government: Excerpts from the OECD Report "The e-government imperative." *OECD Journal on Budgeting, 3*(1), 62-96.

Office of Management and Budget (OMB) (2003, April). *Implementing the president's management agenda for e-government: E-government strategy.* Retrieved July 30, 2004, from http://www.whitehouse. gov/omb/egov/2003egov_strat.pdf

Osborne, D., & Gaebler, T. (1992). *Reinventing government: How the entrepreneurial spirit is transforming the public sector.* New York: Plume.

Pacific Council on International Policy (2002). Roadmap for e-government in the developing world: 10 questions e-government leaders should ask themselves. *Report of the Working Group on e-government in the developing world.*

Poostchi, M. (2002). *Implementing e-government: Potential impact on organization structure, business processes, and costs.* MBA Thesis. Carleton University.

Rais Abdul Karim, M. (Ed.). (1999). *Reengineering the public service: Leadership and change in an electronic age.* Subang Jaya, Malaysia: Pelanduk Publications.

Reddick, C.G. (2004). A two-stage model of e-government growth: Theories and empirical evidence for U.S. cities. *Government Information Quarterly, 21*, 51-64.

Somogyi, E.K., & Galliers, R.D. (1987). Applied information technology: From data processing to strategic information systems. *Journal of Information Technology, 2*, 30-41.

UK Cabinet Office (2000, April). *E-government: A strategic framework for public services in the information age.* Central IT Unit.

United Nations World Public Sector Report 2003: E-government at the crossroads (2003). Retrieved April 2004, from http://unpan1.un.org/intradoc/groups/public/ documents/un/unpan012733.pdf

Ward, J., & Peppard, J. (2002). *Strategic planning for information systems. Wiley Series in information systems.* West Sussex, UK: John Wiley & Sons.

World Markets Research Centre (2001). *Global e-government survey.* Providence, RI: Brown University.

ADDITIONAL REFERENCES

E-Government Vision Documents and White Papers

Malaysia
Electronic government flagship applications (2002). Retrieved June 2002, from http:// www.mampu.gov.my/mampueng/Ict/flagship.htm

Electronic procurement (internal supply chain). Retrieved July 2002, from http://www.mampu.gov.my/mampueng/Corporat/profile/eg/ep.htm

Human resources management information system. Retrieved July 2002, from http://www.mampu.gov.my/mampueng/Corporat/profile/eg/hrmis.htm

ISP framework version 1.0. Retrieved December 2002, from http://www.mampu.gov.my/mampueng/ICT/ISPlan/ISPlan.htm

ISP template version 1.0. Retrieved December 2002, from http://www.mampu.gov.my/mampueng/ICT/ISPlan/ISPlan.htm

PMO office: Generic office environment. Retrieved July 2002, from http://www.mampu.gov.my/mampueng/Corporat/profile/eg/goe.htm

Malta

Government portal architecture. Retrieved July 2002, from http://www.cimu.gov.mt/eGovWPcontents.asp

Maltese exchange. Retrieved July 2002, from http://www.cimu.gov.mt/eGovWPcontents.asp

National email. Retrieved July 2002, from http://www.cimu.gov.mt/eGovWP_contents.asp

White paper on the vision and strategy for the attainment of e-government (n.d.). Retrieved July 2002, from http://www.cimu.gov.mt/htdocs/content.asp?c=34

South Africa

e-governemnt policy, second draft 2001 version 3.2. Department of Public and Administrations. Republic of South Africa. Retrieved July 2002, from http://www.dpsa.gov.za/e-gov/2001docs/e-govpolicyFramework.htm

PIT – Public information terminal. Retrieved July 2002, from http://www.dpsa.gov.za/e-gov/2001docs/e-govpolicyFramework.htm, and http://www.dpsa.gov.za/e-gov/e-govindex.htm

Smart card and population registry. Retrieved July 2002, from http://www.dpsa.gov.za/e-gov/2001docs/e-govpolicyFramework.htm, and http://www.dpsa.gov.za/e-gov/e-govindex.htm

Transportation information services. Retrieved July 2002, from http://www.transport.gov.za

United States

Consumer portal. Retrieved July 2002, from http://www.consumer.gov

Core process identification and high payoff initiatives. Retrieved July 2002, from http://www.firstgov.gov

Department of Labor Web site. Retrieved July 2002, from http://www.ajb.org

E-government strategy: Simplified delivery of services to citizens (2002). Office of Management and Budget. Retrieved July 2002, from www.whitehouse.gov/OMB

Federal business opportunities. Retrieved July 2002, from http://www.FedBizOpps.gov

First gov your first click to the US Government (2002). Retrieved July 2002, from http://www.firstgov.gov

United Kingdom

Department of Trade and Industry (1999). Building the Knowledge Driven Economy. United Kingdom. Retrieved June 2002, from http://www.dti.gov.uk/comp/competitive/wh_intl.htm

Electronic government services for the 21ˢᵗ century (2000). Retrieved June 2002, from http://www.cabinet-office.gov.uk/innovation/2000/delivery/intro.htm

Parliament Web TV. Retrieved July 2002, from http://www.parliamentlive.tv

Postal services. Retrieved July 2002, from http://www.consignia.com

UK e-commerce services for the 21ˢᵗ century (2001). Retrieved June 2002, from http://www.cabinet-office.gov.uk/innovation/1999/ecomm.html

UK online action plan (2001). Retrieved December 2002, from http://www.e-envoy.gov.uk/ukonline/progress/actplan/table.htm

APPENDIX A:
KEY E-GOVERNMENT APPLICATION AREAS

Service Automation and Information Provision

This refers to efforts that are primarily concerned with automating existing government services. Typically, existing services are duplicated to provide an alternate communication channel. Additionally, implementation programs are skewed towards the online aggregation and publishing of materials and information. The default standard is towards information quantity and richness versus organization for usage.

Interactive Services

These constitute development efforts that are implemented for providing a broad range of services and a high level of functionality. Initiatives focus on providing information and content that is transactional in nature and that offer a higher level of interaction. Communication capability is performed in duplex mode (i.e., both citizens and government have the capacity to provide feedback to one another).

CRM Development

Another refinement in service delivery is to add citizen centricity to the design and development effort. Constituent Relationship Management (CRM) techniques, such as focus groups, need analysis feedback and field-testing, which are integral parts of the action plan. Constituent or user targeting and segmentation efforts are also prevalent, and sites are structured around the needs and requirements of citizens and business. Not only are services offered, but applications also offer value-added services and may provide proactive advisory capabilities, as well. Service integration and user-friendly interfaces also characterize CRM service development.

Collaboration and Partnership Programs

Advances in fostering cooperation and joint initiatives between internal agencies and external organizations are the focus. Partnerships are encouraged and the risks and rewards are shared. Often, service delivery and maintenance are distributed between government and private industry. External stakeholders can also have a significant role in determining and plotting out vision strategies and objectives. Stakeholders also work cooperatively to implement and realize the vision.

Infrastructure Consolidation and Standardization

Internal transformation efforts relate to the growth and implementation of initiatives that aid in reorganizing internal processes to improve efficiency and decision-making effectiveness. Core processes are analyzed and optimized for online delivery. Organizational changes are also brought about to enable these efforts and include modifying reward programs, evaluation procedures, and procedures for resource allocation. Redundant process and information are also reduced or eliminated.

eDemocracy and eParticipation

Citizens are informed and educated about the decision-making process and programs to increase the transparency and responsiveness of government as a whole. Citizen feedback and involvement in day-to-day governance is encouraged as much as possible. Additionally, access to legislation and the decision-making process is more prevalent, and efforts seek to bring government closer to the population and to as wide an audience as possible.

Marketing E-Government

This overlaps to some degree with eDemocracy and citizen centricity objectives. Citizens and business again are informed and educated. However, developments in this area are targeted at promoting and marketing the visions and services. Comprehensive plans to introduce and advocate electronic government services and technology are put into place. Consumer confidence and trust are key objectives, and dedicated resources are allocated to the overall strategy. The measuring of service and CRM performance is another key feature.

Global Business Development

The principal thrust of globalization is to increase global connectivity. A high level of partnership and fostering of relationships internationally are central to these efforts. A main activity is the development and encouragement of e-commerce and business ventures. Programs also reflect a high degree of effort towards establishing links and contacts across physical and state boundaries.

This article was previously published in the *Journal of Global Information Management,* 13(1), pp. 1-30, © 2005.

Chapter V

Culture and Trust in the Adoption of Electronic Voting:
A Look at the USA and South Africa*

David Gefen, Drexel University, USA

Gregory M. Rose, Washington State University, USA

Merrill Warkentin, Mississippi State University, USA

Paul A. Pavlou, University of California, USA

ABSTRACT

Trust is a cornerstone of society, and it enables democratic institutes. It captures people's expectations about others' (the trustees) socially-acceptable behavior. In the context of information technology (IT) adoption, trust also increases the perceived usefulness (PU) of IT associated with the trustee's agency. One way of increasing this trust is through greater sociocultural similarity. Extrapolating based on previous research to the realm of electronic voting, this chapter posits that because trust is culture-dependent, it should decrease considerably as cultural diversity and differentiation increases. To investigate the role of trust in IT adoption in different cultures where dissimilar concepts of socially-acceptable behavior exist, this study

* This project is in cooperation with Accenture South Africa (www.accenture.co.za)

compares trust-related perceptions of an emerging IT, namely electronic voting, between the United States of America (USA) and the Republic of South Africa (RSA). More specifically, the question was addressed by comparing the unique circumstances of the cultural changes in the RSA with the more socially-integrated mainstream USA culture. In both cultures, perceived sociocultural similarity between the individual and the agency in charge of the electronic voting IT contributed to both the establishment of trust and to an increase in the perceived usefulness of the IT, supporting and extending the extrapolations of past propositions to this new realm. However, only in the USA did trust contribute to the PU of the IT. The results suggest that when cultural diversity is large, trust becomes of lesser importance, perhaps because it can no longer reduce social uncertainty. Implications for researchers and governmental voting agencies are discussed, and future research directions are proposed.

INTRODUCTION

Electronic Government (e-government) is the ability of citizens to interact with a government organization using electronic technology, primarily the Internet. Because of the extensive use of technology, it is beneficial to examine e-government adoption by regarding citizens as also IT users, which is actually in accordance with previous research. According to Taylor and Todd (1995), IT adoption not only encompasses hardware and software use, but also the use of services that surround the technology, as well as the people and procedures to support that technology.

Viewing e-government adoption as IT adoption brings trust into the story. Trust is a central issue that facilitates IT adoption, when the IT is a social medium through which individuals interact or transact business with other people or organizations (Gefen, 2000, 2002a, 2002c; Gefen, Karahanna, & Straub, 2003; Jarvenpaa, Tractinsky, & Vitale, 2000; McKnight, Choudhury, & Kacmar, 2002; Pavlou, 2003). The e-government medium is an instance where trust should have a prominent role.

Of course, IT adoption also depends on the ITs Perceived Usefulness (PU), originally defined as "the individual's assessment of the ability of a specific IT to increase his or her performance at some task or activity" (Davis, 1989). In the case of e-government processes, such as electronic voting (e-voting), this definition would narrowly address how well the IT manages the activity of casting and counting votes. In this study, however, we adopt a broader definition of the term as it has been applied by more recent research in e-commerce (Gefen et al., 2003). In e-commerce, as in e-voting, the IT is only a conduit to a much broader process which includes organizational activity beyond what the Web site reveals. Accordingly, PU is herein defined as "perceptions that the IT increases the productivity of the overall *process* of which the voting machines are a conduit." In other words, the PU of e-voting deals with both the usefulness of the IT itself in handling the voting activity, and with the usefulness of the whole voting process done through the IT beyond its limited technological perspective.

In this broader definition of PU, related research in e-commerce and enterprise resource planning (ERP) implementation has shown that trust increases the positive assessment of IT usefulness because that assessment depends on whether the personnel deploying and managing the voting process, of which the IT is the starting point, are trustworthy, and whether they will fulfill their socially expected roles, as is the case with e-commerce.[1] In the case of e-voting, these socially expected roles include activities beyond the limited interaction that the voters have with the IT, including the honest and proper management of the whole voting and counting processes. Similar to e-commerce, trust is likely to increase PU in e-voting. Since many of the benefits from an e-voting system depend on the agency behaving in a socially acceptable manner, citizens, assessing the situation rationally, should expect more usefulness from e-voting when the agency and its personnel can be presumed to be trustworthy.

Another aspect of IT adoption is culture. Unfortunately, most empirical research in e-commerce and e-government has dealt exclusively with the United States of America (USA) and similar Western cultures. Moreover, even when that research was not conducted in USA, it still involved mainly educated young adults (frequently students) in cultures where sectarian influences are small. However, theory suggests that trust depends on cultural characteristics, and its effects and importance should hence vary among cultures (Fukuyama, 1995; Hofstede, 1980).

Accordingly, the objective of this study is to examine whether the importance of trust varies when comparing the USA culture with a strongly sectarian nescient non-Western democracy, such as that of the Republic of South Africa (RSA). Since there are eleven national languages and distinct cultural characteristics in the RSA, data from a broad section of these cultures was compared with a USA sample.

This study highlights a central aspect of cross-cultural differences on trust and IT adoption, namely the salience of *cultural diversity within a community*. Further, it argues for a direct link between cultural diversity and trust. The study also argues for an interaction effect, following the foundations of trust theory (Fukuyama, 1995; Zucker, 1986) and Social Identity Theory (SIT) (Hogg & Terry, 2000; Tajfel, 1970, 1978; Turner, 1985). Where the effect of trust on PU may be culture-dependent, trust should be a lesser predictor of the expected usefulness of the IT in cultures with a high degree of cultural diversity. These propositions were examined by comparing a wide cultural array of potential electronic voters in RSA with a less diverse group in the USA. In showing this interaction effect, this study also extends previous theory on this relationship which has shown that a potential adopter's perceptions of cultural similarity to those individuals in charge of implementing and managing an IT will affect their acceptance.

These results are significant also on a practical level. E-voting is an emerging form of IT which is of increasing practical importance. Gaining broad participation in voting is a primary democratic objective. Thus e-voting in its own right is a topic of particular interest in the context of both the USA and the RSA. Voter turnout for the last 20 years in the USA has been low (approximately 50% in presidential and 35% in congressional elections) when compared with other nations like Italy, Canada, Brazil, and the UK.[2] Similarly, voter participation in the RSA has been disturbingly low in a country that fought hard to give the right to vote to its citizens. While national elections have broad participation (87-89% in 1994 and 1999), municipal elections have consistently drawn participation rates around 48% (in 1996 and 2000).[3] Likewise, the size of the RSA combined with its current economic difficulties makes e-voting a particularly inviting option, especially with the current dearth of culture-specific research in RSA (Hugo, 2000, 2002).

This study also addresses the urgent need presented in a 2000 manifesto by Jacques Hugo, the chair of the Association for Computing Machinery Special Interest Group on Computer Human Interaction (ACM SIGCHI) in South Africa (called CHI-SA). Hugo called for IT research focused on user needs, and specifically for taking the new culture of the RSA and its subcultures into consideration (Hugo, 2000). Addressing this need is even more necessary considering how two years later, almost no culture-specific research had yet been conducted into understanding how IT should be built for the nation of the RSA as a whole when contrasted with other nations or for the various users of information systems in RSA (Hugo, 2002).

THEORY AND HYPOTHESES

Electronic Voting

Computer-based and Internet-based voting is in use in some form in both the USA and the RSA. In the USA, computer-based voting is hoped to be commonplace for the 2004 presidential elections (Heichler, 2003). Moreover, USA Federal Government plans call for a pilot test of Internet-based voting for the 2004 election for 100,000 overseas voters.[4] While RSA citizens still cast their votes in traditional ways and cannot vote *directly* over the Internet, all of their votes are tallied and submitted remotely over the Internet by voting officials. As of 2000, all polling stations have their votes transmitted to a central Web server that collects voting data, making the RSA one of the most technologically advanced nations in their use of Internet-supported voting. Each of 550 stations is connected in the government's wide area network via a satellite dish to the Internet (Microsoft, 2000). As a result of the success of these services, prototype kiosk-based e-voting systems have been developed and proposed for beta testing in the RSA (Accenture, 2002). Since the infrastructure and programming for back-end computing and data entry are already in place for Internet voting, all that is needed is citizen-accessible interfaces. Therefore, once the government decides to make it available, the RSA should be capable of rolling out a working e-voting system in a very short time. Because of the near term possibility of these services being tested and potentially adopted in both the USA and the RSA, there is greater urgency in studying e-voting issues.

According to industry sources, a central issue impeding the successful implementation of these plans is the concern about fraud and voter privacy (Gross, 2003; Heichler, 2003). The same type of concerns have made trust crucial for companies operating Web sites (Gefen, 2000). Extrapolating from previous e-commerce research and from such industry reports, the ongoing assumption of this study is that trust should be central to citizens' e-voting adoption decision. Examining this assumption, while integrating sociocultural similarity into the model, is the purpose of this research. The research model, presented in Figure 1, is discussed next.

Trust

Trust is the belief that another person or organization on whom one depends will behave in a socially-acceptable manner, namely, they will be honest, caring, and capable (Gefen, 2002c; Giffin, 1967; McKnight et al., 2002), and in doing so will fulfill the trusting party's expectations (Gefen, 2002a; Gefen et al., 2003; Lewis & Weigert, 1985; Mayer, Davis, & Schoorman, 1995; Pavlou & Gefen, 2004). Trust is critical in many economic and social interactions, especially in an electronic (Internet) environment where visual and other social cues are notably missing (Reichheld & Schefter, 2000). One of the reasons why trust is so central is that it provides a subjective sense of reduced social complexity (Gefen, 2000). In other words, trust lets one assume away the possibility of opportunistic behavior by the person or organization they trust, and in doing so, it reduces the overwhelming social complexity involved in assessing others' motives and behaviors (Lewis & Weigert, 1985; Luhmann, 1979). One of the results of this is an increased belief that the expected benefits from the interaction will be fulfilled (Kelley, 1979).

Past research has shown that, at least with regard to e-commerce, trust increases the PU of an IT in cases where part of the benefits from the IT depends on the agency personnel. This phenomenon is true in such cases of e-commerce where the benefits from a Web site also depend on the organization behind the IT, in that case the Web site (Gefen et al., 2003). The relationship between trust and PU is based on the broader meaning of PU. In adopting the meaning of PU in e-commerce (Gefen et al., 2003), PU in e-voting relates to both the IT itself as a *technology* and to the *process* that the IT is designed to support (Kelley, 1979). As such, the PU of these intertwined aspects of the IT should be related to trust in the agency implementing the e-voting system, in a manner parallel to that found in e-commerce. While some technology aspects of the IT are not related to trust (because they do not depend on the human side of the organization), the process aspects of the IT do relate to trust because they depend on the organization doing its part of the voting process to achieve the PU of the IT.

In general, trust is crucial for economic transactions because it reduces the risk of falling victim to opportunistic behavior (Fukuyama, 1995; Williamson, 1985). Accordingly, research has shown that trust in the agency personnel has a strong effect on the use and appreciation of an IT (Gefen, 2000, 2002a, 2002c; Gefen et al., 2003; Jarvenpaa

Figure 1. Research model

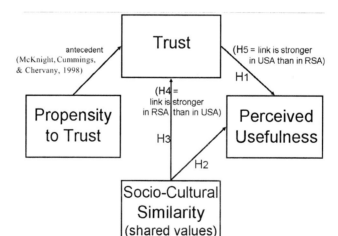

& Tractinsky, 1999; Jarvenpaa, Tractinsky, & Vitale, 2000; McKnight & Chervany, 2002; Pavlou, 2003). The same effect of trust applies to virtual communities where trust in other people with whom one interacts through the IT also increases the appreciation and use of the IT (Ridings, Gefen, & Arinze, 2002). Along the same lines, trust in those implementing an IT directly and strongly affects the PU and intended use of the IT (Gefen, 2004).

Past information systems (IS) research (Gefen, 1997; Gefen et al., 2003) has explained the central role of trust based on Social Exchange Theory (SET) (Blau, 1964; Kelley, 1979; Kelley & Thibaut, 1978; Thibaut & Kelley, 1959). According to SET, people take part in an interaction with others based on a cost-benefit analysis of whether their expected benefits from the interaction justify the costs involved. Trust is central in this process because in a social exchange, there are no rules to guarantee the expected future benefits. Trust affects PU even when there are rules and regulations that govern the interaction, as in the case with e-commerce or contracting IT vendors, because there is always a gray zone not fully covered by the rules and regulations, and because the cost of litigation might be prohibitive and may not fully compensate for the damage caused (Gefen, 2004). In other words, one's justification for investing current costs in an interaction depends to some extent also on the degree of trust one has in realizing expected benefits from the other individuals or organizations. This theory base ties indirectly into another theory underlying trust, namely Luhmann's (1979) theory, in which trust serves to reduce social uncertainty, that is, to subjectively regulate the expected favorable behavior of others.

Accordingly, trust affects PU of an IT because users that have little warranty that the organization behind the Web site will provide their expected benefits are forced to trust the organization (i.e., accept on faith that it will behave in a socially acceptable manner). This relationship is especially strong among users experiencing a specific Web site for the first time, because their experience with that specific IT (the Web site) is minimal . Nonetheless, even among experienced users, trust strongly affects both user assessment of the IT and their expected use of it (Gefen, 2004; Gefen et al., 2003).

Extrapolating to the realm of e-voting, the literature implies that trust should also play a central role in the decision to use IT to vote online. Not only is trust critical in IT adoption, but trust is a central determinant of political behavior in general (Fukuyama, 1995). Specifically in this study, the usefulness of e-voting should depend in part on whether the voting agency can be trusted to manage the entire voting process, including the process aspects of e-voting which go beyond the limited interaction the voter has with the e-voting system, with honesty, appropriate capability, and caring for the voters' interests as far as their voting online is concerned. Indeed, industry reports note privacy, as well as technical issues, as primary concerns standing in the way of e-voting adoption (Gross, 2003; Heichler, 2003). It is because the PU of the voting system as a whole depends not only on the technology but also on the process beyond the Web site, that trust should be a significant predictor of PU, as it is for the same reasons with e-commerce (Gefen et al., 2003). If the agency is dishonest, that is, it cheats or does not keep its promises, or if the agency cannot show adequate capability, then there is hardly reason for voters to expect much usefulness from the Web site. On the other hand, if the agency is honest, that is, it plays by the rules and keeps its promises, and if the agency has the capability to manage the Web site properly, then there is good reason for voters to expect increased usefulness from the Web site, because such a Web site should be inherently useful, presuming it performs properly.[5] This need to trust is a serious practical concern considering the known vulnerability of current systems to hackers and to privacy violations (Jefferson, Rubin, Simons, & Wagner, 2004; Vijayan, 2004).

Accordingly, trust should increase PU also in these settings. The inherent usefulness of e-voting is evident in places where it was adopted it through the services of trustworthy agencies, including in nine districts in England (Peterson, 2002) and in the 2000 Democratic Party presidential primary in Arizona (Burke, 2000). However, since true e-voting (user interaction with an online voting system) has not yet been implemented in the RSA or in the USA state of Mississippi where the data were collected, the hypothesis addresses the expected usefulness of the IT.

Hypothesis$_1$: Trust in the agency administering the e-voting process will increase citizens' assessment of the perceived usefulness of the IT supporting it.

The hypothesis is consistent with what was observed in a British e-voting pilot that took place in 2002. Public perception of e-voting by nonusers in the pilot election was that it was not trustworthy, even though mechanisms were adopted to assure it was (see Peterson, 2002, for details of procedures). As such, those individuals who deemed the process untrustworthy did not find the technology useful enough to adopt. Though these are not measures of PU, this finding indicates that trust was a major indicator of attitudes and intentions toward these services.

Cultural Diversity and Socio-Cultural Similarity

The relationship between trust and PU is based on SET, a calculative theory of behavior. But trust is not the only way in which people address the uncertainty involved in the behavior of others. Social influences are also crucial. When making a decision, individuals often rely on members of their perceived social group with whom they identify. People in this group are viewed in a much more favorable manner than others are. The reasons for this are anchored in Social Identity Theory (SIT) (Hogg & Terry, 2000; Tajfel, 1970, 1978; Turner, 1985), which argues that human behavior can be explained in part by viewing people as irrationally but naturally biased in favor of those whom they perceive as belonging to the same sociocultural group, that is, others who are perceived as sharing the same values (Hogg & Terry, 2000; Tajfel, 1970, 1978; Turner, 1985), and biased against those who are perceived as belonging to different groups. The belief in having shared values is a major determinant of whether people feel that others belong to the same sociocultural group as they do (Hogg, 1996). See Gefen and Ridings for a detailed discussion of the application of SIT to IT adoption management.

At the basis of SIT is the recognition that people's self-identity is in part the product of their perception of what social groups they belong to. Such perceptions relate to vocation (Hogg and Terry, 2000), gender and race (Bhattacharya, Rao, & Glynn, 1995; Mehra, Kilduff, & Brass, 1998), nationality (Hogg, 1996) and ethnicity (Grier & Deshpande, 2001). As a result of this perception of belonging to a certain social group and not to another, what SIT labels categorization, people apply a self-enhancement bias. People will assess others of their own social group more highly and people of other social groups less so, because of the way this perception reflects positively also on their own self-esteem (Brown, 1996; Hogg & Terry, 2000), because it allows them to take part and feel pride in the achievements of their own group (Bhattacharya et al., 1995), and because it increases people's sense of solidarity (Lembke & Wilson, 1998). People will exaggerate and even create imaginary differences to justify this self-enhancement bias (Hogg & Terry, 2000).

Applying SIT to the realm of IT adoption, Gefen and Ridings show how reduced perceptions of belonging to different social groups increase users' positive assessments of an IT. Gefen and Ridings also show how reduced perceptions of belonging to the different social groups also increase users' perceptions of having shared values with the IT agency. This perception of shared values also has a strong effect on users' positive assessments of an IT based on a rational, rather than only SIT, basis of less misunderstandings about how to use the IT. Extrapolating this to e-voting, implies:

Hypothesis$_2$: Increased e-voter perceptions of shared values with the e-voting agency personnel will result in increased assessment of the perceived usefulness of the IT.

Trust and Diversity

Where SET and SIT interact is in the creation of trust. Such perceptions of sociocultural similarity should also contribute to the creation of trust because people generally have greater trust in those with whom they have shared values (Zucker, 1986). These perceptions are one of the three major trust-building mechanisms, according to Zucker. Increased perceived social similarity builds trust by reducing the social uncertainty that is related to how people of different cultural backgrounds perceive what acceptable social behavior means. Presumably, one knows better what to expect of people from the same social background. In part, this is a very rational assessment. Having shared values means lesser misunderstandings about what constitutes appropriate social behavior (Gefen, 2004). This relationship is of practical value in the e-voting context because a citizen might have more realistic expectations when dealing with someone with similar culturally determined beliefs and values. In other words, individuals would be expected to trust others who share the same values more because they know better what to expect.

Hypothesis$_3$: Increased e-voter perceptions of sociocultural similarity with the e-voting agency personnel will result in increased e-voter trust in the agency.

Varying Effects of Diversity

The SIT perspective of IT adoption adds a cultural aspect to the aforementioned research on trust. Though social differences may be present, previous research has been conducted in established democratic societies where tribal rivalries are nonexistent and where society has had generations to establish what constitutes acceptable social behavior. But what happens when the society is only a nascent democracy and where tribal loyalty still takes precedence over other issues? A unique opportunity to examine this case exists in the RSA.

Because the RSA is a more socially-fragmented country, as can be seen in the wide range of national languages spoken there (see Table 2)[6], and formally began the integration process in 1994, it might be expected that perceived shared values with the agency personnel might have an even greater effect on perceptions of how trustworthy the e-voting agency is. As suggested by Hypothesis$_3$, if one thinks agency personnel have a different mindset or worldview, one might be less inclined to regard them as one's own group and thus be less inclined to trust in them. This proposition is supported by Zucker's (1986) observations about the USA economy and Gefen's (2004) results examining ERP adoption. Accordingly, assuming Hypothesis$_3$ holds and recognizing the inherently-greater cultural diversity, as reflected through linguistic diversity, in the RSA compared with the USA,[7] the following is implied:

Hypothesis$_4$: The effect of sociocultural similarity on trust (Hypothesis$_3$) will be stronger in the RSA.

The inherently greater cultural (i.e. linguistic, tribal, etc.) diversity in the RSA should also affect the degree to which trust in the agency affects the perceived usefulness of the e-voting IT. At the heart of the argument for Hypothesis$_1$ was the recognition that trust, by reducing misunderstandings of what constitutes appropriate social uncertainty, should increase the perceived usefulness of the IT, as in other IT (Gefen et al., 2003; Pavlou, 2003). This has been shown in the USA.

In the RSA, on the other hand, historical events have created an elaborate scheme of tribal alliances and rivalries. These alliances differentiate not only white from black, but historically also among the Afrikaans and British whites and among the various black tribes, especially the Zulus who came from the north, and the local tribes. Contributing more to the segmentation were additional waves of immigration to the RSA, namely Indians who came at the peak of the British Empire and gold miners from around the globe. Whereas the USA's "melting pot" culture served to deemphasize such ethnic alliances and has generally created a legal environment conducive to the assimilation of minorities ever since the Civil War, the same did not take place in the RSA until a decade ago. In the RSA, under the Apartheid system, which was legally enforced from 1948 until 1991, these tribal alliances and rivalries were enhanced through legal measures. In effect, segregation between white, "coloured,"[8] and black existed long before 1948, as did the tribal segregation and wars among the blacks. Segregation was an integral part of RSA culture and history for centuries prior to 1991. This segregation was also practically evident on a linguistic level, because each of the various peoples had its own language and related culture. The Apartheid system created legally-segregated public facilities and school systems, with better equipment and higher standards for whites; limited the vocation of blacks and coloureds; and forbade many types of social contacts crossing racial lines (Dowling, 2002). This segregation accentuated existing tribal and racial boundaries, reflected accurately by the use of different languages, within the RSA.

Needless to say, the Apartheid system created a sense of revolt against and distrust in the government and its agencies by the non-whites. Viewed in the perspective of SIT, the Apartheid system, by emphasizing group boundaries within society, should have effectively created a sense of intense rivalry among its elements. Typically, increasing the sense of group boundaries results in a greater sense of the lack of shared values and common ground (Hogg, 1996) and, arguably, should make it harder to establish what constitutes acceptable social behavior. Indeed, in cultures where there is an inherent sense of low trust, people trust their family but avoid trusting strangers (Fukuyama, 1995). The USA, by contrast, is a high-trust culture, where people generally place trust in the government, the police, the legal system, and many other public and private institutions, such as banks and other businesses.

As a result of what is commonly known as "*the Transition*" (Wines, 2003), a society that had been made up of many fragmented and physically isolated cultures living within a shared national border has become an embryonic, unknown, and multifaceted culture. In 1994, multiracial elections were held, and all adults in the RSA were eligible to vote regardless of race. New laws have enabled this integration to occur in physical living, educational, social, business, financial, and government environments. Once forbidden to partake in the opportunities available only to white men, new laws now enable non-whites to vote in elections, become members of the managerial workforce, join the now desegregated educational system as both students and instructors, and participate in majority numbers in the government and leadership.[9]

While the group boundaries have been legally erased in the RSA, the USA experience suggests that these changes take generations until they take effect, if at all. In the USA at the aftermath of the Civil War, the thirteenth (1865) and fourteenth amendments (1868) to the Constitution also attempted to legally erase group boundaries within society. But biases and distrust among the races continued for generations, especially among many whites in the South (the Confederacy) who lost their previously leading position in society with the reincorporation of the South into the Union. Drawing a parallel with the whites in the South, this study assumes that, as in the USA, the social group boundaries in the RSA, which were so prevalent, will take time to disappear, especially as in the case of the RSA, the tribal boundaries, including among the Afrikaners and British, have been there for hundreds of years. As in the USA, when a social group is discriminated against or feels disenfranchised, it tends to rely more on its own members than on the government. In other words, the need to trust in the government as a precondition for taking part in governmental programs should be of lesser weight in these groups because of their greater reliance on the inner workings of their own social group.

Hypothesis$_5$: The effect of trust in the agency on perceived usefulness of e-voting (Hypothesis$_1$) will be stronger in the USA.

Supporting this proposition are clues from Hofstede's study. His results find that the USA scores highest of all countries in individualism (USA = 91). While Hofstede's work does not provide measures for the new RSA, indications are that Africans should be more collectivist than Americans. White RSA in the 1970's had a score of 65, which was well below the USA value, and majority-black African nations in East and West Africa had scores of 27 and 20, respectively. This indicates that for members of both the black and white cultures of Africa, there is a predisposition to trust their own group, whereas the Americans (who don't have "their own group" on which to rely) would generally look toward an agency as a target of trust.

Control Variable: Disposition to Trust

Based on Gefen (Gefen, 2000) and on McKnight et al. (1998), it is also assumed that because voters have not yet had any interaction with the electronic voting governmental agency, that disposition to trust should also be a factor contributing to trust in the agency. Generally, disposition to trust is a major antecedent of trust when people encounter a new person or agency for the first time, that is, they have not had enough experience to base their trust on actual experience (McKnight et al., 1998).

RESEARCH METHODOLOGY

In order to test the hypotheses and explore cultural differences between the USA and the RSA, data were collected from voters and potential voters in the USA and from diverse subgroups of RSA citizens who are eligible to register to vote. The RSA groups were deliberately chosen so we could get a reasonable representation of the major population segments. Overall, the USA sample was 35% female, while the RSA dataset was 53% female.

To evaluate the research questions, data were collected from a culturally diverse group of 219 RSA voters and a sample of 375 educated young USA voters. While the data collected was a convenience sample, care was taken when choosing the RSA sample to include in the sample representatives of the major groups in the population, namely educated and uneducated blacks and educated whites.

When compared to the RSA demographics, USA voters are linguistically, and hence presumably also culturally, less diverse. See Table 2 with details of the languages sampled in the RSA. Citizens of the USA largely speak one language, attend the same schools, watch the same media, and are subject to similar influences, even when they are ethnically diverse. The contrast between so-called first-world and third-world individuals so evident in the RSA situation is absent in the USA environment. This dichotomy between the USA and the RSA with respect to the level of sociocultural similarity or diversity provides an ideal laboratory for analysis of trust and IT adoption

The RSA data were collected from three distinct groups. The first group of RSA participants was comprised of university students at a major university in a large urban center – these subjects were primarily white of the former dominant socioeconomic class in the country. The second group was of black participants living in the former rural homelands. We have been unable to identify any other IT research that has included rural RSA blacks. Accessing this population is difficult and likely is the cause of this omission in the current literature. In this group, rural adults were targeted for inclusion because they represent a very large segment of the society. This group is made of people who are largely functionally and computer illiterate, but would constitute a majority of the population impacted by e-voting at the proposed centralized kiosk locations such as post offices and at polling stations (as projected by Accenture, 2002). To access these participants, field workers were hired to travel to villages, interview citizens orally, and document their responses. To minimize bias, ten different subjects were interviewed from each of ten villages (n = 100) requiring a total of 336 km of travel.

The third RSA group is of black young adults attending a special school in a rural area within a former black homeland. The school is the Siyabuswa Education Improvement and Development Trust (SEIDET). SEIDET was developed as a school where students in the rural areas could learn advanced skills beyond what was available at their public schools and thus prepares them better for a career in the sciences. Likewise, it is a place where research could be conducted with its students in an effort to understand and improve their lives. One of the resources available to students at SEIDET is a computer lab with Internet access. With permission of the school elders, guardians, and the students themselves, access was granted to collect data from those students between 18-23 years old. These students represent the first generation of black South Africans that has been permitted to acquire an education in preparation for university studies. This group is computer and functionally literate, yet they live and grew up in the villages. They represent the new South Africa and, as such, were included for analysis. While the RSA sample cannot be thought to represent the rich diversity of RSA's 45 million citizens, we believe it provides previously unavailable insight into the greater RSA population.

The USA sample was obtained from volunteers at a large, ethnically-diverse public university. Subjects were all of legal voting age, and the sample population was approximately 17% black and 78% white, with a small number of others. By including a USA sample group, those characteristics that are common within the three RSA groups can be tested to see if they are idiosyncratic to the greater RSA culture, or if they are consistent across an international sample. The USA sample consisted of 375 voting-age young adults attending a large, public, comprehensive land grant university in a rural location. Students volunteered to complete the survey, and anonymity was maintained.

Survey instruments have been constructed using validated measures where possible. The PU scale was adapted from Davis (1989), and the propensity to trust scale was adapted from Gefen (2000). The sociocultural similarity scale was adapted from another paper (currently under review by an author, identity withheld for anonymity). The trust scale captures integrity, ability, and predictability. This scale did not include a benevolence item because there is no aspect of benevolence by the government to citizens when providing the service, given that the agency is providing a service to the government rather than to the citizens. Sociocultural similarity is measured by four scale items which elicit the respondents' perceptions of shared values with the personnel of the voting agency (see Table 1).

Although PU was the target of the study, Behavioral Intent to Use (BI) and perceived ease of use (PEOU), the other two central components of the Technology Acceptance Model (Davis, 1989) were not included because the RSA system is not yet operational. As such, it is meaningless to ask how easy a nonexistent e-voting is to use. Similarly, BI cannot be realistically assessed because the e-voting IT has only been proposed in RSA at the time of data collection. On the other hand, PU can be more easily assessed based on shared values and understanding of what such an IT should do; it is the most appropriate measure in the context of this research effort.

The instrument begins with a description of Internet-based voting (see Appendix A). The items used in the study are shown in Table 1. Demographic details were also collected including nation of origin, ethnic origin, gender, language, age, and number of times voted in the last three years.

Extensive pilot testing on a large group of comparable study subjects prior to the actual data collection allowed the research team to assess and evaluate each instrument item in the context of the target audience. Each item was discussed with the pilot test group to ensure that the proper meaning was conveyed. Further, measures of construct validity were utilized to ensure that the items measured the intended constructs. Content validity was evaluated through interviews with other academics who were not involved in the study to verify that the items were understood as intended. The psychometric properties of the measures were examined after the pilot data were collected. The convergent and discriminant validity of the scales was examined through a principle

Table 1. Items used in study

Disposition to Trust
In general, one can get better outcomes by treating others as though they are able.
In general, one can get better outcomes by treating others as though they are honest.
Overall, I believe in people's goodness.
I generally believe that people are well-meaning.
Socio-Cultural Similarity (shared values)
The election agency is made up of people like me.
The election agency is made up of people who have my values.
The election agency is made up of people who believe as I do.
The election agency is made up of people who have the culture I do.
Trust
Promises made by the election agency are likely to be reliable.
The election agency is competent.
I am quite certain what to expect from the election agency.
Perceived Usefulness (PU)
Computer and Internet-based voting would be useful.
Computer and Internet-based voting will improve my performance in voting.
Computer and Internet-based voting would enhance my effectiveness in voting.
Computer and Internet-based voting would increase my speed in voting.

components factor analysis in which it was verified that the items loaded highly, above .60, only on their expected factors and low, below .40, on all other factors. The nomological validity of the scales was examined through the correlations that the constructs had with each other, verifying that constructs that should be related to each other in theory are significantly correlated to each other while being either insignificantly correlated or correlated with a much lower coefficient to constructs they are expected to be only weakly correlated to in theory. The reliability of the constructs, shown through Cronbach's Alpha, were also within the accepted range of above .70.

DATA ANALYSIS

The data were first analyzed with a Principle Components factor Analysis (PCA) with Varimax rotation to assess the factorial validity of the two samples. The two PCA with descriptive statistics are shown in Appendices B and C. Both PCA show four eigenvalues above one and a clean pattern of loadings, indicating good convergent and discriminant validity. The two tables also show the acceptable reliability of the four scales in both cultures.

The data from the RSA is a mixture of 36% rural young blacks, 22.4% from SEIDET, and 41.6% from a prominent white university. Language distribution was diverse among the RSA sample participants as is shown in Table 2. Comparison of means is shown in Table 3. RSA data show very significant differences among the three groups regarding social-cultural similarity. As would be expected, this difference carries over to trust;

Table 2. Languages in the RSA sample

	Frequency	Percent
Ndebele	57	26.0
Swazi	3	1.4
Shangaan	3	1.4
Afrikaans	56	25.6
Tswana	10	4.6
Xhosa	2	.9
Zulu	15	6.8
Venda	2	.9
North Sotho	39	17.8
South Sotho	4	1.8
English	27	12.3
Other	1	.5
Total	219	100.0

Table 3. Comparison of construct means

	Comparison Between Countries		Comparison Among Groups in RSA			
Construct	USA	RSA as a whole	RSA Rural blacks Mean (STD)	RSA SEIDET	RSA Mostly white university	Difference among the groups in RSA F-value (p-value)
Social-cultural similarity	4.21 (1.02)	4.11(1.15)	4.19 (1.13)	3.97 (1.18)	3.06 (1.28)**	20.240 (<.001)
Trust	4.39 (1.09)	4.11 (1.22)	4.41 (1.17)	4.38 (1.14)	3.69 (1.18)**	9.771 (<.001)
Perceived Usefulness	5.05 (1.26)	5.39 (1.30)**	5.55 (1.31)**	5.14 (1.24)	5.91 (.98)**	2.992 (.086)
Disposition to Trust	4.93 (1.09)	4.91(1.44)	4.91 (1.16)	4.92 (1.13)	4.63 (1.25)**	1.525 (.220)

* means significantly different from the USA at the .05 level
** means significantly different from the USA at the .01 level

however, it does not carry over to perceived usefulness. The RSA data also shows insignificant differences among the three groups regarding disposition to trust. The differences in the means between the USA and the RSA sample as a whole are significant for PU only. But when examined by each of the three RSA sectors, it is striking that while the two black samples are mostly insignificantly different from the USA sample, the mostly white university sample shows remarkably significant differences from the USA sample. The significant differences between the white RSA sample and the USA sample, as opposed to the mostly insignificant differences between the black RSA samples and the USA sample, may be because the white RSA sample came from people who felt disenfranchised by the new RSA much as the whites in the South felt after the Civil War in the USA.

Table 4. Linear regression results

Country or Group	Dependent Variable	Independent Variables	Beta (p-value)	R-square
RSA data as a whole	PU	Socio-cultural Similarity	.17 (.039)	5%
		Trust	Not significant	
	Trust	Socio-cultural Similarity	.49 (<.001)	31%
		Disposition to Trust	.15 (.018)	
RSA rural blacks alone	PU	Socio-cultural Similarity	.30 (.018)	8%
		Trust	Not significant	
	Trust	Socio-cultural Similarity	.23 (.036)	26%
		Disposition to Trust	.37 (.001)	
RSA SEIDET students	PU	Socio-cultural Similarity	.39 (.008)	26%
		Trust	Not significant	
	Trust	Socio-cultural Similarity	.37 (.008)	22%
		Disposition to Trust	Not significant	
RSA white university	PU	Socio-cultural Similarity	.26 (.014)	6%
		Trust	Not significant	
	Trust	Socio-cultural Similarity	.65 (<.001)	38%
		Disposition to Trust	Not significant	
USA	PU	Socio-cultural Similarity	.18 (.002)	8%
		Trust	.13 (.028)	
	Trust	Socio-cultural Similarity	.37 (<.001)	31%
		Disposition to Trust	.27 (<.001)	

The hypotheses were then analyzed with linear regression. These results are shown in Table 4. The beta of the path from sociocultural similarity to trust in the RSA data, representing Hypothesis$_3$, is significantly bigger than the path in the USA data (t=14.505, p-value < .001), supporting Hypothesis$_4$. The beta of the path from Trust to PU, representing Hypothesis$_1$ in the USA data, is significantly larger than in the RSA data (t=23.662, p-value < .001), supporting Hypothesis$_5$. The comparison of the betas was performed based on Keil, Tan, Wei, and Saarinen (2000). The analysis is summarized in Figure 2. All research hypotheses were supported by the analysis of the data. When examined by each group alone, however, the results show that the significance of Hypothesis$_4$ is primarily due to the white RSA sample. Nonetheless, even when examining each RSA group separately, Hypothesis$_5$ is supported. Only in the USA does trust increase PU.

KEY FINDINGS AND DISCUSSION

Comparing citizens from the RSA and the USA provides researchers with a unique opportunity to examine the varying interaction between cultural diversity and trust. The RSA is a nescient democracy where legal equality for all citizens came only recently. Accordingly, tribal identification is still very strong. In contrast, the USA is a more established democracy, similar to many nations in Europe and the Americas.

Trust is an essential ingredient in IT adoption where the IT is a medium connecting the user (consumer or citizen) to other organizations or agencies. In such IT, trust directly and strongly affects perceptions about the PU of the IT (Gefen, 2002b; Gefen et al., 2003), because trust in general affects people's perception about the value of their relationships with others (Fukuyama, 1995). Trust affects perceptions and behavior because it lets

Figure 2. Supported hypotheses

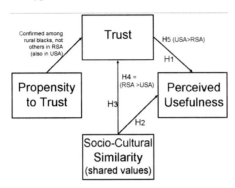

people rule out socially undesirable but possible behavior of others, based on the belief that the trusted party will adhere to socially-acceptable behavior (Gefen, 2000; Luhmann, 1979). But what happens when this concept is examined in a multicultural environment, where different concepts of socially-acceptable behavior prevail? Answering this question was a primary motivation for this study.

The question was addressed by comparing the unique circumstance of the cultural changes in the Republic of South Africa with the more socially-integrated mainstream USA culture in the context of an emerging new IT, namely e-voting. The study found that while both trust and sociocultural similarity were predictors of PU in the USA, only similarity was a predictor in RSA. Nonetheless, in both cultures sociocultural similarity contributed to an equivalent degree to the creation of trust, supported by significantly larger beta in both RSA and USA data analysis result (RSA= 0.49, p<.001; USA= 0.37, p<.001). This supports the past assertions (Gefen & Ridings, 2002). Also in support of the hypotheses, the data show that sociocultural similarity had a greater effect on trust in the RSA, while trust had a greater effect in the USA.

Interestingly, and perhaps rather disturbingly, the data also show a distinct difference within the RSA data. While both black samples are mostly insignificantly different from the USA sample, the mostly white university sample shows remarkably significant differences from the USA sample. Considering the leading position that whites had in society and in the government prior to the transition, and considering the takeover by the majority black population since then, the data tentatively implies a possible unforeseen side effect. While prior to the transition, arguably, the whites felt a close social bond with the governmental agencies (a bond made stronger by being in the same social class as the minority who lead the country), after the transition this position changed, with the whites becoming a minority and not in power. Moreover, the data suggest that the effect of sociocultural similarity on trust might be related to the perception of belonging to the leading social group. This difference is most pronounced when comparing the USA sample with the white RSA sample, which represents the segment of RSA population which was in command but now feels marginalized. Apparently, the transition may have caused a sense of alienation among the whites.

Implications and Conclusions

The results of this study provide several contributions to practice and research. First, it begins the exploration of culture and IT in RSA per Hugo's (2000, 2002) call to arms. The existing dearth of research is problematic because developers of systems for the RSA (including both those from within and outside of RSA) have difficulty "understanding the needs of a user from (their) own culture, let alone from a very different culture whose language, customs, values, prejudices, fears, and preferences are totally unknown" (Hugo, 2000). As a result, Hugo and CHI-SA called for research into understanding the diverse users in "South Africa with its mix of first and third-world components – culture, language, race, education, economy, and technology" because South Africa could "no longer afford to exclude any individual or any sector of society from access to, and benefiting from information technology" (Hugo, 2000). While understanding culture and IT has been recognized as important throughout the IT community (see such studies as Ford, Connelly, & Meister (2003) or Gallupe & Tan (1999) for a large review of culture and IT literature), it is all the more critical in the RSA because of the unique history and persistent raw scars left by Apartheid. Specifically, *"without proper understanding of the cultural variables involved, [information systems and technology threaten to expand, rather than resolve, certain cultural conflicts"* (Hugo, 2000).

Research into culture and IT is finally beginning to enter the mainstream and much of cross-cultural IT work relies on bootstrapping the work of anthropologists and sociologists. Notably, work from researchers such as Hofstede (see Ford (2003) for a review) and Hall (e.g., Rose, Evaristo, & Straub (2003); Straub, Loch, & Hill (2001)) in these reference disciplines have been extended into the IT realm. What is problematic for conducting cultural research in RSA is that the seminal research describing the new culture of RSA has yet to be conducted. Because the work of researchers such as Hofstede and Hall took place prior to the 1980's, IS research cannot easily use these familiar crutches to understand this newly-formed Rainbow Nation.[10] This study contributes to Hugo's vision of an RSA that takes cultures into consideration. Further, as a relative leader in IT adoption, RSA could be a model for the rest of Africa. The RSA is the most wired and technologically advanced nation in Africa (Anonymous, 2000),[11] and the government and non-government organizations are considering expanding the reach of Internet services by providing more networked computers in the rural areas in locations such as schools (Coning, 2002) and post offices, as well as developing cell phone-accessible applications (Accenture, 2002) to further extend these services.

Based on the exploratory results of this study, governments both in the RSA and elsewhere where there is a high degree of sociocultural diversity, should be aware of the effects that sociocultural diversity has on citizen trust and ultimately on citizen assessments of government-sponsored IT, in this case of e-voting. Many other voting units around the world, such as India and the European Union, face multi-ethnic sociocultural diversity. Taking steps to reduce this tension (e.g., through advertising and joint interracial activities), could be a necessary step toward convincing citizens of the value of these IT. The disturbing results of the sample of white students highlight the potential problems that governments may be facing.

The strong effect of sociocultural similarity on trust is another aspect of this study that governments may want to consider. Building citizen trust is arguably a crucial aspect of nation building, and is an imperative requirement for proper governmental functioning.

President Lincoln put it beautifully in the Gettysburg Address in 1863 when he said, "government of the people, by the people, for the people." As the data imply, handling perceptions of sociocultural dissimilarity, and through it building trust in governmental agencies and in their IT, is an imperative to achieving such a noble goal.

Related to this, the study provides some insight into how to improve the PU of e-voting, and in doing so presumably also increase participation rates in the RSA. By understanding what motivates or deters RSA voters, the government's Independent Election Committee (IEC) can formulate strategies to make voting more inclusive for all the people of South Africa. Based on our analysis, the PU of e-voting differs greatly among segments of the population and is closely related to the degree of sociocultural similarity. The government of the RSA may need to invest more to achieve such perceptions of inclusion.

The second major contribution of this study is in adding a theoretical insight into the interaction between sociocultural similarity and trust. Research has established the need to create trust as a crucial aspect of IT adoption across IT types. The varying degrees of how this trust affects assessments of an IT, based on the varying degrees of sociocultural similarity, is a new and somewhat disturbing aspect of this relationship. If sociocultural similarity actually overrides the effect of trust, as shown in $Hypothesis_5$, then new perspectives of how people handle social uncertainty need to be added to existing models and to managerial implications of IT management. Gefen and Ridings (2002) showed how creating a sense of oneness between the users and the agency handling the IT is a central aspect of managing an IT. Perhaps as the data show here, this sense of oneness is even more imperative because it not only creates trust but also determines the effect of this trust on user perceptions about the IT.

Belonging to a social group is a central part of self-identity. As this study has shown, the sense of belonging to the same sociocultural group as those in the governmental agency has a strong effect on both creating citizen trust in this governmental agency as well as in positively assessing its IT, at least as shown with e-voting. Even more alarming, the study shows how this sense of belonging affects whether citizen trust in the governmental agency will determine their assessments of its usefulness. Managing citizens' sense of belonging should be a central aspect of managing governmental IT.

Limitations and Future Research

As with all research, this study has limitations that must be recognized in an effort to both spell out future research opportunities as well as caution against extrapolation from the results except where appropriate. As noted by Hugo (2000, 2002), there has been almost no culture-specific IT research in the RSA. While our study begins the process of understanding the role culture plays in system adoption and use in the RSA, it is just that, a beginning. Future studies should extend beyond the narrow focus of this study and look at other variables where culture may play a role in IT development, adoption, and use. Certainly, much more work needs to be done in understanding this nascent culture.

Alternate explanations for these results, utilizing additional constructs, should also be pursued. For example, to what extent do educational differences, IT accessibility, and IT proficiency impact perceived usefulness? What differences can be identified between rural blacks, urban blacks, and whites in RSA, and what would explain these differences in their levels of trust or perceived usefulness of e-government technology? Additionally, the study took some steps toward integrating trust and SIT. Additional research could examine whether this relationship can be expanded beyond the relationships suggested by Zucker (1986). It may be that belonging to a social group builds trust in the other group members, as suggested by the literature and examined here, but also serves independently to reduce social uncertainty.

Future work should also be conducted with other research subjects. Finding diverse subjects in the RSA was challenging, time-consuming, and expensive. Likewise, it is difficult to find a pool of subjects willing to participate in the USA. While our goal was to have a sample representative of both cultures, each was a convenience sample and, as such, may limit our external validity. Subsequent research should be conducted with different subject groups in both the USA and the RSA in an effort to triangulate this study and test its validity. Specifically, groups such as black RSA university students and functionally-illiterate USA subjects should be included. Further, it would be worthwhile to test for any differences between registered and unregistered voters to establish any potential bias between those who actively vote and those who have chosen not to participate in the voting process. Lastly, different subject groups should also be sought in the RSA in an effort to validate our *post hoc* findings of cultural differences between black and white South Africans.

REFERENCES

Accenture (2002, April). Electronic elections: Overview. *Internal White Paper Accenture.*

Anonymous (2000). South Africa nears 2 million Internet users. *CyberAtlas.com.* Retrieved April 2002, from http://cyberatlas.internet.com/big_picture/geographics/article/0,1323,5911_380361,00.html

Bhattacharya, C. B., Rao, H., & Glynn, M. A. (1995). Understanding the bond of identification: An investigation of its correlates among art museum members. *Journal of Marketing, 4*(59), 46-58.

Blau, P. M. (1964). *Exchange and power in social life.* New York: Wiley.

Brown, R. (1996). Tajfel's contribution to the reduction of inter-group conflict. In W. P. Robinson (Ed.), *Social groups and identities: Developing the legacy of Henri Tajfel* (pp. 69-190). Oxford, UK: Butterworth-Heinemann.

Burke, L. (2000). Arizona vote: Not who but how. Retrieved April 2002, from http://www.wired.com/news/politics/0,1283,34911,00.html

Coning, S. D. (2002). *Department of informatics celebrates 10 years of Siyabuswa community project.* Retrieved April 2002, from http://www.up.ac.za/announce/1610021e.html

Davis, F. D. (1989, September). Perceived usefulness, perceived ease of use, and user acceptance of information technology. *MIS Quarterly, 3*(13), 319-340.

Davis, F. D., Bagozzi, R. P., & Warshaw, P. R. (1989). User acceptance of computer technology: A comparison of two theoretical models. *Management Science, 8*(35), 982-1003.

Dowling, M. (2002). *The electronic passport to Apartheid.* Retrieved April 2002, from http://www.mrdowling.com/610-apartheid.html

Ford, D. P., Connelly, C. E., & Meister, D. B. (2003). Information systems research and Hofstede's culture's consequences: An uneasy and incomplete partnership. *IEEE Transactions on Engineering Management, 1*(50), 8-25.

Fukuyama, F. (1995). *Trust: The social virtues and the creation of prosperity.* New York: The Free Press.

Gallupe, R. B., & Tan, F. (1999). A research manifesto for global information management. *Journal of Global Information Management, 3*(7), 5-18.

Gefen, D. (1997). *Building users' trust in freeware providers and the effects of this trust on users' perceptions of usefulness, ease of use, and intended use.* Dissertation, Georgia State University.

Gefen, D. (2000). E-commerce: The role of familiarity and trust. *Omega, 5*(28), 725-737.

Gefen, D. (2002a). Customer loyalty in e-commerce. *Journal of the AIS,* (3), 27-51.

Gefen, D. (2002b). Nurturing clients' trust to encourage engagement success during the customization of ERP systems. *Omega: The International Journal of Management Science, 4*(30), 287-299.

Gefen, D. (2002c). Reflections on the dimensions of trust and trustworthiness among online consumers. *The DATABASE for Advances in Information Systems, 3*(33), 38-53.

Gefen, D. (2004). What makes ERP implementation relationships worthwhile: Linking trust mechanisms and ERP usefulness. *Journal of Management Information Systems, 21*(1), 275-301.

Gefen, D., Karahanna, E., & Straub, D. W. (2003). Trust and TAM in online shopping: An integrated model. *MIS Quarterly, 1*(27), 51-90.

Gefen, D., & Ridings, C. (2002). Implementation team responsiveness and user evaluation of CRM: A quasi-experimental design study of social exchange theory. *Journal of Management Information Systems, 1*(19), 47-63.

Giffin, K. (1967). The contribution of studies of source credibility to a theory of interpersonal trust in the communication process. *Psychological Bulletin, 2*(68), 104-120.

Grier, S. A., & Deshpande, R. (2001, May). Social dimensions of consumer distinctiveness: The influence of social status on group identity and advertising persuasion. *Journal of Marketing Research, 28*, 216-224.

Gross, G. (2003). Electronic voting vendors band together. *Computerworld.* Retrieved April 2002, from http://www.computerworld.com/governmenttopics/government/story/0,10801,88064,00.html

Heichler, E. (2003). Criticism of electronic voting machines' security is mounting. *Computerworld.* Retrieved December 15, 2003, from http:// www.computerworld.com/databasetopics/data/story/0,10801,8198,00.html

Hofstede, G. (1980). *Culture's consequences: International differences in work related values.* London: Sage Publications.

Hogg, M. A. (1996). Group structure and social identity. In W. P. Robinson (Ed.), *Social groups and identities: Developing the legacy of Henri Tajfel* (pp. 65-94). Oxford, UK: Butterworth-Heinemann.

Hogg, M. A., & Terry, D. J. (2000). Social identity and self-categorization processes in organizational contexts. *Academy of Management Review, 1*(25), 121-140.

Hugo, J. (2000). *South Africa's first HCI conference: CHI-SA 2000 — A rainbow of opportunity.* First Conference on Human Computer Interaction in Southern Africa, South Africa.

Hugo, J. (2002). *HCI and multi-culturalism in Southern Africa.* Retrieved April 2002, from http://www.chi-sa.org.za/articles/HCIculture.htm

Jarvenpaa, S. L., & Tractinsky, N. (1999). Consumer trust in an Internet store: A cross-cultural validation. *Journal of Computer Mediated Communication, 2*(5), 1-35.

Jarvenpaa, S. L., Tractinsky, N., & Vitale, M. (2000). Consumer trust in an Internet store. *Information Technology and Management, 12*(1), 45-71.

Jefferson, D., Rubin, A. D., Simons, B., & Wagner, D. (2004). A security analysis of the Secure Electronic Registration and Voting Experiment (SERVE). *servesecurityreport.* Retrieved January 20, 2004, from http://www.servesecurityreport.org/

Keil, M., Tan, B. C. Y., Wei, K. K., & Saarinen, T. (2000). Cross-cultural study on escalation of commitment behavior in software projects. *MIS Quarterly, 2*(24), 299-325.

Kelley, H. H. (1979). *Personal relationships: Their structure and processes.* New York: Lawrence Erlbaum Associates.

Kelley, H. H., & Thibaut, J. W. (1978). *Interpersonal relations: A theory of interdependence.* New York: John Wiley & Sons.

Lembke, S., & Wilson, M. G. (1998). Putting the "team" into teamwork: Alternative theoretical contributions for contemporary management practice. *Human Relations, 7*(51), 927-944.

Lewis, J. D., & Weigert, A. (1985, June). Trust as a social reality. *Social Forces, 4*(63), 967-985.

Luhmann, N. (1979). *Trust and power.* London: John Wiley & Sons.

Mayer, R. C., Davis, J. H., & Schoorman, F. D. (1995). An integrative model of organizational trust. *Academy of Management Review, 3*(20), 709-734.

McKnight, D. H., & Chervany, N. L. (2002). What trust means in e-commerce customer relationships: An interdisciplinary conceptual typology. *International Journal of Electronic Commerce, 2*(6), 35-53.

McKnight, D. H., Choudhury, V., & Kacmar, C. (2002). Developing and validating trust measures for e-commerce: An integrative typology. *Information Systems Research, 3*(13), 334-359.

McKnight, D. H., Cummings, L. L., & Chervany, N. L. (1998). Initial trust formation in new organizational relationships. *Academy of Management Review, 3*(23), 473-490.

Mehra, A., Kilduff, M., & Brass, D. J. (1998). At the margins: A distinctiveness approach to the social identity and social networks of under-represented groups. *Academy of Management Journal, 4*(41), 441-452.

Microsoft (2000). South Africa elections: Technology revolutionizes electoral process in South Africa. *Microsoft.* Retrieved April 2002, from http://www.microsoft.com/resources/casestudies/CaseStudy.asp?CaseStudyID=12266

Pavlou, P., & Gefen, D. (2004). Building effective online marketplaces with institution-based trust. *Information Systems Research, 1*(15), 37-59.

Pavlou, P. A. (2003). Consumer acceptance of electronic commerce – Integrating trust and risk with the technology acceptance model. *International Journal of Electronic Commerce, 3*(7), 69-103.

Peterson, S. (2002). England tests e-voting. *Government Technology.* Retrieved April 2002, from www.govtech.net/magazine/story.phtml?id=29354

Reichheld, F. F., & Schefter, P. (2000). E-loyalty: Your secret weapon on the Web. *Harvard Business Review, 4*(78), 105-113.

Ridings, C., Gefen, D., & Arinze, B. (2002). Some antecedents and effects of trust in virtual communities. *Journal of Strategic Information Systems, 3-4*(11), 271-295.

Rose, G. M., Evaristo, R., & Straub, D. (2003). Culture and consumer responses to Web download time: A four-continent study of mono- and polychronism. *IEEE Transactions on Engineering Management, 1*(50), 31-44.

Straub, D., Loch, K., & Hill, C. (2001). Transfer of information technology to developing countries: A test of cultural influence modeling in the Arab world. *Journal of Global Information Management, 4*(9), 6-28.

Tajfel, H. (1970). Experiments in inter-group discrimination. *Scientific American, 5*(223), 96-102.

Tajfel, H. (1978). Social categorization, social identity, and social comparison. In H. Tajfel (Ed.), *Differentiation between social groups* (pp. 61-76). London: Academic Press.

Taylor, S., & Todd, P. A. (1995). Assessing IT usage: The role of prior experience. *MIS Quarterly, 4*(19), 561-570.

Thibaut, J. W., & Kelley, H. H. (1959). *The social psychology of groups.* New York: John Wiley & Sons.

Turner, J. C. (1985). Social categorization and the self-concept: A social cognitive theory of group behavior. In E. L. Lawler (Ed.), *Advances in group processes: Vol. 2* (pp. 77-122). Greenwich, CT: JAI Press, Inc.

Vijayan, J. (2004). Panel members find security flaws in Internet voting system. *Computerworld.* Retrieved January 22, 2004, from http://www.computerworld.com/securitytopics/security/story/0,10801,89290,00.html?nas=AM-89290

Williamson, O. (1985). *The economic institutions of capitalism.* New York: The Free Press.

Wines, M. (2003). A mean scrum on playing fields of South Africa. *New York Times Online.* Retrieved December 2003, from http://www.nytimes.com/2003/09/12/international/africa/12AFRI.html

Zucker, L. (1986). Production of trust: Institutional sources of economic structure, 1840-1920. *Research in Organization Behavior, 1*(8), 53-111.

ENDNOTES

[1] In this chapter, we refer to the individuals who create and deploy an organization's IT, including its Web site, as "agency personnel." In this context, the term "agency" will be used to connote an organization deploying an interactive Web site, such as a government unit responsible for managing the voting process. The term "agency personnel" shall also include managers who set policies related to Web site interaction. For example, such policies may determine how a governmental voting agency safeguards sensitive citizen data.

[2] See http://www.prcdc.org/summaries/voting/voting.html

[3] See http://www.localelections.org.za/turnout/turnout.htm

[4] See http://www.sfgate.com/cgi-bin/article.cgi?file=/chronicle/archive/2004/01/22/MNGQF4F7J31.DTL

[5] The benevolent dimension of trust is not part of this study because it is farfetched to expect governmental agencies to actually show benevolence. Governmental agencies are guided by regulations and are expected to fulfill these regulations in an honest and capable manner. Showing benevolence beyond what the regulations say would, in many cases, be unacceptable.

6   Afrikaans, English, Zulu, Xhosa, Swazi, Ndebele, Southern Sotho, Northern Sotho, Tsonga, Tswana and Venda.

7   Cultural diversity is measured in this study through linguistic diversity. Language is, after all, a major aspect of culture. There are 11 primary languages in the RSA but only one in the USA, English, or maybe two including Spanish. Nonetheless, it should also be pointed out that the types of tribal ties in the RSA are not a factor in this context in the USA, given that there is a ubiquitous exposure to national culture through media and other factors. Moreover, the prevailing national tradition and policy in the USA was a melting-pot culture. In contrast, for centuries prior to 1991, the prevailing tradition and governmental policy in the RSA was one of emphasizing ethnic differences among the many different peoples, including the many black peoples of the RSA.

8   "Black," "White," and "Coloured" were legal terms in the RSA legal system with specific official meaning.

9   See http://www.isiswomen.org/pub/wia/wiawcar/affirmative.htm for a summary of the conditions and legal changes.

10   Hofstede did include South Africa in his research in the 1970's at IBM. However, by law, black South Africans would not have been working with whites and, as such, it is safe to assume no non-whites were included.

11   Collectively, South Africa has over 3 million Internet users as of 2003. Likewise, cell phone adoption in RSA is very high (14.4 million users in a country with 44 million people, of whom only roughly 4.5 million are white), per http://www.mobileoffice.co.za/stats/statistics_south_africa.htm and http://www.library.uu.nl/wesp/populstat/Africa/safricag.htm which indicates wireless computing services could reach a large and diverse population. Moreover, e-government applications are available for such functions as electronic filing, http://www.mytax.co.za/html/home.asp, and distribution of application forms, http://www.gov.za/documents/index.html

APPENDIX A: DESCRIPTION OF INTERNET-BASED VOTING

RSA Data	PU	Social-cultural similarity	Disposition to Trust	Trust	Communalities
PU1	**.818**	.009	.001	.064	.674
PU2	**.811**	.088	.170	.013	.695
PU3	**.773**	.072	.025	-.010	.603
PU4	**.768**	.088	.007	.051	.601
SCS1	.038	**.827**	.108	.076	.623
SCS2	.080	**.798**	.165	.305	.764
SCS3	.125	**.726**	.219	.179	.702
SCS4	.086	**.658**	.075	.390	.598
DIS1	.163	.002	**.778**	.203	.674
DIS2	.087	.044	**.756**	.191	.618
DIS1	-.041	.225	**.750**	-.042	.616
DIS2	-.001	.271	**.715**	.074	.590
TRUST1	-.017	.273	.219	**.764**	.706
TRUST2	.014	.229	.083	**.747**	.618
TRUST3	.082	.146	.081	**.727**	.563
Eigenvalue	4.525	2.373	1.672	1.076	
Explained variance	30.169	15.819	11.149	7.174	
Cronbach's Alpha	.81	.83	.77	.71	

There is a possibility of voting using a computer connected to the Internet instead of using paper ballots. Some government election agencies around the world are considering allowing citizens to vote using computers attached to the Internet. This service is not currently available in the USA.

Paper-based voting traditionally takes place with written votes on paper ballots that are put into boxes that are then collected and moved to a central location. Internet-based voting would be different in many ways. For example, Internet-based voting could take place at any computer anywhere that was connected to the Internet. Examples include computers at schools, in homes, and at central locations such as post offices. Votes are sent over the Internet directly to a central location as each person votes.

APPENDIX B: RSA DATA AFTER PCA WITH VARIMAX ROTATION AND WITH DESCRIPTIVE STATISTICS

USA Data	PU	Social-cultural similarity	Disposition to Trust	Trust	Communalities
PU1	**.895**	.000	.093	.113	.823
PU2	**.861**	.031	.111	.102	.765
PU3	**.839**	.197	.078	.109	.760
PU4	**.792**	.137	.127	-.016	.662
SCS1	.070	**.835**	.205	.163	.771
SCS2	.005	**.822**	.162	.157	.727
SCS3	.146	**.779**	.148	.166	.678
SCS4	.167	**.736**	.204	.202	.653
DIS1	.082	.148	**.858**	.115	.778
DIS2	.101	.065	**.839**	.201	.758
DIS1	.144	.296	**.732**	.119	.659
DIS2	.140	.313	**.722**	.240	.696
TRUST1	.129	.127	.209	**.859**	.814
TRUST2	.081	.200	.233	**.822**	.776
TRUST3	.061	.312	.115	**.622**	.501
Eigenvalue	5.699	2.404	1.517	1.201	
Explained variance	37.994	16.025	10.112	8.005	
Cronbach's Alpha	.88	.86	.85	.74	

APPENDIX C: USA DATA AFTER PCA WITH VARIMAX ROTATION AND WITH DESCRIPTIVE STATISTICS

USA Data	PU	Social-cultural similarity	Disposition to Trust	Trust	Communalities
PU1	**.895**	.000	.093	.113	.823
PU2	**.861**	.031	.111	.102	.765
PU3	**.839**	.197	.078	.109	.760
PU4	**.792**	.137	.127	-.016	.662
SCS1	.070	**.835**	.205	.163	.771
SCS2	.005	**.822**	.162	.157	.727
SCS3	.146	**.779**	.148	.166	.678
SCS4	.167	**.736**	.204	.202	.653
DIS1	.082	.148	**.858**	.115	.778
DIS2	.101	.065	**.839**	.201	.758
DIS1	.144	.296	**.732**	.119	.659
DIS2	.140	.313	**.722**	.240	.696
TRUST1	.129	.127	.209	**.859**	.814
TRUST2	.081	.200	.233	**.822**	.776
TRUST3	.061	.312	.115	**.622**	.501
Eigenvalue	5.699	2.404	1.517	1.201	
Explained variance	37.994	16.025	10.112	8.005	
Cronbach's Alpha	.88	.86	.85	.74	

Chapter VI

Globalization and E-Commerce:
A Cross-Cultural Investigation of User Attitudes

John Sagi, Anne Arundel Community College, USA

Elias Carayannis, The George Washington University, USA

Subhasish Dasgupta, The George Washington University, USA

Gary Thomas, Anne Arundel Community College, USA

ABSTRACT

Many authors argue that information and communications technology (ICT) in this New Economy is causing a globalized, unified society. Others take the opposite stand, viewing local factors such as national culture as very important to the success of information technology (IT). Research indicates that related factors such as gender may also play important roles in the use and acceptance of IT. This chapter uniquely examined these by using electronic commerce as the common technology. Business students from the U.S., Greece, and England expressed opinions on the important issues of National Control, Privacy Cost, Property Rights, and Consumer Preferences. Using Analysis of Variance (ANOVA), sufficient evidence was found to conclude that there are statistically significant differences in attitude about e-commerce among cultural groups, but not with gender groups. This research found support for several studies indicating the importance of culture on attitudes about technology, and postulated that common attitudes about Privacy Cost and Consumerism may be among indicators of a "technology veneer".

INTRODUCTION

Although the last few years have witnessed an explosive growth in electronic commerce activities in many parts of the world, very little is known about the exact nature, dynamics, and impact of this phenomenon. There is a certain paucity of systematic investigations reported in the literature. (Lee, M., 2001, p. 3)

In this age of information, researchers postulate that information technology (IT) is providing a new medium to finally unite society. According to the futurist Francis Fukuyama (1992), the end of the cold war signals a shift towards a "normative integration of principles and institutions". Todd (1986) states that technology provides ever-narrowing approaches to social problems, and these approaches are reducing social options. He notes that an "unnatural" selection process caused by technology results in a loss of diversity in human society. Volti (1992) discusses a "convergence theory" where opportunities and demands presented by modern technology promote the convergence of all societies towards a single set of social patterns and individual behaviors, due in part to the requirements of technology for a common set of development and implementation steps, and for common organization constraints. Rosabeth Moss Kanter (1995), in her classic *World Class*, predicts that internationalism will prevail over "nativism". That is, for future corporate profitability, the boundaries of national identity must be subsumed to the need for quality products and global goodwill.

Greider (1997) writes of *One World, Ready or Not*, with mobile phones as the "universal artifact of the revolution". He predicts that there will be four major competitive factors: labor, national governments, multinational corporations, and financial investors. Hope and Hope (1997) discuss the "third wave" leading to more homogeneous global marketing patterns. Cairncross (1997) observes that time zones and language groups will soon define distance, rather than mileage. She further notes that the credit card is the certain symbol of a unified world currency. Kevin Kelly (1998), editor of *Wired* magazine, in his *New Rules for the New Economy*, writes that technology has "been able to infiltrate into our lives to the degree it has become more like us...Technology has become our culture" (p. 33).

On the other hand, however, some argue that a globalization of society has not, and perhaps will not occur. Ferkiss, in *Technological Man* (1969), claims that the existence of technology change presupposes cultural acceptance, and that a single culture, "embracing both the famine-stricken world and the well-fed nations is obviously impossible...cultural variation is likely to be the rule" (p. 171). Volti (1992) observes that technologies developed and implemented in one culture or society may fail when taken to a different setting. Nelson and Clark (1994) note that European firms commonly develop differing computer systems for different nations. Hamel and Prahalad (1994), in their classic *Competing for the Future*, warn firms to address and work with global differences; that global markets emerge at differing speeds; and that global differences will continue to be a challenge. Doremus, Keller, Pauly, and Reich (1998) note that corporate governance is closely linked to national culture, and boldly claim that the global corporation is a myth. Fine (1998) cautions managers to be more sensitive to the effects of national business mores, values, standards, laws, and cultures. Bowers (2000) claims that the most dominant characteristic of computers is their culturally-mediating and transforming effect, but that computers are viewed as a destructive form of Western colonization. "Members of other cultures are aware that when they use computers, they must adapt themselves to radically-different patterns of thought and deep culturally-bound ways of knowing" (p. 22).

Castells (2001) observes that "core economic, social, political, and cultural activities throughout the planet are being structured by and around the Internet… (yet) its logic, its landscape, and its constraints are not well understood beyond the realm of strictly technological matters" (p. 3). He further writes of a large digital divide within a globalized Internet between developed and developing nations; and of a resulting number of challenges, including ownership and control of data; and the exclusion of groups by virtue of education, technology, and national culture. Albrow (2000) discusses several facets of globalization, including values related to daily behavior of many groups (also called "globalism"), universally-available information and commodities ("globality"), communications technologies used to maintain relationships ("time-space compression"), and worldwide institutional arrangements permitting personal mobility and local lifestyles ("disembedding")(p. 199). This research was concerned with personal values, information, and technologies, using globalization under those contexts.

The late Michael Dertouzos (1997) predicted that the "homogenizing forces" of information technologies can "only go so far, because of the overwhelming power of ethnicity… Most likely, the Information Marketplace will superimpose a cultural veneer of shared experiences on top of the individual cultures of the world" (p. 283). Berger and Huntington (2002) write about differing and separate globalization processes. "The emerging global culture is diffused through both elite and popular vehicles" including a business-oriented "Davos" culture and an academic-oriented "faculty club" culture (p. 3). Dubois (2004) observes that there are still numerous risks to the seamless exchange of global goods and services.

Further, globalization encompasses ideologies other than culture, such as environmentalism and feminism. The International Telecommunications Union (ITU) identified gender differences as important to global technology policies. In a recent paper, they observe that technology is not gender neutral, and that there is a statistically significant correlation between the gender of Web users and the global UN Development Program (UNDP) Technology Achievement Index (Hafkin, 2003). Several Internet statistical monitors also claim that the number of female Internet users in the US now equal males.

Thus there are conflicting theories about globalization, with issues often embracing a broader group of ideologies than national culture. The purpose of this research is to investigate and understand the extent of globalization by studying attitudes about electronic commerce. It will show whether the world is truly coming together as prophesied by Fukuyama, Volti, Greider, Kelly, and others. It will also identify certain global differences about e-commerce, in spite of the common technology. Also, given the recent increases in female Internet users, this research investigates the effects of gender on these attitudes.

LITERATURE REVIEW

E-commerce relies heavily upon information and communications technology (ICT). The Internet, and specifically the World Wide Web, is being used by businesses worldwide to manage day to day transactions and as an integral part of their marketing strategy. E-commerce, as a global transaction system, must fall under the same multicultural scrutiny and research as previous ICT projects. The success of e-commerce across national borders is a function of several variables, including the national economy, national literacy, national culture, telecommunications availability, and Internet technology penetration and acceptance (Pitkow & Kehoe, 1996; Tillquist, 1997). Still, little research has been conducted that examines the extent of globalization on Web usage and the associated social implications.

From a comparative analysis of cross-cultural studies, Ein-Dor, Segev, and Orgad (1993) observe that economic, demographic, and socio-psychological factors affect information systems. They integrate these into a framework of research and write that cultural differences may present a greater impact on the technical and procedural aspects of information systems. Deans and Ricks (1993) provide an agenda for research linking IS and International Business. They write that, from an IB perspective, the role of IS may be viewed as a facilitator of information flows across national borders, and that IB offers theoretical underpinnings that may be relevant for international IS research.

National Culture

Straub (1994) studies the globalization of IT using e-mail and fax in the U.S. and Japan. He concludes that while U.S. companies exploit the advantages of IT, the Japanese do not, and that a strong sense of uncertainty avoidance and the use of complex language symbols make fax a more useful tool in the Japanese culture. Straub, Keil, and Brenner (1997) test the Technology Acceptance Model (TAM) on e-mail use with airline employees in Japan, Switzerland, and the U.S. They find that the cultural works of Geert Hofstede (1983, 1997) are not strong predictors of technology use across all cultures. They write that cultural differences alone may not explain differing results. In Japan, cultural tendencies towards uncertainty avoidance (UAI), greater power distance (PDI), and collectivist sentiments may limit e-mail use and disassociate the TAM concept of perceived usefulness (PU) from actual technology use. Hasan and Ditsa (1999) interview managers in Australia, West Africa, and the Middle East to study the impact of culture on the global adoption of IT. They question the belief that technology is culturally neutral, and also use Hofstede (1997) to explain differences in attitudes. They confirm that many aspects of IT are not culturally neutral, and conclude that IT products should accommodate the cultural, economic, social, and other characteristics of a particular group. Kim, Leung, Sia, and Lee (2004) find that Hofstede's cultural traits of Individualism and Uncertainty Avoidance are important in understanding global Internet shopping behavior. Markus and Soh (2002), in studying the structural influences on global e-commerce activity, find that national cultural differences alone do not provide a satisfactory explanation. Karahanna, Evaristo, and Srite (2005) posit that behavior is influenced on several levels of culture, including supranational, national, professional, organizational, and group. Research by McLeod, Kim, Saunders, Jones, Scheel, and Estrada (1997), Rose and Straub (1998), Dasgupta, Agarwal, Ioannidis, and Gopalakrisnan

(1999), Al-Khaldi and Wallace (1999), Cheung and Lee (2001) and Carayannis and Sagi (2001) also find differences across the nations in IT use and attitudes.

Gender

Several of the aforementioned studies note that cultural differences do not provide sufficient explanation for differences in attitudes and use of IT. One of these other factors is gender. Harris and Davison (1999) research global anxiety and technology involvement, and their influence upon attitudes towards computers in developing societies. Using computer students in China, Hong Kong, Malaysia, New Zealand, Tanzania, and Thailand, they find that many differences are attributable to gender and computer experience. Hoxmeier, Nie, and Purvis (2000) study the impact of culture, gender, and other variables on user confidence in e-mail. They report that gender differences may diminish through technical education and experience. In a study of national level culture and global Internet diffusion, Maitland and Bauer (2001) write that economic factors were strong predictors of IT adoption; that cultural variables are slightly less powerful predictors; and that gender plays a significant role. Simon (2001) studies Web site perceptions, and finds that there are both cultural and gender factors involved. Zhang, Chen, and Wen (2002) study the characteristics of Internet users and privacy concerns, surveying U.S. undergraduate students and Chinese graduate students, university professors and managerial professionals. They observe that female respondents are more concerned with the unauthorized use of personal information and the possible misuse of credit card information than are male respondents. In a study of 227 U.S. Midwestern shoppers, Rodgers and Harris (2003) report that emotional factors and trust are strong influencers in female online shopping. Doolin, Dillon, Thompson, and Corner (2005) find that New Zealand males are more likely than females to purchase online.

RESEARCH MODEL AND HYPOTHESES

From the literature, it is clear that there are aspects of e-commerce which can be explored to understand globalization. Straub (1994), Straub et al. (1997), Hasan and Ditsa (1999), Markus and Soh (2002), Kim et al. (2004) and others find cultural differences in IT use. Harris and Davison (1999), Hoxmeier et al. (2000), Maitland and Bauer (2001), Simon (2001), Zhang et al. (2002), Rodgers and Harris (2003), and Doolin et al. (2005) also report gender differences in cross-cultural studies. Thus, this study chose cultural groups and gender and their influence upon attitudes about a globalized e-commerce, with the following research questions:

1. What aspects of e-commerce may be influenced by national culture?
2. What aspects of e-commerce may be influenced by gender?

The independent variables were national culture and gender, while the dependent variables were attitudes about e-commerce. These are shown in the Research Model, Figure 1.

To test the extent of globalization based upon differences in attitude among the independent variables of culture and gender, given the previously-discussed research, several hypotheses were created (Table 1). These hypotheses were developed from

Figure 1. Research model

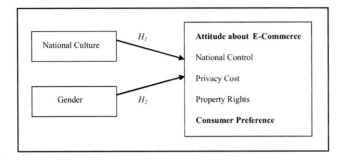

Table 1. Research hypotheses

H1: Cultural groups will differ significantly in attitudes about eCommerce.

   H1A: Cultural groups will differ significantly about attitudes towards National Control of data.
   H1B: Cultural groups will differ significantly about attitudes towards Privacy Cost.
   H1C: Cultural groups will differ significantly about attitudes towards Property Rights.
   H1D: Cultural groups will differ significantly about attitudes towards Consumer Preferences.

H2: Genders will differ significantly in attitudes about eCommerce.

   H2A: Genders will differ significantly about attitudes towards National Control of data.
   H2B: Genders will differ significantly about attitudes towards Privacy Cost.
   H2C: Genders will differ significantly about attitudes towards Property Rights.
   H2D: Genders will differ significantly about attitudes towards Consumer Preferences.

issues about electronic commerce described in Turban, Lee, King, and Chung (2004). These issues include national control of data across borders, the individual cost of privacy, property rights, and consumer preferences.

RESEARCH METHODOLOGY

Instrument Creation, Validity, and Reliability

This research developed an instrument that measured the attitudes about e-commerce. Students were chosen as a convenience sample, and they provide a uniform group of educated samples, with common technology access and education, representing the future leadership in technology (Harris & Davison, 1999). Zmud and Boynton (1991) state that Likert-scale self-reporting questionnaires are very important to information systems research. The design of this research was a cross-sectional study to probe attitudes about major issues of e-commerce. The questions were opinion ques-

Table 2. Factor analysis

Rotated Component Matrix[a,b,c]

	Component						
	1	2	3	4	5	6	7
national control	.861						
control	.771		-.368	.310			.316
give up privacy	.768						-.383
privacy cost	.684	-.626					
own name		.891					-.280
pay for less ads		.864					
more connected			.888	.245		-.311	
right to resell	.354	.276	.769				.208
copy ok	-.213		.745		-.255	.217	-.415
good friends				.844			-.333
reliable web info	.215	-.226		.769			
subsidized access		.328			.809	.270	
domain names			.248	.501	.713		
licensed sites	.534	-.330			.617	.233	
private email		.476	.312	-.464	.477		-.252
new privacy laws						.952	
access rights	.319			.350		.808	
buy from store		-.247					.859
return problems	-.443	.254		-.255			.587

Extraction Method: Principal Component Analysis.
Rotation Method: Varimax with Kaiser Normalization.

a. Rotation converged in 14 iterations.

b. Only cases for which class = Pilot are used in the analysis phase.

c. class = Pilot

tions asking the subjects what they think about an event. Opinions are the verbal expressions of attitude (O'Sullivan & Rassel, 1999). This study built upon previously-unpublished research conducted in October, 2000, at Anne Arundel Community College (AACC), Arnold, Maryland (Sagi, 2000). In that study, business students in an electronic commerce course identified major issues and developed a list of 43 Likert-scale questions related to these issues. The students were directed to develop questions on both the national and macro economic levels, and to include personal issues such as Napster and commercial trust. Demographic and behavioral questions about age, gender, prior Web purchases, and number of hours online were added to the instrument. The researchers and several faculty members edited the questions for content validity.

Validity was further improved by a literature scan for similar questions, techniques, and issues. The research of Doll and Torkzadeh (1988) was helpful in understanding the measurement of end user attitude. The work of Harris and Davison (1999) and Hoxmeier et al. (2000) were used as excellent examples of the cross-cultural survey instrument development and use, and of Analysis of Variance (ANOVA) methodology. The revised questions were then given to a pilot group of business students (N=17). Cronbach's alpha was an acceptable .7281 for this pilot group. According to Harris and Davison (1999) who develop a similar instrument, an alpha above .7 is satisfactory. Factor analysis was used to reduce the questions to express one or more concepts. All of the variables (43 questions) were originally considered, and a correlation matrix was constructed.

Several stronger correlations appeared to express similar attitudes about similar issues. These correlations were rotated using Varimax rotation. According to George and Mallery (1999), the process is highly subjective. The results are shown in Table 2.

Component 1 (Eigenvalue = 21.6) represents two e-commerce issues, national control and privacy. Hofstede's (1983, 1997) research identifies both of these with the index Individualism (IDV). However, these are differing and unique aspects of e-commerce. Thus in this study Component 1 represents two variables, National Control (national control, control) and Privacy Cost (give up privacy, privacy cost). Component 3 (Eigenvalue = 14.6) also contains two questions and represents the construct Property Rights (right to resell, copy ok). Finally, Component 7 (Eigenvalue = 5.8) factors two questions that were chosen to form the construct Consumer Preferences (buy from store, return problems).

It is not unusual in information technology research to rely upon two questions as the basis for operationalizing a research construct. For example, in their seminal work on studying the measurement of end-user computer satisfaction and a model for this current study, Doll and Torkzadeh (1988) rely upon two questions in an 18-item instrument to operationalize one of their major study factors. Lederer, Maupin, Sena, and Zhuang (2000) use two questions for the construct Information Focus, and Jiang, Hsu, and Lin (2000) have two questions comprising the construct Internet Experience. The results of the factor analysis provided the constructs and their associated instrument questions as shown in Table 3.

Dependent Variables

According to Shields (1996), "the Internet raises challenging policy issues of access, privacy, copyright, and regulation. It poses cultural problems as information is made available regardless of social and cultural boundaries" (p. 1). Cairncross (1997) observes that national attitudes "differ enormously, reflecting the extent to which citizens in different countries trust their governments and private industries" (p. 196). She also asserts that the "culture and not just the language of the Internet is also strikingly American. Its quirky blend of technocratic individualism, egalitarianism, and passionate resistance to government control all seem to many foreigners quintessentially American" (p. 95). For example, in the 1990's, the U.S. government provided a *Framework for Global Electronic Commerce* which stated that the private sector should lead and governments should avoid "undue restrictions". Wresch (2002), in a study of less developed nations, finds that national technical capability has a direct impact upon e-commerce.

National Control and Privacy Cost

Hofstede (1997) sees national control of data and the concept of personal privacy as culturally similar under a national index "Individualism" (IDV). He postulates that IDV influences control and the acceptance of government influence, and has an impact upon attitudes about privacy and individual rights. Tavani and Moor (2001), however, distinguish between these concepts. They define privacy in terms of protection from intrusion and information gathering, and control in terms of framing policies that provide privacy protection. They postulate that privacy is best defined in terms of restricted access, and is fundamentally about protection from intrusion and information gathering

Table 3. Research constructs

National Control
NC1. The government should control the Web to better protect the consumer from fraud.
NC2. A nation should be able to control the Web content that crosses its borders.

Privacy Cost
PC1. I'll gladly give up some privacy information for cheaper prices on the Web.
PC2. Loss of privacy is a cost of new technology benefits.

Property Rights
PR1. Web sites should have the right to resell *any* user information that is freely given
PR2. It is ok to save a copy of anything on the Web.

Consumer Preferences
CP1. I surf the Web for product information, but I usually prefer to buy from a store.
CP2. Returning a purchase is still a problem on the Web.

by others. Control, on the other hand, plays a critical role in the management of privacy and should be understood under that framework. They observe that virtually all societies establish normative situations, which vary across cultures. Further, they recommend that e-commerce should be designated as an international "zone of privacy", as per the intent of the European Union's directive on privacy discussed previously. Thus this study separates these concepts.

Rose (2001) writes that the Internet is at a "crossroads" between the ability to collect and relate personal data, and the potential for misuse. Citing research, he also notes a common hesitancy for consumers to provide personal data, the common practice of providing erroneous data and marketing's increasing desire to utilize the potential for data analysis provided by new technology. He notes several common definitions of privacy: "The right to be left alone", "the right to control...", "the degree of access others have to us", "freedom from the judgment of others", and "a means for creating social context in relationships with others". Rose concludes that consumer confidence must be established and maintained to get any value from the data obtained and manipulated by technology. National government may play a role in this.

Etzioni (1999) identifies a "privacy paradox". He observes that privacy is often preferred, in the U.S., over the common good, and national government is often perceived or characterized as the victimizer. Yet, according to Etzioni, the threats to privacy are more often from the commercial private sector. "When privacy is threatened by the private sector in our culture, policies and doctrines provide a surprisingly weak defense" (p. 10). The solution, he offers, is a greater focus on the corresponding social responsibility and commitment to the common good that was, according to Etzioni, lost after 1965.

Kizza (1998) writes, "Individuals are forced to give up some of their rights in order to protect individual privacy." He discusses the problems with the private sector and with data collection, similar to the issues raised by Etzioni (1999). According to Kizza, nations enact laws to protect from the loss of privacy, and that the Internet has heightened the awareness of the potential privacy loss due to technology. He notes that privacy can be protected by information control, property control, and the use of anonymity of addresses in Internet communications.

Ferkiss (1969), in his early work defining the *Technological Man*, observes that privacy will present a future problem, based upon both the potential for a large increase in population and the possibility for absolute surveillance. "Spheres of privacy" may be defined, but the threat of absolute surveillance may be prohibitably costly when compared with the benefits. Volti (1992) writes that technology often leads to a "restructuring of power relations, the redistribution of wealth and income, and an alteration of human relationships" (p. 18). Kelly (1998) notes that society clearly has a need for anonymity and privacy in communications. He then offers some direction in his seminal *New Rules for the New Economy*: "One of the chief chores in the network economy is to restore the symmetry of knowledge." He discusses this idea by formulating privacy as a type of conversation between two trusted parties. "Firms should view privacy not as some inconvenient obsession of customers... but more as a way to cultivate a genuine relationship" (p. 134). However, questions remain over the role of governments in the national control of data and the price that users are willing to pay.

Property Rights

The right of a Web site to sell information and of a user to freely copy data from the Web are prominent issues in e-commerce and the topic of national legislation. Recent intellectual property rights (IPR) law applying to e-commerce includes the international *Trade-Related Aspects of Intellectual Property* (TRIPS) agreement, ratified in 1994 by over one hundred nations. TRIPS provides international IP standards, and specifically provides copyright protection for computer programs as intellectual creations. The U.S. *Anticybersquatting Consumer Reform Act* (ACRA) of 1999 makes it illegal for a person to "register, traffic in, or use" domain names under certain conditions of "bad faith intent". The *Digital Millennium Copyright Act* (DMCA) of 1998 restricts the circumvention of encryption software and absolves the Internet Service Provider (ISP) of liability for certain copyright infringement violations by its users. Disputes are resolved by the *Uniform Dispute Resolution Policy* (UDRP) of the *Internet Corporation for Assigned Names and Numbers* (ICANN) and the United Nations' *World Intellectual Property Organization Arbitration and Mediation Center* (WIPO).

Consumer Preferences

The propensity to prefer the store as the purchase location instead of the Internet, and the expectation that those Internet purchases are subject to issues with returns, are also common issues in e-commerce. Cairncross (1997) addresses the drivers of the Internet and the resulting new business models, and elaborates about the increased confidence required for consumers to embrace this technology. "The overall low percentage (of Internet sales to total commerce) suggests that the vast majority of customers are perfectly happy to buy at real-world stores" (p. 130). Trust and confidence with this new technology may be factors, as well as differences in consumer location and in buying habits among nations. Doolin et al. (2005) find that a loss of social interaction correlates with reduced online spending. Rural consumers or consumers in nations where face-to-face agreements are considered important, such as the Middle East, may cause consumers to prefer stores over the Internet. Further, rural customers may not be able to return items purchases on the Web to a store as easily as the urban customer. Thus, the impact of culture and other sociologic factors on these consumer attitudes is not entirely understood.

Population Sampling

The respondents were 195 business students at colleges in the U.S., Greece, and England. Business students were particularly good subjects because of their homogeneity of education, familiarity with the Internet and e-commerce topics, their availability for study, and their potential for future leadership in the Internet and e-commerce. Students were used as subjects in many similar studies referenced in this chapter, including Stylianou, Robbins, and Jackson (2003), Simon (2001), Jiang et al. (2000), Hoxmeier et al. (2000), and Harris and Davison (1999). The institutions were chosen based upon previous relationships between the researchers and the schools, and compare as shown in Table 4.

Anne Arundel Community College (AACC) serves the Maryland county of Anne Arundel, on the western shore of the Chesapeake Bay. Total enrollment exceeds 13,000 students, with over 7,000 full time equivalent students (FTE). The School of Business, Computing, and Technical Studies prepares students to enter the job market with expert skills and training. Hands-on courses provide experience and realistic simulations of the work environment. Transfer options prepare students for entry into four-year institutions. AACC offers Associate degrees in business, accounting, and law, among others. Business students have access to over 160 PCs in eight classroom-laboratories. Personal computer (PC) instruction is mandatory for all students.

Athens Laboratory of Business Administration (ALBA) was founded in 1992, through a joint initiative of the Federation of Greek Industries, the leading Employers' Union in Greece, and the Hellenic Management Association. ALBA was originally funded by the European Commission and local Athens contributions. ALBA offers MBA and law degrees. The computer network consists of approximately 100 PCs configured with the latest software versions. More than half of the PCs are available to the students at study rooms, the Computer Laboratory and the Library, as well as in the classrooms and amphitheaters, to be used during lectures and case study/projects presentations. Students have free 24-hour access to the Internet. ALBA is located in the suburb of Vouliagmeni, about 25 kilometers southeast from the center of Athens.

Southwark College is in a suburb on the South Bank of the Thames, opposite London. Southwark is a working-class neighborhood. The college's 3,000 FTE and 7,000

Table 4. School profiles

School	Anne Arundel Community College (AACC)	Athens Laboratory of Business Administration (ALBA)	Southwark College
Location	Arnold, Maryland, USA	Athens, Greece	London, England
Class	Undergraduate	Graduate	Undergraduate
Business Enrollment	1000	200	500

Table 5. Sample descriptive statistics

Item	US		UK		GR	
	Count	Percent	Count	Percent	Count	Percent
Male	44	59%	46	54%	23	66%
Female	31	41%	39	46%	12	34%
Totals	75	100%	85	100%	35	100%
Education	Undergraduate		Undergraduate		Graduate	
Age < 20	34	45%	69	81%	0	0%
20-25	18	24%	8	10%	6	17%
26-30	10	13%	2	2%	16	46%
31-40	11	15%	4	5%	9	26%
> 40	2	3%	2	2%	4	11%
Online Hours / wk						
< 3	23	31%	31	36%	5	14%
4-10	20	27%	33	39%	13	37%
11-20	17	23%	16	19%	8	23%
20-30	8	11%	4	5%	6	17%
> 30	7	8%	1	1%	3	9%

part time students use the college's three campuses, all within the immediate area. Southwark maintains close relations with and often serves as a feeder school for several nearby universities, including the University of London. Students have access to a large research facility containing about 100 new Internet-able PCs and current software. There are also several computer technology labs. Most students have PCs at home and rely on the school facilities primarily for class-related activities. The descriptives for the samples are shown in Table 5.

Analysis

Multivariate Analysis of Variance (MANOVA) was used to test the hypotheses since there was more than one dependent variable (survey questions) under study. MANOVA tests are interpreted by examining the significance level of the F-ratio, which is the comparison of the "Between-groups Means Square" and the "Within-groups Mean Square". As the means of the treatment groups (cultural groups and gender) become similar, the F-ratio approaches 1. The significance is based upon the distribution and the degrees of freedom. Significance is interpreted as the chance of making a Type I error. For this research, the acceptable significance for assuming a difference in treatment groups was $< .05$.

RESULTS

Note from Table 6 that the significance .012 was $<.05$ for hypothesis H1. The null hypothesis, that the means of the treatment groups are similar, could be rejected, and the hypothesis that there are culture differences in attitude could be supported. However,

Table 6. MANOVA analysis

Test: If the F ratio > 1 and its significance level at the degrees of freedom for the two mean squares is < .05, the null hypothesis, that the means are the same, can be rejected.							
Hypothesis	**Source of Variance**	**Sum of Squares**	**df**	**Mean Square**	**F**	**Sig.**	**Result**
H1: Cultural groups will differ significantly in attitudes about eCommerce.	Between groups.	87.477	2	43.739	4.547	.012*	Supported.
	Within groups.	1741.242	181	9.620			
H2: Genders will differ significantly in attitudes about eCommerce.	Between groups.	22.907	1	22.907	2.309	.102	Not Supported.
	Within groups.	1805.811	182	9.922			

*Indicates statistically significance

Table 7. ANOVA for cultural groups

Test: If the F ratio > 1 and its significance level at the degrees of freedom for the two mean squares is < .05, the null hypothesis, that the means are the same, can be rejected.				
Hypothesis	**F**	**Significance**	**Differences**	**Result**
H1A: National Control	9.622	.000*	UK (4.04) > US (3.15)* GR (3.88) > US (3.15)*	Supported.
H1B: Privacy Cost	2.470	.087		Not Supported.
H1C: Property Rights	6.656	.002*	UK (2.58) > GR (1.88)* UK (2.58) > US (1.99)*	Supported.
H1D:Consumer Preferences	1.441	.239		Not Supported.

*Indicates statistically significant at $p < 0.05$

the significance .102 of H2 led to the conclusion that there were no statistically-significant differences in gender attitude.

From Table 7, it was noteworthy that national culture was not an influence on the constructs of Privacy Cost and Consumer Preferences. ANOVA generates a significance value indicating whether there are differences among the treatments. This does not indicate, however, what the differences are when the number of treatment groups exceeds

Table 8. ANOVA for gender

Test: If the F ratio > 1 and its significance level at the degrees of freedom for the two mean squares is < .05, the null hypothesis, that the means are the same, can be rejected.				
Hypothesis	F	Significance	Differences	Result
H2A: National Control	2.457	.119		Not Supported.
H2B: Privacy Cost	3.822	.052		Not Supported.
H2C: Property Rights	1.030	.312		Not Supported.
H2D: Consumer Preferences	2.691	.103		Not Supported.

* Indicates statistically significant at $p < 0.05$

2. To identify the differing treatments in this situation, this research uses Scheffe's Bivariate Comparison test. There were differences among cultural groups in several constructs. UK (μ=4.04) and GR (μ=3.88) students were more likely to agree with National Control of the Web than their U.S. (μ=3.15) counterparts.

All respondents in this study generally disagreed with giving up privacy as a cost of technology (μ=2.31). Both U.S. (μ=1.99) and GR (μ=1.88) students disagreed with the idea that Web sites should have the right to resell any user information. UK (μ=2.58) students, on the other hand, also disagreed but were less sure about that construct. Cultural groups generally concurred with the construct of Consumer Preferences (μ=3.92), preferring to buy from a store and expecting problems with their purchases.

From Table 8, the general agreement between genders is interesting. Genders were close to disagreement about Privacy Cost (sig. = .052) as females (μ=2.11) tended disagree more than males about giving up privacy as a cost of technology.

DISCUSSION

Certainly the world is not in common agreement about e-commerce. Ferkiss, Clark, Hamel and Prahalad, Dertouzos and others expected cultural groups to differ. It is particularly interesting that this research found differences in National Control given the previously-discussed cultural work of Hofstede (1983, 1997), and no differences in Consumer Preference given the variety of business models and distribution channels among the nations. Areas of agreement and difference were anticipated by Mittleman (2000) who writes "...The architecture of globalization is too high to perceive as a whole, but if one moves to a finer scale — more discreet issues — the structures become discernable" (p.13).

On differences in National Control, Castells (2001) discusses Singapore as an example of a government proactive in Internet control. "Attempting to steer a narrow path between (embracing technological modernization and maintaining a sophisticated authoritarian regime), the government of Singapore has tried to expand the use of the

Internet among its citizens, while retaining political control over this by censoring Internet service providers" (p.164). Further, the nations of the European Union are developing the "Directive of Distance Selling", a mandate of standards for Web sites to protect the consumer from fraud. Sheff (2002) discusses the emergence of China as an economic power but also as an unpredictable government having the dual role of both expanding the Internet while attempting to regulate and censor it. Zhang et al. (2002) also discuss Chinese research subjects, and report that respondents are more likely to support an increased government involvement for greater privacy protection. Gajewski (2004) notes that the Cuban government is moving to control Internet access for the "social good".

On the common attitudes towards Privacy Cost, this may be important to e-commerce site developers and certainly refutes the common idea that "privacy is dead". Castells (2001) also writes "Most people waive their rights to privacy in order to be able to use the Internet" (p.174). Clearly any waiving of rights is not done consciously. Zhang et al. (2002) report that among their Chinese respondents, those with online shopping experience were more likely to trade their personal information for free merchandise and for targeted advertisements. The U.S. and GR strong common disagreement with selling Web information is interesting, and is another message to developers about the nature of e-commerce expected by those nations. That all three cultural groups concurred with Consumer Preferences is also interesting given the diverse business models and different commercial distribution channels present in each nation.

On gender, we hypothesize that the level of education reported by the respondents may be related to this lack of difference. The subjects here were all college students. Other possible factors may include age and technology access, which are areas for further research. Hoxmeier et al. (2000) report that, although gender plays a role in confidence in technology use, the role of gender greatly diminishes with education and with experience. The nearly significant differences in attitudes about Privacy Cost are similar to the findings of Zhang et al. (2002) who report that their female respondents were more concerned with unauthorized use of personal information by Web sites than were males. Similar findings are reported by Rodgers and Harris (2003). This also correlates with recent studies by British Telecom (BT PLC). While over half of UK males purchase some form of content online, only one fourth of females were willing to pay for content (*Internet Works*, Autumn, 2002, p. 13). Simon (2001) reports that gender may also have different influences in different nations. Stewart, Shields, and Sen (2001) find gender differences in the use of Internet communications. Further, Htun (2000) observes that, while culture is an essential concept, it does not alone explain gender issues.

Limitations

Markus and Soh (2002) discuss structural influences on global e-commerce, including financial (electronic payment systems, credit financing), legal and regulatory (consumer protection, taxes), national policies about promoting or regulating the Internet usage and e-commerce, space and logistics (home size, distance to shopping, transportation, warehousing), telecommunications, IT penetration and use, local business practices (purchasing, payment, financing), language, education, firm size, structure, and control systems, and industry concentration. Markus and Soh conclude that structural conditions may vary widely across countries, and are not fully captured in measures of national culture. This conclusion is supported by the work of Bin, Chen, and Sun (2003) and Wresch (2003). This research attempted to control as many of these as possible. The subjects were students, with similar interests (business), technology access (via school computers), and language (instruction in English). Many of the structural influences were reasonably not applicable to the subjects. Others may result from culture and physical resources, such as national policies, legal and regulatory infrastructures, and local business practices.

From Table 5, it is clear that gender ratios and the self-reported online hours are reasonably similar across cultural groups. Several other factors may arguably have presented a bias and a limitation to this research. Subject age is not commonly considered in IT research. Harris and Davison (1999) report that age is not a factor in PC anxiety. Doolin et al. (2005) find no significant association between age or education and Internet purchasing behavior. Education is commonly reported in research but level differences are not often noted. Harris and Davison (1999) also use both graduate and undergraduate students in their study. Zhang et al. (2002) find that education level is not an issue in attitudes about online privacy. The use of student subjects is criticized for its limited generalizability to the population. However, students are often used (Hoxmeier, 2000; Jiang et al., 2000; Simon, 2001; Zhang et al., 2002) in IT research. The use of students is supported by their potential as managers and are often more strongly associated with technology utilization. However, the results obtained from such a study of students should be generalized with caution. The difference in sample size may be a limitation in the findings. Harris and Davison (1999) also have similar differences among the six cultural groups in their study. Pelto and Pelto (1981) note that differences may be more difficult to identify with smaller sample sizes. The assumptions for ANOVA do not include equality of sample sizes, but that the samples are independently drawn and selected with some degree of randomness.

It is certainly possible that one group is more culturally homogenous than another. Many researchers who use cultural groups to study technology rely upon national borders to determine those groups (Harris and Davison, 1999; Hasan and Ditsa, 1999; Jiang et al. 2000; Kim et al., 2004; Straub, 1994; Stylianou et al., 2003; Zhang et al., 2002) . Straub et al. (2001) tested the survey responses against home of birth and report no correlation. That is, while respondents may report other nations as home of birth, their attitudes towards technology are more similar to those in their residence nation than those within their home nation. Harrison and Huntington (2000) discuss this rather pointedly and write that "The diversity — the vast number of subcultures — is undeniable. But there is a foundation of shared values, attitudes, and institutions that binds together the nations… analogous to that of Great Britain … no one would question the existence of a British culture" (p. 67). Finally, the instrument was developed within one culture and administered to two others. There may be an inherent bias in the wording or interpretation of the questions that was unforeseen and that influenced the responses. However, since the topic was mostly the use of technology, and since the shared language was English, this bias is not expected to be influential. While noting differences in age and education level, and the possibility of bias from national cultural heterogeneity and from the instrument, these are not considered major limitations to the findings of this study.

Recommendations for Research and Business

It is recommended that future researchers expand this study to other cultural groups to better identify cultural traits corresponding to the use of e-commerce. Researchers should study other populations and subjects with this research model, such as managers and technology workers. Other factors such as the national infrastructure conditions, electronic payment systems, consumer protection, home sizes, distance to stores, and information technology penetration should be investigated. Researchers may test the influence of gender on the attitudes expressed by cultural groups, age groups, and those with differing technology access. Although this research attempted to provide a common sample, the results may have been influenced by factors such as local business customs, personal income, and credit card access. Nonetheless, businesses must identify national culture as influential on the acceptance of e-commerce and know that nations may differ on controls and access to this technology. Businesses must also recognize that consumer attitudes about information technology may differ across nations. Not all cultures may react the same way to the need to develop and control the Internet infrastructure, for example. They must pay particular attention to the influence of culture on attitudes about National Control and Property Rights. That is, businesses must remain aware that nationalities may expect governments to control various aspects of e-commerce and the Internet; that ideas about data and software ownership may be different; and that the citizens of other nations may differ on opinions about wholesale Web access and control of facets of the Internet structure such as domain naming.

CONCLUSIONS

This study found that globalization and common technology have not resulted in common attitudes about e-commerce. It also uniquely revealed several interesting facts about the nature of globalization as perceived by various cultural groups and genders. This study found that culture influenced attitudes about e-commerce, yet gender did not. It was clear that cultural groups differed in attitude about National Control and Property Rights. However, and very important, culture played no role in influencing attitudes about Privacy Cost and Consumer Preference. This study found that U.S. e-commerce users were less tolerant of government control of the Web. Gender did not play a statistically-significant role in attitudes about e-commerce. It may be that gender differences diminish with education. However, it was noted that females were more concerned about giving up privacy.

One possible explanation of shared attitudes towards aspects of privacy and consumer behavior may be the work of Dertouzos (1997, 2001). He writes of the "Information Marketplace" as exerting a "blending and levelling force on the local and global cultures..." (p. 283). He postulates a "thin but universal cultural layer" but casts doubt upon a single universal culture due to local conditions and the "overwhelming power of ethnicity". Similarly, Berger and Huntington, (2002) write of cultural "globalization" or synchronomy and of cultural "localization" or autonomy. This study postulates that aspects of privacy and consumer behavior may be early indicators of Dertouzos "veneer" layer, and of the "middle ground of cultural homogeneity" discussed by Berger and Huntington.

Table 9. Culture group reactions

Culture Reactions	Research Constructs	F-ratios	Significant Differences
Acceptance.	Consumer Preferences.	1.441	None.
	Privacy Cost.	2.470	
Modification	Property Rights.	6.656	UK (2.58) > GR (1.88) UK (2.58) > US (1.99)
and	National Control.	9.622	UK (4.04) > US (3.15) GR (3.88) > US (3.15)
Rejection.			

Berger and Huntington also postulate several possible consequences for the intersection of globalizing forces and indigenous cultures. These include replacement of the local culture with the new, coexistence of the local and new cultures, synthesis of the new and the local resulting in a modified local culture, and total rejection of the new. It was interesting to note the correspondence between the work of Berger and Huntington and this research, leading us to uniquely postulate that the constructs of Privacy Cost and Consumerism may be areas of global agreement, while Property Rights and National Control may be areas of local modification across cultures as shown in Table 9.

REFERENCES

Albrow, M. (2000). Travelling beyond local cultures. In F. Lechner & J. Boli (Eds.), *The globalization reader* (pp. 118-125). Oxford: Blackwell.

Al-Khaldi, M., & Wallace, R. (1999). The influence of attitudes on personal computer utilization among knowledge workers: The case of Saudi Arabia. *Information and Management, 36*, 185-204.

Berger, P., & Huntington, S. (Eds.). (2002). *Many globalizations: Cultural diversity in the contemporary world.* Oxford: Oxford University Press.

Bin, Q., Chen, S., & Sun, S. (2003). Cultural differences in e-commerce: A comparison between the U.S. and China. *Journal of Global Information Management, 11*(2), 48-56.

Bowers, C. (2000). *Let them eat data: How computers affect education, cultural diversity, and the prospects of ecological sustainability.* Athens, GA: University of Georgia Press.

Cairncross, F. (1997). *The death of distance.* Boston: Harvard Business School Press.

Carayannis, E., & Sagi, J. (2001). Dissecting the professional culture: Insights from inside the IT "black box". *Technovation, 21*, 91-98.

Castells, M. (2001). *The Internet galaxy: Reflections on the Internet, business and society.* Oxford: University Press.

Cheung, C., & Lee, M. (2001, July-September). Trust in Internet shopping: Instrument development and validation through classical and modern approaches. *Journal of Global Information Management*, 23-35.

Dasgupta, S., Agarwal, D., Ioannidis, A., & Gopalakrisnan, S. (1999, July-September). Determinants of information technology adoption: An extension of existing models to firms in a developing country. *Journal of Global Information Management*, 30-40.

Deans, P., & Ricks, D. (1993, Winter). An agenda for research linking information systems and international business: Theory, methodology and application. *Journal of Global Information Management*, 6-19.

Dertouzos, M. (1997). *What will be: How the new world of information will change our lives.* NY: Harper Collins.

Dertouzos, M. (2001). *The unfinished revolution: Human-centered computers and what they can do for us.* NY: Harper Collins.

Doll, W., & Torkzadeh, G. (1988, June). The measurement of end-user computing satisfaction. *MIS Quarterly*, 259-273.

Doolin, B., Dillon, S., Thompson, F., & Corner, J. (2005). Perceived risk, the Internet shopping experience and online purchasing behavior: A New Zealand perspective. *Journal of Global Information Management*, 13(2), 66-89.

Doremus, P., Keller, W., Pauly, L., & Reich, S. (1998). *The myth of the global corporation.* Princeton: Princeton University Press.

Dubois, F. (2004). Globalization risks and information management. (Editor's comments). *Journal of Global Information Management*, 12(2), i-iii.

Ein-Dor, P., Segev, E., & Orgad, M. (1993, Winter). The effect of national culture on IS: Implications for international information systems. *Journal of Global Information Management*, 33-44.

Etzioni, A. (1999). *Limits of privacy.* New York: Basic.

Ferkiss, V. (1969). *Technological man: The myth and the reality.* New York: Braziller.

Fine, C. (1998). *Clock speed: Winning industry control in the age of temporary advantage.* Reading, PA: Perseus Books.

Fukuyama, F. (1992). *The end of history and the last man.* New York: Free Press.

Gajewski, K. (2004, March-April). A new Cuban law tightens control over Internet access. *The Humanist*, 45.

George, D., & Mallery, P. (1999). *SPSS for Windows.* Boston: Allyn and Bacon.

Greider, W. (1997). *One world, ready or not: The manic logic of global capitalism.* New York: Simon & Schuster.

Hafkin, N. (2003). Some thoughts on gender and telecommunications. *Proceedings of the 3rd World Telecommunications/ICT Indicators Meeting.* Retrieved February 21, 2006, from http://www.itu.int/ITU-D/pdf/5196-007-en.pdf

Hamel, G., & Prahalad, C. (1994). *Competing for the future.* Boston: Harvard Business School Press.

Harris, R., & Davison, R. (1999, January-March). Anxiety and involvement: Cultural dimensions of attitudes toward computers in developing societies. *Journal of Global Information Management*, 26-38.

Harrison, L., & Huntington, S. (Eds.). (2000). *Culture matters: How values shape human progress.* New York: Basic.

Hasan, H., & Ditsa, G. (1999, January-March). The impact of culture on the adoption of IT: An interpretive study. *Journal of Global Information Management,* 5-15.

Hofstede, G. (1983). National cultures in four dimensions. *International Studies of Management and Organization, 9*(1-2), 46-74.

Hofstede, G. (1997). *Cultures and organizations: Software of the mind.* New York: McGraw Hill.

Hope, J., & Hope, T. (1997). *Competing in the third wave: The ten key management issues of the information age.* Boston: Harvard Business School Press.

Hoxmeier, J., Nie, W., & Purvis, G. (2000, October-December). The impact of gender and experience on user confidence in electronic mail. *Journal of End User Computing,* 11-20.

Htun, M. (2000). Culture, institutions, and gender inequality in Latin America. In L. Harrison & S. Huntington (Eds.), *Culture matters: How values shape human progress* (pp. 189-199). New York: Basic.

Jiang, J., Hsu, M., & Lin, B. (2000). E-commerce user behavior model. *Human Systems Management, 19*(4), 265-277.

Kanter, R. (1995). *World class: Thriving locally in the global economy.* New York: Simon and Schuster.

Karahanna, E., Evaristo, J., & Srite, M. (2005). Levels of culture and individual behavior: An integrative perspective. *Journal of Global Information Management, 13*(2), 1-20.

Kelly, K. (1998). *New rules for the new economy.* New York: Viking.

Kim, K., Leung, K., Sia, C., & Lee, M. (2004, November). Is e-commerce boundary-less? Effects of individualism-collectivism and uncertainty avoidance on Internet shopping. *Journal of International Business Studies,* 545-560.

Kizza, J. (1998). *Ethical and social issues in the information age.* New York: Springer-Verlag.

Lederer, A., Maupin, D., Sena, M., & Zhuang, Y. (2000). The technology acceptance model and the World Wide Web. *Decision Support Systems, 29,* 269-282.

Lee, M. (2001, July-September). The adoption and diffusion of electronic commerce. Editorial. *Journal of Global Information Management,* 3.

Maitland, C., & Bauer, J. (2001). National level culture and global diffusion: The case of the Internet. In C. Ess (Ed.), *Culture, technology, communication: Towards an intercultural global village* (pp. 87-128). New York: SUNY Press.

Markus, M., & Soh, C. (2002, January-March). Structural influences on global e-commerce activity. *Journal of Global Information Management,* 5-12.

McLeod, R., Kim, C., Saunders, C., Jones, J., Scheel, C., & Estrada, M. (1997, Summer). Information management as perceived by CIOs in three Pacific Rim countries. *Journal of Global Information Management,* 5-16.

Nelson, K., & Clark, T. (1994, Fall). Cross-cultural issues in information systems research: A research program. *Journal of Global Information Management,* 19-29.

O'Sullivan, E., & Rassel, G. (1999). *Research methods for public administrators.* New York: Addison Wesley Longman.

Pelto, P., & Pelto, G. (1981). *Anthropological research: The structure of inquiry.* Cambridge, UK: Cambridge University Press.

Pitkow, J., & Kehoe, C. (1996). Emerging trends in WWW user population (GVU Tech. Rep. No. GIT-GVU-96-11). *Communications of the ACM.* Retrieved February 21, 2006, from http://www.gatech.edu/user_surveys/papers/cacm.pdf

Rodgers, S., & Harris, M. (2003, September). Gender and e-commerce: An exploratory study. *Journal of Advertising Research,* 322-330.

Rose, E. (2001, March). Balancing Internet marketing needs with consumer concerns: A property rights framework. *Computers and Society,* 17-21.

Rose, G., & Straub, D. (1998, Summer). Predicting general IT use: Applying TAM to the Arabic world. *Journal of Global Information Management,* 39-46.

Sagi, J. (2000). *Inside the new economy: Business students and issues of e-commerce and the Web.* Unpublished manuscript, School of Business, Computing and Technical Studies, Anne Arundel Community College, Arnold, MD.

Sheff, D. (2002). *China dawn.* New York: Harper Collins.

Shields, R. (1996). *Cultures of Internet.* London: Sage.

Simon, S. (2001, Winter). The impact of culture and gender on Web sites: An empirical study. *The DATA BASE for Advances in Information Systems,* 18-37.

Stewart, C., Shields, S., & Sen, N. (2001). Diversity in online discussions: A study of culture and gender differences in listserves. In C. Ess (Ed.), *Culture, technology, communication: Towards an intercultural global village.* NY: SUNY Press.

Straub, D. (1994, March). The effect of culture on IT diffusion: E-mail and FAX in Japan and the U.S. *Information Systems Research,* 23-47.

Straub, D., Keil, M., & Brenner, W. (1997). Testing the technology acceptance model across cultures: A three-country study. *Information and Management, 33,* 1-11.

Straub, D., Loch, K., & Hill, C. (2001, October-December). Transfer of information technology to the Arab world: A test of cultural influence modeling. *Journal of Global Information Management,* 6-28.

Stylianou, A., Robbins, S., & Jackson, P. (2003). Perceptions and attitudes about e-commerce development in China: An exploratory study. *Journal of Global Information Management, 11*(2), 31-47.

Tavani, H., & Moor, J. (2001, March). Privacy protection, control of information, and privacy-enhancing technologies. *Computers and Society,* 6-11.

Tillquist, J. (1997, Fall). Managing the global impacts of IT: Standing on conceptual quicksand. *Journal of Global Information Management,* 6-8.

Todd, J. (1986). A modest proposal. In A. Teich (Ed.), *Technology and the future.* NY: St. Martin's Press.

Turban E., Lee, J., King, M., & Chung, H. (2004). *Electronic commerce: A managerial perspective.* Upper Saddle River, NJ: Prentice Hall.

Volti, R. (1992). *Society and technological change.* New York: St. Martin's Press.

Wresch, W. (2003). Initial e-commerce efforts in nine least developed countries: A review of national infrastructure, business approaches, and product selection. *Journal of Global Information Management, 11*(2), 67-79.

Zhang, Y., Chen, J., & Wen, K. (2002). Characteristics of Internet users and their privacy concerns: A comparative study between China and the United States. *Journal of Internet Commerce, 1*(2), 1-16.

Zmud, R., & Boynton, A. (1991). Survey measures and instruments in MIS: Inventory and appraisal. In *Harvard Business School Research Colloquium* (pp. 149-180). Boston: Harvard Business School.

Chapter VII

The Evolution of IT Governance Structures in Dynamic Environments

Pauline O. Chin, Florida Atlantic University, USA

ABSTRACT

Information technology (IT) governance structures focuses on the distribution of the IT decision-making process throughout the enterprise to achieve the strategic IT goals of the organization. The development of an effective IT governance structure that is flexible and will meet the needs of a complex and dynamic environment is a challenging task. This is particularly the case in organizations that have achieved growth through mergers and acquisitions. When the acquired organizations are geographically located in different regions than the host enterprise, the factors affecting this integration and the choice of IT governance structures are quite different than when this situation does not exist. This study performs an exploratory examination of the factors that affect the choice of IT governance structures in organizations that grow through mergers and acquisitions in developing countries with transitional economies using the results of a case study of an international telecommunications company. In addition to the commonly recognized factors such as government regulation, competition and market stability, organizational culture, and IT competence, top management's predisposition toward a specific business strategy and governance structure can profoundly influence the initial choice of IT governance in organizations. The case also finds that IT governance structures are not static, but are continuously evolving in dynamic environments. Managerial implications are discussed.

INTRODUCTION

Rapid technological innovation has had a significant impact on every aspect of human life and this has resulted in significant changes in the way the world communicates, learns, and does business. The business environment has also become increasingly complex and competitive due to globalization of the world economy over the last two decades. In order to survive and to compete on a global scale, organizations have sought to increase their market share through mergers and acquisitions (M&A), both locally and internationally. In a publication by the Bureau of Census (2002) on mergers and acquisitions in over 41 industries for the year 1998, it was reported that there were 3,882 cases of U.S. companies acquiring other U.S. companies. This data also indicated that there were 483 cases of foreign companies' acquisitions of U.S. companies at an estimated value of US$233 billion, and 746 cases of U.S. companies acquiring foreign companies at an estimated value of US$128 billion.

The trend toward mergers and acquisitions has been clearly demonstrated within the telecommunications industry worldwide (Oh, 1996; Ramamurti, 2000; Trillas, 2002; Wilcox, Chang, & Grover, 2001). Over the last several years, telecommunications companies in North America, Europe, and Asia have looked toward acquisitions and mergers for their survival and growth. During the last decade there have been an increasing number of local and foreign investments in the industry (Oh, 1996; Ramamurti, 2000), due primarily to the deregulation of the telecommunications markets as well as the move toward total or partial privatization of telecommunications companies within developing regions (Gutierrez & Berg, 2000; Melody, 1999).

Foreign investments in developing countries within Latin America and the Caribbean have increased tremendously over the last twenty years due largely to changes in the regulatory policies within these regions. Historically, companies in Latin America and the Caribbean were owned primarily by the local states. This changed dramatically in the mid-1980s to 1990s as the increasing economic and financial demands on the industry forced companies in the region to look toward foreign investments in order to stay competitive. Gutierrez and Berg (2000) reported that between the mid-1980's to mid-1990's 14 out of the 24 telecommunications firms in the region privatized their companies. This strategy is also credited with setting into motion the current trend in a majority of the region's telecommunications companies toward increased partial or total privatization (Gutierrez & Berg, 2000; Ramamurti, 2000).

As a consequence of this massive privatization and merger-and-acquisition movement in the telecommunications industry, the role of IT in these organizations has changed significantly over the last decade. The traditional relationship of IT providing support services to individual departments within an organization has evolved into one where IT now plays a broader role in achieving the overall strategic goals of the organization via a focus on global enterprise-wide support that encompasses not only multiple departments, but often different countries and cultures as well. As a result, IT governance in the dynamic and complex business environment has been pushed to the forefront of critical issues facing the management of these organizations, in spite of the fact that little research exists on IT governance that attempts to identify and explain the multiple factors that may affect the choice of IT governance structures in the context of mergers and acquisitions in developing regions. In order to address these issues, this chapter examines the evolution of a governance structure within a global telecommunications network organization, based on a framework developed from the extant literature on corporate and IT governance theories and practices. The chapter addresses the general research question: In the process of merging foreign subsidiaries into the host company, what are the factors that influence the choice of IT governance structure? The primary purpose of the chapter is to contribute to a broader understanding of the evolution of IT planning and governance structures within a multinational organization operating in a dynamic environment.

The remainder of the chapter is structured as follows: The theoretical background of this research is explored, and the research framework is developed based on a literature review of governance structures and factors affecting the choice of these structures in organizations. A description of the case research methodology used in the chapter follows, and the findings of the study are then presented and discussed. The chapter concludes with a discussion of the managerial implications and the limitations of the study, as well as future research directions.

THEORETICAL BACKGROUND

IT Governance Structure

Peterson (2004) indicates that integration of the business and IT competencies is important for effective IT governance structures that are flexible and will meet the needs of a complex and dynamic environment. IT governance can be defined as "an integral part of enterprise governance and consists of the leadership and organizational structures and processes that ensure that the organization's IT sustains and extends the organization's strategies and objectives" (IT Governance Institute, 2001, p. 9). An alternative definition of IT governance focuses on "the structure of relationships and processes to develop, direct, and control IS/IT resources in order to achieve the enterprise's goals through value-adding contributions, which account for balancing risk versus return over IS/IT resources and its processes" (Korac-Kakabadse & Kakabadse, 2001, p. 9). The underlying theme running through both of these definitions is a focus on the relationship between corporate governance and IT governance, the alignment of IT strategy with the organization's strategy, and the concept of evaluating opportunities and risk versus returns on IT investments. Some researchers have suggested an extension of the traditional models of governance to include partners, service providers, and internal as well as external communities of practices (Robbins, 2004).

Three basic structures of IT governance within organizations have emerged over the last two decades. These structures essentially follow the basic concepts of a "centralized," "decentralized," and "hybrid" structure that represents a combination of the two (Brown, 1997; Sambamurthy & Zmud, 1999; Sohal & Fitzpatrick, 2002). Within the centralized structure, the decisions regarding the IT infrastructure and application software development and deployment, as well as the management of IT projects, are all made by corporate IT management (Sambamurthy & Zmud, 1999; Sohal & Fitzpatrick, 2002). This is usually achieved through the use of steering committees consisting of the organization's top-level management. In this model, IT governance is seen to come under the mandate of the board of directors and the senior management of the organization (IT Governance Institute, 2001; Sohal & Fitzpatrick, 2002). Centralized IT governance has the advantage of allowing an organization to benefit from economies of scale and scope by leveraging the planning process, the acquisition and deployment of IT resources, and the establishment and control of enterprise-wide standards and procedures. The drawback of this structure is that the individual business units may perceive IT systems as being rigid and less than optimal due to the lack of local control and/or ownership of the systems (Sohal & Fitzpatrick, 2002).

In the decentralized structure, the decisions regarding IT infrastructure and application software development and deployment, as well as the management of IT projects, are made at the divisional and the business unit levels. This structure has the advantage of placing ownership of the systems in the hands of the business units that are using them. This may in fact also ensure that IT is more in tune with the needs of the business units. The disadvantage is that this may result in a loss of economies of scale and scope, resulting in increased IT costs and a reduced level of integration of IT resources across business units (Sambamurthy & Zmud, 1999; Sohal & Fitzpatrick, 2002).

In the hybrid structure, the decisions regarding the overall IT infrastructure are made at the corporate level, and decisions regarding application development and deployment, as well as the management of IT projects, are made at the division and business unit levels. This structure attempts to give the organization the benefits of both the centralized and decentralized structures by ensuring that a corporate-wide synergy is maintained while facilitating a measure of responsiveness to the individual business units' IT needs. In the hybrid structure, these benefits are achieved by keeping activities such as the development of the overall IT strategy and decisions regarding enterprise information systems, operating platforms, data management and storage, and network infrastructures, as well as research and development, centralized in order to benefit from economies of scale and corporate-wide skill sets. At the business unit level, the functions related to the development of IT plans and infrastructures for each business unit are the responsibility of the individual business unit. Weill and Ross (2005) propose that the effectiveness of organizations' IT governance structures can be assessed by examining how IT delivers on four objectives: cost effectiveness, asset utilization, business growth, and business flexibility. IT governance structures are dynamic and tend to change as the organization attempts to evaluate their effectives. Weill and Ross (2005) found in their research that companies with fairly effective governance changed some aspect of that governance structure approximately once annually, while companies with less effective governance structures changed these structures up to three times annually. Rau (2004) also indicates that an effective IT governance structure is not easily developed and implemented; rather it is an evolutionary process spanning several years and utilizing organizational learning to modify the structure as necessary.

Factors Influencing IT Governance

A significant amount of research has brought to light factors that affect the choice of IT governance structures within organizations. This body of research can be classified into two categories: research focusing on the impact of a single factor, such as firm size (e.g., Ahituv, Neumann, & Zviran, 1989; Brown & Magill, 1994; Tavakolian, 1989), and research utilizing the underlying principles of contingency theory to identify the combination of factors that impact IT governance decisions within organizations (e.g., Brown, 1997; Brown & Magill, 1998; Sambamurthy & Zmud, 1999). A review of the literature suggests that the following five categories of factors are commonly recognized to be influential on IT governance: corporate governance structure, government regulations and policies, global and local market competition and stability, organizational culture, and organizational IT competence.

Corporate Governance Structure

Corporate governance structures can have a significant impact on the IT governance structures of organizations (Brown, 1997; Brown & Magill, 1994; Ein-Dor & Segev, 1982; Olson & Chervany, 1980; Sambamurthy & Zmud, 1999). It is argued that IT governance and corporate governance are integrally related to such a degree that IT governance is viewed as a subset of the corporate governance because "successful enterprises will need to be able to integrate the IS/IT contribution with the strategies, culture, and desired ethics of the enterprise in order to attain business objectives, optimize information value, and capitalize on the utilization of technology" (Korac-Kakabadse & Kakabadse, 2001, p.10). In a study of the organization of information systems in multinational corporations, King and Sethi (1999) found that firm characteristics such as the degree of centralization, dispersal, and coordination are differentially reflected in the IT configurations of these firms. It is thus logical to argue that factors identified to have significant impact on corporate governance will have a cascading effect on IT governance. As a consequence, the literature on corporate governance becomes relevant to studies of IT governance.

Studies on corporate governance structures usually focus on the characteristics and roles of members of the board as well as the development of processes and organizational structures necessary for facilitating achievement of corporate strategies (Argyres, 1995; Korac-Kakabadse & Kakabadse, 2001). Reuer and Zollo (2000) developed a framework of factors that affect adoption of governance structures within strategic alliances. They identified environmental conditions that include factors such as competition for market share as well as conditions in the host country of the acquired firms. The second set of attributes identified includes partner capabilities and alliance experience. Partner capabilities were defined as consisting of such things as the differences in cultures and management styles of the organizations, quality problems, and the competitive environment in which the organization operates. Alliance experience addresses one firm's prior alliance with a specific partner. The third factor identified is alliance attributes that focus on the skill sets and other assets that each alliance possesses.

Several corporate governance structures have been identified in the literature. These can be defined based on the decision-making processes along mechanistic versus organic lines. Mechanistic organizational structures tend to have high centralized control of the decision-making processes, whereas organic structures tend to have more decentralized decision-making processes (Brown, 1997). Other research literature defines organizational structures based on reporting lines. Some of the more common ones include organizational structures grouped around functional departments, products, processes, geographical regions, and the matrix structure, usually characterized by multiple reporting lines and consisting of both vertical integration of functional activities and the horizontal integration of processes (Board, 1998).

Organizational structures usually have an impact on the choice of corporate governance, which in turn impacts the choice of IT governance structures (Brown & Magill, 1994; Lainhart IV, 2000; Sambamurthy & Zmud, 1999; Tavakolian 1989). Most of the discussion on the relationship between corporate governance and IT governance in the literature has been in the context of a single organization. Few studies have addressed this issue in the context of multinational corporations with global foreign subsidiaries. This leads us to the first research question of the case study: In the M&A process, how does the corporate governance structure influence the IT governance structure of the host company and its foreign subsidiaries?

Government and Regulatory Policies

When consumers and producers choose freely in the market, *Pareto Optimum* is achieved and social welfare is maximized. Government and regulatory policies designed to achieve these goals are, therefore, extremely important. In developing countries, the legal and institutional foundations for the proper functioning of markets are extremely weak or absent. These foundations include a legal system that enforces contracts and validates property rights, a stable and trustworthy currency, an infrastructure of roads and utilities, a well-developed system of banking and insurance, formal credit markets that select projects and allocate loanable funds on the basis of relative profitability, and norms and behavior that facilitate successful long-term business relationship (Todaro, 2003, p. 69).

Government and regulatory policies have traditionally heavily governed the telecommunications industry both locally and globally. The regulatory policies related to the telecommunications industry in the U.S. are very similar to those in other North American regions such as Canada (Lehn, 2002; Melody, 1999) but significantly different from those in Europe, which are subject to more political constraints (Trillas, 2002). Telecommunications policies in place in developing countries are, however, quite different from their North American and European counterparts, partially attributable to the fact that telecommunications companies have traditionally been owned by the governments of those regions. These state-owned companies have typically not been driven by the commercial practices common in privately-owned firms throughout North America and Europe, but rather by political and bureaucratic factors (Gutierrez & Berg, 2000; Lehn, 2002).

The inception of the deregulation of the telecommunications industry in the 1990s generated dramatic changes and reforms in various countries around the globe (Melody, 1999). Research has shown that countries with a primarily state-owned telecommunications sector, as is the case in most of the developing countries, seem to be going through this transformation process more slowly than their counterparts in the more developed regions (Melody, 1999; Ramamurti, 2000). As a result of the differing speeds in the transformation process from a regulated to a deregulated environment, regulatory policies currently vary dramatically across countries. Some countries have made the transformation fairly quickly, while others are still going through the process.

The overall effect of the deregulation process in the telecommunications sector is the removal of many traditional restrictions. This has resulted in much more competitive telecommunications markets by giving telecommunications companies more leverage in pricing their products and services, making use of new technologies, and expanding into new markets, either through alliances or mergers and acquisitions. These new policies, in turn, lead to changes in the corporate governance structures in order to accommodate and facilitate the resulting changes in the relationships among external and internal stakeholders and the new management structures (Lehn, 2002). King and Sethi (1992) noted that regulatory policies at industry and country level could significantly influence the competitiveness of the markets in which multinational corporations operate, and that in turn could affect the IT structures and IT strategies of these firms.

This leads to the second research question of this study: In the M&A process, what role does government regulations and policies play in the evolution of the corporate and IT governance structures of the host company and its foreign subsidiaries?

Global and Local Market Competition and Stability

Estrin (2002, p. 101) states "Improved company performance must be at the heart of any successful transition from a command to a market-oriented economy. The standard pattern in the transition economies has been to seek improved companies by heightening competition and sharpening corporate governance in various ways; through privatization of state-owned firms ; by allowing and encouraging new firms and competition among existing firms; and via the withdrawal of government subsidies so that firms must face their own profits and losses...". However, Estrin goes on to indicate that this methodology has had mixed success based on the organizational environment as well as the policies implemented.

The competitive environment has changed significantly for the global telecommunications market (Pentzaropoulos & Giokas, 2002). One of the main drivers of the transformation process within the telecommunications industry is the need to be able to compete for survival and growth, both locally and globally. Reuer and Zollo (2000) suggested that on the global scale, competition for market share by forging new alliances through mergers and acquisitions may have an impact on the governance structure chosen by an organization. On the local level, increased competition as a result of lifting the restrictions with regard to the number and monetary value of foreign investments into local markets may also have an impact on the governance structure chosen (Reuer & Zollo, 2000). With the deregulation of the global telecommunication industry, competition has increased from global telecommunications companies who are trying to get into the markets of developing countries (Ramamurti, 2000).

The research literature also indicates that previous exposure to competitive environments makes business units more responsive to changes and improvements in business processes than those who operate in monopolistic environments protected by the state (Henderson & McAdam, 2001). Tavakolian (1989) studied the relationship between a firm's competitive strategy and its IT governance structure in the computer component industry. He divided the sample firms based on three competitive strategy categories: defenders, analyzers, and prospectors. The results show that the degree of centralization of IT function is significantly related to the type of competitive strategy a firm adopts: IT functions of an organization with a conservative competitive strategy, such as defenders, are more centralized than those of the organizations with a more aggressive competitive strategy, such as prospectors.

The literature also recognizes the impact of global and local market stability on corporate governance. The telecommunications industry has, in recent times, faced turbulent and adverse market conditions. Deregulation, increased competition, overcapacity, and a number of other factors during the last five years have also resulted in severe downfalls in certain parts of the industry. This is evidenced by the fact that many telecommunications companies have filed for bankruptcy and insolvency, the most noteworthy of which is the bankruptcy of WorldCom, one of the largest in the corporate history of the U.S. This situation has additional ramifications for other telecommunications companies that provided services to these bankrupt or insolvent companies. Brown (1997) identified many indicators of instability and linked them with IT governance. She found that organizations operating in unstable environments have greater local information processing needs and thus a tendency toward decentralized IT governance. In the reverse scenario, organizations operating in a stable environment tend to have a centralized IT governance structure.

However, there is limited research literature on the influence of market conditions on the corporate and IT governance structures of organizations that have adopted a strategy of growth through mergers and acquisitions. This leads to the third research question of the case study: In the M&A process, what influence does global and local market conditions, such as competition and stability have on the corporate and IT governance structures of the host company and its foreign subsidiaries?

Organizational Culture

The evaluation of the culture component is extremely relevant to studies of mergers and acquisitions, because the realization of any benefits of an M&A strategy requires the collaboration and cooperation of executives from different countries and different business units with different cultural backgrounds. The collaboration and cooperation often lead to modifications in the corporate governance structures, which in turn significantly affect the IT governance structures.

While culture can be defined in general as "the collective programming of the mind which distinguishes one group or category of people from another" (Hofstede, 1980, p. 25), cultural factors are often examined at several different levels, including country and regional cultures, industry cultures, and organizational cultures and subcultures. Country and regional cultures can, in turn, heavily influence organizational cultures, which can be defined as "the social or normative glue that holds an organization together and that expresses the values or social ideals and beliefs which organizational members come to share" (Cooper, 1994, p. 18). One of the factors that affect organizational culture is the degree of intervention from the state, as demonstrated by the degree and nature of the regulations to which an organization is subjected. Organizational cultures and subcultures have, therefore, evolved as a result of country and regional culture, industry culture, organization history, and market environment (Schneider & Barsoux, 1997).

Research on organizational culture suggests that the cultural artifacts, and even the art of management itself, provide a powerful symbolic means of communication in the sense that they can be used to build organizational commitment, convey the philosophy of management, rationalize and legitimize activities, motivate employees, and facilitate socialization (Smircich, 1983). Thus, it is not surprising that scholars have linked country and organization culture to many aspects of information systems, including its impact on IT governance (Brown, 1997; Cooper, 1994; Olson & Chervany, 1980).

A useful framework is developed by Quinn and Rohrbaugh (1983) in which organizational culture is analyzed based on two dimensions: One depicts the desired amount of organizational order versus flexibility, and the other depicts the desired focus for an internal versus external view of the organization. These two dimensions of organizational design create four types of organizational culture (Cooper, 1994): 1) *Survival culture* represents an open-systems view where organizational effectiveness is defined in terms of survival, with criteria including growth, new market development, and resource acquisition; 2) *Productivity culture* represents the rational goal model where organizational effectiveness is defined in terms of production or economic goals such as profit maximization; 3) *Stability culture* is based on the internal-process model and largely ignores the environment, and organizational effectiveness is measured to the extent that it is in control, stable, and internally efficient; and 4) *Human-relations culture* represents an organizational environment where informal behavioral structures (interpersonal systems of power, status, communications, and friendship) are emphasized over formal structures (rules, positions, and procedures).

Even though organizational culture has been the focus of many studies, few have examined the impact of culture on IT governance in the context of mergers and acquisitions and the integration of multi-country subsidiaries. This leads to the fourth research question of the case study: In the M&A process, what is the role of organizational culture in the evolution of corporate and IT governance structures of the host company and its foreign subsidiaries?

Organizational IT Competence

The level of IT competency possessed by the host organization in a merger and acquisition will affect the division of labor between the firms and the scope of any collaborative activity. If the host organization does not possess high IT competencies, then a centralized IT governance structure will likely not materialize. On the other hand, if the subsidiaries are weak in their capabilities of planning and managing IT infrastructures and applications, a decentralized IT governance structure is less likely. In a more general sense, IT competency can be considered as a special case of an organization's absorptive capacity, which is defined as the ability of an organization's employees to develop relevant knowledge bases, recognize valuable external information, make appropriate decisions, and implement effective work processes and structures (Cohen & Levinthal, 1990). From this perspective, Sambamurthy and Zmud (1999) argue that the choice of IT governance structure can be significantly influenced by the level of IT-related knowledge possessed by business managers across the organization and their willingness to accept IT decision-making responsibilities. To that extent, an organization's capability to effectively implement and sustain a decentralized structure for IT governance can be largely predicated upon the extent to which the line managers throughout its operating units possess the requisite level of IT-related absorptive capacity.

Figure 1. Research framework of factors influencing the selection of IT governance structure

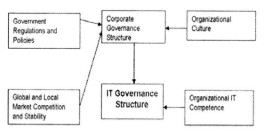

This line of discussion on IT competency leads us to the fifth and final research question of this case study: In the M&A process, how does the IT competence of subsidiaries influence the evolution of the IT governance structure of a host company and its foreign subsidiaries?

Research Framework

The discussion of the influential factors of IT governance and the research questions presented above can be summarized in the following research framework, as shown in Figure 1. The essence of this framework is that the IT governance structure of any given organization is dynamic rather than static, contingent upon the complex interactions among a number of internal and external constraining factors to which the organization is subjected. Based on the literature, we posit that government regulations and policies, global and local market competition and stability, and organizational culture all have significant influence on the IT governance structure of the host company and its foreign subsidiaries created through mergers and acquisitions. However, such influences are mediated through the corporate governance structure that emerged during the mergers and acquisitions. On the other hand, IT competency of the host company and its foreign subsidiaries will have a direct influence on the final IT governance structure selected following the completion of the mergers and acquisitions.

As discussed in the previous sections, the effect of each of the individual factors on IT governance structure has been investigated in one or more previous studies under various organizational contexts. What we aim to do in this case study is to address these research questions by exploring the real-world process of IT governance changes experienced by an international telecommunications company during its aggressive growth through merger and acquisition in a turbulent time that was marked by increasing global competition and deregulation of the telecommunications industry in many developing countries.

RESEARCH METHODOLOGY

The main objective of this research is to conduct an examination of the emergence of an IT governance structure in an organization that has grown through mergers and acquisitions. In order to achieve this, an explanatory case study research approach (Yin, 1994) is used. The goal of the case study research in this context is to expand and generalize theories, that is, analytical generalization, by posing competing explanations and developing new ones. A case study methodology is preferred when "a 'how' or 'why' question is being asked about a contemporary set of events over which the investigator has little or no control" (Yin, 1994, p. 9). This methodology allows us to examine this phenomenon within its "real-life context." An embedded case-study-design approach was used since the focus of the study is on the corporate level of the organization as well as its major subsidiaries. Case study methodologies have been frequently used in IS research (e.g., Benbasat, Goldstein, & Mead, 1987; Brown, 1997; Levina & Ross, 2003; Sambamurthy & Zmud, 1999).

The Target Organization Before and After Integration

ECW[1] is a United Kingdom (UK)-based company with subsidiaries around the world. It has been in the telecommunications business for over a century. ECW is, in effect, a holding company with direct or indirect investments in foreign subsidiaries, with total assets in excess of US$24 billion at the time of this study. The strategy undertaken by ECW in the 1990s consisted of an intensified program of acquisitions, disposals, and investments. The overall acquisition of the various subsidiaries within the group occurred at different times, some as far back as the late 19th Century.

Under the directions of a chief executive who was appointed in 1999, ECW adopted a regionalized corporate strategy in 2000. This resulted in the ECW group of companies being subdivided into two units: ECW Global (ECW-G) and ECW-Regional (ECW-R). ECW-G consisted of the group's operations in Europe, the U.S., and Japan. The ECW-R division at the start of this study consisted of subsidiaries in thirty-three territories in three main regions: the Caribbean, Middle East, and Asia Pacific. ECW-R, with net operating profits of approximately US$600 million and $350 million respectively for the years ended March 31, 2001, and 2002, was the more profitable of the two units. At the conclusion of the initial study and over the next year, ECW suffered severe losses from its Global businesses and decided to withdraw its operations from the United States. As a result of this and increasing competition in the dynamic environments within which ECW was operating, this regional structure, which heralded the initial integration process within the Caribbean, was subsequently modified. A new group CEO of ECW was appointed in 2003 and further restructuring took place over the next couple years with the removal of the original regional and global structures and the implementation of a new country-based structure.

ECW was chosen for this research because it provided a unique opportunity to study the phenomenon of the restructuring process undertaken by an organization that has grown through mergers and acquisitions in the dynamic environments of developing regions and to examine the IT governance structures that have evolved as a result of this restructuring. Another factor considered in the selection of ECW as the target organization was the association of the author with the company, which in turn helped to open the doors to conduct interviews, gather documents, and perform direct observations of some of the business transition processes.

The study was conducted using the three largest territories within ECW-R in which ECW has controlling interest or management control and can therefore affect the governance structures. This consisted of the Caribbean, Panama, and Macau. These territories were selected because collectively they generate over 85% of the revenue earned by ECW-R and employ over 80% of the employees within the regional unit. The Caribbean territories generate over 55% of the total revenue earned in the region, with Jamaica generating over 40% of the total Caribbean revenue. Panama and Macau each have a single business unit, whereas the Caribbean has business units in fourteen different territories. As a result of these factors and also due to space limitation, the focus of this chapter will be on the analysis of the initial integration and further restructuring process and the IT governance transformation of ECW and its Caribbean territories as a result of mergers and acquisitions.

Data Collection and Analysis

Initial data collection took place between April 2002, and January 2003. Two years after the initial data collection, a more moderate data collection phase was undertaken utilizing published sources such as company press releases to gain insights on the progress of the organization to date. Following Yin's (1994) case study methodology, a

Table 1. Data collection procedures

Sources of Evidence	Description
Literature Review	Existing literature on corporate governance, IT governance, and the trends within the telecommunications industry was reviewed.
Documentation	All relevant documentation, such as proposals, progress reports, and other internal organizational documents highlighting the integration and restructuring process were collected.
Archival records	Organizational charts as well as the results of a survey/questionnaire conducted by a major consultancy firm were obtained.
Semi-Structured/ Unstructured Interviews	Interviews conducted with the CIO ECW Caribbean as well as other key employees provided useful insights.
Participant observation	The historical connection of the author with the organization afforded the opportunity to obtain insights that would not have otherwise been available.
Published sources	Newspaper articles, press releases, and other publicly available financial statements and filings by the company were also collected.

variety of techniques were utilized, including the collection of relevant documentation such as proposals, progress reports, and other internal documents; archival records such as organizational charts and survey data previously collected about the organization; semi-structured and unstructured interviews; participant observation; published sources; as well as physical artifacts such as manuals and reports. Table 1 shows the data collection methods used in this study.

An initial semi-structured two-hour interview was conducted with the CIO of ECW Caribbean. Unstructured interviews were also conducted with other key managers and employees within the organization. Archival data was also collected in the form of the summary results of a review conducted by an external consultancy firm for the organization that was initially designed to assist in the transformation process of the information systems department in the largest business unit of the group located in Jamaica.

CASE STUDY FINDINGS

Corporate and IT Governance Structure Before the Integration

At the time when the acquisitions of these foreign subsidiaries were completed, the majority of them operated in a monopolistic environment as independent and autonomous units. Each subsidiary had individual functional and support departments that provided the skills necessary for that business unit to perform its tasks. A hierarchical reporting structure existed in these companies, with each territory having its own President/CEO who reported directly to the CEO of ECW-R, the host company.

The Caribbean region is somewhat unique because it is made up of many different territories of varying sizes and resources. In response to the challenges of the new telecommunications industry environment, the decision was made to establish the Caribbean unit as a single entity under a new CEO of ECW Caribbean (ECW-C) position, and this heralded the start of the integration process for the foreign subsidiaries located in fourteen different countries in that region. Panama and Macau continued to function independently, with their individual CEOs reporting to the CEO of ECW-R. The functions being performed within each of the fourteen foreign subsidiaries in the countries involved were then evaluated, and the transformation process to achieve vertical and horizontal integration along functional lines began in May 2001, and became fully effective by the end of 2002.

In the area of IT governance, prior to the integration a regional business IT steering committee existed at the ECW-R corporate level, that examined overall strategic technology and systems issues on a quarterly basis. This process, however, did not include active user involvement throughout the foreign subsidiaries, and therefore did not effectively impact the information systems planning process at the subsidiary level. Each of the larger foreign subsidiaries had an Information Systems (IS) manager who reported to the CEO/President of that subsidiary. The local IS Department (ISD) handled the IT needs of the individual subsidiary either internally or through outsourcing. At the start of this study and prior to the integration, there was no formal corporate IT governance structure to assess IT opportunities and agree on priorities across subsidiaries. Consequently, the IT needs of each subsidiary were largely managed on a project-by-project basis. There was also no sharing of IT resources across the subsidiaries. Thus, the IT governance before the integration was effectively a decentralized structure, consistent with the corporate governance structure at the time.

Corporate and IT Governance Structures After the Integration

The acquisition of these foreign subsidiaries, with their differing business cultures and legacy systems, brought with it the associated challenge of transforming them from independent autonomies into a cohesive and collaborative group. In order to effectively handle this transition, two significant changes in corporate governance occurred in 2001 – 2002. The CEO of ECW-C position was created to handle the integration of the business units in the 14 territories of the Caribbean region. The second major change was that the board director responsible for Group Finance and who also had the dual role of CEO of ECW-R was directed to pass his finance role over to a new director effective July 1, 2002, so that he could focus totally on the management, development, and integration of the foreign subsidiaries within ECW-R.

The corporate governance structure that emerged as a result of the integration process was that a CEO position was created for each of the three major regional territories, each of which reported directly to the CEO of ECW-R. ECW-R also has a Chief Operations Officer with reporting lines from the finance, regulatory affairs, human resource, network operations, marketing, e-commerce, purchasing, fraud, and revenue assurance functions serving the subsidiaries within the region.

In May 2002, shortly after its transformation in corporate governance, EWC-C created the position of Chief Information Officer (CIO) with a direct reporting relationship to the CEO of ECW-C. The CIO indicated that this new position facilitated his participation in the strategic planning process at the regional level and allowed him and his team to provide strategic IT direction and coordination to the Caribbean region as a whole. The CIO also stated that this position enabled the management function to participate in the implementation and support of corporate applications common across several territories. The CIO's responsibilities included directing the information and data integrity of ECW-C for all Caribbean region information technology functions, including shared services for all the business units inclusive of all software applications, hardware acquisitions, data centers, technical services, user support, enterprise-wide area networks, security, application development, and system operations.

The IT division, under the management of the new CIO, was restructured into three strategic groups in July 2002: Infrastructure and User Support, Applications Management, and Delivery. These groups are aligned across the fourteen geographical boundaries. The CIO indicated that the aim of the restructuring was to achieve a flatter and broader structure that would facilitate the sharing of data, applications, and IT expertise across subsidiaries. The CIO also indicated that this new structure was designed to facilitate better services and communications with the business representatives while improving the relationship between the business unit management and the IT division. As a result of this integration process, within the Caribbean region the IT governance structure became centralized. The Caribbean IT division therefore consisted of the integration of the IT functions across the fourteen subsidiaries, and eliminated the independent IT functions at the individual subsidiary levels.

As indicated in the research literature, the governance structures of organizations are continuously evolving. Over the last couple years, 2003 to 2005, after the initial integration took place, ECW decided to remove the global and regional divisions in order to reduce overheads and allow for greater flexibility and a more effective transfer of knowledge and skills between business units in all regions.

This latest change in corporate governance structure resulted in the elimination of the following positions: CEO of ECW-G, CEO of ECW-R, and CEO of ECW-C. The decision was taken to have the Chief Executives of the individual business units in the various geographical locations reporting to the Chief Operating Officer (COO) of ECW. The impact of this change on the IT governance structure was the subsequent elimination of the position of CIO of ECW-C and a shift from a hybrid-centralization to a hybrid-decentralization of the IT functions within the Caribbean countries.

Government and Regulatory Policies

In the majority of the developing countries where ECW has controlling stake, the ability to provide telecommunications services is largely dependent on receiving and maintaining licenses and authorizations from the local governments of those countries. For the last 40+ years, ECW has been able to enter the telecommunications market in the majority of these developing countries with the security of exclusive licenses ranging in timeframe from 10 to 25 years, and in some cases indefinitely but with a termination provision after a minimum period of time. This exclusivity began to change dramatically in the late 1990's, as is evidenced by the following press release:

It's the end of an empire. Even if it has to be done brick by brick, political and business leaders in the English-speaking Caribbean countries are determined to dismantle the telecom monopoly held by [ECW] in their region. These nations are demanding that [ECW] open its networks to spur competition and liberalization, and they are fighting against a superpower reluctant to let go of what took it years to build. Although [ECW] has held exclusive operating rights in these nations for 130 years, long before the removal of the British colonial government, the company is facing a revolution that it probably won't be able to quell. (McKay, 2001, p. 1)

The majority of the countries in this region that belong to the World Trade Organization (WTO) have committed to a phased approach to the deregulation of their markets. Although most of their commitments originally indicated completion by 2010-2013, the point at which most of the exclusive licenses held by ECW would have expired, deregulation has actually occurred at a much faster pace than anticipated. ECW managers estimate that by the end of 2005 more than 90% of their revenues will come from competitive markets within the region.

Global and Local Market Competition and Stability

The deregulation in the global telecommunications industry has resulted in many of these countries transforming the telecommunications sector in the region through the introduction of "regulated competitive markets." This term is used because in the majority of these countries, regulatory bodies still control the maximum rates that can be charged by the company for its products and services. The move towards competition is captured in the following press release:

The movement to support competition has picked up steam, spreading from island to island over the last three to five years, with the influence of the World Trade Organization (WTO), which has been working to open competition in developing nations. (McKay, 2001, p. 1)

In the majority of these markets, ECW, as the original dominant carrier with ownership of the telecommunications infrastructure, is required to provide network access to its competitors. The flip side of this scenario is that ECW obtains revenue from this because their competitors become their customers through interconnection payments. The rates charged to customers for telecommunications services are still heavily regulated and controlled in most of the countries in the region. The reason for this is that one of the major challenges of the deregulation process is the rebalancing of prices charged for services with the cost of these services, as would normally occur in a competitive environment. Many of the territories have not yet accomplished this task. This new competitive environment has also had a significant impact on the IT governance structures, as it is well stated by the CIO of ECW-C in an interview for this research:

One need not be reminded how fast and radically IT is changing in today's organizations. What was essentially a centralized backbone has become an organization's lifeblood, running throughout it and supplying each department with the information needed for survival. Accordingly, the job has changed from ensuring the efficient operation of the central mainframe, to supporting IT functions of users throughout an entire Enterprise, which ranges across several countries...Therefore, in order to deliver the quality products and services required by the business divisions to stay ahead of their competition, the proposed organizational structure (integrated IT) will be required to accomplish these tumultuous divisional tasks. If IT cannot deliver, then business divisions will be left no choice than to outsource to outside vendors.

In the majority of the developing countries where ECW has presence, businesses were operating in some highly regulated environments. Over the years, this has resulted in an unstable market as the terms and conditions of operations are changing at various points in time due to economic, social, and political instabilities in these countries. Changes in regulatory decisions or government policies can have severe adverse effect on the business operations and practices. This is particularly so in areas where ECW is the sole provider of telecommunications services and products, and has been reaping the benefits derived from a monopolistic environment.

Over the past several years, ECW has sought to expand product and service offerings into the area of Internet-related services. The demand for these services can neither be easily predicted nor guaranteed, thus adding more to the instability of the market environment (Standage, 2003). Additionally, a large percentage of the revenue obtained by ECW is from foreign investments outside of the United Kingdom, which means that fluctuations in the currency exchange rates between these countries and the pound sterling further add to the market instability. Approximately one year since the integration was completed, the U.S. dollar has devalued more than 7% approximately against the sterling and the Jamaican dollar by more than 13% against sterling, and the rates are continuing to decrease.

The progression of the liberalization process within the Caribbean territories over the last couple years has brought with it challenges in three major areas: the rebalancing of international rates, new entrants in mobile, and more demanding customers. The current CEO of ECW has therefore mandated a more proactive approach through active communication with local regulators; more extensive cost and capital expenditure monitoring; more aggressive sales and marketing; greater service innovation; and a greater focus on the mobile market.

Organizational Culture

In order to manage the turbulent market changes in the wake of deregulations and globalization, ECW has adopted a survival culture both at the host country and subsidiary levels. This is evidenced by the number of acquisitions it has negotiated over the period, and is in line with the general defensive strategies now being adopted by many telecommunications companies globally in order to survive. As a result of the increasing competition in the three major subsidiary regions in this study, and also because of the changes that have occurred globally in the telecommunications industry, the companies in these regions can also be seen as operating under a survival culture. This is evidenced in a report in the *Troubled Company Reporter* (2002), which indicated that ECW-C may experience reduced growth in cash flow as a result of tougher-than-expected competition in the market. The report went on to state that since the start of the deregulation process, ECW-C has lost the mobile market in Jamaica to one of its competitors in the region who now holds 65% of the mobile market share.

In the period mid-January to mid-March 2001, the CIO of ECW-C, who during that time was Senior Vice President of IT ECW-Jamaica, commissioned a formal review of the local IT department. This review was conducted as a result of the situation that he encountered when he took up this position. In order to fully understand the situation as well as to have the documentation he needed to make his case for transformation to senior management, the CIO decided to conduct a formal review with an independent third party. This task was carried out by a major consulting firm in cooperation with internal employees.

Before the integration, the general consensus in the company was that the IT department was not in tune with its business needs and requirements. This was highlighted in the findings of the review. The report pointed out that there was a "monopoly supplier culture" in the IT department and that there existed a lot of informality and inconsistency of working methods that put more emphasis on handling problems than on the use of good, quality, upfront planning to prevent the problems in the first place. Senior vice presidents from the functional divisions such as marketing were interviewed for this review, and following are some excerpts from what they had to say about the Information Systems Department (ISD) before the transformation and integration:

- ISD does not have a customer service culture at all.
- ISD has a major and fundamental lack of appreciation of the impact on the business of their actions.
- You wonder if ISD knows what is going on in the external market place.

As a result of this report, the need for a strategy whereby ISD is better able to deliver the optimum value for the money was identified as being critical to the survival of the business because of the increasing competition and commercialism across the business. As the move towards integration unfolded, the CIO also indicated that the perceptions identified in the review also existed in the majority of the other territories. As a result of this and in accordance with the new corporate strategy of achieving regional synergies and economies of scale in order to survive in this new competitive environment, the decision was made to integrate the business units in the fourteen foreign subsidiaries along functional lines, therefore creating a centralized IT division that would serve the needs of the entire Caribbean region. The stated objective of this is to facilitate the sharing of both physical and human resources across subsidiaries and eliminate the incremental operating costs associated with having to manage and maintain smaller systems in some of the smaller foreign subsidiaries.

In the last couple years after this integration was completed, some further modifications have been made to the operational processes. The organization through its new strategy is making it clear that the gains obtained from integration and economies of scale and scope are to be retained, while at the same time recognizing that each of the markets in which the National Telecommunications businesses operate are at varying stages of liberalization with differing customer profiles, but with very similar competitive challenges.

Organizational IT Competence

The CIO indicated that at the beginning of his tenure he noticed a lack of coordination between the IT department and the functional business divisions. Business plans were being developed without utilizing or integrating IT opportunities into these plans. He also indicated that strategic planning by the functional business divisions and the IT department was conducted largely independently. The general consensus was that the functional business divisions treated the IT department as a "back office, overhead" function that provided application support, rather than as an asset that could add value to the functions of the individual divisions and the overall company. These observations were further confirmed in the findings of the review. The following highlights some of these findings:

[IT governance] Although at the business unit level there existed a centralized IT governance structure, local business departments often independently initiated IT activities and either did not involve the IT department at all, or involved them very late in the process.

[Information systems planning] Driven by the individual functional department's systems requirements. Lack of alignment of projects with the overall strategic plans of the organization. Lack of integration of business and IT strategic plans.

[Dissemination of IT policy] No standard way of tracking the dissemination and understanding of IT policies on issues such as computer/ information security and corporate email by the employees.

The CIO also commissioned informal observations and reviews in the other thirteen business units. It was observed that the issues previously highlighted were consistent throughout the region. A strategic plan to alleviate these deficiencies was therefore implemented. The main objective of the strategic plan as defined by the CIO, during an interview for this research, is to:

Provide a leading-edge, high-quality IT infrastructure to support the provisioning and maintenance of new and existing services and help drive revenues and margins from business and consumer (internal and external) customers in the most cost-effective and efficient way through the use of technology, innovation, and best practices.

The broad IT strategy as outlined by the CIO is designed to achieve a 360 degree organization. This is to be accomplished by leveraging the network, the Internet, and

Table 2. ECW-C – IT structure and operational plan after integration

Groups	Departments	Functions
Infrastructure and User Support	IT Technology and Platforms	Enterprise Security
		Operations
		LAN/ WAN
		Business Continuity
		Database Administration
	End User Computing and Common Services	IT Help Desk
		PC/Notebook, e-mail and LAN/WAN applications support
Applications Management	Enterprise Resource Planning and Business Productivity	Finance/ Accounting Systems
		Human Resources and Payroll Systems
		Procurement
		Integration
	Customer Management and Revenue Applications	Customer Care, Billing and Revenue Systems
		Group Information Systems
	E-Enablement and Business Intelligence	Business Intelligence, Knowledge Management
		Intranet / Enterprise Portals
Delivery	IT Business Alignment and Project Management	Define, Measure and Monitor IT Objectives
		Monitor Accounting/ Financial Performance of IT Division
		Assess Risks & Benefits of IT projects

technologies to provide services and interact with customers, employees, and suppliers in order to sustain competitive advantage. The overall plan is to build an IT framework that supports the delivery of the business requirements and assists the organization in achieving its priorities in the areas of increasing revenues, operation efficiencies, employee productivity, and customer satisfaction.

In an interview with the CIO, he described the new IT structure as outlined in Table 2. The infrastructure and user support group is in charge of all technology infrastructure and end-user computing issues. The applications management group handles the functions of software development and maintenance, and the delivery group has the responsibility of ensuring strategic alignment of IT objectives with the business as well as ensuring proper project governance. In general, the Delivery area acts as the liaison between the IT division and the internal user community to ensure that all IT and business initiatives are properly coordinated. The CIO also indicated that the IT division is being positioned as a service provider that competes with external service providers for the company's business. The services provided are then charged back to the business units that requested them. The CIO refers to this model as "staff services for sale."

The further transformation to the structure which has taken place has resulted in a more decentralized day-to-day operational process while still maintaining the centralized components for systems that will affect all ECW national telecommunications businesses. This move was done to improve the flexibility of the national telecommunication businesses to handle increasing competition in a very dynamic environment.

DISCUSSIONS

The main findings of the study are highlighted in Table 3. These findings show that many of the influential factors identified in the previous research, such as government regulatory policies, global and local market competition and stability, organizational culture, and IT competency, have indeed played significant roles in shaping the corporate and IT governance structures of the ECW-R division and its subsidiaries in the period January 2001-August 2005. ECW-R adopted an organic corporate structure to fit its growth and survival through merger-and-acquisition strategy, resulting in an overall hybrid corporate and IT governance structure. The turbulence of deregulation of the telecommunications industry, coupled with the entrance of the new competitors in the previously monopolistic telecommunications markets and the dynamic changes in these local markets in the Caribbean countries, hastened the adoption of the hybrid corporate and IT governance structures in the ECW-R territories, lending support for the overall research framework. In terms of the effect of organizational culture on the IT governance structure, ECW-R adopted a survival culture and restructured the business and IT governance structures of its subsidiaries from a completely decentralized governance to a more integrated and hybrid structure amid the turbulent market conditions. However, as indicated by the research literature, as the organization learned from its new structure and business processes, the decision to modify the structure to one which would give more flexibility and autonomy to the national telecommunications companies to handle increasing competition was subsequently adopted.

Table 3. Summary of case findings

Influential Factors	ECW Case Evidence
Corporate Governance Structure	Before the integration process, the host organization ECW engaged in merger and acquisition for survival and growth. The corporate and IT governance structure across the host company and the foreign subsidiaries was completely decentralized.
	After the integration process, ECW adopted an organic organizational governance, which largely contributed to the formation of a hybrid corporate and IT governance structure across the host company and the foreign subsidiaries. Approximately one year after that, the corporate governance structure changed with the removal of the Global and Regional divisions, resulting in a more decentralized hybrid corporate and IT governance structure.
Government Regulations and Policies	Before the integration process, each of the subsidiaries of ECW-R and the fourteen ECW-C units existed in territories that were highly regulated and the IT governance structure across the host company and the foreign subsidiaries was completely decentralized.
	After the integration process, the business units in the fourteen Caribbean subsidiaries were integrated to form ECW-C and all IT functions in these units were subsequently integrated. However, the IT divisions of Panama and Macau are still operated largely independently. This effectively created a centralized hybrid corporate and IT governance structure across the host company and the subsidiaries. The removal of the Global and Regional divisions resulted in a decentralized hybrid corporate and IT governance structure with the CEOs of each of the Caribbean business units, as well as all other business units in the Group, now reporting to the COO of ECW.
Global and Local Market Competition and Stability	Before the integration process, each of the subsidiaries of ECW-R operated as a monopoly in their respective countries, and the IT governance structure across the host company and the foreign subsidiaries was completely decentralized.
	After the integration, even though the local markets became competitive, the CEOs of ECW-R and ECW-C decided to integrate all the IT functions in the Caribbean territories for better alignment with business strategies and better utilization of the IT resources, yet still kept Panama and Macau largely independent. Dynamic environments and increasing competition has resulted in a subsequent modification of this model to a more decentralized hybrid governance structure.
	Before the integration process, each of the subsidiaries of ECW-R operated as a monopoly with a closed-market and stable regulative environment in their respective territories. The IT governance structure across host and subsidiaries was completely decentralized.
	As a result of deregulations and mergers and acquisitions, the local telecommunications markets in the regions of ECW-R subsidiaries became extremely volatile, yet instead of maintaining the decentralized governance structure, ECW-R instituted an integration effort of the fourteen Caribbean territories, while keeping Panama and Macau decentralized, resulting in the centralized hybrid corporate and IT governance structure. This hybrid structure has been modified to allow more flexibility and better sharing of knowledge and skills across all units while retaining the benefits obtained through centralization.
Organizational Culture	Before the integration process, the dominant organizational culture in the telecom subsidiaries in each of the regions for a long time was stability, and the governance structure was decentralized. However, due to deregulation and increased global and local competition, the companies began to move towards a survival culture.
	After the integration process, with deregulation, the dominant culture in ECW-R was survival. A centralized hybrid corporate and IT governance structure was adopted across the host company and the foreign subsidiaries. Dynamic environments and increasing competition, however, resulted in a modification of that model to a more decentralized hybrid model.
Organizational IT Competence	Before the integration process, at the subsidiary level, an internal review of IT competence revealed many areas of deficiencies in the fourteen subsidiaries that make up ECW-C, prompting the CIO to institute a centralized IT governance structure in ECW-C to enhance the performance of the IT division and improve the utilization of IT resources and skills across the subsidiaries. However, Panama and Macau were not part of the centralization process.
	After the integration process, with the perceived enhanced performance of the corporate and IT division as a result of the integration of ECW-C resources and skills, a centralized hybrid corporate and IT governance structure was implemented across the host company and the foreign subsidiaries. With the removal of the Global and Regional Divisions, it was felt that a decentralized hybrid model would better allow for the sharing of knowledge and skills across all business units within the company while giving the business units more flexibility to deal with dynamic environments and increased competition.

This case study also revealed some interesting issues. The most prominent is, perhaps, why ECW-R initially decided to move from a completely decentralized IT governance structure immediately after the completion of mergers and acquisitions in Panama, Macau, and the Caribbean territories to a centralized-hybrid governance structure, even though the prevailing thought in the literature would suggest to stay completely decentralized due to the highly competitive and volatile local markets and the geographically dispersed operational structures. Approximately one year later, the decision was taken to modify that structure and move to a decentralized-hybrid governance structure. In this section, we attempt to shed some light on this issue.

The Impact of Management Predisposition and Dynamic Environments on Corporate and IT Governance Structures

The prevailing literature suggests that firms are likely to adopt a decentralized or hybrid corporate and IT governance structure in a highly competitive global and local market environment. In the case of the ECW-R, even though its Caribbean subsidiaries operated in an increasingly competitive market, the management decided to move from a completely decentralized to a more centralized hybrid IT governance structure. The decision to centralize the IT functions of the Caribbean subsidiaries was largely made at the corporate level by the CEO of ECW-R in conjunction with the CEO of ECW-C. This resulted in the initial integration of the Caribbean subsidiaries along functional and support lines. The IT division was initially classified as a support line in the strategic plan of the organization. The overall result of this process is the initial emergence of a centralized-hybrid corporate and IT governance structure with decisions being made at both the host company level, ECW-R, and at the Caribbean subsidiary level, ECW-C, demonstrating a strong influence of corporate governance on the IT governance structure.

The factual materials gathered in the case suggests that the emergence of the initial centralized-hybrid corporate and IT governance structure in ECW-R can also be attributed to a large degree to the predisposition of the CEO and senior executive levels of the organization to achieve regional synergies through the integration of corporate resources and skills. This predisposition as it relates to the IT division was largely influenced by the good professional relationship between the then CEO as well as other senior executives and the CIO. Prior research has indicated that the nature of the professional relationship between the CIO and the CEO can have a significant impact on the successful use of IS for strategic purposes (Jones, Taylor, & Spencer, 1995). The essence of this business relationship is that the CIO should have a global understanding of the functions of the business and that the CEO should have an understanding of the value-adding potential of IT and makes appropriate use of various IT opportunities. The reporting structure of the CIO directly to the CEO facilitated effective communications between the CIO with the CEO in order to make appropriate use of IT within the organization. An internal review of the IT division conducted by a consulting firm indicated that there was a fair amount of satisfaction among senior executives with the vision and activities of the CIO.

The relationship between the predisposition of top management to a certain business strategy and the choice of corporate and IT governance structure has rarely been investigated. As is clearly demonstrated in this case, ignoring such a relationship may result in incomplete or even incorrect predictions about the choices of governance structures in organizations. Future research should pay more attention to this aspect of the influential factors of corporate and IT governance. The predominance of a change in corporate governance and a dynamic competitive environment subsequently resulted in some modifications to this initial structure. The organization recognized that there were certain benefits to be derived from centralization which they had seen in the Caribbean region over the period since integration; however, the dynamic environments in which these companies were operating necessitated more flexibility to be able to respond quickly to increasing competition and to consumer demands. In an attempt to gain the best of both worlds, the organization decided to move to a more decentralized hybrid governance structure.

The Impact of Homogeneity of Products, Services, and Culture on Corporate and IT Governance

Another factor that might have facilitated the initial transition from fourteen decentralized IT units into one centralized IT unit in ECW-C is the fact that all of the Caribbean subsidiaries offered similar products and services, and the territories, though geographically dispersed, have similar cultures due to historical reasons. There is a high level of homogeneity of products and services across the subsidiaries since the majority of ECW-R's holdings are companies offering telecommunications products and services to the local markets. The countries making up the English-speaking Caribbean also enjoy the added feature that their cultures are very similar. As a result, the top management of ECW-R and ECW-C capitalized on the unique environment of the Caribbean markets and created an overall centralized corporate and IT governance structure in order to realize the benefits of economies of scale and scope across subsidiaries. Most of the decisions regarding the major IT investment projects were made at the corporate regional level and communicated in the form of business cases, with the three major subsidiaries IT managers handling the execution and implementation of the decisions. The subsequent move to a decentralized hybrid structure has retained some of these functions while giving each business unit manager more local autonomy and enabling the sharing of knowledge and skills across all territories.

Evolution of the Centralized-Hybrid and the Decentralized-Hybrid IT Governance Structures

The consequences of the factors discussed above are the emergence of two unique IT governance structures over a period of approximately two years. The initial structure was implemented in the original ECW-R unit: This consisted of a highly centralized yet still hybrid structure labeled in this chapter as the centralized-hybrid structure. Under such governance structure, any IT infrastructure/application software decisions that affected all three major subsidiaries, that is, the Caribbean, Panama, and Macau, were made at the ECW-R corporate level, with the implementation being handled at the individual subsidiary levels. This hybrid decision and execution process was further facilitated by the use of third-party companies for software acquisition, with customization and implementation being done in conjunction with the vendors and the individual subsidiaries. IT infrastructure/applications decisions that affect only a specific subsidiary was usually handled within the IT division of that subsidiary.

In the Caribbean, as it affected all of the fourteen subsidiaries in that region, these decisions were handled by the centralized IT division of ECW-C. Depending on the size of the budget of a proposed IT investment project, corporate approval may still have to be obtained by the foreign subsidiary even if the project only affects that business unit. Once again, the enforcement of the centralized-hybrid governance structure was clearly demonstrated. The implementation of a decentralized-hybrid structure has changed those functions somewhat. Top level IT infrastructure/application decisions for all individual subsidiaries would be made at the ECW corporate level under the COO, with local implementation.

CONCLUSIONS

This study has examined the emergence of IT governance structures that have evolved within an existing organization: ECW, a global telecommunications company operating in dynamic environments, which has grown primarily through mergers and acquisitions in foreign subsidiaries. A set of factors have been highlighted that had significant influence on the corporate and IT governance structures that evolved as a result of the initial integration process as well as the dynamic environments of liberalization and competition. The experience of ECW is fairly consistent with the findings of the previous studies on corporate and IT governance in the sense that the commonly-recognized influential factors, such as government regulation and policy, market competition and stability, organizational culture, and IT competence, all have significant impact on an organization's IT governance structure, either directly or indirectly, through the corporate governance structure. The modification of the initial governance structure approximately one year after being implemented is also consistent with the literature.

In addition and perhaps more significantly, the findings that top management predisposition toward a specific business strategy or governance structure can significantly impact the course of the emergence of IT governance structures within an organization. In the case of ECW-R and ECW-C, for instance, instead of a more decentralized IT governance structure as predicted by the research propositions of the literature, a hybrid and more centralized IT governance structure emerged as a result of the strong predisposition of the top management team towards integration and synergy and the strong business relationship between the CEO and CIO. Interestingly, this is consistent with the findings of another case study (Roche, 1992) that multinational corporations with decentralized organizational structure might adopt a centralized IT structure in order to take advantage of the economies of scale and achieve better alignment with corporate strategies. A modification of this as a result of dynamic environments is also consistent with the findings of another case study (Weill & Ross, 2005) which indicated that companies with fairly effective governance changed some aspect of that governance structure approximately once annually.

The results of this research offer a conceptual framework to identify and understand the evolution of IT governance structures for organizations that have grown through mergers and acquisitions. Several other studies have identified factors that affect an organization's choice of IT governance formations. However, research that identifies the factors and explains the process to be taken into consideration within the context of mergers and acquisitions is limited. The significant contribution of this study is, therefore, the investigation of the evolutionary process and the identification of the influential external and internal factors that affect governance structures within dynamic environments.

Managerial Implications

The findings of this study could have several important managerial implications. First, the predisposition of individual managers toward business strategies and IT strategies could have profound impact on the IT governance structure. In the case of ECW-R and ECW-C, even though the regulatory and market conditions called for a distributed IT governance structure, the organization eventually moved away from a decentralized structure to a hybrid and relatively centralized structure because the top management team at the time strongly believed that an integrated IT infrastructure and the resulting economies of scale would better serve the competitive strategies that the organization has adopted.

Second, the relationship and trust between the CIO and the top management team could be critical to the successful transformation of previously-independent and relatively weak IT units into an integrated and strong IT department for the entire new organization during and after the merger and acquisition. Throughout our interviews and in reviewing company documents, it is evident that the then CIO of ECW-C had the full support of the top management team of ECW-C and its parent company, ECW-R. This support enabled the CIO to implement his vision for the integrated IT department for all territories of the ECW-C organization in alignment with the organization's competitive strategies.

Third, the hybrid IT governance seems to be the most appropriate for organizations that operate in multiple geographical regions and have grown rapidly through mergers and acquisitions. The case of ECW-R and its subsidiaries demonstrates that adopting a hybrid IT governance created minimal initial disruption to the operations of the acquired business units by keeping decentralized operations and semi-centralized decision-making mechanisms. However, as the case demonstrates, eventually senior management in any organization that has grown through mergers and acquisitions will have to reevaluate the governance and operational structure and consider integrating and even centralizing some of the IT operations in order to take advantage of the economies of scale and achieve better alignment between organizational business strategies and IT strategies while decentralizing certain functions to maintain flexibility within a dynamic competitive environment.

Fourth, the IT competence of business units in a multi-division organization may have the most profound influence on the emergence of the IT governance structure. In the case of the ECW-R and ECW-C, the integration and centralization of the most important IT functions and services would have been difficult had the IT departments of the individual companies within the Caribbean subsidiaries been highly competent and regarded as strategic by their business counterparts. The fact that these IT units were deemed as nonstrategic by business managers provided strong justification for the establishment of a stronger and more responsive IT department with integrated infrastructure and operations. Some of these functions will still be retained, and there will be a broader sharing of knowledge and skills across all the subsidiaries of the company, with clearer accountabilities.

Finally, the integration process and governance structure should be chosen with the objective of ensuring alignment between the organization's IT strategies and investments and its business strategies. An effective IT governance structure should also provide the organization with the ability to capitalize on benefits and take full advantage of opportunities. The governance structure should also provide a means of accountability that ensures that the organization uses its IT resources responsibly. The risks associated with IT decisions should also be appropriately managed within this context. As has been shown in the case evidence, the driving force behind many of the strategic moves of ECW was to create and enhance such alignment.

Limitations and Future Research

Like many case studies, this study inevitably has its limitations. The first of these is the ability to generalize the findings due to some unique situations in this case. For instance, the relationship between the CIO and top management team and the broad business and IT management experience of the CIO in the Caribbean region may have masked many issues that might occur in other integration processes after mergers and acquisitions. However, the issues raised by this study, such as the roles of management predisposition toward IT governance, the relationship between CIO and top management in the evolution of IT governance structures, and the impact of dynamic environments on the choice of governance structures are worth future investigation in a broader range of organizations. The cultural factors in the evolution of the corporate and IT governance structure in a multinational organization such as ECW deserve more in-depth investigation and analysis. And finally, the impact of top management's predisposition toward business and IT strategies on IT governance structure offers an intriguing topic to explore in future studies.

REFERENCES

Ahituv, N., Neumann, S., & Zviran, M. (1989). Factors affecting the policy for distributing computing resources. *MIS Quarterly, 13*(4), 389-401.

Argyres, N. S. (1995). Technology strategy, governance structure, and interdivisional coordination. *Journal of Economic Behavior and Organization, 28*, 337-358.

Benbasat, I., Goldstein, D. K., & Mead, M. (1987). The case research strategy in studies of information systems. *MIS Quarterly, 11*(3), 369-386.

Board, B. H. (1998). Redesigning the IT organization for the information age. *Information Systems Management, 15*(3), 23-30.

Brown, C. V. (1997). Examining the emergence of hybrid IS governance solutions: Evidence from a single case site. *Information Systems Research, 8*(1), 69-94.

Brown, C. V., & Magill, S. L. (1994). Alignment of the IS function with the enterprise: Toward a model of antecedents. *MIS Quarterly, 18*(4), 371-403.

Brown, C. V., & Magill, S. L. (1998). Reconceptualizing the context-design issue for the information systems function. *Organization Science, 9*(2), 176-194.

Bureau of Census (2002, January). Mergers and acquisitions by industry: 1998. *Statistical Abstract of the U.S.: 2001* (Table, p. 493). LexisNexis Statistical Database. Retrieved March 9, 2003, from http://www.lexusnexus.com

Cohen, W. M., & Levinthal, D. A. (1990). Absorptive capacity: A new perspective on learning and innovation. *Administrative Science Quarterly, 35*(1), 128-152.

Cooper, R. B. (1994). The inertial impact of culture on IT implementation. *Information & Management, 27*(1), 17-31.

Ein-Dor, P., & Segev, E. (1982). Organizational context and MIS structure: Some empirical evidence. *MIS Quarterly, 6*(3), 55-68.

Estrin, S. (2002, Winter). Competition and corporate governance in transition. *Journal of Economic Perspectives, 16*(1), 101-124.

Gutierrez, L. H., & Berg, S. (2000). Telecommunications liberalization and regulatory governance: Lessons from Latin America. *Telecommunications Policy, 24*, 865-884.

Henderson, J., & McAdam, R. (2001). Decision making in the fragmented organization: A utility perspective. *Management Decision, 39*(5/6), 461-469.

Hofstede, G. (1980). *Culture's consequences: International differences in work-related values.* Beverly Hills, CA: Sage Publications.

IT Governance Institute (2001). *Board Briefing on IT Governance.* Retrieved February 11, 2003, from http://www.ITgovernance.org/

Jones, M. C., Taylor, S. G., & Spencer, B. A. (1995). The CEO/CIO relationship revisited: An empirical assessment of satisfaction with IS. *Information & Management, 29*, 123-130.

King, W. R., & Sethi, V. (1992). A framework for transnational systems. In P. Palvia, S. Palvia, & R. Zigli (Eds.), *The global issues of information technology management* (pp. 214-248). Harrisburg, PA: Idea Group Publishing.

King, W. R., & Sethi, V. (1999). An empirical assessment of the organization of transnational information systems. *Journal of Management Information Systems, 15*(4), 7-28.

Korac-Kakabadse, N., & Kakabadse, A. (2001). IS/IT governance: Need for an integrated model. *Corporate Governance, 1*(4), 9-11.

Lainhart IV, J. W. (2000, July-August). Why IT governance is a top management issue. *Journal of Corporate Accounting and Finance, 11*(5), 33-40.

Lehn, K. (2002). Corporate governance in the deregulated telecommunications industry: Lessons from the airline industry. *Telecommunications Policy, 26*, 225-242.

Levina, N., & Ross, J. M. (2003). From the vendor's perspective: Exploring the value proposition in information technology outsourcing. *MIS Quarterly, 27*(3), 331-364.

McKay, J. P. (2001, October 15). Trouble in paradise. *Telecom.* Retrieved January 12, 2003, from http://www.teledotcom.com/article/TEL20011015S0012

Melody, W. H. (1999). Telecom reform: Progress and prospects. *Telecommunications Policy, 23*, 7-34.

Oh, J. (1996). Global strategic alliances in the telecommunications industry. *Telecommunications Policy, 20*(9), 713-720.

Olson, M. H., & Chervany, N. L. (1980). The relationship between organizational characteristics and the structure of the information services function. *MIS Quarterly, 4*(2), 57-68.

Pentzaropoulos, G. C., & Giokas, D. I. (2002). Comparing the operational efficiency of the main European telecommunications organizations: A quantitative analysis. *Telecommunications Policy, 26*, 595-606.

Peterson, R. (2004). Crafting information technology governance. *Information Systems Management, 21*(4), 7-22.

Quinn, R. E., & Rohrbaugh, J. (1983). A spatial model of effectiveness criteria: Towards a competing values approach to organization analysis. *Management Science, 29*(3), 363-377.

Ramamurti, R., (2000). Risks and rewards in the globalization of telecommunications in emerging economies. *Journal of World Business, 35*(2), 149-170.

Rau, K. G. (2004, Fall). Effective governance of IT: Design objectives, roles, and relationships. *Information Systems Management, 21*(4), 35-42.

Reuer, J., & Zollo, M. (2000). Managing governance adaptations in strategic alliances. *European Management Journal, 18*(2), 164-172.

Robbins, S. (2004, Fall). IS governance. *Information Systems Management, 16*(4), 81-82.

Roche, E. M. (1992). Managing systems development in multinational corporations: Practical lessons from 7 case studies. In P. Palvia, S. Palvia, & R. Zigli (Eds.), *The global issues of information technology management* (pp. 630-654). Harrisburg, PA: Idea Group Publishing.

Sambamurthy, V., & Zmud, R. W. (1999, June). Arrangements for information technology governance: A theory of multiple contingencies. *MIS Quarterly, 23*(2), 261-290.

Schneider, S. C., & Barsoux, J. (1997). *Managing across cultures.* Hempstead, Hertfordshire: Prentice Hall, Europe.

Smircich, L. (1983). Concepts of culture and organizational analysis. *Administrative Science Quarterly, 28*(3), 339-358.

Sohal, A. S., & Fitzpatrick, P. (2002). IT governance and management in large Australian organizations. *International Journal of Production Economics, 75*, 97-112.

Standage, T. (2003, October 11). Beyond the bubble: A survey of telecoms. *The Economist, 369*(8345), [special section] 3-7.

Tavakolian, H. (1989). Linking the information technology structure with organizational competitive strategy: A survey. *MIS Quarterly, 13*(3), 309-317.

Todaro, M. (2003). *Economic development.* Reading, MA: Addison Wesley.

Trillas, F. (2002). Mergers, acquisitions, and control of telecommunications firms in Europe. *Telecommunications Policy, 26*, 269-286.

Troubled Company Reporter (2002). Europe, December 13, 3(247). Retrieved February 11, 2003, from http://www.bankrupt.com/TCREUR_Public/021213.mbx

Weill, P., & Ross, J. (2005, Winter). A matrixed approach to designing IT governance. *MIT Sloan Management Review, 46*(2), 26-34.

Wilcox, H. D., Chang, K., & Grover, V. (2001). Valuation of mergers and acquisitions in the telecommunications industry: A study on diversification and firm size. *Information & Management, 38*, 459-471.

World Bank (2002). *World Development Indicators, 2002.* Issued By: International Bank for Reconstruction and Development.

Yin, R. K. (1994). *Case study research: Design and methods.* Beverly Hills, CA: Sage Publications.

ENDNOTE

[1]   The name of the company has been disguised for confidentiality.

Chapter VIII

Collaborative Software Requirements Engineering Exercises in a Distributed Virtual Team Environment

H. Keith Edwards, University of Hawaii at Hilo, USA

Varadharajan Sridhar, Management Development Institute, India

ABSTRACT

Round-the-clock work cycle, low cost of software development, and access to specialized skills have prompted many companies in the USA, Canada, and Europe to outsource some or part of their software development work to off-shore centers in countries such as India. While design, development, and testing phases that are traditionally off-shored require less interaction between clients and the off-shore consultants, phases such as requirements engineering require close co-ordination and interaction. The clients and consultants in such off-shored projects often work in a virtual team environment. In this research, our endeavor is to understand the complex issues in such a virtual project environment during the requirements definition phase of the software development cycle. In particular, we conducted an exploratory research study, involving 24 virtual teams based in Canada and India, working collaboratively on defining business requirements for software projects, over a period of 5 weeks. The study indicates that trust between the teams and well-defined task structure positively influence the performance, satisfaction, and learning level of such distributed virtual teams.

INTRODUCTION

In the past two decades, the world has witnessed significant globalization of the process of software development. Development of software has increasingly moved away from the traditional co-located model, often called on-site development, to the off-shoring model. Cost of programmers and analysts are significantly lower in India than in the U.S., Canada, or Europe. Consequently, it makes economic sense to do a significant portion of software projects in countries such as India. Bates, Davis, and Haynes (2003) argue that using staff in low-wage countries such as India and China can cut cost of development of applications by as much as 50 to 70%.

The other benefit of increasing the offshore component of software development is that it reduces uncertainties due to government regulations regarding visas. Further, using geographically distributed development teams in a "follow the sun approach" enables an almost 24-hour software development cycle, thereby cutting down project duration (Carmel, 1999).

Given these opportunities, the delivery models used in Indian software export have seen a significant shift from the on-site to the offshore model over the past five years. For example, India has a dominant offshore software development industry with revenue of about $16.7 billion, which is growing at the rate of more than 30% per year (NASSCOM, 2005). This industry has more than 2,800 software export firms, and employs approximately 600,000 software professionals (NASSCOM, 2004).

The percentage of offshore revenue in the Indian software industry has increased from 34% in 1999-2000, to 64% (Sridhar, 2005). There has been a corresponding decrease in on-site revenue from 57% to 36%. Improved infrastructure, especially telecommunications, and the fact that Indian software companies have now beome very proficient at the global delivery model, have led to clients becoming more   and more comfortable with off-shoring. Coordination and communication problems typically encountered in offshore development, as discussed in Battin, Crocker, Kreidler, and Subramanian (2001), have been mitigated by the use of excellent processes and tools for software configuration management and project management adopted by Indian software companies.

In addition to clients contracting out software development projects to third-party software firms, off-shoring has also increasingly been practiced for captive purposes. Multinational companies such as Adobe, Motorola, Microsoft, and Oracle have followed this model and have set up their own Software Development Centers (SDCs) in and around major Indian cities such as Bangalore, Hyderabad, and Delhi. Battin, et al (2001) describes how a 3G Trial project was done using global engineering team at Motorola with one of the SDCs being in Bangalore, India.

Several large Indian software houses such as Infosys, Wipro, TCS, and Satyam have followed such an offshore development model successfully for over a decade. Interestingly, even within the off-shoring model, several variants exist. In the extreme case, the entire team could be based in India, and the client would be in Europe or the USA. In other words, all the interaction between the client and the software firm would be in "virtual team" mode, using various online modes of communication. This extreme case would hopefully lead to maximum cost advantage to both the parties. In reality, however, we might have a small number of analysts from the software firm based in the client's premises, and therefore the project would be a hybrid, rather than a purely virtual team project. The importance of physically locating some team members from the software company in the client's premises to liaison with the client is well documented in Battin et al. (2001). However, organizations are increasingly looking at minimizing liaisons to reduce costs further. Therefore, it is interesting to study the process of collaboration between teams at geographically dispersed locations operating purely in virtual mode.

The Distributed Virtual Teams (DVTs) are primarily linked through computer and telecommunications technologies across national boundaries. Dube and Pare (2001) outline several of the problems and challenges faced by DVTs. They indicate that cultural diversity of the global teams distributed across many countries, while providing potential richness to the team constitution, also represents an enormous challenge for DVTs. Communication and language barriers, as well as discrepancies in technological proficiency among team participants are also factors that influence the effectiveness of DVTs.

Several researchers have examined these issues in an academic setting. Faculties in many universities and business schools have set up distributed software engineering laboratories, and have conducted virtual team exercises in their courses. This approach has two benefits. Firstly, it makes available several teams that work in parallel, and therefore creates a rich amount of data, based on which conclusions can be drawn. Secondly, it equips and trains students of software engineering to understand and to handle the challenges of working in global software teams. Favela and Pena-Mora (2001) have conducted exercises that helped students better understand the distributed collaborative software development process.

Nath, Sridhar, and Malik (2005) argue that in future, major software firms in India will take on software contracts from clients in the U.S. or Europe, and execute the first phase including requirements analysis of this contract within their software facilities in India. Subsequently, the next phase consisting of design and development shall be further outsourced by the Indian firm, to a second software firm, typically in a country such as China or Vietnam. To understand issues in such a two-phase off-shoring environment, Nath et al. (2005) conducted an exploratory research study, involving student teams based in India and Netherlands, working on the requirements and analysis phases of software development projects.

In this work, it was also our endeavor to provide a simulated global virtual team environment to potential business managers and software developers to enable them to better understand the software industry's globalization. In addition, we present the findings from conducting such a distributed virtual team project exercise between student teams from the University of Western Ontario, Canada (UWO) and the Indian Institute of Management, Lucknow, India (IIML).

ISSUES IN A COLLABORATIVE SOFTWARE REQUIREMENTS ENGINEERING EXERCISE IN A DISTRIBUTED VIRTUAL TEAM ENVIRONMENT

A software engineering project involves a number of different activities such as requirements specifications, analysis, design, coding, testing, and implementation. The requirements definition phase of the software development life cycle is often cited as the most critical of the phases (Maciaszek, 2001). This is due to the fact that mistakes made during the requirements analysis phase cascade into the latter phases of the software development life cycle, including functional specifications, code development, and implementation. Previous research has shown that mistakes made during the requirements phase can cost as much as hundred times those caused by coding errors (Sommerville & Kotonya, 1998). Thus, it is critical to have an exceedingly well-defined requirements document in order to ensure a successful project that meets the three concurrent metrics of on time, within budget, and in conformance to requirements.

Modern approaches to the requirement definition stage emphasize cross-functional teams, group collaboration, and consensus decision-making techniques (Gorton & Motwani, 1996). In the requirements definition phase of the software development life cycle, co-located teams comprised of users, business analysts, and system analysts work closely to define the requirements definition artifacts. Gorton and Motwani (1996) argue that if virtual teams are used in the requirements definition stage, the teams can exploit the overnight gain effect due to the time difference between the locations where the teams are deployed, which will reduce the cycle-time. It is also reported that apart from overnight gain effect, the teams can leverage the expertise of the different DVTs, in developing robust requirements artifacts. They further argue that for projects that are intended to be used in a global scale, cross functional teams from different parts of the world can capture the international requirements more aptly at the very beginning of the software development life cycle.

However, specifying requirements is a communication-intensive collaborative activity and hence is affected when performed across geographical, cultural, language, and time zone boundaries. Damian and Zowghi (2002) studied the interplay between culture and conflict and the impact of distance on the ability to reconcile different viewpoints with respect to requirements and requirements engineering processes. Damian, Herlea, Eberlein, Shaw, and Gaines (2000) studied the effect of the distribution of various stakeholders in the requirements negotiation process. They found that the configuration where the customers were remotely located from one another was perceived to be less emotional, allowing the group to focus on the task and hence to perform better in the negotiation process.

It is also to be noted that most of the offshore development centers such as those located in India and other developing countries are involved in coding, testing, and bug fixing phases of the software development life cycle because of low-cost advantage. These are inherently low-value added activities. Heeks, Krishna, Nicholson, and Sahay (2001) argue that clients and software developers need to move their global outsourcing relationships up the value chain to reap greater benefits. One way for companies involved in software outsourcing business to move up the value chain is to undertake turnkey projects starting at the requirements definition stage and continuing until implementation. In this context, it is important to study whether the early stages of the software development process can be carried out at offshore centers using virtual teams.

In this exploratory study, we conducted distributed virtual team projects to develop software requirements definitions of business information systems. Our objective was to analyze the factors that significantly affect the quality of the requirements definition artifacts prepared by the virtual teams and to examine the effectiveness of the global virtual teams in performing these projects. While this study was conducted over a short period of time in an academic context, we hope that some of the conclusions from this simulated virtual team environment may be applicable to virtual teams in a professional setting.

The rest of this chapter is organized as follows: In the next section, we describe the experimental design and the model used for analyzing the performance of virtual teams. Then, we present details of the conducted survey and construct measurement. Limitations of this study and implications of the study for practitioners and for curriculum development are discussed next. The last section lists the future research directions.

DESIGN OF THE EXPERIMENT
AND MODEL USED

The purpose of this exploratory study was to have the students at IIML and UWO work together with their virtual team counterparts to develop requirements for a business information system. The project description specified that students were to choose a business information system that fulfilled a real business or organizational need. This was significantly different from previous course experiences where the computer science students had modeled trivial systems such as university enrollment or library systems. This project allowed students the opportunity to work with a system that closely mirrored one in a real business environment.

The project also featured distinct roles between the groups that further reflected a real business environment. Typically, the requirements engineering process consists of requirements elicitation, requirements analysis and negotiation, requirements documentation, and requirements validation. The students at IIML would assume responsibility for the conception of the business motivation behind the project and requirements elicitation while the UWO students would apply their skills in requirements analysis to define the system and to document it using Unified Modeling Language (UML). Thereafter, both groups would perform validation of the requirements mutually. The demographic profile of both the teams is given in Table 1.

The virtual team projects were carried out over a period of five weeks. The project milestones and deliverables are indicated in Table 2. During the evaluation of the deliverable of the projects, the instructors for both courses communicated regarding the quality of the documents and grades for the projects. After the completion of the requirements document, the UWO group was required to create the functional specifications and a prototype of their system for customer review. While the teams were no longer

Table 1. Demographic profile of the teams

	IIML	**UWO**
Sample size	116	85
Gender	Male=102; Female=14	Male=64; Female=21
Average Age	22.91	24.08
Average full-time work experience (in months)	12.54	16.64

Table 2. Project milestones and deliverables

Project Milestone / Deliverables	**Due**
Formation of groups at IIML/UWO. At IIML, 25 groups should be formed with not more than 5 in a group	Middle of week-1
Pairing of IIML and UWO groups. Exchange of email addresses of paired groups	First half of week-2
Project Topic and a brief description of 250 word abstract of the project mutually accepted by the groups, posted on the designated course web site	Second half of week-2
User population, Use Cases, Important Data/Data Dictionary, Functional Requirements, User Interface, Security/Privacy Requirements, Portability requirements, Reliability Needs, Response Time and Disk Space mutually accepted by the groups, posted on the designated course web site	First half of week-5
Project Report containing the requirements document and an analysis of technologies used, and relevant experiences	Middle of week-5

Figure 1. Model for assessing the performance of global virtual team projects

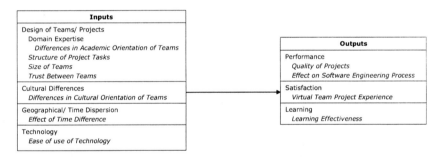

Constructs used in the survey are shown in *italics*

required to stay in direct contact, several of the UWO teams informally contacted their peer teams at IIML for verification of functional specifications.

In order to analyze the effect of various input parameters on the output of the experiment, we derive our model from the input-process-output model presented in Powell, Piccoli, and Ives (2004), which is shown in Figure 1. The following is a look at the output variables measured in this research.

Performance: The virtual team research on outputs or outcomes has focused on the performance and effectiveness of the team. Powell et al. (2004) point out that previous research have examined more specific aspects of performance such as decision quality, number of ideas generated, and/or time it took team members to reach a decision. Lurey and Raisinghani (2001) present an empirical study, in which the extent to which the virtual teams' outputs, product, or service, meets the required standards. They also point out that the teams' output can be measured based on the actual amount of output or quality of the product/service generated by the team. We determine the "quality" of the project using the marks awarded to the requirements definition artifacts prepared by the virtual teams. We have added a variable to measure the "impact of virtual team exercise on the software engineering process". This can be used to determine whether the virtual team exercise has brought any efficiency gain or loss in the requirements definition stage of the software development process.

Satisfaction: Lurey and Raisinghani (2001) point out that teams will not be effective if the team members themselves are not satisfied with the way the team functions in a virtual setting. Hence, team member satisfaction should be considered as one of the outcome variables. Powell et al. (2004) point out that satisfaction with the virtual team experience is the ultimate performance of the virtual team. In our model, the "project experience" is a measure of how satisfied/dissatisfied the team members are with the virtual team exercise.

Learning: In the academic setting in which the experiments were conducted, we were interested in exposing the students of the software development and software engineering courses to the issues in global software development. We also expected student teams to train each other in nuances of software development process including the many artifacts apart from what they learned in their classrooms. We consider the "effectiveness of the learning process" as one of the outcome variables. It is reasonable to expect that the learning effectiveness may be correlated positively with project experience and that the software engineering process improvement correlated positively with the quality of the projects. Inputs given in Figure 1 represent the design and composition characteristics of the virtual team and the endowment of resources, skills, and abilities with which the teams begin their work.

Design of Teams/ Projects: Powell et al. (2004) point out that the design of the virtual team and the structuring of its interactions have been found to impact the development of a shared language and shared understanding by team members. Hence, the design also has a consequence on the output and quality of the deliverables.

Domain Expertise: As pointed out earlier, one of the objectives of distributed teams is to effectively use available domain expertise from different locations. Capturing the software requirements involves a functional team, which knows the business requirements of the organization, and the technical team, which translates the requirements into technical specifications. One of the objectives of this exercise is to explore whether the business domain expertise of the management students at IIML can be supplemented with the technical expertise of the computer science students at UWO in preparing requirements definition artifacts. We felt that having teams from technical and managerial disciplines would not only enrich the quality of projects, but would also mirror the realities of practical software development environment, especially in the requirements definition stage of the system development life cycle.

IIML students were in the first year of the master's degree program in business administration, while the students at UWO were pursuing a four-year undergraduate degree in computer science with a specialization in software engineering. Herein, we find two major distinctions. First, the students at IIML were graduate students and were thought to possess a larger degree of business experience than their counterparts at UWO. Second, the diversity in academic orientation mirrored the business scenario where both functional business managers and software system developers are involved in preparing the requirements definition documents.

Based on the arguments above, we can expect that the "differences in academic orientation" between peer teams would have positive associations with all the outcome variables.

Structure of Project Tasks: The importance of coherence in task allocation where the work is split up according to feature content is cited as a critical activity for better performance of global teams (Ebert & De Neve, 2001). The task structure for the virtual team exercises are given below.

The deliverable for this specific project was a professional requirements document that reflected the expertise and collaboration between the two groups. In particular, the requirements document had several components similar to the ones used in industrial context (Maciaszek, 2001). In particular, this document featured several distinct sections including, but not limited to:

- Business use cases using UML to describe how the users were expected to use the system after its implementation.
- Business level class diagrams using UML. Business class diagrams are object-oriented classes with a selected set of attributes and the relationships between them. Typically, analysts do not specify operations and parameters for the classes until the design phase.
- A data dictionary describing the important data that the users will require in the application.
- A high level description of the user interface using either a prose format or screen mock-ups.
- Portability, security, and reliability needs for the application based upon its proposed industrial utilization.
- Estimates of performance metrics such as response time, throughput and disk space utilization.

In addition to the requirements document deliverable, the project had several learning objectives relating to the virtual teams experience that were distinct from the requirements document. Both instructors communicated the following learning objectives to the students through lectures and handouts:

- To participate in a collaborative virtual team project with the students from another university and culture in defining the requirements of a business information system.

- To experience the spirit of global software development and to appreciate temporal, cultural, and other differences that exists in such an environment.
- To experiment with synchronous and asynchronous collaborative technologies.
- To document and to analyze the experience of the virtual team project.

Better-structured projects as measured using the construct "structure of project tasks" are likely to have positive impact on both the quality of the projects and on the software engineering process itself.

Size of the Teams: Powell et al. (2004) point out the importance of determining appropriate size and skill composition of virtual teams for different project types. Larger teams require more co-ordination and control. However, as the team size increases beyond a threshold level, more formal methods and robust tools for communication and management of the projects tend to get used. On the other hand, because of higher overhead, smaller teams often tend to use informal methods and may find it difficult to complete the project activities before the deadline. Hence, size of the teams is related to the outcome variables.

In our study, we formed 24 distinct teams from IIML and UWO to work together in a collaborative virtual team environment. Each team of five to six members from IIML was paired with a counterpart at UWO consisting of about three to four members.

Trust between Teams: Trust has been cited as a single most important factor, especially in the context where the parties involved in a business partnership do not see each other. There is wealth of research, which systematically examines the effect of trust in the context of electronic commerce (Cheung & Lee, 2001). However, the existing literature lacks an analysis of the effect of trust on the effectiveness of global virtual teams. Hence, we have included "trust" as one of the predictor variables that measures the extent to which the peer teams trusted the capabilities at the beginning and during the course of the project. It is expected that as trust improves, all the outcome variables can be expected to improve as well.

Cultural Differences: Distributed Virtual Teams that are dispersed across organizational, space, or time boundaries are often cross-functional in nature (Gorton & Motwani, 1996). Culture is a difficult concept to define. Hofstede (1991) identifies five dimensions of national culture: power distance, uncertainty avoidance, individualism versus collectivism, masculinity versus femininity and long-term versus short-term orientation. Favela and Pena-Mora (2001), in their distributed software development exercise, cite that the American students exhibited more individualism than their Mexican counterparts. Cultural differences include work ethic, work hours, preferred method of communication, individualism versus collectivism, and concern for quality. The other related aspect is the willingness of the teams to adjust and to accommodate for any of the above-mentioned differences in the virtual setting. It is reported in Favela and Pena-Mora (2001) that the Mexican students reinforced each other's work and were more accommodative. They sought to build consensus among the entire team before proceeding with a decision during the course of their virtual team exercise. Students from India, with higher scores in power distance and long term orientation, along with corresponding lower scores in individualism and uncertainty avoidance, were expected to be more accommodative than their Canadian counterparts.

One of the reasons behind having teams from two very different countries was to explore the impact of national and cultural differences on the interaction between the virtual teams as exposed by Hofstede (1991). In particular, the interaction between India and Canada allowed us to explore the impact of cultural factors such as the need for structure, attitudes towards hierarchy, sense of time, and communication styles, while maintaining a common language of English for communication (Herbsleb & Moitra, 2001).

We measured how the peer teams perceived "cultural differences across peer teams" during the course of the project. It is expected that even though cultural differences may not affect significantly the quality of the project, it may have positive or negative influence on the virtual team project experience of the team members.

Geographical/Time Dispersion: The development teams working in a global context have some advantages such as the ten-and-a-half-hour time difference between North America and India, which can facilitate a near continuous software development cycle. The positive effects of time difference on software project management to introduce "software shift work" have been well documented (Gorton & Motwani, 1996). However, time difference also introduces demands on coordination and communication activities. Espinosa and Carmel (2004) modeled the effect of coordination and communication costs under the consequences of time separation.

India and Canada are located in opposite hemispheres of the world and feature a 10 hour and 30 minute difference between them. This enabled us to measure the impact of the geographical and associated time differences on the performance of global virtual teams as this large geographic distance made co-location amongst teams a virtual impossibility. Hence the "effect of time difference" on the outcome variables is ambiguous because of reasons cited above.

Technology: The criticality of coordination and communication for the performance of virtual teams is mentioned in Carmel and Agarwal (2001). Coordination and communication gaps across peer teams in a virtual setting can sometimes be bridged using suitable technologies. Kobitzch, Rombach, and Feldmann (2001) cite the requirement of advanced communication infrastructure for implementing distributed software development processes. In our experiment, virtual team members were encouraged to use both synchronous communication technologies such as chat and document sharing and asynchronous technology such as e-mail. However, the Internet bandwidth availability and the reliability of Internet services are different across the two countries in which the experiment was conducted. Andres (2002) discusses ways to assess the relative effectiveness of video conferencing technology to support distributed software design teams. He suggests that with innovate methods, video conferencing could be a substitute for face-to-face meetings.

To facilitate communication, each side hosted Web sites that featured electronic mail addresses and photographs of each team. Each deliverable was also posted on both the Web sites. However, the teams were left to use technologies suitable for them. Powell et al. (2004) cites that irrespective of their access to various technologies, effective virtual teams appear to be able to adapt the technology and match it to communication requirements of the task at hand. If the team members feel comfortable in using appropriate technologies for coordinating and communicating during the project as encapsulated using the construct "ease of use of technology", then it is expected that it will have positive impact both on the quality of the projects, and on the team members' learning effectiveness and satisfaction levels.

Survey Data and Construct Measurement

A survey instrument containing measurement items, which fit into the constructs defined in the model shown in Figure 1, was constructed. Survey responses for 61 items were generated at the end of the virtual team project exercise, from the 116 IIML students and the 85 UWO students who participated. All items were measured on a seven-point Likert-type scale, where one indicated strong disagreement while seven meant strong agreement with the construct item. Demographic and experience items were measured through direct questions.

We performed various statistical analyses at the individual level rather than by teams. The larger sample size of $N = 201$ at the individual level minimizes the subjective bias in the outcome variables and reduces the chances of missing real relationships, compared to doing analysis on a smaller sample size of 24 at the team level. Factor analysis was performed on the pooled sample to assess construct validity. Principal components extraction method was used with Varimax rotation. The items, which did not load well on the constructs, were removed. Reliability of the constructs was further validated by computing reliability coefficients for each construct. The reliability statistics are given in Table 3. All the constructs have a Cronbach's alpha closer to or greater than 0.70 and hence prove construct validity (Cheung & Lee, 2001). Quality of projects were measured using the marks given to the projects, and hence is not listed in Table 3. "Size of the teams" and "Structure of project teams" each had one item and hence are not listed.

Table 4 shows the correlation amongst the four outcome variables. The correlation matrix indicates that there are significant positive associations between learning effectiveness, virtual team project experience, and the software engineering process outcome as expected. However, quality of the projects as measured by marks awarded did not have any positive association with the other outcome variables. One possible explanation could be that since these projects were done for a short duration and focused on just one aspect of the software development process, there was not enough effect of the global virtual environment on the project outcome.

The students were also asked to specify how many hours they spent on this virtual team exercise during the five weeks of project duration. Significant positive correlations

Table 3. Reliability statistics of the constructs

Constructs (Number of items)	Reliability Coefficient
Learning effectiveness (3)	0.8308
Virtual team project experience (10)	0.8415
Effect on software engineering process (7)	0.7068
Ease of use of technology (2)	0.7193
Effect of time difference (4)	0.6760
Trust between teams (4)	0.6971
Difference in academic orientation of teams (3)	0.7613
Difference in cultural orientation of teams (3)	0.8332

Table 4. Correlation between the outcome variables

	Quality of projects	Learning effectiveness	Virtual team project experience	Effect on software engineering process
Quality of projects	1.000	0.004	0.042	0.069
Learning effectiveness		1.000	0.783**	0.711**
Virtual team project experience			1.000	0.773**
Effect on software engineering process				1.000

(All Pearson correlations reported are for two-tailed tests. **correlation significant at the 0.01 level)

were observed between hours spent on the project and the outcome variables such as quality of projects, learning effectiveness, and virtual team project experience. However, the plot of the outcome variables against number of hours spent on the project did not exhibit a definite linearly increasing pattern. One reason again could be the short time duration of the projects, which minimized the effect of these associations.

ANALYSIS

To test our various hypotheses about the causal relationship between the outcome and predictor variables, Pearson's product-moment correlation matrix was constructed and is given in Table 5. Time and cultural differences as well as the size of teams did not have any significant correlations with any of the outcome variables. To further analyze the causal relationship, four regression models, one for each outcome (dependent) variable, with the corresponding significant predictor (independent) variables were then constructed. Results of regression analysis are presented in Table 6.

The F-statistic results for all the regression equations are significant at $p < 0.05$, indicating the significant association of at least one of the independent variables with the corresponding outcome variables. From the results in this table, we see the following two significant results for the performance of virtual teams:

- Trust between the peer teams alone has significant positive association with the quality of the projects.
- Both the structure of the project and trust between peer teams have significant positive association with virtual team project experience of the students, the learning effectiveness of the team members, as well as the efficiency of the software engineering process itself.

The above two results confirm our initial research questions. Though it is difficult to quantify trust levels, regression estimates indicate that each unit increase in trust level increases the quality of projects by as much as 17%. Similarly unit improvement in structure of the projects increases the effectiveness, satisfaction and efficiency of projects by 17%, 28% and 28% respectively.

Table 5. Correlation between predictor and outcome variables

Predictor Variable	Learning effectiveness	Quality of projects	Project experience	Effect on software engineering process
Ease of use of technology	0.156*	0.049	0.246**	0.213**
Structure of project tasks	0.277**	0.077	0.432**	0.429**
Effect of time difference	0.079	-0.014	0.010	0.101
Trust between teams	0.398**	0.172*	0.546**	0.551**
Difference in academic orientation of teams	-0.098	-0.004	-0.218**	-0.191**
Difference in cultural orientation of teams	-0.107	-0.138	-0.134	-0.067
Size of the teams	0.007	-0.017	0.022	-0.014

*(All Pearson correlations reported are for two-tailed tests. * correlation significant at the 0.05 level; ** correlation significant at the 0.01 level)*

Table 6. Regression models for the outcome variables (N=199)

	Standardized Beta	t-value	Significance
Learning effectiveness (R^2-adj = 0.170; F = 14.533; significance = <0.001)			
Ease of use of technology	0.023	0.338	0.736
Structure of project tasks	*0.169*	*2.458*	*0.015*
Trust between teams	*0.341*	*5.064*	*<0.001*
Quality of projects (R^2-adj = 0.025; F = 6.033; significance = <0.015)			
Trust between teams	*0.172*	*2.456*	*0.015*
Project experience (R^2-adj = 0.376; F = 30.833; significance = <0.001)			
Ease of use of technology	0.062	1.051	0.295
Structure of project tasks	*0.280*	*4.698*	*<0.001*
Trust between teams	*0.428*	*6.867*	*<0.001*
Difference in academic orientation of teams	-0.077	-1.313	0.191
Effect on software engineering process (R^2-adj = 0.366; F = 29.605; significance = <0.001)			
Ease of use of technology	0.023	0.393	0.695
Structure of project tasks	*0.284*	*4.733*	*<0.001*
Trust between teams	*0.447*	*7.118*	*<0.001*
Difference in academic orientation of teams	-0.038	-0.642	0.522

Though the association between trust and the other outcome variables is strong, the causal relationship between them has to be viewed with caution. Since the trust levels were measured at the end of the project duration, it is quite likely that the success of the project might have caused an improvement in trust level than the other way around. In order to establish a stronger causal relationship, the trust level needs to be monitored at various stages of the project.

However, difference in academic orientation between the peer teams, in fact, has a negative association with the project experience of the team members and the efficiency of the software engineering process. The association, though present in the correlation matrix, is not significant in the regression analysis. It is opposite to our expectation. The research question that heterogeneous teams actually can contribute positively in a global virtual team setting needs further examination. As expected, ease of use of technology, when taken alone, has significant positive associations with the learning effectiveness, virtual team project experience, and the efficiency of software engineering process. All the other correlations were of expected sign as discussed before, though the associations were not strong.

To analyze whether there are any significant differences in the perception of outcome and predictor variables across teams, an ANOVA was performed. The mean scores of the predictor and outcome variables for the two teams, along with ANOVA results, are presented in Table 7. ANOVA results where there are significant differences in mean values ($p < 0.05$) across IIML and UWO teams are highlighted. From the table, we can draw several conclusions.

The UWO team found the activities and milestones of the project to be significantly less structured compared to IIML team. This is surprising, since the average age and work experience (see Table 1) that are indicative of maturity and hence the potential to operate in an unstructured environment were higher for UWO team members than that of IIML team members. One possible explanation could be that the management curriculum at IIML, as is typical of the MBA programs, encourages work in an unstructured environment compared to the undergraduate computer science curriculum at UWO. This might have enabled IIML students to better cope with gaps in the structure of the project exercise.

Both sets of teams felt that the difficulties and challenges due to time difference were more than average. Furthermore, both sets of teams exhibited higher than average level of trust between them in carrying out their projects. However, the trust level of UWO teams was significantly lower than that of IIML teams. One explanation could be that the UWO teams were expected to carry on with further phases of system development life cycle including prototype development. These activities very much depended on the requirements generated during the virtual team exercise. Since the project stakes were higher for the UWO teams, the team members might have felt a little bit uneasy about the peer team members and that resulted in a lower level of trust. The UWO teams experienced differences due to academic orientation (business versus computer science) and culture (Indian versus Canadian) significantly more than the IIML teams.

IIML teams felt that their learning process was strengthened by the virtual team exercise while the UWO teams were more moderate in their response. The same holds true for the overall experience about the virtual team exercise. The grades for the virtual team exercise were equal for both IIML and UWO teams. However, since IIML team did not take part in the subsequent phases of the project, their stakes were limited. Due to

Table 7. Mean scores and ANOVA results

Variables	Mean Scores		ANOVA Results
	IIML	**UWO**	**F (p)**
Predictor Variables:			
Ease of use of technology	4.2500	4.2143	0.038 (0.0845)
Structure of the project tasks	4.6261	3.5529	**21.601 (<0.001)**
Effect of time difference	4.6875	4.8029	0.456 (0.500)
Trust between teams	5.2371	4.8000	**8.824 (0.003)**
Difference in academic orientation of teams	3.7813	4.4156	**10.937 (0.001)**
Difference in cultural orientation of teams	2.6339	3.2946	**11.601 (0.001)**
Size of the teams	3.7632	3.9059	0.373 (0.542)
Outcome Variables:			
Learning effectiveness	5.7531	4.6194	**47.733 (<0.001)**
Virtual team project experience	5.5000	4.2746	**83.875 (<0.001)**
Effect on software engineering process	4.8617	4.1504	30.614 (0.845)
Marks awarded to the project	77.18	77.59	0.147 (0.702)

Table 8. Supporting questions and the mean scores of the teams

Survey Questions	Mean Scores		ANOVA Results
	IIML	**UWO**	**F(p)**
Using voice communication (Internet Telephony, phone calls, etc) would have improved the co-ordination of the project.	5.84	4.36	44.471 (<0.001)
Using video communication (Internet based video conferencing) would have improved the co-ordination of the project.	5.67	3.96	57.835 (<0.001)
We feel that course credit/grade given to the virtual team project is more.	2.26	3.89	62.994 (<0.001)
I don't mind working at odd hours, and doing extra work for the virtual team project.	5.43	4.41	21.800 (<0.001)
Virtual team project should include teams from more than two countries.	4.94	3.38	38.833 (<0.001)
I would like to work with a virtual team from another country in a future course.	5.86	4.58	42.175 (<0.001)

commitment to the subsequent phases of the project, the UWO teams might have perceived more risk and found the project to be more complex. Hence, they may have rated the effectiveness of the virtual team exercise lower.

Additional supporting questions in the survey and the responses are given in Table 8. Both the teams are of the opinion that synchronous technologies such as voice and video conferencing would have improved the coordination of their projects. There is a strong affirmation that the students wanted to work with another country doing a similar exercise in future. From the ANOVA results in Table 7 and Table 8, we can conclude that the UWO teams were moderately poised, whereas the IIML teams were more positively poised in their view towards the virtual team exercise.

DISCUSSIONS

Limitations of the Study

While this exploratory study makes some initial observations into the nature of global virtual teams during the requirements definition phase of software engineering projects, there are limitations of the study. The controlled academic environment in which the exercises were carried out imposes more structure and discipline to the global virtual team exercise compared to real-world projects. Further, since UWO students were informed that they would be involved in the subsequent phases of the software development process after the virtual team exercise, their stake in the project was much higher compared to IIML students and hence may have affected the way in which they performed and perceived the exercise. However, this is more akin to reality as most of the outsourcing partners are involved only during part of the software development life cycle.

Our projects lasted only for 5 weeks compared to 32 weeks for the distributed software engineering laboratory exercises conducted by Favela and Pene-Mora (2001). Powell et al. (2004) lists the disadvantages of short-term projects involving student teams. Hence results from this exercise have to be carefully transformed to longer duration projects in practical settings. We only dealt with requirements engineering phase of the software development life cycle during the virtual project time duration. This is limiting since offshore business consultants often deal with the subsequent phases such as analysis, design, and implementation. The teams mostly used asynchronous technologies such as e-mail and Web interfaces in their projects. Voice and video conferencing technologies, configuration management tools, and code development tools were not used in these exercises. Hence results of the study do not take in to account the possible effects of these technologies.

With these limitations in mind, we discuss below the lessons from our virtual team exercise for practitioners in the industry and for the course instructors in educational institutions.

Lessons for Practice

The use of virtual teams in the construction of industrial software is becoming more and more commonplace as corporations seek to take advantage of lower costs and to utilize a follow-the-sun approach to software development. In this research, we sought to examine the factors that impact the quality and performance of distributed virtual teams engaged in the requirements definition phase of the software development life cycle. The study yields several interesting conclusions that can assist organizations in creating and managing their global virtual team projects more effectively. Even though this study was limited to the requirements definition phase of the project, the phase is very critical for the quality of the software product and requires effective communication between the business process teams and systems analysis teams. Although realities of global software development environment were simulated as closely as possible using heterogeneous teams spread across the globe, generalizations to professional teams in business settings should still be made cautiously.

Our experiment indicates that trust between peer teams significantly affect the performance, satisfaction, and learning of the virtual teams. It has been observed that in global software teams, trust level is lower at the start of the project, leading to reluctance to share information (Herbsleb & Grinter, 2001). This may be because of insecurity or because the teams did not look at themselves as partners working towards a common goal. Over the course of the project, trust develops between the teams. In our project, even though the duration was very short, the teams trusted each other to the same degree with the trust level found to be high. Prevalence of a high amount of trust indicates that, given a suitable environment (e.g., a university environment where creativity is encouraged and there is no power hierarchy), it is possible to promote a good trust level between the virtual teams, which in turn affects positively the outcome variables. As Herbsleb and Grinter (1999) point out, businesses engaged in virtual team projects should arrange face-to-face meetings of team members at regular intervals to build the trust level of the team members.

Another conclusion is that well-structured projects positively affect the performance, satisfaction, and learning of the virtual teams. The bulk of successful offshore outsourcing activities are mostly centered around testing and maintenance as these are well structured. However, as software companies, especially in emerging countries such as India, move into the area of information technology consulting, activities become less structured. One solution could be the use of tools for code development, configuration management, and version control. These tools allow hand-off controls to be implemented, which provide structure and control of different project activities. Our exercise also reveals that technical members of global virtual teams will have to be given training to operate in a less structured uncertain environment before being inducted into virtual team projects.

Since the ease of use of technologies positively affect the outcome variables, virtual teams should be encouraged to use them. Carmel and Agarwal (2001) argue that despite the power of today's asynchronous technologies for dispersed work, there are powerful reasons for synchronous communication. Our study also reveals that use of voice and video communications would have improved the coordination of the projects. Countries such as India now have the requisite telecommunications infrastructure, thanks to competition and technology advancements. Offshore software development centers in these countries now can afford to have synchronous technologies to complement the asynchronous communication facilities to improve the quality of virtual team projects. As pointed out by Carmel and Agarwal (2001), offshore centers should also adopt other technology solutions such as software configuration management to improve communication and coordination between peer teams. As technology itself is a moving target and is continuously evolving, this study indicates a reference point from which various managerial issues of deploying different levels of technologies can be assessed in a practical setting.

Lessons for the Classroom

This research work built a platform similar to Favela and Pena-Mora (2001) and a large number of student projects as mentioned in Powell et al. (2004) to help a new set of software developers better understand the nature of working in distributed collaborative software engineering environment. As part of the software engineering and information systems curriculum, the global virtual team projects were perceived positively by the students. Students also evinced interest in working on similar virtual team projects in future. Hence we recommend that such exercises can be given to the students in the Management Information Systems courses in the business curriculum or Software Engineering courses in the computer science curriculum. These projects will enrich students' learning of the subject and also provide them the experience of working in a simulated real-world distributed software engineering setup.

In addition, there are significant positive associations between learning effectiveness, virtual project experience, and the software engineering process outcome. The project exercises also gave the students exposure to the realities of global software development environment. However, our experiment indicates that if the risks (mainly related to marks awarded to the exercises), deliverables, and the time of involvement are less, then global virtual team exercise will be more favored by the students. The faculty administering the virtual team projects in their courses should keep this in mind while designing the project particulars.

Apart from software engineering, instructors of courses in other disciplines also can adopt virtual team exercises spanning regions of the world in their classes to improve the skills, competitiveness, and capacity of their students in a global setting. For example, Internet- based interdisciplinary simulation tools such as "Mikes Bikes" can be used in areas such as business strategy, management accounting, organizational behavior, marketing, and advertising courses to conduct competitive simulation games in an international virtual team setting (Smartsims, 2004). These exercises help students understand differences and similarities between virtual and face-to-face group processes, in particular, group decision-making. They also help students develop personal skills for initiating, developing and maintaining relationships without the aid of face-to-face interactions.

FUTURE RESEARCH DIRECTIONS

There are several potential directions for future research. First, a subsequent experiment can be conducted that examines the outcomes of such an experiment where the software development team is located in India, which is often the case due to low software development cost, and the management functions are located in Canada. Virtual team facilitators are often the nexus of a virtual team, facilitating communications, establishing team processes, and taking responsibility for task completion (Pauleen & Yoong, 2001). Pauleen and Yoong (2001) also note that the ultimate challenge for facilitators, particularly in long-term and ongoing virtual teams, is to work at merging the individual culture of the team members into a team culture. It would be an interesting extension to add a project management team in the virtual team exercise, to assume the roles and the responsibilities of facilitators, and then study its impact on the outcome variables. This would more closely mirror the process used in real world development environments. Finally, as indicated earlier, we could not see clearly the impact of the time investment by the virtual teams on the outcome variables. It would be interesting to study this trend, as this would help businesses involved in virtual team projects to allocate optimal man-hours to maximize quality, efficiency, and effectiveness of the projects.

As organizations try to move their outsourcing relationship up the value chain to include all phases of system development, they incur costs and risks as indicated by Heeks, Krishna, Nicholson, and Sahay (2001). An interesting extension of this exercise would be to conduct projects in which the different phases of the system development life cycle are distributed amongst multiple non-co-located virtual teams. Quantifiable metrics should be developed to assess the performance of the teams across the different phases. This can help in devising ways by which companies can minimize risks and reap maximum benefits by selectively outsourcing the phases of software development projects. The project also can illustrate how domain expertise can be tapped across the globe by integrating the management and process knowledge with software expertise available at distant locations as discussed by Battin et al. (2001).

REFERENCES

Andres, H. (2002). A comparison of face-to-face and virtual software development teams. *Team Performance Management, 8*(1/2), 39-48.

Bates, M., Davis, K., & Haynes, D. (2003). Reinventing IT services. *The McKinsey Quarterly, 2*, 143-153.

Battin, R., Crocker, R., Kreidler, J., & Subramanian, K. (2001, March/April). Leveraging resources in global software development. *IEEE Software*, 70-77.

Carmel, E. (1999). *Global software teams*. Upper Saddle River, NJ: Prentice-Hall.

Carmel, E., & Agarwal, R. (2001, March-April). Tactical approaches for alleviating distance in global software development. *IEEE Software*, 22-29.

Cheung, C., & Lee, M. (2001). Trust in Internet shopping: Instrument development and validation through classical and modern approaches. *Journal of Global Information Management, 9*(3), 23-35.

Damian, D., Herlea, D. E., Eberlein, A., Shaw, M. L. G., & Gaines, B. R. (2000, May). The effects of communication media on group performance in requirements engineering. *IEEE Software*, 28-36.

Damian, D., & Zowghi, D. (2002). The impact of stakeholders' geographical distribution on requirements engineering in a multi-site development organization. *Proceedings of the 10th IEEE International Conference on Requirements Engineering*, Essen, Germany (pp. 319-328). Piscataway, NJ: IEEE.

Dube, L., & Pare, G. (2001). Global virtual teams. *Communications of the ACM, 44*(12), 71-73.

Ebert, C., & De Neve, P. (2001, March/April). Surviving global software development. *IEEE Software*, 62-69.

Espinaso, J., & Carmel, E. (2004). The impact of time separation on coordination in global software teams: A conceptual foundation. *Software Process Improvement and Practice, 8*, 1-19.

Favela, J., & Pena-Mora, F. (2001, March-April). An experience in collaborative software engineering education. *IEEE Software*, 47-53.

Gorton, I., & Motwani, S. (1996). Issue in co-operative software engineering using globally distributed teams. *Information and Software Technology, 38*, 647-655.

Heeks, R., Krishna, S., Nicholson, S. B., & Sahay, S. (2001, March-April). Synching or sinking: Global software outsourcing relationships. *IEEE Software*, 4-60.

Herbsleb, J., & Grinter, R. (1999, September-October). Architecture, coordination and distance: Conway's law and beyond. *IEEE Software,* 63-70.

Herbsleb, J., & Moitra, D. (2001, March-April). Global software development. *IEEE Software*, 16-20.

Hofstede, G. (1991). *Cultures and organizations: Software of the mind.* London: McGraw Hill.

Kobitzsch, W., Rombach, D., & Feldmann, R. (2001, March-April). Outsourcing in India. *IEEE Software*, 78-86.

Lurey, J., & Raisinghani, M. (2001). An empirical study of best practices in virtual teams. *Information & Management, 38*, 523-544.

Maciaszek, L. (2001). *Requirements analysis and systems design: Developing information systems with UML.* Toronto: Addison-Wesley.

Nath, D., Sridhar, V., & Malik, A. (2005). Effectiveness of the two-phase software offshoring model. *Proceedings of the First International Conference on Management of Globally Distributed Work* (pp. 159-170). Bangalore, India: GDW Consortium.

National Association of Software and Service Companies (NASSCOM). (2004). *Indian IT industry.* Retrieved June 24, 2004, from http://www.nasscom.org/

National Association of Software and Service Companies (NASSCOM). (2005). *Indian IT industry.* Retrieved March 3, 2005, from http://www.nasscom.org/

Pauleen, D., & Yoong, P. (2001). Relationship building and the use of ICT in boundary-crossing virtual teams: A facilitator's perspective. *Journal of Information Technology, 16*, 205-220.

Powell, A., Piccoli, G., & Ives, B. (Winter, 2004). Virtual teams: A review of current literature and directions for future research. *The DATABASE for Advances in Information Systems, 35*(1), 6-36.

Smartsims (2004). *MikesBikes advanced: An advanced business simulation.* Retrieved June 21, 2004, from http://www.smartsims.com

Sommerville, I., & Kotonya, G. (1998). *Requirements engineering: Processes and techniques.* Toronto: John Wiley & Sons.

Sridhar, V. (2005) IT: Look for competitive advantage. *The Hindu Business Line.* Retrieved March 11, 2005, from http://www.blonnet.com

Section II: Regional Themes

Chapter IX

Determinants of Online Purchasing Behaviour

Bill Doolin, Auckland University of Technology, New Zealand

Stuart Dillon, University of Waikato Management School, New Zealand

James L. Corner, University of Waikato Management School, New Zealand

ABSTRACT

This chapter presents a research model of the determinants of online purchasing behaviour. The model assesses the importance of various dimensions of perceived risk and the Internet shopping experience in the online purchasing behaviour of Internet users. The model was tested using a survey of some 700 New Zealand Internet users. Both the perceived risk and perceived benefits of Internet shopping were found to be significantly associated with the amount and frequency of online purchases made. Loss of social interaction in Internet shopping was associated with reduced online spending. The results of the study suggest that Internet retailing Web sites should include features that enhance customer service and reduce perceived risk.

INTRODUCTION

Business-to-consumer (B2C) electronic commerce involves the use of the Internet and World Wide Web to market and sell products and services to individual consumers. These technologies offer consumers an additional channel for information, service, and purchasing, as well as potentially increased choice, convenience, competition among retailers, and cost savings.

B2C electronic commerce is increasing annually in the U.S., traditionally the top region for electronic commerce revenue, as well as Europe, Japan, and the Asia/Pacific region (George, 2002; IDC, 2002a). Increasing numbers of new buyers, as well as existing buyers, who are moving a larger proportion of their spending online, are contributing to this trend (IDC, 2002b). The relatively small percentage of total retail sales contributed by online sales suggests plenty of scope for increasing the amount of shopping which could be performed using this mode (Ward & Lee, 2000).

Nevertheless, making a success of online retailing has proven more difficult than initially predicted. Internet retailers need to understand online consumer purchasing behaviour in order to design and support effective retail Web sites that match the preferences of their target market (Vijayasarathy & Jones, 2000).

A number of prior studies have attempted to identify various factors that either encourage Internet users to engage in B2C transactions or create resistance to such activity. Many of these studies were undertaken in the mid to late 1990s; these were surveys of students, or relied upon secondary data generated in other surveys, such as the periodic GVU (Georgia Institute of Technology "Graphics, Visualization, and Usability") Survey of Internet Usage. As adoption of the Internet continues and demographic differences in the Internet user population diminish, there is a need to update and extend these studies. Experience with, and education about, the Internet are growing, and this might reasonably be expected to be reflected in changing user behaviour online, including Internet shopping.

Jarvenpaa and Todd (1997) describe a technology-centred approach to understanding consumer acceptance of Internet shopping that focuses on technological factors encouraging or inhibiting adoption of this innovation, and a consumer-centred approach that focuses on the perceptions, attitudes, and beliefs of consumers in relation to online shopping. This study extends prior consumer-centred research by examining the association of consumer perceptions of risk and the Internet shopping experience with online purchasing behaviour. Much of this prior research has examined attitudes or intentions towards Internet shopping, and utilised secondary data or student samples. In contrast, this study is intended to provide data on the actual online shopping behaviour of actual Internet users. Further, it addresses the general lack of research on this aspect of Internet commerce in New Zealand, and provides an initial analysis of its similarities and differences with Internet shopping in other countries.

The main objective of the study was to discover whether consumers' perceived risk of Internet shopping and the Internet shopping experience were associated with online purchasing behaviour. The intention was to provide empirical evidence of this to inform the design and operation of Internet retailing, in line with the need to develop Web site functionality that matches consumer requirements (rather than vice versa). The subject of the study was the online purchasing behaviour of individual New Zealand Internet users. By sampling actual Internet users, we were able to exclude factors affecting access to and use of the Internet, and focus on those factors relevant to online purchasing itself.

The study contributes to the general body of empirical evidence about Internet shopping behaviour (Saeed, Hwang, & Yi, 2003), as well as providing a picture of Internet shopping behaviour in New Zealand, a small but developed economy. As of August, 2002, 53% of the New Zealand population was online (Nua, 2006). In addition, by the end of 2003, 25% of regular Internet users in New Zealand had made an online purchase that year. Between 2002 and 2004, Internet purchasing increased by 32% (Watkin, 2004). New Zealanders have a track record of relatively rapid adoption and high utilisation of consumer electronic technologies, including the concept of electronic transactions inherent in automatic teller machines, telephone banking, and electronic funds transfer at point of sale (EFTPOS) (Howell & Mariott, 2001; MED, 2000). As such, New Zealand provides a useful point of comparison to other studies of this nature.

The structure of the chapter is as follows. First, we review the relevant literature on perceived risk and the Internet shopping experience, and develop a research model of their association with actual online purchasing behaviour. In doing so, we propose a number of hypotheses. The next part of the chapter describes the Web-based survey instrument which we developed and distributed in order to test the hypotheses. We then present the results of the survey and discuss the implications of these findings for Internet retailers.

PERCEIVED RISK IN ONLINE PURCHASING

Prior research has indicated a relationship between the risk perception of a new shopping channel and the choice of purchasing using that channel (Bhatnagar, Misra, & Rao, 2000). While consumers perceive risk in most purchasing decisions, non-store purchase decisions tend to have a higher level of perceived risk associated with them. Online purchasing over the Internet is a more recent information technology-related form of direct marketing, and is similarly perceived as higher risk by consumers (Tan, 1999). Tan (1999) found that risk-averse consumers are less likely to use Internet shopping. Jarvenpaa and Todd (1997) reported that perceived risk influenced attitudes toward online shopping, but not the intention to shop online. However, Vijayasarathy and Jones (2000) found that perceived risk influenced both attitudes towards online shopping and intention to shop online. Other studies similarly found that perceived risk negatively influenced consumers' attitude or intention to purchase online (Liu & Wei, 2003; van der Heijden, Verhagen, & Creemers, 2003). Huang, Schrank, and Bubinsky (2004) observed, not surprisingly, that online shoppers were found to have less perceived risk than non-online shoppers. Interestingly, Forsythe and Shi (2003) found that risks perceived by Internet shoppers did "not significantly influence Internet patronage behaviours among current Internet shoppers in an extensive and systematic way" (p. 874). Moreover, they also found Internet browsers to be more sensitive to perceived risks than actual shoppers.

Various types of risk are perceived in purchase decisions, including product risk, security risk (Bhatnagar & Ghose, 2004; Kolsaker, Lee-Kelly, & Choy, 2004), and privacy risk (Garbarino & Strahilevitz, 2004; Kolsaker et al., 2004). Product risk is the risk of making a poor or inappropriate purchasing decision. One aspect of product risk is the risk of a poor economic decision through an inability to compare prices, being unable to return a product, or not receiving a product which has been paid for (Jarvenpaa & Todd, 1997; Vijayasarathy & Jones, 2000). Another aspect involves product performance, and is associated with the risk that a product will not function as expected (Bhatnagar et al., 2000; Cho, 2004; Forsythe & Shi, 2003; Jarvenpaa & Todd, 1997; Tan, 1999; Vijayasarathy

& Jones, 2000). Partly, this relates to the lack of opportunity to examine products prior to purchase (Tan, 1999). Bhatnagar et al. (2000) suggest that the likelihood of purchasing on the Internet decreases with increases in product risk. Also, Bhatnagar and Ghose (2004) found that while product risk decreases with increased age, use of the Internet, and product categories high in search attributes, security risk decreases with increased levels of education. Counter intuitively, Huang et al. (2004) observed that perceived security risk actually increased with the presence of a product's brand name. Finally, Pires, Stanton, and Eckford (2004) found that the perceived risk for products purchased online is higher than that for services, although perceived risk is higher when much decision making activity is required pre-purchase, be it for products or services bought online.

Other dimensions of perceived risk concern the medium of the Internet itself, rather than the consequences of purchasing a particular product. They are related to consumers' perceptions and beliefs about the Internet as a trustworthy shopping medium (Bhatnagar et al., 2000; Garbarino & Strahilevitz, 2004; Lee & Turban, 2001; Lim, 2003). For example, a common perception among consumers is that communicating credit card information over the Internet is inherently risky due to the possibility of credit card fraud (Ahuja, Gupta, & Raman, 2003; Bhatnagar et al., 2000; Furnell & Karweni, 1999; George, 2002; Hoffman, Novak, & Peralta, 1999; Jarvenpaa & Todd, 1997; Jones & Vijayasarathy, 1998; Liebermann & Stashevsky, 2002). George (2002) found that beliefs about the trustworthiness of the Internet were associated with positive attitudes toward Internet purchasing. In a survey of U.S. online shoppers, Ranganathan and Ganapathy (2002) found that security was a major factor in discriminating between high and low intentions to purchase online. However, Swaminathan, Lepkowska-White, and Rao (1999) reported that consumers in their study seemed less concerned about the security of online transactions. Kolsaker et al. (2004) concluded that "risk perceptions are associated with the structural assurance of the web itself rather than any particular vendor or site's appearance" (p. 301).

Apart from concerns about the security of Internet transactions, Internet trustworthiness seems also to relate to consumers' concerns about privacy (George, 2004). These concerns include the unauthorised acquisition of personal information during Internet use or the provision of personal information collected by companies to third parties (Furnell & Karweni, 1999; George, 2002; Hoffman et al., 1999; Lim, 2003; Wang, Lee, & Wang, 1998). Forsythe and Shi (2003) use the term "psychological risk" to encompass the disappointment, frustration, and shame that might be experienced if one's personal information is disclosed. The available literature on Internet purchasing and privacy suggests that a large number of Internet consumers do not trust Web providers enough to exchange personal information with them (Hoffman et al., 1999; Liebermann & Stashevsky, 2002). Hoffman et al. (1999) suggest that with increasing privacy concerns, the likelihood of purchasing online decreases. Similarly, George (2002) found that a belief in the privacy of personal information was associated with negative attitudes toward Internet purchasing. Swaminathan et al. (1999) found that consumers who purchased more on the Internet were more concerned about the creation of privacy laws. However, Pires et al. (2004) found that experience factors did not seem to affect perceived risk. Additionally, Garbarino and Strahilevitz (2004) found that, while men and women equally perceive the probability of loss of privacy while using the Web, women think the consequences of lost privacy will be more severe than do men. They also found that women will reduce their perceptions of risk more than will men, when receiving online buying recommendations from friends. Overall, the preceding discussion leads to the following hypothesis:

H_1:   Consumers who place importance on the perceived risk of Internet shopping are less likely to purchase online.

THE INTERNET SHOPPING EXPERIENCE

For many consumers, shopping is an important personal and social activity. Attributes of the shopping experience that influence shopping behaviour include enjoyment, convenience, and social interaction (Jarvenpaa & Todd, 1997). Consistent with the earlier study of Jarvenpaa and Todd (1997), Vijayasarathy and Jones (2000) found that the Internet shopping experience was significantly associated with attitudes to Internet shopping and intentions to shop online. Both studies measured shopping experience across items related to enjoyment, convenience, and compatibility with consumer lifestyles. In addition, Koivumaki (2001) found a positive relationship between the Internet shopping experience and the amount of purchases which are made. Lee, Pi, Kwok, and Huynh (2003) found that shopping enjoyment and purchasing convenience were positively associated with online customer satisfaction.

The perceived convenience offered by Internet vendors is often presented as a significant influence on the decision to purchase online (Ahuja et al., 2003; Rohm & Swaminathan, 2004). Convenience includes the time and effort saved by consumers (Cho, 2004; Ranganathan & Ganapathy, 2002; Swaminathan et al., 1999). Kim, Cho, and Rao (2000) analysed data from the October 1998, GVU Survey of Internet Usage. They found that a time-constrained lifestyle was positively associated with Internet purchasing behaviour. They measured this time orientation by items related to saving time and effort. Swaminathan et al. (1999) also examined the October, 1998, GVU Survey of Internet Usage. They found that consumers who valued convenience tended to use the Internet to make purchases more often and to spend more money doing so. Similarly, Li, Kuo, and Russell (1999) reported that frequent Internet shoppers were convenience-oriented. Similarly, Rohm and Swaminathan (2004) included the convenience shopper as one of the four main types of online shopper. Other studies have also reported that limited discretionary time has a strong influence on a consumer's decision to purchase online (Bellman, Lohse, & Johnson, 1999; Vijayasarathy & Jones, 2000).

Despite the perceived benefits in online shopping, there are a number of possible negative factors associated with the Internet shopping experience. These include the loss of sensory shopping or the loss of social benefits associated with shopping (Vijayasarathy & Jones, 2000). For example, Swaminathan et al. (1999) suggest that a consumer's social or behavioural orientation to shopping plays an important role in his or her propensity to engage in Internet shopping. In particular, so-called recreational shoppers, motivated by the social aspects of shopping, might find the Internet a less attractive medium for shopping since it generally allows for limited interaction compared to other retail formats. In their research, Swaminathan et al. (1999) found that the lack of social interaction in Internet shopping deterred consumers who preferred dealing with people or who treated shopping as a social experience from purchasing online.

The findings discussed above lead to the following hypotheses:

H₂: Consumers who place importance on the perceived benefits of Internet shopping are more likely to purchase online.

H₃: Consumers who place importance on the loss of social interaction in Internet shopping are less likely to purchase online.

CONSUMER CHARACTERISTICS

Prior research suggests that various demographic variables, such as gender, income, age, level of education, and computer or Internet experience, are often associated with both Internet usage patterns and shopping motivation (Chang & Samuel, 2004; Katz & Aspden, 1997; Sorce, Perotti, & Widrick, 2005; Swaminathan et al., 1999; Teo, 2001). These variables tend not to form a coherent theoretical group, and are often treated as control variables in studies of Internet purchasing behaviour (Lee & Turban, 2001). Bellman et al. (1999) further suggest that while demographics influence whether a person is online in the first place, they have little influence on their online purchasing behaviour. Indeed, in the study by Li et al. (1999), demographic variables accounted for only four percent of the variance in the online buying behaviour. Teo (2001) found that demographic variables contributed only two percent in the variation of Internet purchasing activities.

Bhatnagar et al. (2000) examined the April, 1997, GVU Survey of Internet Usage and found that the effect of gender on the likelihood of Internet purchasing was mixed, and tended to vary with product category (depending on whether men or women are likely to have greater experience with a particular product). Li et al. (1999) found in their study that men were more frequent online purchasers than women. A U.S. study by Sorce et al. (2005) showed that younger online shoppers search for more products than do older shoppers, but that the age groups purchase about the same amount. In a Singapore study, Teo (2001) also found that males were more likely to engage in Internet purchasing. Forsythe and Shi (2003) observed that older Internet users were likely to be shoppers, whereas younger users (particularly those in the 11-20 age range) were more likely to be browsers.

Age and educational level have often been associated with levels of computer usage. Both tend to be related by researchers to computer anxiety. For this reason, age is often considered to be negatively related to usage, while education is considered to mitigate the effect of computer anxiety (Teo, 2001). In terms of the Internet, Katz and Aspden (1997) found that long-time Internet users were younger than average and very well-educated. Bhatnagar et al. (2000) found that older consumers were more open to purchasing on the Internet, and Bellman et al. (1999) found that the higher a person's age and education, the more likely that person will buy online. However, Teo (2001) failed to find a significant association between age or educational level and Internet purchasing.

Kim et al. (2000) included current household income as a factor in their analysis of the October 1998, GVU Survey of Internet Usage. They found that income showed a strong positive relationship with Internet purchasing behaviour. A similar result was reported by Koivumaki (2001). Li et al. (1999) found that consumers with higher incomes were more likely to be frequent online purchasers, as did Bellman et al. (1999).

Bellman et al. (1999) note that measures of past behaviour are probably more important for predicting online shopping behaviour. Studies by Bhatnagar et al. (2000) and Corbitt, Thanasankit, and Yi (2003) found that the likelihood of purchasing online increased as a consumer's experience on the Internet increased. Kim et al. (2000) also reported a positive association between experienced Internet users and online purchasing behaviour. George (2002) found that more Internet experience was associated with more frequent Internet purchasing. Park and Kim (2003) found that a buyer's commitment toward a given online store was largely a function of past experience with that store.

As mentioned earlier, online purchasing over the Internet is a more recent form of direct marketing. As such, it might be expected that Internet users already inclined to purchase from non-store channels would be adopters of Internet shopping. Indeed, early work by Jones and Vijayasarathy (1998) suggested investigating the influence of past direct purchasing behaviour on consumers' attitudes to Internet shopping. Jarvenpaa, Tractinsky, and Vitale (1999) measured direct shopping experience in their study of Internet retailing, focusing on frequency of purchasing from television infomercials and print catalogues. They found a correlation between direct shopping experience and willingness to buy from an Internet store.

As Internet adoption increases, the influence of demographic differences is likely to further decline (Korgaonkar & Wolin, 2002; Swaminathan et al., 1999). However, Lee and Turban (2001) do not rule out the possibility and value of individually testing demographic variables as part of a research design. The preceding review of consumer characteristics leads to the following hypotheses:

H_4:   Males are more likely than females to purchase online.

H_5:   Older consumers are less likely to purchase online.

H_6:   Consumers with higher education are more likely to purchase online.

H_7:   Consumers with higher incomes are more likely to purchase online.

H_8:   Consumers with Internet experience are more likely to purchase online.

H_9:   Consumers that shop using other direct marketing channels are more likely to purchase online.

ONLINE PURCHASING BEHAVIOUR

The dependent variable examined in this study is online purchasing behaviour. Prior studies of online purchasing have variously considered the association of independent variables with consumers' attitudes towards online shopping (e.g., Van der Heijden et al, 2003; Vijayasarathy & Jones, 2000), their intentions to shop online (e.g., Liu & Wei, 2003; Vijayasarathy & Jones, 2000) and their willingness to shop online (e.g., Jarvenpaa et al., 1999). Other studies have used measures of actual purchasing behaviour, such as the frequency of online purchases or the amount spent on online purchases in a certain prior period. This period is usually the last 6 months, 12 months, or both (e.g., Kim et al.,

2000; Korgaonkar & Wolin, 2002; Ranganathan & Ganapathy, 2002; Swaminathan et al., 1999). Consistent with these latter studies, this study measures actual behaviour using both frequency and amount of online purchases over the previous 12 months.

RESEARCH MODEL

A research model based on the above literature review of perceived risk in online purchasing, the Internet shopping experience, and consumer characteristics is presented in Figure 1. Three constructs are proposed to measure aspects of risk and the Internet shopping experience: perceived risk, perceived benefits (of Internet shopping), and loss of social interaction (in Internet shopping). Following Teo (2001), in this study we also examine the direct association of a range of demographic variables based on consumer characteristics. The research model and the developed hypotheses attempt to examine the association between these consumer-centred factors and online purchasing behaviour.

DEVELOPMENT OF THE
SURVEY INSTRUMENT

Despite the relatively large number of prior studies of Internet shopping behavior, their diversity meant that it was difficult to use items from previous instruments to operationalise the constructs in the research model in a consistent way. Accordingly, most of the items were specifically developed for this study based on the literature reviewed earlier in the chapter.

Perceived risk was conceptualised as a multidimensional construct comprising economic, product performance, security, and privacy risks. The composite risk con-

Figure 1. Research model

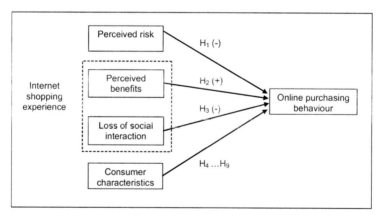

struct was measured using five items adapted from prior studies. A further five items were used to measure the two dimensions of Internet shopping experience presented in the research model, perceived benefits and loss of social interaction. Table 1 shows each item and its antecedents. Respondents were asked to identify the importance of each item in purchasing a product online. Respondents rated each item on a 5-point scale, where 1 represented "not important" and 5 represented "very important".

Online purchasing behaviour was measured using two items: the frequency of online purchases in the last 12 months, and the amount spent on online purchases in the last 12 months (Table 1). Both items used categorical ranges to capture the relevant data.

Other questions in the survey instrument collected demographic data, including single measures of gender, age, education level, household income, and Internet

Table 1. Constructs, items, and antecedents

Perceived risk	
Inability to inspect product	Cho (2004), Corbitt et al. (2003), Liebermann & Stashevsky (2002), Tan (1999)
Inability to compare price or quality of similar products	Corbitt et al. (2003), Tan (1999)
Risk of making a poor purchase decision	Jarvenpaa & Todd (1997), Tan (1999), Vijayasarathy & Jones (2000)
Risk of credit card abuse	Ahuja et al., (2003); Forsythe & Shi (2003), Huang et al. (2004) Kim et al. (2000), Liebermann & Stashevsky (2002), Vijayasarathy & Jones (2000)
Risk of compromising personal information	Ahuja et al., (2003); Forsythe & Shi (2003), Jarvenpaa & Todd (1997), Garbarino & Strahilevitz (2004), George (2004), Liebermann & Stashevsky (2002), Limayem et al. (2000), Vijayasarathy & Jones (2000)
Perceived benefits	
Convenience of online shopping due to effort involved	Ahuja et al., (2003); Cho (2004), Limayem et al. (2000), Rohm & Swaminathan (2004), Swaminathan et al. (1999), Tan (1999)
Convenience of online shopping due to time saved	Ahuja et al., (2003); Jarvenpaa & Todd (1997), Kim et al. (2000), Limayem et al. (2000), Swaminathan et al. (1999)
Enjoyment of online shopping	Jarvenpaa & Tractinsky (1999), Limayem et al. (2000), Teo (2001)
Loss of social interaction	
Loss of personal contact	Liebermann & Stashevsky (2002), Swaminathan et al. (1999)
Loss of social shopping experience	Swaminathan et al. (1999), Tan (1999)
Online purchasing behaviour	
Frequency of online purchasing in last 12 months	Kim et al. (2000), Korgaonkar & Wolin (2002), Ranganathan & Ganapathy (2002), Swaminathan et al. (1999)
Amount purchased online in last 12 months	Kim et al. (2000), Korgaonkar & Wolin (2002), Ranganathan & Ganapathy (2002), Swaminathan et al. (1999)

experience. Direct shopping experience was measured using the amount of direct purchases made through mail order or television sales in the last 12 months. With the exception of gender, which was a dichotomous variable, these items used categorical ranges to capture the relevant data. Data on the types of products and services purchased online were also collected. A summary of the items used in the survey is appended.

DATA COLLECTION

A Web-based survey was deliberately chosen in order to access a sample of Internet users. A Web-based survey offered a comparatively cheap distribution mechanism, the retrieval of survey responses in a digital form, and rapid response times compared to conventional mail surveys (Boyer, Olson, & Jackson, 2001; Dillman, 2000; Vehovar, Manfreda, & Batagelj, 2000).

A New Zealand Internet service provider (ISP) agreed to send an e-mail to customers that had elected to receive electronic newsletters from them. The e-mail discussed B2C electronic commerce in New Zealand and encouraged customers to participate in the survey. Recipients of the e-mail from the ISP were informed that the survey was part of a University research study on online shopping in New Zealand. The e-mail contained a URL that linked to a survey form stored on a University Web server. Confidentiality of responses was emphasised. Respondents had the option to enter an e-mail address with their response if they wished to receive a summary of the survey results. An e-mail link for one of the researchers was included in the survey form to allow respondents to comment on the survey if they wished. The survey was pilot-tested for both technical performance and respondent use. Minor adjustments were made on the basis of the feedback which was received.

The survey form was created using a combination of HTML and Javascript. Form elements used to collect responses included radio buttons, check boxes, and text boxes. On submission of the form, the form data was subjected to some preliminary processing and then automatically e-mailed to one of the researchers. As expected, the rate at which responses were received was approximately logarithmic. Fifty percent of the responses were received within 12 hours of the invitation e-mail being distributed by the ISP. The rate of responses received decreased after that, with 92% of the responses being received within one week. We stopped response collection after three weeks. The survey form was removed from the Web server and replaced with an acknowledgement thanking people for their interest and informing them that a summary of the results would be posted at the same URL when available.

The ISP estimated that the e-mail inviting participation in the survey was sent to 7,000 customers, and 749 responses were received within the three-week data collection period. The data were extracted from the e-mailed responses and imported into a spreadsheet for subsequent analysis. Once in the spreadsheet, the data comprising each response were carefully checked as it was apparent that a number of responses were duplications of the same response. This checking was achieved through visual inspection and comparison of the data in each record, together with the time each e-mail was generated and any e-mail address or free text data included by the respondents. After this process, 698 usable responses remained, giving an estimated response rate of 10%. Sample characteristics are shown in Table 2.

Based on those respondents that reported their gender, there was a slight imbalance of female respondents (54%) over male respondents (46%). This is consistent with recently reported statistics of New Zealand Internet users (Cullum, 2003). The age distribution of the sample was older than that observed in recent U.S. surveys, where 50 to 60% were aged between 20 and 30 years (Korgaonkar & Wolin, 2002; Ranganathan & Ganapathy, 2002). In our sample, only 18% of respondents reporting their age were 35 years or younger. In contrast, some 65% of respondents were aged between 36 and 60 years. This reflects the age demographic of the ISP customer base, of which 58% are in a similar age bracket.

Sixty-five percent of the sample had used the Internet for three or more years. Some 60% had made an online purchase in the last 12 months, spending varying amounts. Internet shopping was still a relatively infrequent event, with only 11.5% of respondents shopping at least monthly. Some 90% of respondents had access to a credit card, and 90% said they were most likely to shop online from home (9% from work). The products purchased online by our respondents were consistent with previous studies of Internet shopping in other countries (Figure 2). Books and magazines were the most commonly purchased items, with 47% of those respondents who had purchased online having purchased these. Other commonly purchased products were computer software (35%), travel and accommodation (33%), CDs, DVDs, videos, and music (25%), and clothing (22%).

Table 2. Sample characteristics

Characteristic	%	Characteristic	%
Gender (n=671)		*Age (years)* (n=686)	
Male	45.8	Under 18	0.5
Female	54.2	18-25	3.5
		26-35	14.3
Gross household income (NZ$) (n=664)		36-45	24.9
Under 15,000	3.6	46-60	39.8
15,000-25,000	7.4	Over 60	16.9
25,001-35,000	12.3		
35,001-50,000	22.0	*Education level attained* (n=686)	
50,001-75,000	23.3	No formal qualification	2.6
75,001-100,000	15.7	High school	23.2
Over 100,000	15.7	Other vocational qualification	12.8
		Some tertiary study	32.4
Internet experience (years) (n=697)		University graduate	19.7
Under 0.5	4.3	Postgraduate	9.3
0.5-1	9.5		
1-2	21.2	*Employment status* (n=685)	
3-5	41.9	Full time	60.0
Over 5	23.1	Part time	17.8
		Not in paid work	5.1
Amount spent on online purchases		Retired	12.8
in last 12 months (NZ$) (n=698)		Student	4.2
Nil	39.8		
1-50	7.3	*Frequency of online purchases in last*	
51-100	13.5	*12 months for online shoppers* (n=417)	
101-200	9.6	Once or twice	47.5
201-500	13.0	3-6 times	41.0
501-1,000	7.7	Monthly	10.1
Over 1,000	9.0	At least weekly	1.4

The survey was specifically targeted at Internet users in order to control for the effect of variables such as access to Internet shopping. It is possible that, as respondents were self-selected, the sample may reflect some response bias. For example, respondents might be individuals more likely to respond to Web surveys and thus be more likely to shop online. However, the sample displays a reasonable distribution of online purchasers versus non-purchasers, as well as experienced versus less-experienced Internet users. Future surveys could measure the amount of Internet use per week of respondents in order to better understand response bias in this form of survey.

CONSTRUCT VALIDITY AND RELIABILITY

One of the items, that relating to the risk of credit card abuse, was unable to be measured. A programming error in the Web-based survey form meant that all responses for this item returned the same value. Unfortunately, this error was not detected in the analysis of the pilot testing exercise. Reference to perceived risk in the discussion of the results of this study does not, therefore, include this aspect of security risk.

A principal component factor analysis with Varimax rotation was used to assess the validity of the perceived risk (consisting of the remaining four items), perceived benefits, and loss of social interaction constructs. The analysis converged in four iterations, extracting three factors with an eigenvalue of greater than one, which accounted for 70.2% of the total variance. A conventional factor loading of 0.50 or better allowed the unambiguous assignment of all items to one of the three factors (Lee and Turban, 2001;

Figure 2. Most commonly purchased products in this study

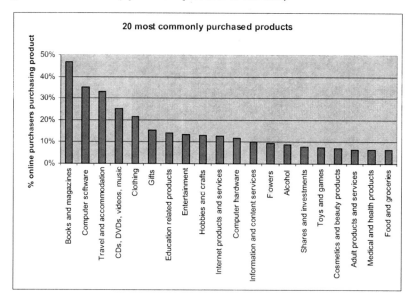

Table 3. Factors, alpha values, items, and loadings

	Factor 1	Factor 2	Factor 3
Cronbach's alpha	0.77	0.76	0.85
Perceived Risk			
Risk of making a poor purchasing decision	0.85		
Inability to compare price	0.81		
Inability to inspect the product	0.76		
Risk of compromising personal information	0.56		
Perceived Benefits			
Convenience of online shopping due to time saved		0.89	
Convenience of online shopping due to effort involved		0.89	
Enjoyment of online shopping		0.68	
Loss of Social Interaction			
Loss of personal contact			0.90
Loss of social shopping experience			0.90

Teo, 2001; Vijayasarathy & Jones, 2000). Table 3 shows the three factors, their items, and loadings. Factors are presented in eigenvalue sequence, and items are shown in order of factor loading within factors. All items loaded onto the appropriate construct. The reliability of the three constructs was assessed using Cronbach's alpha (Table 3). The alpha value for each of the factors exceeded the acceptance level of 0.70 (Cheung & Lee, 2001; Lee & Turban, 2001; Teo, 2001).

RESULTS

The results for the three constructs and the demographic variables (gender, age, education, income, Internet experience, direct shopping experience) are summarised in Table 4. To explore the possible association between the three constructs and the demographic variables, a correlation analysis was performed. Table 5 shows the intercorrelation matrix with Pearson's correlation coefficients. Significant correlations ($p < 0.01$) are shown in bold in Table 5 and are discussed briefly below. The two dependent variables used in the study, frequency and amount of online purchasing, were highly correlated with a Pearson's correlation coefficient of 0.841 (2-tailed significance 0.000).

Age and gender were negatively correlated, with male respondents being older than female respondents. Age was negatively correlated with Internet experience and positively correlated with perceived risk, suggesting that older respondents had used the Internet for less time and were more likely to be risk averse in shopping through this medium. The correlations between gender and income, Internet experience and direct shopping experience suggest that male respondents tended to have been Internet users longer and to have more purchasing power, while female respondents were more likely to have shopped using other direct marketing channels. Female respondents were also more likely to place importance on the perceived risks, perceived benefits and loss of social interaction in shopping online. The results presented in Table 5 also suggest that

Table 4. Summary statistics

	n	Min	Max	Mean	Std dev
Frequency of Online Purchasing	695	1	6	1.99	0.99
Amount of Online Purchasing	698	1	7	3.08	2.10
Perceived Risk	630	1	5	3.67	0.94
Risk of making a poor purchasing decision	654	1	5	3.72	1.23
Inability to compare price	647	1	5	3.42	1.22
Inability to inspect the product	642	1	5	3.43	1.26
Risk of compromising personal information	659	1	5	4.15	1.20
Perceived Benefits	635	1	5	3.44	1.05
Convenience of online shopping due to time saved	653	1	5	3.66	1.27
Convenience due to effort involved	645	1	5	3.75	1.20
Enjoyment of online shopping	643	1	5	2.88	1.36
Loss of Social Interaction	634	1	5	2.13	1.17
Lack of personal contact	647	1	5	2.19	1.26
Lack of social shopping experience	643	1	5	2.09	1.27
Gender (1=male 2=female)	671	1	2	1.54	0.50
Age	686	1	6	4.51	1.07
Education Level	686	1	7	3.73	1.37
Household Income	664	1	7	4.64	1.62
Internet Experience	697	1	5	3.70	1.06
Direct Shopping Experience	696	1	7	2.88	1.76

Table 5. Intercorrelation matrix

	1	2	3	4	5	6	7	8	9
1 Perceived Risk	1.00								
2 Perceived Benefits	.071	1.00							
3 Loss of Social Interaction	**.379**	**.115**	1.00						
4 Gender (1=male 2=female)	**.144**	**.230**	**.119**	1.00					
5 Age	**.112**	-.038	.041	**-.127**	1.00				
6 Education Level	**-.181**	-.018	**-.107**	-.067	-.047	1.00			
7 Household Income	**-.164**	.073	**-.164**	**-.115**	.013	**.219**	1.00		
8 Internet Experience	**-.254**	-.023	**-.220**	**-.216**	**-.119**	**.294**	**.198**	1.00	
9 Direct Shopping Experience	-.006	.096	-.048	**.101**	.029	**.128**	**.244**	.068	1.00

Correlations significant at the 0.01 level (2-tailed) are shown in **bold**

as education level, income and Internet experience increased the importance of perceived risk and loss of social interaction in Internet shopping tended to decrease. As might be expected, there were significant positive correlations between education level and income, Internet experience and direct shopping experience.

In order to test the nine hypotheses associated with the research model, multiple regression analyses were performed to examine the association between the constructs and demographic variables and the two dependent variables that measured online purchasing behaviour (Lee & Turban, 2001; Swaminathan et al., 1999; Teo, 2001; Vijayasarathy & Jones, 2000). Two models were used. The first model used frequency of online purchases as the dependent variable, and the second model used amount of online purchases as the dependent variable. Table 6 shows the results of the regression analyses.

The explanatory power of the models, as indicated by the adjusted $R2$ values shown in Table 6, is 23% for Model 1 and 21% for Model 2. The regression analyses were initially run with only the demographic variables entered so as to examine their effect on online purchasing behaviour. The demographic variables contributed 14% (adjusted $R2 = 0.144$) of the variation in online purchasing behaviour in Model 1 (frequency of Internet purchases), and 16% (adjusted $R2 = 0.156$) of the variation in Model 2 (amount of Internet purchases). In contrast, the three constructs used in the overall regression analysis (Table 6) contributed 8% and 5% of the variation, respectively.

Model 1 shows that both the perceived risk and the perceived benefits of Internet shopping are significantly associated ($p < 0.01$) with the frequency of online purchasing. As expected, for perceived risk this is a negative association, while the perceived benefits construct is positively associated with frequency of online purchasing. Loss of social interaction in Internet shopping is not associated with frequency of online purchasing. However, the results for Model 2 show that all three constructs are significantly associated ($p < 0.05$) with the amount of online purchasing. Loss of social interaction is negatively associated with online purchasing amounts.

With respect to the demographic variables included in the analyses, gender and Internet experience were the only consumer characteristics to have a significant association ($p < 0.01$) with the frequency of online purchasing (Model 1). In Model 2, both these variables were also significantly associated ($p < 0.001$) with the amount purchased online. Income and experience with other direct shopping channels displayed some association with the amount of online purchasing (Model 2). Age and level of education were not associated with online purchasing behaviour in either model.

Overall, the results show that H_1 (consumers who place importance on the perceived risk of Internet shopping are less likely to purchase online) and H_2 (consumers who place importance on the perceived benefits of Internet shopping are more likely to purchase online) are supported. There is some support for H_3 (consumers who place importance on the loss of social interaction in Internet shopping are less likely to purchase online) with respect to the amount of online purchasing.

The remaining hypotheses related to various consumer characteristics. H_4 (males are more likely than females to purchase online) and H_8 (consumers with Internet experience are more likely to purchase online) were both supported. There was weak support of H_7 (consumers with higher incomes are more likely to purchase online) and H_9 (consumers that shop using their direct marketing channels are more likely to purchase online) with respect to the amount of online purchasing. H_5 (older consumers are less likely to purchase online) and H_6 (consumers with higher education are more likely to purchase online) were not supported.

Table 6. Regression results

Model 1: Dependent variable *Frequency of online purchases*			
	df	Sum of squares	Mean square
Regression	9	139.985	15.554
Residual	598	453.000	0.758
F = 20.533 Significance of F = 0.000			
	Standardised Beta	t	p <
Perceived Risk	-0.281	-7.020	0.000
Perceived Benefits	0.108	2.907	0.004
Loss of Social Interaction	-0.031	-0.794	0.428
Gender	-0.130	-3.363	0.001
Age	-0.016	-0.425	0.671
Education Level	0.034	0.884	0.377
Household Income	0.067	1.726	0.085
Internet Experience	0.202	5.078	0.000
Direct Shopping Experience	0.056	1.482	0.139
R^2 = 0.236 Adjusted R^2 = 0.225			

Model 2: Dependent variable *Amount of online purchases*			
	df	Sum of squares	Mean square
Regression	9	591.115	65.679
Residual	598	2094.234	3.502
F = 18.755 Significance of F = 0.000			
	Standardised Beta	t	p <
Perceived Risk	-0.194	-4.815	0.000
Perceived Benefits	0.095	2.534	0.012
Loss of Social Interaction	-0.085	-2.141	0.033
Gender	-0.162	-4.142	0.000
Age	0.014	0.390	0.697
Education Level	0.027	0.707	0.480
Household Income	0.076	1.944	0.052
Internet Experience	0.208	5.167	0.000
Direct Shopping Experience	0.078	2.058	0.040
R^2 = 0.220 Adjusted R^2 = 0.208			

Note: df = degrees of freedom

DISCUSSION

Overall, it seems that the perceived negative consequences of Internet shopping, specifically product and privacy risk, and the loss of social interaction, are closely associated with online purchasing behaviour. Perceived risk seems to deter Internet users from shopping online frequently and from spending significant amounts of money. Prior findings on the influence of perceived risk on Internet purchasing are mixed. Of the six studies summarised in Table 7, only half found a significant association between these two variables. However, consistent with Swaminathan et al. (1999), this current study found that consumers who place a high value of importance on personal contact and the social benefits of shopping are likely to spend less online than their counterparts who place less value on the social shopping experience.

The perceived benefits of Internet shopping were also found to be significantly associated with online purchasing behaviour. Consumers who value the convenience and enjoyment of Internet shopping tend to purchase more online and more often. This is consistent with prior studies of this factor (Table 7), including recent findings from Hong Kong (Lee et al., 2003).

Despite the diminishing gender differences between Internet users in New Zealand and elsewhere (e.g., Howell & Mariott, 2001), which was reflected in the survey sample where 54% of respondents were female, gender continued to show a significant association with online purchasing behaviour. Consistent with studies in Singapore (Teo, 2001) and the U.S. (Li et al., 1999) (Table 7), male respondents were likely to spend more on online purchases and shop online more frequently than were female respondents.

The significant positive correlation between gender and both perceived risk and loss of social interaction (Table 5) suggests that this may partly reflect a tendency for female consumers to place more importance on the risks and social benefits of Internet shopping. However, gender was significantly correlated with perceived benefits, suggesting that female consumers also value the convenience and enjoyment offered by Internet shopping. These results confirm Swaminathan et al.'s (1999) finding that males are less motivated than females by social interaction in Internet shopping, but contradict their other finding, that males are more convenience-oriented than females in this medium. Female respondents in this study were also likely to have less Internet experience and less income, both of which (to different and varying extents) were positively associated with online purchasing behaviour.

The type of products purchased by male and female respondents may also influence the association between gender and the amount and frequency of online purchasing (Bhatnagar et al., 2000). An analysis of products purchased by gender revealed that, compared to female respondents, male respondents were significantly more common purchasers of 6 of the 12 most commonly purchased product categories shown in Figure 2 (books and magazines; computer software; CDs, DVDs, videos, music; Internet products and services; computer hardware; information and content services). Clothing was the only product in this group that women were significantly more common purchasers of.

Consistent with other studies of Internet shopping in the U.S. and New Zealand (Table 7), this study found that the frequency of shopping online and the amount spent online are positively associated with the Internet experience of consumers. One explanation is the negative correlation between Internet experience and the perceived risk construct (Table 5). It appears that as Internet experience increases, perceived product risk and personal risk decreases, suggesting that experience with using the Internet generates confidence in its trustworthiness as a shopping medium. Income was also negatively correlated with perceived risk. It is possible that consumers with higher household incomes are less concerned about the inability to inspect products or compare prices when shopping online. Internet experience was also significantly associated with the loss of social interaction construct, the importance of which decreased as Internet experience increased. One interpretation is that as consumers become more experienced with using the Internet, the absence of social benefits in online shopping appears less important.

Earlier studies of Internet purchasing in the U.S. found that as the age of consumers increased (Bellman et al., 1999; Bhatnagar et al., 2000) and their level of education increased (Bellman et al., 1999), so did their Internet purchasing (Table 7). However,

Table 7. Comparison of findings with prior studies of online purchasing

Factor	Present study	Prior studies
Perceived risk	Consumers who place importance on the perceived risk of Internet shopping are less likely to purchase online	**Vijayasarathy & Jones (2000)** US Consumer risk negatively influences attitude towards Internet shopping and intention to shop online **Kim et al. (2000)** US No significant association between perceived risk and online purchasing **Liu & Wei (2003)** Singapore Perceived risk has an inverse effect on intention to shop online **Van der Heijden et al. (2003)** Netherlands Perceived risk negatively effects attitude towards online purchasing **Jarvenpaa et al. (1999)** Australia Perceived risk of Internet shopping did not affect willingness to buy from an Internet store **Pires et al. (2004)** Australia Experience factors do not appear to reduce perceived risk. **George (2004)** US Trustworthiness of the web is related to purchase behavior **Forsythe & Bi (2003)** US Perceived risk does not significantly affect the patronage behaviour of current shoppers **Cho (2004)** US Security concerns do not have a statistically significant influence on the likelihood to abort a transaction **Huang et al. (2004)** US The presence of a brand name had a negative effect on the perceived risk of online shopping security **Corbitt et al. (2003)** NZ Perceived risk is not significantly correlated with participation in Internet shopping
Perceived benefits	Consumers who place importance on the perceived benefits of Internet shopping are more likely to purchase online	**Swaminathan et al. (1999)** US Consumers who value convenience shop online more frequently and spend more **Kim et al. (2000)** US Time-constrained lifestyle is positively associated with Internet purchasing behaviour **Vijayasarathy & Jones (2000)** US Internet shopping convenience, lifestyle compatibility and fun positively influence attitude towards Internet shopping and intention to shop online **Lee et al. (2003)** Hong Kong Enjoyment and convenience are positively associated with customer satisfaction with online purchasing **Rohm & Swaminathan (2004)** US The convenience shopper is one of four broad types of online shopper **Cho (2004)** US Better product and value offerings, control in information search and effort saving evoke positive attitudes towards online shopping
Loss of social interaction	Consumers who place importance on the loss of social interaction in Internet shopping are likely to spend less online	**Swaminathan et al. (1999)** US Consumers who value the social shopping experience shop online less frequently and spend less

consistent with Teo's (2001) Singapore study, this study found no significant association between Internet purchasing and age or education. This probably reflects the relatively high age and education levels of respondents in this study (the most common age group was 46-60 years, and over 60% of respondents had at least some tertiary level education (Table 2)) and the declining influence of these demographic variables as Internet use increases in the general population.

Table 7. (continued)

Gender	Males are more likely than females to purchase online	**Li et al. (1999)** US Men are more frequent online purchasers than women **Bhatnagar et al. (2000)** US Effect of gender on Internet purchasing is mixed, and tends to vary with product category **Teo (2001)** Singapore Males are more likely to purchase online than females **Forsythe & Shi (2003)** US Men are slightly more likely than women to be heavy online shoppers **Chang and Samuel (2004)** Australia Online shoppers who shop frequently tend to be male
Age	No significant association between age and Internet purchasing	**Bellman et al. (1999)** mainly US The higher a person's age, the more likely that person will buy online **Bhatnagar et al. (2000)** US Older consumers are more open to Internet purchasing **Teo (2001)** Singapore No significant association between age and Internet purchasing **Sorce et al. (2005)** US Older shoppers search less online but purchase equal amounts **Chang and Samuel (2004)** Australia Frequent online shoppers tend to be middle-aged (aged 24 to 44)
Education	No significant association between educational level and Internet purchasing	**Bellman et al. (1999)** mainly US The higher a person's education, the more likely that person will buy online **Teo (2001)** Singapore No significant association between education level and Internet purchasing
Household income	A weak association between income and amount spent online	**Li et al. (1999)** US Consumers with higher incomes are more likely to be frequent online purchasers **Bellman et al. (1999)** mainly US The higher a person's income, the more likely and frequently that person will buy online **Kim et al. (2000)** US Consumers with more disposable income are more likely to purchase online **Forsythe & Shi (2003** US The higher the household income, the greater the likelihood of being a moderate or heavy online shopper **Chang and Samuel (2004)** Australia Online shoppers who shop very frequently tend to have higher incomes

Prior studies that examined the association between income and Internet purchasing (Table 7) show that disposable income tends to affect the likelihood or frequency of shopping online. However, this study found only a weak association between household income and the amount spent online. This suggests that , similar to age and education, income was most influential in providing access to Internet shopping, and that its influence on the likelihood of online purchasing is diminishing as Internet use becomes

Table 7. (continued)

| Internet experience | Consumers with Internet experience are more likely to purchase online | **Kim et al. (2000)** US
Internet-oriented lifestyle is positively associated with Internet purchasing behaviour
Bhatnagar et al. (2000) US
Consumers with more Internet experience are more open to Internet purchasing
George (2002) US
Internet experience is associated with more frequent Internet purchasing
Corbitt et al. (2003) New Zealand
Internet experience is positively correlated with participation in Internet shopping
Forsythe & Shi (2003 US
Internet users with more Internet experience are more likely to purchase online |
| Direct shopping experience | Consumers that shop using other direct marketing channels are likely to spend more online | **Jarvenpaa et al. (1999)** Australia
Extent of other direct shopping experience is positively correlated with willingness to buy from an Internet store |

more mainstream. We would still expect some association between income and the amount spent online to continue as disposable income potentially influences spending in any form.

This study also found support for the idea that consumers who make purchases using other direct marketing channels, such as television or mail order, are likely to spend more online. This is somewhat consistent with an earlier study of Australian Internet users by Jarvenpaa et al. (1999), who correlated direct shopping experience with willingness to buy from an Internet store. We suggest that the possible relationship between direct shopping experience and Internet purchasing deserves further exploration.

IMPLICATIONS FOR INTERNET RETAILERS

We now highlight the implications of our findings for Internet retailing vendors through a discussion of a range of Web site features under the control of Internet vendors that can potentially mitigate negative consumer perceptions or enhance positive consumer perceptions of the Internet shopping experience.

To minimise perceived risk, consumers often resort to various risk-reduction strategies. In terms of product risk, these can include using brand awareness or vendor reputation as a guide to product quality, or relying on vendor offers such as money-back guarantees to mitigate the risk of making a poor purchasing decision, partially overcoming the inability to physically inspect a product in an online shopping transaction (Jarvenpaa & Tractinsky, 1999; Lee & Turban, 2001; Lim, 2003; Liu & Wei, 2003; Talaga & Tucci, 2001; Tan, 1999; Ward & Lee, 2000). Past experience with a particular product might also be expected to reduce the perceived risk of purchasing that product online. With regard to security and privacy risk, the presence of a secure transaction facility tends to reduce a consumer's perceived security risk in making an Internet purchase (Bellman et al., 1999; Furnell & Karweni, 1999; Ranganathan & Ganapathy, 2002). There is also some evidence that the inclusion of a clear policy on the privacy of customer information on a Web site might mitigate consumers' perceived privacy risk (Hoffman et al., 1999).

A variety of vendor-related Web site features might also be expected to influence purchasing behaviour in relation to the Internet shopping experience. For example, Ranganathan and Ganapathy (2002) discussed the importance of design and information content factors in effective B2C Web sites as perceived by online consumers. These factors include complete information on products and services, access to information through search tools, decision aids for evaluating alternatives, speed of Web page loading, ease of navigation and aesthetic appeal. Koivumaki (2001) also noted that navigational experience is one of the main components in overall Internet shopping experience, while Swaminathan et al. (1999) emphasised the importance of rich information. Vijayasarathy and Jones (2000) suggested that Internet shopping is likely to become popular because of quick access to extensive product information and the ability to make more price comparisons. Lohse and Spiller (1999) suggested that extra product information, navigation, and interactive customer service are important features of Internet stores. Kim and Lim (2001) also included customer service in their list of Web site attributes important to Internet shoppers.

The survey used in this study also asked respondents to evaluate the importance of 12 vendor-related Web site features that could act as risk-relieving strategies for Internet shoppers or otherwise influence purchasing behaviour in relation to the shopping experience. The results are shown in Table 8. The features are listed in rank order based on the percentage of respondents that rated a specific feature as important (4 or 5 on a 5-point Likert scale with 1 representing "not important" and 5 representing "very important").

The results presented in Table 8 indicate that despite the increase in Internet retailing experience since earlier studies, security and privacy concerns still remain prevalent in consumers' perceptions of online shopping. The three most important risk-relieving features found in this study were the presence of a secure transaction capability, a clear policy on privacy of customer information, and a money-back guarantee. The latter would act to mitigate the risk of making a poor purchasing decision. Vendor reputation was also ranked relatively high as a way of relieving product risk.

In terms of vendor-related Web site features that are likely to influence the Internet shopping experience, ease of Web site navigation and detailed product information were the two most highly ranked features. This reinforces the suggestion by Koivumaki (2001) and Ranganathan and Ganapathy (2002) among others, that information content and navigational experience are major components in the overall Internet shopping experience. The next three most important Web site features were online customer support, speed of page loading, and a product search capability. Interestingly, a product comparison facility, a feature commonly associated with the comparative advantage of Internet shopping, was not ranked particularly high in importance in this survey.

The results of this study suggest that, despite the increase in Internet retailing experience since earlier studies, concerns about risk remain prevalent in consumers' perceptions of online shopping. The study confirms the need for Internet vendors to invest in risk reduction measures in order to encourage consumers to shop online (Corbitt et al., 2003; Lim, 2003). Web site features that reduce perceived risk, whether related to product purchase, security, or privacy concerns, continue to be an important aspect of Internet retailing design. As Limayem et al. (2000) suggest, security and privacy measures should be publicised to in order to reassure nervous online shoppers. The findings of this study reinforce the need for Internet vendors to foster online consumer trust across multiple dimensions (Tan & Sutherland, 2004).

In terms of the Internet shopping experience itself, this study found that the perceived convenience and enjoyment benefits of Internet shopping are associated with increased online purchasing, as are the loss of social interaction benefits. Consumers who place a high degree of importance on the lack of personal contact or social benefits in Internet shopping are likely to spend less online. Thus, in terms of vendor-related Web site features that are likely to improve the Internet shopping experience, ease of Web site navigation, speed of Web page loading, and quick access to detailed product information are critical. Customisation to provide information necessary for a purchase decision and streamlining the transactional process should increase the convenience benefits perceived by online consumers (Bellman et al., 1999; Limayem et al., 2000).

Improving customer service may be one way in which Internet retailers can overcome the loss of personal contact in online shopping (Kim & Lim, 2001; Lohse & Spiller, 1999). Synchronous or asynchronous computer-mediated communication (e.g., Web chat or electronic mail contact with a customer service representative) offers one

Table 8. Importance of vendor-related Web site features

Rank	Feature	% respondents ranking feature as 'important'
	Risk-relieving strategies	
1	Secure transaction capability	88
2	Money back guarantee	80
3	Privacy policy	78
4	Vendor reputation	71
5	Product is known	58
6	Product brand	56
	Shopping experience	
1	Ease of navigation	81
2	Product information	78
3	Online customer support	74
4	Speed of page loading	70
5	Product search capability	70
6	Product is immediately available	52

approach to doing this. Online communities, discussion groups, chat rooms, and customer reviews are all mechanisms that some Internet retailers are using to encourage interaction between customers. They allow shoppers to interact as they search for information and recommendations, make buying decisions, and report feedback on their experiences (Swaminathan et al., 1999). Other social dimensions of shopping could be simulated online using the Internet to connect multiple shoppers in different geographic locations within a virtual showroom.

CONCLUSIONS

This study developed a research model of online purchasing behaviour based on consumer perceptions and beliefs about Internet shopping. Three main constructs were used as the independent variables. These were perceived risk, and the positive and negative aspects of the Internet shopping experience. Perceived risk measured various dimensions of perceived risk in Internet shopping relating to product and privacy risk. The two Internet shopping experience constructs focused on the perceived convenience and enjoyment benefits of Internet shopping and on the loss of social interaction in the shopping experience. The model also considered the possible association of a range of consumer characteristics, including gender, age, education level, household income, Internet experience, and other direct shopping experience, with online purchasing behaviour.

The contribution of this study lies in the confirmation of the importance of consumers' perceptions of the risk and benefits of Internet shopping in encouraging online purchasing. The study also found that consumers who value social interaction in shopping are likely to spend less online. The implication is that Internet retailers need to continually adjust their virtual storefronts to the needs and attitudes of their target customers. This study places renewed emphasis on reproducing the perceived security and customer service of traditional shopping channels. In particular, attention should be paid to Web site navigation; the provision of detailed product information and the use of a money-back guarantee; a clear policy on privacy of customer information and a secure transaction capability; and the development of interactive online customer support and engagement.

Despite suggestions that demographic variables are becoming less significant in Internet shopping, this study found that the gender and Internet experience of online shoppers remain significantly associated with their purchasing behaviour. Male consumers are still more likely to shop online than female Internet users, and experienced Internet users also shop more online, and spend more online, than their less experienced counterparts. To a lesser extent, higher income was associated with the amount spent online, and consumers who purchased through other direct marketing channels were also likely to spend more online.

This study focused on consumer-related aspects of Internet shopping. We do not deny the importance of other factors that might be associated with consumer decisions to make Internet purchases, such as the availability and relative price of products or technical aspects of Internet retailing. It is also important to note that this study was based on a sample of older Internet users than previous studies, and that the perceived risk of credit card abuse was not included in the eventual perceived risk construct.

The New Zealand context provides a useful extension of and comparison with prior studies conducted using consumers in other countries. The results of this study confirm similar findings from studies conducted in the U.S., South East Asia, and Australasia. Further research is needed to confirm the results of this study in countries with a similar population and Internet uptake, perhaps in Europe. Research is also needed on online purchasing behaviour in developing economies and in the rapidly growing economies of the wider Asia region. The changing pattern of Internet adoption in the populations of all countries ensures continued interest in such research.

ACKNOWLEDGMENT

The authors would like to acknowledge the contribution of Fiona Thompson to this study.

REFERENCES

Ahuja, M., Gupta, B., & Raman, P. (2003). An empirical investigation of online consumer purchasing behaviour. *Communications of the ACM, 46*(12), 145-151.

Bellman, S., Lohse, G. L., & Johnson, E. J. (1999). Predictors of online buying behaviour. *Communications of the ACM, 42*(12), 32-38.

Bhatnagar, A., & Ghose, S. (2004). Segmenting consumers based on the benefits and risks of Internet shopping. *Journal of Business Research, 57,* 1352-1360.

Bhatnagar, A., Misra, S., & Rao, H. R. (2000). On risk, convenience, and Internet shopping behaviour. *Communications of the ACM, 43*(11), 98-105.

Boyer, K. K., Olson, J. R., & Jackson, E. C. (2001). Electronic surveys: Advantages and disadvantages over traditional print surveys. *Decision Line, 32*(4), 4-7.

Chang, J., & Samuel, N. (2004). Internet shopper demographics and buying behaviour in Australia. *Journal of the American Academy of Business, 5,* 171-176.

Cheung, C. M. K., & Lee, M. K. O. (2001). Trust in Internet shopping: Instrument development and validation through classical and modern approaches. *Journal of Global Information Management, 9*(3), 23-35.

Cho, J. (2004). Likelihood to abort an online transaction: Influences from cognitive evaluations, attitudes, and behavioural variables. *Information & Management, 41,* 827-838.

Corbitt, B. J., Thanasankit, T., & Yi, H. (2003). Trust and e-commerce: A study of consumer perceptions. *Electronic Commerce Research and Applications, 2,* 203-215.

Cullum, C. (2003). New Zealand online: Report one 2003 highlights. *Phoenix Research.* Retrieved from http://www.phoenix.co.nz/about/articles/nzonline.html

Dillman, D. A. (2000). *Mail and Internet surveys: The tailored design method.* New York: Wiley.

Forsythe, S. M., & Shi, B. (2003). Consumer patronage and risk perceptions in Internet shopping. *Journal of Business Research, 56,* 867-875.

Furnell, S. M., & Karweni, T. (1999). Security implications of electronic commerce: A survey of consumers and business. *Internet Research, 9*(5), 372-382.

Garbarino, E., & Strahilevitz, M. (2004). Gender differences in the perceived risk of buying online and the effects of receiving a site recommendation. *Journal of Business Research, 57,* 768-775.

George, J. F. (2002). Influences on the intent to make Internet purchases. *Internet Research, 12*(2), 165-180.

George, J. F. (2004). The theory of planned behaviour and Internet purchasing. *Internet Research, 14*(3), 198-212.

Hoffman, D. L., Novak, T. P., & Peralta, M. (1999). Building consumer trust online. *Communications of the ACM, 42*(4), 80-85.

Howell, B., & Mariott, L. (2001). *The state of e-New Zealand: 12 months on.* New Zealand Institute for the Study of Competition and Regulation. Retrieved February 28, 2006, from http://www.iscr.org.nz/documents/12_months_on.pdf

Huang, W., Schrank, H., & Bubinsky, A. J. (2004). Effect of brand name on consumers' risk perceptions of online shopping. *Journal of Consumer Behaviour, 4*(1), 40-50.

IDC (2002a). Internet and e-commerce, 2001. *Internet Commerce Market Model (ICMM) version 7.3, 2002.*

IDC (2002b). *European Internet commerce to surpass $1,500 billion by 2005, says IDC.* Press release, January 7, 2002. Retrieved September 14, 2002, from http://www.idc.com/getdoc.jhtml?containerId=pr2002_01_07_102535

Jarvenpaa, S. L., & Todd, P. A. (1997). Consumer reactions to electronic shopping on the World Wide Web. *International Journal of Electronic Commerce, 1*(2), 59-88.

Jarvenpaa, S. L., & Tractinsky, N. (1999). Consumer trust in an Internet store: A cross-cultural validation. *Journal of Computer-Mediated Communication, 5*(2). Retrieved February 28, 2006, from http://jcmc.indiana.edu/vol5/issue2/hairong.html

Jarvenpaa, S. L., Tractinsky, N., & Vitale, M. (1999). Consumer trust in an Internet store. *Information Technology & Management, 1*(1&2), 45-72.

Jones, J. M., & Vijayasarathy, L. R. (1998) Internet consumer catalog shopping: Findings from an exploratory study and directions for future research. *Internet Research, 8*(4), 322-330.

Katz, J., & Aspden, P. (1997). Motivations for and barriers to Internet usage: Results of a national public opinion survey. *Internet Research, 7*(3), 170-188.

Kim, D. J., Cho, B. & Rao, H. R. (2000). Effects of consumer lifestyles on purchasing behavior on the Internet: A conceptual framework and empirical validation. *Proceedings of the 21st International Conference on Information Systems* (pp. 688-695). Atlanta, GA: Association for Information Systems.

Kim, S. Y., & Lim, Y. J. (2001). Consumers' perceived importance of and satisfaction with Internet shopping. *Electronic Markets, 11*(3), 148-154.

Koivumaki, T. (2001). Customer satisfaction and purchasing behaviour in a Web-based shopping environment. *Electronic Markets, 11*(3), 186-192.

Kolsaker, A., Lee-Kelly, L., & Choy, P. C. (2004). The reluctant Hong Kong consumer: Purchasing travel online. *International Journal of Consumer Studies, 28*(3), 295-304.

Korgaonkar, P., & Wolin, L. D. (2002). Web usage, advertising, and shopping: Relationship patterns. *Internet Research, 12*(2), 191-204.

Lee, J., Pi, S., Kwok, R. C., & Huynh, M. Q. (2003). The contribution of commitment value in Internet commerce: An empirical investigation. *Journal of the Association for Information Systems, 4,* 39-64.

Lee, M. K. O., & Turban, E. (2001). A trust model for consumer Internet shopping. *International Journal of Electronic Commerce, 6*(1), 75-91.

Li, H., Kuo, C., & Russell, M. G. (1999). The impact of perceived channel utilities, shopping orientations, and demographics on the consumer's online buying behavior. *Journal of Computer-Mediated Communication, 5*(2). Retrieved February 28, 2006, from http://www.ascusc.org/jcmc/vol5/issue2/hairong.html

Liebermann, Y., & Stashevsky, S. (2002). Perceived risks as barriers to Internet and e-commerce usage. *Qualitative Market Research, 5*(4), 291-300.

Lim, N. (2003). Consumers' perceived risk: Sources versus consequences. *Electronic Commerce Research and Applications, 2*, 216-228.

Limayem, M., Khalifa, M., & Frini, A. (2000). What makes consumers buy from the Internet? A longitudinal study of online shopping. *IEEE Transactions on Systems, Man, and Cybernetics – Part A: Systems and Humans, 30*(4), 421-432.

Liu, X., & Wei, K. K. (2003). An empirical study of product differences in consumers' e-commerce adoption behaviour. *Electronic Commerce Research and Applications, 2*, 229-239.

Lohse, G. L., & Spiller, P. (1999). Internet retail store design: How the user interface influences traffic and sales. *Journal of Computer-Mediated Communication, 5*(2). Retrieved February 28, 2006, from http://jcmc.indiana.edu/vol5/issue2/lohse.htm

Ministry of Economic Development (2000). *E-commerce: A guide for New Zealand business*. Retrieved February 28, 2006, from http://www.med.govt.nz/templates/MultipageDocumentTOC____9842.aspx

Nua Internet Surveys. (2006). *How many online?* Dublin: ComputerScope. Retrieved February 28, 2006, from http://www.nua.ie/surveys/how_many_online/asia.html

Park, C. -H., & Kim, Y. -G. (2003). Identifying key factors affecting consumer purchase behavior in an online shopping context. *International Journal of Retail & Distribution Management, 31*(1), 16-29.

Pires, G., Stanton, J., & Eckford, A. (2004). Influences on the perceived risk of purchasing online. *Journal of Consumer Behavior, 4*(2), 118-131.

Ranganathan, C., & Ganapathy, S. (2002). Key dimensions of business-to-consumer Web sites. *Information & Management, 39*(6), 457-465.

Rohm, A., & Swaminathan, V. (2004). A typology of online shoppers based on shopping motivations. *Journal of Business Research, 57*, 748-757.

Saeed, K. A., Hwang, Y., & Yi, M. Y. (2003). Toward an integrative framework for online consumer behaviour research: A meta-analysis approach. *Journal of End User Computing, 15*(4), 1-26.

Sorce, P., Perotti, V., & Widrick, S. (2005). Attitude and age differences in online buying. *International Journal of Retail & Distribution Management, 33*(2), 122-132.

Swaminathan, V., Lepkowska-White, E. & Rao, B. P. (1999). Browsers or buyers in cyberspace? An investigation of factors influencing electronic exchange. *Journal of Computer-Mediated Communication, 5*(2). Retrieved February 28, 2006, from http://jcmc.indiana.edu/vol5/issue2/swaminathan.htm

Talaga, J. A., & Tucci, L. A. (2001). Consumer tradeoffs in online textbook purchasing. *Journal of Consumer Marketing, 18*(1), 10-20.

Tan, F. B., & Sutherland, P. (2004). Online consumer trust: A multi-dimensional model. *Journal of Electronic Commerce in Organizations, 2*(3), 41-59.

Tan, S. J. (1999). Strategies for reducing consumers' risk aversion in Internet shopping. *Journal of Consumer Marketing, 16*(2), 163-180.

Teo, S. H. T. (2001). Demographic and motivation variables associated with Internet usage activities. *Internet Research, 11*(2), 125-137.

van der Heijden, H., Verhagen, T., & Creemers, M. (2003). Understanding online purchase intentions: Contributions from technology and trust perspectives. *European Journal of Information Systems, 12*, 41-48.

Vehovar, V., Manfreda, K. L., & Batagelj, Z. (2000, June 19-21). Sensitivity of e-commerce measurement to survey instrument. *Proceedings of the 13th International Bled Electronic Commerce Conference, Bled, Slovenia, 2000* (pp. 528-543). Kranj, Slovenia: University of Maribor.

Vijayasarathy, L. R., & Jones, J. M. (2000). Print and Internet catalog shopping: Assessing attitudes and intentions. *Internet Research, 10*(3), 191-202.

Wang, H., Lee, M. K. O., & Wang, C. (1998). Consumer privacy concerns about Internet marketing. *Communications of the ACM, 41*(3), 63: 70.

Ward, M. R., & Lee, M. J. (2000). Internet shopping, consumer search, and product branding. *Journal of Product & Brand Management, 9*(1), 6-20.

Watkin, T. (2004, June 5). Netting big bargains. *The New Zealand Listener*, 18.

Chapter X

An Investigation of Revenue Streams of New Zealand Online Content Providers

Prateek Vasisht, Air New Zealand, New Zealand

Jairo A. Gutiérrez, University of Auckland, New Zealand

ABSTRACT

This chapter describes an empirical investigation into the revenue streams of online content providers in New Zealand. It extends previous academic literature by taking a broader scope and a unique geographic focus (New Zealand). Framed according to a proposed integrated classification of revenue streams and supporting features, which identifies six revenue streams and four supporting features, the study investigates the satisfaction levels of content providers with the revenue stream(s) they use, the issues faced in generating revenue and whether the supporting features support the revenue generating capacity of content sites. After applying certain eligibility criteria, 36 sites comprised the target population of which 11 were represented. Web site examinations coupled with a mixture of face-to-face and e-mail interviews with senior managers comprised the data collection instruments. Respondents used all six revenue streams to monetize their online content. A profile of revenue stream usage, satisfaction levels with revenue stream performance, the issues surrounding revenue generation and the contributions of supporting features are presented.

INTRODUCTION

The magic word these days is to monetize, or convert customer satisfaction and loyalty at a Web site into a commercially viable relationship (Rayport, 1999). The reality for content providers however has been rather harrowing; revenue models are in a flux, and contradictory experiences with revenue generation have further confused practitioners: for instance, while a subscription-based approach seemingly works for the WSJ, the subscription-oriented National Business Review (NZ) site consistently hemorrhaged money before converting to a free offering (Gallaugher, Auger, & BarNir, 2001; Greenstein, 2000; Tomsen, 2000; Hutchinson, 2001). Motivated by the currency of the topic and this apparent environment of confusion, this research examines the revenue streams of online content providers. Related previous research has focused on the profit strategies of online newspapers (Mensing, 1997) and revenue streams of online magazines (Gallaugher et al., 2001). By studying content providers and including indirect sources of revenue, this research takes a broader perspective and for the first time, focuses on the experiences of New Zealand content providers. An exploratory study, it empirically gauges the satisfaction levels of New Zealand content providers with their revenue streams and elicits the issues surrounding revenue generation to create a first understanding of content revenue streams in New Zealand. Consequently, existing literature is extended in terms of scope and geographic focus.

INTEGRATED CLASSIFICATION

Online content providers use the Internet to distribute copyrighted content like news, movies, and other types of information (Eisenmann, 2002). To get a comprehensive overview of the main revenue streams used by online content providers, the classifications of five authors (Eisenmann, 2002; Tomsen, 2000; Zerdick et al., 2000; Gallaugher et al., 2001; Mensing, 1997) who categorized the revenue streams of content providers, online media firms, online magazines and newspapers, were selected from the literature. These were then synthesized to propose the integrated classification (Figure 1). The bottom row depicts the subcategory of content providers the respective classifications relate to. Revenue streams are listed in a way that groups equivalent definitions together. The rightmost column depicts the categories[1] identified by the mapping process.

The proposed integrated classification of revenue streams and supporting features identifies six revenue streams (advertising, subscription, pay-per-view, sales & affiliate programs, syndication, wireless) and four supporting features (newsletters, communities, registration, personalization). It encompasses the main revenue streams used by content providers, indirect revenue sources, and the latest revenue stream — wireless. Building on Mensing (1997), the integrated classification distinguishes between subscription-based access to site content and premium services. Arrangements under which sites offer free content but charge for premium offerings (like newsletters and community areas) are grouped with pay-per-access arrangements (like paid archives) under the pay-per-view category. As the title reflects, pay-per-access arrangements are the *primary focus* of this category and premium offerings the secondary focus. The integrated classification also amalgamates merchandise sales and affiliate programs, mainly because many affiliate programs belong to e-tailers, an arrangement which is essentially

Figure 1. Integrated classification

(Eisenmann, 2002)	(Tomsen, 2000)	(Zerdick et al., 2000)	(Gallaugher et al., 2001)	Mensing (1997)	INTEGRATED CATEGORY	
Ad revenue	Advertising	Advertising	Advertising	Advertising	**ADVERTISING**	Main Revenue Streams
Paid content	Subscription	Subscription	Subscription	Subscriptions	**SUBSCRIPTION**	
	Pay per access		Per unit charge for online content	Premium services	**PAY-PER-VIEW**	
		Transaction	Sale of additional merchandise		**SALES & AFFILIATE PROGRAMS**	
		Commission	Affiliate	Transaction Potential		
Licensing	Syndication		Syndication		**SYNDICATION**	
					WIRELESS	
	Registration	and Newsletters - included independently			*Supporting Features*	Supporting Features
	Personalization					
	Communities					
Content Providers	**Content Providers**	**On-line Media**	**Online magazines**	**Online newspapers**	***CONTENT PROVIDERS***	

equivalent to *selling* merchandise. While the revenue potential of wireless content provision has been acknowledged, it has not been formally included in a revenue stream classification of content providers. The integrated classification categorizes wireless as a distinct revenue stream. Tomsen (2000) classifies registration, online communities and personalization as Web site features and describes how they can augment site revenues. Following that idea, registration, communities and personalization are classified as revenue-supporting features. Newsletters are also independently posited as revenue-supporting features.

Advertising: Content providers generate revenue by charging advertisers wanting to access site visitors; and, since ad payments are usually proportional to audience size, online content providers maximize revenue by maximizing their user base — which often means providing free content (Eisenmann, 2002). Advertising is a vital source of revenue as consumers continue to demand free content (Gallaugher et al., 2001). However, given its popularity, competition is fierce and ad revenues remain disproportionately concentrated among a handful of top sites (PWC & IAB, 2002). The branding versus click through debate is a key issue facing the advertising model. When it began on the Internet, advertising was mainly seen as a direct response tool (eMarketer, 2002). While direct response metrics (click-through) are easy to observe and indicate an immediate interest in the advertisement, they underestimate exposure: click-through may not have occurred but exposure to the advertisement may have promoted brand awareness (Briggs & Hollis, 1997; Mullarkey, 2001). Indeed, studies now show that online advertisements enhance brands (Briggs, 2001; Briggs, Sullivan, & Webster, 2001). Branding nevertheless remains hard to "sell" as most people dealing with online advertising are direct response oriented (Smith, 2002b). Newer technologies like rich media ads (using animation and video) and broadband are expected to promote greater user engagement and increase the time spent online (Eisenmann, 2002; eMarketer, 2002; Tomsen, 2000). These projections hold promise for the advertising model.

Subscriptions: Advertising is about leveraging a large audience base for ad revenue. Firms implementing subscription models, however, ask — can we garner greater benefit from a smaller paying population than from a larger base attracted by free offerings (Gallaugher et al., 2001)? The Internet started out as an open community to encourage the free exchange of information, and users steeped in this tradition continue to demand free information (Hutchinson, 2001; Mings & White, 2000). Indeed, according to a recent Jupiter survey, 70% of online adults polled "could not understand why anyone would pay for online content" (Jupiter Research, 2001). Philosophical idiosyncrasies aside, easily available free substitutes are a major disincentive to pay. Another reason for user reluctance to pay arises from the fact that information goods are experience goods and as Shapiro and Varian (1999) exemplify — how do you know whether today's newspaper is worth 75 cents until you have read it? Success with subscriptions has generally been rare and the winners rely on providing unique content in a specialist field (Kennerdale, 2001). As Smith (2002a) succinctly notes, fee-based approaches are likely to succeed or fail on a case-by-case basis, sector-by-sector and brand-by-brand basis.

Pay-per-View: Enabled by the low distribution costs offered by the Internet and micro-payment technologies, disaggregating strategies such as per-use fees enable sellers to maximize their profits by price discriminating when consumers are heterogeneous (Bakos & Brynjolfsson, 2000). Pay-per-view schemes allow content providers to generate revenue from visitors who would not pay for a subscription but would pay for immediate access to selected content (Gallaugher et al., 2001). Publishers however may find pay-per-view schemes unattractive for four reasons: users are reluctant to pay for content, revenues are less predictable compared to subscriptions, volume of revenue generated is small and more importantly, attempts to implement efficient micro-payment collection and processing systems have generally floundered (Anders, 2001; McGarvey, 2001; Miller, 2001b; Shirky, 2000). In fact, a chicken and egg scenario operates in the latter case: firms hesitate to install micropayment systems unless merchants using them share in the costs; merchants hesitate to share costs until more customers use the system and customers hesitate to use micropayments until more merchants are online (VanHoose, 2003). Indeed, a lack of critical mass in terms of consumers and merchants was one reason behind the failure of early micropayment systems (Crocker, 1999).

Sales and Affiliate Programs: Since visitors to content sites are often segmented by interest and able to be easily targeted, content providers implement merchandise sales initiatives to leverage the site visitor's immediate interest in a subject with the Internet's instant ability to link buyers and sellers (Alster, 1999; Gallaugher et al., 2001). Selling content related merchandise allows content providers to benefit from a symbiosis with e-tailers who wish to present their products to an audience drawn to their content (Eisenmann, 2002). E-tailers can widen their user base, content providers can collect revenue from transactions, and users benefit from the integrated marketplace of content and commerce based on their interests (Tomsen, 2000). Non-merchandise based affiliate programs also exist. The volume of revenue earned from sales and affiliate programs however remains low (Mensing, 1997; Smith, 2002c), and for content providers interested in selling directly, adding e-commerce capabilities can pose technical challenges (Greenstein, 2000).

Syndication: Syndication only works with information goods because unlike physical goods, information is never "consumed" and can therefore be used infinitely (Werbach, 2000). Sites often seek syndicated content to supplement their commercial offerings and by doing so conveniently offer the multiple distribution points required for successful syndication (Gallaugher et al., 2001; Werbach, 2000). Apart from generating revenues, syndication also drives traffic to the site and strengthens brand awareness (Eisenmann, 2002; Posnock, 2001). Indeed, while syndication provides a source of revenue, increased exposure is the principal motivation for some content providers (Hicks, 2001). Content providers however must beware of overexposing their content and take measures to counter the risk of visitors going to the distributor's site to get information rather than to their site (Eisenmann, 2002; Hicks, 2001; Posnock, 2000; Tomsen, 2000).

Wireless: Unlike the free culture of the Internet, wireless users expect to pay for content (Fitzgerald, 2001). This is a facilitating factor in wireless revenue generation. Content providers generally have three revenue-generating options: subscriptions, advertising, and revenue sharing arrangements with wireless carriers (Fitzgerald, 2001; Gren, Maor, & Ubinas, 2001; Rabasca, 2001). Content providers, network operators and device makers contend for controlling relationships with wireless customers, and each has different capabilities relative to the three assets of content, customers and technology platform (Gren et al., 2001). The real contention however is between content providers and network operators. While network operators currently hold the biggest advantage by virtue of owning the physical networks, they typically lack content development skills and this is where content providers become important (Bamrud, 2000; Bricken, 2001; Gren et al., 2001). Technical issues surrounding wireless content provision may, however, present roadblocks to wireless revenues (Fitzgerald, 2001; Rabasca, 2001; Steiner, 2001).

Supporting Features: Registration, newsletters, community areas and personalization are four features that can be used to support revenue generation. Through *registration*, content providers can more precisely target advertisers' messages to consumers' needs, and hence charge advertisers higher rates (Outing & Coats, 2002). The information gained can also be used to target products and/or content according to user demographics and to implement fee-based offerings (Tomsen, 2000). *Newsletters* help drive traffic to the site, generate ancillary revenue, increase customer loyalty, build brands, and build e-mail databases (Clientize, 2001). They are indispensable direct and viral marketing tools and can be used to test new product concepts and identify finer niches in a given audience base (Miller, 2001a; Sewell, 1999). By *personalizing* content on a Web site to individual tastes and preferences content providers can increase site loyalty, learn more about their audiences, identify new opportunities for content enhancement, facilitate targeted advertising and aid the development of pay-per-view or subscription offerings (Hanson, 2000; Lasica, 2002; Tomsen, 2000). *Community areas* give members the opportunity to interact electronically with like-minded people to create and consume relevant and mutually interesting content (Weill & Vitale, 2001). Apart from generating traffic and driving up page views, communities help increase stickiness, customer loyalty and word-of-mouth referrals (Eisenmann, 2002; Ryan & Whiteman, 2000; Sherman, 2001; Tomsen, 2000). Since community areas benefit from network effects, finding and retaining a critical mass is imperative to their success (Weill & Vitale, 2001).

METHODOLOGY AND DATA COLLECTION

The research answers three questions: (a) which of the six revenue streams are NZ content providers using, (b) how satisfied are they with the performance of the revenue streams they use and what are the issues involved in generating revenues from these streams and (c), do supporting features really support revenue generation.

New Zealand Web directories and the Audit Bureau of Circulation listings were referenced to create a list of New Zealand online content providers. The research limited content providers to online newspapers, pure-play news sites, online magazines, and pure-play information sites. Sites not fitting this definition were excluded. Furthermore, to qualify, a site needed to have a *reasonable* amount of content online and there had to be some indication that the site was generating revenues from any one of the six revenue streams mentioned in the integrated classification. A comprehensive search, covering over 120 sites, was conducted, of which 36 sites met the eligibility criteria and therefore comprised the target population. Interviews were chosen as the data collection methodology because apart from providing the mainly qualitative information required to answer the research questions, they offered the ability to probe and the flexibility to adapt questions while proceeding with the interview process (Daymon & Holloway, 2002; Sekaran, 2000). Face-to-face and e-mail interviews (conducted by exchanging e-mail messages) were used to gather data. Compared to face-to-face interviews, which take personal time and are not very efficient for covering wide geographic areas (Sekaran, 2000), asynchronous e-mail interviews are a practical way to collect information from geographically distant respondents who may find it difficult to work on a face-to-face basis (Mann & Stewart, 2000). Given the small size of the eligible population, maximizing response rate was critical. E-mail interviews were therefore also offered with the intention of bolstering response rates. An information pack, consisting of an information sheet, a consent form and a glossary, was posted to invite a senior manager at the each of the 36 eligible sites to participate in an interview. The glossary conveyed the *research specific definitions* formulated for revenue streams and supporting features; and hence reduced the potential for misunderstandings. The initial mail out was followed up by e-mail and phone. Eleven senior managers agreed to participate in an interview, yielding a 30% response rate. Eight of these interviews were conducted via e-mail and three were face-to-face interviews. Semi-structured interviews were conducted: each respondent was asked the same questions in the same manner, and when required, relevant leads were probed (Sekaran, 2000). While interviews were the *principal* data collection tool, a site search was also conducted to help create a profile of revenue stream usage for the population.

With a dual mode of data collection, ensuring consistency was paramount. The interviews lasted 45 minutes, hence requiring a similar time commitment from face-to-face and e-mail respondents. Being less spontaneous, e-mail interviews allow respondents

Figure 2. Revenue stream profile

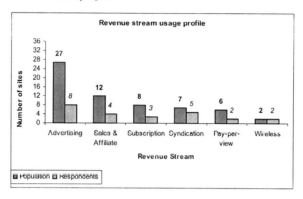

to be more reflective and send in more considered responses (Daymon & Holloway, 2002; Mann & Stewart, 2000). To counter the inconsistency created by the aforementioned notion, face-to-face interviewees were given the transcripts of the interview, which allowed them to "reflect" upon their responses. For e-mail interviewees, the e-mail was the "transcript". The qualitative data obtained from the interviews was analyzed using the strategies outlined in Miles and Huberman (1994). The interview transcripts were read and codes were assigned to pieces of data dealing with similar topics. These codes were then clustered into aggregate categories, which provided the qualitative information required to answer the research questions. The 26 tactics described by Miles and Huberman (1994) for generating meaning and verifying conclusions (e.g., making contrasts, weighing the evidence, checking out rival explanations) guided the analysis process.

RESULTS AND DISCUSSION

The information collected from interviews with respondents was collated with the information gathered by examining the Web sites of non-respondents to create a profile of the revenue streams New Zealand's online content providers use. Figure 2 presents the revenue stream profile of the population and respondents. At least a third of the total known users of each stream are represented in the study (respondents). With 27 of the 36 eligible sites using it, advertising was the most popular revenue stream with New Zealand content providers. A third of the sites (12/36) sold merchandise and employed affiliate programs. Affiliate programs were the predominant component in this category and arrangements with both e-tailers and other types of sites were seen. Eight sites offered subscription based access. Interestingly, one site (non-participant) also operated on a barter basis where users could contribute articles in lieu of a subscription fee to access site content. Paid archives, reports and newsletters made up the six entries

Table 1. Satisfaction levels

REVENUE STREAM	SATISFACTION LEVELS								Median Score
	VS	S	SS	N	SD	D	VD	DN	
Advertising	1	1	2	1	2	1			Somewhat satisfied / neutral
Subscription		1				2			Dissatisfied
Pay-per-view	1				1				Somewhat satisfied / neutral
Sales & affiliate			2	1		1			Somewhat satisfied / neutral
Syndication		2	2	1					Somewhat satisfied
Wireless	1	1							Very satisfied / satisfied
LEGEND: VS = Very Satisfied; S = Satisfied; SS = Somewhat Satisfied; N = Neutral; SD = Somewhat Dissatisfied; D = Dissatisfied; VD = Very Dissatisfied; DN = Don't know									

under the pay-per-view and premium services category. One site (non-participant) also sought voluntary donations through the Paypal online payment system. At least seven sites syndicated content and at least two sites generated revenue from wireless initiatives (in addition, one was planning to implement wireless initiatives). Since they are hard to detect from a site search alone, syndication and wireless numbers are expected to be higher. Moreover, wireless revenue streams are expected to grow as mobile usage increases.

Table 1 presents the satisfaction levels reported for each revenue stream along with the median satisfaction scores. Except for wireless, and syndication, satisfaction with the performance of revenue streams generally varied. Wireless yielded the highest median satisfaction score (between "very satisfied and satisfied") followed by syndication, a three way tie between advertising, pay-per-view and sales & affiliate programs, and then, subscriptions. Interestingly, seven responses were received for the dissatisfaction categories (VD, D, SD) compared to 14 for the satisfaction categories (VS, S, SS).

Advertising: Responses from three respondents suggested that a direct response orientation existed and that the branding potential of online advertising was still not fully understood. Nevertheless, they anticipated things to change, especially in the light of newer studies showing the positive influence of online advertising on brand building, and a growing expectation that the Internet will become part of the mix for brand advertisers. In fact, another respondent was predominantly getting branding oriented campaigns. The increased credibility of the Internet was also seen as facilitating factor. As one respondent noted, "new media take time to build credibility, trust… the fact that both the medium and some of the individual properties have been around for sometime is now helping [the advertising model]. In line with the literature, two respondents cited the high competition for ad dollars as an impeding factor. Regarding the role of new technologies, the findings suggested that increased broadband penetration, newer ad formats and the anticipated convergence with wireless advertising would change the shape of online advertising and facilitate the growth of the model. Conversely, the barrier posed by ad-blocking software was also mentioned. Technological advances thus exert facilitating and impeding influences on the ad model.

Subscriptions: While one respondent mentioned the free culture as an impediment, the other two, who emphasized the uniqueness of their offerings, did not. This contradicted initial expectations of the free culture being the overriding impediment to subscription models. More responses however are required to produce firmer conclusions about the true impact of the free culture on subscription models. One respondent noted how reputation facilitated the initial growth of their subscription site. Overall, experiences of respondents with the subscription model varied and findings, in line with Smith (2002a), suggest that success will be on a "case-by-case" basis. While differences in the type of content offered and the target audience plays an influential role, an initial indication is that unique content backed by good reputation/brand can be used to bypass the impediments posed by the free culture and availability of free substitutes. The site with the "barter" arrangement contained scientific content. It would be interesting to appraise such arrangements from a revenue perspective.

Pay-per-View: The free culture, free content provision by competing providers, and lack of a micro-payment system were cited as impediments. As one respondent said, before there is a substantial change in the free culture attitude, a *valid, secure, commercial infrastructure* needs to be built into the Web to enable *easy payment* and *micro-transactions*. Building on that, another respondent (did not have a pay-per-view initiative) opined that the spread of wireless would provide the payment infrastructure required to overcome the current limitations posed by the lack of efficient micro-payment systems; and, once established, those systems would present opportunities for niche pay-per-view content provision. Another respondent, who was thinking of introducing a pay-per-view product, was also watching the development of payment systems like Amazon's Honor System with interest. Voluntary donation schemes were a novel finding. It will be interesting to see how widely they are used, the types of sites that use them, and the revenue they generate.

Sales and Affiliate Programs: In line with the literature, the findings suggest that sales & affiliate programs are predicated on a sound business rationale: "merchandising by content providers makes sense — products can be offered that are tightly targeted, based on the content". Indeed, research at one site showed that their visitors got information from their site and a good proportion then went to e-tailers, giving the site a good reason to be affiliated to these e-tailers. For another site, affiliation increased the scope of their offering, thus adding value. Equally, the findings indicate that affiliate revenues earned must be balanced against the effort required to implement and maintain these programs, image, and branding issues. As one respondent opined, affiliation may create "image problems" vis-à-vis users who may feel that the site is "desperately trying to scrape in cash from everywhere". Overall, the findings suggest that while revenues from sales & affiliate programs may not be sizeable for all, their strategic benefits would ensure their continued usage. Implementing affiliate programs in particular seems to be more about improving market positioning than purely earning revenues.

Syndication: As the positive satisfaction ratings reflect, respondents saw syndication as an important activity. However, as anticipated from the literature, overexposure of content was identified as a pitfall to avoid: "unique content is in demand and the more licensing one does, the less unique it gets therefore lessening demand". An inference is that syndication has a "capped potential" and after a point, the risks negate the benefits of syndication. On a related note, one respondent also mentioned the risk of cannibalizing traffic to Web sites of syndicates. Content piracy emerged as an important issue, with respondents talking about how it reduced the ability to monetize demand for content and its adverse implications for branding. While only two respondents mentioned it, others would have shared this concern. Some sites also did free syndication deals to maximize exposure to their content. Syndication was thus being used for tangible and intangible gains.

Wireless: The willingness of consumers to pay for wireless content and the ability to charge for micro-transactions of mobile data were seen as facilitating factors, which increased the revenue potential of wireless media compared to the Internet. Content providers often share revenues with network operators. The reported "equal" relationship with network operators is thus a facilitating factor. While respondents noted that network operators were advantaged by virtue of "controlling the technology" and "holding the delivery mechanism," they indicated that the content side was equally important. Contrary to the expectation from the literature, there was insufficient evidence to suggest the existence of technical impediments in creating wireless content/sites. The high cost of providing wireless data was cited as a major impediment. Building on that, one respondent noted how wireless was an expensive area to enter and a very young branch of media. Uncertainty, high costs, and learning curves are hence likely to await early movers in this area.

Reflecting their popularity with content providers, seven respondents used newsletters, two of whom generated revenue from newsletter advertising. The business purposes of newsletters (categories taken from Clientize, 2001) in decreasing order of (average) importance were: increasing customer loyalty, driving traffic to the site, building customer database, building Internet brand and generating additional revenue. Interestingly, the two respondents who charged for newsletter ads rated generating additional revenue as the top priority. All others voted it as the least important purpose. However, as more respondents start accepting newsletter ads, generating ancillary revenue is expected to become increasingly popular. As anticipated from the literature, newsletters were seen as effective communication, advertising, direct marketing and viral marketing vehicles. Overall, offering newsletters makes positive tangible and intangible contributions to the revenue generating capacity of content sites. The four respondents using community-building features indicated that these features drove traffic, improved the offering ("it is giving people another option on what they can do with your Web site") and helped build site-visitor and visitor-visitor bonds. As one respondent succinctly summarized: "It is all part of things like the average time spent on site, all contribute to your credibility with advertisers and it helps create traffic". Three of the four respondents felt that communities augmented the revenue generating potential of their sites. The respondent who disagreed offered free e-mail accounts, a service whose take-up was very low. Notably, despite seeing no benefit from offering the free e-mail facility, the respondent persisted with the feature because it was a "part of the site make-up". In line with Weill and Vitale (2000), this shows how important healthy adoption rates are for realizing the benefits of community areas and indeed, the benefits of other supporting features as well. The site offering personalization options cited enhanced capability for target advertising as a key benefit. No site required registration (defined as up-front registration, like NY Times Online). This was surprising given the popularity of registration based access in recent years.

From a practitioner perspective, the research provides an empirical account of what was until now largely anecdotal knowledge. The integrated classification, satisfaction levels and the findings may be valuable for practitioners currently using or planning to implement revenue streams and/or supporting features. From an academic perspective, literature in this field has remained scarce. Being an exploratory study with a different geographic focus, scope, methodology and research questions, the findings cannot be compared to previous academic literature. This research created a new first understanding about the revenue streams of New Zealand content providers and the influence of indirect revenue sources on the revenue generating potential of content providers. Plus, a broader scope meant that the findings were reported at a higher level of abstraction (content providers). The research is thus another piece in the puzzle, which has shed first light on hitherto unexplored areas.

CONCLUSIONS

An exploratory study, this research empirically investigated the experiences of New Zealand content providers with the revenue streams they use and formulated some answers to the fundamental inquiries on this topic, represented by the three research questions. Framed according to a proposed integrated classification, which categorized the revenue streams along with the Web site features that indirectly support revenue generation, the research found that New Zealand content providers used all six revenue streams and three of the four supporting features. Experiences with revenue streams varied, although wireless, and to an extent, syndication got uniformly positive reviews. Some issues facing revenue generation were also unearthed. Furthermore, the findings suggested that supporting features augmented the revenue-generating potential of sites. Two limitations were identified. Even though a third of the population was studied, some streams remained underrepresented. This hindered the ability to make firmer conclusions about revenue stream performance and create a more detailed inventory of issues surrounding revenue generation. To avoid jeopardizing response rates, financial data, which is often confidential, was not collected. Like Gallaugher et al. (2001), the authors feel that the performance of revenue streams would have been better quantified and evaluated had financial data been available. Another caveat is that a different pool of participants might have yielded different results. Content providers operate in a very dynamic environment. With the growth in Internet access, the arrival of high-speed connections and the roll-out of mobile data services, the content provider industry, and consequently, their online revenue streams, will see major changes. The results can be used as a reference point for longitudinal studies on this dynamic field. The contributions of supporting features to the bottom line could also be quantified (dollar value). Benchmarking studies on costs and revenues can also be useful. Furthermore, revenue streams and supporting feature can be researched individually to present more targeted insights. Comparative studies with non-English speaking countries could be conducted in order to contrast the revenue stream profiles and experiences.

REFERENCES

Alster, N. (1999). The quest for real money. *Upside, 11,* 140-154.

Anders, G. (2001). Nickeled-and-dimed to death. *FastCompany.* Retrieved November 24, 2002, from http://www.fastcompany.com/online/52/untangle.html

Bakos, Y., & Brynjolfsson, E. (2000). Aggregation and disaggregation of information goods: Implications for bundling, site licensing, and micro payment systems. In B. Kahin & H.A. Varian (Eds.), *Internet publishing and beyond: The economics of digital information and intellectual property.* MIT Press.

Bamrud, J. (2000). Fighting for revenues. *The Feature.* Retrieved September 10, 2002, from http://www.thefeature.com/article.jsp?pageid=7063

Bricken, K. (2001). Making money from wireless data. *Wireless Week Supplement: 2002 Buyers Guide and Databook, 7,* 26-27.

Briggs, R. (2001). *Measuring success: An advertising effectiveness series from the IAB.* IAB.

Briggs, R., & Hollis, N. (1997). Advertising on the Web: Is there response before click-through. *Journal of Advertising Research, 37*(2), 33-45.

Briggs, R., Sullivan, J., & Webster, I. (2001). *New Zealand online advertising effectiveness study 2001: Summary.* ACNielsen. Retrieved August 25, 2002, from http://www.acnconsult.com

Clientize. (2001). *Excerpts from e-newsletters: An industry benchmarking study.* Retrieved from www.clientize.com.

Crocker, S. (1999). *The siren song of Internet micropayments.* Retrieved October 25, 2002, from http://www.cisp.org/imp/april_99/04_99crocker.htm

Daymon, C., & Holloway, I. (2002). *Qualitative research methods in public relations and marketing communications.* London: Routledge.

Eisenmann, T.R. (2002). *Internet business models: Text and cases.* New York: McGraw-Hill.

eMarketer. (2002). *Online advertising update: A review of research data measuring the growth and effectiveness of online advertising in the U.S.*

Fitzgerald, M. (2001). Papers' e-content with profit. *Editor & Publisher, 134.*

Gallaugher, J.M., Auger, P., & BarNir, A. (2001). Revenue streams and digital content providers: An empirical investigation. *Information and Management, 38,* 473-485.

Greenstein, J. (2000). *Content in search of profits.* Retrieved February 27, 2002, from http://www.thestandard.com/article/display/0,1151,20480-0,00.html

Gren, F., Maor, D., & Ubinas, L.A. (2001). Late edition: Another chance for newspapers on the web. *The McKinsey Quarterly, Special Edition* (2), 74-81.

Hanson, W. (2000). *Principles of Internet marketing.* USA: South-Western College Publishing.

Hicks, M. (2001). Syndicate or die. *EWeek, 18,* 49.

Hutchinson, M. (2001). *Web media: Free for all or pay as you go?* Retrieved February 25, 2002, from http://www.adventurer.co.nz/collection/MISarchive/MIS-pay-per-view.html

Jupiter Research. (2001). Press release: Bumpy road from free to fee: Paid online content revenues to reach only $5.8 billion by 2006. *Jupiter Research.* Retrieved August 28, 2002, from http://jmm.com/xp/jmm/press/2002/pr_031802.xml

Kennerdale, C. (2001). *Model behavior: Content subscription models are and uphill battle.* Retrieved November 24, 2002, from http://www.econtentmag.com/Magazine/Columns/model8_01.html

Lasica, J.D. (2002). The second coming of personalized news. *Online Journalism Review.* Retrieved November 29, 2002, from http://www.ojr.org/ojr/lasica/1017779244.php

Mann, C., & Stewart, F. (2000). *Internet communication and qualitative research: A handbook for researching online.* Surrey: Sage Publications.

McGarvey, R. (2001). Small change. *EContent, 24,* 18-21.

Mensing, D.H. (1997). *Prospects for profit: The economics of online newspapers.* Unpublished Master of Arts thesis, University of Nevada, Reno.

Miles, A., & Huberman, A.M. (1994). *Qualitative data analysis: An expanded sourcebook* (2nd ed.). CA: Sage Publications.

Miller, M. (2001a). The e-newsletter explosion. *Folio: The Magazine for Magazine Management, 30,* 31-34.

Miller, M. (2001b). Will consumers pay for online content? *Folio: The Magazine for Magazine Management, 30,* 76.

Mings, S.M., & White, P.B. (2000). Profiting from online news: The search for viable business models. In B. Kahin & H.A. Varian (Eds.), *Internet publishing and beyond: The economics of digital information and intellectual property.* MIT Press.

Mullarkey, W.G. (2001). *Advertising exposure quality on the World Wide Web: An empirical examination of webpage exposure duration and its applicability to online media planning.* Unpublished MCom thesis, University of Auckland.

Outing, S., & Coats, R. (2002). *To charge or not to charge.* Retrieved November 27, 2002, from http://poynter.org/content/content_view.asp?id=11174

Posnock, S.T. (2000). Cashing in on content. *Folio: The Magazine for Magazine Management, 29,* 39-41.

Posnock, S.T. (2001). Low risk revenue streams. *Folio: The Magazine for Magazine Management, 30,* 33-35.

PWC & IAB. (2002). *PricewaterhouseCoopers LLP/IAB Internet advertising revenue report.* PriceWaterhouseCoopers and Interactive Advertising Bureau.

Rabasca, L. (2001). Wireless: The strategies. *NAA.* Retrieved September 10, 2002, from http://www.naa.org/artpage.cfm?AID=1756&SID=106

Rayport, J.F. (1999). *The truth about Internet business models.* Retrieved September 1, 2002, from http://www.strategy-business.com/press/article/?art=14631&pg=0

Ryan, J., & Whiteman, N. (2000). Using community to build advertising effectiveness. *Clickz.com.* Retrieved August 27, 2002, from http://www.clickz.com/article.php/828971

Sekaran, U. (2000). *Research methods for business: A skill building approach* (3rd ed.). USA: John Wiley & Sons.

Sewell, H.J. (1999). Online newsletters see increased interest. *Connect Direct.* Retrieved March 16, 2002, from http://www.connectthe.com/articles/newsletters.html

Shapiro, C., & Varian, H.A. (1999). *Information rules: A strategic guide to the network economy.* Boston: Harvard Business School Press.

Sherman, C. (2001). Eight essential strategies for repurposing content for the Web. *EContent, 24,* 20-30.

Shirky, C. (2000). The case against micropayments. *O'Reillynet.com.* Retrieved April 15, 2003, from http://www.oreillynet.com/pub/a/p2p/2000/12/19/micropayments.html

Smith, S. (2002a). *The free lunch is over: Online content subscriptions on the rise.* Retrieved November 24, 2002, from http://www.econtentmag.com/bs1/2002/smith2_02.html

Smith, S. (2002b). Online advertising: The big slow sell. *EContent, 25,* 42-43.

Smith, S. (2002c). A trickle from your tchotchokes. *EContent, 25,* 44-45.

Steiner, I. (2001). Serving up the wireless Web. *Online, 25,* 26-33.

Tomsen, M. (2000). *Killer content: Strategies for Web content and e-commerce.* NJ: Addison-Wesley.

VanHoose, D.D. (2003). *E-commerce economics.* Ohio: Thomson Learning.

Weill, P., & Vitale, M.R. (2001). *Place to space: Migrating to ebusiness models.* Boston: Harvard Business School Press.

Werbach, K. (2000). Syndication: The emerging model for business in the Internet era. *Harvard Business Review, 78*(3), 84.

Zerdick, A., Picot, A., Schrape, K., Artope, A., Goldhammer, K., Lange, U.T., et al. (2000). *E-conomics: Strategies for the digital marketplace.* Germany: Springer.

ENDNOTES

[1] **Inclusion criteria:** At least three of the five authors had to mention a revenue stream. A majority-based cut-off ensured that only widely acknowledged revenue streams were represented.

This article was previously published in the *Journal of Global Information Management,* 12(4), pp. 75-88, © 2004.

Chapter XI

Pursuing Radical Transformation in Information Age Government:
Case Studies Using the SPRINT Methodology

Peter Kawalek, University of Manchester, UK

David Wastall, University of Manchester, UK

ABSTRACT

This article is concerned with the pursuit of radical organizational transformation in information age government. It focuses on three cases, each of which used the SPRINT (Salford Process Reengineering Involving New Technology) process reengineering method. This method was designed specifically for e-government projects with the objective of inculcating radical change. Although each reported case can be described as successful in some measure, this chapter questions why none of the cases seeds a process of ongoing innovation, and why all settle on a set of changes that is less radical than the vision set out within the originating project. Each case sees the remaking of processes within an accepted set of goals, and not the remaking of these goals themselves. This restriction is reported, using the concept of organizational alignment with a declared set of goals. It is shown how in each case the organization favors the less radical amongst a set of alternative proposals. It is argued that in the end, SPRINT, which places great value on its participative ethos, is also constrained by that ethos. This paper reflects the implications for e-government projects more widely.

INTRODUCTION

E-government has been defined in various ways. Many definitions pivot upon access channels to government, a focus that is reflected in the UK government's widely cited performance indicator, BVPI157 (Cabinet Office, 1999). For example, Luling (2001) defines e-government as online government services (i.e., Internet-enabled interaction with government). This is perhaps a limited view, identifying e-government with access to services rather than the refashioning of the services themselves. Others take a more complex position, identifying tension between bold and cautious interpretations of its concerns (Holmes, 2001; Traunmuller & Wimmer, 2003) However, there are also more confident interpretations. Deakins and Dillon (2002) refer to e-government as an arrangement of IT capabilities, competencies, and organizational practice spanning both business-to-business and business-to-consumer activities. Dow et al. (2002) argue that it will transform not only the way in which most public services are delivered, but also the fundamental relationship between government and citizens. In this, e-government is seen as a more general concern with the technological and organizational refurbishment of traditional government bureaucracies. As such, it can be partially aligned with the literature on business transformation (Venkatraman, 1994). However, its distinctiveness is preserved by the combination of issues that come within its gamut; as well as the common concerns of process redesign, organizational structuring, and so forth; there are questions of governance, voting, and community access to information (Heeks, 2001).

The SPRINT method is a public domain resource (SPRINT, 2004) aimed at an audience of UK local government (i.e., cities, boroughs, counties, and districts). It is concerned with the analysis and design of e-government projects. It has been adopted by more than 18 councils in England and Wales, although its origins lie with just one, Salford. SPRINT forms a key element in the City's Information Society Strategy (Salford, 1999). The Strategy's aim is to harness the potential of ICT in order to enhance local service delivery and democratic processes, and to enhance the social and economic well being of the people of Salford through improved service delivery, greater social inclusion, and development of the local economy. To underpin the initiatives, a strategic methodology was required that focused on the innovative use of ICT to realize radical transformation; one of the work programs was explicitly targeted at the development of such a methodology, within which lies the genesis of SPRINT.

This chapter is motivated by the problematical definitions of e-government. It describes e-government as being concerned with IT enabled change, with an aspiration to bring about radical change. This is problematic from two points of view: that this aspiration is not shared by all, and that there are practical limitations as to what may be achieved. It follows from this that process change methodology might assist the change process. This chapter, therefore, focuses on this question: to what extent can such a methodology facilitate radical change in a problematic context?

This chapter includes six sections. In Section Two, the literature review describes the basis and context of e-government. The methodological dimension is represented by SPRINT, set out in Sections Three and Four. These give the reader a detailed account of SPRINT, allowing insight into its features in order to support the analysis of the cases that follows. In Section Three, the general precepts and underlying positions are set out. In Section Four an overview of its structure and techniques is presented. In Section Five, three case studies of the use of SPRINT are set out, each telling how a radical set of proposals was considered alongside less radical, but still productive, possibilities. These cases are then discussed in Section Six, which identifies a tendency towards caution in each of the reported cases, linking it to the organizational dialogues and the participative nature of the underlying method. It then broadens the debate to consider how a radical interpretation of e-government might be supported by process change methodology.

LITERATURE

This chapter focuses on the reality of e-government as a radical, transformational artefact. This transformational focus connects e-government with the wider literature on ICT, wherein it has been frequently argued that ICT can inculcate novelty, process innovation, and large-scale reorganization. This potential is most clearly articulated in the discourse of business process reengineering (BPR), which explicitly champions the potential of IT to effect revolutionary change in organizational structures and processes. Davenport (1992) speaks of "process innovation" in order to highlight the radical, transformational potency of IT. Yet, despite this rhetoric, much IT-enabled change results in failure, and the ideas underpinning BPR have been questioned (Chang & Powell, 1998; Tissan & Heikkilä, 2001; Wastell, 1999).

Nonetheless, the central themes of BPR find some resonance in later literature on the idea of the disruptive technology that permits radical shifts in organizations and markets (Christensen, 1997; Markus, 2004). Moreover, the key tenets of BPR have been explicitly embraced within UK e-government programs, and funding has been made available for BPR methodology (ODPM, 2004). Clearly, there remains the conviction that ICT can be used to enable radical transformation in government. The ideas underpinning all of this can be traced to that the information age itself. This notion that society is entering or has entered a post-industrial state has been proposed by a number of writers (Arthur, 1990; Bell, 1973) with the kernel of the argument being that the highly efficient transfer and management of information places a new premium on the value of that information and enables new forms of organization to exploit the information (Downes & Mui 1998; Haeckel, 1999). At the same time, marketplaces themselves change and become increasingly irascible as the easy movement of information catalyses both local entrepreneurship and globalization. This thesis is subject to ongoing scrutiny. The boom and bust of the dot coms provide ammunition for convert and sceptic alike. A sober post-boom assessment suggests that the significance of the information age will vary from sector to sector (BusinessWeek, 2001, 2003). Manufacturers may use the Internet to smooth their supply chains, but they still will have to make high-quality products. Travel companies may utilize the Internet to enhance their yield management, but they still will have to provide the right destinations and hassle-free journeys. On the other hand, the entertainment industry will be more deeply transformed as it increasingly sells its products in digitized format. Financial transactions also will be digitized. Banks will do more business over the Internet and less over the counter. Many government agencies that trade primarily in information will become leaner and better integrated.

It follows that a radical agenda is manifested in some interpretations of e-government. Others report a more complex picture, wherein powerful and ambitious systems have failed to convince both internal and external stakeholders of the potential of e-government (Traunmuller & Wimmer, 2003). This kind of dichotomy essentially replays the debate over ICT as a sustaining technology against an interpretation of it as a discontinuous or disruptive technology (Christensen, 1997). In the former case, the technology serves the existing goals of the organization. In the latter case, it has the potential to question and reconstruct these goals. Herein lies an innate tension. The need for alignment of information systems and organizational goals has been a consistent theme in management and information systems literature (Beer, 1985; Checkland & Scholes, 1991; Ciborra, 1997). Recent debates about the information age, e-business, and e-government have added to this by stressing the need for innovation and ongoing adaptability (Downes & Mui, 1998; Haeckel, 1999; Moss Kanter, 2001). It is argued that this fresh emphasis on innovation and change is inconsistent with traditional approaches wherein the goals of an organization are devised and passed outwards in a top-down fashion. Such traditional models generally depict goals as arising from senior management and being cemented into the rest of the organization through rational planning and change management, a process through which the whole organization is cast in the image of these goals (Kotter, 1996). A contrasting view is that ongoing innovation percolates from different levels in the organization. It may be as readily bottom-up as it is top-down. Thus, the organization seeks to remake itself around new ideas from whatever their source. It is this intrinsic malleability of organization and goals that gives vitality and viability. This kind of highly adaptive structure stands in stark contradistinction to the older model of a top-down bureaucracy whose credibility lies in the concreteness of its goals and the rigor of their implementation.

In essence, then, as the question of the radical potential of e-government is pursued, it leads to a set of questions about the nature of the process that fosters innovation in an organization. This is essentially a methodological aspect to the debate and shall be returned to. It is related to the whole question of IS and organizational alignment, an important and recurring issue through much of the general discourse on IS and organizational transformation (Henderson & Venkatraman, 1993; Venkatraman, 1994). Increasingly, as wider attention is given to the fundamental potential of IT, there is increasing awareness of the complexity of the relationship between business goals and IS functionality. It is in part a two-way street (Hirschheim & Sabherwal, 2001). Not only does business strategy dictate what IT must accomplish, but IT also shapes business strategy. A number of managerial implications follow from this, including the possibility of the problematic misalignment of IS and business strategy and the need for explicit recognition of such misalignment. It is reasonable to suggest that such issues affect the government agency seeking the alignment of IS and goals in an e-government setting. Increasingly, e-government is best depicted as a set of competing tensions or potentials to be played out within any given organization. Each of these organizations will be engaged in a struggle to comprehend the possibilities of ICT and to consider the virtue of one set of goals over another. Hence, again, process change methodology might have a key role in shaping how e-government is realized in an organization.

SPRINT: GENERAL PRECEPTS

The SPRINT method is a public domain resource (SPRINT, 2004) aimed at an audience of UK local government (i.e., cities, boroughs, counties, districts). It has been adopted by more than 18 councils in England and Wales, although its origins lie with just one, Salford. SPRINT, which was jointly developed by Salford City Council and university partners. It forms a key element in the City's Information Society Strategy (Salford, 1999). The strategy's aim is to harness the potential of ICT in order to enhance local service delivery and democratic processes, and to enhance the social and economic well being of the people of Salford through improved service delivery, greater social inclusion, and development of the local economy. To underpin the initiatives, a strategic methodology was required that focused on the innovative use of ICT to realize radical transformation; one of the work programs was explicitly targeted at the development of such a methodology, within which lies the genesis of SPRINT.

Before discussing the practical aspects of the SPRINT methodology, the main philosophical principles underpinning SPRINT will be described. SPRINT has been designed to be sympathetic to a public-sector culture of well founded and collegial, participative decision-making. It has the following key characteristics:

Breadth of Vision and Depth of Understanding

E-government projects are inherently complex in that many groups and individuals within the organization will be directly or tangentially impacted. Recognizing this, SPRINT stresses the importance of seeking out and examining all stakeholder perspectives in order to appreciate the complexity of the problem and the different views that people hold. SPRINT also advocates the development of a rigorous evidence-based understanding of processes. It is important to know what goes on now, why things are the way they are, and what the important contextual factors are. Ethnographic methods (i.e., detailed, immersive investigation) are recommended to achieve this depth of understanding (Martin, Bowers, & Wastell, 1997).

Learning and Knowledge Management

E-government projects are regarded as opportunities for organizational innovation. Thus, learning and knowledge management are seen as a key to successful change, and the methodology actively aims to stimulate innovative thinking and to nurture radical ideas. Following Wastell (1999), SPRINT projects are regarded as transitional spaces (i.e., supportive learning environments in which users are encouraged to reflect critically on current processes and experiment with new process designs using various modelling techniques). To support the management of knowledge within and across change projects, extensive use is made in SPRINT of intranet technology. A Web site is created for each SPRINT project and acts as a shared repository for the project's working documentation, allowing access to the experience and knowledge gained in other projects.

An Emphasis upon Innovation through Participation

Localized innovation and learning become more important as certainty decreases (Haeckel, 1999; Moss-Kanter 2001). The design of SPRINT recognizes that a key part of any transformation project may be to overturn a traditional ethos of top-down management and to implant a new culture of innovation, based upon the insights of staff at all levels in the organization. The SPRINT expert practitioners from the IT team might be part of the transitional space as the organization makes this change. As end-users become skilled with SPRINT, they will become more able to develop ideas independently, and more eager to implant them in their organization. Therefore, a participative approach is indispensable to the effectiveness of SPRINT as a means of seeding innovation. In this, SPRINT reflects a sociotechnical approach to IS design (Mumford, 1986; Warboys et al., 1999; Wastell & Newman, 1996).

Designed-In Strategic Alignment

It follows that while SPRINT places considerable emphasis on the achievement of recognizable business benefits, it eschews a classical top-down approach to achieving business alignment. We concur with recent critics of the rational paradigm (Ciborra, 1997; Hackney & Little, 1999) who stress the emergent, practice-based nature of the strategy process. Alignment is seen as an integral part of the ongoing process of change, not as something in advance of and separate from the design work itself. In Ciborra's terminology, alignment is something that should be taken care of throughout the design process. Haeckel (1999) makes a similar argument, proposing that strategy should be seen as a Design for Adaptation, which is fulfilled by the ensuing process of organizational development. SPRINT contributes to this by exhorting change participants to address themselves to business goals at all stages in a BPR project, from goal identification in the analysis phase to goal development and the establishment of rigorous mechanisms to track and manage the achievement of business benefits (Serafeimidis & Smithson, 2000) in the implementation phase.

A Multi-Level Change Model

ICT projects are often associated with the idea of large-scale, rapid change. However, the idea that organizations change can proceed on a one-shot Lewinian basis (unfreeze-change-freeze) has been called into serious question (Macredie & Sandon, 1999). The demands on the organization are potentially huge in terms of human and technical resources (Benjamin, 1993), and the risk of resistance is high (especially in a public sector organization with strong collective traditions). SPRINT rejects the idea of change as a discrete, convulsive event imposed on the organization. Instead, the approach draws in part upon inspiration from the improvisational change model of Orlikowski and Hofman (1997). At an initial level, change should not be determined by a top-down plan, but rather guided by a set of business objectives and enacted through a series of incremental steps emphasizing continuous reflection and adaptation to changing circumstances. Each step should be seen as a learning experiment in which a new ICT-enabled process is implemented, evaluated, and refined. The ethos should be one of excitement, even of fun, but not of fear. It goes without saying that a participative approach is key, with users leading the prototyping process and colleagues involved in giving feedback. Of course, a plan is required, but only as a coordinating device and as a means for managing progress; the plan does not drive the change. Then, more profoundly, the improvisational change process might question the objectives themselves. This process of questioning might be supported, for example, through the use of the Design Studio, a component of SPRINT that draws upon theory from various sources (Christensen, 1997; Downes & Mui, 1998; Hammer, 1990). In this way, SPRINT seeds a multilevel approach to change. At one level, it seeks the creative exploration and development of ideas that conform to a set of objectives. At another level, it invites the redefinition of these objectives.

Flexibility and Extensibility

A danger with methodologies is that they can become an end in themselves, with users following the method's prescriptions in a slavish fashion rather than thinking for themselves (Wastell, 1997). To guard against this, SPRINT has been designed deliberately with a minimum of procedural structure; in essence, it comprises a toolbox of recommended techniques within a loose, general framework of tasks and phases. Users should be familiar with SPRINT's structure, tasks, and tools, but they are encouraged to interpret and adapt the methodology according to the particular circumstances of the project they are undertaking. For instance, if they think that some new tool or method is ideally suited to solving a particular problem, they are encouraged to adopt it and bring it into the framework.

AN OVERVIEW OF SPRINT

This section provides a practical overview of SPRINT, focusing on its key phases. Further, information about its project structure, roles, and phases can be gained through reference to SPRINT (2004).

At the outset, SPRINT recommends that two groups be established to manage a change project: a Steering Group and the Change (BPR) team. The former should include: the departmental director for all operational areas impacted by the project, the BPR project manager and a Lead Consultant, and senior representatives from Human Resources (HR) and ICT services. Leadership at such a senior level is critical; given the potentially radical nature of the change process, it is vital that such commitment be made from all those departments that will be directly impacted.

Membership of the Change Team is comprised of a Senior User at deputy director level, who plays the role of Project Manager; a Lead BPR Consultant and supporting consultants; and HR and ICT experts. Early projects required that operational groups whose work will be directly affected by the initiative should be represented on the Team by one or more Practice Representatives.

Phase 1: Understanding Process Context

SPRINT comprises three main phases (see Figure 1). Each phase is defined in terms of a set of aims, and there is a set of tasks within each phase intended to help the realization of these aims. Although the impression may be gained of a tightly defined structure, this is emphatically not the case. The division into phases and tasks is merely to provide a

Figure 1. Schematic overview of SPRINT showing phases and tasks

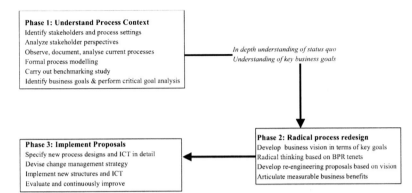

loose organizational framework to allow the work to be structured and divided up amongst the Change Team. There is no requirement, for instance, for tasks to be performed in strict sequence, and there are no dogmatic injunctions on the use of particular techniques.

Phase 1 is essentially one of analysis. The aims are:

- to understand the business context of the project by considering all relevant perspectives and to analyze the effectiveness and efficiency of current processes in this broader context;
- to generate preliminary ideas for process improvements (technical and organizational); and
- to help develop the business vision on which the detailed proposals in Phase 2 will be founded.

The emphasis on understanding the business context is crucial. This forces the Change Team to stand back from the original remit that may focus too narrowly on a particular process or processes. "Zooming out" in this way will assist in identifying and understanding the real business goals that should be addressed and will lead towards the identification of more radical re-engineering opportunities.

Of the various tasks carried out in Phase 1, two require further comment. The construction of formal process models is a key feature of SPRINT. To this end, a modelling method known as Role Activity Diagramming (RAD) is proposed as the technique of choice. The authors' previous BPR experience has demonstrated the accessibility and the efficacy of this simple method that makes use of a small number of relatively straightforward constructs (primarily Roles, Activities, and Interactions). For a detailed description see Warboys et al. (1999).

Critical goal analysis (CGA) is another important technique. This task constitutes the crux of Phase 1, as it is the primary means for addressing the alignment issue. CGA focuses all strands of inquiry on two pivotal questions: What are the business goals relevant to the process context? and How well are they supported by the current processes and support systems? For each business goal, some of the following key issues must be addressed: What is the goal? Who are the primary stakeholders? How does it relate or divert from the strategic aims of the organization, and especially to broader themes of the Information Society? How well is the goal currently achieved and how should it be measured (i.e., what metrics could be used)? SPRINT recommends the use of a Goal Network Diagram to depict the set of goals and their interrelationships. An example is shown in Figure 2.

Phase 2: Radical Process Redesign

The analytical work of Phase 1 constitutes essential preparation for the second phase of SPRINT, the aim of which is to devise a set of process re engineering proposals. These will embrace the use of ICT to underpin new processes aimed at dramatic improvements in the organization's performance in relation to its general strategic objectives and the specific aims of the initiative. The first task in Phase 2 is to develop a business vision in terms of key goals and critical success factors for achieving the goals. It is vital to assess the importance of each goal and the effectiveness of current process support. Although the articulation of a clear business vision might suggest a conventional top-down IS design and planning process, this is not how the business vision is intended to function. Its role is simply to provide a panoramic view of the organization's key goals as currently understood and to enable a set of priorities to be established to guide subsequent design work. Initially, the Change Team leads the work, although key stakeholders also participate and increasingly take over this important alignment activity. A high priority goal is one that is judged to be important to the organization but not well supported in terms of current processes. Figure 2, from the first of the featured case studies, furnishes an example.

Having established a clear business context, the next task requires the Change Team to reflect, in a radical way, on re-engineering opportunities. The aim is to change the way the organization operates by taking full advantage of the potentials of ICT to enable new ways of working, however radical they may be. Innovative thinking can be stimulated in a number of ways: via literature research, through the results of best practice investigations, by existential reflection, and in a Design Studio activity. Although it cannot be reduced to technique, SPRINT provides a set of "re-visioning heuristics" based on Hammer's (1990) early work to aid in the search for new ideas.

The end point of Phase 2 is a set of design proposals that embody new process designs (again using the RAD notation wherever appropriate) enabled by the innovative application of ICT. Crucially, each proposal must be supported by a detailed business case, including the specification of a set of metrics (ideally quantitative) to aid in the delivery of real business benefits and to establish an ongoing feedback loop to facilitate continuous process improvement.

Phase 3: Implementation and Continuous Improvement

The aim of the third phase of SPRINT is to implement the change proposals developed in Phase 2. As noted above, the original Change Team remains in place in order to supervise this stage, although the overall team will typically become much larger via

Figure 2. Part of the goal network diagram for the decision making case study (links between goals are either positive (arrows) or inhibitory (diamonds))

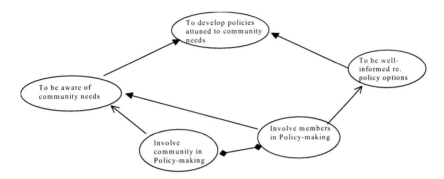

the co-option of additional individuals (e.g., training specialists, ICT specialists, relevant line managers, user representatives) in order to carry out the detailed changes that are required to implement the proposals. Implementation can be a long, arduous process, and strong user leadership is absolutely essential at this stage to carry through the desired changes into working practice. Many tasks are entailed.

- An incremental implementation plan is required to provide an overall organizational framework. It must be determined whether the proposals are to be implemented serially or concurrently, if there are important areas of synergy and sufficient resources available.
- The process designs must be re-examined and translated into new working structures and procedures.
- Training must be addressed, courses and documentation devised, and staff trained.
- Requirements for new ICT must be elaborated in appropriate detail to allow the development of the necessary ICT systems by whatever method is deemed appropriate (i.e., in-house development, packages, etc.).
- Crucially, a positive attitude towards evaluation must be established and appropriate mechanisms put in place to gather whatever data are required to provide feedback on the new systems and processes, whether it be soft data (e.g., interview feedback) or quantitative metrics. It is vital that the ethos of learning, experimentation, and further innovation be maintained through out.
- In principle, this final phase continues indefinitely; the new process designs should be the subject of continuous monitoring and critical evaluation (assisted by the metrics framework). SPRINT thus recommends that the Change Team remain in place on an ongoing basis, considering incremental improvements or, indeed, radical process changes (akin to the original change effort).

CASE STUDIES

SPRINT has been deployed on numerous projects across many local government authorities in the UK. Three of these, all from Salford, are described below in order to give details of the difficult pressures that develop around the pursuit of radical change. They are summarized in Table 1. The descriptions follow in chronological order of project start.

In each case, an Action Research (AR) approach was taken (Greenwood & Levin, 1998; Reason & Bradbury, 2001). This involved university academics working jointly with Salford Council staff. A project diary was maintained; the academics sought to synthesize lessons from the different aspects of the projects and their deployment of SPRINT. The strengths and limitations of the approach are discussed in this context by Wastell et al. (2004). Broadly, the accounts developed here benefit from close engagement with the projects and contain insights gained firsthand. It can be argued that AR is highly appropriate to a highly contextual issue, such as methodology and change in e-government (Baskerville & Wood-Harper, 1998). In all cases, opinions are substantiated by evidence and comments from practitioners involved in the study.

The Decision-Making Project

Profound changes to the nature of local government in the UK form the background to the decision-making (DM) project. At the behest of national imperatives, local government engaged in a process of democratic renewal, wherein the decision-making process is the subject of fundamental change (Wilson & Game, 1998). The traditional method of decision-making involved a set of committees, chaired and staffed by elected representatives, with a committee devoted to each area of the Council's work (Housing, Social Services, etc.). The most common model replacing this method is that of cabinet-style government. This involves the constitution of a small, centralized decision-making body of "Lead Members" (the Cabinet) and a considerably extended system of delegation of power through the executive. Each Lead Member has decision-making power for a given operational area; in effect, they resemble ministers in the Westminster system of government.

In early 1999, a conventional ICT project had been instigated to address issues of IS support for the administrators who would service the new structure. This came to focus upon the issue of text retrieval — the ICT search facilities used by administrators when responding to requests for information made by elected members. Over a period of time, concerns developed that this project was too narrow, that it had failed to address the broader issues regarding the enhancement of local democracy embodied in the Information Society vision. At best, text retrieval could only achieve marginal improvements to the existing administrative process. What was needed was a wider and deeper study that would coalesce a more radical vision of change as a precursor to defining a more fitting ICT solution. The decision thus was made for members of a then nascent BPR team to deploy SPRINT on the project. It was the first SPRINT project ever undertaken. The method was used to facilitate a broad inquiry among all concerned stakeholders about how the decision-making structure should work, and how it could be supported through ICT.

Interviews with key stakeholders (e.g., elected members, council officers, community representatives) were carried out, supplemented by a detailed ethnographic observation of the administrative process supporting the committee decision-making system, which was still operating at that time. Essentially, the support process was paper-based, involving the circulation of agenda packages in advance of committee meetings. These packages included an agenda, the minutes of the previous meeting, and a set of detailed reports relevant to the agenda items.

A Role Activity Diagram for the support processes was constructed, and a Critical Goal Analysis was carried out. This promoted a highly productive discourse among stakeholders about how the existing process operated and its relationship with the goals of the organization. This was important, as it forced stakeholders to confront the fact that the existing support mechanisms were not effective. Very few of the Council's goals regarding effective and responsive decision-making were effectively supported by the existing process; few, indeed, were even tangentially addressed. For instance, effective decision-making was impeded by the fact that large volumes of documentation would be delivered to Council members just a few days before a committee meeting. How were they expected to read it all in such a short time? How were they expected to identify the parts relevant to their constituents? Equally, the need to involve the community in the decision-making process was severely inhibited by lack of ready access to documentation. It was clear that here was a process that was severely out of alignment with its goals.

Phase 2 led to the rapid formulation of a design proposal that had the potential to profoundly affect the decision support processes and the roles of committee support

Table 1. Comparative summary of the three cases

	The Decision-Making Project	Births, Deaths, Marriages	Social Services
Project Outline	Reengineering of the support process for a new structure of decision-making in the Council as a whole.	Reengineering of processes for registration of births, deaths, and marriages.	Development of a radical vision for the reorganization of social services.
Key Personnel	SPRINT authors Committee Support Staff Elected Members	SPRINT consultant Two service managers	"E-envoys" – social services staff chosen to lead the design process. Supporting SPRINT consultants. Other social services staff.
Radical Change Proposal	Comprehensive Information Repository (CIR) to support electronic filing and distribution. New Information Management function. Authors to directly load reports onto the CIR.	Cross-departmental bereavement support service. This proposal emerged after the official project.	Fundamental restructuring of the service around new self-contained practices. The development of a new, independent, Internet-based information service for the sourcing and maintenance of care information (e.g., care home vacancies).
Implemented Solution	Comprehensive Information Repository (CIR) to support electronic filing and distribution.	Call-centre support for the provision of basic information and appointment making. E-mail	Refinements to the existing process (e.g., changing the ways in which social services staff are alerted to new cases).

staff. The design centered on the creation of a comprehensive information repository (CIR) for the Council and the transformation of the role of the committee support staff to that of information managers. All documents (e.g., reports, agendas, minutes) would in the future be stored in the CIR directly by their authors. They would be indexed rigorously in terms of the policy issues they addressed and the areas of Salford to which they related. The committee support staff would no longer simply act as "paper pushers," but would take responsibility for ensuring that documentation was correctly classified; they would also monitor the quality of reports and actively seek out additional material. In short, the BPR proposal envisaged the creation of an information management (IM) function within the Council. This would underpin major changes to the processes of information dissemination and retrieval. This would promote better alignment with the goals of the process by providing a speedier and customizable service. Documents would be circulated to elected members electronically, thus reaching them more quickly. Members also would be able to register their interests (e.g., policy issues, their ward), and information would be proactively supplied to them based upon this profile. Retrieval also would no longer depend upon the committee support staff; elected members could search for electronically held documents using the indexes provided for them. Thus, from its original concerns with text retrieval, the use of SPRINT had enlarged the scope of the project to consider the whole process of decision-making more broadly and the related HR, business process, and ICT issues. The project was considered a success by many of those involved and, crucially, by all the key sponsors. Nonetheless, implementation proceeded slowly, and it was sometime before the CIR was fully operational. It was named SOLAR, for Salford Online Archive and Retrieval. A review of the project followed the completion of SOLAR and found that although some benefits had been derived (e.g., a marked shortening of the time that it took to distribute information to elected members), in many ways the project had not achieved its potential. In particular, the roles of administrators had not fundamentally changed. They had rejected the IM role set out for them in SPRINT Phase 2, and instead had concentrated on recreating their former role, albeit in the changed context of an electronic information repository. This meant that authors of documents were not actually being allowed to enter reports directly, but had to send them to the administrators for checking prior to release on the CIR. However, if one were to judge the project, many saw it as a success. It was also clear that its most radical vision had not been achieved.

Births, Deaths, and Marriages

A later engagement for SPRINT followed in the area of the registration of births, deaths, and marriages (BDM). One SPRINT consultant took primary responsibility for the engagement, working closely with two managers of the service (one a senior manager). The BDM service in Salford is located in a large, converted Victorian house about one mile away from the City Council's main offices. It houses a reception desk where members of the public come in to report for appointments (e.g., to register a death) and to make ad hoc queries. The majority of transactions, however, feature a telephone call. The office receives close to 34,500 telephone calls per annum. Many of these relate to appointments, with copies of certificates and family history being other prominent service requests.

It became clear that the short walk between the City Council's main office and the BDM office was associated with a marked contrast in available technology. The BDM office had no e-mail facilities, and fee payments could only be accepted by cash or cheque. PC-based records for births, deaths, and marriages existed only for the years following 1994.

Staff reported problems with overstretch at peak times. Queues would build at the service counters and on the telephone lines. An interesting problem would be posed by individuals researching family history, a fast-growing area of activity. They might come into an office or make a telephone inquiry with a friendly, long-winded, and time-consuming set of questions about their ancestors. Behind them in the queue might be the traumatized relatives of a recently deceased person.

The inquiry into service goals and alignment identified a number of important service metrics that related to times taken to answer queries from the public. All targets were being met, although the targets themselves were not always ambitious (i.e., customers coming in to the office should be seen by reception staff within 30 minutes). Looking forward, the discussion highlighted a set of proposals made at the national level by the National Audit Office (NAO, 2002). This focused on service developments around the needs of families and individuals. It highlighted the need to be open to the prospect of partnerships within the public sector (e.g., hospitals) and beyond to the private sector (e.g., local wedding or funeral services, family history services). Another set of ideas from central government for modernization was also influential. This was the idea that government services in general could be increasingly organized around "life events." This proposal suggested that much of the public's engagement with government is predictable, taking place in response to defined life episodes. Births, deaths, and marriages are three such life events. It was likely that in the future the act of registering one of these events would initiate a network of information exchanges with the benefit being that the customer needs to engage only once with government over this particular episode.

Beyond a general discussion of these central government initiatives, the discussion of service goals faltered. There were pressing objectives and a number of popular proposals that focused on the use of the corporate call centre to provide basic information and appointment making services (thereby freeing the specialist resources in the BDM centre), and the provision of e-mail for communications within the Council. However, these were clearly incremental in nature, designed to fix existing service deficiencies. The existing goals of the service were not called into question, and there was no obvious realignment of the service around the modernizing agenda of central government. The agenda, and all of its radical potential, remained distant. Instead, it was acknowledged that the SPRINT project set the groundwork for more extensive service reorganization, but the timescale and means for achieving these more fundamental changes were not established. Once again, from many perspectives, the project was described as a success, although the modesty of its ambition was to become an increasing source of frustration (see Table 1).

Social Services

The third case study is the most recent. It reflects a growing awareness that while SPRINT was being used to successfully deliver change to the organization, it was falling short as a means of inculcating more radical change. It was argued that, in part, this might be due to difficulties in securing sufficient participation from staff of affected services.

Although SPRINT is avowedly participative in nature, in practice, staff was often unable to take part in SPRINT projects in a rigorous way. Usually, this was due to the demands of their normal work activity. As a result, the SPRINT project in social services reinvigorated the participative element by introducing a new concept, that of the "e-envoy." The e-envoys were volunteers from an operational area who came to work on the Change Team full-time for the life of the project. The mission of the e-envoy was to think creatively about change possibilities and to represent these ideas to the operational division. Staff was asked to apply for the post prior to the commencement of the BPR study. As part of this application process, they were asked to include a statement describing their feelings and ideas about e-government and service innovation.

The advertisement of an e-envoy position in Social Services brought forward two applicants, both qualified social workers. One had substantial Internet experience. Neither had taken an active part in major organizational change programs. After consultation, it was decided that both should be appointed to the post, with two temporary staff being brought in to provide cover. Following an initial period working on the SPRINT analyses, it was also decided to extend the period of the e-envoys' SPRINT activity to five months. By this stage, it also was clear that the core Change Team would play only a supervisory role in the Social Services project, a position that was a significant retrenchment from that taken in the Decision Making and BDM projects. The social workers quickly became adept at using SPRINT and soon found their way to generating some noteworthy innovations.

The social services case was an interesting one, for, in some ways, it was the most potentially radical of all the SPRINT projects reported here. Among the many ideas developed by the e-envoys was the restructuring of the service around self-contained practices (analogous to local medical practices) and the development of a new, independent, Internet-based information service, which would be responsible for the sourcing and maintenance of care information (e.g., care home vacancies). These ideas aligned with the overriding goals of the social care function — to provide high quality care to members of society. However, they deviated sharply from some deeply entrenched goals of the organization itself — to maintain itself as an entity and to retain control over the information its uses. This radicalism was sometimes the source of tension within the SPRINT project itself. The Change Team insisted on promoting alignment, using SPRINT to ensure that the social workers think about the existing goals of the service and whether any particular innovation conforms to or diverts from them. The social workers worked differently, instinctively seeing the virtue of an innovation and then giving a post hoc view of how the innovation does or does not fit in with the goals of the organization. They viewed SPRINT's requirement that they pre-think alignment issues in Phase 1 as a restriction on their creative operation. "I don't know who owns this process," complained one social worker, "but it's not us." At one stage, colleagues of the social workers in the Social Services directorate also raised concerns about the innovative nature of the ideas. They sought to remind the e-envoys about legacy issues arising from a recently sourced software package. They argued that they should not propose any initiative that was inconsistent with the functionality of this software.

As the project progressed, the redesign ideas of the e-envoys became increasingly well focused and well described. The ideas lost none of their radicalism but were accompanied by a number of less profound, more incremental changes (see Table 1).

However, ultimately, it was only these less radical ideas that were implemented. The more radical ideas of self-contained, local practices and Internet-based sourcing were placed on-hold. From the point of view of the e-envoys, this meant that the project was unsuccessful. Ultimately, as the project neared its conclusion, they had faced the problem of selling their radicalism back to their colleagues in Social Services. They were unable to build sufficient support for their radical vision. This is interesting, given that the appointment of e-envoys was originally motivated by the wish to source ideas directly from operational staff and to build a focus for ongoing innovation in the operational division. It seems that radicalism is still radicalism and will be difficult to sell, whatever its source.

DISCUSSION

This chapter questions the extent to which process redesign methodology can achieve radical change in the complex context of e-government. The discussion is organized in two parts. The first addresses the main research question, and the second develops the implications for practice.

Theoretical Issues: The Tendency Towards Caution

Under analysis, the projects perhaps can be considered successful, or as accomplishing change, only up to a point. All three have been associated with changes in the departments concerned, and yet in each case we see the projects aligning with the more cautious of an alternative set of goals.

In the Decision Making project, the SPRINT consultants took a hands-on approach to the development of the new design. They worked closely and shared responsibility with end users and managers. They clearly demarcated ownership of the project; it resided with the manager of the committee staff. The result was a successful implementation of SOLAR, giving rise to a number of business benefits (e.g., more rapid dissemination of reports). However, the most radically innovative ideas were left on the shelf. The idea of reconstituting the committee support function as an information management function was not implemented. Neither was the proposal that authors of documents should input them directly to SOLAR. Both of these innovations would have enhanced the alignment of the service with its declared goal of supporting policy development. This would be achieved by further speeding the process and by ensuring the development of a rigorously catalogued library of reports for further policy development. Retracing the steps of the project reveals that Change Team members proposed both of these fundamental ideas. They were supported by the Senior Manager and his staff. Nonetheless, the failure to implement speaks eloquently. Judged against this challenge (promoting alignment), the Decision Making project only was partially successful. Perhaps what we are describing exemplifies the difference between formal service goals and the tacit goals of those carrying out the service. Yes, all sides agreed that the radical innovations would improve the contribution of the service to its formal goals, but how well accepted are these goals? Do they conflict with another set of goals, the internalized goals of the service providers themselves? These internalized goals might dictate that service innovations are kept within a comfort-zone of current process and technology know-how. Hence, in this case, the very idea of understood and accepted business goals has proved to be an oversimplification, which has important ramifications for the challenge of developing a radical concept of e-government. The SPRINT ethos of participative organizational development will not necessarily dislodge the caution of the project owners. Instead, it seems that the organization will migrate towards the goals it holds most closely, and not necessarily the goals expressed most explicitly (Jackson, 2003; Scott, 2001).

In the case of births, deaths, and marriages, we again see a SPRINT expert taking a hands-on approach to the development of design ideas. However, again, following the SPRINT prescription, ownership resided with the manager of the BDM function. The SPRINT consultant worked closely with this manager and her subordinate staff. The radical agenda was identified (to some extent it is prepackaged), as it was partially described in a governmental vision for service development incorporating partnership, utilizing the concept of life events as a new portal for government services. This redefined the goals of the service. Ultimately, the SPRINT project did no more than prepare the groundwork for this new vision. This radical vision remained remote, with only the most pressing needs being met by the change project. If this is a sensible outcome, it is also conservative. The idea of introducing e-mail and call centre support facilities is not bold. Perhaps the most glaring shortcoming is the fact that the study has not brought forth a plan for building on this groundwork. Yet, an interesting footnote is that, in this case, the SPRINT consultant admitted to a sense of frustration. She saw the opportunity to develop a new model around integrated services. Taking bereavement as an example, the function of registering a death could have cross-departmental implications and could embrace social services, housing, and other relevant areas. By providing a range of services, staff would be able to sort out a number of difficulties for bereaved friends and relatives in one single counselling session. When asked why this idea did not figure in the SPRINT design activity, she replied that she felt constrained to work with the needs and preferences of the client. From their technologically disadvantaged position, even the introduction of e-mail felt radical. In summary, then, while a radical vision and radical set of goals were agreed upon, the participants in the study prioritized their own internal, team goals. It was towards this more comfortable set of goals that the project aligned.

These first two cases show how apparently successful projects can still fall short when judged against the challenge of promoting alignment with a revised set of goals. The third case adds a further twist. Here, some operational staff members were selected for their innovative thinking and given a special status of e-envoy. A role reversal took place. In the BDM case, the SPRINT consultant had been unable to develop some radical ideas because the operational managers owned the study. These operational managers were content with more mundane initiatives. This time, it was the e-envoys who felt frustrated as the Change Team and the SPRINT process itself appeared, at least for a time, to act as a brake on their ambition. Quite early on, one e-envoy complained about the ownership of the study. Nonetheless, progress was made, and the e-envoys developed their proposals. A radical vision emerged, which served a refreshed set of goals for the function as a whole. However, in the end, conservatism again won out. The e-envoys struggled to sell their proposals to their departments. The fact that they were insiders and that they belonged to the affected department mattered little, it seems, when the proposals involved a significant realignment of organization and goals. A familiar theme emerges: What are the goals that are most valued by the participants?

Based on Hirschheim and Sabherwal (2001), these cases seem to constitute a struggle to control the direction of alignment. In each case study, we see a complex dynamic in which alignment is contested between different stakeholders with different goals. Those who act as guardians of the SPRINT process take the most radical positions, whether they are experts in the method or staff co-opted into the process (as in the case of Social Services). From whichever position they originate, and however radical their vision, these SPRINT consultants have to negotiate the final outcome with the participating stakeholders in the organization. This negotiation is not necessarily done explicitly and rationally. Clearly in the Decision Making process, implicit agendas dominate. This is a two-way street of a different kind. Instead of a push and pull between a technological and business-led strategy, we see a contest between those charged with developing a vision and those who participate in the process of creating this vision, but are one step removed. Ultimately, this gap between the SPRINT consultants and the participant stakeholder base is crucial. Key points of difference do emerge, and different weightings are given to different elements of the design. The process of handover from the consultants back to the organization will always mean that the changes are implemented to the degree that they have been understood and purchased by this wider group of participants.

Methodological Implications: Pursuing Radical Transformation

It follows that the successes in these case histories are tempered by the view that they fail to exemplify the potentially radical nature of e-government. It is not even as though the radical possibilities of each project were unappreciated. In each case, we see the SPRINT project being able to set up a range of design options, but each time it is the more conservative options that are implemented. Seemingly, the process focus of the intervention does not dislodge the core values and shared identity of the participants. The most institutionalized values remain intact (Scott, 2001). Essentially, then, these SPRINT projects constitute effective ICT-oriented change of a familiar flavor, and not a visionary, new e-government prescription.

So what lies beyond these projects, and what, if anything, can engender a spirit of change that matches the ambition of the e-government literature? How might BPR methodology support the bolder concept of e-government? The general management literature provides many relevant clues. Arguably, in none of the cases do we see the sense of urgency, the belief that the organization must change, that is often set out as a condition of successful change projects (e.g., Kotter, 1996). Equally, it is arguable that insufficient attention is paid to quick wins and to new reward structures (e.g., Moss-Kanter, 2001). Such prescriptions seem to have a ready applicability to the cases recounted here, yet in practice their application may be problematic. Difficulties may stem from the conversion of these ideas that originate in private sector change to the domain of government. Hence, it may be appreciably more difficult to create the sense of urgency, the feeling that the organization must change or die, and to revise reward structures so as to generate an innovative culture in a government agency rather than in a private sector company. Perhaps, here is the kernel of the problem for the radical concept of e-government — the problem of fit between good practice in change management and the structures and expectations of the public sector.

Moreover, going beyond this change literature, another still more fundamental set of lessons may be drawn by researching the history of discontinuous change in business. These have interesting methodological implications. Christensen's depiction of product innovation suggests an alternate strategy in the change process, building new satellite service operations and allowing them to run alongside, and potentially take over, the older structures (Christensen, 1997). One consequence of Christensen's findings is that the organization serving new goals must be separated from the existing organization and its prior goals. Christensen's argument pivots on this point. If the change is a threat to the prevailing organizational interests, then its future cannot be entrusted to these interests. It must be established and run separately. If this lesson is indeed transferable to the domain of e-government, then perhaps it suggests that in all normal circumstances a participative approach will not be radical. Thus far, perhaps SPRINT has been restricted by its own participative ethos. Its underlying precepts and inclusive, narrative-building techniques might ultimately encourage the status quo to be represented within its many episodes and structures. It follows that perhaps e-government must adopt an unorthodox change strategy, if it truly is to challenge the existing alignment of organizational interests and goals (Kawalek & Temren, 2004). The radical agenda seems to pivot on this seemingly intractable problem: to develop change methods that are appropriate to the public sector, encouraging the engagement of stakeholders and yet being freed from the caution associated with participative approaches.

CONCLUSIONS

The cases exemplify just how difficult it is to meet the challenge of remaking government for the information age. The rhetoric suggests that radical solutions should be the norm and that new technology should be a catalyst amidst a range of organizational and cultural changes. In fact, we tend to find a different outcome. We have reported on projects that start with high ambition but then slip backwards to a positive, but appreciably more modest, result.

It would be easy to fashion these experiences into a typical tale of top-down managerial philosophy versus bottom-up innovative thinking. In one corner, we might see the conservatism of managers, and in the other, the freethinking potential unruliness of more junior staff. This tale of two perspectives would be a highly misleading depiction. Neither alignment nor innovation, conservatism nor radicalness, wholly resides in the gamut of management or junior staff. Each has the potential to promote alignment and to promote innovative radicalism, as each is able to disrupt alignment and dampen innovation. Instead, we see a collective decision across the organizational strata, and in each case, the outcome favors the less radical of the visions that the SPRINT project develops.

Instead, it is more insightful to address the general implication that these cases hold for e-government itself. They highlight the problematic nature of e-government as it was introduced in this chapter. For some, it is a bold and radical vision. Yet, can this vision be attained? The evidence gathered here suggests the negative. What then is the real nature of e-government, and does it amount to anything more than good practice in ICT-enabled change?

This general concern for the problematic nature of e-government brings with it a methodological dimension. Essentially, if a radical vision remains for e-government, how is it to be achieved? This problem can be addressed by looking at the shortcomings of SPRINT as they are manifest here. The key is to understand the implicit change process in these SPRINT projects. Using the SPRINT method, the participants are asked to think explicitly about the goals of the service and to identify process changes that seek alignment with these goals. They are contemporaneously invited to review and revise the goals and then to develop a new set of more radical changes. Essentially, the process divides into two streams governed by a four-step process — articulate goals, seek alignment, review and revise goals, and seek alignment with new goals. In each of the reported cases, this leads to a radical vision being created and then discarded. From this comes the suggestion that the participative nature of SPRINT, which is arguably a key strength, might also serve to weaken its ability to deliver the radical agenda. Looking forward, a key methodological issue concerns the management of radical change in e-government. How might SPRINT and other methods deliver the bolder articulation of e-government?

The problematic scope of e-government that is discussed in the Introduction seems, in the end, to reverberate through to the outcomes of these projects. Are we seeing something new and challenging, or is it something more modest, perhaps no more than an incremental step onward in IT deployment and process redesign? However, it is ultimately reported, with e-government we see again that organizational transformation is a fundamentally challenging prospect. The literature in public and private sectors is replete with cases of failure (Cabinet Office, 2000; Davenport, 1993); then, when change does take root, the financial and organizational costs can be high (BusinessWeek, 2001). In this light, perhaps we should be prepared to accept that the birth of the so-called information age government will be made up of a huge number of change projects as people try to apply new technologies and ideas to their organizations. A few of these projects will be heralded as great successes. Some will be seen as dramatic failures. Many will, in some way, be between these poles — modest success or modest failure. As evidence continues to build around e-government, perhaps it is only in the grand sweep that we will begin to see the occasional radical success that becomes its hallmark.

REFERENCES

Arthur, B. (1990, February). Positive feedbacks in the economy. *Scientific American*.

Baskerville, R. & Wood-Harper, A.T. (1998). Diversity of information systems action research methods. *European Journal of Information Systems*, 7, 90-107.

Beer, S. (1985). Diagnosing the system for organizations. Chicheter, UK: John Wiley & Sons.

Bell, D. (1973). *The coming of post-industrial society*. New York: Basic Books.

Benjamin, R. (1993). Managing information technology enabled change. In Avison et al. (Eds.), *Human, organisational and social dimensions of information systems development* (pp. 381-398). North Holland: IFIP.

Chang, L.-J., & Powell, P. (1998). Towards a framework for business process re-engineering in small and medium-sized enterprises. *Information Systems Journal*, 8, 199-215.

Checkland, P., & Scholes, J. (1991). *Soft systems methodology in action.* Chichester, UK: Wiley.

Christensen, C.M. (1997). *The innovators dilemma: When new technologies cause great firms to fail.* Boston: Harvard Business School Press.

Ciborra, C. (1997). De profundis? Deconstructing the concept of strategic alignment. *Scandanavian Journal of Information Systems, 9,* 67-82.

Davenport, T. (1992). Process innovation: Reengineering work through information technology. *Harvard Business School Press.*

Deakins, E., & Dillon, S.M. (2002). E-government in New Zealand: The local authority perspective. *The International Journal of Public Sector Management, 15*(5), 375-398.

Dow, N., Teicher, J, & Hughes, O. (2002). E-government: A new route to public sector quality. *Managing Service Quality, 12*(6), 384-393.

Downes, L., & Mui, C. (1998). *Unleashing the killer app.* Boxton: Harvard Business School Press.

E-biz surprise (2003, May 12). *BusinessWeek.*

e.gov electronic services for the 21st century, performance and innovation unit (2000, September). Her Majesty's Stationery Office.

Greenwood, D.J., & Levin, M. (1998). *Introduction to action research: Social research for social change.* London: Sage.

Hackney, R., & Little, S. (1999). Opportunistic strategy formulation for IS/IT planning. *European Journal of Information Systems, 8,* 119-126.

Haeckel, S.H. (2000). Adaptive enterprise: *Creating and leading sense and respond organizations.* Boston: Harvard Business School Press.

Hammer, M. (1990, July-August). Reengineering work: Don't automate, obliterate. *Harvard Business Review,* 104-112.

Heeks, R. (2001). Reinventing government in the information age, international practice in IT-enabled public sector reform. *Routledge Research in Information Technology and Society.*

Henderson, J.C., & Venkatraman, N. (1993). Strategic alignment: Leveraging information technology for transforming organizations. *IBM Systems Journal, 31*(1), 4-16.

Hirschheim, R., & Sabherwal, R. (2001). Detours in the path to strategic information systems alignment. *California Management Review, 44*(1) 87-108.

Holmes, D. (2001). *EGOV: E-business strategies for government.* London: Nicolas Brealey Publishing.

Jackson, M.C. (2003). *Systems thinking: Creative holism for managers.* Chichester, UK: Wiley-VCH.

Kawalek, P., & Temren, Y. (2004). *Innovation, CRM national project.* Retrieved from http://www2.salford.gov.uk/icrm

Kotter, J.P. (1996). *Leading change.* Boston: Harvard Business School Press.

Luling, D. (2001). Taking it online: Anyway, anyplace, anytime … Tennessee anytime. *Journal of Government Financial Management, 50,* 42-49.

Macreadie, R.D., & Sandon, C. (1999). IT-enabled change: Evaluating an improvisational perspective. *European Journal of Information Systems, 8,* 247-259.

Markus, L. (2004, March). Technochange management: Using IT to drive organizational change. *Journal of Information Technology, 19*(1), 4-20.

Martin, D., Wastell, D., & Bowers, J. (1998). An ethnographic systems design method: The development and evaluation of an Internet-based electronic banking application. *Proceedings of the 8th European Conference on Information Systems*, Aix-en-Provence, France.

Modernising government (1999, March). Cabinet Office, Her Majesty's Stationery Office.

Moss-Kanter, R. (2001). *Evolve, succeeding in the digital culture of tomorrow.* Boston: Harvard Business School Press.

Mumford, E. (1986). *Using computers for business success: The ETHICS method.* Manchester: MBS Press.

National Audit Office (2002). *Using call centres to deliver public services.* Value For Money Report, National Audit Office.

ODPM (2004). *eGov@Local, e-government strategies for local government.* Office of the Deputy Prime Minister. Retrieved from www.localegov.gov.uk

Orlikowski, W., & Hofman, J.D. (1997). An improvisational model for change management: The case of groupware technologies. *Sloan Management Review, 38*, 11-21.

Reason, P., & Bradbury, H. (2001). *Handbook of Action Research.* London: Sage.

Rethinking the Internet (2001, March 21). *BusinessWeek.*

Salford City Council (1999). *People not technology.* Internal report.

Scott, R. (2001). *Institutions and organizations.* London: Sage Publications.

Serafeimidis, V., & Smithson, S. (2000). Information systems evaluation in practice: A case study of organisational change. *Journal of Information Technology, 15*, 93-105.

Simonsen, J. (1999). How do we take care of strategic alignment: Constructing a design approach. *Scandanavian Journal of Information Systems, 11*, 51-72.

SPRINT (2004). *Salford process reengineering involving new technology.* Retrieved from www.sprint.gov.uk

Tissan, T., & Heikkilä, J. (2001). Successful re-engineering-learning by doing. *International Journal of Logistics: Research and Applications, 4*, 329.

Traunmuller, R., & Wimmer, M.A. (2003). E-government at a decisive moment: Sketching a roadmap to excellence [Lecture]. *Electronic Government, Second International Conference, EGOV*, Springer, Berlin.

Venkatraman, N. (1994). *IT-enabled business transformation: From automation to business scope redefinition.* MIT Sloan School of Management, Reprint 3526.

Warboys, B.C., Kawalek, P., Robertson, I., & Greenwood, R.M. (1999). *Business information systems: A process approach.* London: McGraw-Hill.

Wastell, D. (1999). Learning dysfunctions and information systems development: Overcoming the social defences with transitional objects *MIS Quarterly, 23*, 581-600.

Wastell, D.G., Kawalek, P., Langmead-Jones, P., & Ormerod, R. (2004, in press). Information systems and partnership in multi-agency networks: An action research project on crime reduction. *Information and Organisation.*

Wastell, D., & Newman, M. (1996). Information systems design and organisational change in the ambulance services: A tale of two cities. *Accounting, Management and Information Technologies, 6*, 283-300.

Wastell, D., White, P., & Kawalek, P. (1994). A methodology for business process redesign: Experiences and issues. *Journal of Strategic Information Systems, 3*(1), 23-40.

Wilson, D., & Game, C. (1998). *Local government in the United Kingdom.* Macmillan.

This article was previously published in the *Journal of Global Information Management,* 13(1), pp. 79-101, © 2005.

Chapter XII

A Disconnect in Stakeholders' Perceptions from Emerging Realities of Teledensity Growth in Africa's Least Developed Countries

Victor W. Mbarika, Louisiana State University, USA

Peter N. Meso, Georgia State University, USA

Philip F. Musa, The University of Alabama at Birmingham, USA

ABSTRACT

With the dynamic and meteoric rise in teledensity diffusion across Sub Saharan Africa, one would expect a departure in the perceptions of stakeholders as they relate to the Bernt and Weiss framework that identifies organizational, financial, technological, and geographical factors as the key impediments to teledensity growth. The findings of this research show that there is disconnect between current happenings and perception of stakeholders. Specifically, there is no change in stakeholders' perceptions with respect to the framework mentioned above. However, historical and recent teledensity data from Africa's Least Developed Countries illustrate that the model is inconsistent with the emerging realities in these countries, and that it may be getting obsolete. This leads us to conjecture that in this new dispensation, there may be some emerging factors, issues, constraints, and opportunities that may be of greater importance to understanding telecommunications capabilities in these countries and the world at large.

INRODUCTION

Recent world growth in network infrastructure and tele-accessibility reflects the important role telecommunications plays in social and economic growth. The global diffusion of mobile Information and Communication Technologies (ICTs) has been unprecedented in the past three to four years, expanding from fifty million to over one billion by the end of 2002 (UNCTAD, 2002; ITU, 2002). This has especially been the case in the least developed countries (LDCs) where, for decades, consumers have experienced limited access to ICTs for a myriad of reasons (de Vreede et al., 1998; Meso & Duncan, 2000; ITU, 2002). In these countries, mobile ICTs have increased telephone access by a factor of above six in less than three years and by the end of 2001, 28 out of 49 LDCs had more mobile than fixed subscribers (UNCTAD, 2002; ITU, 2002).

It should be pointed out that fixed-line teledensity in most of Sub-Saharan Africa remains below one (Uneca, 2003). Conversely, the growth rate in mobile telephony in Africa has been accelerating and was the highest of all continents in 2001 (UNECA, 2003). Africa now has more than 25 million mobile ICT users (see appendix 1). By the end of 2001, 28 of Africa's 54 countries had more mobile-phone than fixed-line subscribers, a higher percentage than any other continent (ITU, 2002; Mbarika et al., 2002c). Not only is mobile telephony quickly overcoming the diffusion gaps endeared by fixed line phone networks, but that the rising mobile phone teledensities are showing positive signs of influence on the indices of economic and social development (UNECA, 2003).

Teledensity remains a key factor of interest in the developmental potential of Sub-Saharan Africa. First, the telephone infrastructure is the core backbone upon which the region can implement and develop information-age services such as e-commerce, m-commerce, telemedicine and e-government. Second, it enables and empowers vast numbers of users to access telephone and in Internet-based communication services such as e-mail, Web browsing, instant messaging, and text messaging among others. Adequate communications infrastructure enables citizens to access the global resource pools of knowledge, information, finances and markets that empower them to effectively engage in capacity building, income generation and skills-acquisition activities beneficial to the local communities in which they belong. Third, enhanced teledensity provides the means by which many more citizens can become actively involved in the governance process and contribute effectively to governance issues of the day. As such, enhanced teledensity has the potential for leveraging the quality of governance, long acknowledged as lacking or being very poor in most counties of this region (World Bank, UNDP, etc.). Fourth, growing teledensity holds the promise of enabling Sub-Saharan countries to effectively and significantly participate in the global financial, securities, and commodities markets. Presently, participation in these highly digitized markets requires extensive levels of high-bandwidth teledensity.

While there has been a growing interest in researching ICTs and teledensity in Sub-Saharan Africa, most of the published research has concentrated on the economics and regulation of telecommunications (Alleman et al., 1994; Kenny, 2000; Wallsten, 2001; Mureithi, 2003; Makhaya & Robberts, 2003; McCormick, 2003; Cogburn, 2003; Wilson & Wong, 2003; Kibati & Kraijit, 1999). Few studies have studied ICTs in Sub-Saharan areas from the context of management information systems (Adam & Wood, 1999; Adam, 1996; Mbarika et al., 2002; Darley, 2001; Kenny, 2000; Nidumolu, 1996; de Vreede et al., 1998). Even among these, most have focused on the diffusion of Internet technologies and have largely adopted a quantitative analysis approach to measuring the extent of diffusion and the impacts of these diffusions on economic indices (examples Mbarika et al., 2002; Darley, 2001; Kenny, 2000). Studies on stakeholder perceptions remain few. Even fewer are studies that specifically address teledensity within the context of sub-saharan Africa. A search for peer-reviewed articles containing the terms *teledensity* and *Africa* yielded only four articles, three being by the same author (Madden & Savage, 2000; Mbarika et al., 2000, 2002a, 2002b).

In this regard, the study is conducted within the context of Sub-Saharan Africa for several reasons. First, there is a dearth of information systems and ICTs research that focuses on Sub-Saharan Africa. A search in three top-ranked journals dedicated to research in IS (*MIS Quarterly, Information Systems Research,* and *Journal of MIS*) as well as Journal of the AIS, the flagship journal of the Association for Information Systems, conducted under the guidelines obtained from two recent publications on IS journal rankings (Mylonopoulos & Theoharakis, 2001; Whitman & Townsend, 1999), yielded only a single article (in JMIS) related to SSA (de Vreede et al., 1998). Second, the region has witnessed meteoric growth in ICT density in the past three to five years and is credited with having the fastest teledensity growth in the world (UNCTAD, 2002; ITU, 2002). The impacts of ICT use on society may therefore be more magnified and easily visible here more than in other parts of the world where the marginal utility from ICT use is plateauing. Third, ICTs are said to have significant impacts on social and economic development. The Sub-Saharan region, being home to the vast majority of Least Developed Countries (LDCs) becomes an area of genuine interest regarding assessing the effects of ICTs on society, individuals and business entities.

The premise of our study is to take a step back to understand why Africa's LDCs are so behind the rest of the world in enjoying the full potential of sound telecommunications infrastructures. In essence we want to challenge researchers and practitioners to reexamine the obstacles these countries face before getting into the excitement of complex technologies in a bid to mimic ongoing 'high-tech' trends of the developed 'West.' No known study has sought to address the congruence, if any, in stakeholder perceptions of these obstacles and emerging realities with a focus on sub-Saharan Africa.

Given the potential benefits that could come with adequate telecommunications capabilities, and given that teledensity has been typically used as a measure of a country's telecommunications infrastructure (Gille, 1986; Saunders et al., 1994), the questions in this research are:

- What are the stakeholders' perceptions with respect to teledensity growth obstacles in Africa's LDCs?
- How do the stakeholders' perceptions reflect the realities of teledensity growth in Africa's LDCs today?

To address these questions, we conduct an empirical study of stakeholders' perceptions as to the relevance and criticality of the obstacles to teledensity growth pulled from existing literature. Based partly on the evidence of recent exponential growth in wireless technologies in the region, even in the absence of significant capital investments, we seek to contrast the stakeholder opinions to the realities of Africa's LDCs today.

This paper is organized as follows: First, key obstacles to teledensity growth are identified from existing literature. We then gather stakeholders' perceptions of these obstacles using a validated survey instrument. The data from the survey are then analyzed using confirmatory factor analysis and Friedman's rank order methods. We then investigate if there are any differences in the stakeholders' perceptions relative to current trends in teledensity growth in Sub Saharan Africa. Implications of the findings and suggestions about possible emerging factors that may call for future research are then presented.

Literature Review

Since the early 1960s when most African countries became independent, organizational, financial, technological, and geographical reasons have been sited as the key limitations to teledensity growth in the region (ITU, 1965; U.N., 1969, Hardy, 1980; Maitland Commission, 1984; Jussawalla, 1988). Many African countries today still do not have clearly articulated comprehensive policy frameworks on telecommunications (UNECA, 2003). For instance, until the mid-1970s, Ghana's telecommunications infrastructure was based on the model bequeathed by the former colonial government (Boafo & Kwame, 1991). It is possible that Africa's telecommunications policy makers' perceptions have been shaped by longstanding experiences with unreliable, underdeveloped, and expensive telecommunications infrastructure. They may have also bought into the belief that teledensity growth is limited by the four factors cited above, and that their countries would require huge capital investments to develop their telecommunications capabilities.

The African continent, which is three-and-a-half times the size of the United States of America, consists of 54 countries with a total population of 770 million people. It is also home to the largest concentration of the least developed countries of the world. One of the major prerequisites of economic integration in a modern, complex society is the development of sound telecommunications infrastructure. The establishment of a modern, reliable, and rapidly expanding telecommunications infrastructure contributes considerably to the promotion of a variety of activities of economic expansion (World Bank, 1991). Some researchers have associated the level of a country's telecommunications infrastructure to teledensity (Gille, 1986; Saunders et al., 1994). Teledensity refers to the number of main telephone lines for every 100 inhabitants. In this study, we examine obstacles to teledensity growth in LDCs.

There is a great disparity between the level of teledensity of Least Developed Countries (LDCs) and that of developed countries. For example, the average teledensity for LDCs is about 0.29, whereas it is 11.57 for the world, 31.95 for Europe, 68.2 for Sweden, and 70.0 for the United States (ITU, 2002; Mbarika et al., 2002a). The total number of telephone main lines in the 48 LDCs is about 1.5 million, which is about 1% of the total number of lines in the United States (Rorissa, 1999). Least Developed Countries are defined as low-income countries suffering from long-term constraints against growth. In particular, these growth constraints include low levels of human resource development and severe structural, economical, social, and political weaknesses (Austin, 1990). Currently, there are 48 LDCs as defined by the United Nations, of which 30 (or greater than 60%) are in Africa. A criteria for LDCs classification is presented in Appendix 1.

Researchers have shown that there is a high correlation between the level of telecommunications infrastructure represented by teledensity and the level of economic power represented by the national per capita Gross Domestic Product (Saunders et al., 1994). Other studies have established a relationship between the telecommunications infrastructure and the national economy (Hardy, 1980), and also that growth of telecommunications technologies promote resource mobilization through improved division of labor, and hence, an agent of development (Jussawalla, 1988).

The ability of the telecommunications sector to provide an internationally competitive network for transferring information within an emerging global economy has significant implications for trade and socioeconomic development. Benefits of efficient delivery of telecommunications services to a nation's economy abound. Modern telecommunications infrastructure reduces the costs of acquiring information, and improves the efficiency of product and factor markets. They are also known to increase information flows across countries, thereby integrating domestic and international markets. Telecommunications infrastructures also provide nations with the potential for human capital development, and enable nations to enhance their capacity for the delivery of social, health and educational services to citizens remotely removed from physical delivery points. Further, they are known to generate direct productivity benefits for information intensive sectors such as the finance, wholesale trade, tourism, and transportation, and demonstrate strong positive correlations strongly with economic development indices (Meso & Duncan, 2000; Jussawalla & Lamberton, 1982; Greenstein & Spiller, 1995; Mbarika et al., 2002c; Cronin et al., 1993; Jipp, 1963; Alleman et al., 1994; Madden & Savage, 2000; Antonelli, 1991).

Telecommunications-infrastructure-enabled knowledge-intensive products and services have become a major source of economic growth in the more developed countries (Tisdell, 1972). The lesser-developed countries are beginning to realize the significant impacts that extensive telecommunication infrastructures could bear on the development of their economies. Many have placed deliberate emphasis in the development of these infrastructures as driving forces in their national development plans (European Bank for Reconstruction and Development — EBRD, 1995; Organisation for Economic Cooperation and Development — OECD, 1996; Spiller & Cardilli, 1997).

The political leaders and administrators who emerged in post-independence Africa were mainly what Boafo and Kwame call "nationalist-politician-journalists" who led their people in the fight for independence. Once the nationalist leaders assumed the reins of government, they tended to move into their new roles as policy-makers and political leaders — with little or no clear vision to improve the telecommunications infrastructures of their countries. Boafo and Kwame (1991) provides a useful perspective of this scenario:

Prominent independence leaders such as Kwame Nkrumah of Ghana, Nnamdi Azikiwe of Nigeria, Jomo Kenyatta of Kenya, Felix Houphouet Boigny of Ivory Coast, and Leopold Senghor of Senegal were leading journalists who established or edited newspapers and other publications used to express nationalist sentiments, criticize colonial telecommunications policies, and advocate political independence. Upon the attainment of independence, these nationalist leaders became political leaders and policy makers. They moved into government with their newspapers and exercised excessive control over the media in the generally professed interest of nation building, political unity, and national consciousness. The new political leaders and administrators made very little genuine modification in the structure, utilization, and orientation of telecommunications infrastructure to make them effective and meaningful instruments for development.

In general, these countries have continued to suffer from a poor state of telecommunications infrastructure when compared to other parts of the world. Sub-Saharan Africa is the only major area of the world that does not have its own satellite (Mbarika, 2001). This part of the world continues to lag behind other parts of the world in terms of the state of telecommunications development and various other measures of development.

To examine the obstacles to growth of teledensity in Africa's LDCs, we borrow from the Bernt and Weiss (1993) framework, which groups international telecommunications issues into four categories: organizational, technological, financial, and geographical. Organizational issues include governmental monopoly versus competition, deregulation, and privatization. Financial issues include availability of appropriate funding needed to develop a country's telecommunications infrastructure. Technological issues refer to the purchase and maintenance of telecommunications related equipment, including personal computers, while geographical issues concerns universal service policies which involve the provision of telecommunications infrastructure for both urban and rural areas within a country, as well as issues related to regional cooperation among groups of countries. We used the same framework, but with teledensity diffusion placed at the core. Doing this is plausible, given the high correlation between teledensity and telecommunications infrastructure cited earlier (Gille, 1986; Saunders et al., 1994). Figure 1 presents a modified version of the Bernt and Weiss framework. The model shows four major obstacles that are hypothesized to hinder the growth of teledensity in Africa's LDCs followed by a discussion of each obstacle.

Organizational Obstacles

The regulatory frameworks of most African LDCs indicate that the governments still have monopoly power over these countries' telecommunications infrastructure. Access to communications channels is largely controlled by state monopolies. In a World Telecommunications Development Report, the ITU points out that a major obstacle to the telephone line penetration in LDCs was that telephone services are provided by monopolized, government-run organizations, limiting the incentives for better performance (ITU, 1998).

The government monopolies of many LDCs lack basic knowledge of key global trends in information technology (Jensen, 1995). Although the governments of these countries do not directly control the penetration of Internet hosts in these countries, they do have control over the number of telephone lines.

Figure 1. Modified version of Bernt and Weiss framework for growth of teledensity

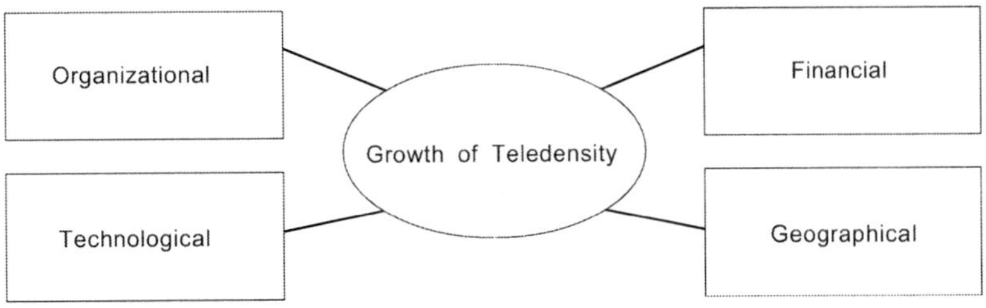

FINANCIAL OBSTACLES

Africa's LDCs are faced with very weak economic structures. The financial obstacles include low Gross Domestic Product (GDP), low GDP per capita, and insufficient financial autonomy of the operating entities. These financial constraints pose major problems for LDCs that generally have a very low average per capita income of only about US$283 per year. This amount just 7% of the global average income of US$3,980 per year. Also, the insufficient financial autonomy of operating entities results in even stronger government control, leading to serious inefficiencies and unnecessary 'red tape.'

As evident in other sectors, there is a perpetual scarcity of foreign exchange for private sector investments in the telecommunications sector (Wellenius, 1989). This makes the cost of importing computing and telecommunications equipment almost unaffordable. Furthermore, the poor state of the LDCs' banking systems makes it difficult for African LDCs to carry out telecommunications transactions that may necessitate the use of credit cards and other financial-related transactions that require the use of a banking institution (Mbarika et al., 2000).

Technological Obstacles

Technological issues are major concerns in providing adequate growth of teledensity in Africa's LDCs; the city of New York or the Tokyo conurbation has more telephone lines than the whole continent of Africa (Boafo & Kwame, 1991; Williamson, 1991). Because the telephone systems in Africa's LDCs were most likely placed to serve the needs of government, they tended to be confined to major cities. This has left most of the rural population of Africa's LDCs (which is at least 70% of the total population) without any form of telephone access. As a result a good proportion of Africans living in the LDCs, especially the rural areas, have never made a phone call, let alone surfed the Web.

In the World Telecommunications Development Report (ITU, 1994), the ITU reports that LDCs use outdated equipment needed to provide the connection lines. The equipment is also inadequately maintained, resulting in poor quality of service and loss of revenues. In many cases, manufacturers abroad have stopped producing old systems that are still widely used in LDCs, making the maintenance of the already obsolete systems even more daunting.

In some countries malfunctioning telephone equipment could wait for months before a maintenance team arrives to attempt any repairs. Even after problems are identified, the maintenance process is generally slow, partly because the technicians mandate bribes.

Geographical Obstacles

Various geographical barriers to remote areas as well as lower monetary returns from those areas reduce incentives to extend telecommunications-related infrastructures to those areas. Therefore, most private investors have little or no incentive to establish technology links in rural areas where most of the people live. The Maitland Commission (1984) argues that such geographical barriers to remote areas are a major problem to most telecommunications-related issues for developing countries in general.

An ITU world development report (ITU, 1998) shows that government monopolies of LDCs lack a universal access policy, which explains why many rural areas do not have any form of telecommunications access.

Exploring the Perceptions of Africa's Telecommunications Stakeholders

The telecommunications stakeholders in Africa are made up of governmental and non-governmental stakeholders. The governmental stakeholders include government and parastatals, and telecommunication operators (government controlled). The non-governmental stakeholders include telecommunication operators (non-government controlled), academia, research centers and IT experts, and international/regional organizations. Both the governmental and non-governmental stakeholders have typically played a major role in the implementation of IT at national levels in most developing countries (Montealegre, 1999).

These stakeholders have typically suggested different strategies to solve the various telecommunications-related problems of their countries (Bruce, 1989; Foreman-Peck & Muller, 1988). For instance, some stakeholders believe the telecommunications operator should be a government-controlled monopoly for reasons of national security. On the other hand, some stakeholders believe the telecommunications operator should be liberalized to allow for free entry, thereby promoting competition, which will benefit the national economy and improve on the status of telecommunications activity (Mbarika et al., 2002a). Some stakeholders — international development organizations — charged with assisting LDCs, regard highly developed telecommunications infrastructures as an urban luxury (Hudson, 1983). On the other hand, academicians have argued on the fundamental importance of having universal services in order to close the gap between telecommunications infrastructures of urban areas and those of rural areas (Saunders, 1982).

In this paper, we explore the perceptions of telecommunications stakeholders in Africa's LDCs. Using a list of experts from an ITU/UN database, a sample of the stakeholders was asked to rate some telecommunications-related constraints and strategies in terms of perceived criticality. We then analyzed the data to determine if significant differences in perceptions existed compared to actual trends in the growth of teledensity in recent years. The analyses helped shed some light on the research questions presented in this paper earlier.

SURVEY INSTRUMENT
AND ADMINISTRATION

Quantitative and qualitative data were collected from Africa's telecommunications stakeholders to identify the main obstacle to the growth of teledensity and to examine some possible strategies to overcome the obstacle. The stakeholders were asked to analyze the strategies identified in the literature, and to modify, enhance, or add new insights. The stakeholders were asked to rank the four obstacles presented to them, based on the perceived relative criticality of the obstacles (or constraints). They were also asked to rank the possible strategies for overcoming the various obstacles that came from the literature.

A survey instrument was developed that listed obstacles and strategies found in past literature. The items for the obstacles and strategies were derived from a comprehensive review of academic literature and publications of development organizations. The items for the survey questionnaire were ranked using a Likert scale from 1 (strongly disagree) to 7 (strongly agree). Respondents were given the opportunity to provide comments on how they felt about the suggested obstacles and strategies. Some of the comments are included in the discussion section of this paper.

A pilot test of the questionnaire was conducted by randomly selecting 15 participants from the list provided by the ITU. However, participants were unaware of their role in the pilot test. We asked the stakeholders to give comments on the understandability of the items for the different obstacles and strategies. Questions that were unclear were rewritten to make them more meaningful and certain redundant questions were thrown out of the survey. Lists of the items used in the survey are presented in Table 1.

The survey was administered with the option of using both traditional (paper-based) and Web-based methods. The importance of data collection using multiple techniques that inherently have differing advantages and disadvantages has been suggested (Alreck & Settle, 1996; Brancheau & Borton, 1999; Yin, 1994). More recently, some researchers have argued in favor of using Web-based survey, noting improved response time while still sustaining the reliability and validity of data obtained through such an approach (Alreck & Settle, 1996; Kueng & Wettstein, 1999). As far as the traditional approach to data collection used in this research, respondents were provided a fax number to which they could return the survey. The option of mailing back their responses using traditional snail-mail systems was also available.

SURVEY ANALYSIS AND RESULTS

Of the 212 questionnaires sent to individuals, 71 responses were returned. This equated to a response rate of 33.5%. We were limited to this sample size because our target sample included participants (stakeholders) that had a major level of control over their specific institutions (for the non-governmental stakeholders), and ministries or governmental organizations (for governmental stakeholders). Sixty-one percent of the respondents were from Africa, and 24% from North America. A regional distribution of the responding participants is shown in Figure 2.

Distributions of the participants across group and affiliation are summarized in Table 2. Twenty-nine participants that responded were governmental stakeholders, and

Table 1. Descriptions of obstacles to growth of teledensity

Obstacle	Description of Issues Related to Obstacle
Organizational/ Policy-Oriented obstacle	There seems to be insufficient management autonomy of the telecommunications operators in African LDCs. Telephone services are still provided by certain government monopoly-run organizations, which may be bureaucratic and often counter productive.
Technological-Oriented obstacle	Many African LDCs operate outdated equipment and tend to have inadequate maintenance for their equipment. African LDCs typically have difficulties finding and keeping technically qualified maintenance personnel, which may result in poor quality of service and loss of revenues
Financial-Oriented obstacle	African LDCs seem to have low levels of internal and external investments in telecommunications. In terms of external investments, the devaluation of some African LDCs currencies seems to limit the availability of foreign exchange. There exist very high exchange rates with major currencies that may be needed to purchase telecommunications equipment and other telecommunications services from abroad.
Geographical-Oriented obstacle	Certain policy makers in African LDCs seem to regard telecommunications as an urban luxury. Policy makers in African LDCs limit telephone services to mostly cities and urban areas. In many African LDCs, the rural life styles of people scattered throughout a wide geographical area result in the requirements for very heavy investment to give service to very small numbers of people. Very heavy investments to provide telecommunications services in rural areas may not be commercially justifiable and may present a huge burden for the telecommunications operator.

Table 2. Participants in the survey

STAKEHOLDER AFFILIATION	STAKEHOLDER GROUP	
	Governmental	Non-Governmental
Telecommunications Operator	6 (21%)	8 (19%)
Telecommunications Regulator	20 (69%)	4 (10%)
Academia, Research Centers, Development Agency	3 (10%)	30 (71%)
Total	*29 (100%)*	*42 (100%)*

Note. Percentages enclosed in parentheses are rounded up to whole numbers.

Figure 2. Distribution of participants

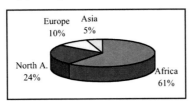

Table 3. Worldwide rank order of means for obstacles to growth of teledensity

Rank	Mean Rank	Overall Mean	Std. Deviation	Obstacle
1	2.67	5.48	1.47	Financial
2	2.59	5.38	1.68	Technological
3	2.46	5.19	1.90	Organizational/Policy
4	2.28	4.78	1.87	Geographical

$\mu^2 = 46.41;\ d.f. = 2;\ Significance = .000^{++}$

forty-two participants were non-governmental stakeholders. Most of the respondents from regions outside Africa were academics and research organizations concerned with telecommunications diffusion in Africa's LDCs.

Scale Assessment and Reliability

Cronbach's alphas were computed for all items under the four obstacles to teledensity growth in Africa's LDCs. Similar computations were done for the possible strategies identified to help spur teledensity growth in the region. In all cases, the Cronbach alphas were well above 0.60, which is the generally acceptable lower limit in exploratory research (Robinson et al., 1973, 1991). The values obtained also showed evidence of internal consistency among the items in each construct.

Rank Order for Each Category of Obstacle

The survey participants were asked to assess the relevance and criticality of each obstacle in the effort to promote growth of teledensity in Africa's LDCs. All data from governmental stakeholders and non-governmental stakeholders were compiled. First, a rank order and Asymptotic Significance of each category of strategies was evaluated using Friedman's Test. The Asymptotic Significance test is considered significant if the value is less than 0.05 (Green et al., 1997).

Second, means and standard deviations were computed for each obstacle. All four obstacles had high means (ranging from 4.78 to 5.48), indicating the stakeholders' belief that these obstacles were highly relevant and critical to teledensity growth. The results revealed that the Financial-Oriented obstacle was ranked the highest, followed by the Technological-Oriented obstacle, and then the Organizational/Policy-Oriented obstacle. The Geographical-Oriented obstacle was ranked the lowest. Table 3 shows the rank orders of the mean scores for the four categories.

Table 4. MANOVA results for obstacles to growth of teledensity

Effect	F-value	P-value
Affiliation	.29	.966
Group (governmental stakeholders vs. non-governmental stakeholders)	1.98	.121
Affiliation * Group	1.97	.062

Note. F and P values used are based on Pillai's test.

Similarities and Differences of Perceptions

One of the main purposes of data analysis in this study was to examine the potential differences in perceptions of teledensity growth obstacles based on stakeholder affiliation. As shown earlier in Table 2, there are three possible affiliations: 1) telecommunications operator, 2) telecommunications regulator, and 3) academia/research centers/development agency. In terms of groups, a stakeholder could be governmental stakeholders or non-governmental stakeholders.

In Table 4, we present the results of the data analysis that was done using a 3x2 factorial multivariate analysis of variance (MANOVA) to investigate possible differences based on stakeholder affiliation or group, and to see if there was any evidence of significant interactions between affiliation and group. The results show that there is no significant difference in the perceptions of stakeholders (regardless of group or affiliation) with regards to the order of the four obstacles to teledensity growth presented to them.

DISCUSSION AND IMPLICATIONS FOR FUTURE RESEARCH

Summary of Results

The means all four obstacles pursued in this study range from 4.78 to 5.48, with the Financial-Oriented obstacle considered the most critical. This was followed by the Technological-Oriented obstacle, and then the Organizational/Policy-Oriented obstacle. The Geographical-Oriented obstacle was perceived by the stakeholders to be the least critical of the four.

In ranking the financial obstacle highest, the stakeholders seem to suggest that African LDCs suffer from low levels of internal and external investments in telecommunications. In terms of external investments, the devaluation of some African LDCs' currencies further limits the availability of foreign exchange. This is a difficult obstacle to overcome, considering the poor state of the LDCs' banking systems and high levels of foreign debts that make it difficult for these countries to attract new capital (World Bank, 2003).

The stakeholders also perceived technological factor as being a critical obstacle in this study. Many African LDCs operate outdated equipment and tend to have inadequate maintenance for the equipment. These countries typically have difficulties finding and keeping technically qualified maintenance personnel. This leads to poor quality of service.

For the organizational obstacle, the stakeholders seem to suggest that there is insufficient autonomy of the telecommunications operators in African LDCs. In essence, the telecommunications services in most of these countries have been controlled and provided by government monopolies, which tend to be bureaucratic and often inefficient.

With regards to the Geographical obstacle, the stakeholders' apparently perceive that policy makers in African LDCs have come to regard telecommunications as an urban luxury. The vast majority of the urban dwellers have not been able to afford these services. As for the populace who live in rural areas, a whopping 70% or more of the region's populace, telecommunications services have been unavailable (Mbarika et al., 2002; Musa et al., 2003). The stakeholders seem to suggest that substantive development will continue to elude Africa until the realities that curtail improvements in technology infrastructure are addressed.

In addition to the quantitative data gathered from the survey, many of the stakeholders offered some qualitative remarks. These remarks corroborate the longstanding belief that financial, organizational, technological, and geographical factors are the key impediments to teledensity growth. Select comments from stakeholders regarding each of the obstacles include:

Probably the major obstacle is the ability to raise foreign exchange to pay for the external services rendered by suppliers and foreign experts.

Investors prefer stable countries and liberal telecommunications environments.

[Acquiring] equipment constitutes a major component of technology-oriented obstacle...and required maintenance are often lacking.

We are actually in a dilemma. It's a waste, to install complex communication systems in some rural areas, where they are very underutilized, but at the same time, we want to ensure that those in the rural areas can communicate without such complex systems. If the resources were available, those in the rural areas would most likely opt for some other things; such as electricity, water, hospitals, schools, etc.

These remarks corroborate the findings from the survey. The findings are also consistent with the Bernt and Weiss framework that identifies financial, organizational, technological, and geographical obstacles as being the main impediments to telecommunications capabilities.

Recent Trends in Teledensity Growth: Wireless Takes Africa by Storm

While the results from this study are valid, recent trends in teledensity growth in Africa's LDCs raise questions as to whether or not the four obstacles are indeed as crucial as they have been in the past four decades (when most of these countries gained independence). In particular, the diffusion of wireless technology has produced an exponential increase in levels of teledensity across the region to the point that the African continent has become the world's largest birthing ground for the wireless telephone industry. Recent statistics indicate that:

- At the end of 2001, 28 African nations — or over half the region's countries — had more mobile phone than fixed-line subscribers. The fixed-line teledensity was 0.79 and the mobile density was 1.13, a higher fixed-line to mobile ratio than any other continent (ITU, 2002).
- The number of mobile subscribers in 30 Sub-Saharan Africa countries, not including South Africa, rose from zero in 1996 to 1.7 million in late 2001 (UNCTAD, 2002).
- The rate of growth for the entire continent has been more than 82% a year, much faster than the 33% growth rate in the U.S. In many African countries, such as Cameroon, Kenya, Senegal and Tanzania, annual cellular growth rates are running in excess of 300% (York, 2002).
- As of January 2003, most African LDCs still had a teledensity of less than 1. However, at that same period, more than half of these countries had a mobile density greater than 1 (ITU, 2002).

These recent trends indicate a possible paradigm shift in the strategic impediments to telecommunications capability development in this region. It should be noted that this recent exponential growth in telecommunications capabilities has occurred despite little if any improvements in the conditions that mitigated teledensity growth for decades across the region. This leads us to conjecture that there may be some emerging factors, issues, constraints, and opportunities that may be of greater importance to understanding telecommunications capabilities in these countries and the world at large.

Directions for Future Research

Wireless telecommunications infrastructure holds a lot of promise for the socioeconomic advancement of both urban and rural areas in Africa's LDCs. Research on wireless telecommunications infrastructure in the region is important. We need a better understanding of the implications of this technology on the diffusion of e-commerce, m-commerce, computer-based business applications, education, health, entertainment, leisure, etc. We also need a better understanding of the forces that could impede the diffusion of these technologies. This is especially so, since these technologies are proving to be resilient to the traditional factors that hitherto impeded the growth in telecommunications capabilities in the region.

While mobile teledensity levels have risen significantly in the recent past, issues of accessibility, affordability, scope of application, etc., point to new inhibitors to telecommunications penetration. These emerging inhibitors could curtail the realization of the potential benefits that these technologies could bring about. Therefore studies that would help identify these inhibitors and their effects are necessary.

CONCLUSIONS

This study examined two research questions. The first related to telecommunications stakeholders' perceptions of the factors traditionally believed to be the key obstacles to growth in telecommunications capabilities. The second question had to do with how stakeholders' perceptions compare to recent trends in telecommunications capabilities growth in the region.

Based on the data gathered from the telecommunications stakeholders from Africa, there is no change in their perceptions with respect to the Bernt and Weiss framework. The findings also show that there is disconnect between current happenings and perception of stakeholders. This led us to conjecture that in this new dispensation, there may be some emerging factors, issues, constraints, and opportunities that may be of greater importance to understanding telecommunications capabilities in these countries and the world at large. Although the analysis was done using data from African stakeholders, it is possible to extend the study to other developing countries to see if the approach is generalizable.

The apparent disconnect between stakeholders' perceptions and emerging realities in the region, as demonstrated in this research, suggest a paradigm shift. It also points to the need for policy makers to understand the emerging dynamics at play with respect to telecommunications capabilities, and their relationships to traditional inhibitors, while developing blueprints for socioeconomic development.

REFERENCES

Achterberg, R. (2002). Competition policy and regulation: A case study of telecommunications. *Development Southern Africa, Sep2000, 17*(3), 357.

Adam, L. (1999). An investigation of the impact of information and communication technologies in sub-Saharan Africa. *Journal of Information Science, 25*(4), 307.

Adam, L. (1996). Electronic communications technology and development. *Information Technology for Development, 7*(3), 133.

Alleman, J., Hunt, C., Mueller, D., Rappaport, P., & Taylor, L. (1994). *Telecommunications and economic development: empirical evidence from Southern Africa*. 10th Biennial International Telecommunications Society Meeting, Sydney.

Alreck, P.L., & Settle, R. (1996). *The survey research handbook*. Chicago: Irwin/McGraw-Hill.

Antonelli, C. (1991). *The diffusion of advanced technologies in developing countries*. Organisation for Economic Co-operation and Development, Paris.

Austin, J.E. (1990). *Managing in developing countries: Strategic analysis and operating techniques*. NY: The Free Press.

Babbie, E. (1989). *The practice of social research* (5th ed.). Belmont, CA: Wadsworth.

Barnett, C. (1998). The contradictions of broadcasting reform in post-apartheid South Africa. *Review of African Political Economy, 25*(78), 551.

Bernt, P., & Weiss, M. (1993). *International telecommunications*. Carmel, IN: Sams.

Black, P., & Baird, P. (1997). Ownership and competition in South African telecommunications. *South African Journal of Economics, 65*(2), 226.

Boafo, S., & Kwame T. (1991). Communication technology and dependent development in sub-Saharan Africa. In G. Sussman & J. Lent (Eds.), *Transnational communications: Wiring the third world*. London: Sage Publications.

Brancheau, J., & Borton, R. (1999). *Information technology adoption and implementation: A longitudinal multi-method approach*. University of Colorado: Boulder Colorado.

Braun, R. (1996). Educating engineers for telecommunications in South Africa. *IEEE Communications Magazine, 34*(3), 2.

Braun, R. (1997). South Africa's telecommunications to undergo major changes in next five years. *IEEE Communications Magazine, 34*(1),3.

Braun, R. (1997). Telekom Malaysia and SBC buy into Telkom South Africa. *IEEE Communications Magazine, 35*(6), 3.

Bruce, R. K. (1989). Restructuring the telecommunications sector in developing countries: New options for policymakers. *IEEE Technology and Society Magazine*.

Cogburn, D. (2003, February-March). Governing global information and communications policy: Emergent regime formation and the impact on Africa. *Telecommunications Policy*.

Cogburn, D. (1998). Globalization and state autonomy in the information age: Telecommunications sector restructuring. *Journal of International Affairs, 51*(2), 583.

de Vreede, G.-J., Jones, N., & Mgaya, R.J. (1998). Exploring the application and acceptance of group support systems in Africa. *Journal of Management Information Systems, 3*(15), 197.

EBRD (1995), *Transition Report Update*. London: EBRD.

Forman-Peck, J., & Muller, J. (1988). *European Telecommunications Organizations*. Baden Beden: Nomos Verlagsgesellschaft.

Gary, M., & Savage, S. (2000). Telecommunications and economic growth. *International Journal of Social Economics, 27*(7-10), 893.

Gille, L. (1986). Growth and telecommunications. In *Information, Telecommunications and Development* (pp. 25-61). Geneva: ITU.

Green, S., Salkind, N., & Akey, T. (1997). *Using SPSS for Windows*. NJ: Prentice Hall.

Greenstein, S.M., & Spiller, P.T. (1995). Modern telecommunications infrastructure and economic activity: An empirical investigation. *Industrial and Corporate Change, 4*, 647-65.

Hacten, W.A. (1971). *Muffled drums: The communications media in Africa*. Iowa State University Press.

Hamilton, J. (2003). Are main lines and mobile phones substitutes or complements? Evidence from Africa. *Telecommunications Policy, 27*(1/2), 109.

Hardy, A. P. (1980). The role of the telephone in economic development. *Telecommunications Policy, 4*, 278-286.

Hodge, J. (2002). Liberalizing communication services in South Africa. *Development Southern Africa, 17*(3), 373.

Hudson, H. E. (1983). The role of telecommunications in development: A synthesis of current research. In O. H. Gandy, P. Espinosa, & J. Ordover (Eds.), *Proceedings of The Tenth Annual Telecommunications Policy Research Conference* (pp. 291-307). Norwood, NJ: Ablex.

International Telecommunications Union (1994). *World Telecommunications Development Report*. Geneva: ITU.

International Telecommunications Union (1998). *World Telecommunications Development Report.* Geneva: ITU.

International Telecommunications Union (2002). *World Telecommunications Development Report.* Geneva: ITU.

Jensen, M., (1995). *Telematics in a global context.* Discussion Paper, Africa Regional Symposium on Telematics for Development, Addis Ababa.

Jipp, A. (1963, July). Wealth of nations and telephone density, *Telecommunications Journal,* 199-201.

Jussawalla, M., & Lamberton, D.M. (1982). Communications economics and development: An economics of information perspective. In M. Jussawalla and D. Lamberton (Eds.), *Communications economics and development.* Potts Point, PA: Pergamon Press.

Jussawalla, M. (1988). Information economies and the development of Pacific countries. In M. Jussawalla, D. M. Lamberton, & N. D. Karunaratne (Eds.), *The cost of thinking: Information economies of ten Pacific countries* (pp. 15-43). Norwood, NJ: Ablex.

Karikari, J., & Gyimah-Brempong, K. (1999). Demand for international telephone services between US and Africa. *Information Economics & Policy, 11*(4), 407.

Kenny, C. (2000). Expanding Internet access to the rural poor in Africa. *Information Technology for Development, (9)*1, 25.

Kibati, M., & Krairit, D. (1999). The wireless local loop in developing regions. *Communications of the ACM, 42*(6), 60.

Kueng, P., & Wettstein, T. (1999). Measuring customer satisfaction using IT: A case study. *Proceedings of the Sixth European Conference on Information Technology Evaluation.* Uxbridge (UK).

Madden, G., & Savage, S. (2000), Telecommunications and economic growth. *International Journal of Social Economics, 27*(7-10), 893.

Maddy, M. (2000, May/June). Dream deferred. *Harvard Business Review, 78*(3), 56.

Maitland Commission, The (1984). The missing link. *ITU Independent Commission for World Wide Telecommunications Development,* Geneva.

Makhaya, G., & Roberts, S. (2003). Telecommunications in developing countries: Reflections from the South African experience. *Telecommunications Policy, 27*(1).

Matungul, P., Lyne, M., & Ortmann, G. (2001). Transaction costs and crop marketing in the communal areas of Impendle and Swayimana, KwaZulu-Natal. *Development Southern Africa, 18*(3).

Mbarika (2001). *Africa's least developed countries' teledensity problems and strategies.* ME & AGWECAMS.

Mbarika, V. (2002). Re-thinking information and communications technology policy focus on Internet versus teledensity diffusion for Africa's least developed countries. *The Electronic Journal on Information Systems in Developing Countries, 9*(1), 1-13.

Mbarika, V., Byrd, T. A., Raymond, J., & McMullen, P. (2000). Investments in telecommunications infrastructure are not the Panacea for least developed countries leapfrogging growth of teledensity. *International Journal on Media Management, 2*(3), 133-142.

Mbarika, V., Byrd, T. A., & Raymond, J. (2002a). Growth of teledensity in least developed countries: Need for a mitigated euphoria. *Journal of Global Information Management, 10*(2),14-27.

Mbarika, V., Jensen, M., & Meso, P. (2002c). Cyberspace across sub-Saharan Africa: Association for computing machinery. *Communications of the ACM, 45*(12), 17-21.

Mbarika, V., Musa, P., Byrd, T. A., & McMullen, P. (2002b). Teledensity growth constraints and strategies for Africa's LDCs: 'Viagra' prescriptions or sustainable development strategy? *Journal of Global Information Technology Management, 5*(1), 25-42.

McCormick, P.K. (2003). Telecommunications reform in Southern Africa: The role of the Southern African development community. *Telecommunications Policy, 27*(1/2), 95.

Meso, P., & Duncan, N. (2000). Can national information infrastructures enhance social development in the least developed countries? An empirical investigation. *Journal of Global Information Management, 8*(4), 30-42.

Minges, M. (1999). Mobile cellular communications in the Southern African region. *Telecommunications Policy, 23*(7/8), 585.

Montealegre, R. (1999). A temporal model of institutional interventions for information technology adoption in less-developed countries. *Journal of Management Information Systems, 16*(1), 207-232.

Mureithi, M. (2003). Self-destructive competition in cellular: Regulatory options to harness the benefits of liberalization. *Telecommunications Policy, 27*(1).

Musa, P. F., Meso, P., & Mbarika, V. (2003), Toward a model of interactions of technology adoption factors vis-à-vis socio-economic development issues in Sub-Saharan Africa. *Information Technology and Organizations: Trends, Issues, Challenges and Solutions, Proceedings of the Information Resource Management Association (IRMA 2003) International Conference*, Philadelphia.

Myers, J. (1998). Human rights and development: Using advanced technology to promote human rights in sub-Saharan Africa. *Journal of International Law, 30*(2/3), 343.

Mylonopoulos, N., & V. Theoharakis (2001). On-site: Global perceptions of IS journals. *Communications of the ACM, 9*(44), 29-33.

Nidumolu, S., & Goodman, S. (1996). Information technology for local administration support: The governorates project in Egypt. *MIS Quarterly, 20*(2), 197.

OECD (1996). *Employment and growth in the knowledge-based economy.* Paris: OECD.

Onwumechili, C. (2000). Telecommunications in Africa (book review). *Journal of Communication, 50*(2), 172.

Pfeifer, K. (1999). Parameters of economic reform in North Africa. *Review of African Political Economy, 26*(82), 441.

Robinson, J. P., & Shaver, P. R. (1973). *Measures of psychological attitudes.* Ann Arbor: Survey Research Center Institute for Social Research, University of Michigan.

Robinson, J. P., Shaver, P. R., & Wrightsman, L. S. (1991). Criteria for scale selection and evaluation. In J.P.Robinson, P. R. Shaver, & L. S. Wrightsman (Eds.), *Measures of personality and social psychological attitudes.* San Diego, CA: Academic Press.

Rorissa, A. (1999). *The impact of introduction of electronic communication in Ethiopia: A survey.* Ethiopian Scientific Society Conference.

Saunders, R. J. (1982). Telecommunications in developing countries: Constraints on development. In M. Jussawall & D.M. Lamberton (Eds.), *Communication economics and development* (pp. 190-210). Honolulu, HI: The East-West Center.

Saunders, R. J., Warfbrd, J. I., & Welienius, B. (1994). *Telecommunications and economic development* (2nd ed.). Baltimore: John Hopkins University Press.

Spiller, P.T., & Cardilli, C.G. (1997). The frontier of telecommunications deregulation: Small countries leading the pack. *Journal of Economic Perspectives, 11*, 127-38.

Taaffe, J. (2001). Credit where credit is due. *OECD Observer, 224*, 29.

Tisdell, C. (1972). *Microeconomics: The theory of economic allocation.* Sydney, Australia: John Wiley & Sons.

Tisdell, C. (1981). *Science and technology policy: Priorities of governments.* London: Chapman & Hall.

UNCTAD — United Nations Conference on Trade and Development (2002). *E-Commerce and Development Report.* United Nations: New York and Geneva.

UNECA (2003). *The ICT Maps of Africa, Promoting Information and Communication Technologies for Development.* Retrieved June 2003 from http://www.uneca.org/disd/ictmaps. htm

Wallsten, S. (2001). An econometric analysis of Telecom competition, privatization, and regulation in Africa and Latin America. *Journal of Industrial Economics, 49*(1), 1.

Wellenius, B. (1989). The impact of modern telecommunications. *IEEE Technology and Social Magazine, 8*(4), 3-6.

Whitman, M., Hendrickson, A., & Townsend, A. (1999). Research commentary. Academic rewards for teaching, research and service: Data and discourse. *Information Systems Research, 2*(10), 99-109.

Williamson, J. (1991). The crisis in Africa's telecommunications infrastructure. *Telephony, 22*(1).

Wilson III, E., & Wong, K. (2003). African information revolution: A balance sheet. *Telecommunications Policy, 27*(1/2).

World Bank (1991). *Telecommunications sector reports.* Washington, DC: World Bank.

World Bank (2003). *World Bank Development Indicators 2003.* Washington, DC: World Bank.

Yin, R. (1994). *Case study research: Design and methods* (2nd ed.). Thousand Oaks, CA: Sage.

York, T. (2002, June). Wireless taking African sub-continent by storm. *Mpulse Magazine.*

Appendix 1

Criteria for Inclusion to the list of Least Developed Countries

Old criteria for inclusion

The original set of criteria for constructing a list of countries classified as LDCs was adopted in 1971. This includes:

- Per capita income per year: less than US $200. This figure, revised periodically, stood at US $600 in 1998.

- Share of industrial production in the Gross National Product (GNP): under 10 percent.

3. Adult literacy rate: less than 20 percent.

New criteria for inclusion

New criteria for determining LDCs was established in 1994:

1. Population: less than 75 million.

2. Per capita Gross Domestic Product (GDP): less than US $700 (averages 1990-92).

3. Augmented physical quality of life index (APQLI): less than 47.[1]

4. Economic diversification index (EDI): less than 26.[2]

---

[1] APQLI comprises four indicators: life expectancy at birth, per capita calorie supply, school enrolment ratio, and adult literacy rate.

[2] EDI comprises the share of manufacturing in GDP, the share of employment in industry, per capita electricity consumption, and the export concentration ratio.

This article was previously published in the *Journal of Global Information Management*, 12(3), pp. 1-20, © 2004.

Chapter XIII

Evaluating the Factors Affecting DSS Usage by Senior Managers in Local Authorities in Egypt

Ibrahim Elbeltagi, Wolverhampton University Business School, UK

Neil McBride, De Montfort University, UK

Glenn Hardaker, Huddersfield University Business School, UK

ABSTRACT

The study of factors influencing the adoption and use of information systems in less-developed countries is an important area to address since differences in culture, social structure, and business approaches may have significant effects on the benefits derived from importing Western-influenced IT technology, concepts, and management approaches. This study examines the usage of a decision support system (DSS) in Egyptian local authorities using an adapted Technology Acceptance Model (TAM). The centrally-developed DSS had been rolled out to 27 governorates in Egypt for use by chief executive officers. The results demonstrated that TAM could be applied to a specific system within a developing country. Both perceived ease of use (PEU) and perceived usefulness (PU) had a significant direct effect on DSS usage. PEU dominated over PU whose effect on DSS usage was negative.

CHAPTER COVERAGE

TAM was extended by defining nine external variables: Task Characteristics, Cultural Characteristics, Environmental Characteristics, DSS Characteristics, Internal Support, External Support, Top Management Support, Organizational Characteristics and Decision Maker Characteristics. Top Management Support and Organizational Characteristics exerted the greatest effect, while Environmental Characteristics and Task Characteristics had a negative effect on DSS usage.

The successful use of a DSS requires that the user has a significant amount of independence and autonomy in the decision-making process. However, the organizational structure of Egyptian government is hierarchical with long chains of command and only the top level able to make decisions. In conjunction with interviews, the quantitative results suggest that the perceived usefulness of the DSS is reduced in an environment where there is a lack of autonomy, a command and control culture, and little requirement for decision making in implementing centrally-made decisions.

This study indicates the importance of taking into account external factors when examining IT technology adoption globally. In particular, many aspects of culture, including the background and characteristics of the decision maker, will strongly influence the perception of management support systems.

INTRODUCTION

The usage and non-usage of IT within the developed and non-developed world poses challenging problems for IS researchers and practitioners. While IT usage in the developed world has been well studied (Alavi & Joachimsthaler, 1992; Al-Gahtani & King, 1999; Boynton, Zmud, & Jacobs, 1994), the study of strategic usage of IT in the developing world is a relatively new field in which research is only just being established (Kamel, 1995; Rose & Straub, 1998).

In some countries, poverty, trade barriers, and lack of infrastructure constitute massive constraints to IT usage (Goodman & Green, 1992; Krovi, 1993; Lu, Hsieh, & Pan, 1989). However, the usage of IT is not always constrained by resources alone. Where resources are available, whether local or imported, non-usage of IT is still prevalent (Ibrahim, 1985; Nidumolu & Goodman, 1993; Shibanda & Musisi-Edebe, 2000). Local usage of global systems may be affected by local politics and culture. For example, local usage of Geographical Information Systems in India is affected by cultural attitudes to maps and cartography. Using maps is not seen as important in a country where it is usually easier to ask someone for directions (Walsham, 2001). In China, a reliance on intuition and informal approaches to managerial decision making debilitates the effective use of management information systems (Hempel & Kwong, 2001). In Malaysia, the cultural view of computer systems as symbols of power limits their use to senior figures in authority (Walsham, 1993).

Since effective usage of IT is important for economic advancement in developing countries and the delivery of benefits from IT deployment in organizations, and IT usage is clearly affected by local cultural conditions, it is important to develop an understanding of the factors that drive local usage in order to benefit from global information systems. Quantitative and qualitative models are needed which are transferable between countries and cultures. Such models should be standardized to such an extent that the instrument and its outcomes are globally comparable.

The Technology Acceptance Model (TAM) (Davis, 1989) has the potential to become a standard model for predicting IT adoption and, through extension, for analyzing IT usage. TAM explains the extent of adoption of an information system in terms of the perception of the ease of use (PEU) and perceived usefulness (PU) of the IT, concepts which may be investigated simply through items on a questionnaire. The concepts may be used to predict adoption or to explain subsequent usage, as is the case in this study.

TAM has been extensively applied in the developed world (Boudreau, Gefen, & Straub, 2001; Legris, Ingham, & Collerette, 2003). However, until recently, little work has been done on the application of TAM to developing countries. Rose and Straub (1998) established the transferability of TAM to less-developed countries, particularly focusing on Arabic countries. Using a sample of professional knowledge workers from five Arabic countries, including Egypt, they demonstrated that TAM successfully predicted general computer technology adoption in these Arabic cultures. Recently, Brown (2002) applied TAM to the use of Web-CT in South Africa, and Kamel and Assem (2003) described the application of TAM to the introduction of electronic banking in Egypt.

This study builds on the work of Rose and Straub (1998). First, it confirms the conclusion of Rose and Straub (1998) that TAM successfully transfers to Egypt. Second, it applies TAM to a homogenous population of professionals in the public sector. While Rose and Straub used a sample of managers and professionals in the airline, public, and health sectors, surveying attitudes to general IT, this study uses a sample of chief executive officers and their supporting DSS unit managers within Egyptian governorates. Furthermore, this study addresses the actual use of, rather than intention to use, a decision support system developed in Egypt by the central government and distributed to local government centers.

This study further extends the work of Rose and Straub (1998) by identifying and modeling the antecedents which influence PEU and PU. Identifying the antecedents may increase the explanatory power of the model and lead to the identification of suitable strategies for encouraging information system adoption and effective usage which, while globally applicable, are sensitive to local culture and conditions.

Following a description of the information system and its context, the use of TAM in the developing world is briefly reviewed, and the rationale for its extension, modification, and use to study this specific system in Egypt is provided. The derivation of the antecedents is then discussed and the model established. Results are briefly described, and we conclude that the relative importance of PEU is higher than PU suggesting that the usability of DSS may have a significant effect on its use for decision making in local authorities in developing countries. Analysis of the antecedents suggested that PEU was greatly influenced by cultural characteristics and the effect of external support, raising some important implications for the construction of research models of information technology adoption.

DSS WITHIN THE EGYPTIAN GOVERNORATES PROJECT

Egypt is a developing country of 70 million inhabitants where IT penetration and adoption is relatively advanced. The Egyptian government has a history of pursuing IT initiatives and promoting IT usage in the public and private sectors. Recently, it has begun to pursue e-government and geographical information system projects. One such government-initiated project is the Information and Decision Support Centre (IDSC) or Governates project (El Sherif, 1990; Kamel, 1998; Nidumolu, Goodman, Vogel, & Danowitz, 1996). This centrally-initiated project provided resources for each governorate to establish decision support centers (DSCs) consisting of units for computer resources, decision support, library, publications, and statistics. These DSCs were to provide coherent electronic information to senior management to support public sector decision making.

To ensure standardization, a suite of decision support applications was developed for the governorates by central government, within a cabinet IDSC, and then rolled out to governorates. The systems developed centrally covered various sectors of the Egyptian economy (Nidumolu et al., 1996) including population, health, and housing. Governorates then established multiple DSCs at a lower district level. Senior managers could then draw information from district DSCs or from the governorate DSCs which collated information from district DSCs. By 1998, 1,202 DSCs were located across the 27 Egyptian governorates, employing 7,300 staff (Table 1). DSCs support the centrally-provided applications providing reports to senior executives.

The centrally-developed DSS provided a focus for the study of DSS usage by senior managers within a developing country. A focus on usage, particularly the constructs provided by TAM, was particularly salient when a pilot study suggested that only 33% of executives actually made use of the output of the DSS. This raised the question of why usage of DSS by executives is so limited despite the extensive government investment and support for the system.

ADAPTING AND EXTENDING THE TECHNOLOGY ACCEPTANCE MODEL

The basic Technology Acceptance Model was adapted in this study to reflect the fact that the DSS was already in use and to support the investigation of factors influencing PU and PEU.

Since the DSS was already in use, the attitude and intention to use constructs were omitted and effort was concentrated on the link between PEU, PU, and actual systems usage. Systems usage was derived from self-reported estimates of percentage use of the DSS in strategic decisions, level or depth of use, and frequency of use. Statements used in this research to operationalize the PEU and PU were adapted from Davis's (1989) study, with minor changes in wording and the addition of one item to PU: *lower cost*, which reflects the developing world's environment where cost is an important factor in using DSS.

In order to expand understanding of why DSS are used in developing countries, this study extended TAM by specifying the external variables which may influence PEU and PU. The Technology Acceptance Model demonstrates that a significant amount of system usage behavior can be explained in terms of the user's perception of usefulness (PU) and ease of use (PEU). External constructs are characteristics of the environment or the system that influence the user's perception. If executives perceived the DSS as difficult to use, what influenced their perception? Some studies have investigated some of the influencing variables (Keil & Konsynski, 1995; Phillips, Calantone, & Lee, 1994; Taylor & Todd, 1995a, 1995b; Venkatesh, 2000), but they do not relate these variables to TAM.

For each selected variable, the hypothesis was that the effect of the variable on DSS usage was entirely dependent on PU and PEU. Figure 1 depicts the research model employed in the study.

Task Characteristics

Most strategic decisions are characterized by uncertainty and complexity (Kivijarvi & Zmud, 1993). Increasingly complex decisions require significant expertise, insight, and intuition and may be made more effective using information systems. However, with highly complex decision situations, "the answers are obtained through subjective opinions rather than from objective data" (Daft & Lengel, 1986, p. 557). Previous studies in end-user computing have shown that PU and PEU are influenced by task/tool fit (Keil & Konsynski, 1995).

In laboratory studies, the effectiveness of DSSs increased with increasing task complexity (Webby & O'Connor, 1994). Blili, Raymond, and Rivard (1998) found that the

Figure 1. Conceptual DSS usage model for SDM in Egypt

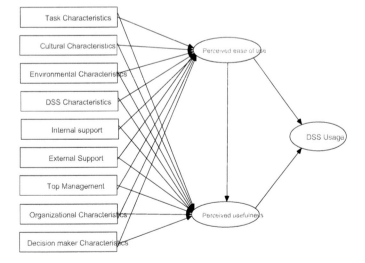

more complex the task, the more alleviation would be sought using end-user computing (EUC). However, they also suggest that increased task uncertainty reduces the perceived importance of EUC. So, if the decision makers perceived DSS as a supporting tool in complex and uncertain situations, their usage of the systems will increase, especially if they realize that the system is easy to use. Based on this, it is reasonable to assume that task characteristics will influence PU and PEU. Hence:

H1:   Perceived ease of use and perceived usefulness of decision support systems fully mediate the influence of task characteristics variables on usage of DSS.

Cultural Characteristics

Cultural factors are increasingly cited as significant influences on IT adoption. Leidner, Carlsson, and Elam (1995) suggested that cultural differences need to be understood before IT developed in one country can be implemented in another. Group Decision Support Systems were not as well received in an Asian country as in the United States because of different attitudes toward the appropriateness of expressing disagreement. A comparative analysis of management information systems success between the US and Latvia suggested that Latvian managers with extensive experience under the Soviet management model were less likely to participate in information system development for fear of being seen as incompetent (Ishman, Pegels, & Sanders, 2001). From studying the transfer of IT to the Arab world, Straub, Loch, and Hill (2001) suggest that specific components of Arab culture have an influence on how IT is viewed and the extent to which it might be utilized. Kambayashi and Scarbrough (2001), in a comparative survey of managers in UK and Japanese firms, found a greater willingness to use information sharing systems in the UK than in Japan. They conclude that national cultural attributes may influence managerial preferences for the use of information.

In studying cultural effects, Hofstede's (1997) four dimensions of culture provide an influential benchmark. Straub, Keil, and Brenner (1997) applied the four cultural dimensions of power-distance, uncertainty avoidance, individualism, and masculinity to predict whether TAM would transfer across different cultures represented by the US, Switzerland, and Japan. Here, the cultural dimension served to provide a cultural classification rather than any causal link to TAM. Their findings suggested that TAM might not transfer across cultures since it appeared not to predict technology acceptance in Japan. Veiga, Floyd, and Dechant (2001) propose extending TAM using individualism, uncertainty avoidance, and power-distance, together with Hofstede's fifth construct, short/long-term orientation as constructs influencing PEU and PU. They argue that cultural characteristics will influence the core variables of TAM.

Since the adoption of IT in a non-Western culture is a core theme of this paper, it seems sensible to suggest that cultural influences will affect PU and PEU. Hofstede's (1997) dimensions of culture were used as a basis for testing this construct, since they are widely accepted. Hence:

H2:   Perceived ease of use and perceived usefulness of decision support systems fully mediate the influence of cultural characteristics variables on usage of DSS.

DSS Characteristics

Previous studies have found that certain DSS characteristics seem to have an important influence on the effectiveness of the systems: user-friendliness, ease of use, size (cost) of DSS, range of alternatives, timeliness, accuracy, and relevancy of output (Igbaria, Pavri, & Huff, 1989; Udo & Davis, 1992a, 1992b). Also some researchers attempting to measure IS success have put forward factors related to DSS characteristics like system quality, information quality, information use, and user satisfaction with the information (DeLone & McLean, 1992; Li, 1997). The technical quality of the DSS may influence DSS usage. Indeed, it is clear that the quality and accessibility of the information provided by the DSS is important (Kraemer et al., 1993). Low technical quality, whether real or imagined may influence DSS usage. Gupta, Nemati, and Harvey (1999) highlight the operational integrity, performance, and reliability of a DSS as important factors affecting successful implementation. Whether perceptions of technical quality are gained through rumors or through formal evaluation processes, inadequate data storage, modeling capacity, processing speed, accessibility, and reliability may influence PEU and PU, hence:

H3: Perceived ease of use and perceived usefulness of decision support systems fully mediate the influence of DSS characteristics variables on usage of DSS.

Environmental Characteristics

In local authorities, the political environment represented by centrally-imposed laws, strategies, and policies is of great significance. The government plays a major role in local authorities in both developed and developing countries, as regulator and/or investor (Blanning, Bui, & Tan, 1997). In Egypt, the government dominates the shape of IT development in the country, so control over the computing infrastructure has frequently been associated with the political control of information, particularly to reinforce the power of the government (Nidumolu et al., 1996). The government in Egypt is highly centralized, and the public administration system is still dominant. So, the heads of cities ought to closely follow the central government plans and priorities, and therefore most of the important decisions are made centrally. Because of lack of incentive to use the systems by decision makers in local authorities, ease of use might play an important role as internal incentive to use the system. Both *favorable government policies* and *uncertainty in environment* have been identified as key facilitators of the strategic use of IT (King & Teo, 1996). Hence, environmental characteristics were proposed as an antecedent:

H4: Perceived ease of use and perceived usefulness of decision support systems fully mediate the influence of environmental characteristics variables on the usage of DSS.

Organizational Characteristics

Many studies have investigated the influence of organizational attributes on the effectiveness of information systems in general (Cheney, Mann, & Amoroso, 1986; Lind, Zmud, & Fischer, 1989) and DSS in particular (Guimaraes, Igbaria, & Lu, 1992; Sanders

& Courtney, 1985). Nidumolu et al. (1996) noticed that, in the governorates project, training associated with computers and problems analysis had to be centralized in Cairo because of lack of local computer training facilities and trainers. Organizational characteristics may also include extent of centralization of management structure, hence, also of planning and the level of communication of information occurring within the organization. Hence:

H5: Perceived ease of use and perceived usefulness of decision support systems fully mediate the influence of organizational characteristics variables on usage of DSS.

Internal Support Characteristics

Internal support given to decision makers within the organization, either through training within the organization or other sources of support, may be a significant influence on PE and PEU. That internal support may come from formal channels, such as IT training, or informal support from other colleagues who are using the system. Aladwani (2002) found that in Kuwait internal computing support did not positively influence end-user computing. Furthermore, Young and Watson (1995) did not find that the level of internal support influenced EIS acceptance. We would suggest that internal support including the availability of experienced DSS staff, training opportunities, and a network of supportive colleagues would be a significant influence on the executive perception of the usefulness of the DSS and its ease of use, and hence it might affect the level of DSS usage. Based on this, it is reasonable to assume that internal support characteristics will influence PU and PEU. Hence:

H6: Perceived ease of use and perceived usefulness of decision support systems fully mediate the influence of internal support characteristics variables on usage of DSS.

External Support Characteristics

Due to insufficient internal technical expertise, especially in developing countries, the availability and quality of external support may be an important determinant of DSS effectiveness in strategic decision making. Recommendations from outside consultants were found to be an important variable in using IT strategically (Neo, 1988). Past research suggests that when new computer-based technology is complex and the related knowledge is difficult to transfer, mediators (i.e., vendors and consultants) play an important role in the diffusion of the technology (Attewell, 1992). Good relationships with external vendors or consultants are a facilitator of success in end-user computing (Shayo, Guthrie, & Igbaria, 1999). Good vendors may act as surrogate IT departments, providing business-specific advice and technical support. Perceptions of usefulness may be influenced by the rhetoric and comments of both government agencies and suppliers; this in turn might increase the effective usage of DSS. Based on this, it is reasonable to assume that external support characteristics will influence PU and PEU. Hence:

H7: Perceived ease of use and perceived usefulness of decision support systems fully mediate the influence of external support characteristics variables on usage of DSS.

Decision Maker Characteristics

The importance of decision maker characteristics as determinants of information systems success has been emphasized by several authors (Guimaraes et al., 1992; Igbaria et al., 1989; Sanders & Courtney, 1985). Babcock, Bush, and Lan (1995) concluded that organizations that enjoy a higher level of IT use tend to have managers who have positive attitudes toward IT. They concluded that this positive attitude did not grow with age but was obtained through education. Chen and Lee (2003) emphasize the importance of decision makers' cognitive style, beliefs, and assumptions about how the world works. Decision makers' attitudes to DSS are likely to be expressed in terms of their perception of usefulness and ease of use. This is turn may affect their level of usage. Hence:

H8:   Perceived ease of use and perceived usefulness of decision support systems fully mediate the influence of decision maker characteristics variables on the usage of DSS.

Top Management Support Characteristics

It is important that top management participation be active, not merely symbolic. Simply giving the go-ahead for the DSS implementation in the organization is not sufficient (Ang & Teo, 1997). Some of the ways that top management can demonstrate its support could be by providing the necessary resources and leadership, by setting goals and policies for DSS, and showing interest by participating in DSS design and development (Ang & Teo, 1997; King, 1996). In one case study of EIS implementation, the managing director of a communications company perceived EIS to be useful and encouraged its development and adoption by senior executives, since it suited his management style. His successor, whose focus was on marketing rather than trend analysis, did not see any value in an EIS and soon halted its use (McBride, 1997). Senior management support is recognized as an important factor in IT adoption. For example, Nasirin and Birks (2003) report that senior management awareness of the benefits of DSS was a leading factor in ensuring smooth system implementation. The pilot study found that some heads of cities became hands-on users of the DSS while others depended on reports from the system provided by IT specialists. In both cases, the exposure to the DSS influenced their perception of the usefulness of the DSS and their judgment of the business benefits of the DSS, hence, the extent of their support for the use of the DSS within their organization. Since the importance of top management support is widely recognized, it features in this model:

H9:   Perceived ease of use and perceived usefulness of decision support systems fully mediate the influence of top management characteristics variables on usage of DSS.

RESEARCH METHOD

Preparing the Questionnaire

Items to measure the selected external variables were developed from a synthesis of a combination from the extant literature and interviews carried out during an early pilot

Table 1. Profile of DSS units in local governorates

No.	Governorate	DSS Unit	Employees	Computers
1	Ministry of village development	3	17	21
2	Trustee of Local Management.	1	10	10
3	Cairo	41	386	146
4	Giza	44	352	167
5	Kalubya	60	363	94
6	Alexandria	25	208	124
7	Beheira	96	624	191
8	Matrough	18	86	39
9	Menouffia	35	300	77
10	Gharbeya	79	512	45
11	Kafr El Sheik	59	373	98
12	Damietta	24	197	68
13	Dakhlia	76	616	146
14	North Sinai	33	142	92
15	South Sinai	20	04	37
16	Port Said	20	82	67
17	Ismailia	40	163	116
18	Suez	18	80	65
19	Sharkia	73	371	155
20	Bani Suef	31	192	45
21	Fayoum	29	186	79
22	Menia	39	232	114
23	Assiut	97	477	169
24	New Valley	22	137	49
25	Red Sea	13	62	55
26	Souhag	76	411	199
27	Kena	67	344	101
28	Aswan	48	232	120
29	Luxor	15	61	38
Total		1202	7300	2668

study in Egypt. Discussion with academic and IT practitioners led to the development of draft questions for each construct, which were validated by academicians who were interested in the area of DSS in five universities in America, Australia, UK, Israel, and Egypt. The revised questions were then translated into Arabic using the back translation technique (Brislin, 1986). Further revision of the questionnaire occurred following a pilot study conducted on a number of senior executives and IT managers in local government in Egypt.

Sample and Procedure

The revised questionnaire was sent to a sample derived from the directory of DSS units in the local governments issued by IDSC which included all local authorities and units of DSS in each governorate all over Egypt as indicated in Table 1.

Over a two-month period, 450 questionnaires were personally delivered to governorates across Egypt. Some questionnaires were posted to remote governorates. This effort resulted in a high response rate (68%). Of 309 questionnaires returned, 294 (about 73.5%) were valid and 12 incomplete. To ensure that the valid responses were representative of the larger population, a non-response bias test was used to compare the early and late respondents. χ^2 tests showed no significant difference between the two groups

Table 2. Cronbach's coefficient for constructs

Factors	α
DSS usage (3 items)	0.70
PEU (6 items)	0.69
PU (7 items)	0.72
Task characteristics (5items)	0.65
Cultural characteristics (4 items)	0.78
DSS characteristics (12 items)	0.68
Environmental characteristics (4 items)	0.71
Organisational characteristics (7 items)	0.78
Internal support characteristics (5 items)	0.74
External support characteristics (3 items)	0.81
Decision maker characteristics (12 items)	0.68
Top management support (6 items)	0.79

Table 3. Fit measures for the research model

Fit Measure	Research model characteristics
Discrepancy (CMIN)	245.21
Degrees of freedom	226
P	0.18
Number of parameters (NPAR)	123
Discrepancy / df (CMINDF)	1.084
NFI	0.66
GFI	0.95
Adjusted GFI	0.91
Parsimony-adjusted GFI	0.65
Normed fit index (NFI)	0.68
Relative fit index (RFI)	0.55
Incremental fit index (IFI)	0.96
Tucker-Lewis index (TLI)	0.94
Comparative fit index (CFI)	0.95
Parsimony ratio (PRATIO)	0.75
Parsimony-adjusted NFI (PNFI)	0.50
Parsimony-adjusted CFI (PCFI)	0.72
RMSEA (PCLOSE)	0.02
P for test of close fit	1.00

of respondents at the 5% significance level, implying that non-response bias is not a concern. Additionally, 12 interviews were undertaken with the CEO and IT staff in local governments in Egypt to validate the data collected by questionnaires.

Data Analysis

Cronbach's coefficient α was used to assess the reliability of all multi-item scales. All scales showed reasonable reliability (Ramaprasad, 1987), ranging from 0.65 for task characteristics to 0.81 for external support characteristics (Table 2). It should be noted that not all exceed Nunnally's (1967) generally accepted alpha level of 0.70.

Following Taylor and Todd (1995a) because of sample size limitations, multi-item constructs for the external variables were measured using a summated scale derived as the average value of all items pertaining to these constructs. The AMOS 4.0 program (Arbuckle & Wothke, 1999) was used to test the hypothesized linear effect of each group of variables on PEU, PU, and DSS usage.

The hypothesized research model is shown in Appendix 2. The goodness of fit measures for this model, summarized in Table 3, indicated a significant $\chi^2 = 245.207$, df $= 226$, $p = 0.181$. This result indicated a good fit, as the probability level was above the generally accepted critical value $p = 0.05$, hence, supported the research hypotheses.

Each construct was individually tested in the model. The results are shown in Table 4, indicate a significant fit, and support the hypotheses. Additionally, the parameter estimates and their T-values are shown in Appendix 3.

The results of this research showed that PEU's total, direct, and indirect effect on DSS usage was 2.36 (variance 1.5) while PU was -0.41 (variance 1.5) (Table 5). Additionally, three external factors had a negative impact on DSS usage. The implications of these results are discussed below.

DISCUSSION

The purpose of this study was twofold. First, the study confirmed the validity of the adapted TAM in a developing country. In contrast to previous studies, a specific application was selected which was developed in the developing country and then rolled out across the country to all districts. This focus enabled the study of a more homogenous population of users of a single application while accessing a relatively large population. The application was in use by staff whose tasks were influenced by it, hence, actual use could be measured, rather than intention to use. Second, the study extended TAM by identifying and exploring a set of external variables which may determine PU and PEU. Once PEU and PU are confirmed as determinants of system usage, the study of the factors which influence the user's perception is essential to explaining why a particular user perception of usefulness and ease of use should develop and what, practically, can be done to alter that perception. The nine antecedents selected are considered the most probable influences, but the list of factors is neither definitive nor exhaustive.

Validating Adapted TAM in Egypt

Rose and Straub (1998) point out that a majority (more than 70 studies) of TAM studies have been done in the developed world. A few studies have used TAM outside the developed world (Doll, Hendrickson & Deng, 1998; Ghorab, 1997). Therefore, there is a need to accumulate further studies to indicate the general applicability of TAM.

This study confirmed Rose and Straub's finding that TAM transferred successfully to the Arab world. Furthermore, Perceived Usage (PU) and Perceived Ease of Use (PEU) showed a significant direct effect on DSS usage at 0.001 and 0.10 levels and in consequence confirmed all earlier cited studies about TAM (Davis, 1989; Igbaria et al., 1997). As TAM proposes, both PU and PEU are important in technology acceptance and usage. However, their relative importance in the acceptance process has been shown to be different in previous studies. For instance, Davis (1993) found that usefulness

Table 4. Hypotheses testing results

Hypothesis	χ^2	probability	DF	Variance
Task characteristics	77.604	0.310	169	1.6
Cultural characteristics	159.859	0.237	148	1.4
DSS characteristics	283.041	.239	267	1.05
Environmental characteristics	166.829	.300	158	1.2
Organisational characteristics	201	.402	197	1.2
Internal support characteristics	173.021	.442	171	1.00
External support characteristics	168.819	.077	144	.96
Decision maker characteristics	292.842	.124	266	1.10
Top management characteristics	199.883	.231	186	1.10

Table 5. Total effect of factors on DSS usage

Perceived Ease of Use	2.36
Top Management Support	0.188
Organisational characteristics	0.112
Decision maker characteristics	0.076
Internal Support characteristics	0.017
External Support characteristics	0.012
Cultural characteristics	0.002
Environmental characteristics	-0.02
Task characteristics	-0.091
DSS characteristics	-0.116
Perceived Usefulness	-0.41

dominated ease of use, whereas Adams, Nelson, and Todd (1992) found ease of use to be more influential than usefulness. In this study, the fitness of the model was substantially reduced when the link between PEU and PU was removed. This indicates that PEU dominated PU.

Furthermore, the application of an adapted TAM to the actual use of a DSS in a large organization extends the validity of TAM since most empirical studies of TAM have examined relatively simple end-user technologies, often in controlled environments.

The contrasting positive effect of PEU (2.36) on DSS usage and negative effect of PU (-0.41) may suggest that decision-making managers in local authorities are more likely to use DSS technologies on the basis of ease of use and user-friendliness rather than because of the functions it performs for them. Decision makers with difficulties in using the system might, as a consequence of their lack of skills training, be discouraged from using the system and may not be able to observe the potential benefits. This emphasizes the importance of having features and services to support the usability of an information system. This result is also consistent with Agarwal and Prasad (1999) where ease of use predicted usefulness. A bias toward seeing the DSS more as a vehicle for publicity and increasing the political prestige of senior managers, rather than seeing it as technically useful, may explain the dominance of PEU. This result is also consistent with Nidumolu et al. (1996).

Factors Affecting DSS Usage

The study showed that the external variables played a significant role in explaining DSS usage in the context of the model, mediated by PEU and PU. It suggested that top management support, organizational characteristics, decision maker characteristics, internal support characteristics, external support characteristics, and cultural characteristics, in order, were the most positive significant influences of DSS usage.

Environmental characteristics and task characteristics had a negative effect on DSS usage. The function of a DSS is to provide relevant information to enable decision makers to determine considered solutions for less structured problems. The use of a DSS assumes that decision makers have a significant amount of independence in using their judgment to make decisions. If that autonomy is absent or limited, then the DSS usefulness is substantially reduced. So, the DSS depends on a particular type of organizational environment which may in itself be culturally influenced. A DSS may not only require an organizational environment which encourages individualism and autonomy, but may also catalyze autonomy, in that it provides information which reduces the decision maker's dependence on organizational structures.

Interviews suggested that most of the important decisions were made by the centralized government, and local decisions were quite simple, although qualitative in nature. The organizational structure of Egyptian government is based more on a hierarchy of power vested in individuals. This culture, which reflects Egyptian culture, means that decisions are handed down a chain of command and expected to be implemented. Indeed, the spread of the DSS in this study was influenced by the culture of command and control. Hence, there is a paradox, in that an information system which needs individualism to be effective is being rolled out in a culture that is characterized by a lack of autonomy and significant power-distance. In such an environment, task complexity may be low, since a significant element of local management involves implementing centrally-made decisions; hence, the perceived usefulness of the DSS is reduced.

An analogous initiative in Egypt's Ministry of Education, Technology Development Center, involved establishing multimedia centers and computer laboratories in secondary schools. These centers were rarely used, except for special occasions (Warschauer, 2003). The Egyptian educational system is extremely hierarchical with long chains of command and only the top level able to make decisions. In one case, a request from a visiting teacher to see a copy of a CD used in the school could only be granted permission by the Vice Minister of Education. Technology was serving the purpose of hierarchy and transmission, rather than horizontal networking (Warschauer, 2003).

If strategic decisions are being made by stakeholders higher up the hierarchy and being transmitted to the executives, then the executives' involvement concerns interpretation of that decision, rather than making it. In that context, information held in the DSS will have little bearing on the outcome of the decision-making process. This may explain this negative relationship between PU and top management support. Hence, the study suggests that the championing of a DSS by top management may not be effective unless subordinates are given sufficient managerial autonomy to justify its use. Encouragement to use a DSS, involving marketing the system, providing the resources to buy the system, and providing technical support, will not be fruitful unless the business environment which catalyzes its use is also provided.

A DSS not only carries in it assumptions about who will make decisions and their autonomy, but also assumptions about how decisions will be made and in what business context. The DSS may encourage, if not assume, the rationalization of the decision-making processes, such that decisions result from an objective analysis of the provided information. If the local, culturally determined, decision making style is less formal, more subjective, and depends on power hierarchies and social influence, then the perceived usefulness of the DSS may be low.

Egyptian culture is less inclined to use systematic and formal planning procedures than its Western counterparts. Decision makers will rely more on extrapolations from experience and intuition. Strategic decisions in most of the Egyptian cities are made by powerful individuals (rather than groups) who frequently rely on personal knowledge and intuition rather than objective criteria or formal and quantitative methods (Moores & Gregory, 2000; Seliem et al., 2003). One of the DSS staff expressed his negative feelings about the way that decision makers made their decisions, stating that:

Most managers seek the information that they need in their own personal way. Much of this information remains in a soft form, in the mind of the manager, and is verbally communicated mainly in private meetings rather than written memos or reports. In the formal meetings, employees will compete for privileged confidence of the boss and manoeuvre to get close to him by [expressing] agreement with what he is saying and the decision will be in the end what the boss thinks is right and suitable according to his viewpoint.

The DSS studied here had been developed indigenously within Egypt and was not commercial off-the-shelf (COTS) software imported from the West. However, the development was led by a western-trained software engineer (El Sherif, 1990; El Sherif & El Sawy, 1988). Rose and Straub (1998) highlight the fact many students from developing countries attend Western universities and then go back to their home countries. As such, Western philosophies concerning business processes, formal decision making, the software development process, and the purpose of the information system are imported into the development and implementation of the DSS. Such local technical leaders, on returning from Western universities and commercial companies, transmit cultural assumptions about technology. Heeks (1999) suggests the need to develop indigenous software development in which the cultural sensitivities of the local environment are reflected in the software.

If the DSS reflects ways of thinking which are basically foreign to the Egyptian nationals and places a value on the formalization of information and decision making which is foreign to the Egyptian civil servants, then those executives, feeling culturally lost when faced with using the DSS, are likely to look outside their own organization for support. Hence, the extent of external support, which will essentially be providing cultural education in the Westernizing of business and decision-making processes, will strongly influence whether the system is useful and can indeed be used at all. Results suggested that external support was seen as more influential than internal support.

External support may not be subject to the cultural norms which drive the organization internally. Advice from an external consultant may be more easily accepted than internal advice, particularly in a hierarchical organization where status and position is of significant importance. Interviews suggested that, internally in the organization, there were significant cultural barriers arising from the power distance between chief executives and more junior IT managers. The head of one city council stated:

DSS and IT in general is like a sledge hammer waiting to fall on our heads. We have managers that think they know how to use it and don't. They trained the IT staff to use this system but not the city managers. And if any one is going to train me around its use, it is better to be an experienced head of city council who has used the system. I don't understand why we needed it, what it can do for us, so I have no intention to use it.

Furthermore, the effectiveness of internal support may be limited by resources as well as cultural norms. While in some private organizations, internal computing support may be a significant positive factor, the same may not apply in public institutions, particularly in developing countries, where staffing may be inadequate and skill levels low. It may be that such a lack of formal support forces users to rely on their own personal networks. One participant suggested that he depended totally on his own self development in relation to DSS and he "*used his own personal connections to get the facilities for his department*".

However, interview participants expressed dissatisfaction with vendor support. One of the participants said:

We were wrong to depend on the help that we get from the vendors, because all what they care about is to get the goods delivered and that's it in most cases. This may be because most of them are agencies serving many manufacturers. So they are all salesmen and do not have real expertise.

It is reasonable to assume that the experiences, attitudes, and management styles of DSS users will influence their perception of the DSS, the extent to which they use the DSS and the usefulness of the DSS in producing effective strategic decisions. Like many information systems, the benefits attained from a DSS may be limited by inadequacies in the user.

The role of the military is significant as a socialization agent and in managing public sector activities (Gotowicki, 1997). The decision makers in local government in Egypt tend to be ex-military staff, appointed centrally, with little awareness of IT. One ex-army city executive stated:

As you see I am in my early fifties. At the time when I graduated from university none of this type of knowledge was available. According to my experience, I used to make decisions according to rules and regulations. When I heard about DSS I read a book about it and I did not feel that it could do much for me. I am willing to learn even at this age but when I find the proper way of doing that.

If the attitudes of the users are influenced by their background and by the national culture, the background and culture will influence their perception of the value of the DSS.

CONCLUSIONS

This study confirmed the validity of extending the applicability of the adapted TAM to predict the actual usage of DSS in this type of environment. The study showed that managers in local authorities are more likely to use DSS on the basis of PEU rather than PU. This emphasizes the importance of having services within and outside the organization to support the usability of information systems. The study also contributes to a move in TAM research away from confirming the relevance of PEU and PU to technology adoption toward identifying the influences on the participants' perceptions of ease of use and usefulness. This study identified some of the influencing external factors that could affect the usage of DSS in local authorities in less-developed countries, mediated by PEU and PU. Top management support, organizational characteristics, decision maker characteristics, internal support characteristics, external support characteristics, and cultural characteristics were all influential in encouraging DSS usage. In contrast, environmental and task characteristics negatively affected DSS usage.

In conjunction with interviews, the quantitative results suggest that there is a mismatch between the autonomy and independence in decision making that the DSS supports and the hierarchical command and control culture prevalent within the Egyptian public sector. Furthermore, the nature of Egyptian culture may inhibit junior staff from seeking internal support.

This study indicates the importance of taking into account external factors when examining IT technology adoption globally. In particular, many aspects of culture, not only defined as cultural characteristics, but also influenced through top management support, organizational characteristics, and the background and characteristics of the decision maker, will strongly influence the perception of management support systems.

LIMITATIONS

Further development of the instrument used in this study would be desirable. Although validated, results suggest some difficulty with measuring task, DSS, and decision-maker characteristics. Rose and Straub (1998) raise concerns about culturally-dependent bias in Arab respondents which may apply to this study. In addition, no attempt was made to differentiate between the response of chief executives of local authorities and DSS managers. Interviews suggested they may sometimes take different views of DSS usage. Furthermore, generalization of the results for Egypt to the rest of the Arab community should not be taken for granted. While Hofstede (1997) grouped all Arab countries in one category, each country still has its own unique social, political, and cultural structure.

FUTURE RESEARCH

This study suggests a range of implications for further research. First, both the quantitative and qualitative aspects of this study indicated the importance of cultural influences on DSS usage. As significant work is developed in this area and applied to TAM (Straub et al., 1997; Veiga et al., 2001) there will be a need to expand the repertoire and depth of cultural models which provide the basis for exploring IT adoption among different countries. The variables described by Hofstede (1997) provide a coarse model on which would be unwise to depend. Such universal measures are crude and sweep the subtleties of cultural difference under the carpet (Walsham, 2001, p. 188). A whole raft of other cultural attributes, such as criticism avoidance, respect, consideration, and patronage need to be considered. Hence, attention should be paid to developing richer cultural constructs which may give deeper understanding of the cultural determinants of IT adoption and usage. In addition, models of power should be explored and power constructs developed in order to understand and test the influence of power on IT adoption across cultures.

Second, the unidirectional nature of the model, in which the external variables influence PU and PEU, and PU and PEU influence DSS usage omits the interaction between external variables and any feedback from actual DSS usage. Culture may influence organizational characteristics, which in turn influence the decision maker's characteristics. Top management may influence the culture. The external influences on TAM may be better portrayed as a web of influences, which would require more complex models to represent. There is a clear need to understand the interaction between variables, which may in themselves be closely coupled.

Third, there is a need to study the culture of the software itself. The way it represents information and dictates processes may be culturally determined. This needs to be recognized when software is being distributed globally. The culture of the software may be compared to the local culture in order to identify points of conflict and understand the issues which may result in local nonacceptance of the globally distributed software.

Finally, an understanding of the interaction between local and global factors may be a key element in global information management studies. IT adoption may be affected by both global networks of interacting factors and local networks. Studies which focus on the interface between global and local influences on IT adoption may help in identifying what managerial and technical actions are needed to make globally distributed software sensitive to local requirements arising from culture, business processes, and attitudes to technology.

ACKNOWLEDGMENTS

The authors would like to thank Felix Tan, the associate editor, and the three anonymous reviewers for thoughtful and insightful comments during the revision process.

REFERENCES

Adams, D.A., Nelson, R.R., & Todd, P.A. (1992). Perceived usefulness, ease of use, and usage of information. *MIS Quarterly, 16*(2), 227-248.

Agarwal, R., & Prasad, J. (1999). Are individual differences germane to the acceptance of new information technologies? *Decision Sciences, 30*(2), 361-391.

Aladwani, A.M. (2002). Organisational actions, computer attitudes, and end-user satisfaction in public organisations: An empirical study. *Journal of End-User Computing, 14*, 42-49.

Alavi, M., & Joachimsthaler, E.A. (1992). Revisiting DSS implementation research: A meta-analysis of the literature and suggestions for researchers. *MIS Quarterly, 16*(1), 95-117.

Al-Gahtani, S.S., & King, M. (1999). Attitudes, satisfaction and usage: Factors contributing to each in the acceptance of information technology. *Behaviour & Information Technology, 18*(4), 277-297.

Ang, J., & Teo, T. (1997). CSFs and sources of assistance and expertise in strategic IS planning: A Singapore perspective. *European Journal of Information Systems, 6*, 164-171.

Arbuckle, J.L., & Wothke, W. (1999). *AMOS 4.0 User's guide*. Chicago: Smallwaters Corporation.

Attewell, P. (1992). Technology diffusion and organisational learning: The case of business computing. *Organization Sciences, 3*(1), 1-19.

Babcock, T., Bush, M., & Lan, Z. (1995). Executive use of information technology in the public sector: An empirical examination. *Journal of Government Information, 22*(2), 119-130.

Blanning, R.W., Bui, T.X., & Tan, M. (1997). National information infrastructure in Pacific Asia. *Decision Support Systems, 21*(3), 215-227.

Blili, S., Raymond, L., & Rivard, S. (1998). Impact of task uncertainty, end-user involvement and competence of the success of end-user computing. *Information and Management, 33*, 137-153.

Boudreau, M.-C., Gefen, D., & Straub, D. (2001). Validation in IS research: A state-of-the-art assessment. *MIS Quarterly, 25*, 1-24

Boynton, A.C., Zmud, R.W., & Jacobs, G.C. (1994). The influence of IT management practice on IT use in large organizations. *MIS Quarterly, 18*(3), 299-320.

Brislin, R. (1986). The wording and translation of research instruments. In W. Loner & J. Berry (Eds.), *Field methods in cross-cultural research*. Thousand Oaks, CA: Sage.

Brown, I.T.J. (2002) Individual and technological factors affecting perceived ease of use of Web-based learning in a developing country. *Electronic Journal of Information Systems in Developing Countries, 9*, 1-15.

Chen, J.Q., & Lee, S.M. (2003). An exploratory cognitive DSS for strategic decision making. *Decision Support Systems, 36*, 147-160.

Cheney, P.H., Mann, R.I., & Amoroso, D.L. (1986). Organizational factors affecting the success of end-user computing. *Journal of Management Information Systems, 3*(1), 65-80.

Daft, R.L., & Lengel., R.H. (1986). Organizational information requirements, media richness and structural design. *MIS Quarterly, 32*(5), 554-572.

Davis, F.D. (1989). Perceived usefulness, perceived ease of use, and user acceptance of information technology. *MIS Quarterly, 13*(3), 319-340.

Davis, F.D. (1993). User acceptance of information technology: Systems characteristics, user perceptions and behavioral impacts. *International Journal of Man-Machine Studies, 38*(3), 475-487.

DeLone, W.H., & McLean, E.R. (1992). Information systems success: The quest for the dependent variable. *Information Systems Research, 3*(1), 60-95.

Doll, W.J., Hendrickson, A., & Deng, X. (1998). Using Davis's perceived usefulness and ease-of-use instruments for decision making: A confirmatory and multigroup invariance analysis. *Decision Sciences, 29,* 839-869.

El Sherif, H. (1990). Managing institutionalisation of strategic support systems for the Egyptian cabinet. *Interfaces, 20*(1), 97-114.

El Sherif, H., & El Sawy, O.A. (1988). Issue-based decision support systems for the Egyptian cabinet. *MIS Quarterly, 12*(4), 551-570.

Ghorab, K.E. (1997). The impact of technology acceptance considerations on system usage, and adopted level of technological sophistication: An empirical investigation. *International Journal of Information Management, 17*(4), 249-259.

Goodman, S., & Green, J.D. (1992). Computing in the Middle East. *Communications of the ACM, 35*(8), 21-25.

Gotowicki, S.H. (1997). *The role of the Egyptian military in domestic society.* Foreign Military Studies Office, Fort Leavenworth, US. Retrieved December 22, 2004, from http://fmso.leavenworth.army.mil/fmsopubs/issues/egypt/egypt.htm

Guimaraes, T., Igbaria, M., & Lu, M. (1992). The determinants of DSS success: An integrated model. *Decision Sciences, 23*(2), 409-431.

Gupta, B., Nemati, H.R., & Harvey, J.D. (1999). Organisational factors affecting successful implementation of decision support systems: The case of fuel management system at Delta Airlines. *Journal of Information Technology Cases and Applications, 1*(3), 4-25.

Heeks, R. (1999). Software strategies in developing countries. *Communications of the ACM, 46*(6), 15-20.

Hempel, P.S., & Kwong, Y.K. (2001). B2B e-commerce in emerging economies: I-metal.com's non-ferrous metals exchange in China. *Journal of Strategic Information Systems, 10,* 335-355

Hofstede, G. (1997). *Cultures and organisations: Software of the mind.* New York: McGraw-Hill.

Ibrahim, R.R. (1985). Computer usage in developing countries: Case study Kuwait. *Information & Management, 8,* 103-112.

Igbaria, M., Pavri, F.N., & Huff, S.L. (1989). Microcomputer applications: An empirical look at usage. *Information & Management, 16*(4), 187-197.

Igbaria, M., Zinatelli, N., Cragg, P., & Cavaye, A.L.M. (1997). Personal computing acceptance factors in small firms: A structural equation model. *MIS Quarterly, 21*(3), 279-305.

Ishman, M.D., Pegels, C.C., & Sanders, G.L. (2001). Managerial information systems success factors within the cultural context of North America and a former Soviet republic. *Journal of Strategic Information Systems, 10,* 291-312.

Kambayashi, N., & Scarbrough, H. (2001). Cultural influences on IT use amongst factory managers: A UK-Japanese comparison. *Journal of Information Technology, 16*, 221-236.

Kamel, S. (1995). IT diffusion and socio economic change in Egypt. *Journal of Global Information Management, 3*(2), 4-17.

Kamel, S. (1998). *Decision support systems and strategic public sector decision making in Egypt* (Working Paper No. 3). Manchester: University of Manchester, Precinct Centre.

Kamel, S., & Assem, A. (2003). Assessing the introduction of electronic banking in Egypt using the technology acceptance model. *Annals of Cases on Information Technology, 5*, 1-25.

Keil, M.B., & M. Konsynski, B.R. (1995). Usefulness and ease of use: Field study evidence regarding task considerations. *Decision Support Systems, 13*, 75-91.

King, W.R. (1996). Strategic issues in groupware. *Information Systems Management, 13*, 73-76.

King, W.R., & Teo, T.S.H. (1996). Key dimensions of facilitators and inhibitors for the strategic use of information technology. *Journal of Management Information Systems, 12*(4), 35-53.

Kivijarvi, H., & Zmud, R.W. (1993). DSS implementation activities, problem domain characteristics and DSS success. *European Journal of Information Systems, 2*(3), 159-169.

Kraemer, K.L., Danziger, J.N., Dunkle, D.E., & King, J.L. (1993, June). The usefulness of computer-based information to public managers. *MIS Quarterly*, 129-148.

Krovi, R. (1993). Identifying the causes of resistance to IS implementation: A change theory perspective. *Information & Management, 25*, 327-335.

Legris, P., Ingham, J., & Collerette, P. (2003). Why do people use information technology? A critical review of the technology acceptance model. *Information and Management, 40*, 191-204.

Leidner, D., Carlsson, S., & Elam, J. (1995). A cross-cultural study of executive information systems. *Proceedings of the 28th Annual Hawaii International Conference on Systems Sciences* (Vol. III, pp. 91-100). IEEE Publications.

Li, E.Y. (1997). Perceived importance of information system success factors: A meta-analysis of group differences. *Information & Management, 32*(1), 15-28.

Lind, M.R., Zmud, R.W., & Fischer, W.A. (1989). Microcomputer adoption: The impact of organizational size and structure. *Information & Management, 16*(3), 157-163.

Lu, M.-t., Hsieh, C.-c., & Pan, C.-c. (1989). Implementing decision support systems in developing countries. *IMDS, 7*, 21-26.

McBride, N. (1997). The rise and fall of an executive information system: A case study. *Information Systems Journal, 7*, 277-287.

Moores, T., & Gregory, F. (2000). Cultural problems in applying SSM for IS development. *Journal of Global Information Management, 8*(1), 14-29

Nasirin, S., & Birks, D.F. (2003). DSS implementation in the UK retail organisations: A GIS perspective. *Information and Management, 40*, 325-336.

Neo, B.S. (1988). Factors facilitating the use of information technology for competitive advantage: An exploratory study. *Information & Management, 15*, 191-201.

Nidumolu, S.R., & Goodman, S.E. (1993). Computing in India. An asian elephant learning to dance. *Communications of the ACM, 36*(6), 15-22.

Nidumolu, S.R., Goodman, S.E., Vogel, D.R., & Danowitz, A.K. (1996). Information technology for local administration support: The governorates project in Egypt. *MIS Quarterly, 20*(2), 197-221.

Nunnally, J.C. (1967). *Psychometric theory*. New York: McGraw-Hill.

Phillips, L.A., Calantone, R., & Lee, M.-T. (1994). International technology adoption: Behavior structure, demand certainty and culture. *Journal of Business and Industrial Marketing, 9*(2), 16-28.

Ramaprasad, A. (1987). Cognitive process as a basis for MIS and DSS design. *Management Science, 33*(2139-148).

Rose, G., & Straub, D. (1998). Predicting general IT use: Applying TAM to the Arabic world. *Journal of Global Information Management, 6*(3), 39-46.

Sanders, G.L., & Courtney, J.F. (1985). A field study of organisational factors influencing DSS success. *MIS Quarterly, 9*(1), 77-94.

Seliem, A.A., Ashour, A.S., Khalil, O.E., & Millar, S.J. (2003). The relationship of some organisational factors to information systems effectiveness: A contingency analysis of Egyptian data. *Journal of Global Information Management, 11*(1), 41-56.

Shayo, C., Guthrie, R., & Igbaria, M. (1999). Exploring the measurement of end user computing success. *End User Computing, 11*(1), 5-14.

Shibanda, G.G., & Musisi-Edebe, I. (2000). Managing and developing the strategy for Africa information in global computerization. *Library Management, 21*(5), 228-234.

Straub, D., Keil, M., & Brenner, W. (1997). Testing the technology acceptance model across cultures: A three country study. *Information & Management, 33*(1), 1-11.

Straub, D.W., Loch, K.D., & Hill, C.E. (2001). Transfer of information technology to the Arab world: A test of cultural influence modelling. *Journal of Global Information Management, 9*, 6-28.

Taylor, S., & Todd, P. (1995a). Assessing IT usage: The role of prior experience. *MIS Quarterly, 19*(4), 561-570.

Taylor, S., & Todd, P.A. (1995b). Understanding information technology usage: A test of competing models. *Information Systems Research, 6*(2), 144-176.

Udo, G.J., & Davis, J.S. (1992a). Factors affecting decision support system benefits. *Information & Management, 23*, 359-371.

Udo, G.J., & Davis, J.S. (1992b). A comparative analysis of DSS user-friendliness and effectiveness. *International Journal of Information Management, 12*(3), 209-224.

Veiga, J.F., Floyd, S., & Dechant, K. (2001). Towards modelling the effects of national culture on IT implementation and acceptance. *Journal of Information Technology, 16*, 145-158.

Venkatesh, V. (2000). Determinants of perceived ease of use: Integrating control, intrinsic motivation, and emotion into the technology acceptance model. *Information Systems Research, 11*(4), 342-365.

Walsham, G. (1993). *Interpreting information systems in organisations*. Chichester: John Wiley & Sons.

Walsham, G. (2001). *Making a world of difference: IT in a global context*. Chichester: John Wiley & Sons.

Warschauer, M. (2003). Dissecting the "Digital Divide": A case study in Egypt. *The Information Society, 19*, 296-304.

Webby, R., & O'Connor, M. (1994). The effectiveness of decision support systems, the implications of task complexity and DSS sophistication. *Journal of Information Technology, 9*, 19-28.

Young, D., & Watson, H. (1995). Determinates of EIS acceptance. *Information and Management, 29*, 153-164.

APPENDIX 1

Questionnaire Items Used to Measure Antecedent Constructs Influencing PEU and PU

For each statement, respondents were asked to indicate their agreement that the characteristic influences the use of the DSS in making strategic decisions on a 5-point Likert scale from strongly disagree (1) to strongly agree (5).

1. *Task characteristics*
   - Complexity of problem or issue recognition
   - Complexity of analysis and evaluation of alternatives in strategic decisions
   - Complexity of choice and implementation in strategic decisions
   - Strategic decision processes as a whole are too complex to be computerized
   - Strategic decision making tasks are too "person centered" to be computerized

2. *Cultural characteristics*
   - Individualism (extent to which people act solely in their own interest)
   - Masculinity (extent to which assertive behavior is desired over modest behavior)
   - The cultural gap among decision makers and DSS staff (education, training, experience, and background)
   - Uncertainty avoidance (extent to which people feel uncomfortable with uncertainty)

3. *DSS characteristics*
   - Overall cost effectiveness of DSS
   - Ease of use of DSS
   - Adequacy of DSS's data storage capacity
   - Adequacy of DSS's modeling capacity
   - Adequacy of DSS's processing speed
   - Accessibility of DSS
   - Ease of use of built-in help facility for assistance
   - Usage of DSS is voluntary/compulsory
   - DSS meets the requirements of decision makers
   - DSS reliability
   - Ease of finding the required data
   - Tangible/intangible benefits of DSS usage

4. *Environmental characteristics*
- Competition among local governments
- Favorable government policies
- Uncertainty in local government environment
- Favorable market conditions

5. *Organizational characteristics*
- Size of the organization
- Location of DSS staff /department in the organizational structure
- Degree of decentralization
- Information intensity
- Integration among departments in relation to data/information exchange and sharing experience
- Planning integration between using DSS and overall planning process
- Computer facilities

6. *External support characteristics*
- Recommendations from outside consultants
- Advice and support from the vendors
- Support from government agencies

7. *Decision-maker characteristics*
- Years of experience
- Cognitive style (analytical/heuristic)
- Self-efficiency
- Attitudes toward DSS
- Involvement in the development of DSS
- Level of training and education
- Innovativeness of decision maker
- Fear from using DSS in making strategic decisions
- Familiarity with DSS usage
- Ability to interpret DSS output
- Ability to change and use new methods to make strategic decisions
- Confidence in DSS usage

8. *Internal support characteristics*
- Training/consultation within organization
- Advice provided by other colleagues/friends
- Providing library (books and software manuals)
- Access to help desk or hotline
- Experience of DSS staff in implementation of DSS technology and supporting decision makers

9. *Top management characteristics*
- Top management understanding of DSS
- Rewarding efforts of using DSS to meet set goals at sectional, department, divisional, and corporate level

- Setting policies and goals for DSS
- Offering funds
- DSS design and development
- Developing a core of internal experts who will train others (local resident expert)

This chapter was previously published in the *Journal of Global Information Management,* 13(2), pp. 42-65, © 2005.

Chapter XIV

Understanding Internet Banking Adoption and Use Behavior:
A Hong Kong Perspective

Sui-cheung Chan, Lingnan University, China

Ming-te Lu, Lingnan University, China

ABSTRACT

This study investigates adoption/use behavior within the context of Hong Kong Internet Banking services. A research framework based on the extended Technology Acceptance Model (TAM2) and Social Cognitive Theory is developed to identify factors that would influence the adoption and continue use of Internet Banking. Structural Equation Modeling (SEM) is employed to examine the entire pattern of inter-correlations among the eight proposed constructs, and to test related propositions empirically. A survey involving a total of 499 university students is conducted and confirmatory factor analysis used to determine the measurement efficacies. The results reveal that both subjective norm and computer self-efficacy indirectly play significant roles in influencing the intention to adopt Internet Banking. Perceived ease of use has a significant indirect effect on intention to adopt/use through perceived usefulness, while its direct effect on intention to adopt is not significant.

INTRODUCTION

Hong Kong is an international financial center well known for its efficiency and its ability to adapt and keep up with the times. Recently, however, the Hong Kong banking industry has been losing competitive advantages in some areas, with the adoption of Internet Banking being one of them. Hong Kong banks have been slower than some other international banks in joining the e-commerce evolution, which first emerged in the United States in mid-90s. Financial institutions in the U.S. have introduced and promoted online banking to provide better customer services. Many property and stock investment firms in Hong Kong have also jumped on the bandwagon and adopted the Internet as a channel for providing better and more efficient services to their clientele. However, Hong Kong's banks are still quite slow in providing Internet Banking services that many overseas customers take for granted. This is certainly uncharacteristic of Hong Kong's economic development.

Courtier and Gilpatrick (1999) recommend that financial institutions regularly survey or gauge customers' needs and desires before introducing any banking strategies on the Internet. Moreover, customers' expectations and acceptance of the new technology and their beliefs in their ability to use it directly influence their needs and desires to adopt it. This study follows this line of thought. Specifically, the main objectives of this study are to identify factors influencing the adoption and use of Internet Banking; to investigate whether differences exist between the determinants of adopting and using Internet Banking; and to examine the degree of mediating effects of the two constructs in the Technology Acceptance Model (TAM) between the antecedents and intention to adopt/use Internet Banking via a structural equation model in the Hong Kong context.

Following the approach taken by Karahanna, Straub, and Chervany (1999), this study combines innovation attributes and attitude theories in a theoretical framework to examine potential and early adopters' reasons for adopting and using Internet Banking. This study also attempts to provide a better theoretical understanding of the antecedents of user acceptance and user resistance to adoption and continue using Internet Banking in Hong Kong. In addition, it extends TAM by adding perceived risk and computer self-efficacy as external variables for perceived usefulness and perceived ease of use.

Perceived risk is an external variable first introduced in marketing research in the study of innovation diffusion and adoption (Frambach, 1993, 1995; Ostlund, 1974). The importance of perceived risk has also been examined in IS research, especially in Internet Banking literature (Bhimani, 1996; Cockburn &Wilson, 1996). The perceived lack of security and privacy over the Internet has been a recognized obstacle in people's adoption of electronic commerce. Thus, customers will adopt Internet Banking only when they perceive it as being low-risk. Computer self-efficacy is adopted from the widely accepted model of individual behavior in social sciences research, or as it is better known, Social Cognitive Theory (Bandura 1977a, 1977b; Bandura 1978, 1982, 1986). Evidence of the relationship between self-efficacy and using a computer can be found in a variety of studies (Burkhardt & Brass, 1990; Gist, Schwoerer, & Rosen, 1989; Hill, Smith, & Mann, 1986; Hill, Smith, & Mann, 1987; Webster & Martocchio, 1992, 1993). Users of Internet Banking need to have the necessary knowledge to operate a computer and use the Internet. Therefore, computer self-efficacy helps to explain the adoption and rejection decisions of the users. It is with the above observations in mind that the present researcher has decided to incorporate risk perception and computer self-efficacy in order to give a more in-depth analysis of adoption/use behavior of Internet Banking.

Consequently, this study has two theoretical contributions. It is the first study to empirically examine the different influences of technology acceptance constructs, together with risk perception and self-efficacy, on both the adoption and use behavior of Internet Banking. Second, it provides a theoretical framework that differentiates adoption and usage based on theories of social psychology and attitude formation. Aside from theoretical values, knowing which criteria are important for adoption and which are important for continue-use will enable systems developers and banks to employ more targeted implementation efforts when introducing Internet Banking. Furthermore, results of the study should provide insight on Internet Banking adoption behavior in Hong Kong, an environment which is culturally quite different from developed economies in the West that have been subjects of most studies on technology adoption behavior. It is also hope that both the methodology used and findings obtained will assist future research on Internet Banking adoption behavior in those regions similar to Hong Kong in terms of Internet penetration, per capital income, and banking institutions such as South Korea, Taiwan, and Singapore.

Following the Introduction section, literature review of the prior research which contributes to the theoretical framework of the study is presented. Next, research methodology for the study is described. The fourth section provides the results of data analysis which include a confirmatory factor analysis to assess the validity and reliability of the proposed instruments and the details of the empirical tests of the proposed model; then the Discussion section follows. Finally, implications and limitations of the study are discussed in the Conclusion.

LITERATURE REVIEW

This study lies at the intersection of two issues. The first is the technology adoption decision-making process. The second is the determinants of information technology acceptance and utilization among users. This section presents a review of existing literature on these two areas. Literature of five widely validated models/theories is reviewed and linked to the adoption of Internet Banking, which forms the theoretical background of this research.

Social Psychology

Information systems researchers have suggested intention models from social psychology as a potential theoretical foundation for research on the determinants of user behavior (Swanson, 1982). Fishbein and Ajzen's (1975) Theory of Reasoned Action (TRA) is an especially widely validated intention model that has been proven successful in predicting and explaining behavior across a wide variety of domains. TRA is concerned with the determinants of consciously intended behaviors (Ajzen & Fishbein, 1980; Fishbein & Ajzen, 1975) composed of attitudinal, social influence, and intention variables to predict behavior. TRA hypothesizes that an individual's Behavioral Intention (BI) to perform a behavior is jointly determined by the individual's Attitude Toward performing the Behavior (ATB) and Subjective Norm (SN), which is the overall perception of what relevant others think the individual should or should not do. The TRA has been successfully applied to a large number of situations to predict the performance of behavior and intentions (Prestholdt et al., 1987; Fredricks & Dossett, 1983; Timko, 1987).

Despite the predictability of TRA being strong across studies, it becomes problematic if the behavior under study is not under full volitional control. To deal with these problems, Ajzen (1985, 1991) extended TRA by including another construct called perceived behavioral control, which predicts both behavioral intention and behavior. The extended model is called the Theory of Planned Behavior (TPB). TPB expands the boundary conditions of TRA to more goal-directed actions. TPB has been successfully applied to various situations in predicting the performance of behavior and intentions (Mathieson, 1991; Young et al., 1991; Madden, Ellen, & Ajzen, 1992; Man, 1998; Cheung, Chan, & Wong, 1999). Empirical results (Mathieson, 1991; Taylor & Todd, 1995) show the appropriateness of using these two theories for studying the determinants of IT usage behavior. Nevertheless, many have found that TPB has a better predictive power of behavior than TRA (Madden, Ellen, & Ajzen, 1992; Man, 1998; Cheung, Chan, & Wong, 1999).

Information Technology Acceptance

The Technology Acceptance Model (TAM), introduced by Davis (1989), is an adaptation of TRA specifically for modeling user acceptance of information systems. It attempts to provide an explanation of the determinants of computer acceptance that is general, and is capable of explaining user behavior across a broad range of end-user computing technologies and user populations. TAM posits that two particular behavioral beliefs, Perceived Usefulness (PU) and Perceived Ease Of Use (PEOU), are of primary relevance for computer acceptance behavior, and that the effect of external variables on intention are mediated by these two key beliefs. IS researchers have used TAM to examine the possible antecedents of PU and PEOU toward microcomputer usage (Igbaria, Guimaraes, & David, 1995; Igbaria, Iivari, & Maragahh, 1995). However, one criticism of the current TAM studies is that there are very few investigations that target the study of the factors (i.e., the external variables) that affect PU and PEOU (Gefen & Keil, 1998). In order to address this issue, Venkatesh and Davis (1996) used three experiments to investigate the determinants of PEOU. The results showed that general computer self-efficacy significantly affected PEOU at all times, while objective usability of the system affected users' perceptions after they had direct experience with the system.

Venkatesh and Davis (2000) added a number of determinants to TAM to develop and test an extended TAM (TAM2). TAM2 explains PU and usage intention in terms of social influence processes (Subjective Norm, Voluntariness, and Image) and cognitive instrumental processes (Job Relevance, Output Quality, Result Demonstrability and PEOU). The results showed that all the above-mentioned social influences and cognitive instrumental processes significantly influence user acceptance of systems.

Risk Perception

Frambach (1993, 1995) contends that the speed of adoption is negatively related to the level of Perceived Risk (PRISK). The perceived risk surrounding an innovation might cause a potential adopter to postpone the decision to either adopt or reject the innovation. PRISK is defined as the uncertainty that customers face when they cannot foresee the consequences of their purchase decisions. The definition highlights two relevant dimensions of PRISK: uncertainty and consequence. PRISK can take many forms, depending on the product and consumer characteristics. The degrees of risk that consumers perceive and their own tolerance of risk taking are factors that influence their purchase strategies. It should be stressed that consumers are influenced by risks that they perceive, whether or not such risks actually exist.

Ostlund (1974) introduced risk as an additional measurement in IT adoption. A common and widely recognized obstacle to electronic commerce adoption has been the lack of security and privacy over the Internet (Bhimani, 1996; Cockburn & Wilson, 1996; Quelch & Klein, 1996). This has led many people to view e-commerce and even Internet applications as risky undertakings. Therefore, it is expected that only individuals who regard Internet Banking as a low risk undertaking would have a tendency to perceive it as useful.

Social Cognitive Theory: Self-Efficacy

Social Cognitive Theory (SCT), (Bandura, 1977, 1978, 1982, 1986) also called Social Learning Theory (SLT), is a widely accepted model of individual behavior. A key element in SCT is the concept of self-efficacy (SE), which refers to an individual's belief in his or her own capability to perform a specific task. Estimations of SE are formed through a gradual and dynamic weighting, integration, and evaluation of complex cognitive, linguistic, social, and/or enactive experiences.

Several studies (Burkhardt & Brass, 1990; Gist, Schwoerer, & Rosen, 1989; Hill, Smith, & Mann, 1986, 1987; Webster & Martocchio, 1992, 1993) have examined the relationship between SE with respect to computer use and a variety of computer studies. These studies found evidence in the relationship between SE and the adoption of high technology products (Hill, Smith, & Mann, 1986), registration in computer courses at universities (Hill, Smith, & Mann, 1987), and technology innovation adoption (Burkhardt & Brass, 1990), as well as performance in software training (Gist, Schwoerer, and Rosen, 1989; Webster & Martocchio, 1992, 1993). All these studies urge the need for further research to explore fully the role SE has in computing behavior.

Although there is a limited amount of work examining the determinants of ease of use beliefs in TAM, in a recent study Venkatesh and Davis (1996) presented empirical support for SE as a key antecedent. SE generalizability also reflects the degree to which judgment is limited to a particular domain of the activity. Within a computing context, these domains might reflect different hardware and software configurations. Thus, individuals with high Computer Self-Efficacy (CSE) are expected to be able to compe-tently use different software packages and computer systems, while those with low CSE would perceive their capabilities as limited to particular software packages or computer systems.

METHODOLOGY

The Research Framework

The attitude literature, including social psychology and technology acceptance, provides the theoretical framework needed to define the linkages between beliefs about adopting and using Internet Banking, while TAM2 provides the underlying structure for the theoretical model of the study. The proposed conceptual model of Internet Banking adoption for this study is shown in Figure 1. The model is based on TPB (Ajzen, 1985),

Figure 1. Proposed Internet banking adoption/continue-to-use model

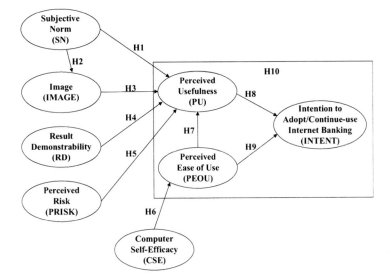

TAM (Davis, Bagozzi, & Warshaw, 1989) and TAM2 (Venkatesh & Davis, 2000). PRISK is considered one of the determinants for the construct of PU of Internet Banking. CSE, which is derived from Social Cognitive Theory's self-efficacy, is employed to help analyze the PEOU of adoption behavior with regard to Internet Banking. The construct of job relevance and output quality are dropped from TAM2 due to their irrelevance to this study. Moreover, the actual usage behavior is not employed as a dependant variable in the research model for two reasons. One is that Internet Banking in Hong Kong is still in an introductory stage. The number of people adopting Internet Banking has not yet reached a critical mass and thus it is difficult to measure usage behavior. The second reason is that the path from intention to actual usage behavior has been widely validated in prior research of different contexts and information systems/technologies; therefore, a positive and direct relationship between intention and actual usage behavior of Internet Banking is expected.

All the constructs are redefined in terms of adopt/continue-to-use Internet Banking. SN, Image (IMAGE), PEOU, PU, and Result Demonstrability (RD) are adapted from TAM2, while CSE is adapted from SCT. Table 1 presents a summary of the brief definitions for the selected research constructs adapted from TAM2 and SCT.

Development of Hypotheses

Early studies by Davis failed to show significant relationships between SN and use. Thus SN is not generally included in TAM. However, Thompson, Higgins, and Howell

Table 1. Definitions of research constructs

Constructs	Definition
CSE	a potential adopter's (or user's) perception of his/her ability to use the computer to accomplish a task
IMAGE	the degree to which adoption/continue-to-use of Internet banking is perceived to enhance one's image or status in one's social system
PEOU	the degree to which Internet banking is perceived as easy to understand and use
PRISK	the uncertainty that a potential adopter (or user) faces when he/she cannot foresee the consequences of his/her adoption/continue-to-use decisions
PU	the degree to which a potential adopter (or user) views Internet banking as offering advantages over previous ways of performing the banking transactions
RD	the degree to which the results of using Internet banking are observable and communicable to others
SN	a potential adopter's (or user's) beliefs that the salient referent thinks he/she should or should not adopt /continue-to-use Internet banking

(1991) found a relationship between SN and PC utilization in a large manufacturing company, whereas Hartwick and Barki (1994) found weak associations between SN and other variables in an empirical study of participation. For this study, classmates and friends are likely to have influence on potential adopters and users of Internet Banking, thus SN is included in the research model. The direct relationship between SN and INTENT in TRA and TPB is based on compliance. The TAM2 (Venkatesh & Davis, 2000) encompasses two additional theoretical mechanisms by which SN can influence INTENT indirectly through PU — internalization and identification. In the case of internalization, SN has an indirect effect on INTENT through PU, as opposed to a direct compliance effect in INTENT. In Hong Kong Chinese cultures, with higher power distance and a more centralized structure, staff waited for directives from superiors about specific work duties. In the present context, if a superior or a co-worker suggests that a particular system (Internet Banking) might be useful, a person may come to believe that it actually is useful, and in turn form an intention to use it. Therefore, the following hypothesis is tested:

H1: Subjective Norm has a positive direct effect on Perceived Usefulness of Internet Banking.

Moore and Benbasat (1991, p.195) define IMAGE as "the degree to which use of an innovation is perceived to enhance one's status in one's social system." If important members of a person's social group believe that he/she should adopt a behavior (using Internet Banking), then adopting it will tend to elevate his/her standing within the group (Blau, 1964; Kiesler & Kiesler, 1969; Pfeffer, 1982). The increased power and influence resulting from elevated status provides a general basis for greater productivity. An individual may thus perceive that using such a system will lead to improvements in his/her job performance (which is the definition of PU) indirectly due to image enhancement, over and above any performance benefits directly attributable to system use. This identification effect is captured in TAM2 by the effect of SN on IMAGE, coupled with the effect of IMAGE on PU. Thus, this study postulates that:

H2:   Subjective Norm has a positive effect on Image.

H3:   Image has a positive effect on Perceived Usefulness of Internet banking.

Even effective information technologies can fail to garner user acceptance if people have difficulty attributing gains in their performance specifically to their use of the technology. Therefore, TAM2 (Venkatesh & Davis, 2000) theorizes that RD, defined by Moore and Benbasat (1991, p. 203) as the "tangibility of the results of using an information technology," will directly influence PU. Based on empirical research, Agarwal and Prasad (1997) found a significant correlation between usage intentions and RD. The relationship between RD and PU is also consistent with the job characteristics model, which emphasizes knowledge of the actual results of work activities as a key psychological state underlying work motivation (Hackman & Oldham, 1976; Loher et al., 1985). Therefore, the following hypothesis is tested:

H4:   Result Demonstrability has a positive effect on Perceived Usefulness of Internet Banking.

A common and widely recognized obstacle to electronic commerce adoption has been the lack of security and privacy over the Internet (Bhimani, 1996; Cockburn & Wilson, 1996; Quelch & Klein, 1996). This has led many people to view Internet commerce and even using Internet applications as a risky undertaking. Therefore, it is expected that only individuals who perceive using Internet Banking as a low risk undertaking would have a tendency to perceive it as useful, and it follows that:

H5:   Perceived Risk has a negative effect on Perceived Usefulness of Internet Banking.

From an empirical standpoint, social psychologists have found that self-efficacy tailored to a computer/information technology context is an important determinant of the perceptions of users about such technologies (e.g., Burkhardt & Brass, 1990; Gist, Schwoerer, & Rosen, 1989; Hill, Smith, & Mann, 1986; Hill, Smith, & Mann, 1987). It is often believed that solely usability features, which in turn form the basis for acceptance or rejection, determine perceptions about the ease of use of a system. However, Venkatesh and Davis (1996) have suggested that users strongly anchor ease of use perceptions about any system to their computer self-efficacy. Consequently, this research attempts to explore and understand acceptance of Internet Banking as a function of an underlying situation of high computer self-efficacy of the target user groups, thus the current research framework posits that:

H6:   Higher Computer Self-Efficacy has a positive effect on Perceived Ease of Use of Internet Banking.

As suggested by both TAM and TAM2, PEOU is a direct determinant of PU (Davis, Bagozzi, & Warshaw, 1989; Venkatesh & Davis, 2000), since, all else being equal, the less effortful a system is to use, the more using it can increase the performance. There is empirical evidence that has accumulated over a decade that suggest PEOU is significantly linked to INTENT, both directly and indirectly via its impact on PU (Davis, Bagozzi, & Warshaw, 1989; Venkatesh, 1999; Venkatesh & Davis, 2000). Consistent with past results, it follows that:

H7:   Perceived Ease of Use has a positive effect on Perceived Usefulness of Internet Banking.

H8:   Perceived Usefulness has a positive effect on Intention to Adopt/Continue-to-use of Internet Banking.

H9:   Perceived Ease of Use has a positive effect on Intention to Adopt/Continue-to-use of Internet Banking.

A central tenet of TAM is that beliefs mediate the influence of all other factors in the environment that exhibit effects on individual acceptance of a new information technology, whereas the beliefs-attitude-intentions relationships in TAM have been subjected to extensive empirical scrutiny. However, little research has been done to focus on the actual mediating role of beliefs. The current research attempts to address the inconclusive results on mediation of external variables by examining this issue from a different theoretical perspective, utilizing the social psychology and technology acceptance theories and the Social Cognitive Theory (Bandura, 1977). As a consequence, the last hypothesis tested here is:

H10: Perceived Usefulness and Perceived Ease of Use fully mediate the influence of selected variables on Intention to Adopt/Continue-to-Use of Internet Banking.

Questionnaire Design

The questionnaire is based on guidelines given by both TRA and TPB, which suggest that belief-based measurements should be constructed by analyzing the most frequent responses from open-ended questions used in an elicitation study. These questions were specific and consistent with respect to action (adoption or continue-to-use), target (Internet Banking services), context (an individual's beliefs), and time (in the next six months). Theoretical constructs were operationalized using validated items from prior research and based on the results of the elicitation study. The measurement of SN was adapted from Taylor and Todd (1995). Measures of IMAGE and RD were adapted from Moore and Benbasat (1991). Measures of CSE were adapted from Compeau and Higgins (Compeau & Higgins, 1995a; Compeau & Higgins, 1995b). The TAM scales of PU, PEOU, and INTENT were measured using items adapted from Davis (1989), Davis, Bagozzi, and Warshaw (1989), Moore and Benbasat (1991), and Karahanna, Straub, and Chervany (1999). Several items of these three constructs were adapted from the results of the elicitation study. Measures of PRISK were adapted from Bhimani (1996), and Cockburn and Wilson (1996); two items were developed based on the results of the elicitation study. A seven-point Likert scale was employed to ensure statistical variability among survey responses for all constructs. To ensure that measurement scales were adapted and developed appropriately to the current context, qualitative interviews were conducted with two academic professionals. This resulted in minor wording changes, which were implemented before three pilot tests were carried out.

Respondents

The population of interest is defined as current and potential users of Internet Banking in Hong Kong. Both undergraduate and graduate students at all seven government-funded universities in Hong Kong constitute the sampling frame for this research (There are no private universities in Hong Kong.) Hong Kong university students are considered appropriate as a sampling frame for the research because they are current Internet users and will, in all likelihood, be Internet users after graduation; and the fact that basically all university students in Hong Kong have their own bank and credit card accounts.

Hong Kong's high Internet penetration percentage at 59.58% of the population and that, for people 16 or above, fully 73% have current Internet access (www.nielsen-netratings.com) support the claim that Hong Kong university students will continue to have access to the Internet with their higher level of computer literacy and income. The fact that close to 30% of those surveyed turned out to be Internet banking customers also lend strong support to the notion that these university students have the same psychological behavior as real Internet banking customers. It appears that banks in Hong Kong also regard this as the case, for they have targeted university students as potential Internet banking customers in marketing campaigns in recent years. The use of university students as the sampling frame, meanwhile, decreases the effect of computer literacy variances.

Data collection was conducted from February to the middle of April, 2001. Eight hundred questionnaires were distributed, of which 634 were completed and returned (79.25% response rate). Of these, 183 were Internet Banking users and 451 were potential adopters of Internet Banking. Fifty-nine of the 451 potential adopters had no knowledge of Internet Banking. Their responses, therefore, were withdrawn from the study. After cases with missing data were eliminated, the final sample consisted of 499 observations, of which 147 were users and 352 were potential adopters of Internet Banking. Male respondents account for 51.5% (257 males: 80 users and 177 potential adopters), while female respondents account for 48.5% (242 females: 67 users and 175 potential adopters). All students in the sample are already Internet users. Among the users of Internet Banking, nearly 60% (88) of the users spent over 30 hours on the Internet per week. Of the potential adopters, one-third of them (32.96%, 140) were online over 30 hours per week.

DATA ANALYSIS

Model Testing

In order to test the measurement model of adoption of Internet Banking, the 45 items used to measure the acceptance/continue-to-use of Internet Banking as a whole was subjected to confirmatory factor analysis using LISREL 8.30. The first step in operationalizing the model was to clarify exactly what relationships the model proposes. The first-order factor structure with eight proposed constructs as the latent factors was assessed. The factor variances were fixed at unity and all latent factors were allowed to correlate freely. The parameters were estimated using the Maximum Likelihood (ML) method with the covariance matrix produced by PRELIS 2.30.

Although the LISREL output suggests that all the estimated parameters in the hypothesized eight-factor model are significant (the χ^2 associated with the model is also significant, $\chi^2/df = 4.8$, which is < 5 and RMSEA = 0.087, which is <0.10), the comparative fit indices are outside the bounds that indicate a good fit to the data (e.g., NFI and CFI <0.90). Faced with results like these, the researcher may well be tempted to engage in a post hoc specification search to improve the fit of the measurement model. Items that had squared multiple correlations with the latent variables of less than 0.40 were dropped from the analysis (Bollen, 1989). Information derived from these exploratory and confirmatory factor analyses of the model constructs led the researcher to conclude that items IMAGE3, RD4, PRISK4, CSE1, CSE2, CSE3, CSE6, PU5, PU7, INTENT4, and INTENT6 may be inappropriate for use. Most of these items were indicators newly developed by the researcher for the proposed research model. Therefore, it is possible for these items to have lower factor loadings and thus lower the constructs' empirical reliability. As a consequence, the researcher re-specified the model with these eleven items deleted. The final eight-factor first-order model was then tested with the remaining 34 items, and this resulted in a fairly good fit ($\chi^2 = 1626.07$, $df = 499$, $p < 0.00$, CFI = 0.93, $\chi^2/df = 3.26$) (Table 2). Table 3 shows the measurement properties of all eight constructs. All the factor loadings were fairly high and significant at an alpha level of 0.01. Moreover, all construct reliabilities were much higher than the acceptable level of 0.70. Thus, together with NFI = 0.90, the convergent validity of the measurement of each construct is supported (Anderson and Gerbing, 1988).

Constructs Reliability and Validity

Typically, a causal-indicator model is specified and analyzed for each theoretical construct individually (Ahire, Golhar, & Waller, 1996; Venkatraman, 1989). The researcher followed these guidelines for all constructs with four or more indicators. Constructs with fewer indicators were pooled together and analyzed in order to provide adequate degrees of freedom for estimation of the model parameters. In this study, three constructs (SN, RD, and IMAGE) were pooled together and analyzed. As shown in Table 4, the GFI indices for all eight constructs are higher than the recommended level of 0.90. These results suggest that all eight scales are unidimensional.

Both Cronbach's α and Werts Linn Jöreskog ρ_c tests were used to access the reliabilities of the eight scales. Table 4 indicates that the ρ_c values are well above the threshold of 0.70 for all scales. Cronbach's alpha values were also found to be greater than 0.70. These results suggest that all eight scales are reliable. The Bentler-Bonnet coefficient represents the ratio of the chi-square value of the specified measurement model to that of a null model, which has no hypothesized item loadings on a construct. The Bentler-Bonnet Δ for all eight scales are greater than 0.90, strong convergent validity of scales was demonstrated.

Analysis for the Structural Path Model

The proposed research model was tested separately with the samples of users and potential adopters of Internet Banking via the structural path model. The partial

Table 2. Fit indices for the final CFA model

χ^2	df	χ^2/df	GFI	AGFI	RMSEA	NFI	CFI	PNFI	PGFI
1626.07	499	3.26	0.84	0.81	0.067	0.90	0.93	0.80	0.70

Table 3. Standardized parameter estimates for the final CFA model

Factor	First-Order CFA		
	Construct Reliability	Factor Loading *	R^2
Subjective Norm	0.936		
SN1		0.92	0.85
SN2		0.86	0.73
SN3		0.95	0.91
Image	0.919		
IMAGE1		0.94	0.89
IMAGE2		0.90	0.81
Result Demonstrability	0.889		
RD1		0.85	0.72
RD2		0.87	0.75
RD3		0.84	0.71
Perceived Risk	0.878		
PRISK1		0.73	0.53
PRISK2		0.91	0.83
PRISK3		0.85	0.72
PRISK5		0.71	0.50
Computer Self-Efficacy	0.938		
CSE4		0.85	0.72
CSE5		0.83	0.69
CSE7		0.86	0.73
CSE8		0.82	0.67
CSE9		0.86	0.74
CSE10		0.86	0.74
Perceived Usefulness	0.924		
PU1		0.85	0.72
PU2		0.85	0.72
PU3		0.89	0.80
PU4		0.86	0.74
PU6		0.76	0.57
Perceived Ease of Use	0.917		
PEOU1		0.78	0.61
PEOU2		0.80	0.64
PEOU3		0.79	0.63
PEOU4		0.82	0.67
PEOU5		0.79	0.62
PEOU6		0.73	0.53
PEOU7		0.77	0.59
Intention to Adopt/Continual Usage	0.920		
INTENT1		0.81	0.66
INTENT2		0.81	0.66
INTENT3		0.90	0.81
INTENT5		0.92	0.84

* All factor loadings are significant at an alpha level of 0.01

Table 4. Assessment of unidimensionality, reliability and convergent validity

| Construct | No. of items | Unidimensionality Goodness of fit index [GFI] | Reliability | | Convergent Validity Bentler-Bonnet Δ |
			Cronbach's α	Werts Linn Jöreskog ρ_c	
Subjective Norm	3	0.97	0.93	0.94	0.98
Image	2	0.97	0.92	0.92	0.98
Result Demonstrability	3	0.97	0.89	0.89	0.98
Perceived Risk	4	0.98	0.87	0.88	0.98
Computer Self-Efficacy	6	0.95	0.94	0.94	0.97
Perceived Usefulness	5	0.98	0.92	0.92	0.98
Perceived Ease of Use	7	0.90	0.92	0.92	0.92
Intention to Adopt/Continual Usage	4	0.99	0.92	0.92	0.99

aggregation approach was employed to reduce the level of random error. The results are as follows.

Users of Internet Banking

Standardized parameter estimates for the revised model are presented in Figure 2. As shown, INTENT was predicted by SN ($\beta = 0.47$, $p < 0.01$) and PU ($\beta = 0.53$, $p < 0.01$), which in turn was predicted by IMAGE ($\beta = 0.11$, $p < 0.10$), RD ($\beta = 0.40$, $p < 0.01$), and PEOU ($\beta = 0.48$, $p < 0.01$). PEOU was predicted by CSE ($\beta = 0.63$, $p < 0.01$). Image was predicted by both SN ($\beta = 0.39$, $p < 0.01$) and RD ($\beta = 0.40$, $p < 0.01$). The model explained substantial item variance: 34% of the variance in INTENT, 28% in PU, 60% in PEOU, and 52% in IMAGE.

Potential Adopters of Internet Banking

For potential adopters of Internet Banking (see Figure 3), INTENT was predicted by IMAGE ($\beta = 0.42$, $p < 0.01$), SN ($\beta = 0.25$, $p < 0.01$), and PU ($\beta = 0.15$, $p < 0.05$). PU was predicted by PEOU ($\beta = 0.58$, $p < 0.01$), SN ($\beta = 0.16$, $p < 0.01$), IMAGE ($\beta = 0.10$, $p < 0.05$), and PRISK ($\beta = -0.22$, $p < 0.01$). PEOU was predicted by CSE ($\beta = 0.71$, $p < 0.01$). IMAGE was predicted by both SN ($\beta = 0.19$, $p < 0.01$) and RD ($\beta = 0.53$, $p < 0.01$). The above model also explained substantial item variance; 53% in INTENT, 34% in PU, 49% in PEOU, and 58% of variance in IMAGE. Table 5 shows a summary of research results for both users and potential adopters of Internet Banking.

DISCUSSION

Intention to Adopt/Use of Internet Banking

PU ($\beta = 0.53$ for users and $\beta = 0.15$ for potential adopters) is significantly positively related to INTENT, with 34% of variance of Intention to Continue-to-use and 53% of variance of Intention to Adopt accounted for. This result is consistent with previous

Figure 2. Standardized parameter estimates for users

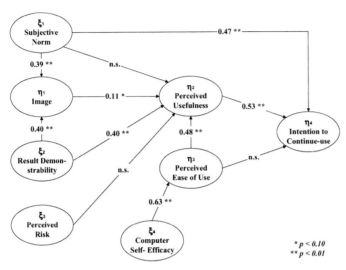

Figure 3. Standardized parameter estimates for potential adopter

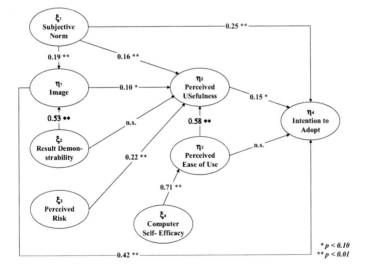

Table 5. Summary of research results

	Hypotheses	Users	Potential Adopters
H1	Subjective Norm will have a positive direct effect on Perceived Usefulness	Not Supported	Supported
H2	Subjective Norm will have a positive effect on Image	Supported	Supported
H3	Image will have a positive effect on Perceived Usefulness	Supported	Supported
H4	Result Demonstrability will have a positive effect on Perceived Usefulness	Supported	Not Supported
H5	Perceived Risk will have a negative effect on Perceived Usefulness	Not Supported	Supported
H6	Higher Computer Self-Efficacy will have a positive effect on Perceived Ease of Use	Supported	Supported
H7	Perceived Ease of Use will have a positive effect on Perceived Usefulness	Supported	Supported
H8	Perceived Usefulness will have a positive effect on Intention to Adopt/Continue-use	Supported	Supported
H9	Perceived Ease of Use will have a positive effect on Intention to Adopt/Continue-use	Not Supported	Not Supported
H10	Perceived Usefulness and Perceived Ease of Use will fully mediate the influence of selected variables on Intention to Adopt/Continue-use	Not Supported	Not Supported

studies on TAM. It implies that if users/potential users perceive Internet Banking to be useful, they will be more likely to continue-to-use/adopt the innovation. Therefore, the result supports H8. The data also revealed that the effect of PU on intention was stronger for users than for potential users. This may be due to the fact that users have direct hands-on experience with Internet Banking, which leads to a better knowledge of its usefulness.

On the other hand, PEOU is not significantly related to INTENT (H9), contradicting expectations. This finding concurs with the original TAM, but contradicts the results of many previous studies (Lu and Gustafson, 1994; Moore and Banbasat, 1991), where ease of use was a significant determinant of intention to use a computer technology. A plausible reason for this is that as IT innovation becomes more user-friendly, learning to use it becomes much easier, especially for Internet technology. Davis (1989) also reported that, while PEOU was found to be significantly correlated with usage, when controlling for usefulness, the effects of ease of use on usage were non-significant. He suggested that "perceived ease of use may actually be a causal antecedent to perceived usefulness, as opposed to a parallel, direct determinant of system usage" (Davis, 1989, p. 319).

Furthermore, SN showed a significant positive relation to INTENT. This means that users feel more positive about using Internet Banking when the social environment encourages its use. This finding concurs with the extended Triandis Model by Cheung, Chang, and Lai (2000), and the extension of TAM by Venkatesh and Davis (2000). However, the setting was different from studies by Venkatesh and Davis, in that the current context (Adopt/Continue-use of Internet Banking) is not mandatory.

The findings also suggest that the effect of SN on intention was stronger for existing users than for potential users of Internet Banking. However, this contradicts the findings of Karahanna, Straub, and Chervany (1999), who revealed that the relationship between SN and behavioral intention was stronger for potential adopters than for users. Triandis (1971) also suggests that subjective norm will have a more pronounced effect in determining behavior when the behavior is new (as in adoption). This influence on behavior decreases when users become more experienced.

In addition, IMAGE ($\beta = 0.42$) was found to be the most significant factor affecting INTENT. It is interesting to note that IMAGE perceived by the potential adopters was very important; it may be due to Hong Kong people's fondness of high technology communication devices, such as mobile phones. Internet Banking, unlike other IT innovations, is less observable. No one, with the exception of close peers, knows whether an individual is an Internet Banking user or not. This is largely because very few people use Internet Banking facilities in front of others, because banking and finances are very personal matters that require privacy. However, within a close peer group, it is relatively easy for any one person to know who else in the group uses Internet Banking. Once individuals feel that Internet Banking is trendy among peers; they may perceive themselves as being looked down upon if they have not yet adopted it. Therefore, as the study has shown, IMAGE and SN were the main factors affecting INTENT for potential adopters.

Perceived Usefulness

Looking at the antecedents of PU, only IMAGE was significantly positively related to PU for both users and potential adopters of Internet Banking. The results support H3, that Image has a positive direct effect on PU of Internet Banking. For potential users, SN and PRISK were respectively significantly positively and negatively related to PU, that is, both H1 and H5 are supported. However, H1 and H5 are not supported for users of Internet Banking. It could be argued that once users have adopted Internet Banking, their perceived usefulness is based mainly on their own personal evaluation of the technology, rather than SN.

As for the different results of H5, PRISK ($\beta = -0.22$) was significantly negatively related to PU for potential users. This implies that if potential users perceive Internet Banking as having a security risk, they will be more likely to perceive it as being less useful. Similar arguments appear in the Internet Banking literature (Bhimani, 1996; Cockburn & Wilson, 1996; Quelch & Klein, 1996), claiming that the perceived security and privacy risk associated with banking on the Internet is a major factor influencing its adoption. Users may not perceive any risk after their adoption of Internet Banking. Thus, no significant relationship was found between PRISK and PU for users.

The finding of RD ($\beta = 0.40$) implies that if Internet Banking produces effective/positive results desired by the users, they are more likely to understand how useful Internet Banking is. Therefore, H4 is supported for users. However, potential users may not be aware of these effective or positive results, or they may have no idea whether these results would be positive or negative. Therefore, they are less likely to understand how useful Internet Banking may be. So, there is no support for H4 for potential users.

Furthermore, PEOU ($\beta = 0.48$ for users and $\beta = 0.58$ for potential adopters) was found to be the most significant factor affecting PU, although it had no statistically significant influence on INTENT. This result is consistent with most prior studies (Lu & Gustafson,

1994) and is easy to explain. For voluntary use of Internet Banking, since individuals usually explore a number of basic features first, the technology's ease of use plays an important role in this stage. The individuals' assessment of the usefulness of the innovation is thus influenced by the innovation's ease of use, all of which supports H7.

Perceived Ease of Use

CSE (β = 0.63 for users and β = 0.71 for potential adopters) was found to be a statistically significant factor of PEOU, and 49% and 60% of variance of PEOU was accounted for potential adopters and users respectively. The finding implies that individuals with higher CSE will perceive Internet Banking as easier to use. This concurs with the suggestion by Venkatesh and Davis (1996) that users strongly anchor ease of use perceptions about any system to their CSE. Therefore, H6 is supported. The data also reveal that the effect of CSE on PEOU was stronger for potential adopters than for users.

Image

H2 is supported. Both SN and RD were significantly positively related to IMAGE for both users and potential adopters of Internet Banking, and a large variance (52% for users and 58% for potential adopters) in IMAGE was explained in the final model. The first part of the results conformed to prior studies of TAM2 (Venkatesh and Davis, 2000), which theorize that SN positively influences image.

Limitations of the Study

There are limitations in this research. First, Internet Banking in Hong Kong is still in its infancy with a scarcity of information on its use at the time of the study. Thus, relevant literature inevitably comes from countries such as the United States and the United Kingdom; such literature may not accurately describe the phenomenon and situation in Hong Kong, especially with regard to cultural differences. Second, Internet Banking adopters should have been surveyed rather than adopters and potential adopters. However, due to confidentiality and other reasons, the leading banks refused the researcher lists of names of Internet Banking users. Furthermore, since Internet Banking is relatively new in Hong Kong, the pool of adopters may not have been large enough during the period of this study. Therefore, their comments may not be reliable. Also, the subjects of this study being university students, this sampling frame, although overlaps the target population to a large degree, is not sufficiently comprehensive in its coverage of all current and potential Internet Banking customers. Last but not least, Byrne (1998) stated that "fit indices provide no guarantee whatsoever that a model is useful ... they can in no way reflect the extent to which the model is plausible; this judgment rests squarely on the shoulders of the researcher." Statistical analysis only provides numerical relationships for the constructs of the proposed research model. Interpretation of these numbers is the researcher's subjective appraisal. Care should be exercised when generalizing these results to other settings. However, consistent results with previous studies and theories, such as SCT and TAM, have enhanced the validity of the empirical findings.

CONCLUSIONS

This study has identified the factors influencing the adoption/continue-use of Internet Banking in the Hong Kong context. It also provides empirical support for a research model that modified the well-known TAM. The results reveal that CSE plays an indirect, but significant role in influencing both intentions to adopt and continue-use of Internet Banking. Differences are found between the determinants of adopting and continuing to use Internet Banking. Risk perceptions of potential adopters hindered the adoption of Internet Banking. Therefore, banks providing Internet Banking could do something to deal with these matters. To boost confidence and enhance self-efficacy in using Internet Banking services, demonstrations via video presentations and Internet kiosks could be made at bank branches to showcase the user-friendliness of such services. These initiative activities will help customers familiarize themselves with the bank and its Internet Banking services. New technology, like all things that are unfamiliar, requires initiation. This is an important criterion in helping potential adopters selecting the bank that offers Internet Banking.

The majority of IS research in the belief/attitude tradition to date has focused on beliefs and attitudes related to usage of IT. Hence, our understanding of beliefs, attitudes, and norms leading to IT adoption and how these are modified over time is limited. Preliminary evidence from the current study suggests that perceptions of image enhancement induce initial adoption, while sustained usage decisions are based solely on beliefs of PU and SN. That means banks should make a better effort in promoting Internet Banking (59 of the 451 potential adopters had no knowledge of Internet Banking). When more people are aware of the availability of Internet Banking, they are more likely to increase discussing the advantages and disadvantages of Internet Banking. Once people perceive that its positive aspects outweigh the negative effects, they are more likely to become users of Internet Banking. Issues such as fear of the lack of privacy and security, together with relative advantages of using Internet Banking should be highlighted to educate potential customers. However, to attract potential adopters that rely more on references (such as friends, colleagues, and family members), member referral rewards programs can be employed. These results represent a vital step toward a deeper understanding of the temporal evolution of beliefs, attitudes, norms, and behavior across different phases of the adoption process. Moreover, the degree of the mediating effect of PU is very high in continue-to-use intention, whereas it is not strong when explaining the adoption intention. PEOU is found to be an important antecedent of PU; however, its mediating effects on both adoption and continue-use intentions are not significant.

This research provides a new perspective and a refined theoretical framework in applying TAM beyond the organizational limit. It may be used as an example for future research on Internet Banking to address the role of other direct determinants of adoption/ usage intentions and behavior. Since this research focuses on the phenomenon and situation of Hong Kong, which has a unique culture, findings in the study should shed light for Hong Kong and overseas banks interested in implementing Internet Banking strategies in Hong Kong by emphasizing the relevant criteria at each phase necessary for a successful adoption process. In addition, the same theoretical framework may also be applied in the adoption of other e-commerce applications in Hong Kong or regions similar to Hong Kong in terms of culture and Internet penetration, by MNCs and dot.coms. Cross-cultural studies may also be carried out using the same theoretical framework. It would be interesting to see how different cultures would exhibit different effects of SN and IMAGE. Several avenues for future work remain, and we hope this study will stimulate others to extend this line of research.

REFERENCES

Agarwal, R., & Prasad, J. (1997). The role of innovation characteristics and perceived voluntariness in the acceptance of information technologies. *Decision Science, 28*(3), 557-582.

Ahire, S.L., Golhar, D.Y., & Waller, M.A. (1996, Winter). Development and validation of TQM implementation constructs. *Decision Sciences, 27*(1), 23-56.

Ajzen, I. (1985). From intentions to actions: A theory of planned behavior. In J. Kuhland & J. Beckman (Eds.), *Action control. From cognition to behavior* (pp. 11-39). Heidelberg: Springer.

Ajzen, I. (1991). The theory of planned behavior. *Organizational Behavior and Human Decision Processes, 50,* 179-211.

Ajzen, I., & Fishbein, M. (1980). *Understanding attitudes and predicting social behavior.* Englewood Cliffs, NJ: Prentice-Hall.

Anderson, J.C., & Gerbing, D.W. (1988). Structural equation modeling in practice: A review and recommended two-step approach. *Psychological Bulletin, 103*(3), 411-423.

Bandura, A. (1977). Self-efficacy: Toward a unifying theory of behavioral change. *Psychological Review, 84*(2), 191-215.

Bandura, A. (1977). *Social learning theory.* Englewood Cliffs, NJ: Prentice-Hall.

Bandura, A. (1978). Reflections on self-efficacy. In S. Rachman (Ed.), *Advances in behavioral research and therapy* (pp. 237-269). Oxford, UK: Pergamon Press.

Bandura, A. (1982). Self-efficacy mechanism in human agency. *American Psychologist, 37*(2), 122-147.

Bandura, A. (1986). *Social foundations of thought and action: A social cognitive theory.* Englewood Cliffs, NJ: Prentice-Hall.

Bhimani, A. (1996). Securing the commercial Internet. *Communications of the ACM, 39*(6), 29-34.

Blau, P.M. (1964). *Exchange and power in social life.* New York: John Wiley.

Bollen, K.A. (1989). *Structural equations with latent variables.* New York: Wiley.

Burkhardt, M.E., & Brass, D.J. (1990). Changing patterns or patterns of change: The effects of a change in technology on social network structure and power. *Administrative Science Quarterly, 35*(1), 104-127.

Byrne, B.M. (1998). *Structural equation modeling with LISREL, PRELIS and SIMPLIS: Basic concepts, applications and programming.* Mahwah, NJ: Lawrence Erlbaum Associates.

Cheung, S.F., Chan, K.S., & Wong, S.Y. (1999). Reexamining the theory of planned behavior in understanding wastepaper recycling. *Environment and Behavior, 31*(5), 587-612.

Cheung, W., Chang, M.K., & Lai V.S. (2000). Prediction of internet and world wide web usage at work: A test of an extended triandis model. *Decision Support Systems, 30,* 83-100.

Cockburn, C., & Wilson, T.D. (1996). Business use of the world-wide web. *International Journal of Information Management, 16*(2), 83-102.

Compeau, D.R., & Higgins, C.A. (1995). Application of social cognitive theory to training for computer skills. *Information Systems Research, 6*(2), 118-143.

Compeau, D.R., & Higgins, C.A. (1995). Computer self-efficacy: Development of a measure and initial test. *MIS Quarterly, 19*(2), 189-211.

Courtier, E., & Gilpatrick, K. (1999). Home banking issteps? *Credit Union Management, 22*(3), 10-12.

Davis, F.D. (1989). Perceived usefulness, perceived ease of use, and user acceptance of information technology. *MIS Quarterly, 13*(3), 318-339.

Davis, F.D., Bagozzi, R.P., & Warshaw, P.R. (1989). User acceptance of computer technology: A comparison of two theoretical models. *Management Science, 35*(8), 982-1003.

Fishbein, M., & Ajzen, I. (1975). *Belief, attitude, intention, and behavior: An introduction to theory and research.* Reading, MA: Addison-Wesley.

Frambach, R.T. (1993). An integrated model of organizational adoption and diffusion of innovations. *European Journal of Marketing, 27*(5), 22-41.

Frambach, R.T. (1995). Diffusion of innovations in business-to-business markets. In M. Bruce & W. G. Biemansm (Ed.), *Product development: Meeting the challenge of the design-marketing interface* (pp. 249-265). New York: John Wiley.

Fredricks, A.J., & Dossett, D.L. (1983). Attitude-behavior relations: A comparison of the fishbein-ajzen and the bentler-speckart models. *Journal of Personality and Social Psychology, 45*, 501-512.

Gefen, D., & Keil, M. (1998). The impact of developer responsiveness on perceptions of usefulness and ease of use: An extension of the technology acceptance model. *The Database for Advances in Information Systems, 29*(2), 35-49.

Gist, M.E., Schwoerer, C., & Rosen, B. (1989). Effects of alternative training methods on self-efficacy and performance in computer software training. *Journal of Applied Psychology, 74*, 884-891.

Hackman, J.R., & Oldham, G.R. (1976). Motivation through the design of work: Test of a theory. *Organization Behaviour and Human Performance, 16*, 250-279.

Hartwick, J., & Barki, H. (1994). Explaining the role of user participation in information system use. *Management Science, 40*, 440-465.

Hill, T., Smith, N.D., & Mann, M.F. (1986). Communicating innovations: Convincing computer phobics to adopt innovative technologies. In R.J. Lutz (Ed.), *Advances in consumer research* (pp. 419-422). Provo, UT: Association of Consumer Research.

Hill, T., Smith, N.D., & Mann, M.F. (1987). Role of efficacy expectations in predicting the decision to use advanced technologies: The case of computers. *Journal of Applied Psychology, 72*, 307-313.

Igbaria, M., Guimaraes, T., & Davis, G.B. (1995). Testing the determinants of microcomputer usage via a structural equation model. *Journal of Management Information Systems, 11*(4), 87-114.

Igbaria, M., Iivari, J., & Maragahh, H. (1995). Why do individuals use computer technology? A Finnish case study. *Information and Management, 29*, 227-238.

Karahanna, E., Straub, D.W., & Chervany, N.L. (1999). Information technology adoption across time: A cross-sectional comparison of pre-adoption and post-adoption beliefs. *MIS Quarterly, 23*(2), 183-213.

Kiesler, C.A., & Kiesler, S.B. (1969). *Conformity.* Reading, MA: Addison-Wesley.

Loher, B.T., Noe, R.A., Moeller, N.L., & Fitzgerald, M.P. (1985). A meta-analysis of the relation of job characteristics to job satisfaction. *Journal of Applied Psychology, 70,* 280-289.

Lu, H-P., & Gustafson, D.H. (1994). An empirical study of perceived usefulness and perceived ease of use on computerized support system use over time. *International Journal of Information Management, 14*(5), 317-329.

Madden, T.J., Ellen, P.S., & Ajzen, I. (1992). A comparison of the theory of planned behavior and the theory of reasoned action. *Personality and Social Psychology Bulletin, 18,* 3-9.

Man, K. (1998). Predicting unethical behavior: A comparison of the theory of reasoned action and the theory of planned behavior. *Journal of Business Ethics, 17,* 1825-1834.

Mathieson, K. (1991). Predicting user intentions: Comparing the technology acceptance model with the theory of planned behavior. *Information Systems Research, 2,* 173-191.

Moore, G.C., & Benbasat, I. (1991). Development of an instrument to measure the perceptions of adopting an information technology innovation. *Information Systems Research, 2*(3), 192-222.

Ostlund, L.E. (1974). Perceived innovation attributes as predictors of innovativeness. *Journal of Consumer Research, 1,* 23-29.

Pfeffer, J. (1982). *Organizations and organization theory.* Marshfield, MA: Pitman.

Prestholdt, P.H., Lane, I.M., & Matthews, R.C. (1987). Nurse turnover as reasoned action: Development of a process model. *Journal of Applied Psychology, 72,* 221-227.

Quelch, J.A., & Klein, L.R. (1996). The internet and international marketing. *Sloan Management Review, 37*(3), 60-75.

Swanson, E.B. (1982). Measuring user attitudes in MIS research: A review. *OMEGA, 10*(2), 157-165.

Taylor, S., & Todd, P.A. (1995). Assessing IT usage: The role of prior experience. *MIS Quarterly, 19*(4), 561-570.

Taylor, S., & Todd, P.A. (1995). Understanding information technology usage: A test of competing models. *Information Systems Research, 6,* 144-176.

Thompson, R.L., Higgins, C., & Howell, J.M. (1991). Personal computing: Toward a conceptual model of utilization. *MIS Quarterly, 15*(1), 125-143.

Timko, C. (1987). Seeking medical care for a breast cancer symptom: Determinants of intentions to engage in prompt or delay behavior. *Health Psychology, 6,* 305-328.

Triandis, H.C. (1971). *Attitude and attitude change.* NY: John Wiley.

Venkatesh, V. (1999). Creation of favourable perceptions: Exploring the role of intrinsic motivation. *MIS Quarterly, 23*(2), 239-260.

Venkatesh, V., & Davis, F.D. (1996). A model of the perceived ease of use: Development and test. *Decision Sciences, 27*(3), 451-481.

Venkatesh, V., & Davis, F.D. (2000). A theoretical extension of the technology acceptance model: Four longitudinal studies. *Management Science, 46*(2), 186-204.

Venkatraman, N. (1989). The concept of fit in strategy research: Toward verbal. *Academy of Management Review, 14*(3), 423-444.

Webster, J., & Martocchio, J.J. (1992). Microcomputer playfulness: Development of a measure with workplace implications. *MIS Quarterly, 16*(2), 201-226.

Webster, J., & Martocchio, J.J. (1993). Turning work into play: Implications for microcomputer software training. *Journal of Management, 19*(1), 127-146.

Young, H.M., Lierman, L., Powell-Cope, G., Kasprzyk, D., & Benoliel, J.Q. (1991). Operationalizing the theory of planned behavior. *Research in Nursing and Health, 14*, 137-144

This article was previously published in the *Journal of Global Information Management,* 12(3), pp. 21-43, © 2004.

APPENDIX

Instrument for Potential Adopters of Internet Banking

Subjective Norm	
	My decision to adopt Internet Banking is influenced by:
SN1	my friends
SN2	my family/relatives
SN3	my colleagues/peers

Image	
IMAGE1	If I were to adopt Internet Banking, it would give me higher status among my peers.
IMAGE2	If I were to adopt Internet Banking, I would be more prestigious among my peers than people who have not yet adopted it.
IMAGE3	Having Internet Banking is trendy among my peers.

Result Demonstrability	
RD1	I have no difficulty telling others about the results of using Internet Banking.
RD2	I believe I could communicate to others the advantages and disadvantages of using Internet Banking.
RD3	The results of using Internet Banking are apparent to me.
RD4	I would have difficulty explaining why using Internet Banking may or may not be beneficial.

Perceived Risk	
PRISK1	I am not confident over the security aspects of Internet Banking in Hong Kong.
PRISK2	Others will know information concerning my Internet Banking transactions.
PRISK3	Others can tamper with information concerning my Internet Banking transactions.
PRISK4	Advances in Internet security technology provide for safer Internet Banking.
PRISK5	It is very easy for my money to be stolen if using Internet Banking.

Computer Self-Efficacy	
	I would be confident in using Internet Banking
CSE1	even if there is no one around to show me how to use it.
CSE2	even if I have never used a system like it before.
CSE3	even if I have only the online instructions for reference.
CSE4	if I see someone else using it before I try it myself.
CSE5	if I can call someone for help if I get stuck.
CSE6	if someone else would help me get started.
CSE7	if I have sufficient time to complete the transaction for which the system provides.
CSE8	if I have the built-in online "help" function for assistance.
CSE9	if someone shows me how to use it first.
CSE10	if I had used a similar system before this one to do the same transactions.

Perceived Usefulness	
PU1	Internet Banking makes it easier for me to conduct my banking transaction.
PU2	Internet Banking gives me greater control over my finances.
PU3	Internet Banking allows me to manage my finances more efficiently.
PU4	Internet Banking is a convenient way to manage my finances.
PU5	Internet Banking is more user-friendly than other existing channels, including Bank Branches, ATMs, and Phone Banking.
PU6	Internet Banking eliminates time constraint; thus I can use the banking services at any time I like.
PU7	Internet Banking eliminates geographic limitation and increases flexible in mobility; thus I can bank any place that has Internet connection.

Perceived Ease Of Use	
PEOU1	Internet Banking is easy-to-use.
PEOU2	Internet Banking is an easy way to conduct banking transactions.
PEOU3	Learning to operate Internet Banking would be easy for me.
PEOU4	It is easy for me to remember how to perform tasks with Internet Banking.
PEOU5	I believe it would be easy to get Internet Banking to do what I want it to do.
PEOU6	Using Internet Banking does not require a lot of mental effort.
PEOU7	Internet Banking provides a clearer interface (visual) than Phone Banking (audio).

Intention to Adopt	
	If Internet Banking is available at your bank(s), how likely would you
INTENT1	plan to experiment with or regularly use Internet Banking during the next six months?
INTENT2	be interested in using wireless Internet Banking (mobile banking) within the next six months?
INTENT3	be interested in using securities trading via Internet Banking within the next six months?
INTENT4	be interested in using insurance services via Internet Banking within the next six months?
INTENT5	be interested in using investment fund services via Internet Banking within the next six months?
INTENT6	be interested in using MPF services via Internet Banking within the next six months?

Chapter XV

IS Change Agents in Practice in a US-Chinese Joint Venture

Dorothy G. Dologite, City University of New York, USA

Robert J. Mockler, St. John's University, USA

Quinghua Bai, Tonji University, China

Peter F. Viszhanyo, City University of New York, USA

ABSTRACT

This chapter presents a case study that documents how information systems (IS) principals in China strategically shifted to different change agent roles to accommodate various IS implementation contingencies in the organization. The case concerns a US-Chinese joint venture, located in China. The change agent models hypothesized by Markus and Benjamin (1996) serve as a lens to interpret the case. Based on observations of how these roles emerged in different phases of implementing packaged software, a meta-category called "adaptor" is offered to visualize what the data revealed and to contribute to this emerging research area. Implications for practitioners and researchers are addressed.

INTRODUCTION

On a research trip in China, the first two authors were invited to do a case analysis of a US-Chinese joint venture (JV) that was implementing packaged software (Dologite et al., 1999). This was in 1996 when this kind of IS implementation was not expected to be found in a typical provincial manufacturing organization in central China.

In a more recent revisit of the data from this case, a story about the struggle to successfully implement the packaged software captivated our interest. In particular, our focus was drawn to how the Chinese IS principals flexibly adopted various change agent roles to handle the challenges encountered as the implementation process progressed.

In a conceptual paper, Markus and Benjamin (1996) identify three, fundamentally different, models of the change agent role performed by IS specialists. They are the traditionalist, the facilitator, and the advocate, presented in the three models identified in the Appendix. After a full discussion of each model, Markus and Benjamin (1996) conclude with a single statement about an "as yet unconfirmed, hypothesis" that "the most effective IS specialists are those who can shift rapidly from one model to another depending on the circumstances" (pp. 400-401).

The Markus and Benjamin's hypothesis, if demonstrated, could be relevant to better understand and explain the change agent phenomenon. What is currently missing in the IS literature is a study that documents and illustrates how IS implementers adopt various change agent roles to deal with the contingencies of installing IS in an organizational setting. This research seeks to fill this gap by contributing an empirical example, with the US-Chinese JV case. In doing this, the study sheds light on a phenomenon that is central to develop emerging theory and its related body of knowledge.

The following discussion begins with a review of the literature relevant to this research. It is followed by a description of the research methods used to construct this case study. Then follows the chapter's main focus, the case study itself. Finally, a discussion, followed by implications for practitioners and researchers, concludes the chapter.

BACKGROUND THEORY

Organizational change implies the presence, or absence for that matter, of resistance to change. Best (1985) defines resistance to organizational change as a natural response, from individuals as well as work groups, which attempts to reduce the impact of change to a less stressful level. To decrease resistance and increase awareness of the need for, and receptivity to change, a skilled change agent would not only implement isolated changes but also persuade the whole organization to view change as normal and necessary.

In an IS context, Markus and Benjamin (1996) propose that change agentry will most likely become the most important part of the IS specialist's work in an organization. They view organizations as moving toward outsourcing application development, computer operations, and even IS management in an effort to cut costs and streamline operations. Information technology (IT) implementation, however, is perceived as work that requires organization specific knowledge (as opposed to pure technical knowledge) and, therefore, will be kept in-house (Markus & Benjamin, 1996).

IS specialists alone cannot bring about the success of a new IT implementation. A large body of research (for example, Baroudi et al., 1986; Joshi, 1991; Majchrzak, 1992; Markus & Benjamin, 1996; Markus & Keil, 1994) shows that managers as well as end users of a system must bring their contribution to the process. An IS specialist skilled in change management could, however, serve an important role to reconcile competing interests as well as obtain the support of key participants.

Change Agents

The role of a change agent, and for that matter any organizational role, is the product of interactions between the individual and the organizational environment as represented by others, the interests of different groups, and the shared values and beliefs conferred by the organizational culture (Markus & Benjamin, 1996; Rogers, 1995).

In their conceptual paper, Markus and Benjamin outline three "ideal types" of change agents hypothesized to exist among in-house IS specialists (1996, p. 387). The models are identified in the Appendix and are briefly described next.

Traditional Model

The perception of the IS professional as an agent of organizational change, presented in the traditional model, reflects the views of many practicing IS specialists (Markus & Benjamin, 1996). It holds that because technology can be relied on to make change, IS specialists do not have to "do" anything to make change other than build systems or install technology (McWhinney, 1992, in Markus & Benjamin, 1996).

Further, traditionalists advocate that management should set specific objectives of the technological change. Consequently, IS professionals can distance themselves from bearing any responsibility for unintended or negative consequences of the system on the organization. Management, on the other hand, tends to blame IS specialists for failing to foresee and eliminate undesirable impacts (Markus & Benjamin, 1996).

Facilitator Model

The facilitator model is mostly reflected in the organizational development literature and holds that people, as opposed to technology, initiate organizational change (Cummings & Huse, 1989; Schwarz, 1994, in Markus & Benjamin, 1996). It finds that individuals make informed choices regarding their actions and behavior based on valid information. Consequently, people have to accept responsibility for their actions including outcomes of actions taken to create and initiate organizational change.

The IS specialist is an agent of change when helping people make choices by providing necessary information (Markus & Benjamin, 1996). From an ethical standpoint, the IS specialist feels obligated to increase people's ability for making a choice by acting as a process facilitator. This implies that the IS specialist has expertise in group dynamics and various aspects of human behavior in addition to technical skills. Moreover, the IS professional would feel obligated to serve the interests of the organization even when these interests are in conflict with particular interests of management or the specialist's own personal or professional interests (Schwarz, 1994, in Markus & Benjamin, 1996).

Advocate Model

The advocate model finds support in the innovation, management, and change politics literatures (e.g., Beath, 1991; Kanter et al., 1992; Rogers, 1995; Semler, 1993, in Markus & Benjamin). "The distinguishing feature of this model is that change advocates work to influence people's behavior in particular directions that the change agents view as desirable, whether or not the change "targets" themselves hold similar views" (Markus & Benjamin, 1996, p. 397).

As an agent of change, the advocate does not hesitate to use symbolic communication, persuasion, and manipulation or even to exercise formal power or authority to achieve the desired outcome (Buchanan & Boddy, 1992, in Markus & Benjamin, 1996).

IS specialists adopting the advocate perspective add business value by advocating process change and user skill training as key components of IS-enabled organizational performance improvement (Markus & Benjamin, 1996).

Structural Conditions Related to IT Implementation

Markus and Soh (2002) "remind the IS community not to neglect the structural conditions (Orlikowski, 1992; Markus & Benjamin, 1996) within which IT use occurs." More specifically, Markus and Benjamin (1996) find that structural conditions define and reinforce the change agent role undertaken by the IS specialist in an organization. It influences the processes of IS work and the outcomes of these processes (Orlikowski, 1992, in Markus & Benjamin, 1996). In this context, structural conditions are defined as different aspects of organizational culture, such as formal and informal channels of communication, company policies, standard operating procedures, and shared values and beliefs of employees. They also include the formal hierarchical structure of the company that is either directly or indirectly linked to IS work and its outcome. All are important as they enable the IS specialist to identify areas of difficulty when initiating organizational change, and to launch appropriate interventions. An intervention might be changing company policies related to IS in order to improve organizational success (Markus & Benjamin, 1996).

Focus of Change Agents in this Study

By providing an empirical example of change agents in practice, this study fills a gap in the literature. It documents and illustrates how IS implementers adopt various change agent roles to deal with the contingencies of installing IS in an organizational setting. This contributes to a better understanding of the change agent phenomenon in organizations.

The study further supports the Markus and Benjamin (1996) hypothesis that a flexible combination of models best describes the process of change agentry during an IS implementation. To make this concept more visible, this study offers a modification to the Markus and Benjamin (1996) framework. The modified framework includes a meta-model, the "adaptor," that incorporates the other three models. The revision has the potential to make the complexity of the change agent phenomenon more visible, especially in IS environments that involve installing packaged software.

RESEARCH METHODS

Our research approach is to use a case study to illustrate and explain how the change agent process evolves in an organization that is implementing an IS. The method provides insight into the processes and problems of functioning as a change agent in an IS

Figure 1. Evolution of change agent roles observed in Chinese IS team

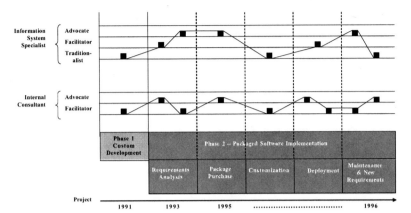

implementation involving packaged software. Yin (1994) recommends the case study as the preferred strategy when "the focus is on a contemporary phenomenon within some real-life context" (p. 1).

The general analytic strategy is to rely on the propositions found in the Markus and Benjamin (1996) framework to organize the case discussion within the packaged software implementation phases (Yin, 1994). The packaged software implementation phases derive from Hoffer (2002), as well as from the first author's industry and research experience, published in Dologite (1982, 1985). These phases are identified in the column definitions found in Figure 1.

Employing a case in this positivist fashion requires attention to construct validity, internal validity, reliability, and external validity (Kirk & Miller, 1986; Yin, 1994).

Construct Validity

Using multiple sources of case evidence supports construct validity (Benbasat et al., 1987; Yin, 1994). In this study, data are mainly based on participants' own reconstructed interpretations of past events and processes that are assumed to reasonably reflect an external reality (Kirk & Miller, 1986; Niedumolu et al., 1996).

The Chinese researcher was on-site for most of the IS implementation effort in a training support role. His presence was essential to triangulate the findings that began with a full-day on-site session in China. The session included open-ended interviews as well as roundtable discussions in English. Three of the authors were present, in addition to eight organization and IS principals and users involved in the IS implementation. We observed systems in use as well as demonstrations that were conducted for our benefit. We collected company and product literature, which was later translated into English. We also had informal social contact with principals. E-mail then served as the continuing bridge among the principals and researchers as the study evolved.

To increase construct validity, key informants reviewed a draft of the case study report. They included the Chinese internal consultant, who had both managerial and "hands-on" views of the IS project, and the Chinese IS specialist in charge of implementing the project. Many sources (for example, Creswell, 1998; Lincoln & Guba, 1985; Miles & Huberman, 1994) recommend member checking, or going back to those who were studied to receive feedback, as a method to ensure the validity of study results.

Construct validity is indirectly supported by the research experience of the investigators. For example, the first two authors have been studying IS implementations in China since 1991 through five on-site research trips. The results of some of their findings have been published in Dologite et al. (1997, 1998, 1999) and Mockler et al. (1995, 1996, 1999). It is further strengthened by the first author's intimate knowledge of packaged software gained from almost 10 years of employment in the US computer industry developing and deploying packaged software with a software development organization. Her published work on this topic appears in Dologite (1982, 1985).

Internal Validity

According to Yin (1994), the concern over internal validity for case study research extends to the broader problem of making inferences. He offers three analytic tactics, which are used in this study, to address internal validity. They are pattern-matching, the main tactic recommended for dealing with this issue, along with two related analytic tactics, explanation-building and a subset of time-series analysis, which is repeated observations.

The pattern-matching technique supports analysis, in this case, at both the embedded units of analysis, which are the phases and steps in the implementation effort, as well as the "whole" case (Yin, 1994). In the embedded units of analysis, the dramatically different patterns observed provide the most simple, or perhaps, gross-level, comparison with the conceptual models offered by Markus and Benjamin (1996).

At the whole-case level, pattern matching is again employed to draw a conclusion about the discovery of an overall "adaptor" pattern evidenced throughout the implementation effort.

The second analytic tactic used, explanation building, according to Yin (1994), is a special type of pattern-matching, where the goal is to analyze the case study data by building an explanation about the case. In most case studies, as in this one, it occurs in narrative form and reflects the development of the central hypothesis. In this study it relates to an unfolding demonstration of the adaptor type of change agent.

The third analytic tactic used to reinforce internal validity is repeated observations. In this single case study, repeated observations occur within every embedded unit of analysis.

Reliability

Reliability is demonstrated by the appropriate use of case study protocol (Yin, 1994).

Our case study strategy largely followed the established case study protocol identified by Yin (1994). It involved organizing and documenting the data collected into a database consisting of the following items:

- Case study notes that were the result of on-site open-ended interviews, observations, and document analysis.
- An audio taped narrative recorded immediately after on-site visits. This enabled the investigators to document their observations and interpretations that connected the specific pieces of evidence with the various issues that emerged. It is worth noting that this was most valuable to the investigators because it was almost impossible to conduct interviews in a way one would be comfortable doing in the West. The Chinese are very suspicious of visible note taking and any form of formal interrogation. Therefore, it was important to establish the research nature of a visit beforehand, but conduct the site visit as informally as possible. So the audio-taped narratives were essential.
- Word-processed transcriptions of the audio-taped narrative. These transcriptions, as well as field notes, were analyzed and the data were entered into tables, using techniques recommended by Miles and Huberman (1994). The tables helped organize core thematic categories, such as those identified on the X and Y-axis of Figure 1.

External Validity

External validity establishes the domain to which a study's finding can be generalized (Yin, 1994). Outsider checking helped corroborate our analysis. Individuals in positions to pass judgment evaluated the final report for this study. Among them are several consultants who have experience implementing packaged software and guiding resident change agents. One is a partner in a major international consulting organization who works in Southeast Asia and provides mainly IS consulting services to companies investing in China.

Nonetheless, our case remains a study of a single IS project in a single organization. Although significant insight can be gained from such research (Yin, 1994), further examination of the change agent concept in other contexts should be pursued to enhance external validity.

CASE STUDY

The US-Chinese JV case study is now addressed as an example of how the change agent processes and functions evolve in an organizational context. First, an overview of the context, foreign-Chinese JVs, the packaged software installed, and the JV participants, is given to provide perspective to the rest of the case. The subsections that follow discuss the change agent roles of the US partner and the Chinese IS team.

Context: Foreign-Chinese Joint Ventures and Their IT Dimension

While the contractual arrangements, as well as the advantages and disadvantages, of foreign-Chinese JVs is beyond the scope of this chapter, some insights on JVs and their IT dimension is relevant.

In many cases, Western companies have found that IT, and a demonstrated commitment to bring this technology into a JV, facilitated the timely completion of their requests with authorities for setting up a new company (Glasser & Pastore, 1998). The Chinese have been known to call this "technology for market," which is to ask foreign companies to transfer technology in exchange for access to Asia's exploding marketplace (Kranhold, 2004).

China has been inviting foreign joint ventures ever since it opened to the West in 1978 and simultaneously lessened the role of central planning to encourage the natural growth of market forces (Chao et al., 1997).

In opposition to such interest, Chinese management frequently perceives IT as a cost center partly because manual-processing labor is very cheap (Dologite et al., 1997, 1998; Glasser & Pastore, 1998). The prevailing belief is that it is difficult to justify spending money on something that, in management's view, could be solved by assigning more people to the task.

In addition, in the Chinese business culture, managers strictly control access to information. Information is often treated as an individual, rather than an organizational resource (Martinsons, 1991). Discretionary power is preserved through the delicate control of critical information, which is made available selectively to subordinates instead of being distributed widely among organizational members (Martinsons, 1991). Formal codification of critical information inside a computer system in order that others can access it would involve substantial changes to the culture of information and its personal value (Davison, 2002).

Patience and the ability to effectively convey the importance of IT in establishing advanced managerial practices in a company have helped foreign managers to persuade their Chinese counterparts to allocate the necessary funds for IT investment (Glasser & Pastore, 1998).

The appropriate level of IT investment, as perceived by multinationals engaged in JVs, ranges from the latest, cutting edge systems to packaged software (Glasser & Pastore, 1998). Advocates of the former base their arguments on the mission criticality of the new venture and need for integration into the parent company's global network. In the latter case, the financial resources of the JV, as well as the expected payback period, may dictate limited investment in new IT. Further, the technological sophistication of end users as well as that of IS professionals, who are to implement a new system, might argue for an off-the-shelf software package purchased from a local vendor that provides initial training and continued technical support (Glasser & Pastore, 1998).

PACKAGED SOFTWARE INSTALLED: MRP AND MRPII

The software package the JV installed is material requirements planning (MRP). Basically, it is an inventory and production control system that enables a manufacturer to schedule material acquisitions to meet future production demand (Sum et al., 1997; Wong & Kleiner, 2001). Theoretically, the software enables the company to acquire raw materials and components, timed precisely, to achieve just-in-time deliveries and zero inventory levels. The inaccuracy of bills of materials and inventory records and the occurrence of unanticipated events, however, result in a certain level of inventory and material shortages. The literature specifies desirable MRP targets of 95% inventory accuracy and 98% bill of material accuracy (Turbide, 1996).

Manufacturing resource planning (MRPII) is a more advanced software package that integrates MRP into a whole set of supporting applications, such as production and capacity planning, accounting and financial applications, customer service, management information systems, and electronic data interchange (EDI) (MRP II, 2004; Wong & Kleiner, 2001). These functions are built around a relational database management system to share data and are completely interdependent. The software package's primary goal is to collect and disseminate information from and across different functional areas of the company in order to achieve efficient allocation of resources and coordination of processing activities (Turbide, 1996).

Research Site

The JV that represents the site for this study was set up in 1986 after the governor of a central China province visited the US and invited the US company to invest in China. The new enterprise is located in a city within the governor's province that has particularly become attractive to foreign companies looking to establish a JV. After 1992, it was granted the right to offer tax and investment incentives to foreign companies. Figure 2 presents a timeline that summarizes the US-Chinese JV key events that emerged from our study.

The US side owns 52% of the venture, while the remaining 48% is equally divided between two Chinese state-owned enterprises. The JV employs about 150 people and

Figure 2. Timeline of key case study events

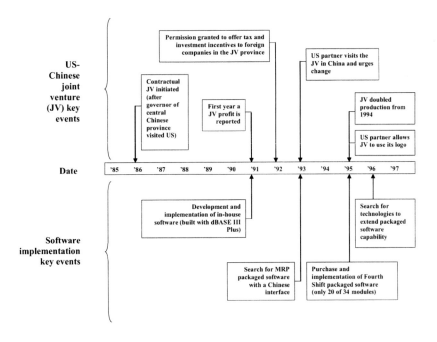

manufactures small gasoline engines. The Chinese partners provided the land and buildings from an existing operation while the US partner transferred production technology and imported manufacturing equipment from the US In the first years of the operation, the JV experienced difficulty in transferring the Western production technology and quality control procedures to the new entity. The patience exercised throughout this period by the US partner demonstrated its commitment to the success of the venture. Personnel from the US were sent to China to train employees in the proper sequence of production steps, in the implementation of contemporary sales and marketing concepts, and in the principles of total quality management. The JV finally turned a profit in 1991 and nearly doubled its production in 1995 (compared to 1994) after the acquisition and subsequent successful implementation of Fourth Shift — a commercial software package designed around the concepts of MRPI (http://www.fs.com). After the implementation of the software package the quality of the finished products improved to such an extent that the US partner allowed the JV to use its logo.

The organization of the JV, as well as our observations, reveal that decision-making in the company is highly centralized. It is centered on the general manager (GM), who functions as a CEO in Chinese enterprises. Although there are four levels of management under the GM, our concern is with the first level. It consists of internal consultants to the GM. One functioned as the main operational decision maker, who also served as an informal liaison and supporter of the IS group.

There was no formal IS department. IS was considered a staff function and reported to a fourth-level manager of the General Office. Our concern is with an IS specialist in the IS group who worked with the internal consultant to realize the packaged software implementation.

JV Participants

The JV participants of this study were purposely recruited on the basis of their position in the company and their knowledge of IS on the one hand, and that of operations and management attitudes toward the IS implementation process on the other. The subjects were directly involved in the whole process of initiation, selection and development of the IS.

At the time of the IS implementation, the chief engineer of the JV was promoted to be an internal consultant to the GM. He knew the technology from both the management and the IS viewpoints. He was an older person whom everyone treated with respectful deference. He spoke fluent English and conducted himself and our meetings with the demeanor and the depth of technical, as well as strategic-level, knowledge normally identified with the CEO of US small business organizations. His place in the organization was highly visible; for example, in publicity photos he is always positioned standing next to the GM.

The main resident IS specialist was a young engineering graduate of a local university who also spoke fluent English. He was the technical person who researched the packaged software and learned how to use it from English manuals. He was the one who modified the package so that it could be used throughout the JV's four production lines and the assembly workshop. He was part of a small group of technical people responsible for implementing IT in the organization.

Analysis of US-Chinese JV

The following analysis of the US-Chinese JV considers the change agent roles of, in turn:

- The US partner who initiated fundamental organizational change in the new JV, but who remained largely US-bound. While this change agent role is unremarkable and follows well-documented practice in the IS literature, it is given here to provide insights for the exposition of the Chinese participants.
- The Chinese participants who were on-site in the JV to carry out the organizational change initiated by the US partner.

Role of the US Joint Venture Partner

Since its inception, the Chinese operation had been disturbed by substantial problems in production, quality control and inventory management, characteristics common to traditional Chinese state-owned enterprises. The problems are amply documented in the popular as well as professional literature (Chen, 1995; China Survey, 2000; Dologite et al., 1998; Franz et al., 1991; Harding, 1997; Nafziger, 1997; Norton, 2003; Thornhill, 2002). The US JV partner recognized that Chinese labor-intensive operational processes prevailed, because in China labor is very cheap (Bin et al., 2003). Also, the lack of adequate training for the labor force, and unsystematic management practices, caused much of these problems. The transfer and implementation of Western operational practices to the JV would be important far beyond the requirement to satisfy contractual obligations. The very existence of the JV had come to depend on it, since the operation was losing money since 1986, and was unsuited to take over the production of cast iron engines from the US plant, the strategic reason behind the establishment of the JV.

US management determined that the implementation of an MRPII software package would initiate needed organizational change that could help transform inefficient Chinese production processes, planning and control, which remained from its days as a state-run institution. The US partner repeatedly urged the Chinese management of the JV to implement material requirement planning concepts in day-to-day operations.

Consequently, in 1991 the JV developed in-house MRP software using dBASE III Plus software. The impact on ameliorating the problems of the organization was, however, only marginal. The software did not include the latest developments in MRP concepts, such as integrated sales and financial support, reflected in the MRPII concept.

Eventually, in 1993 the president of the US partner visited the JV (for only the third time in seven years) to participate at a two-day board meeting and urge organizational change to meet Western quality standards for products and production. Later that year the Chinese partner initiated contact with a software vendor in Shanghai to get information about the Fourth Shift software package. This application software was recommended by the US management and is a microcomputer-based client/server approach to MRPII. Its 34 modules provide manufacturing, sales and financial support as well as EDI and decision support.

The company purchased the software two years later from a new authorized, local distributor. Then it implemented the software in a matter of months throughout the four production lines and in the financial department. The staff from a local university provided 40 hours of training to the 30 people who use and maintain the system.

Those who had to learn how to use the system were given an exam at the end of the training period. For high scores on the exam, employees received a bonus. For low scores, they were told that in the event of an economic downturn they would be the first to be laid off. Such an employee mandate would be considered heresy, at the time, in a pure Chinese state-owned enterprise whose "cradle-to-grave" welfare practices provided employment for life, including full pension care (Chen, 1995; Dologite et al., 1998; Harding, 1997; Song, 2003; Thornhill, 2002).

The behavior of the US JV-partner closely matches the pattern of the advocate in Markus and Benjamin's (1996) model of change agentry. For example, by his presence at the meeting, the president communicated a clear message about the seriousness of management's intentions regarding quality and the importance attributed to a new IS system. The fact that this was only the third time that he visited the JV elevated this board meeting to a level of importance equal to that of the meetings in which the JV agreements were signed.

The use of shock is demonstrated by the fact that the president himself participated at the board meeting where the decision to purchase the software was adopted. Threat to exercise formal power made sure that every employee who had to use the system really learned it. The reward and punishment system that was instituted, which was unusual in 1996 and not observed elsewhere, is other evidence of the use of formal power by management to achieve the desired outcome.

Additionally, structural conditions match a role orientation pattern compatible with the advocate model. For example, while the US partner had no direct managerial authority or delegated control over the Chinese operations, it had valued resources to dispense. The main one was its supply of orders for an otherwise failing business. It stimulated the Chinese partner to seek a Chinese supplier of the requisite MRPII software, as well as to learn how to install and use the software.

Roles of the Chinese IS Team

Our study finds that the Chinese IS team, consisting mainly of the internal consultant to the GM and the IS specialist, demonstrated various change agent behavior patterns as the project evolved. The pivotal role in the project was carried by the internal consultant, who we found initially performed a facilitator role. As we iterated over our data, we found exceptions to this fixed role. The data showed him variously wearing both facilitator and advocate change agent hats to effect change in the organization. Both these roles were essential to support the work of the subordinate IS specialist.

The IS specialist, on the other hand, demonstrated the most dramatic shifts during the packaged software installation project. His behaviors started in a pattern consistent with a single-dimensioned traditionalist change-agent. This pattern recurred several other times during the evolution of the package implementation. But several deviations from this role caused us to iterate back and forth through the story that the data were telling us and the Markus and Benjamin (1996) models. Eventually, a multidimensional profile surfaced. We traced the IS specialist's role evolving from the IS traditionalist through the facilitator to the advocate change agent. The manifestation of these role patterns with both members of the Chinese IS team is summarized in Figure 1 and described below.

Phase One - Custom Software: Because the US partner mandated the use of IT but did not supply funding or expert support, the IS specialist first built a homegrown version of MRP software using dBASE III Plus. He had no organizational change responsibilities beyond building technology, consistent with a role orientation of the IS traditionalist. The custom-built software ultimately was a failure and follows a pattern consistent with the IS traditional model.

The Chinese operation decided to build custom software because they refused to fund the purchase of packaged software. As previously pointed out, in China, IS is typically looked on as a cost sink. We found, for example, that funds are only available at the start of a new five-year economic plan cycle. There follows a rush to spend IT funds for hardware that is often outdated because it is cheaper. During the rest of the five-year interim until the next cycle, no funds are available for application software to run on the purchased hardware, for staff training to run the hardware, or for hardware maintenance contracts. It was not unusual for the research team at many research sites to find hardware, from IBM mainframes to rooms of PCs, dark and unused because of an inappropriate allocation of funds. Such a mindset existed at the case company to color the funding picture.

During the custom software phase, the internal consultant functioned as a facilitator for both the IS specialist and the organization. He provided a supportive climate that enabled the IS specialist to stay focused on new software development. While he had no formal authority for business results, consistent with his role orientation, he did bear some functional responsibility because his boss, the GM, was a political appointee who remained detached from the daily business of running the company.

Phase Two - Packaged Software: When the in-house produced software proved inadequate to support the expectations of the US partner, the change agent roles of both the IS specialist and the internal consultant changed.

Step One - Requirements Analysis: The internal consultant had to adopt the behavior pattern associated with the advocate change agent to obtain adequate funding and support to buy MRPII packaged software. He had to champion the need for packaged software to his superiors. On the other hand, he remained the organization's facilitator in charge of carrying out the mandate of the JV agreement, which was to bring operating processes and controls up to quality standards that met the approval of the US partner.

Several organization structural conditions were in place to make his facilitator role work. For example, he functioned outside the hierarchical chain-of-command because he was not a client group (or official IS professional) member. He also had a need to:

- Build the IS specialist's capacity in order to increase the project's success and IS credibility.
- Help make his client, the IS specialist, self-sufficient and reduce his resentment at trying to build a system with inappropriate support.

To support the internal consultant, the IS specialist began to experience his role change from that of traditional IS change agent to that of facilitator and advocate. His task became promoting the change by helping to increase management's awareness, from a technical viewpoint, of the requirements for an improved system.

Step Two - Package Purchase: After the Chinese IS team succeeded in making the requirement for packaged MRPII software technically acceptable, they began a quest to purchase the software. Both complemented each other, assuming behavioral roles associated with the advocate change agent, to bring the MRPII package, Fourth Shift, into the organization.

The pair traveled to major Chinese manufacturing cities until they located an organization that had a version of Fourth Shift software, modified with a Chinese language front-end.

Because of low funding, the Chinese IS team could buy only a subset of the full package and had to learn and implement it locally, using English language manuals, without expert support. The new local vendor of the package, at this stage, functioned mainly as a transfer agent.

The team's behavior is consistent with previous studies that find IT champions attach importance to securing resources (Beath, 1991; Frost & Egri, 1991; Nayak & Ketteringham, 1986). The Chinese team, in this case, actively and energetically went about securing organizational resources for their project. As Heng, Trauth, and Fischer (1999) describe it, they can be characterized as a mix of project manager and IT champions.

Step Three - Customization: Once the package was purchased, the internal consultant could settle back into the role pattern characteristic of a facilitator while the IS specialist could resume the traditional IS role by rebuilding, or customizing, the software package.

Because software was purchased for only one instead of the necessary four production lines, and the financial functions were excluded, the IS specialist immersed himself in the software modification task.
In other words, the IS specialist served as management's "pair-of-hands" to build the technology that would cause change, while the internal consultant remained supportive to facilitate the project's progress.

Step Four - Deployment: The deployment phase, when the customized software package was rolled out to the shop floor, required the IS specialist once more to adopt the stance of a facilitator, while the resident consultant wore the hats of both facilitator and advocate for organizational change.

Together, the Chinese IS team created local-language training materials and hands-on workshops to help facilitate the shop-floor implementation of the packaged software. Local university computer science faculty was enlisted by the internal consultant, who advocated for help to leverage in-house deployment efforts and to prepare and deliver shop-floor training modules.

Two other structural conditions, compatible with the internal consultant's advocator role, were in place to help ease the way to a successful package implementation. First, the consultant's position lacked delegated control authority over the change targets. This stance is predicted to have a greater probability of success than if he had direct authority. Second, to spiral down to the shop-floor worker level, it was clear that the internal consultant had unspoken line authority over everyone in the plant and was indeed responsible for achieving business outcomes that would result from the IT deployment project.

Step Five - Maintenance and New Requirements Analysis: Once deployed, the maintenance of the packaged software was an issue overwhelmed immediately by new requirements analysis and a new software development cycle. It thrust the IS specialist into the role pattern identified with an advocate while the consultant exercised his usual dual roles of facilitator/advocate.

The IS specialist was keenly aware, and regretted that, the Chinese JV partner purchased only 20 of the 34 Fourth Shift modules available. The modules for decision support and EDI were not purchased. In other words, the MRPII software could serve only tactical purposes related to production and inventory management and control.

This approach by the Chinese JV partner, however, is consistent with findings that Chinese management makes little use of IS for strategic-level planning purposes (Dologite et al., 1997, 1998; Franz et al., 1991).

In this phase, the IS specialist once again became an advocate who attempted to influence management, mainly the internal consultant, in a direction he viewed as desirable. Matching the behavioral pattern associated with an advocate change agent, he initiated a campaign to research and learn about decision support software in order to enhance the packaged software. As an example, he aggressively interrogated the US authors about the benefits of expert systems to enhance the decision support capabilities of the custom software he is designing. Later, the IS specialist expects to put on his traditionalist hat of the technical expert to build the technology that can cause change.

Throughout this phase, the internal consultant remained an advocate for change by facilitating the IS specialist's quest to enhance the packaged software. As an example, he invited the US researchers on-site in part to learn about Western approaches to enhance software functionality.

DISCUSSION

The perspective on the change agent function analyzed in this study offer insights into the process of how change evolves in an organization implementing new computer technology, in particular package software, and in the particular context of China.

Change Agent Framework

First, the data showed how IS principals flexibly moved through the various change agent roles in response to various contingencies or challenges arising within the organizational context. While the discrete components of the Markus and Benjamin

(1996) framework provided a template to discern identifiable behavior by the IS principals, the framework did not account for everything we uncovered.

The findings in this case lead us to modify the Markus and Benjamin (1996) framework to acknowledge the overwhelming presence of the meta-role, called an "adaptor" role in this study, played by the IS change agent. As presented in Figure 3, the adaptor change agent role identifies and makes visible important relationships that exist among the other three roles. It supports an understanding of what Markus and Benjamin (1996) call the "most effective" type of IS change agent — one who can move flexibly among all three roles.

The expanded framework offers an IS specialist a more representative model to draw on to help guide the change effort while navigating through an IS implementation.

The time dimension evident in Figure 1 highlights a pattern in the changing role of an IS agent as the project evolves from one stage to another. The emergent pattern is that the IS change agent assumes the role of advocate and facilitator to a larger extent in the beginning (project inception) and the end (training and installation) of the project than in the middle of the project (technical development). This pattern reflects a general pattern found in the authors' practical and research experiences, and is identified by Markus and Tanis (2000) when implementing enterprise resource planning software packages. Markus and Tanis (2000) find, for example, that the middle of the project involves typical technical development activities, as found in this study, of "software customization" as well as "integration of software bolt-ons" (p. 192). These activities contrast with the earlier project inception activities, where "selection of software," and later activities, and where "training" and "adding people to accommodate learning" occupy the IS change agent involved with an enterprise resource planning package implementation.

The new adaptor construct theoretically sets up expectations. It implies that all three skill areas potentially are necessary in an IS implementation effort, especially one involving packaged software. It supports the Markus and Benjamin "tentative conclu-

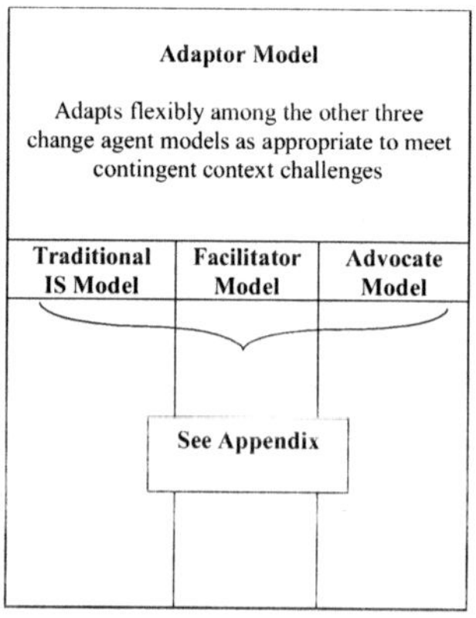

Figure 3. Modification of the Markus and Benjamin 1996 change agent framework

sion that all IS specialists who do or could work with in-house clients need to be intellectually familiar with, and behaviorally skilled in, all three roles in order to be most credible and most able to contribute to organizational success with information technology" (1996, p. 400).

Our study additionally extends the power of the change agent framework beyond its original large-company, internal IS focus by demonstrating its applicability to the area of small business as well as to non-US organizational cultures. All areas would be enriched and strengthened by additional research efforts.

While the intent of this research is to enhance an understanding of the change agent phenomenon within a contextual situation, it is believed that our specific context can be used to inform other studies in other organizational and national contexts.

Implications for Practitioners and Researchers

There are several implications this study offers for both practitioners and researchers. As with any case study, our context and IS implementation are contingent on the organization studied. While this limits the scope for generalization, the intent is to contribute an empirical example to better understand and explain the change agent phenomenon. It is expected that other studies, with different organizational contexts, other IS implementations, and other national contexts, will continue to contribute to the emerging conversation on IS change agents.

Our study adds to a growing body of research that focuses on analyzing the extent and depth of the use of IT in Chinese enterprises in general and JVs in particular. We offer the following propositions tailored to guide practitioners thinking about or already engaged in US-Chinese JVs. Again, we urge IS researchers to consider doing related studies.

- An entrepreneurial and flexible Chinese IS professional team is needed on-site to adapt to varying change agent roles in order to overcome operational and technical contingencies and challenges of the new IS package selection and implementation process.
- A Western change agent, preferably high-level executive, must initiate the change process.

These propositions allow restating our specific findings more generally by deriving general interaction patterns that may be meaningful beyond the confines of the one research site. The same propositions, therefore, can be generalized and restated, by removing context, and offered to further guide practitioners and to encourage IS researchers to validate.

- Entrepreneurial and flexible IS professionals are needed on-site who can adapt to various change agent roles in order to overcome operational and technical contingencies and challenges during a new IS software package selection and implementation effort.
- A change agent, preferably high-level executive, has to initiate an organizational change process.

It is beyond the scope of this study to address how managers and IS specialists of Western companies planning to operate in China will have to overcome, in addition to the cultural differences, the challenges posed by the fundamentally different managerial practices present in the Chinese business environment.

The findings of this study do imply, in addition to the points made above, that:

- The implementation of packaged software can initiate organizational change and may facilitate the transition away from traditional Chinese processes.
- The use of commercial packaged software may enable the rapid implementation of a total solution to a business process, leapfrogging the need for an experienced and extensive Chinese IS development staff and for extensive capital investment in IT.

Recent research demonstrates that knowledge about, and skill in using, software packages continue to rise in the Chinese workforce, and that management considers IT a vital part of an organization's competitive strategy (Stylianou, 2003). On the other hand, recent research warns Asian organizations about the possible difficulty when implementing packaged software because of the differences in cultural, economic, and regulatory context when a package is modeled on European or US industry practices (Soh et al., 2000).

It is possible to explore the practical implications of this study from a broader perspective. One question that surfaces is "How does the experience of implementing packaged software in other emerging economies compare to this study?" If similar results are tracked, they can make a contribution to:

- Demonstrate how IT plays a strategic role in transforming work practices in merging economies.
- Accelerate the progress of transitioning economies that choose to adopt processes and technologies known to be standards in developed economies.

Such an effort would support Hofstede's (1997) notion that "common practices, not common values, are what solve practical problems" (p. xiii).

In the flexibility found in the Chinese IS team lies implications for practice and the education of IS practitioners. The question surfaces, are we training our IS students to competently negotiate the various roles they will be thrust into when implementing packaged software? As we observe a global move to packaged software installations, such as ERP packages (Brown & Vessey, 2003; Kumar & van Hillegersberg, 2000; Markus & Tanis, 2000; Robey, Ross, & Boudreau, 2002; Stevens, 2003), is the next generation of IS graduates ready to cope? Readers are directed to Markus and Benjamin (1996) for a discussion about a "proposed educational program on change agentry" that outlines a plan for educational reform. It advocates for the IS academic community to proactively engage in developing the soft skills necessary for effective change agents.

Future research studies are needed not only to provide a more substantial body of evidence and test our findings, but also to focus on each implementation phase and compare changes within phases. A related issue is whether the change agent construct is more allied with the individual or the situation. Another area of study would answer the question about whether there are gray areas or new models to be explored other than those offered in Markus and Benjamin (1996) or this study. These concerns gain an added dimension from the Markus and Benjamin (1996) observation that the change agent function will most likely become the most important part of the IS specialist's work in the organization, especially as other aspects of this work are outsourced.

REFERENCES

Baroudi, J.J., Olson, M.H., & Ives, B. (1986). An empirical study of the impact of user involvement on systems usage and information satisfaction. *Communications of the ACM, 29*(3), 232-238.

Beath, C.M. (1991). Supporting the information technology champion. *MIS Quarterly, 15*(3), 355-372.

Benbasat, I., Goldstein, D., & Mead, M. (1987). The case research strategy in studies of information systems. *MIS Quarterly, 11*(3), 369-386.

Best, J.D. (1985). The MIS executive as change agent. *Journal of Information Systems Management, 2*(4), 14-18.

Bin, Q., Chen, S.J., Sun, & S.Q. (2003). Cultural differences in e-commerce: A comparison between the US and China. *Journal of Global Information Management, 11*(2), 48-55.

Brown, C.V., & Vessey, I. (2003). Managing the next wave of enterprise systems: Leveraging lessons from ERP. *MIS Quarterly Executive, 2*(1), 65-77.

Buchanan, D., & Boddy, D. (1992). *The expertise of the change agent: Public performance and backstage activity.* New York: Prentice Hall.

Chen, M. (1995). *Asian management systems.* New York: Routledge.

China Survey. (2000, April 8). *The Economist,* 3-16.

Creswell, J.W. (1998). *Qualitative inquiry and research design: Choosing among five traditions.* Thousand Oaks, CA: Sage Publications.

Cummings, T.G., & Huse, E.F. (1989). *Organization development and change* (4th ed.). St. Paul, MN: West Publishing.

Davison, R. (2002). Cultural complications of ERP. *Communications of the ACM, 45*(7), 109-111.

Dologite, D.G. (1982). Evaluating packaged software. *Data Management, 20*(1), 20-25.

Dologite, D.G. (1985). *Using small business computers.* Englewood Cliffs, NJ: Prentice Hall.

Dologite, D.G., Fang, M.Q., Chen, Y., Mockler, R.J., & Chao, C. (1997). Information systems in Chinese state-owned enterprises: An evolving strategic perspective. *Journal of Global Information Management, 5*(4), 10-21.

Dologite, D.G., Fang, M.Q., Chen, Y., Mockler, R.J., & Chao, C. (1998). An information systems view of Chinese state enterprises. *Journal of Strategic Information Systems, 7*(2), 113-129.

Dologite, D.G., Mockler, R.J., Bai, Q., & Viszhanyo, P.F. (1999). A role for packaged software in Chinese joint ventures: Change agent. *Proceedings: Decision Sciences Institute* (Vol. 2, pp. 769-771). New Orleans, LA.

Franz, C.R., Wynne, A.J., & Fu, J.H. (1991). Managing information systems to support functional business requirements in China. *International Journal of Information Management, 11*(3), 203-209.

Frost, P.J., & Egri, C.P. (1991). The political process of innovation. In L.L. Cummings & B.M. Staw (Eds.), *Research in organizational behaviour* (Vol.13, pp. 229-295). Greenwich, CT: JAI Press.

Glasser, P., & Pastore, R. (1998, September 15). West meets East. *CIO, 1*, 32-36.

Harding, J. (1997, June 11). Steelmaker rises as China's national model. *Financial Times*, 4.

Heng, M.S.H., Trauth, E.M., & Fischer, S.J. (1999). Organizational champions of IT innovation. *Accounting, Management and Information Technologies, 9*(3), 193-222.

Hoffer, J.A., George, J.F., & Valacich, J.S. (2002). *Modern systems analysis and design* (3rd ed.). Upper Saddle River, NJ: Prentice Hall.

Hofstede, G. (1997). *Cultures and organizations: Software of the mind.* New York: McGraw-Hill.

Joshi, K. (1991). A model of user's perspective on change: The case of information systems technology implementation. *MIS Quarterly, 15*(2), 228-242.

Kanter, R.M., Stein, B.A., & Jick, T.D. (1992). *The challenge of organizational change: How companies experience it and leaders guide it.* New York: The Free Press.

Kirk, J., & Miller, M.L. (1986). *Reliability and validity in qualitative research.* Beverly Hills, CA: Sage Publications.

Kranhold, K. (2004, February 26). China's price for market entry: Give us your technology, too. *The Wall Street Journal,* A1.

Kumar, K., & van Hillegersberg, J. (2000). ERP experiences and evolution. *Communications of the ACM, 43*(4), 23-26.

Lincoln, Y., & Guba, E. (1985). *Naturalistic inquiry.* Beverly Hills, CA: Sage Publications.
Majchrzak, A. (1992). Management of technological and organizational change. In G. Salvendy (Ed.), *Handbook of industrial engineering* (pp. 767-797). New York: Wiley and Sons.

Markus, M.L., & Benjamin, R.I. (1996). Change agentry - the next IS frontier. *MIS Quarterly, 20*(4), 385-407. This article also appears in Galliers, R.D., Leidner, D.E., & Baker, B.S.H. (1999). *Strategic information management: Challenges and strategies in managing information systems* (2nd ed.). Oxford: Butterworth Heinemann.

Markus, M.L., & Keil, M. (1994, Summer). If we build it they will come: Designing information systems that users want to use. *Sloan Management Review,* 11-25.

Markus, M.L., & Soh, C. (2002). Structural influences on global e-commerce activity. *Journal of Global Information Management, 10*(1), 5-12.

Markus, M.L., & Tanis, C. (2000). The enterprise system experience—from adoption to success. In R.W. Zmud (Ed.), *Framing the domains of IT management: Projecting the future through the past* (pp. 173-207). Cincinnati, OH: Pinnaflex Educational Resources.

McWhinney, W. (1992). *Paths of change: Strategic choices for organizations and society.* Newbury Park, CA: Sage Publications.

Miles, M.B., & Huberman, A.M. (1994). *Qualitative data analysis.* Thousand Oaks, CA: Sage Publications.

Mockler, R.J., Chao, C., Dologite, D.G., Chen, Y., & Fang, M. (1996). Chinese and American entrepreneurs: Common frameworks for managing cross-cultural differences. *Proceedings: International Conference on Cross-Cultural Management*, (pp. 1-6). Hong Kong: Hong Kong Baptist University.

Mockler, R.J., & Dologite, D.G. (1995). Easing information technology across cultural boundaries: A contingency perspective. *International Journal of Computer Applications in Technology, 8*(3/4), 145-162.

Mockler, R.J., Dologite, D.G., Chen, Y., & Fang, M.Q. (1999). Information technology diffusion in developing countries: A study of China. *Journal of Global Information Technology Management, 2*(4), 23-40.

MRP II. (2004). Manufacturing Resource Planning (MRP II): Sources and references. Retrieved March 12, 2004, from: http://www.business.com/directory/management/ operations_management/planning_and_scheduling/ enterprise_resource_planning_erp/manufacturing_resource_planning_mrp_ii/

Nafziger, E.W. (1997). *The economics of developing countries.* Upper Saddle River, NJ: Prentice-Hall.

Nayak, P.R., & Ketteringham, J.M. (1986). *Break-throughs.* New York: Rawson.

Niedumolu, S.R., Goodman, S.E., Vogel, D.R., & Danowitz, A.K. (1996). Information technology for local administration support: The governorates project in Egypt. *MIS Quarterly, 20*(2), 197-221.

Norton, L.P. (2003, April 21). Broken promise. *Barron's, 83*(16), F4-F5.

Orlikowski, W.J. (1992). The duality of technology: Rethinking the concept of technology in organizations. *Organizational Science, 3*(3), 398-427.

Robey, D., Ross, J.W., & Boudreau, M.C. (2002). Learning to implement enterprise systems: An exploratory study of the dialectics of change. *Journal of Management Information Systems, 19*(1), 17-46.

Rogers, E.M. (1995). *Diffusion of innovations* (4th ed.). New York: Free Press.

Schwarz, R.M. (1994). *The skilled facilitator: Practical wisdom for developing effective groups.* San Francisco: Jossey-Bass.

Semler, R. (1993). *Maverick: The success story behind the world's most unusual workplace.* New York: Warner Books.

Soh, C., Kienh, S.S., & Tay-Yap, J. (2000). Cultural fits and misfits: Is ERP a universal solution? *Communications of the ACM, 43*(4), 47-51.

Song, S. (2003). Policy issues of China's urban unemployment. *Contemporary Economic Policy, 21*(2), 258-270.

Stevens, C.P. (2003). Enterprise resource planning: A trio of resources. *Information Systems Management, 20*(3), 61-67.

Stylianou, A.C., Robbins, S.S., & Jackson, P. (2003). Perceptions and attitudes about ecommerce development in China: An exploratory study. *Journal of Global Information Management, 11*(2), 31-47.

Sum, C., Ang, J.S.K., & Yeo, L. (1997). Contextual elements of critical success factors in MRP implementation. *Production and Inventory Management Journal, 38*(3), 77-83.

Thornhill, J. (2002, December 12). Private enterprise seen as way forward. *The Economist*, II.

Turbide, D.A. (1996). *Why systems fail and how to make sure yours doesn't.* New York: Industrial Press.

Wong, C.M., & Kleiner, B.H. (2001). Fundamentals of material requirements planning. *Management Research News, 24*(3/4), 9-12.

Yin, R.K. (1994). *Case study research: Design and methods* (2nd ed.). Thousand Oaks, CA: Sage Publications.

APPENDIX

Agentry Model	Traditional IS Model	Facilitator Model	Advocate Model
Role Orientation (the change agent's attitudes, beliefs, behaviors)	- Technology causes change - IS specialist has no change responsibilities beyond building technology - Specialist is an agent of change by building technology that causes change; specialist is a technical expert - Specialist is an agent of change by serving the objectives of others; specialist is the manager's pair-of-hands - Specialist does not hold self responsible for achieving change or improvements in organizational performance	- Clients make change using technology; technology alone does not - Facilitator promotes change by helping increase clients' capacity for change - Facilitator avoids exerting expert or other power over clients - Facilitator serves interests of all clients, not just funders and direct participants - Facilitator values clients' informed choice about conditions of facilitator's work; works to reduce client dependence on facilitator - Facilitator does not hold self responsible for change or improvements in organizational performance; clients are	- People, including the change advocate, make change - Advocate influences change targets in direction viewed as desirable by advocate - Advocate increases targets' awareness of the need for change - Advocate champions a particular change direction - Advocate tactics include communication, persuasion, shock, manipulation, power - Advocate and change targets are responsible for change and performance improvements - Advocate shares credit or avoids taking full credit for outcomes
Structural Conditions Compatible with Role Orientation	- IS is sole-source provider of services - Clients have limited technical and sourcing options - Low IS budget pressure exists - IS is centralized, responsible for many clients - IS is "staff" function-responsible and rewarded for expert/functional performance, not business performance - IS holds "control" role-with delegated authority over certain processes, decisions, behaviors - IS builds systems	- Facilitator is not a client group member - Facilitator's function lies outside the hierarchical chain-of-command - Facilitator's function is not formally responsible for business results, though some functional responsibility is inevitable	- One type of change advocate has no managerial authority and no delegated control, but may have valued resources to dispense - Another type of change advocate has line authority over the change targets and responsibility for achieving business outcomes - A third type of advocate occupies staff positions in the organizations for which change targets work; those who lack delegated control authority have much greater credibility than those who have it
IS Structural Conditions Incompatible with Role Orientation	- Decentralized IS - Outsourced IS - Purchased systems - Diversity of client technology and sourcing options - Strong IS budget pressure - New technologies that demand different "implementation" activities	- Valuable expertise in technical or business matters - Formal responsibility for business or technical results - Staff control over clients' processes, decisions, behaviors - Concerns about locus of employment	- Absence of managerial authority over target - Staff control over target's processes, decisions, behavior
Consequences of Model Applied to IS Work	- Widespread system failures for social reasons - Key systems success factors defined as outside IS role and influence - Technical organizational change blocked by IS - Low IS credibility - IS resistance to role change	- Greater attention to building user capacity might increase project success and IS credibility - Emphasis on client self-sufficiency would reduce client resentment and increase IS credibility - Many new ITs offer more scope to IS specialists who act as facilitators than to those who act as experts/builders	- Role fits a need in situations where IS specialists have or could have better ideas than clients about effective business uses of technology - Role might increase IS credibility; role emphasizes communication, which is a key factor in credibility

This article was previously published in the *Journal of Global Information Management,* 12(4), pp. 1-22, © 2004.

Chapter XVI

E-Government Implementation:
Balancing Collaboration and Control in Stakeholder Management

Chee-Wee Tan, University of British Columbia, Canada

Eric T.K. Lim, National University of Singapore, Singapore

Shan-Ling Pan, National University of Singapore, Singapore

ABSTRACT

As e-government plays an increasingly dominant role in modern public administrative management, its pervasive influence on organizations and individuals is apparent. It is therefore timely and relevant to examine e-governance, the fundamental mission of e-government. By adopting a stakeholder perspective, this study approaches the topic of e-governance in e-government from the three critical aspects of stakeholder management: (1) identification of stakeholders; (2) recognition of differing interests among stakeholders; and (3) how an organization caters to and furthers these interests. Findings from the case study point to the importance of: (1) discarding the traditional preference for controls to develop instead a proactive attitude towards the identification of all relevant collaborators; (2) conducting cautious assessments of the technological restrictions underlying IT-transformed public services to map out the boundary for devising and implementing control and collaboration mechanisms in the system; and (3) developing strategies to align stakeholder interests such that participation in e-government can be self-governing.

INTRODUCTION

The notion of corporate governance is a topic of intense debate within strategic management literature (Sundaramurthy & Lewis, 2003). Disputes have persisted over the optimal configuration of power in an organization to exploit the collective strength of its stakeholders (see Demb & Neubauer, 1992; Sundaramurthy, 2000; Westphal, 1999).

Strategic management scholars, such as Eisenhardt (1989) and Hawley and Williams (1996), have argued that self-serving opportunism is a predominant trait among stakeholders; they recommended the enforcement of procedural controls to restrain the manifestation of such delinquent behavior. Yet social psychologists suggested otherwise. Observing stakeholders to be inherently inspired by motivational desires of self-actualization (Davis, Schoorman, & Donaldson, 1997), sociologists propose that instead of imposing restrictive perimeters around stakeholders' actions, responsible stakeholders should in fact be empowered to exercise their own judgments and be cherished as partners of the governance system (Donaldson & Davis, 1994). Not surprisingly, these opposite viewpoints have prompted researchers to seek alternative theoretical approaches that go beyond either direction (see Audia, Locke, & Smith, 2000). Among them, Demb and Neubauer (1992) advocate a paradoxical and provocative strategy to corporate governance, one that encapsulates the simultaneous demand for both stakeholder control and cooperation.

Nonetheless, advances in Information Technology (IT) and its assimilation into business processes have further complicated the theoretical framing of corporate governance. Allen, Juillet, Paquet, and Roy (2001) postulated that the emergence of electronic governance (e-governance) goes beyond the mere adaptation of technologies to encompass novel patterns of managerial decision-making, power-sharing, and re-source-coordination. Changes include the induction of adaptive corporate structures, innovative leadership styles, and even a redefinition of business purpose, all of which are made possible and necessary through IT (Allen et al., 2001). In this sense, e-governance may be considered as the embodiment of the challenges facing corporate governance in the realization of an optimal mix strategy of control and collaboration for the maximization of organizational stakeholder value. Aptly, we conceive e-governance as the effective utilization of IT to strategically manage stakeholders for competitiveness. This definition builds upon scholarly predictions that foresee the future of organizations as intimately dependent on their capabilities in exploiting technological innovations to harness competencies in an enhanced network of stakeholders (Guillaume, 1999; Prahalad & Ramaswamy, 2000).

The managerial interpretations of e-governance are not exclusive to the private sector (Allen et al., 2001; Seavey, 1996). Pablo and Pan (2002) noted similar IT-induced reformations in civil administration. With a renewed strategic focus on citizens as partners in the governing process (Wimmer & Traunmuller, 2000), this modernized approach to public management promises expanded functionalities through IT integration, and has been popularly termed "Electronic Government (e-government)" (Stratford & Stratford, 2000). Aichholzer and Schmutzer (2000) noted the fundamental changes in public management brought about by IT, and advised that the e-transformation of established government operations should entail a corresponding re-conceptualization of the underpinning governance system.

The study of e-governance in e-governments thus offers an excellent opportunity to explore fundamental challenges encountered by government agencies in their efforts to redefine their tactics in IT-enabled stakeholder management. This chapter adopts an e-governance perspective to examine the Electronic Tax Filing (e-filing) system, a pioneering e-government initiative of the Singapore government. By means of a case study, we seek to unveil the strategic elements of effective e-governance that will promote economical and efficacious elicitation of stakeholder value. We will further consider the significance of an e-governance vision in developing e-government initiatives and in structuring policy decisions within the public administration.

This chapter comprises seven sections, inclusive of the introduction. The second section offers a conceptual overview of the current status of research in the areas of e-government and corporate governance. It underpins our theoretical impetus for merging knowledge from these domains to better understand stakeholder management in developing e-government initiatives. The following section discusses the rationale and considerations behind the choice of the research methodology used in this study. It covers the reason for the case study method, the research techniques, as well as the data collection and analysis process. The fourth section continues with a breakdown of the events and decisions leading to the conceptualization, development, and implementation of the e-filing system. The fifth section focuses on the analytical discussion of core findings from the case that contribute to the appreciation and management of stakeholders within e-governmental projects. Subsequently, the sixth section emphasizes some implications for managerial practice to be gleaned from this study and highlights future research directions, which manifest from the case findings. Finally, the last section concludes with a discourse on the limitations of this study.

LITERATURE REVIEW

The impact of IT on public administration cannot be understated as governments worldwide rapidly embrace emerging technologies to restructure archaic bureaucratic procedures (Moon, 2002). By redeploying conventional public services through new communication media (Ho, 2002; Milford, 2000), recent IT-driven advancements in civil administration are not merely cosmetic changes. Rather, they represent a paradigmatic shift in basic government functioning (Wimmer, Traunmuller, & Lenk, 2001) as public management is restructured to steer away from conventional bookkeeping functions (Norris, 1999). Increasingly, this phenomenon of adapting IT for the modernization of public administrative practices has been commonly referred to as the dawn of the e-government era. The remainder of this section draws on relevant literature to justify our rationale for subscribing to the stakeholder perspective in examining the concept of e-governance in e-government.

Definitions of E-Government

Despite the relative infancy stage of e-government development, its definitions have already proliferated in contemporary literature. Though it is not the intention of this study to engage in a rigorous debate on a comprehensive definition of e-government, it is still useful to get acquainted with the various terminologies offered by researchers in order to arrive at an intuitive working definition.

From a technological angle, Milford (2000) considered e-government to be the means by which IT is utilized to simplify and to automate transactions between public organizations and its external constituent entities such as citizens, businesses, or even foreign governmental agencies (see also Marchionini, Samet, & Brandt, 2003). Therefore, from the standpoint of technologists, e-government is the process of transacting business between the public and the government through the use of automated computerized systems (Sharma & Gupta, 2003). This, in turn, has popularized the notion that e-government is no different from that of pursuing "electronic commerce" within the context of public services (Stratford & Stratford, 2000).

Tapscott (1996), however, provided an alternative appraisal of the role of IT in revamping public administration. He visualized an "inter-networked government" in which public agencies thrives on the collaborative potential of networking technologies in forging virtual alliances to create strategic value for collaborators (Tapscott, 1996). Zweers and Planque (2001) further expanded on this idea and suggested that e-government is the provision and attainment of information and services through electronic media, by and from any governmental agency, such that extra value is generated for all participating parties. Incidentally, this line of argument parallels the views of Nadler and Tushman (1997) who argued that technology is one of the means but not the ends for e-government.

Amidst these discourses over the technicalities of e-government, there are other scholars who adopted a more societal outlook on its mission. Embracing a citizens' perspective, Lawson (1998) put forward the idea that e-government is the provision of public services in a "one-stop, non-stop" manner where "power is transferred to the people" (p. 10). This is reinforced through the work of other scholars where it is again emphasized that the core responsibility of e-governments is to ensure convenient access to public information and dialogic communication channels for the entire community (Kaylor, Deshazo, & van Eck, 2001; Turban, King, Lee, Warkentin, & Chung, 2002). Quoting O'Neill (2001), "the new technologies will allow the citizen new access to the levers of power in government. As more information reaches the citizen, the greater the potential for them to influence and make informed choices regarding how government touches their lives. That potential gives new meaning to a 'government of the people, by the people and for the people'" (p. 6). Summarizing these social standpoints, Wimmer and Traunmuller (2000) hypothesized that e-government exists as the guiding vision toward a modern genre of public administration and democracy where citizens are substantially empowered to contribute toward policy formulation and legislation. From the above discussion, three major characterizations of e-government have emerged as read in Table 1.

To reconcile the differing positions undertaken by either the technical or the sociological emphasis on the e-government phenomenon, Aichholzer and Schmutzer (2000) conceive the function of e-government as "covering the changes of governance in a twofold manner: (1) the transformation of the business of governance, i.e. improving service quality delivery, reducing costs and renewing administrative processes and; (2) the transformation of governance itself, i.e. re examining the functioning of democratic practices and processes" (p. 379). To their credit, Aichholzer and Schmutzer's (2000) conceptualization captures the duality of e-government as both a transactional mechanism for public services and a legitimized forum to further the mandate of democratic societies. Consequently, it will be espoused as the working definition for this chapter.

Table 1. E-government definitions and their implications

Definitions of e-Government	Implications for Citizens' Involvement
e-Government defined as *IT Artefacts* employed by public institutions to achieve cost-effective business transactions	Citizens are regarded as customers of governmental transactions and the objective of e-government is the delivery of improved products and services through electronic media.
e-Government defined as *Virtual Value Chains* of public institutions and their transactional partners to enhance virtual transacting experience	Citizens are deemed as business partners of governmental agencies and the purpose of e-government is the creation of additional value in any given transaction by exploiting the collective strengths of participants through digital alliances.
e-Government defined as the *Virtual Socialization Process* between public institutions and citizens to create responsive governments	Citizens are viewed as pillars of the democratic system and the aim of e-government is to amplify citizens' voice in the process of governance through easily accessible virtual communication channels.

Based on this definition, the participation of citizens in e-government occurs on two distinct levels: 1) citizens as consumers of public goods and services (Fernandes, Gorr, & Krishnan, 2001; Newcombe, 2000); and 2) citizens as members of a democratic system (Cumming, 2001; Elgarah & Courtney, 2002; Webler & Tuler, 2000).

Furthermore, as mentioned earlier, e-government is different from e-governance. The interchangeable use of both theoretical constructs in some of the existing empirical studies has blurred their conceptual boundaries (see Allen et al, 2001; Tan, Pan, & Lim, 2003). E-governance is the broader definition of the two and symbolizes the adaptation of technologies to give rise to innovative managerial approaches in public-private organizations whereas e-government, on the other hand, is reserved solely for the manifestation of e-governance in the realm of public administration.

Similarly, Pablo and Pan (2002) postulated that the notion of e-governance materializes in governments on four separate dimensions: 1) a transformation in the operational principles of governance by shifting toward increased communication, participation, integrity, and transparency (Schiavo-Ocampo & Sundaram, 2001); 2) a transformation in the internal functions of government by automating public transactions and administrative processes (Backus, 2001; Inter-American Development Bank [IADB], 2001); 3) a transformation in the interactions between governments and their citizens (Csetenyi, 2000; Heeks, 2001; Stiglitz, Orszag, & Orszag, 2002), and finally, 4) a transformation of society itself by crafting and sustaining networks of social relationships through electronic means (IADB, 2001). In other words, the advent of e-governance within public administration denotes a major overhaul of traditional stakeholder management practices to revitalize the long-standing estranged relationship between government agencies and citizens, thus warranting an in-depth investigation. Unless stated otherwise, this chapter is more attuned towards the appreciation of e-governance in public administration, or simply, e-government.

Collaboration vs. Control in E-Governance

Yet, despite the beneficial prospects of infusing e-governance into public administration, scholars have questioned the impact of businesslike transformations embodied in the drive towards e-government. Gregory (1999) and Haque (2001) hypothesized that the convenient transplant of business norms onto public administration will undermine the role of government agencies in representing and fulfilling public interest. A number of articles emphasized the need for e-governments to realign their developmental objectives with stakeholder determinants (see Pardo & Scholl, 2002; Pardo, Scholl, Cook, Connelly, & Dawes, 2000; Scholl, 2001; Tennert & Schroeder, 1999). These studies espouse the view that e-government initiatives hinge on the effective e-governance of stakeholder expectations (Allen et al., 2001).

From above, it is clear that the effectiveness of e-governance translates to substantial advantages for the organization. Benefits include increased operational efficiency in terms of utilizing less time, effort, and material resources while maintaining a constant level of output (due to automation, reengineering, or transformation of processes) as well as increased operational effectiveness (new and better services, enhanced client convenience and satisfaction, and re-engineered processes including those for leadership and decision-making). These operational gains may take the form of financial returns (the monetary equivalent of the time, effort, and other resources saved), political gains (greater participation, a wider base for democracy, and increased empowerment), and more significantly, relational rewards in terms of new and better connections between groups of stakeholders as well as new forms of cooperation, collaboration, linkages, and partnerships (Aichhlozer & Schmutzer, 2000; Allen et al., 2001; Backus, 2001; Csetenyi, 2000; Heeks, 2001; Lenk & Traunmuller, 2000; Stiglitz et al., 2000; von Hoffman, 1999).

There are, however, problems associated with the growing e-governance phenomenon. Giving stakeholders direct access to government transactions via electronic means essentially removes human intermediaries, which may shift some of the transactional burden (such as the interpretation of and search for additional information) to citizen-clients. Such a shift, in turn, requires the adoption of more flexible structures and processes, coordinated change efforts, and an increased cooperation between government units, businesses, and citizen partners (Aichhlozer & Schmutzer, 2000; Csetenyi, 2000; Wescott, 2002). It is precisely because of this increasingly sophisticated web of government-stakeholder relations embedded within the governance system of e-governments that Pardo et al. (2000) noted the importance of identifying stakeholders and incorporating their requirements in the development and maintenance of e-government initiatives.

Unfortunately, strategic management theorists are divided over the most effective mode of governance from which to regulate stakeholders' contributions. Those who support the agency theory, which is founded on financial economics, emphasize the creation of procedures to curb the opportunistic behavior of managers (agents) and align their actions to the wishes of principals (owners) within an organized atmosphere (Eisenhardt, 1989; Hawley & Williams, 1996). They assume that managers share a tendency to appropriate partisan gains at the expense of their shareholders. For instance, Jensen and Meckling (1976) illustrated how investors in listed enterprises incur additional expenses in monitoring and bonding representatives to best serve their business agendas.

Nevertheless, excessive control has been noted to be counterproductive to corporate missions as it transmits a strong signal of distrust towards organizational stakeholders (Ghoshal & Moran, 1996). Frey (1997) reinforced, "the agent may perceive more intensive monitoring by the principal as an indication of distrust, or as a unilateral break of the contract built on mutual trust" (p. 664). Indeed, this growing suspicion among stakeholders has often been blamed for triggering defensive attitudes which inhibit altruistic performance, the very mindset that control is meant to contain (Davis et al., 1997).

Alternatively, departing from the agency approach, stewardship theory details an opposite collaborative stance on stakeholder management (Davis et al., 1997). Drawing on insights from social psychology, proponents of the stewardship theory postulate that managers are "good stewards of the organizations and diligently work to attain high levels of corporate profit and shareholder returns" (Donaldson & Davis, 1994). According to this model, "managers are principally motivated by achievement and responsibility needs [and] given the needs of managers for responsible, self-directed work, organizations may be better served by freeing managers from subservience to non-executive director dominated boards" (Donaldson & Davis, 1994).

Conversely, scholars have also noted the negative effects of an overemphasise on collaboration. Sundaramurthy and Lewis (2003) highlighted that a blind focus on cooperative decision-making and goal alignment could lead to the suppression of tensions which are necessary for the systematic monitoring and critiquing of collective decisions. Indeed, extremely cohesive governance teams may be lulled by the success of their previous collective decisions and fall prey to the common mistakes of groupthink (Janis, 1982) and strategic persistence (Kisfalvi, 2000). In their biased confidence and subjective support for collaborative resolutions (Audia et al., 2000), decision-makers could become susceptible to the downward spiraling effects of denying their own better judgments. Consequently, they may downplay the environmental uncertainties that they are facing, and hesitate to implement the changes that may be much needed in the organization (Hambrick & D'Aveni, 1988). Lindsley, Brass, and Thomas (1995) predicted that over time, such passive governance techniques will result in rigid mental maps in stakeholders, constricting information flow and inducing complacency among them.

The contradictory positions on corporate governance may be traced to an oversimplification of stakeholder identification, categorization, and management. By presuming that the spectrum of organizational stakeholders can be simply partitioned into groups of shareholders and managers, the agency and stewardship ideologies conveniently discount the interplay of broader stakeholder dependencies in shaping corporate performance (Demb & Neubauer, 1992). In effect, the two governance paradigms deem shareholders (or the board) as the only focal point from which all governance praxis should originate.

The two pyramidal governance models are also not applicable in the public sphere as civil administration exists to fulfill its obligations to the larger social community rather than a group of shareholders or the board (Coursey & Bozeman, 1990). Indeed, the developmental cycle of e-government reveals patterns of evolution which emphasize the steady empowerment of partnering stakeholders, especially the traditionally neglected citizens, while preserving the administrative ethics of public agencies (Traunmuller & Wimmer, 2000; von Hoffman, 1999). In light of the maturing e-government development, the appeal by Audia et al. (2000) for the re-conceptualization of governance highlights a research need in the e-government arena.

Stakeholder Theory

Stakeholder theory, with its emphasis on realistic corporate circumstances (Freeman, 1984), offers a logical first step in the search for a viable theoretical alternative for the study of e-government. Departing from the crude distinction between owners and employees as the main categorization to be considered in formulating governance strategies, Stakeholder theory posits that an organization encompasses a sophisticated network of stakeholders operating within the broader framework of the host society that provides the necessary market infrastructure for its business activities (Clarkson, 1994). From this aspect, stakeholder dynamics may extend beyond the narrow dimensions of principals and agents with each identified stakeholder segment warranting a matching relational stratagem.

As defined by Carroll (1989), a stake is "an interest or a share in an undertaking" (p. 56). Therefore, a stakeholder is "any individual or group who can affect or is affected by the actions, decisions, policies, practices, or goals of the organization" (Freeman, 1984, p. 25; see also Greenley & Foxall, 1998; Scott & Lane, 2000). This definition has been further broadened by Donaldson and Preston (1995) to include individuals who are identified through the actual or potential harms and benefits that they experience or anticipate as a result of an organization's actions or inactions.

Intuitively, it can be deduced from these definitions that stakeholders are specific to an organization (Berman, Wicks, Kotha, & Jones, 1999). For example, within the context of e-government, the potential stakeholders for any public agency may include politicians, civil servants, commercial corporations, citizens, and perhaps even foreign government organizations (Traunmuller & Wimmer, 2000). The first step in strategic stakeholder management is thus the listing of all entities that have a stake in the establishment. Freeman (1984) referred to this list as the stakeholder map of an organization.

Once the stakeholders have been identified, Pfeffer and Salancik (1978) recommended that managers "rank or assign weights to them in order to indicate their impact on the organization or the extent to which the organization believes it should moderate its consequences on them" (p. 52), that is, stakeholders should be segmented according to their priorities or impacts on the organization. This will facilitate the efficient allocation of limited organizational resources to cater to the relational requirements of the most salient stakeholders (Frooman, 1999).

In elementary classification schemes, stakeholders can be generally grouped into primary and secondary stakeholders. Primary stakeholders refer to those playing a vital role in the survival of the organization; that is, without the continuing participation of these stakeholders, the organization may suffer serious consequences or even cease to function (Clarkson, 1995; Schneiderman & Rose, 1996). In view of their strategic significance, the terms "critical stakeholders" or "strategic stakeholders" are often synonymously used to refer to primary stakeholders (Demb & Neubauer, 1992; Monks & Minow, 1995; Turnbull, 1997). Conversely, secondary stakeholders are typically those "who influence or affect, or are influenced or affected by the corporation, but they are not engaged in transactions with the corporation and are not essential for its survival" (Clarkson, 1995, p. 107; Schneiderman & Rose, 1996).

Further to the above technique of stakeholder categorization, other characteristics have been proposed as normative factors to separate stakeholders. Amidst the debates

Table 2. A comparison among power, legitimacy, and urgency of stakeholders

Table 2: A Comparison among Power, Legitimacy and Urgency of Stakeholders		
Attribute	**Definition**	**Managerial Concerns**
Power	- Stakeholders have power when managers perceive them to have the ability to impose their will on the organization.	- Because of their potential to acquire legitimacy or urgency or both, management should remain cognizant of such stakeholders and adjust priorities accordingly.
Legitimacy	- Stakeholder legitimacy is a perception or assumption that the actions of an entity are desirable, proper, or appropriate within some socially constructed system of norms, values, beliefs, and definitions.	- There is typically no pressure on managers to engage in an active relationship with such stakeholders. However, by virtue of their legitimacy, the actions taken by these stakeholders will impact the performance of an organization if they were to gain a second attribute.
Urgency	- Stakeholders have urgency when their claims for organizational attention are both time-sensitive and critical to them, and any delays in paying attention to them are unacceptable.	- In general, urgent stakeholders are irksome but not dangerous, bothersome but not warranting more than passing management attention, if any at all. Nevertheless, in the event that these stakeholders are able to attain power or legitimacy in their claims, then they will count amongst some of the topmost priorities in stakeholder management.

on stakeholder differentiations, a noteworthy framework developed by Mitchell, Agle, and Wood (1997) for demarcating stakeholders is founded on the notion that the extent of stakeholders' influence on an organization is subjected to the interplay of the three attributes of power, legitimacy, and urgency (Agle, Mitchell, & Sonnenfeld, 1999; Scott & Lane, 2000). Depending on the combination of attributes possessed by a particular stakeholder, appropriate managerial actions may be necessary. The crux of this argument is summarized in Table 2.

From the table, the message is clear: The assessment of stakeholders' saliency is instrumental to the formulation of relational strategies to co-opt principal stakeholders into the organizational vision (Jawahar & McLaughlin, 2001; Mitchell et al., 1997). This imperative nature of saliency in stakeholder management is reinforced through the seminal work of Frooman (1999), who devised what is known as the typology of relationships between stakeholders and firm. Based on the Resource Dependency Theory (Yuchtman & Seashore, 1967), Frooman's (1999) typology is represented as a 2x2 matrix where each axis reflects the extent of resource dependency or level of power symmetry between the firm and its stakeholders. The gist of this model is presented in Figure 1.

Figure 1. A summary of Frooman's (1999) typology of relationships between stakeholders and firm

		Is the Stakeholder Dependent on the Firm?	
		No	Yes
Iis the Firm Dependent on the Stakeholder?	No	**Low Interdependence** 1. Neither the firm nor the stakeholder depends on each other.	**Firm Power** 2. The stakeholder is dependent on the firm, but the firm is not dependent on the stakeholder.
		Management Strategy Since the firm is not dependent on the stakeholder for resources, it is likely to adopt an indifferent attitude towards stakeholders' concerns, i.e. the firm will be almost oblivious to their needs and expectations	
	Yes	**Stakeholder Power** 3. The firm is dependent on the stakeholder, but the stakeholder is not dependent on the firm.	**High Interdependence** 4. Both the firm and the stakeholder depend on each other.
		Management Strategy Since stakeholders control resources pivotal to the survival of the firm, the firm has an immediate mandate to attend their needs and whenever possible, manoeuvre them to become amiable partners, i.e. shift stakeholders into high interdependent relations.	**Management Strategy** Since both the firm and the stakeholder are reliant on each other for resources, the firm will attempt to negotiate with stakeholders to arrive at mutually acceptable solutions.

In essence, the manifestation of the stakeholder theory in commercial enterprises can be summarized into three basic principles, each corresponding to a specific phase of stakeholder management:

Stakeholder Identification: Firms should always seek to identify their most salient partners, as these stakeholders have the capacity to impact the survival of the organization (Blair, 1995; Freeman, 1984; Greenley & Foxall, 1998; Scott & Lane, 2000).

Stakeholder Categorization: Firms should always be mindful of their most salient partners and prioritize them according to their influence, in order to devise business strategies that align with the interests of these crucial stakeholders (Blair, 1995; Boatright, 2002; Donaldson & Preston, 1995; Porter, 1992).

Stakeholder Management: As long as the stakeholders do not acquire the capability to exert sufficient influence to obstruct organizational operations, there is no necessity to allocate resources to attend to their requirements (Frooman, 1999; Mitchell et al., 1997). In addition, if the balance of power is tilted towards stakeholders, organizations should concoct means by which to maneuver these stakeholders into a mutually dependent relationship so as to level the playing field for both parties (Frooman, 1999; Lawler & Yoon, 1995).

Undeniably, these guidelines in stakeholder management are formulated and well-tuned to the context of commercialization where businesses operate to optimize their responses to deserving stakeholders (Boatright, 2002; Donaldson & Preston, 1995; Schneiderman & Rose, 1996) within a relatively smaller resource scarcity perimeter (Greenley & Foxall, 1998; Scott & Lane, 2000). However, bearing in mind the socio-political distinctions between public-private organizations such as a lower degree of market exposure, the prevalent centralization of power and a wider range of constituents as highlighted above (Rainey, Backoff, & Levine, 1976), it is the proposition of this study that the underlying philosophy of stakeholder management in the private sector is not entirely transferable to the public sphere.

From the preceding discussion, it could be seen that while the stakeholder theory offers a more perceptive and relevant means for exploring the dynamism of strategic stakeholder management within organizational environments, its guiding principles should be reexamined in light of the e-government phenomenon. As such, this study subscribes to the stakeholder perspective as the conceptual lens to unravel the case of the e-filing system to facilitate a holistic appreciation of stakeholder management within the e-government system. Specifically, this study will attempt to decipher how the e-governance of stakeholders in an e-government initiative can be derived from the integration of control and collaborative mechanisms into the three integrative phases of stakeholder management: 1) identification of key stakeholder groups within an organization; 2) recognition of differing interests among groups of stakeholders; and 3) definition of an IT-enabled governance system that caters to and furthers the interests of the stakeholders.

METHODOLOGY

Considering the extensive impact of e-government campaigns on the socioeconomic landscape, an inquiry of e-governance in an e-government initiative should extend beyond the boundaries of tangible implementation efforts to the more intricate surrounding context. This is to allow the underlying intersection between the phenomenon and the social environment to be established. For this reason, this study adopts an in-depth case research approach for data collection and analysis (Strauss & Corbin, 1990).

According to Yin (1994), a case study is "an empirical inquiry that: investigates a contemporary phenomenon within its real-life context, when the boundaries between phenomenon and context are not clearly evident, and in which multiple sources of evidence are used" (p. 23). It is most appropriate in scenarios where the research question is exploratory in nature and focuses on the examination of current events that occur beyond the control of the investigator (Yin, 1994). Moreover, case studies offer a chance to engage in theory-building in an area where there is relatively little prior knowledge (Eisenhardt, 1991; Parkhe, 1993). Therefore, through the case research methodology, this study hopes to reveal unforeseen relationships and generate deeper insights into the interdependencies among the themes uncovered over the course of the investigation (Benbasat, Goldstein, & Mead, 1987).

Researchers and methodologists have articulated both positivist and interpretivist approaches to the design and execution of case studies (see Numigami, 1998; Paré & Elam, 1997; Walsham, 1995; Yin, 1994), with no mention of inherent superiority in either technique. In fact, as observed by Lee (1991), the feasibility of any theoretical angle is essentially a function of the underlying research objectives. In contrast to the structured approach of positivism which is governed strictly by the philosophy of constructing mathematically quantifiable relations between prior theoretically-derived propositions and empirical realities (Ngwenyama & Lee, 1997), the interpretivist perspective believes that reality is only partially observable and comprises relations beyond noticeable facts (Comte, 1971). In other words, from the interpretivist point of view, the collection of objective data is impossible since the investigator interacts with the human subjects involved in the enquiry, and in the process, alters the perceptions of both parties (Walsham, 1995).

Effectively, interpretive studies supply evidence of a nondeterministic perspective, which demonstrates the "intent to increase understanding of the phenomena within a specific cultural and contextual setting, and an examination of the phenomena and the setting from the perspectives of participants" (Walsham, 1995, p. 384; see also Orlikowski & Baroudi, 1991). Inspired by Markus's (1994) defense of individuals as intelligent beings existing in a shared social context, this study postulates that stakeholders are not mere passive receptacles of corporate actions, and that they participate actively in shaping government-stakeholder relations. Consequently, given the research objective, we deem a holistic comprehension of the social environment through the triangulation of multiple perspectives a necessary prerequisite.

Also, taking into account the unique circumstances of this study where everybody, including the investigator, is a target audience of the e-government initiative, the adoption of an interpretivistic perspective of the data collected can be perceived as a logical decision. In another sense, the experience and contextual understanding of the researcher serve to provide complementary background information that is invaluable to the interpretation of the evidence gathered (Lacity & Janson, 1994).

The case study was conducted at the Inland Revenue Authority of Singapore (IRAS) over a period of six months with the use of several methods of data collection (Benbasat et al, 1987). A series of focused interviews (Merton, Fiske, & Kendall, 1990) were conducted with the chief information officer (CIO), the e-filing system design team, the e-filing system implementation team, and the e-filing administrative group to solicit data on the intra-organizational considerations behind the implementation of the e-filing project. The data was triangulated with interviews with perspectives provided through interviews with taxpayers (Orlikowski, 1993). In addition, supplementary data from other sources including meeting minutes, press statements, and a huge pool of archival records from 1995 to the time of research was also solicited. These secondary documents were provided with the understanding that the research findings would contribute to the future development and strategization of the e-filing system. From the 30 hours of interviews and the supplementary archives, the researchers built a qualitative in-depth data collection of data points within the study environment (Lacity & Janson, 1994) that focused specifically on developmental issues pertaining to the e-filing service provided by the IRAS; less emphasis was given to the technicalities of the system (Eisenhardt, 1991).

In conjunction with the data collection stage, thematic analysis (Boyatiz, 1998) was employed for the coding and interpretation of the raw information. Patterns from the transcribed interviews were first identified and then combined and catalogued into sub-themes (Taylor & Bogan, 1984) that were subsequently coded into the main themes of the investigation. The entire research process concluded only when information appeared to have reached saturation.

CASE DESCRIPTION

The Singapore government faced a rising amount of uncollected revenue during the 1980's. Unprocessed tax returns accumulated in the Singapore Income Tax Department, which resulted in administrative backlogs that led to dissatisfaction among department staff and taxpaying citizens. In view of this, the Inland Revenue Authority of Singapore (IRAS) was inaugurated in 1992 to remove the bureaucratic red tape by restructuring the taxation system. This responsibility became the corporate vision guiding the IRAS over the next eight years when the tax administration process was re-engineered into an integrated information system (IS) that resulted in a decrease in the staff turnover rate and a general rise in public satisfaction.

The introduction of direct taxpayer services (phone filing) in 1995 was a milestone in the IRAS' drive towards revolutionizing the tax filing system. Forty-three percent of tax inquiries could then be handled by the automated voice response system, with the remaining 400,000 calls left to tax officers. In the 2000 IRAS survey, 95% of individual taxpayers, 83% of corporate taxpayers and 93% of goods and services taxpayers expressed their satisfaction with the IRAS' services. The IRAS' reputation was given a further boost as reflected in a 2001 survey where 94.1% of individual taxpayers, 89.6% of corporate taxpayers, and 94.6% of goods and services taxpayers expressed their satisfaction with the refurnished e-government services. Also, in a customer service evaluation survey conducted by Forbes Research in October, 2003, 2,466 respondents confessed a high level of satisfaction with the IRAS' services. Over 80% of the respondents agreed that the time and money spent on fulfilling tax obligations were reasonable. The respondents were also asked to rate their satisfaction with the IRAS' service against other organizations. The IRAS was ranked third, after a private bank and another statutory board. In the area of service quality and outcome, individual and business income taxpayers ranked the IRAS second, ahead of the private bank.

The Internet provided an opportunity for the IRAS to expand the user base of its phone filing services. With the launch of the e-filing system on February 16, 1998, taxpayers are able to file their income returns online either through the Internet or over the phone. This new Singapore $1.9 million e-filing system is even accessible to citizens overseas. Since filed returns are entered directly into the IRAS electronic database, the e-filing process is paperless other than the need for a verification receipt. The IRAS has projected that the investment of the e-filing system would be recovered within five years from its implementation if 30% of taxpayers submit their returns electronically. With a reported approximated growth of 100% in the number of e-filers annually, the IRAS is confident of breaking even.

A deciding factor behind the success of the e-filing initiative is its fusion of both control and collaborative mechanisms into the system such that the collective potential of stakeholders (taxpayers and their employers) can be consolidated without an overreliance on checks and balance. Before the implementation of the e-filing system, physical paper returns were used in the report of employment income. This physical filing procedure resulted in an overwhelming demand on both manpower (to sift through each document) and storage capacity (to archive the accumulating tax returns). Moreover, the use of paper folders which had limited the ability of tax officials to access and process the information concurrently; at the same time, it greatly increased the chance of the tax documents being misplaced.

The e-filing system was conceptualized as a digital paperless solution to the problems inherent in its labor-intensive predecessor. Making use of a technologically integrated back-end infrastructure to incorporate taxation calculations and regulations, the e-filing system automates tax processing according to an 80/20 rule, that is, it is crafted on the assumption that 80% of the tax returns are "normal" and do not require additional validation by tax officers. The remaining 20% of tax returns are then automatically routed to the appropriate tax official with the essential skill domain for further verification.

To accommodate the minority group of taxpayers who choose to continue submitting paper returns, the e-filing system provides two points of data entry. If tax returns are filed through the Internet portal, the submitted information will be directly entered into a centralized database. However, if a taxpayer chooses to file a paper tax return, the relevant data fields will be extracted and keyed into the database, and the document is scanned as a digital image for archiving purposes. Basically, through these design specifications, the premise of the e-filing system lies in offering an integrated one-stop digital tax filing option for taxpayers' convenience. The structure of the e-filing system is depicted in Figure 2.

The revamped electronic tax filing system not only boasts symmetrical communication channels for stakeholders to participate in system development and enhancement

Figure 2. Illustration of the contemporary tax administration system of the IRAS

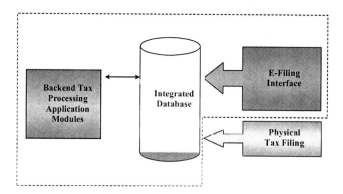

decisions, but at the same time, it incorporates the rigorous administrative controls of its paper-based ancestor. As highlighted by one of the system engineers:

By integrating the front-end data capturing process with back-end tax processing functions, the e-filing system basically represents a whole new perspective on how we interact with our taxpayers...However, in designing the e-filing system, we have also made sure that the new system does not compromise the integrity of the tax filing process but retains the same level of control as the previous paper [-based] system.

In a further bid to make e-filing effortless for taxpayers, the IRAS has established close ties with a number of government agencies and huge business organizations so that they may transfer the relevant tax information of each of their employees directly into the IRAS central database in each tax cycle. Once the information for a particular taxpayer has been uploaded into the system, the taxpayer has only to submit a series of zero returns through the e-filing system.

To date, this auto-inclusion scheme has generated data transfer agreements with a total of 1,197 business organizations or 2% of all Singaporean companies. This small percentage of participating organizations may seem insignificant, but according to statistical approximation, these companies account for an approximate figure of 550,000 or 46% of all employees in the country. Recently, the auto-inclusion scheme has also been broadened to include tax relief and stock dividends. Most importantly, the direct transmission of tax information reduces data capturing efforts and enables controls to be built into the system to validate the accuracy of taxpayers' financial portfolio. Through the solicitation of data directly from the third-party employers, the IRAS is assured of the accuracy of employees' income information.

CASE ANALYSIS AND DISCUSSION

The IRAS' e-filing system demonstrates how a public agency may unleash the capabilities of IT to craft an efficient and robust e-government architecture that serves as a common denominator between the agency and its stakeholders. Given the success of the e-filing system, the case could provide valuable insights into the strategic elements constituting an effective governance of the triangulating relationship constituting government goals, stakeholder involvement, and IT-enabled public service adoption. This study will thus analyze the case of the IRAS according to the three guiding principles discussed in the literature review section and attempt to formulate guidelines for the e-governance of control and collaboration by integrating and refining the three essential elements of strategic stakeholder management.

Identifying Crucial Stakeholders

The identification of critical stakeholders has been described as an indispensable step in effective corporate governance (Demb & Neubauer, 1992; Monks & Minow, 1995). Indeed, scholars have prescribed the need to identify strategic stakeholders, whose presence directly determines a firm's ability to survive (Donaldson & Preston, 1995; Turnbull, 1997). Naturally, most governance researchers agree on the necessity to concentrate organizational resources on specific niches of stakeholders who are consid-

Table 3. Categorization of stakeholders and their corresponding interests in the e-filing system

Table 3: Categorization of Stakeholders and their Corresponding Interests in the e-Filing System	
Stakeholder	**Stakeholder Interests**
Singapore Government	▪ To reduce the bureaucratic red tape in the tax processing system and recover the uncollected revenue accumulated over the years.
IRAS	▪ To repair the tarnished image of its predecessor through streamlining the tax processing system for operational efficiency and effectiveness.
Tax Officials	▪ To eliminate redundant administrative workload on 'normal' tax returns and increase overall productivity while at the same time ensuring taxpayers' compliance.
Taxpayers	▪ To submit tax returns through the most efficient and convenient means possible.
Employers	▪ To resolve the issues of taxable vs. non-taxable income with the tax agency.

ered vital to the organization (Blair, 1995; Freeman, 1984). Typical of the conventional agency (Hawley & Williams, 1996) and stewardship (Donaldson & Davis, 1994) governance models, a corollary of such power centralization on key players is the marginalization of the remaining stakeholders during project development.

In the case of the IRAS, there are five primary categories of stakeholders involved in the administration of the tax filing system, each with differing stakes or interests in the evolution of the taxation process. The details are given in Table 3.

Interestingly, the findings from the case of the IRAS suggest a gradual shift away from the conventional corporate centric mentality of focusing on salient principals as described above. Before the introduction of the e-filing system, taxpayers have often been regarded as compulsory and obligatory participants, with the IRAS being the sole owner of the tax-filing process from which the strategic implementation directions are derived. To institutionalize its dominion, controls in the form of law enforcements were used by the IRAS to guarantee taxpayers' compliance. As recalled by one of the managers:

In the past it was like, taxpayers are people who owe us money. To be honest, we actually need to see taxpayers as customers even though they are bonded by law to pay taxes... In fact, if they don't pay us, we will jail them.

From the quote, it is apparent that taxpayers in the past were not regarded as stakeholders, and minimal attention was given to their interests. Communication was dictatorial as the public agency sought to impose its will on taxpayers (Moon & Bretschneider, 2002). At the same time, taxpayer expectations were not addressed promptly, leading to an oppressive atmosphere and a tarnished public image for the public institution. As an IRAS system engineer commented, "We had difficulty clearing all the returns... Many taxpayers had to wait, and even then, it took us one and a half years to clear the lot, so a lot of people got angry."

In turn, the tensions between the IRAS and taxpayers incurred an unnecessarily high overhead in operational expenditure for the tax agency during each tax cycle. Acknowledging this problem in corporate performance, the IRAS management embarked on an extensive campaign to reinvent its business processes with the aid of IT. A significant feature of this organizational reinvention is the decreased level in the usage of jurisdictional options. Instead, by systematically recognizing and classifying taxpayers into different clusters such that tax services can be tailored specifically to differing requirements, the IRAS believes that taxpayers' compliance may be better achieved through establishing stronger collaborative ties. One of the managers elaborated:

We have a broad base of taxpayers with diverse needs and requirements. It is important to acknowledge them as customers and categorize them according to their needs and requirements...In the IRAS, we believe that through excellent taxpayer service, we can bring about higher levels of compliance.

The Internet has transformed and boosted taxpayers' expectations. With the Internet as a real-time and inexpensive communication medium, citizens are no longer constrained in the means to voice their opinions. Quite the opposite, individuals are empowered substantially through IT to exercise substantial influence over policy formulation (Thomas & Velthouse, 1990). The IRAS CIO highlighted one prominent example of such empowerment:

Taxpayers just send [emails] and they treat it [email communication with the IRAS] like a chat room. They keep sending and sending and they complain of lateness and failure to respond. They think that there is a person there all the time [to answer their queries] and they expect instant replies.

Such occurrences represent a gradual diffusion of power from public administrators to every concerned citizen. Therefore, it becomes imperative to marshal both internal and external commitment in crafting public initiatives. In response to this need, the fusion of IT into public administration is an inevitable phase of development in government services. However, such a development also blurs the conventional governance boundaries separating stakeholders by altering the basis of power distribution from the previous one of legal authority to one of information accessibility. For this reason, public institutions operating in the new information-intensive environment can no longer disengage any seemingly inconsequential stakeholder from policy discourses.

Following the above reasoning, the success of the e-filing system can be attributed to it being a bilateral communication platform that connects taxpayers to the tax agency. It is notable that the e-filing system is being continually enhanced through the objective assessment of taxpayers' feedback gathered after each tax cycle. As mentioned by a customer service executive in relation to the annual post-mortem exercise:

The main purpose is that we want to gather taxpayers' opinions. It is important to put ourselves in their shoes and... incorporate taxpayers' views in whatever we do, so that we can deliver new systems or procedures that taxpayers will be receptive of.

In essence, the identification of stakeholders in the civil administration mentality has adapted from the increasing emphasis on business-IT integration. Unlike prior governance concepts where the mandate of power is vested in the public institution and the utilization of controls is common, the integration of IT into public services has tipped the balance by empowering proactive citizens through the diffusion of information. Consequently, it becomes practically impossible for government agencies to distance citizenries during e-initiative conceptualization. Furthermore, since information accessibility runs parallel to technological advances, the identification of stakeholders has to change from a relatively static procedure to a dynamic process. To encourage acceptance of an e-government initiative, a public agency has to actively seek out relevant stakeholders and continuously strive for their consensual support for the system during its development. In this sense, e-governance in e-government stresses the need for public agencies to relinquish their long-standing preference for control by deploying IT to methodically identify citizen collaborators of e-initiatives.

Recognizing Differing Stakeholder Interests

The recognition and prioritization of differing interests among stakeholders is another essential component of corporate governance. According to Demb and Neubauer (1992), "governance is the process by which organizations are made responsible to the rights and wishes of stakeholders" (p. 9). Hence, Tricker (1994) proposed that effective governance hinges on the ability of the organization to address the issues raised by different interest groups associated with the firm. Similarly, Monks and Minow (1995) highlighted that the relational interests among various partners would ultimately determine the direction and performance of the organization.

In the case of the e-filing system, observations indicate that the mere recognition of differing interests is inadequate in consolidating a unified agreement among stakeholders towards system development. During the conceptualization phase, the IRAS spared no effort in soliciting concerns that the stakeholders might have with the upcoming taxation system. To provide a holistic intra-organizational perspective of the system, the design team consisted of representatives from all tax divisions within the organization. In addition, throughout different phases of system development, taxpayers were invited to take part in focus groups and forums to offer external input on the required functionalities of the e-filing system. Taxpayers' participation even extended into testing a prototype prior to the launch of the system proper. As revealed by one of the system engineers:

We need to go through the whole process and let taxpayers see the way we do it. If we find that we have placed something there that two persons interpret differently, we request for input. When we perform testing, we involve taxpayers and observe the result. Whenever we obtain unexpected results, we ask them why they interpret it in that manner.

Yet, despite efforts to inject stakeholders' interests into the e-filing system, there was still some disagreement between the IRAS and taxpayers over the final product. One primary concern was the lack of transparency in the information management process. In the interviews, most taxpayers expressed limited knowledge of what went on behind the e-filing system. Questions pertaining to the confidentiality of the tax information transmitted to the organization were raised, with suggestions that the IRAS should lay down "explicit rules and guidelines" governing sensitive tax information. Again, such concern over organizational procedures indicates the existence of taxpayers' perception of the presence of control mechanisms erected through information regulation (Tannenbaum, 1967).

These apprehensions over data management integrity may in turn discourage the adoption of the e-filing system. However, as clarified by the CIO, there are strategic considerations and tactical limitations in meeting the expectations of every taxpayer. The IRAS noted that acceding to taxpayers' request to show the resultant tax computations during the e-filing process would mean disseminating sensitive tax information over the public medium of the Internet. Such a step might trigger the possibility of data interceptions, which would in turn translate into additional expenses in implementing security measures within the channel of data transfer. The IRAS maintains that in having a non-transfer policy where data transfer is unidirectional from the taxpayer to the agency, it is in fact looking after the interests of the community. The CIO explained:

A lot of information is already captured by the system, so what we need for e-filing is just asking you to complete the remaining portion. As such, the information [available via the Internet] of the taxpayer is never a complete picture; it would be meaningless to a [hacker] without the rest of the information [kept by the IRAS].

A crucial lesson to be learned from the situation discussed above is that governments, despite a mounting emphasis on citizens' empowerment and involvement, do indeed shoulder a greater responsibility in safeguarding the general welfare of the larger society (see Haque, 2001). The case of the e-filing system shows that although the IRAS values taxpayers' participation in developing the e-initiative, it neither foregoes nor compromises on the integrity expected of public services. Indeed, the infusion of IT into government services may create grey areas of contention where the discharge of public duty comes into conflict with the need for congenial collaborative ties between government agencies and their direct service recipients.

As Foucault (1991) observed, the challenge is to attain equilibrium between individual expectations and the interests of the wider community, so that the organization may avert progress-inhibiting squabbles (Kruckeberb & Starck, 1998). Therefore, in merging IT with government processes, it is a fundamental responsibility of public institutions to evaluate the technological limitations of the e-government services before designing and implementing control and collaboration mechanisms in the system. Specifically, the case evidence indicates that at no time should the e-governance of e-governments be pursued along the extremes of either pure control or unconditional collaboration in satisfying stakeholders' wishes; rather, it requires a delicate balance of the differing expectations of various stakeholders in the anticipated functionalities of the e-government system which is being implemented.

Catering to and Furthering Stakeholder Interests

Indisputably, the eventual objective of sound governance is to enable organizations to formulate plans and management strategies that cater to and further the interests of their stakeholders (Blair, 1995; Clarkson, 1994). Nonetheless, it is frequently documented that stakeholders, acting independently to further partisan interests, hinder the organization from maximizing its potential (Jensen & Meckling, 1976; Shleifer & Vishny, 1996). With the expansion of the stakeholder base in the digital economy, organizations face a more steeply uphill task in catering to the diverse interests of multiple players.

As discussed in previous sections, a critical area of concern in e-government development is the need to retain a certain amount of administrative control while introducing collaborative devices in the e-initiative. To resolve this dilemma, an innovative strategy by the IRAS in pushing for e-filing system acceptance among all stakeholders is to systematically reduce the extent of explicit controls. In place of the controls, the IRAS develop a strategy to align the interests of various stakeholder categories. In traditional system development, usage of the system is encouraged through attempts to satisfy individual stakeholders. In the case of the IRAS, the agency perceives that the alignment of stakeholder expectations will eliminate the need for repressive control measures to sustain the taxation system. In other words, a strategic convergence of interests between the IRAS and its stakeholders may be considered a self-perpetuating motivator (self-governance) in adopting the e-filing system (Turnbull, 1997).

The auto-inclusion scheme described earlier is one strategy that leverages on the integrative capabilities of IT to unite stakeholder interests to craft a mutually beneficial relationship between the IRAS and its stakeholders. The objective of the auto-inclusion scheme is to encourage employers to transfer the employment information of their employees directly into the IRAS central database. From the perspective of the IRAS, such data-transfer agreements are beneficial to organizational operations. An IRAS manager commented, "We prefer it that way [auto-inclusion] because first of all it is very accurate. In fact, sometimes the taxpayers themselves enter the thing wrongly."

However, the nondisclosure of the transmitted employment information made data integrity a taxpayer concern. A taxpayer remarked, "I suppose if there is anything to note here, it is the accuracy of the information. If the employer files it for you, the implication or interpretation may be a bit different."

To tackle these negative sentiments and to facilitate the alignment of stakeholder interest, the IRAS promoted the awareness of mutual benefits through regular dialogue with taxpayers. By strengthening collaborative bonds with different stakeholders, the cooperative benefits to be derived from the auto-inclusion scheme could be better appreciated and more readily accepted by all parties involved. In fact, individual taxpayers became the primary promotional means of the IRAS in encouraging employer participation. As verified by the CIO:

We encourage a lot of them to get their employers to join the auto inclusion scheme because whether an item is taxable or nontaxable, we can arrange with the employer. So taxpayers don't have to crack their heads.

More importantly, the auto-inclusion scheme has also allowed the IRAS to employ imperceptible but effective controls in ensuring the reliability of the tax filing system. The CIO commented:

By getting the information directly from the employer and automatically into the system...I have no worries about whether there is an understatement of income because [now] I source it directly from a third party. I can accept tax information from third parties without worries because it is not in their interest to lie.

The auto-inclusion scheme represents a creative application of IT to preserve or even reinforce the level of control in e-government services without undermining taxpayers' perception of the organization's collaborative position. The case shows that e-government offers novel alternatives of blending the ideals of control and cooperation into stakeholder management for strategic development. In the case study, the IRAS use an integrated e-government solution to engineer a strategic convergence of interests among stakeholders such that a mentality of self-governance becomes the intrinsic motivational driver in e-government service adoption. Specifically, the integrated e-government solution enables the coexistence of control and collaboration by allowing control mechanisms to assume a more discreet nature while giving more prominence to the agency's collaborative intent in encouraging citizen participation. The case of the e-filing system demonstrates that e-governance in e-government can adopt a less intrusive and more engaging approach in stakeholder management by keeping controls subtle and making collaborative intentions more explicit.

E-GOVERNANCE IN E-GOVERNMENT: IMPLICATIONS FOR PRACTICE AND RESEARCH

Findings from the case point to the dawn of a technologically-driven era in public administration where governance is guided by a constant search for the optimal blend of control interjected with increasing emphasis on the element of cooperation (Demb & Neubauer, 1992). This phenomenon, driven partially by the increasing emancipation of citizens from over-relying on authorities for information access, demands refinements to the principles of stakeholder management in corporate governance so that they may remain relevant in an e-governance system of e-government. The revised principles are:

1. Stakeholders can no longer be left out in the development of e-government initiatives, and public organizations should be proactive in identifying all relevant collaborators and working with them. They should also give up their prior preference for punitive controls and instead undertake measures to systematically engage their stakeholders (Pardo & Scholl, 2002; Pardo et al., 2000; Scholl, 2001; Tennert & Schroeder, 1999).

2. In acknowledging stakeholders' expectations, e-government practitioners should not simply give in entirely to stakeholders' demands. Rather, they should cautiously assess the technological restrictions underlying the IT-transformed public service so as to map out the boundary for devising and implementing control and collaboration mechanisms in the system. Most importantly, as noted by Haque (2001), the mandate of any governmental modernization efforts should not omit the responsibility of catering to a broader public community. The choice of technological improvements should be weighed against the larger social cost brought on by their implementations.

3. Instead of futile attempts to integrate the expectations of every stakeholder, government agencies should develop strategies to align stakeholder interests such that participation in e-government becomes self-governing (Turnbull, 1997).

Specifically, to be less invasive and more accommodating to the social community, controls should be subsumed into the back-end infrastructure of the e-government initiative while collaboration is given more prominence.

Indisputably, the proposed requirements of e-governance in e-governments must be investigated further for an understanding of their implications for e-government project development. Future research in e-governance could progress along the following three streams/trajectories:

1. Since information accessibility is a crucial determinant of an organizational stakeholder, studies could be conducted to uncover the means by which desirable behavior of stakeholders can be encouraged through information regulation within e-governance processes.
2. Considering that the success of e-government is governed by the accurate evaluation of technical limitations surrounding IT-inspired public services, subsequent studies could focus on how metrics can be constructed to improve the accuracy of such evaluations.
3. Due to the complexities associated with stakeholder alignment, future research in the area could focus on the discovery of barriers to stakeholder convergence in e-government and how IT can be utilized to overcome these obstacles.

LIMITATIONS AND CONCLUSIONS

This study has approached the topic of e-governance in e-government from the three critical aspects of stakeholder management in corporate governance: 1) identification of stakeholders; 2) recognition of differing interests among stakeholders; and 3) how an organization caters to and furthers these interests. In the case study, the impetus for e-governance in e-government has manifested as an impending need for the public organization to strategize its relationship with stakeholders in order to achieve a convergence of interests for the creation of an ever-expanding IT-driven value network (see Guillaume, 1999; Prahalad & Ramaswamy, 2000; Stratford & Stratford, 2000; Wimmer & Traunmuller, 2000). Also, in line with the original research objective, the case of the e-filing system provides evidence supporting the integration of IT into government processes as a vital facilitator in the fusion of control and collaborative mechanisms into e-government activities.

While our single case study has supplied empirical evidence pointing to the importance of balancing control and collaboration in the understanding of e-governance within e-government, we acknowledge the limitations of our study in providing statistical extrapolation across the board. Nevertheless, the actual value of case-based research, as clarified by Yin (1994), lies in the ability to provide "analytical generalization" as opposed to that of survey research to present "statistical generalization". In analytical generalization, the investigator is "striving to generalize a particular set of results to some broader theory" (p. 36). As such, our study undertaken from this perspective could provide a vocabulary that e-government researchers and practitioners may employ during their examination of e-governance within other public organizations, allowing future public e-transformations to be compared and benchmarked.

In sum, the emergence of organizational e-governance has made obsolete old administrative wisdom about power distribution in public institutions. In its place, there is a rising need to view strategic stakeholder management as an important competitive imperative of e-government. As such, business-IT integration in public administration should evolve along the direction of a strategic convergence of stakeholder interests.

REFERENCES

Agle, B. R., Mitchell, R. K., & Sonnenfeld, J. A. (1999). Who matters to CEOs? An investigation of stakeholder attributes and salience, corporate performance, and CEO values. *Academy of Management Journal, 42*(5), 507-525.

Aichholzer, G., & Schmutzer, R. (2000, September 6-8). Organizational challenges to the development of electronic government. *Proceedings of the 11th International Workshop on Database and Expert Systems Applications* (DEXA'00) Greenwich, London (pp. 379-383). IEEE Computer Society Press.

Allen, B. A., Juillet, L., Paquet, G., & Roy, J. (2001). E-governance & government online in Canada: Partnerships, people, & prospects. *Government Information Quarterly, 18*(1), 93-104.

Audia, P. G., Locke, E. A., & Smith, K. G. (2000). The paradox of success: An archival and a laboratory study of strategic persistence following radical environmental change. *Academy of Management Journal, 43*, 837-853.

Backus, M. (2001). E-governance in developing countries. *International Institute for Communication and Development (IICD) Research Brief No 1*. Retrieved February 17, 2006, from http://www.eldis.org/static/DOC13419.htm

Benbasat, I., Goldstein, D. K., & Mead, M. (1987). The case research strategy in studies of information systems. *MIS Quarterly, 11*(3), 369-386.

Berman, S. L., Wicks, A. C., Kotha, S., & Jones, T. M. (1999). Does stakeholder orientation matter? The relationship between stakeholder management models and firm financial performance. *Academy of Management Journal, 42*(5), 488-506.

Blair, M. M. (1995). *Ownership and control.* Washington, DC: The Brookings Institution.

Boatright, J. R. (2002). Contractors as stakeholders: Reconciling stakeholder theory with the nexus-of-contracts firm. *Journal of Banking and Finance, 26*(9), 1837-1852.

Boyatzis, R. E. (1998). Transforming qualitative information: Thematic analysis and code development. Thousand Oaks, CA: Sage Publication.

Caroll, A. B. (1989). *Business and society.* Cincinnati, OH: South-Western Publishing.

Clarkson, M. B. E. (1995). *A risk based model of stakeholder theory.* The Centre for Corporate Social Performance & Ethics, University of Toronto.

Comte, A. (1971). *A general view of positivism.* Dubuque, IA: Brown Reprints.

Coursey, D., & Bozeman, B. (1990). Decision making in public and private organizations: A test of alternative concepts of "publicness". *Public Administrative Review, 50*(5), 525-535.

Csetenyi, A. (2000, September 6-8). Electronic government: Perspectives from e-commerce. *Proceedings of the 11th International Workshop on Database and Expert Systems Applications* (DEXA'00) Greenwich, London (pp. 294-298). IEEE Computer Society Press.

Cumming, J. F. (2001). Engaging stakeholders in corporate accountability programmes: A cross-sectoral analysis of UK and transnational experience. *Business Ethics: A European Review, 10*(1), 45-52.

Davis, J. H., Schoorman, F. D., & Donaldson, L. (1997). Toward a stewardship theory of management. *Academy of Management Review, 22*, 20-47.

Demb, A., & Neubauer, F. F. (1992). The corporate board: Confronting the paradoxes. *Long Range Planning, 25*(3), 9-20.

Donaldson, L., & Davis, J. H. (1994). Boards and company performance — Research challenges the conventional wisdom. *Corporate Governance: An International Review, 2*(3), 151-160.

Donaldson, T., & Preston, L. E. (1995). The stakeholder theory of the corporation: Concepts, evidence, and implications. *Academy of Management Review, 20*(1), 65-91.

Eisenhardt, K. M. (1989). Agency theory: An assessment and review. *Academy of Management Review, 14*, 57-74.

Eisenhardt, K. M. (1991). Better stories and better constructs. *Academy of Management Review, 16*(3), 620-627.

Elgarah, W., & Courtney, J. F. (2002, August 9-11). Enhancing the G2C relationship through new channels of communication: Web-based citizen input. *Proceedings of 8th Americas Conference on Information Systems* (AMCIS 2002) Dallas, TX (pp. 564-568). Retrieved February 17, 2006, from http://www.aisnet.org

Fernandes, D., Gorr, W., & Krishnan, R. (2001, August 3-5). Servicenet: An agent-based framework for one-stop e-government services. *Proceedings of the 7th Americas Conference on Information System* (AMCIS 2001), Boston, USA (pp. 1590-1594). Retrieved February 17, 2006, from http://www.aisnet.org

Foucault, M. (1991). Governmentality. In G. Burchell, C. Gordon, & P. Miller (Eds.), *The Foucault effect: Studies in governmentality* (pp. 87-104). Chicago: University of Chicago Press.

Freeman, R. E. (1984). *Strategic management: A stakeholder approach.* Boston: Harper Collins.

Frey, B. S. (1997). On the relationship between intrinsic and extrinsic work motivation. *International Journal of Industrial Organizations, 15*, 427-439.

Frooman, J. (1999). Stakeholder influence strategies. *Academy of Management Review, 24*(2), 191-205.

Ghoshal, S., & Moran, P. (1996). Bad for practice: A critique of the transaction cost theory. *Academy of Management Review, 21*, 13-47.

Greenley, G. E., & Foxall, G. R. (1998). External moderation of associations among stakeholder orientations and company performance. *International Journal of Research in Marketing, 15*(1), 51-69.

Gregory, R. J. (1999). Social capital theory and administrative reform: Maintaining ethical theory in public service. *Public Administration Review, 59*(1), 63-75.

Guillaume, G. (1999). *L'empire de réseaux.* Paris: Descartes & Cie.

Hambrick, D. C., & D'Aveni, R. A. (1988). Large corporate failures as downward spirals. *Administrative Science Quarterly, 33*, 1-23.

Haque, M. S. (2001). The diminishing publicness of public service under the current mode of governance. *Public Administration Review, 61*(1), 65-82.

Hawley, J. P., & Williams, A. T. (1996). *Corporate governance in the United States: The rise of fiduciary capitalism, a review of the literature.* Prepared for the Organization for Economic Cooperation and Development, Paris.

Heeks, R. (2002). *Understanding e-governance for development. I-Government Working* Paper Series. Retrieved March 25, 2002, from http://idpm.man.ac.uk/ idpm/ igov11.htm

Ho, A.T -K. (2002). Reinventing local governments and the e-government initiative. *Public Administration Review, 62*(4), 434-44.

Inter-American Development Bank (IADB). (2001). *E-governance.* Retrieved February 17, 2006, from http://www.iadb.org/SDS/itdev/governance.htm

Janis, I. L. (1982). *Groupthink.* Boston: Houghton, Mifflin.

Jawahar, I. M., & McLaughlin, G. (2001). Toward a descriptive stakeholder theory: An organizational life cycle approach. *Academy of Management Review, 26*(3), 397-414.

Jensen, M. C., & Meckling, W. H. (1976). Theory of the firm: Managerial behaviour, agency costs, and ownership structure. *Journal of Financial Economics*, 3, 305-360.

Kaylor, C., Deshazo, R., & van Eck, D. (2001). Gauging e-government: A report on implementing services among American cities. *Government Information Quarterly, 18*(3), 293-307.

Kisfalvi, V. (2000). The threat of failure, the perils of success, and CEO character: Sources of strategic persistence. *Organizational Studies, 21*, 611-639.

Kruckeberg, D., & Starck, K. (1998). *Public relations and community: A reconstructed theory.* New York: Praeger.

Lacity, M., & Janson, M. A. (1994). Understanding qualitative data: A framework of text analysis methods. *Journal of Management Information System, 11*(2), 137-155.

Lawler, E. J., & Yoon, J. (1995). Structural power and emotional processes in negotiation: A social exchange approach. In R. M. Kramer & D. M. Messick (Eds.), *Negotiation as a social process* (pp. 143-165). Thousand Oaks, CA: Sage.

Lawson, G. (1998). *Netstate.* London: Demos.

Lee, A. S. (1991). Integrating positivist and interpretive approaches to organizational research. *Organizational Science, 2*(4), 342-365.

Lenk, K., & Traunmuller, R. (2000, September 6-8). A framework for electronic government. *Proceedings of the 11th International Workshop on Database and Expert Systems Applications* (DEXA'00) Greenwich, London (pp. 271-277). IEEE Computer Society Press.

Lindsley, D. H., Brass, D. J., & Thomas, J. B. (1995). Efficacy-performance spirals: A multilevel perspective. *Academy of Management Review, 20*, 645-678.

Marchionini, G., Samet, H., & Brandt, L. (2003). Digital government. *Communications of ACM, 46*(1), 25-27.

Markus, M. L. (1994). Electronic mail as the medium of managerial choice. *Organizational Science, 5*(4), 502-527.

Merton, R. K., Fiske, M., & Kendall, P. L. (1990). *The focused interview: A manual of problems and procedures* (2nd ed.). New York: Free Press.

Milford, H. S. (2000). Racing to e-government: Using the Internet for citizen service delivery. *Government Finance Review, 16*(5), 21-22.

Mitchell, R. K., Agle, B. R., & Wood, D. J. (1997). Toward a theory of stakeholder identification and salience: Defining the principle of who and what really counts. *Academy of Management Review, 22*(4), 853-886.

Monks, R. A. G., & Minow, N. (1995). *Corporate governance.* Cambridge, MA: Blackwell.

Moon, M. J. (2002). The evolution of e-government among municipalities: Rhetoric or reality? *Public Administration Review, 62*(4), 424-433.

Moon, M. J., & Bretschneider, S. (2002). Does the perception of red tape constrain IT innovativeness in organizations? Unexpected results from simultaneous equation model and implications. *Journal of Public Administration Research and Theory, 11*(3), 327-352.

Nadler, D., & Tushman, M. (1997). *Competing by design: The power of organization architecture.* New York: Oxford University Press.

Newcombe, T. (2000). Customer is king. *NetGov - Supplement to Government Technology*, 8-11.

Ngwenyama, O. K., & Lee, A. S. (1997). Communication richness in electronic mail: Critical social theory and the contextuality of meaning. *MIS Quarterly, 21*(2), 145-67.

Norris, P. (1999). Who surfs? New technology, old voters, and virtual democracy. In E. C. Kamarck & J. S. Nye (Eds.), *Democracy.com? Governance in networked world* (pp. 71-94). Hollis, NH: Hollis Publishing Company.

Numagami, T. (1998). The infeasibility of invariant laws in management studies: A reflective dialogue in defense of case studies. *Organization Science, 9*(1), 2-15.

O'Neill Jr., R. J. (2001). *The levers of power.* In 21st Century Governance, supplement to Government Technology.

Orlikowski, J. W., & Baroudi, J. J. (1991). Studying information technology in organizations: Research approaches and assumptions. *Information Systems Research, 2*(1) 1-28.

Orlikowski, W. (1993). Case told as organizational change: Investigating incremental and radical changes in system development. *MIS Quarterly, 7*(3), 309-40.

Pablo, Z. D. & Pan, S. L. (2002, September 2-4). A multi-disciplinary analysis of e-governance: Where do we start? *Proceedings of the 6th Pacific Conference on Information Systems (PACIS 2002),* Tokyo, Japan (pp. 288-302). Retrieved February 17, 2006, from http://www.aisnet.org

Pardo, T. A., & Scholl, H. J. (2002, January 7-10). Walking atop the cliffs: Avoiding failure and reducing risk in large scale e-government projects. *Proceedings of the 35th Hawaii International Conference on System Sciences* (HICSS 2002), Big Island, HI. IEEE Computer Society Press. Retrieved February 17, 2006, from http://csdl2.computer.org/comp/proceedings/hicss/2002/1435/05/14350124b.pdf

Pardo, T. A., Scholl, H. J., Cook, M. E., Connelly, D. R., & Dawes, S. S. (2000). *New York State central accounting system stakeholder need analysis. Central for technology in government.* Albany, NY.

Paré, G., & Elam, J. J. (1997). Using case study research to build theories of IT implementation. In A. S. Lee, J. Leibenau, & J. I. DeGross (Eds.), *Information systems and qualitative research* (pp. 542-568). London: Chapman and Hall.

Parkhe, A. (1993). Messy research, methodological predispositions, and theory development in international joint ventures. *Academy of Management Review, 8*(2), 227-268.

Pfeffer, J., & Salancik, G. R. (1978). *The knowledge-doing gap: How smart companies turn knowledge into action.* Boston: Harvard Business School Press.

Porter, M. E. (1992). *Capital choices: Changing the way America invests in industry.* Research report presented to the Council on Competitiveness, Co-sponsored by The Harvard Business School, Boston.

Prahalad, C. K., & Ramaswamy, V. (2000). Co-opting customer competence. *Harvard Business Review, 78*(1), 79-87.

Rainey, H. G., Backoff, R. W. & Levine, C. H. (1976). Comparing public and private organizations. *Public Administration Review, 36*(2), 233-244.

Schiavo-Ocampo, S., & Sundaram, P. (2001). *To serve and preserve: Improving public administration in a competitive world.* Manila, Philippines: Asian Development Bank.

Schleifer, A., & Vishny, R.W. (1996). *A survey of corporate governance.* Working paper, National Bureau of Economic Research. Cambridge, MA.

Schneiderman, B., & Rose, A. (1996). Social impact statements: Engaging public participation in information technology design. *Proceedings of The Symposium on Computers and the Quality of Life* (pp. 90-96). New York: ACM Press.

Scholl, H. (2001). Applying stakeholder theory to e-government. In B. Schmid, K. Stanoevska-Slabeva, & V. Tschammer (Eds.), *Towards the e-society: E-commerce, e-business, and e-government* (pp. 735-747). Boston: Kluwer Academic Publishers.

Scott, S. G. & Lane, V. R. (2000). A stakeholder approach to organizational identity. *Academy of Management Review, 25*(1), 43-62.

Seavey, A. C. (1996). Final thoughts on interesting times. *Journal of Government Information, 23*(4), 515-520.

Sharma, S. K., & Gupta, J. N. D. (2003). Building blocks of an e-government - A framework. *Journal of Electronic Commerce in Organizations, 1*(4), 1-15.

Stiglitz, J., Orszag, P., & Orszag, J. (2000). *The role of government in a digital age.* Retrieved April 16, 2002, from http://www.ccianet.org/digital_age/report.pdf

Stratford, J. S., & Stratford, J. (2000). Computerized and networked government information. *Journal of Government Information, 27*(3), 385-389.

Strauss, A.L., & Corbin, J. (1990). *Basics of qualitative research: Grounded theory procedures and techniques.* London: Sage.

Sundaramurthy, C. (2000). Anti-takeover provisions and shareholder value implications: A review and a contingency framework. *Journal of Management, 26,* 1005-1030.

Sundaramurthy, C., & Lewis, M. (2003). Control and collaboration: Paradoxes of governances. *Academy of Management Review, 28*(3), 397-415.

Tan, C. W., Pan, S. L. & Lim, E. T. K. (2005, January 3-6). Towards the restoration of public trust in electronic governments: A case study of the e-filing system in Singapore. *Proceedings of 38th Hawaii International Conference on System Sciences (HICSS 2005),* Big Island (pp. 1-10). IEEE Computer Society Press. Retrieved February 17, 2006, from http://csd12.computer.org/comp/proceedings/hicss/2005/2268/05/22680126c.pdf

Tannenbaum, A. S. (1967). *Control in organizations.* New York: McGraw-Hill.

Tapscott, D. (1996). *Digital economy: Promise and peril in the age of networked intelligence.* New York: McGraw-Hill.

Taylor, S., & Bogdan, R. (1984). *Introduction to qualitative research methods.* New York: John Wiley & Sons.

Tennert, J. B., & Schroeder, A. D. (1999). *Stakeholder analysis.* Presentation at the 60th Annual Meeting of the American Society of Pubic Administration, Orlando, FL.

Thomas, K. W., & Velthouse, B. A. (1990). Cognitive elements of empowerment: An "interpretive" model of intrinsic task motivation. *Academy of Management Review, 15*, 666-681.

Traunmuller, R., & Wimmer, M. (2000, September 6-8). Process — collaboration — norms — knowledge: Signposts for administrative application development. *Proceedings of the 11th International Workshop on Database and Expert Systems Applications* (DEXA'00) Greenwich, London (pp. 1141-1145). IEEE Computer Society Press.

Tricker, R. I. (1994). *International corporate governance.* Singapore: Simon & Schuster.

Turban, E., King, D., Lee, J., Warkentin, M., & Chung, H. M. (2002). *Electronic commerce 2002: A managerial perspective* (2nd ed.). Upper Saddle River, NJ: Prentice Hall.

Turnbull, S. (1997). Stakeholder co-operation. *Journal of Co-operative Studies, 29*(3), 18-52.

Von Hoffman, C. (1999, November 15). The making of e-government. *COI Enterprise Magazine.* Retrieved February 17, 2006, from http://www.cio.com/archive/enterprise/111599_egov.html

Walsham, G. (1993). *Interpreting information systems in organizations.* Chichester, West Sussex, UK; New York: Wiley.

Walsham, G. (1995). Interpretive case studies in IS research: Nature and method. *European Journal of Information Systems, 4*, 74-81.

Webler, T., & Tuler, S. (2000). Fairness and competence in citizen participation — Theoretical reflections from a case study. *Administration & Society, 32*(5), 566-595.

Wescott, C. (2002). *E-government in the Asia Pacific region.* Retrieved on March 27, 2002, from http://www.adb.org/ Documents/Papers/E_Government/default.asp

Westphal, J. D. (1999). Collaboration in the boardroom: Behavioral and performance consequences of CEO-board social ties. *Academy of Management Journal, 42*, 7-24.

Wimmer, M., & Traunmuller, R. (2000, September 6-8). Trends in electronic government: Managing distributed knowledge. *Proceedings of the 11th International Workshop on Database and Expert Systems Applications (DEXA'00),* Greenwich, London (pp. 340-345). IEEE Computer Society Press.

Wimmer, M., Traunmuller, R., & Lenk, K. (2001, January 3-6). Electronic business invading the public sector: Considerations on change and design. *Proceedings of 34th Hawaii International Conference on System Sciences.* (HICSS 2002), Big Island, HI (pp. 1-10). IEEE Computer Society Press.

Yin, R. K. (1994) *Case study research: Design and methods.* London: Sage.

Yuchtman, E., & Seashore, S. E. (1967). A system resource approach to organizational effectiveness. *American Sociological Review, 32*(6), 891-903.

Zweers, K., & Planqué, K. (2001). Electronic government. From an organizational based perspective towards a client oriented approach. In J. E. J. Prins (Ed.), *Designing e-government. On the crossroads of technological innovation and institutional change* (pp. 91 120). The Hague, The Netherlands: Kluwer Law International.

About the Authors

M. Gordon Hunter is currently an associate professor, information systems, in the faculty of management at The University of Lethbridge, Canada. Hunter previously held academic positions at universities in Canada, Hong Kong, and Singapore. He has held visiting positions at universities in Australia, Monaco, Germany, the U.S., and New Zealand. He has a Bachelor of Commerce from the University of Saskatchewan in Saskatoon, Canada, and a doctorate from Strathclyde Business School, University of Strathclyde in Glasgow, Scotland. Gordon obtained a certified management accountant (CMA) designation from the Society of Management Accountants of Canada. He is a member of the British Computer Society and the Canadian Information Processing Society (CIPS), where he has obtained an information systems professional (ISP) designation. Gordon chairs the executive board of The Information Institute, an information policy research organization. He has extensive experience as a systems analyst and manager in industry and government organizations in Canada. Hunter is an associate editor of the *Journal of Global Information Management*. He is the Canadian world representative for the Information Resource Management Association. He serves on the editorial board of the *Journal of Global Information Technology Management*, and the *Journal of Information Technology Cases and Application*. He has published articles in *MIS Quarterly, Information Systems Research, The Journal of Strategic Information Systems, The Journal of Global Information Management, Information Systems Journal*, and *Information, Technology and People*. He has conducted seminar presentations in Canada, the U.S., Asia, New Zealand, Australia, and Europe. Hunter's current research interests relate to the productivity of systems analysts with emphasis upon the personnel component including cross-cultural aspects, the use of information systems by small business, and the effective development of information systems.

Felix B. Tan is a professor of information systems, head of the School of Computer and Information Sciences and associate dean (research) for the Faculty of Design and Creative Technologies at Auckland University of Technology, New Zealand. He serves as editor-in-chief of the *Journal of Global Information Management*. He is on the executive council and is a fellow of the Information Resources Management Association. He served on the council of the Association for Information Systems as the Asia-Pacific representative. He has held visiting positions with the National University of Singapore, The University of Western Ontario, Canada and was visiting professor at Georgia State University (May/June 2005). Dr. Tan is internationally known for his work in the global IT field. Dr. Tan's current research interests are in electronic commerce, global information management, business-IT alignment, and the management of IT. He is actively using cognitive mapping and narrative inquiry methods in his research. Dr. Tan has published in *MIS Quarterly, Information & Management, Journal of Information Technology, IEEE Transactions on Engineering Management* as well as other journals and refereed conference proceedings. Dr. Tan has more than 20 years experience in information systems management and consulting with large multinationals, as well as university teaching and research in Singapore, Canada, and New Zealand.

* * * * *

Qinghua Bai is a professor of management science and management information systems, School of Economics and Management, Tonji University, China. He is the head of the Management Science and Management Information Systems Department. He authored or co-authored eight books and published more than 60 articles in his academic area. His current research interests include implementing MRPII as well as ERP applications in the enterprise, integrating information and organizational requirements, and managing strategic information in the organization.

Elias Carayannis is full professor of management science at the School of Business (SB) of The George Washington University (GWU), as well as director of research on science, technology, innovation, and entrepreneurship for the GWU SB European Union Center and co-founder and co-director of the GWU SB Global and Entrepreneurial Finance Research Institute (GEFRI). Dr. Carayannis received his PhD in technology management and his MBA in finance from the Rensselaer Polytechnic Institute in Troy, New York, and his BS in electrical engineering from the National Technical University of Athens, Greece. He has published more than 50 refereed journal articles and several other papers in innovation and technology management journals (*IEEE TEM, Research Policy, R&D Management, Journal of Technology Transfer, Technovation, IJTM, JETM*) as well as 10 book chapters on technology, innovation and knowledge management, creativity, and entrepreneurship. He has three published and two forthcoming books on strategic technology and innovation management, project management, and entrepreneurship, and is the editor of a four-book series on technology, innovation, and knowledge management by Greenwood Press/Praeger Books and has five book contracts under preparation with MacMillan Press. He is fluent in English, French, German, Greek, and has a working knowledge of Spanish. He is a citizen of the United States of America and the European Union.

Siu-cheung Chan is an instructor in the Lingnan Institute of Further Education, Lingnan University, China. He received his Bachelor of Business Administration in information systems and Master of Philosophy in business from Lingnan University, Hong Kong. He has been teaching for Hong Kong Productivity Council and Hong Kong Management Association. His main teaching responsibilities are in the information technology and electronic commerce area. His current research interests are in the fields of electronic commerce, IT adoption, innovation diffusion, Internet and Internet applications, and Internet banking in Hong Kong.

Derek Chau graduated with an MBA from Carleton University (Canada) with concentrations in information technology and organizational design disciplines (2004). In 1995, he earned a BASc in electrical engineering from the University of Waterloo. His research and professional interests include horizontal IM/IT infrastructure, electronic government, and organizational systems and design. Previous experiences include design and applications support in the high tech industry, business case development, and human resources consulting with public and private sector clients and organizations.

Pauline O. Chin is a faculty member of the Department of Information Technology and Operations Management in the College of Business, Florida Atlantic University (USA). She received her PhD in decision and information sciences at the University of Florida, Gainesville. Her research interests include the adoption and management of information technology in developing and developed regions, specifically in the areas of information technology governance and the influence of information technology on organizational behavior, coordination, and management structures within organizations.

Brian J. Corbitt, PhD, is chair professor of information systems in the School of Information Systems and is also pro vice chancellor (online services) at Deakin University, Melbourne (Australia). He has published widely on policy and IT, and on e-business in journals including the *Journal of Information Technology* and *Prometheus* (information economics) and the *International Journal Mobile Communications*. He has published six books on e-commerce and IT, and has more than 120 scholarly publications. He serves on the editorial boards of numerous IS journals. He has undertaken substantial consultation with both business and government on e-business, development, and policy. His research has included substantial work in Thailand, Malaysia, Singapore, Australia, and New Zealand.

James L. Corner is professor of decision sciences and head of the department at the University of Waikato Management School, New Zealand. He received his BS in mechanical engineering from The University of Virginia (1976), his MBA from The University of Wyoming (1987), and his PhD in management science from Arizona State University (1991). His main area of research is the prescriptive modeling technique known as decision analysis. He has published numerous articles on this topic in journals such as *Operations Research, Management Science, European Journal of Operational Research, Journal of Operational Research Society*, and *Journal of Multi-Criteria Decision Analysis*.

Subhasish Dasgupta is associate professor of information systems in the School of Business of The George Washington University, Washington, DC. He holds BS and MBA degrees from the University of Calcutta, India, and a PhD from Baruch College, The City University of New York. Dr. Dasgupta's research interests include cultural issues in information technology adoption and diffusion, electronic commerce, effectiveness of information technology investments, and knowledge-based systems in group decision-making. He has published on these topics in *Electronic Markets, Logistics Information Management Journal, European Journal of Information Systems, Decision Support Systems, Group Decision and Negotiation*, and the *Journal of Global Information Management*. Dr. Dasgupta has also presented his research in international, national, and regional conferences.

Stuart Dillon is a senior lecturer of electronic commerce at the University of Waikato Management School, New Zealand, where he received his PhD in decision behavior (2002). He has a number of refereed publications in international conferences and journals such as *International Journal of Project Management* and *International Journal of Public Sector Management*. His primary areas of research are e-government and naturalistic decision making.

Dorothy G. Dologite is a professor of computer information systems at the Zicklin School of Business, Baruch College, City University of New York. She wrote 12 books and published many articles related to computer information systems. Her 15 years of computer industry experience before becoming an educator includes positions with computer hardware and software firms. She lectured and conducted workshops on computers in China, Russia, and other countries. As a Fulbright scholar, she helped develop a strategic information system for a Malaysian government agency. Her current research interests include diffusing IT in developing economies, exploring IS-driven change in organizations, and applying knowledge-based and other intelligent systems technology to business and educational environments.

Bill Doolin is the Microsoft professor of e-business at Auckland University of Technology, New Zealand, where he plays a senior role in coordinating teaching and research in this area. His research focuses on the processes that shape the use and adoption of information technologies in organizations. Lately this has involved work on electronic commerce technologies, applications, and strategies. He has over 40 refereed publications in international conferences and journals such as *Journal of Information Technology, Accounting, Management and Information Technologies,* and *Information Systems Journal*.

H. Keith Edwards is an assistant professor at the University of Hawaii at Hilo (USA). He obtained his bachelor's degree in mathematics and creative writing with a minor in comparative literature from the University of Michigan (1993) and his master's degree in mathematics and computer science from Eastern Michigan University (1999). After a wrong turn at the Canadian border in 1999, he earned his PhD from the University of Western Ontario in 2004 under the guidance of Dr. Michael A. Bauer. During that time, he also served as a research fellowship student at the IBM Centre for Advanced Studies in Toronto, Ontario. Dr. Edwards enjoys researching performance measurement method-ologies for distributed systems, applied areas of software engineering, and implementa-tion issues for management information systems. In his spare time outside of academia, he enjoys hiking, playing frisbee, and studying the martial arts.

Phillip Ein-Dor is currently professor *emeritus* at the Faculty of Management, Tel-Aviv University, Israel. His research interests include theory of information systems, natural language processing, information technology and infrastructure, artificial intelligence, and the Internet. Over the past three decades, Dr. Ein-Dor has published about 50 research papers and has written or edited four books in his fields of interest. Ein-Dor is the founding editor of the *Journal of AIS* and has served on the editorial board of *MIS Quarterly*. He currently serves on the editorial or advisory boards of various IS journals. He has served as council member as well as in the organizing, nominating, publications, Fellows and LEO Award committees of AIS. In 2000, he was honored as an AIS fellow. In 2001, he was elected president-elect of AIS, and served as president in 2002-2003.

Ibrahim Elbeltagi, PhD, is a senior lecturer at Wolverhampton University Business School, UK. He received his doctorate in strategic use of DSS in local authorities in both Egypt and the UK from University of Huddersfield. Before he joined Wolverhampton University, he worked as a lecturer at the School of Computing at De Montfort University. His current research interests include ICT in SMEs, knowledge management, decision support systems, and e-commerce.

J. Roberto Evaristo is professor in the Information and Decision Sciences Department, University of Illinois, Chicago. He has published in the *Communications of the ACM, Database, Journal of Engineering and Technology Management, Business Horizons, European Management Journal, Journal of Organizational Computing and Electronic Commerce*, and elsewhere. He also serves on the editorial board of the *Journal of Global Information Management, Information Technology and People, International Journal of E-collaboration*, and the *Journal of Global Information Technology Management*.

David Gefen is associate professor of MIS at Drexel University, Philadelphia, where he teaches strategic management of IT, database analysis and design, and VB.NET. He received his PhD in CIS from Georgia State University and a Master of Science in MIS from Tel-Aviv University. His research focuses on psychological and rational processes involved in ERP, CMC, and e-commerce implementation management. David's wide interests in IT adoption stem from his 12 years of experience in developing and managing large information systems. David is a senior editor for *The DATA BASE for Advances in Information Systems*. His research findings have been published in *MIS Quarterly, Information Systems Research, Journal of Management Information Systems, Journal of Strategic Information Systems, IEEE Transactions on Engineering Management, Electronic Markets, The DATA BASE for Advances in Information Systems, Omega: The International Journal of Management Science, Journal AIS, Communications of the AIS*, and *Journal of End User Computing*, among others. David is also first author of the textbook "Advanced VB.NET: Programming Web and Desktop Applications in ADO.NET and ASP.NET."

Gerald Grant is an associate professor of information systems at the Eric Sprott School of Business, Carleton University, in Ottawa, Canada. He previously taught at the Faculty of Management, McGill University, Montreal, Canada, and in the Department of Information Systems and Computing at Brunel University, Uxbridge, UK. Dr. Grant earned his PhD in information systems from the London School of Economics and Political Science, University of London. He has consulted for the Commonwealth Secretariat (UK) and the COMNET-IT Foundation (Malta) on projects related to national and sectoral IT strategies. His current research interests are in the areas of strategic management of enterprise information systems, IT governance, and e-government. He is the editor of two books published by Idea Group Inc. (Hershey, USA). He serves on the advisory board of the Ottawa Manufacturers Network in Ottawa, Canada.

Jairo A. Gutiérrez is a senior lecturer in information systems at the University of Auckland (New Zealand) and coordinator of its Cisco Networking Academy Program. He has worked in the industry as a research and development manager, systems integration consultant, and information systems manager. His current research topics are in network management systems, viable business models for mobile commerce, programmable networks, and quality-of-service issues associated with Internet protocols. He was recently appointed editor-in-chief of the *International Journal of Business Data Communications and Networking* (Idea Group Inc.). He received a systems and computer engineering degree from The University of The Andes (Colombia, 1983), a master's degree in computer science from Texas A&M University (1985), and a PhD (1997) in information systems from The University of Auckland, New Zealand.

Glenn Hardaker, PhD, is a professor of innovation management and head of the Learning and Teaching Innovation Unit at the Huddersfield University Business School (UK). His books include *Wired Marketing: Energising Business for E-Commerce*, *Re-Formating the Learning Experience* and, most recently, *Creative Destruction*. Glenn has also published numerous book chapters and articles in journals including *Long Range Planning* and the *European Journal of Innovation Management*. He is also editor of the *International Journal of Campus Wide Information Systems* and associate editor of *International Journal of Management Practice*. His research interests focus on promoting social diversity and equality through ICT, e-learning, and e-commerce.

Byron Hill is a lecturer in information systems in the School of Information Systems, Deakin University, Melbourne (Australia). He is a PhD scholar and is studying the impact of the Web on learning processes.

Saranond Inthanond is a PhD scholar in the School of Information Systems, Deakin University, Melbourne (Australia) and was previously a lecturer at Dhurakijpundit University (Thailand). His specialization is in the social construction of information and the ways that meaning is derived from it in different cultural settings. He is particularly interested in the role of diaspora in information creation.

Elena Karahanna is an associate professor of MIS and director of international programs at the Terry College of Business, University of Georgia (USA). Her work has been published in *Management Science*, *Organization Science*, *MIS Quarterly*, and elsewhere. She serves or has served on the editorial boards of the *MIS Quarterly, Information Systems Research, IEEE Transactions in Engineering Management, Journal of AIS,* the *European Journal of Information Systems,* and *Computer Personnel.*

Peter Kawalek is a senior lecturer in information systems at Manchester Business School in the University of Manchester, UK. He has previously held posts at Warwick Business School, UK, and with the Department of Computer Science, University of Manchester. Peter has specialized in projects around government, IT, and organizational change. He has worked with many key agencies at the policy and strategy level in the UK, and has developed a series of action research cases. Dr. Kawalek is the author of two books and numerous research papers. He was organizing chair of the 2004 IFIP WG 8.2 Conference on "Relevant Theory and Informed Practice". He also holds grant awards from the Engineering and Physical Science Research Council (EPSRC) and the Office of the Deputy Prime Minister (ODPM).

Eric T. K. Lim is a graduate student in the School of Computing, National University of Singapore. His research interests include topics such as e-learning, e-government, enterprise systems, knowledge management, and strategic management of public relations. His research has been presented at several international conferences such as the European Conference on Information Systems (ECIS), the IFIP 8.2 Working Conference, the Hawaii International Conference on System Sciences (HICSS) and the Academy of Management Meeting (AoMM). He has also published in several academic journals such as the *Journal of the American Society for Information Science and Technology (JASIST),* the *Journal of Information and Knowledge Management (JIKM),* the *Journal of Global Information Management (JGIM), Decisions Support Systems (DSS),* and the *European Journal of Information Systems (EJIS).*

Ming-te Lu is chair professor of information systems and the chief information officer at Lingnan University (China). He received his BS business from Cheng Kung University in Taiwan, an MS in management science and a PhD in business from the University of Minnesota. Professor Lu's teaching and research interests are IT developments in developing economies, electronic commerce, decision support systems, strategic use of IT, and IT educational issues. He has published more than 90 journal articles and conference proceeding papers in the areas of information systems including those which appeared in *Decision Sciences, Information & Management, Journal of Global Information Management, Journal of End User Computing, Journal of Information Systems Management, Journal of Computer Information Systems, Journal of Systems and Software,* and others.

Victor W. Mbarika is an assistant professor of information systems and decision sciences at the E. J. Ourso College of Business Administration, Louisiana State University (USA). He holds a BS in management information systems (MIS) from the United States International University Nairobi/San Diego, California, an MS in MIS from the University of Illinois at Chicago, and a PhD in MIS from Auburn University. His research in multimedia learning and telecommunications diffusion in developing countries has been published in over 15 academic journals and book chapters, and has also been presented at over 25 national and international conferences on information systems.

Neil McBride, PhD, is the leader of the IT Service Management Research Group at De Montfort University (UK). The group specializes in applying concepts from service management research to IT service management. Dr. McBride's research interests include the management of help desks, IT service strategy, and information systems evaluation. Recent work has applied the chaos theory and actor network theory to information systems research. His publications have appeared in several journals including the *European Management Journal*, *Information Systems Journal*, the *Communications of the AIS*, *Information and Software Technology*, and *Geography*.

Peter N. Meso is an assistant professor of information systems at Georgia State University (USA). His current research deals with the contributions of requirements and software engineering in knowledge management, the processes of system development and implementation, consequences of information systems in underdeveloped nations, and emergent business information systems and infrastructure. He earned his PhD in information systems from Kent State University and holds a BS in information systems and an MBA from the United States International University - Africa. His published works have appeared in the *Journal of Knowledge Management* and the *Journal of Global Information Technology*, among others.

Robert J. Mockler is the Joseph F. Adams professor of management at St. John's University's Graduate School of Business (USA). He received a BA and MBA from Harvard and a PhD from Columbia University. He is a director of the Strategic Management Research Group and its Centers of Knowledge-Based Systems for Business and of Case Study Development. He has authored or co-authored 40 books and monographs, 100 case studies, and over 200 articles, book chapters, and presentations. He has lectured and consulted worldwide, been a Fulbright scholar, received national awards for innovative teaching, and taught MBA and executive courses in Europe, China, and Latin America. His current research interests include multinational strategic alliances, the diffusion of IT in developing economies, and the application of knowledge-based and other intelligent systems in business and educational environments.

Philip F. Musa is an assistant professor of information systems and operations management at The University of Alabama at Birmingham School of Business (USA). He holds a BSEE, MSEE, MBA, and PhD in information systems and quantitative sciences, all from Texas Tech University. He is a licensed professional engineer with process and test engineering experiences in the semiconductor industry. He has published research in the areas of entrepreneurship, problem solving methodologies, systems thinking/system dynamics, and information systems and technology issues in developing countries in various journals and conference proceedings.

Michael Myers is a professor of information systems and associate dean (postgraduate and research) at the University of Auckland Business School, New Zealand. He currently serves as senior editor of *MIS Quarterly Discovery*, associate editor of *Information Systems Research*, editor of the *ISWorld Section on Qualitative Research*, and editor in chief of the *University of Auckland Business Review*. His research articles have been published in many journals and books. He won the Best Paper Award (with Heinz Klein) for the most outstanding paper published in *MIS Quarterly* in 1999. He also won the Best

Paper Award (with Lynda Harvey) for the best paper published in *Information Technology & People* in 1997.

Shan-Ling Pan is an assistant professor and the coordinator of Knowledge Management Laboratory in the Department of Information Systems of School of Computing, National University of Singapore (NUS). Dr. Pan's primary research focuses on the recursive interaction of organizations and information communication and technology (ICT). Dr. Pan's research work has been published in journals such as the *Journal of the American Society for Information Systems and Technology (JASIST); IEEE Transactions on Systems, Man, and Cybernetics (IEEE SMC);* and *Journal of the Academy of Marketing Studies (JAMS).*

Paul A. Pavlou is assistant professor of information systems at the University of California at Riverside (USA). He received his PhD from the University of Southern California in 2004. His research focuses on institutional trust building in electronic commerce and online marketplaces, and information systems strategy in turbulent environments. His research has appeared in *MIS Quarterly, Information Systems Research,* the *Journal of the Academy of Marketing Science,* the *Journal of the Association of Information Systems,* the *International Journal of Electronic Commerce,* the *Journal of Strategic Information Systems,* the *Proceedings of the ICIS Conference,* and the *Best Paper Proceedings of the Academy of Management Conference,* among others. His research has been cited over 400 times in Google Scholar and over 100 times in the Web of Science Institute of Scientific Information (ISI). Paul received the 2003 *MIS Quarterly* "Reviewer of the Year" Award, and the "Best Reviewer" award of the 2005 Academy of Management Conference (OCIS Division). Paul also won the "Best Doctoral Dissertation Award" of the 2004 International Conference on Information Systems (ICIS).

Konrad J. Peszynski is a lecturer in the School of Information Systems, Deakin University, Melbourne, Australia. He is currently completing a PhD on information systems epistemologies and has published book chapters and has previously undertaken research on culture and information.

K. S. Raman is an adjunct professor, Department of Information Systems, National University of Singapore. Prior to this, he has been senior fellow and coordinator of information systems at the University as well as adjunct associate professor. In these appointments, his research covered cross-cultural issues, group support systems, IT in small enterprises, and government IT policies in Asia-Pacific countries. His current research focuses on IT in developing countries. He has published widely on these topics and served on the editorial boards of *MIS Quarterly* and *Information Technology for Development.* Raman has extensive industry experience in planning, design, implementation, and management of information systems, including ERP systems. He has led consulting and research projects for large organizations and government agencies in Asia-Pacific countries and the World Bank.

Gregory M. Rose is assistant professor in the College of Business and Economics at Washington State University (USA). He received his PhD in the CIS Department at

Georgia State University, an MBA from Binghamton University, and a BS in business administration from the University of Vermont. Gregory has more than 20 publications including those in journals such as *MIS Quarterly, IEEE Transactions on Engineering Management, Accounting, Management and Information Technologies, Information Systems Journal, Journal of Global Information Management,* and *Communications of the AIS.* A 1998 ICIS doctoral consortium fellow, he has won multiple teaching awards, a post doctoral fellowship from the University of Jyväskylä (Finland), and was an invited scholar at University of Pretoria (South Africa). He is currently working on research projects involving innovation theory, organizational learning, and global issues in IT. He also serves on the editorial board of the *Journal of Global Information Management.* Prior to entering the Georgia State doctoral program, he worked as a systems integrator.

John Sagi is an associate professorial lecturer of information systems at The George Washington University, Washington, DC, and associate professor of business, Anne Arundel Community College, MD. He holds a BS from the United States Naval Academy, an MS in international business from Johns Hopkins University, Baltimore, and MS and PhD from The George Washington University. Dr. Sagi is a 2004 Fulbright senior scholar to the Russian Federation, teaching e-commerce. His other research interests include global information systems, and the social and philosophical aspects of information technology. He has published on these topics in *Technovation* and in the *Journal of Global Information Management,* and in the proceedings of several international conferences. Dr. Sagi is a former DBA at NATO Headquarters, Brussels, and has worked as IT manager for FMC Corporation.

Varadharajan Sridhar is a professor in information management area at the Management Development Institute, Gurgaon, India. He received his PhD in management information systems from the University of Iowa. His current research interests include telecommunications management and policy, global electronic commerce, and global virtual teams. He has published articles in a number of journals including *Annals of Cases on Information Technology, European Journal of Operational Research,* and *The Journal of Regional Analysis and Policy.* He is associate editor of *International Journal of Business Data Communications and Networking.*

Mark Srite is an assistant professor of MIS at the University of Wisconsin - Milwaukee (USA). His research interests include the acceptance, adoption, and use of information technologies, cross-cultural IT issues, and group decision making. His work has been published in *Decision Support Systems,* the *Journal of Global Information Management,* the *Journal of Computer Information Systems,* and elsewhere.

Chee-Wee Tan is a PhD candidate in the Sauder School of Business, University of British Columbia (Canada) after completing his master's degree from the School of Computing, National University of Singapore. His research interests span across various socioeconomic phenomena such as e-government, enterprise systems, and knowledge management. In particular, he has delved extensively into the management of stakeholder relations within e-government systems. His papers appearing in a number of international conferences such as the Americas Conference on Information Systems (AMCIS), the Hawaii International Conference on System Sciences (HICSS), the Academy of Management Meeting (AoMM), European Conference on Information Systems (ECIS), and the IFIP 8.2 Working Conference. He has also been published in the *Journal of the American Society for Information Science and Technology (JASIST)*, the *Journal of Global Information Management (JGIM)*, and the *International Journal of Information Management (IJIM)*.

Theerasak Thanasankit, PhD, is IT and development manager at Varakit Textiles, Bangkok, and an adjunct professor at Kasetsart University (Thailand). He was formerly a senior lecturer in the School of Information Management and Systems at Monash University and has also taught at Victoria University of Wellington in New Zealand and the University of Melbourne in Australia. He is the author of two books and nearly 30 scholarly papers in journals including the *European Journal of Information Systems* and the *Journal of Systems and Technology*.

Gary Thomas is full professor of business in the School of Business, Computing, and Technical Studies of Anne Arundel Community College, Arnold, MD (USA). He holds an AB from Lycoming College, MEd from Shippensburg University, and PhD from the University of Maryland. Dr Thomas' teaching and research interests include the issues of online synchronous and asynchronous education, business leadership, and personal investment strategies. He has published in the *Journal of Global Information Management*. He is the recipient of a 2002 National Institute for Staff and Organizational Development (NISOD) teaching excellence award.

Prateek Vasisht is a business analyst with Air New Zealand. He has a master's degree in commerce from the University of Auckland (Department of Information Systems & Operations Management) and a Bachelor of Business from Auckland University of Technology, majoring in information technology and management.

Peter F. Viszhanyo received an MBA in international studies at the Zicklin School of Business, Baruch College, City University of New York, where he also did research on packaged software implementations in Chinese joint ventures. He received a BS in electrical engineering from the Technical University of Timisoara, Romania. He has worked for an international organization focusing on packaged software implementations in global installations. Currently he is a manager of client services at a major developer of Web-based infrastructure software.

Merrill Warkentin is professor of MIS at Mississippi State University (USA). He has published over 125 research manuscripts, primarily in e-commerce, computer security management, and virtual teams, in books, proceedings, and journals such as *MIS Quarterly, Decision Sciences, Decision Support Systems, Communications of the ACM, Communications of the AIS, Information Systems Journal, Journal of End User Computing, Journal of Global Information Management*, and others. Professor Warkentin is the co-author or editor of four books, and is currently an associate editor of *Information Resources Management Journal* and the *Journal of Information Systems Security*. Dr. Warkentin has served as a consultant to numerous organizations and has served as national distinguished lecturer for the Association for Computing Machinery (ACM). Previously, Dr. Warkentin held the Reisman Research Professorship at Northeastern

University in Boston, where he was also the director of MIS and E-Commerce programs. Professor Warkentin holds BA, MA, and PhD degrees from the University of Nebraska-Lincoln. For more information, visit MISProfessor.com.

David Wastall is an associate editor of the *European Journal of Information Systems* and is an editorial review board member for *Information and Management*. He has co-edited a special issue of the *Information Systems Journal on eGovernment*. Professor Wastell was joint programme chair for the IFIP WG 8.2 Conference on "Relevant Theory and Informed Practice" which was held in Manchester in July 2004. He was also the organizing co-chair for IFIP WG 8.6 Conference on Technology Transfer in 1997. Professor Wastell has been a programme committee member for conferences including AMCIS 2003; ICIS 98, Helsinki; Joint IFIP 8.2/8.6 Conference, Helsinki (1998); and ICIS 97, Atlanta. He was a visiting professor at MIT in 1999.

Index

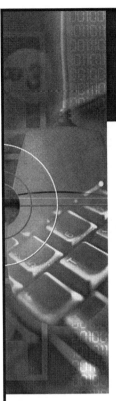

CPSIA information can be obtained at www.ICGtesting.com
Printed in the USA
269701BV00002B/1-2/P